GERMAINE

KRULL

GERMAINE KRULL

MICHEL FRIZOT

Distributed by Yale University Press, New Haven and London

HAZAN

JEU DE PAUME

FOREWORD

The aesthetic and ideological ferment characteristic of photography in Europe in the first half of the 20th century runs parallel to the similarly convulsive geopolitical situation that prevailed in the region at the time. Within this context, modern photography broke away from 19th-century Romanticism and Expressionism in order to boldly explore the possibilities of the medium, from advertising to photo-reportage, propaganda, illustration and publishing.

The key role of women photographers during this period started to become apparent approximately two decades ago thanks to the pioneering endeavours of curators and collectors in their rediscovery of archives and publications. The result of this alternative vision of history, which only a few had the courage to propose, albeit in a brilliant manner, was a number of collective exhibitions on 'women photographers'.

From the starting point of those precedents, which amply promoted the existence of other histories of photography – and other protagonists – it is evident that the art historians, curators and museums of today must now assume the responsibility for continuing to rewrite those histories from multiple perspectives, encouraging detailed, interconnected research that analyses, documents and interprets the individual contributions of each of these women; contributions that were as polymorphic and varied as that of their male counterparts.

The case of Germaine Krull is paradigmatic of this endeavour, as revealed in the present publication and in the outstanding project of research and selection of publications and photographs undertaken by Michel Frizot, the exhibition's curator. As Frizot notes in his text, despite the fact that Krull has been relatively widely recognised since the 1990s, partly due to Christian Bouqueret's excellent work in Paris and the retrospective organised by the Folkwang Museum in Essen, until now there has been no thorough research into her work that was published in books and magazines. This then constitutes the central axis of the present exhibition and its accompanying publication, and is the starting point for Michel Frizot's reflection on the 'economics of photography', its use and dissemination.

The intensity with which Krull lived her life, the events in it, her political commitment, reflections on her personal life and spiritual convictions combine together as convincingly as the totality of her extensive and heterogeneous oeuvre. As another contemporary creative figure, the writer Marguerite Yourcenar, noted: 'il faut presque toujours un coup de folie pour bâtir son destin' (a touch of madness is almost always necessary for constructing a destiny). Germaine Krull moved through life with that rebellious, dissident spirit which knows its own freedom and exercises it to the full, aware of its consequences.

The Jeu de Paume and the Berliner Festspiele with Martin-Gropius-Bau would like to thank all the individuals, private collections and public institutions whose involvement has made this exhibition possible. Our particular and most sincere thanks go to the exhibition's curator, Michel Frizot, for embracing with enormous enthusiasm the simultaneously intellectual and poetic notion that the history of photography can never be taken as written once and for all.

Marta Gili, Director of the Jeu de Paume, Paris
Thomas Oberender, Director of the Berliner Festspiele
Gereon Sievernich, Director of the Martin-Gropius-Bau, Berlin

CONTENTS

LIKE A SONG, WORDS, A CRY 8

'MAD DOG' 14

PHOTOGRAPHER 22

1928: *VU* AND 'MY FERS' 40

REPORTAGE AND MAGAZINES 64

PARIS, PARIS 110

AUTOMOBILES, ON THE ROAD 136

WOMEN 160

MY COLLECTION OF HANDS 194

LE COURRIER LITTÉRAIRE, 1930 210

FREE SPIRIT 218

WAR 240

IN ASIA 248

ORIGINAL TEXTS 254

TIMELINE 256

BIBLIOGRAPHY 257

LIST OF WORKS 260

PHOTOGRAPHIC CREDITS 264

LIKE A SONG, WORDS, A CRY

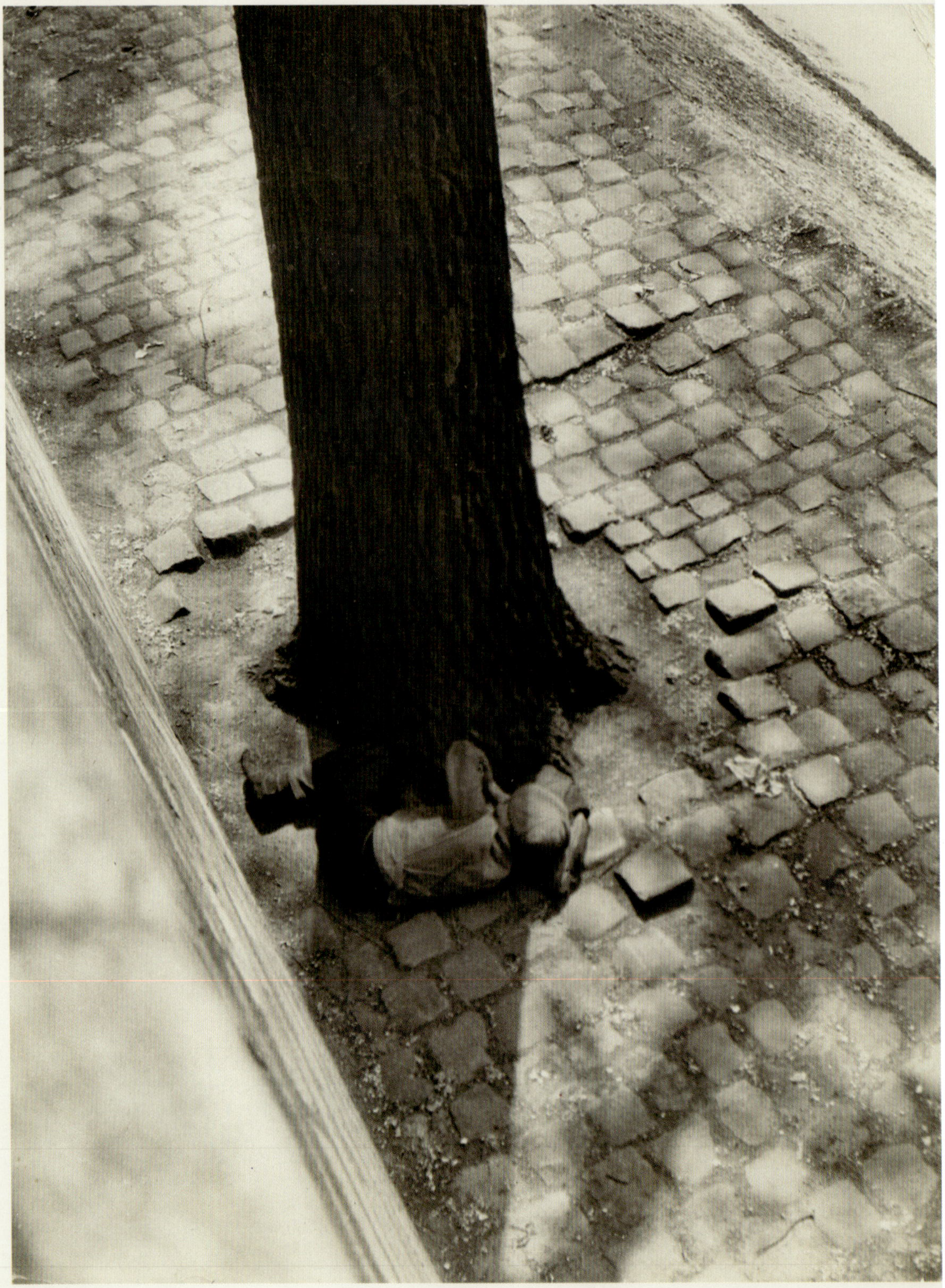

Krull's photography, for example . . . like a detail, a deep, ultimate song, a colour, words, a cry, whose resonance is almost unlimited.
Pierre Mac Orlan, 1931

'THERE ARE MOMENTS when I detest photographs: what have I to do with Atget's old tree trunks, with Pierre Boucher's nudes, with Germaine Krull's double exposures?' Krull is mentioned twice by Roland Barthes in *La Chambre claire* (1980) and the tone is acrimonious, with the author professing himself unreceptive or indifferent to 'contortions of technique' (in her case, those double exposures).[1] Barthes picked on Krull's inhabitual use of this artifice for the sake of contrasting her with the emotional qualities of his favourite photographer, André Kertész, whose work, he argues, 'induces us . . . to think'. In this view of things, Krull is associated with the deformation of the image characteristic of the interwar avant-garde, of which she is seen as a major representative, her position mocking the photography of affects that gives Kertész his particular aura. But the opposition is factitious, based on the incomplete knowledge of the subject in 1980 and the use of hastily constructed categories.

If we look at the year 1928 we see that Kertész and Krull's closeness during the early months of the magazine *VU*, founded in Paris in March that year (when they formed a trio along with Eli Lotar), was not based on avant-garde positions. The challenge they both faced was not to elaborate a formal language for modernist photography – the New Vision – nor to find iconographic expression for their inner movements; it was to work out a new kind of relation between photography and the press, in the form of the 'New Reportage' fostered by *VU* founder Lucien Vogel to 'illustrate' the carefully written, thoroughly researched articles by his 'reporters'. Behind this was the whole question of 'photography as a means of illustration'.[2] This would be crucial for the print media in the 1930s, and has remained so through to the present.

But the parallel with Kertész goes much further than these specific circumstances. Born in 1897 and 1894 respectively, moving to Paris in 1926 and 1925, and both very fond of the city and its unusual visual character, Krull and Kertész died in the same year: 1985. They were forgotten and were rediscovered in the 1960s. Both had long careers in photography, from their early youth to their old age. The only difference is that whereas Kertész was always a loner and a nonconformist, Krull's period of individual eccentricity did not outlast her time in Paris. Established as photographer in Berlin in 1918 but not very active, a sporadic photographer in the Netherlands in 1924–1925, she moved to Paris in 1926. Her work only gained momentum in early 1928 with the creation of *VU* and the publication of her portfolio *Métal*. This was the beginning of a flourishing few years when she worked in reportage and advertising and developed many different aspects of photographic modernism. Her activity began to wane a little in 1931, and by 1935 Krull was a reporter in Monte-Carlo. She was forced to flee during the war in order to join Free France. She then worked as a reporter, first in French Equatorial Africa and later with the liberating armies as they pressed all the way to Alsace. In 1946 she was in Southeast Asia and opened a luxury hotel in Bangkok, which she managed until 1966. Now a Buddhist, she tirelessly photographed the religious heritage of the region, then became actively involved in supporting Tibetan refugees in India, not least through her photography.

Krull (1897–1985) is seldom mentioned in the historical surveys that began to appear in the late 1930s and multiplied in the 1980s. She is not mentioned in the successive editions of *The History of Photography* by Beaumont Newhall (1937, 1949, 1982),[3] nor does she

Nota Bene
Throughout the catalogue the titles of Germaine Krull's manuscripts are abbreviated as follows: *Chien fou*, typescript, 1934, 181 p., Essen, Folkwang Museum, Nachlass Germaine Krull (NGK), abbreviated as CF. *La Vie mène la danse*, typescript, 1981, 272 p., NGK, abbreviated as VMD. *Click entre deux guerres*, typescript, 1976, 134 p., NGK, abbreviated as CEDG.

1 Roland Barthes, *La Chambre claire. Note sur la photographie*, Paris: Cahiers du Cinéma, Gallimard and Seuil, 1980. Trans. Richard Howard, *Camera Lucida*, New York: Hill and Wing, 1982, p. 14, and p. 31: 'Great photographers (Germaine Krull, Kertész, William Klein) have played on these surprises, without convincing me.'
2 This was implicit in 1930 when Carlo Rim, who had a background in drawing and supported the New Photography, introduced photography into the Salon de l'Araignée (for draughtsmen and illustrators). Rim became editor of *Jazz* in 1928 and in 1930 became editor of *VU*.
3 Beaumont Newhall, *The History of Photography from 1839 to the Present*, revised and enlarged edition, London: Secker and Warburg, 1982.

Rest on the Bank, 1927

feature in the Julien Levy collection at the Art Institute of Chicago, which is a bellwether for the spread of European modernism. She does, however, feature in the *New Vision*[4] catalogue of the Ford Motor Company Collection at the Metropolitan Museum of Art, New York in 1989, but only because her *Eiffel Tower* is used to illustrate the introduction. This gives an idea of how difficult it was to assess her role in the major international movement that existed in around 1930 when, looking back in 1989 during celebrations of the 150th anniversary of the invention of photography, an attempt was made to reassess more equitably the importance of European interwar photography.[5] Few collections owned Krull vintage prints at this time.

There have been four exhibitions of Krull's work. The first, held at the Cinémathèque Française in Paris in 1967[6] at the instigation of her friend André Malraux, then Minister of Culture, was more of a homage to her Asian period (she had been living there since 1945), with a mixture of new prints of old photographs and experiments with colour called Silpagrammes (vintage prints were not exhibited in those days). The second, at the Rheinisches Landesmuseum, Bonn, in 1977,[7] followed the same principle with the help of the Galerie Wilde, which had been working to draw attention to Krull's work since the 1960s. The first exhibition to show her oeuvre as such was organised by Christian Bouqueret in 1988–1989, based on his personal collection.[8] He was the first to piece together her career, to resurrect her Parisian period, which is by far its most captivating part, to emphasise the interest of the original prints, and to research the publications Krull had worked for. He restored her to her rightful place in French interwar photography, and for the rest of his life was constantly championing Krull for her dynamism[9] and for her role in developing the photography book.[10] Krull was one of the jewels in Bouqueret's collection, which is now held at the Musée National d'Art Moderne in Paris.[11]

The last big exhibition to date followed the acquisition of Krull's estate by the Folkwang Museum in Essen. She died in Germany in 1985, shortly after her return from Asia. Under the curatorship of Kim Sichel, who wrote the voluminous catalogue[12] and carried out an impressive study of the archives, this exhibition, which travelled to Essen, Munich, San Francisco, Rotterdam and Paris (1999–2000), brought together vintage prints from the archives in Essen and from private and public collections. These reflected the importance of Krull's Parisian period and established her innovative role in the context of the New Photography. At a time when the role of women in photographic modernity was being reassessed – in Essen, this process was driven by Ute Eskildsen[13] – the argument tended to focus on the woman photographer as artist, around significant figures such as Florence Henri, Ilse Bing, Lucia Moholy, Aenne Biermann and many more. This was all the more legitimate in that Krull was 'born in Germany' and educated in photography in that particular artistic context, and herself insisted on this fact.

For this exhibition, part of the Jeu de Paume's ongoing exploration of the work of women photographers (Claude Cahun, Laure Albin Guillot, Florence Henri, Diane Arbus, Lisette Model, Kati Horna, etc.), we have reconsidered Krull's position in the complex and turbulent context of Paris at the time, starting with the reality of her life as a photographer in the capital, principally in the years 1928 to 1931, and bearing in mind the nature of the 'economy of photography', the ways it was seen and used. A photographer like Krull had no other source of income than the royalties on reproductions of her images in magazines and art journals. It was impossible for her to make a living as an artist by selling her 'works', because in those days photographs were only tangentially recognised as artworks, in the odd, occasional exhibition. Krull, who moved in circles frequented by writers, journalists, artists, filmmakers and actors, many of whom were already famous, was well aware that photographers did not have the same prestige. Although they all 'desired intensely to do something',[14] their profession may sometimes have touched on art but it did not enjoy the corresponding status (as sometimes it did in Germany). This was even more the case if the photographer happened to be a woman, and especially if she worked for magazines (woman filmmakers faced a similar struggle to have their

4 *Tour Eiffel*, in Maria Morris Hambourg (ed.), *The New Vision. Photography between the World Wars, Ford Motor Company Collection at The Metropolitan Museum of Art*, exh. cat. (New York, The Metropolitan Museum of Art, 1989), New York: Harry N. Abrams, 1989, p. 95; *Métal* is mentioned on page 97.
5 Unlike Kertész, she did not feature in John Szarkowski's 1989 exhibition 'Photography Until Now' (New York, Museum of Modern Art, 1989; Cleveland Museum of Art, 1990), New York, Museum of Modern Art, 1989, nor in *The Art of Photography, 1839–1989* by Mike Weaver (Houston, Museum of Fine Arts, 1989; Canberra, Australian National Gallery, 1989; London, Royal Academy of Arts, 1989), London: Yale University Press, 1989. Her work was included, however, in *L'Invention d'un art* (Paris, Centre Pompidou, 1989), Paris: Centre Pompidou, 1989.
6 *Germaine Krull*, Paris: Cinémathèque Française–Musée du Cinéma, 1967.
7 *Germaine Krull. Fotografien 1922–1966* (Bonn, Rheinisches Landesmuseum, 1977), Cologne: Rheinland Verlag, 1977.
8 Christian Bouqueret, *Germaine Krull. Photographie 1924–1936* (Arles, Rencontres Internationales de la Photographie, Musée Réattu, 1988; Céret, Musée d'Art Moderne, 1988–1989; Chalon-sur-Saône, Musée Nicéphore Niépce, 1989), Arles: Musée d'Arles, 1988.
9 Christian Bouqueret, *Les Femmes photographes de la Nouvelle Vision en France, 1920–1940*, Paris: Marval, 1998.
10 Christian Bouqueret, *Les Livres de photographie des années 1920 aux années 1950*, Paris: Gründ, 2012.
11 *Voici Paris. Modernités photographiques 1920–1950. La collection Christian Bouqueret* (Paris, Centre Pompidou, 2012), Paris: Centre Pompidou, 2012. The Bouqueret holdings list some six hundred photographs by Krull.
12 Kim Sichel, *Germaine Krull, Photographer of Modernity*, Cambridge, Mass., and London: The MIT Press, 1999.
13 Ute Eskildsen (ed.), *Fotografieren hiess Teilnehmen: Fotografinnen der Weimarer Republik*, Düsseldorf: Richter Verlag, 1994.
14 Abbreviated in the notes as CEDG, p. 11. See note 20.

15 Michel Frizot and Cédric de Veigy, *VU. Le magazine photographique, 1928–1940*, Paris: La Martinière, 2009; *VU, The Story of a Magazine*, New York: Thames and Hudson, 2009.
16 CEDG, p. 14.

legitimacy recognised). The gap between the photographer and artist was the same as between the journalist and writer, a gulf that Krull's friend Titaÿna vainly tried to bridge in around 1928. But a photographer was less exposed to rejection than a writer. Krull gives the impression that the obstacles she came up against were never simply on account of her being a woman (except, as she would ironically observe, for the driving test). Besides, she did not practise her profession alone: her companion Eli Lotar did the printing, and her assistant Marcel did the retouching and looked after the equipment, as Krull repeatedly notes in her memoirs.

Our research began with a set of publications assembled over a long period, especially the issues of *VU*,[15] and considered the reportages illustrated by Krull as the true source of information on the reality of her work from day to day. For however unusual and innovative they may have been, these photographs were assignments rather than the product of personal initiatives motivated by her taste or the desire to stand out. After the 'New Vision' images of *fers*, the iron structures that she had photographed in Holland and Paris and shown in 1928, Krull's new orientation, which would determine the rest of her life, was assigned by Lucien Vogel, the creator of *VU* magazine, a publication based on an entirely new conception, 'packed with photographs' on every page in dynamic juxtapositions. As Krull would acknowledge, '*VU* marked the beginning of a new era for photography.'[16] Nor did it limit her in other ways. In the course of her work she was free to constitute what she would call a 'stock' of photos on subjects of her own choosing and offer them to other publications. *Variétés* (1928–1930), a publication close to the Belgian Surrealists, was very attentive to Krull's work and she became its main contributor. She also took part in exhibitions that accepted the most unusual images. Above all, Krull manifested her freedom and autonomy as a maker of singular, innovative photographs in the field of the 'book of photographs', where her pioneering role was unique, evincing a sense of appropriateness and acuity unmatched by any other photographer at the time. Although Krull's photographs were made for advertisements, promotional purposes and mass publications, and as illustrations (including her photomontages and double exposures), this in no way detracts from their unique and innovative aesthetic qualities, and they should not be underestimated. Krull's work exists only through these publications, magazines and books, which were the raison d'être for her life as a photographer. From *Métal* to *Marseille*, we have identified some 1,300 reproductions of her photographs in magazines and books during the years from 1928 to 1935.

Research for this exhibition also had access to new ensembles which are more accessible now than fifteen years ago. It benefited, in particular, from the reorganisation of various collections, and we are grateful to the Folkwang Museum and to the Ann and Jürgen Wilde Foundation, which has just moved to Munich, for making theirs available to us. The Musée National d'Art Moderne in Paris gave us access to the Krull section of the Bouqueret collection, even though this was being inventoried at the time, while Éric Rémy communicated a number of documents in his possession. The Amsab-Institute of Social History in Ghent generously allowed us access to its complete collection of Krull photographs, and the Bibliothèque Nationale de France, which owns previously unpublished prints, generously communicated a recently acquired manuscript by Emmanuel Berl and Germaine Krull. As a result of having taken part in the study of the Thomas Walther Collection at MoMA, too, I was given access to its Germaine Krull prints.

It is interesting to note that these various collections do not repeat each other. Most of Krull's images seem to have been printed only once. Nor do the known prints all match the reproductions in the magazines mentioned above, which tells us that many original prints were lost, and that many other pictures were never reproduced. With these points in mind, what we have tried to do in this exhibition is to re-evaluate the standard categories, to determine the natural connection between the production and publication of photographs, and, as part of the same dynamic, to link simple topical reportage and imaginative art, the occasional striving for innovation and a number of Krull's abiding interests, notably in hands and shadows.

Another of Krull's singularities proved essential here: she wrote a great deal, hundreds of pages. This, too, sets her apart form most of her contemporaries. And because this writing is essentially autobiographical, it tells us a great deal about what it was like to be a photographer in Paris in around 1930, about the practice of photography, and about Krull's milieu and way of life, and the people she associated with. Kim Sichel, too, has made abundant use of these sources. They comprise three autobiographical accounts, all written in French and existing in the form of corrected typescripts. The first, *Chien fou*,[17] is an autobiographical novel about Krull's childhood and youth in Germany. Its title is the nickname given to her by a friend in Germany in around 1916. Written in 1934 in collaboration with one Gaston Cohen, it was intended for publication but, despite a number of possible contacts and the support of Walter Benjamin, this never happened. In this text Krull gives a very frank account of her political and sentimental adventures, her plans and her mistakes, notably her involvement with the Spartacist uprising in Munich in 1919. *La Vie mène la danse*[18] is more about photography, and ends in a Tibetan centre in India in 1981. This is a more conventional autobiography that describes all the different phases of the photographer's life. To date it has been published only once, in an Italian translation.[19] A third autobiography, *Click entre deux guerres*,[20] dates from 1976, and the text was translated into German for Krull's first catalogue, published in Bonn in 1977. As regards the history of photography, this, I think, is the most fascinating of the three because it is full of information about the circumstances surrounding various photographs, the role of Krull's photographic and literary milieu, and her own engagements and even her doubts about various pieces of work. Such writings are a precious resource, of the kind rarely available to historical researchers. However, the chronological information they provide is not always precise, and they suffer from the writer's faulty memory and, sometimes, her unconscious desire to enhance her role – a natural penchant of all autobiographies. Other memoirs and novels from the African period (Brazzaville, 1943)[21] and the Asian period have also remained unpublished, as have shorter texts, mainly essays and articles, stating a political position.[22] All these writings reflect a remarkable personality, one that cannot be reduced to Krull's profession as a photographer or to her individual adventures or to private matters, or to her socio-political engagements. Rather, they show all these things to be linked.

Given all these considerations, what were the right choices when it comes to showing the full extent of Krull' oeuvre and practice, and its impact at the time? This is a photographer who encourages an open-minded view of modernism and the avant-garde, of photographic 'art' and 'photography as art' – about all the ready-made categories of history whose models are propagated by certain books that, if actually little distributed, are always referred to in historical studies.

Putting matters of aesthetic heterogeneity to one side, as individuals photographers determined their identity in the field, in accordance with their possibilities and their instincts, and not in relation to the movements whose existence they may not even have been aware of, even if they were contributing to shape it. This was especially the case for someone with a 'mad dog' temperament like Krull. A strong, rugged character, she was, according to her companion Joris Ivens, 'free of conventions in every domain' and always ready to follow her intuitions, her tastes and the natural penchant for provocation that was part of her rebellious and independent spirit – always ready as she said to follow her 'idea', her desires and her pleasure. This was a way of living her life through her profession as photographer without obeying slogans or identifying with groups or movements. In her memoirs Krull briefly mentions Lotar, Man Ray, Kertész and Berenice Abbott and describes the distinctive talents of these figures who had in common only the fact of being 'mad dogs' of photography. However, she does not evoke any connections with the Bauhaus artists, nor does her work show her to be aiming for a strict construction of the image around vanishing lines. In fact, it evinces relatively little concern with composition.

17 *Chien fou*, typescript, 1934, 181 p., Essen, Folkwang Museum, Nachlass Germaine Krull (NGK), henceforth CF.
18 *La Vie mène la danse*, typescript, 1981, 272 p., NGK, henceforth VMD.
19 *La Vita conduce la danza*, trans. Giovanna Chiti, Florence, Giunti Grupp Editoriale, 1992.
20 *Click entre deux guerres*, typescript, 1976, 134 p., NGK, abbreviated in the notes as CEDG.
21 *Hallo, Hallo, Brazzaville vous parle*, typescript, n.d.
22 Germaine Krull Ivens, 'Error in Laos', *Far Eastern Survey, American Institute of Pacific Relations*, June 4, 1947, vol. XVI, no. 11, pp. 121–124 ('A French view on colonial relations with a little-known part of Indochina').

23 CEDG, p. 36. See the chapter 'Reportage and Magazines'.
24 Preface to *Études de nu par Germaine Krull*, portfolio, Paris: A. Calavas, 1930.
25 Pierre Mac Orlan [Introduction], *Germaine Krull*, 'Photographes nouveaux' series, NRF, Paris: Gallimard, 1931, p. 7.

The view-finding of her Icarette was crude, in any case, and Krull's way of taking photographs was sometimes abrupt, casual and almost insolent when compared to her closest colleagues. It was as if she was speaking in a kind of photographic slang. For her there was no opposition between high and low, between creative and commercial, or between art and reportage. Where one might have expected the transition from her *'fers'* to *VU* to have been a rupture, for Krull it represented a remarkable opportunity, which meant that in 1928 she could envisage photography as a means of intercession, a way of coming into contact with individuals and situations, of showing different people and ways of doing things, and of sharing what she had seen and captured with those who would later look at her pictures. For her photographs were not made to be shown on a wall; they called for a particular form of distribution. For Krull, this anticipation of the future viewer was part of the method, as reflected in her strong interest in publication and the book form. And such was her confidence in the evocative and suggestive power of photography that she was even planning a novel without text, made up exclusively of photos: 'I thought that it should be possible to make a book consisting solely of photos.'[23] In what was like the shoot for a silent film, she would go from a factory chimney to a tramp, from one view to another, in 'sequence shots' like those of her cineaste friends (Ivens, Ruttmann, Cavalcanti) filming the city (Paris and Berlin). Putting her images together would constitute a kind of retrospective edit of the film that she was unconsciously making.

For Krull, being a photographer certainly meant being attached to her equipment, to the Icarette camera that she cherished just as much as her car, Gisette – and she would lose and miss both – but it also meant being free to do as she liked, staying if need be within the framework imposed by a commission, but also escaping as much as she could into her imagination, the way an artist does. In her only practical text, written in 1930, she affirms that 'the true photographer ... is a reporter.'[24] But what she meant by 'reportage' was a practice that she invented and propagated along with Kertész and Lotar, working in the team at *VU*, and this was something quite different from what was understood by 'reportage' twenty or fifty years later. For Krull, the reporter, this 'witness of each day's events', was no less valid than an artist who makes fleeting appearances in one or two exhibitions. This phase of putting in place a new practice required a real capacity for spontaneity, the ability to let the object of the photograph make itself present rather than constrain it by an assigned framing. This was how Krull was able to photograph the road from her car seat. She was in perfect communion with the Parisian spirit she loved – that constant poetry of the moment, that vibrant proximity of the old and the modern explored by her friend Walter Benjamin and illuminated by another friend, Pierre Mac Orlan, author of *Quai des Brumes,* with the expression that he coined for it: the 'social fantastic'. This quality was epitomised by Krull's work: 'Photography, such as Krull's, adapts itself [to melancholy poetry] like a detail, a deep, ultimate song, a colour, words, a cry, whose resonance is almost unlimited.'[25]

'MAD DOG'

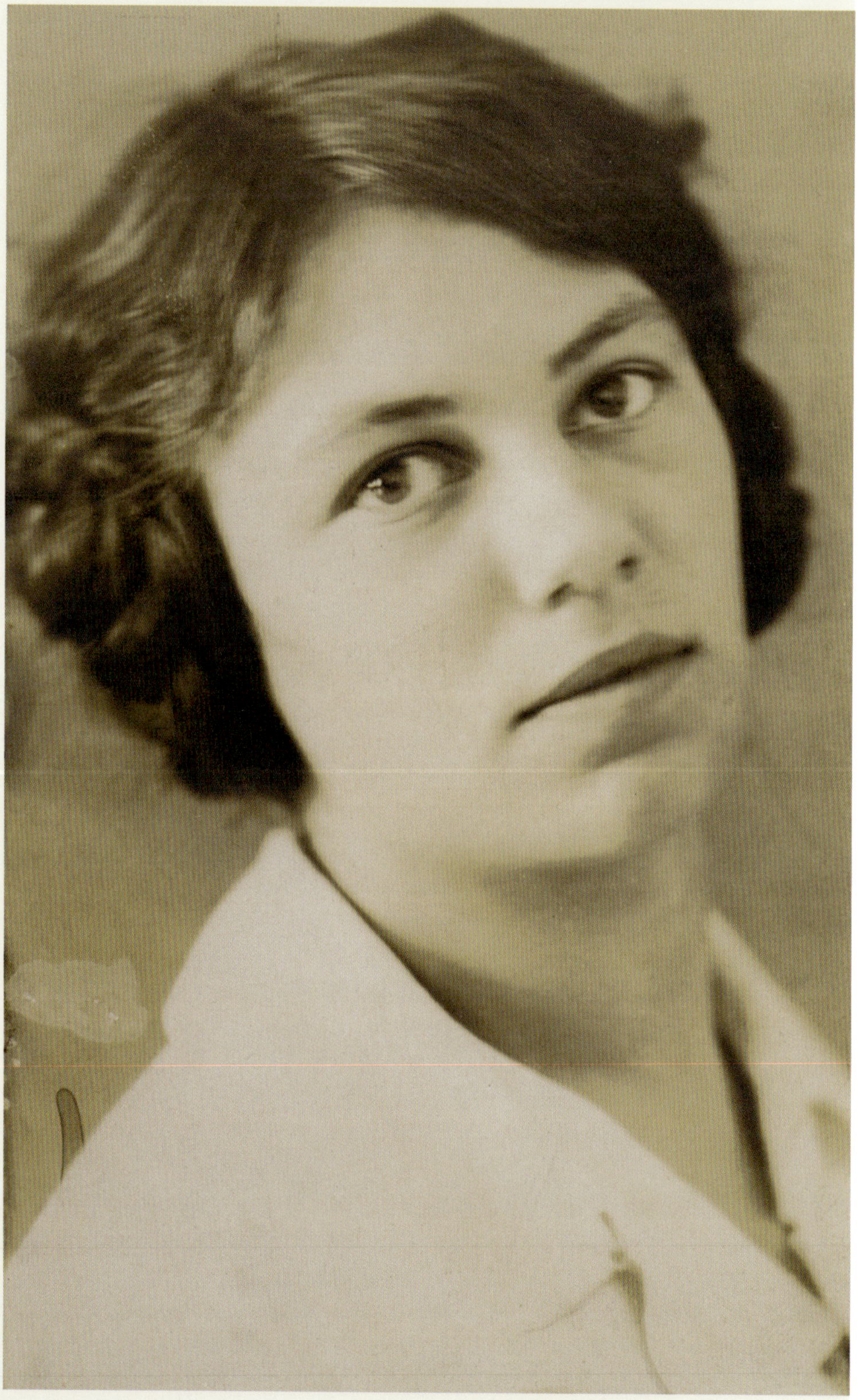

1 VMD, p. 1.
2 CF, pp. 24–25. 'A man defeated and shattered by prison.' These words are attributed to Albertine's brother in CF, p. 28.
3 CF, p. 21.
4 'As Papa saw it, Christ was the first revolutionary . . . but one should not believe it.' VMD, p. 6 (Germaine was five at the time).
5 I have found a reference to a 'patent' taken out on 27 June 1899 for an 'Electric Coin Freed Apparatus' (no. 627,736), but there are no doubt others.
6 The place was a 'two-hour horse ride' from Pettau, for shopping. The residence of Baron Austerlitz, owner of the adjoining lands, was three hours by horse. VMD, p. 18.
7 VMD, p. 24.

THERE IS NO NEED to bring in psychoanalysis to realise that the way Germaine Krull lived her life was shaped by her childhood and adolescence, so vividly do her memoirs paint the picture of a chaotic, rudderless upbringing and distressed adolescence, which were what drove her as a young woman to commit – not without a degree of innocence – to social causes, and to cherish freedom throughout her life. This also has to do with the attitudes of those around her, her father, mother and governesses, and the various forms of instability – both geographical and social – that she experienced. In 1932, when she began working on a semi-autobiographical 'novel' based on her youth – her star as a photographer was now on the wane – she gave it a French title, *Chien fou* (mad dog), an adaptation of 'Zottel' (shaggy), the nickname she was given when she began living independently at the age of eighteen. She turned an adjective inspired by her hair and general appearance into an evocative sobriquet denoting independence of mind, agitation and, also, a consciously accepted masculinity.

'I am told I was born on Monday, 29 November 1897 in Wilda.'[1] This neighbourhood of Poznan, then part of the German Empire (Prussia), was returned to Poland in 1919. Germaine Luise Krull was the daughter of Johann Heinrich Friedrich Krull, an engineer and inventor from Hamburg, and Kunigunde Engelbrecht, from Nuremberg. Krull's 'education' (if it can be called that) and atypical behaviour were due in the first place to the unusual personalities of her parents, which were themselves the result of their own histories. Born into a family of industrialists, her father was sent to the seminary but ran away (hence his ineradicable hatred of religion) and eventually went to work in his father's factory, now entrusted to his brother, which he eventually co-directed. However, unable to overcome chronic disagreement with his sibling, he decided to set up his own factory. As a result of unwise business deals he ended up in prison.[2] He met subsequently Albertine, who became his second wife shortly afterwards. She was nineteen, he was over forty.[3] As the youngest of five children, a late addition to a very wealthy family, she tended to be kept on the edge of things. Friedrich's professional setbacks were no help. A freethinker and virulent atheist,[4] he was also hostile to school and insisted on taking charge of his daughter's education. Considered by some a 'genius' of mechanics and 'mathematician of the first rank', this deviser of 'remarkable inventions'[5] failed in the role obtained for him by his father-in-law as chief engineer in Bosnia. The geographical instability that ensued made its mark on Germaine. She later recalled her successive homes in Italy, in Paris, in Asnières (summer 1906), then in Montreux. They left Switzerland for an isolated farm in the middle of the countryside between Graz and Pettau (Ptuj, in today's Slovenia),[6] which Germaine refers to as 'La Mounia'. There was much local hostility to the 'Prussians'. The family lived there a year and eventually decided to flee when the father was 'shot at' in the country in the winter of 1907–08.[7] Now came Vienna, Switzerland and a move to Bad Aibling in Bavaria, where they opened a family boarding house, the 'Karol'. There, Germaine's father built a ruinous and ineffective solarium, and set up a 'laboratory'. This four-year spell seems to have been the most balanced period in Germaine's youth (she even had a piano teacher). But conflict between her parents ended in separation. Certainly, reading Krull's memoirs it is

Unidentified photographer, **Portrait of Germaine Krull**, 1916 hard to understand her father's real functions, apart from his insistence on registering patents (especially in Paris) that would, he imagined, provide affluence and stability. The couple was living on the money provided to Albertine, first in the form of her dowry, and then from her inheritance from her father, who died when they were in Italy (Albertine insisted on being given cash, which meant that properties had to be sold), and from her mother, who died in 1906. After that, she was supported by her brother.[8] It was Albertine's money that paid for the move to Paris, for the purchase of La Mounia and Bad Aibling, and for the boarding house in Munich. The friction due to Friedrich's dependency was aggravated by his infidelities in the home with maids and governesses, and, outside it, by his partiality to 'little working girls'.[9] The couple argued frequently, whether about money, about the father's frequentations or about Germaine's education. 'Daddy shouting, going away, Mummy left alone for long periods, her eyes often red as if she had been crying. And one day Daddy comes back and again Mummy's shouting and sobbing.'[10] Albertine had her weaknesses, too: in 1906 a little sister, Berthe, was born in Asnières. Friedrich was not the father.[11] Germaine's emotions were turbulent: 'I hated my father and I adored my mother'; 'I started to hate this little sister.'[12]

Germaine's education was chaotic to say the least, what with her father's hostility to school and religion and his deep desire to inculcate a few fixed ideas ('All she needs to know is how a human being should behave, that's all'), and his inability to offer anything more than slogans ('Human history begins with the French Revolution, the rest is not worth the trouble').[13] She knew Goethe and Nietzsche, but her writing was poor.[14] Teachers, governesses, maids and nannies came and went, dismissed on a variety of pretexts. From Paris she remembered fairy tales, the revelations from Henriette who told her all about crimes, and (much to her father's displeasure) the court of the Sun King, and explained graphically how babies are made (which earned her the sack).[15] In Paris there was also a period, apparently lasting two years, when they got into the habit of dressing her as a boy.[16] Germaine was also marked by the spiritualist table-turning sessions held at the boarding house in Bad Aibling every day at 3pm, led by an Italian marquis and with the participation of her father. On one occasion, a moving tablet took dictation from Giordano Bruno! Lucifer now interfered and shuffled the cards when Friedrich suddenly decided to personally baptise his two daughters: 'Dad had become something like the devil himself for me.'[17] Later, Berthe would receive a Catholic education, which made Germaine feel uncomfortably different.

When her parents separated, in 1912, Albertine, who had previously 'dreamed of giving herself',[18] apparently tried to take things in hand. But the father still made frequent appearances, usually to cadge money. During the move, mother and daughter found out that Friedrich had been stealing valuable objects and even toys to sell for cash ('lost treasures that we tried so hard to find').[19] Albertine bought a new boarding house in Munich's university quarter, with four or five rooms to let. Germaine was fifteen. No longer subjected to her father's sexist intolerance, she followed her mother's libertarian inclinations. Soon, she was the mistress of a boarder, one Dr Harbeck ('his caresses were sublime')[20] with the acquiescence of her mother, who nevertheless warned her about getting pregnant – which she did. Thanks to 'all kinds of manipulations' and mixtures,[21] Germaine aborted. She was then seduced by another boarder, a Belgian violinist and composer named Peters. But he had other interests and soon left for Berlin.

Albertine sent her daughter to the Marchese di Tattara in Crespano, Italy, to get over her sorrows.[22] War broke out while she was there and she managed to make her way to Peters in Berlin, travelling via Munich. Her mother disowned her, as did her father, who had also taken refuge in Munich. Peters, 'a rich boy and a good Christian' with a family from 'big industry',[23] offered marriage but then withdrew when Germaine became pregnant. She had a second abortion carried out in atrocious conditions by a lecherous doctor in Berlin, then returned

8 CF, pp. 24–30.
9 CF, p. 29.
10 CF, p. 10.
11 Albertine admits to having 'sinned' (VMD, p. 15) with one 'Uncle Joyce', an 'adviser at the American embassy' (VMD, p. 14). Albertine did consider leaving Friedrich, but gave in to his pressure and stayed 'for Germaine's sake' (VMD, p. 15).
12 VMD, p. 16.
13 CF, p. 8.
14 She struggles with the spelling of Nietzsche in her autobiography and her handwriting is itself difficult to read.
15 VMD, p. 12.
16 VMD, pp. 15 and 25.
17 VMD, p. 29.
18 CF, p. 23.
19 VMD, p. 31.
20 VMD, p. 32.
21 VMD, p. 33.
22 There is a Via Tattara in Oné, near Crespano del Grappa (Treviso).
23 VMD, p. 37.

24 'I might never be able to have a child,' VMD, p. 39.
25 VMD, p. 39.
26 VMD, pp. 39–40.
27 She is mentioned in the *Jahrbuch der Lehr- und Versuchsanstalt für Photographie, Chemigraphie, Lichtdruck und Gravüre zu München, 1915–1916*, Munich, 1916, p. 32 and *Jahrbuch der Lehr- und Versuchsanstalt für Photographie, Chemigraphie, Lichtdruck und Gravüre zu München, 1916–1918*, Munich, 1918, p. 52. See also Pohlmann, Ulrich, Rudolf Scheutle, Hrsg, *Lehrjahre – Lichtjahre: Die Munchner Fotoschule, 1900–2000*, Fotomuseum in Münchner Stadtmuseum, Schirmer/Mosel, Munich, 2000.
28 VMD, p. 40.
29 In CF, p. 126, it is the 'Cubist' painter Marc, a friend of Katja's, who gives her the nickname.
30 VMD, p. 41.
31 VMD, pp. 162–163.
32 See further on.
33 *Der Akt, Zwanzig photographische Aufnahmen weiblicher Körper nach der Natur*, 1918, Erschienen im Einhorn-Verlag in Dachau bei München im fünften Kriegsjahre. 'Prof. J[osef]. Pésci, Bild 1, 3, 10, 14. W[anda]. v. Debschitz-Kunowski, Bild 2, 5, 6, 7, 8, 12, 17, 18, 20. L[ouisa]. G[ermaine]. Krull, Bild 4, 9, 11, 13, 15, 16, 19. Wiedergabe in Kupfer-Handpressendruck. Von Dieser Ausgabe wurden 50 exemplare auf echtem Japan in Halbleber gebunden.' Album in publisher's binding, gravure glued on first board (Pecsi), printed title 'Der Akt' (copy at the Fotomuseum in Stadtmuseum München).

to her mother in Munich, only to be told that she should have kept the child. It was thought that the operation might have made her sterile.[24] It was now winter 1915. She was eighteen, haunted by the image of her 'little bleeding ghost',[25] disconsolate after the inconstancy and betrayals of her parents: 'Mummy had become a stranger to me'; 'Daddy had left me a fine heritage of freedom, but not of knowledge.'[26]

Albertine divorced in order to obtain an inheritance from her brother, made a living by dealing on the black market and 'lived a life of her own that was incomprehensible' to Germaine. Expelled by the university, Germaine now chose to go to a photography school that had begun admitting women in 1905, the Lehr- und Versuchsanstalt für Photographie, Chemigraphie, Lichtdruck und Gravüre in Munich.[27] But she did not do so 'out of taste – on the contrary'.[28] She appears in the student rolls in 1915–16 and 1916–17. For the first time in her life, Germaine was regularly attending an educational establishment. She learned drawing, chemistry and physics, and she made friends, especially Katja and Eyna (credited with the 'mad dog' nickname').[29] She began to distance herself from her stifling family environment and get involved with the intellectual and artistic life of the Schwabing quarter. Munich, we should recall, was an artistically vibrant city in the early twentieth century which witnessed the foundation of the NKVM (Neue Künstlervereinigung München) in 1909 with Kandinsky as its chairman, of the dissident Blaue Reiter in 1911, and of the Neue Sezession with Paul Klee, Alexei von Jawlensky, Wassily Kandinsky and Gabriele Münter (Klee lived in Munich until 1916). Germaine responded 'fervently to everything that could be seen'[30] (Cubism, Futurism) or learned, including theosophy – 'my first contact with Buddhism'. Politically, the situation was volatile. She lived with her mother, had a few encounters ('I missed male warmth') and, during an excursion into the mountains, met Rudi, a forty-year-old painter of seascapes who was receptive to the new painting and taught her 'the subtleties of love'. Against all hope, she managed to obtain her diploma with works including a portrait of her sister Berthe. Rudi set her up with a studio for six months, making her an official studio photographer, a trade whose various facets – portraits, retouching negatives (a vital stage), printing and pictorialist techniques (gum bichromate, no doubt, and velvet-finish paper) – she knew well enough to work in a studio 'in town'. Germaine continued to frequent writers and artists, among them Lotte Pritzel, who made wax dolls, and Rainer Maria Rilke ('the conscience of Schwabing'), whom she appears to have seen on numerous occasions (he lived in Munich until June 1919).[31] She called herself 'the rising star of Schwabing'.

Little is known about her first works. Only a few images remain: a portrait of her father, and two portraits of Kurt Eisner[32] from early and late 1918. With their dark grounds and ambience in which the light picks out the relief of the faces, these photographs reflect the teachings of Frank Eugene, an American pictorialist and contributor to *Camera Work* who lectured at the Lehr- und Versuchsanstalt für Photographie from 1906 to 1913. The finish of the prints is close to effects achieved by drawing (charcoal) and engraving (mezzotint). The main public manifestation of Krull's talent on leaving the school was her inclusion in a book of twenty studies of the female nude, *Der Akt. Zwanzig photographische Aufnahmen weiblicher Körper nach der Natur*,[33] co-published with two renowned photographers and former students of Eugene's at the Lehr- und Versuchsanstalt, Wanda von Debschitz-Kunowski and Josef Pécsi. Her participation does at least tell us that Krull was approved by her peers, and capable of finding her place within a tradition (she was still only twenty-one). Seven of the gravure prints in the book were hers. They are distinguished by their plainness (in three, the body stands out against an unmodulated black ground) and the naturalness of the poses compared to those in the work of her two colleagues, which seems more constrained by fine arts models.

But Krull's photographic oeuvre lay ahead of her. Before considering it, we should dwell on events in Munich and her growing political involvement. War was making life increasingly difficult and her mother was surviving by shady expedients (which would get her into trouble after the armistice). When her father died in Hamburg in the spring of 1917 she went on her own to collect his ashes.[34] Through Ernst, a jilted lover who was also his comrade, she met a Jewish philosopher and journalist at the *Münchner Post*, Kurt Eisner, a member of the SPD (Sozialdemokratische Partei Deutschlands), and became a regular presence in his home. She also met Max Horkheimer (1895–1973), the only son of an industrialist 'who works for the war', a sociologist and 'fervent supporter of Rosa Luxemburg and Karl Liebknecht',[35] as well as Horkheimer's friend Friedrich (Fritz) Pollock (1894–1970), also a Marxist philosopher and sociologist – 'my big brother as long as he lived'.[36] In 1923 the two men went on to found the Institute for Social Research, the cradle of the Frankfurt School. By virtue of their intellectual background and social status, the two men had a real influence on Germaine ('I dreamed of becoming the queen of Schwabing'), but it was the political events triggered by the defeat of 1918 that swept her up in the turbulence of the 'German Revolution'. Although it joined Bismarck's German Empire, Bavaria still had a degree of autonomy and its own king, Ludwig III. Kurt Eisner, the founder of the USPD, a branch of the SPD based in Munich, had been put in prison on 31 January 1918, for encouraging strikes by munitions workers, and freed on 14 October. Germaine marched with him in the great demonstration of the 'November revolution in Munich' on 7 November. On the 8th, Eisner proclaimed the Free Republic of Bavaria and became its Ministarpräsident (prime minister). He was assassinated on 21 February 1919. In April, a Soviet Bavarian Republic was proclaimed, with Ernst Toller of the USPD, another of Germaine's friends ('a simple poet and not a worker'),[37] as its president. This became home to the Spartakists of the KPD (German Communist Party, founded on 30 December 1918) after the assassination of Liebknecht and Luxemburg in Berlin (15 January 1919). The Republic was brought down by the violence of the Freikorps and the 'white terror' directed by the Prussians, costing the lives of some thousand people.[38]

Germaine now embarked on a veritable whirlwind of adventures, worthy of a page-turning novel, a succession of ups and downs described with head-spinning precision in her autobiography. The wild and dangerous life lived by this young woman alongside the Spartakists of the KPD is the antithesis of what one might expect from a 'photographer' aspiring to uninterrupted work. 'Life leads the Dance' is a perfectly appropriate title for the ten-page section relating these extraordinary or unlikely episodes.

It begins with a plot to kill the Kaiser, continues with her being raped by her mother's lover, then comes a meeting with a Soviet commissar who has infiltrated the KPD, Tobias Axelrod,[39] as well as two Spartakists that she hides and helps to escape from Germany. They cross the Alps in the snow, take refuge in Austria, are spotted, arrested and put in prison, then brought back to Germany. Germaine ends up in prison in Garmisch and gets out with the help of her mother and the unfailing support of Horkheimer and Pollock (she is later tried for her role alongside Axelrod, the representative of Moscow, but acquitted). Axelrod himself is arrested and sentenced to fifteen years in prison before finally being 'swapped' for a Soviet diplomat, thanks in part to Germaine's intervention in political negotiations with Paul Levi (head of the KPD), while 'Max very patiently explained Karl Marx' to him.[40]

Germaine zealously defended the Munich Soviets against the causes supported by Moscow in its efforts to centralise the communist movement. 'I felt strong, I thought we should bring all our friends together and go to Moscow, if need be, to explain to them.'[41] At this point she met and fell deeply in love with Samuel Levit, alias Kurt Adler (also nicknamed Mila), a Russian Jewish militant with the KPD-Berlin. As 'handsome as a young god', he was a 'magnificent orator, the best in Berlin'.[42] 'I wanted Mila's child.'[43] She continued her efforts on behalf of Axelrod and was active in the Munich KPD, now riven by internal dissent.

34 'Berthe was the only member of the family to cry for my father.' VMD, p. 47.
35 VMD, p. 48.
36 VMD, p. 48.
37 VMD, p. 50.
38 Kim Sichel, note 29, p. 307.
39 Tobias Axelrod directed the government press office in Moscow in 1918 and was sent to Germany to militate. For all these political figures, see the research done by Kim Sichel before 1999. See also Wikipedia for Ernst Toller, Tobias Axelrod, Eugen Leviné, Kurt Eisner, and Paul Levi.
40 VMD, p. 61.
41 VMD, p. 62.
42 VMD, p. 67.
43 VMD, p. 73.

44 VMD, pp. 65–70.
45 VMD, p. 72.
46 VMD, p. 79.
47 Attributed to one of her accusers at the Lubyanka, VMD, p. 93.
48 VMD, p. 89. The reasons for the sailors' rebellion in Kronstadt are not so far removed from the causes that Levit and Krull came to plead in Moscow: support for the Soviets (in Berlin) rather than obedience to the party.
49 VMD, p. 91.
50 VMD, p. 95.
51 VMD, p. 101.
52 VMD, p. 108.

Both excluded, she and Levit travelled to Budapest, at the height of Béla Kun's Hungarian Soviet Republic (March–August 1919), to attempt to obtain his support for Axelrod and the Munich faction of the KPD. At stake was the autonomy of local revolutions in relation to Moscow.[44]

Returning to Munich, they attempted to organise an internal breakaway. Germaine apparently took part in the debates but must certainly have lacked the political stature of her interlocutors (all men). 'Was it necessary to go to Moscow to make another Internationale?'[45] Levit was arrested and put in prison in Nuremberg and Germaine was banned from Munich because of the Axelrod affair. There remained, too, the question of Germaine's nationality. She was a Hamburger – 'my father's nationality'.[46] She accepted a job as a photographer in Düsseldorf and in March 1920 travelled to Berlin, where she met up with Levit and followed him, out of both political conviction and love (it is thought that they married but there is no proof, although in 1922 she said she had taken his name).

From January 1921 to January 1922 she threw herself into a complex Soviet adventure, still following Levit but seeing herself as his 'inspiration'.[47] They hoped to attend the congress of the Third Internationale, then being prepared, in order to champion the merits of the Munich experiment. They stayed first in Saint Petersburg, where Germaine discovered the absurdity of the mode of social organisation: '"Any person who does not work must not eat": that is the revolution.' She also witnessed the crushing of the Kronstadt rebellion in February 1921 ('all we can do is rage in silence').[48] As a photographer, she was given the inane task of classifying negatives. Transferred to Moscow before the opening of the Congress, well treated as foreign 'delegates', Levit and Krull heard Lenin 'talk for five straight hours about world politics' (she did not understand Russian).[49] The next day, they were interned in the Lubyanka – the prison run by the Cheka secret police – as opponents of Lenin. Levit was seen as a conspirator and Germaine was judged as his companion. In poor health, she was mistreated in hospital and, on her liberation (August or September) realised that Levit, now in the regime's good graces, had betrayed her and was about to leave Russia, unconcerned by her fate. 'Betrayal' is the title of the chapter she devotes to this episode.[50] Germaine was tasked with producing summaries of foreign newspapers, then put in prison again (eleven weeks) and subjected to a fake execution that scarred her for life. After that she met one Hans Basler, a 'parvenu' from Berlin with close links to the Bolsheviks, was interrogated again, and finally expelled as a counter-revolutionary in a 'famine column' riddled with typhus. Seriously ill, she reached Riga in January 1922 and finally made it to Berlin, sick and hairless.

Fritz and Max, her faithful friends, found her a sanatorium and sent her to rest with Kurt Eisner's widow, who offered her some advice ('The past has nothing to give you. You must have the strength to leave the past and you must have the will to live'),[51] and tried to protect her both from her political engagements and from the depressive effects of disillusion. Germaine emerged from it all shattered: 'They have taken my love [Mila] and above all my love for the workers, for the great proletarian family.'[52]

There was no room for thoughts of photography during these three hectic years. Besides, in March 1920 she had lost the studio that was her only foothold in the profession. Because of this mental separation, it never occurred to her to take photographs of the extraordinary events she was witnessing. All that mattered was the boundless commitment 'to the workers' and to the truth she believed she saw in political struggle.

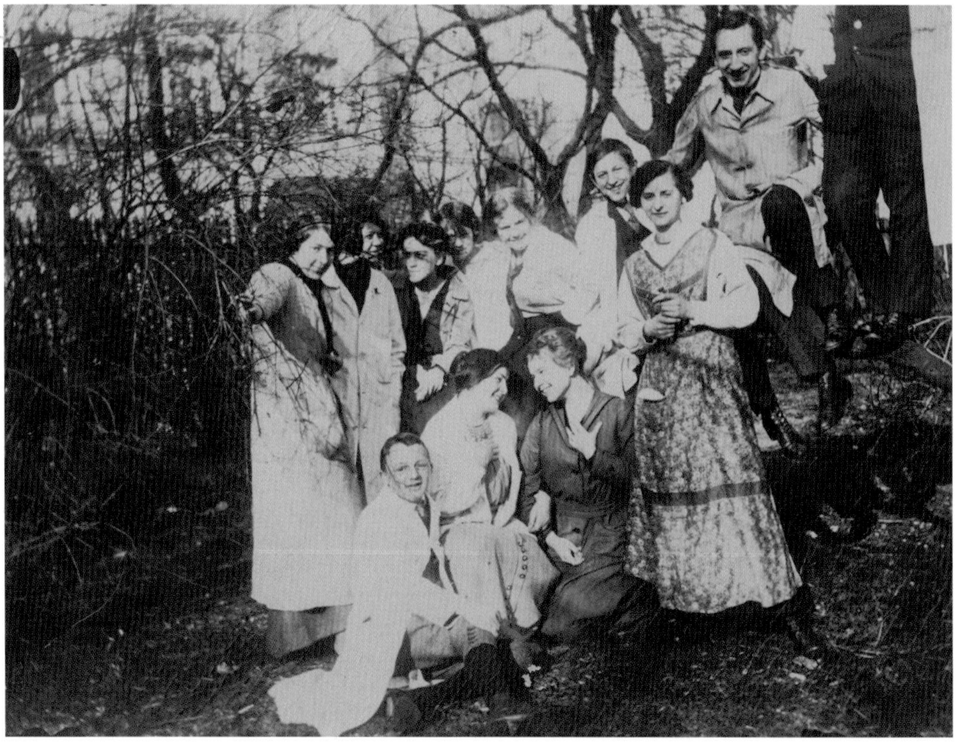

Unidentified photographer, **Group portrait. School of Photography in Munich** (Germaine is standing, second from the left), 1916

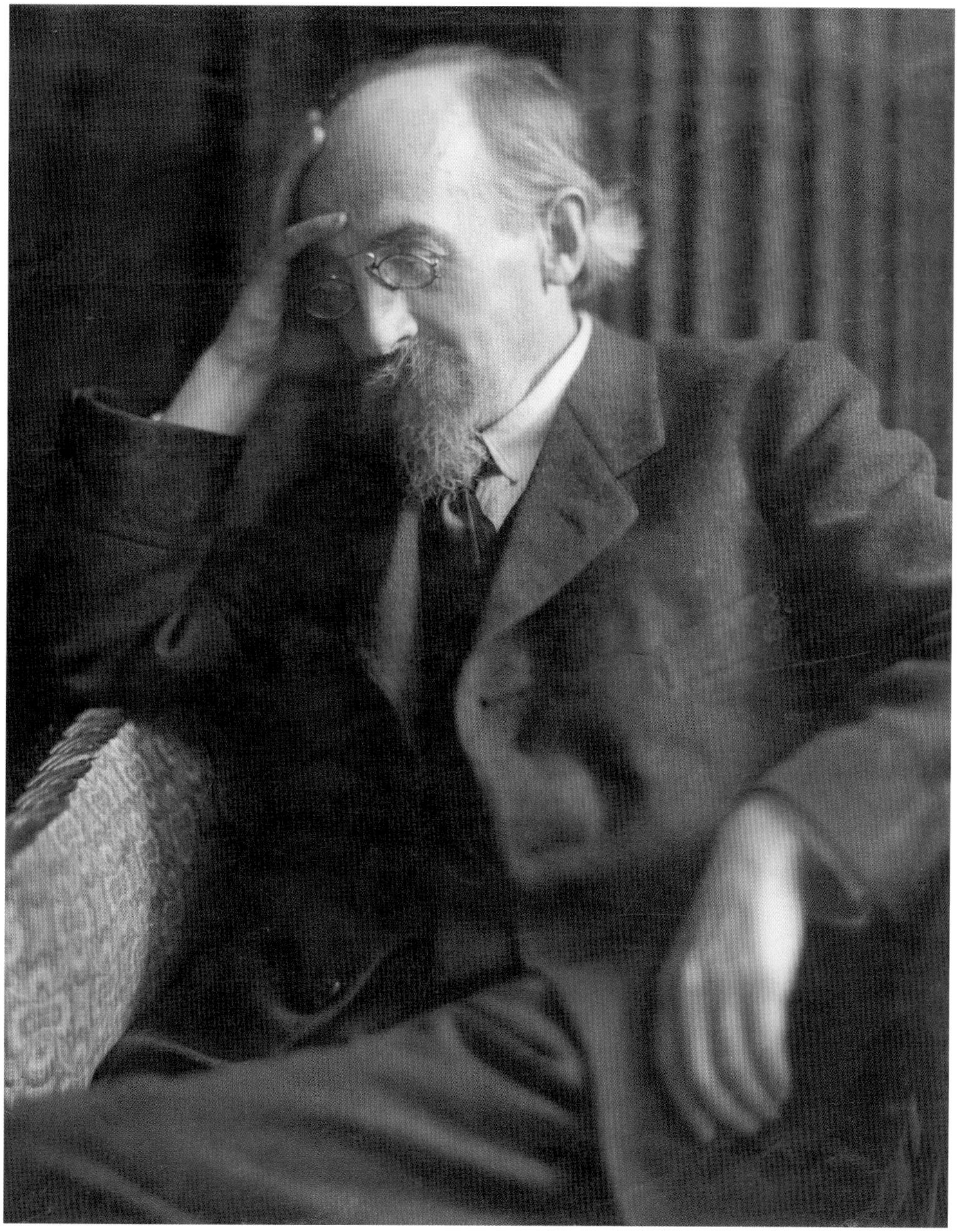

Portrait of Kurt Eisner, 1917–1918

PHOTOGRAPHER

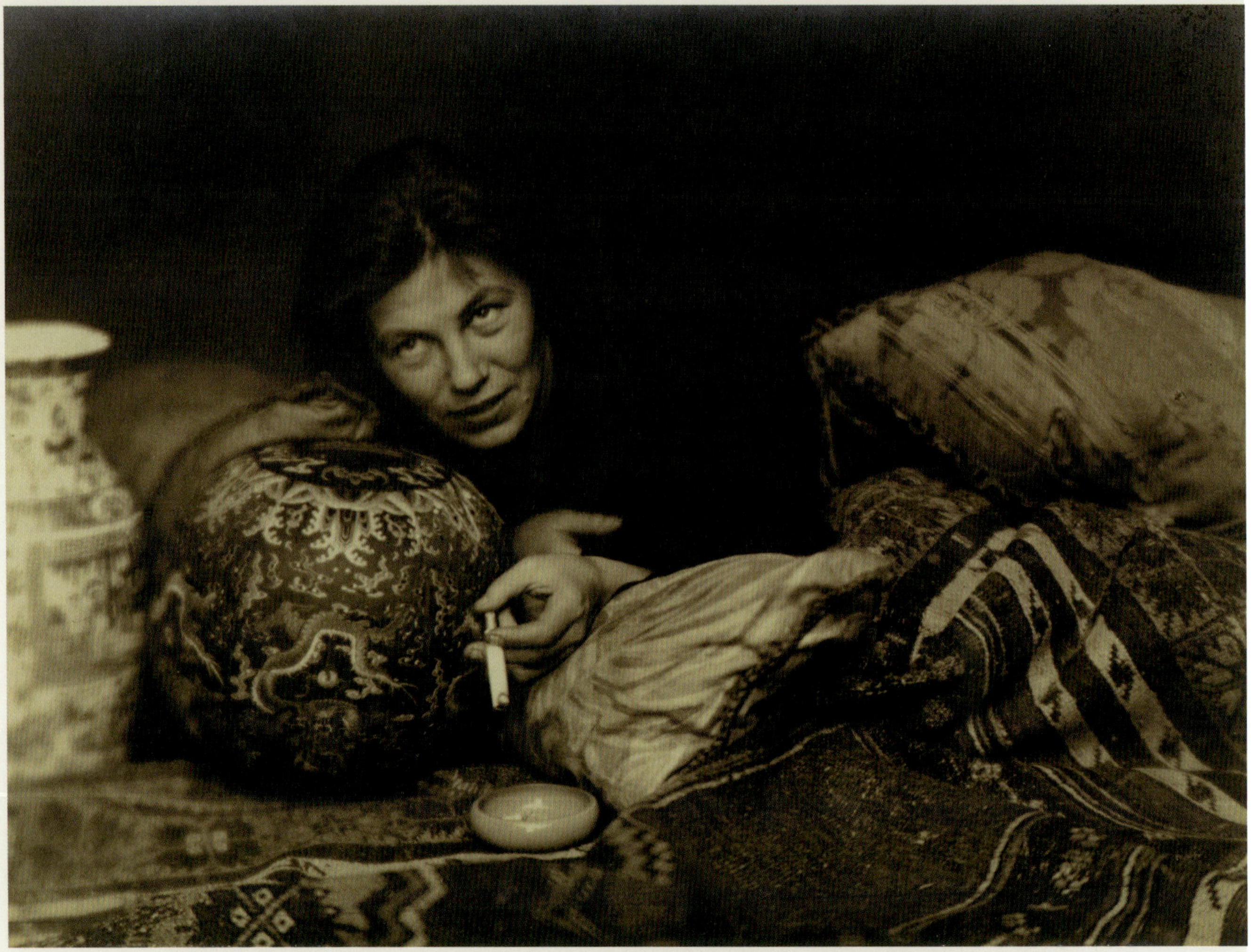

1 Prices increased tenfold between 10 July and October 1922, and again in January 1923, and again tenfold in July, then the rhythm increased. In 1923, the dollar exchange rate could double in a single day (VMD, p. 110).
2 VMD, p. 104.
3 VMD, p. 104.

READING GERMAINE KRULL'S MEMOIRS, it is clear that up until then she had blindly trusted in humankind, just as she had trusted her father, without judging or questioning in any way. And all that came out of it was baseness, treachery, abandonment and betrayal. Krull was twenty-five in 1922. Symbolically, she was no longer called 'mad dog' (Zottel) but was once again 'Germaine'. Not because of her hair, but because of a new lucidity. She returned to Berlin, where she happened to meet Hans Basler again. An operator on the black market and profiteer taking advantage of the hyperinflation that began in 1922,[1] he supported her and paid for her apartment. With his fat cigar, he looked like 'a Georges Grosz caricature'.[2] She let herself become his mistress, against all expectations but with lucidity, for circumstances had changed and she had a new maturity. In complete contrast with her habits and desires, she discovered a world of luxury, of pleasure, of easy money and of a certain refinement, such as 'black linens for the body' or the 'oriental room' that Basler had laid out at his mother's home, with 'big Buddhas, masks, and cushions on the floor'.[3] In spite of the two abortions that were thought to have left her barren, she became pregnant again, and had a third. This time it was legal, because she had typhus.

BERLIN

Above all, though, Basler brought her back to photography by finding her work with the studio of Kurt Hübschmann, which was nicely positioned on the Kurfürstendamm, where he 'loved the laboratory but not at all the studio' (taking photos) and where his wife Gretel did the kind of fashion photography that Germaine loathed. Clearly, she worked on her own initiative and had broken away from academic principles, as can be seen from the fine portrait of Germaine 'signed' by Hans Basler, which she had manifestly prepared, and which showed her as a liberated woman with a resolute gaze, a cigarette between her figures, surrounded by cushions and oriental objects. Nothing is known about her work for the studio's clients, but what we can see is sufficient evidence of a new maturity.

It was no doubt after the unexpected visit to Berlin of her sister Berthe, then only just eighteen (this was 1923), who had been hired by a dubious cabaret from which her sister soon rescued her, that Germaine came back to nude photography, but in a manner very different from the work arising from her time at photography school (*Der Akt*, 1918). This time, Berthe, whose adolescent body was a little too slender for the canons of the day, strikes slightly grandiloquent, theatrical poses in relation to an 'oriental' mask hung on the wall behind her draped with black cloth. This arrangement can be explained by the fact that Berthe Krull was a 'modern dancer' in the tradition of Mary Wigman, the German apostle of 'free dance' (she would make dance her career). The postures could be read as a kind of ritual dance in honour of some primitive divinity, with 'danced' gestures of adoration, supplication, offering, wariness and submission. The mask itself seems indeterminate and could be a fantasy mask provided by Basler. In each picture, its grimace and disturbing authority contrasts with the fragility of the young women, this being one of the structural principles of these compositions. This kind of displacement of 'nude photography' was not unusual in the context of pictorialism, symbolism or even the academic nudes given to painters as a model, the point in all these instances always

Hans Basler, **Portrait of Germaine Krull**, Berlin, 1922

being to find pretexts for representing full nudity – pretexts that varied considerably from one national culture to another, and with the mode of dissemination – broad or limited – intended for the images. The same configuration had already appeared in *The Model and the Mask* by Edward Steichen, published in *Camera Work* in April 1906.[4] This series, which could be given the title 'Berthe with Mask', is known from the Deutsches Tanzarchiv collection in Cologne and was, it seems, available in an *Aktmappe* portfolio.[5] The known copies carry a double signature, G. Krull/Hübschmann, and refer to a publishing house, 'Kara-Kunstdruck-Verlag GMBH Berlin', that was apparently created by Krull and Hübschmann.[6] In keeping with the commercial logic of the day (especially for subjects of this kind), the prints were to be available individually or as a portfolio, with the content potentially variable on request. There is a recently discovered portfolio of eight gelatin silver prints from this series titled *Spuk, 8 Aufnahmen weiblicher Akte*[7] ('Spuk' means spirit, revenant, apparition or ghost, which gives a good idea of the mask's uncertain status). Other prints showing Berthe Krull similar to the ones in *Spuk*, albeit a little too 'choreographic' and directed not towards a mask but at a dark, indeterminate form (black sheets), also came onto the market.[8]

Presented, again, under Krull's name and in a similar form,[9] the portfolio *Dämmerstunden-6 Aufnahmen weiblicher Akte* (Hours of Dawn-6 Photographs of Female Nudes) makes it clear that this was a way of disseminating nudes more widely, even if today we know of only one existing copy of these portfolios. *Dämmerstunden* contains gelatin silver prints and at least one photograph of Berthe Krull (standing, her arm on her head).[10] We may note that some of the images from *Dämmerstunden* were published in postcard form by Verlag der Schönheit, Dresden.[11] Another *Kara-Mappe* portfolio contains six gelatin silver prints of 'artistic' groups of nudes (boys and girls) trained, we are told, by the Berliner pedagogue Adolf Koch.[12] The format of the pull-out, similar to the previous two, and the *Kara-Mappe* (Kara portfolio) title leave us in no doubt as to its origin, the Krull-Hübschmann studio, where Germaine composed her photos. A contemporary of Germaine's, Koch (1896–1970) was an advocate of *Freikörperkultur* (naturism) in the 1920s. This practice was culturally more deeply rooted in northern Germany and was all about living naturally, without sexual connotations. It was abundantly promoted by various publications illustrated by photographs of naked adults and children engaged in various leisure activities.

Naturism was the reason (and sometimes the pretext) for photographic representations of the female or male nude in Germany, just as the artist's model could be in France in and since the nineteenth century. But we cannot make any assumptions about the erotic function of these photographs published in books, magazines or in print format. And we also know that Krull produced a series for private use about Freia (*frei* means free), a young woman shown naked in natural settings – in a wheat field, bathing in a river (this particular image is stereoscopic).[13] These publications by Krull (or Krull-Hübschmann) add an artistic dimension in the form of chiaroscuro, posture and refinement of pose, a slight haziness, the blurring of outlines and details, the positioning of the figure, and the technical care taken over the printing and editing.

But Adolf Koch and his followers cannot be separated from movements of sexual liberation, especially if we bear in mind that he studied at the Institut für Sexualwissenschaft (Institute for Sexual Research) that Magnus Hirschfeld set up in Berlin in 1919, and which Germaine must have known, if only through Koch himself. Hirschfeld had long campaigned for the legal recognition of male and female homosexuality, and of transvestism. In this context, the contents of two other portfolios by Germaine will come as no surprise. They show lascivious scenes involving two women, scenes that (to use the terminology of the day) are clearly sapphic (i.e., lesbian). Even so, the two series constitute two very different propositions. In *Akte* (1924),

4 *Camera Work*, April 1906, VIII, accompanied by two other nudes, VI. *The Cicada* and VII. *In Memoriam*.
5 According to Kim Sichel, note 49, p. 312, the Deutsches Tanzarchiv holds fourteen prints.
6 Kim Sichel, p. 38 and note 49, refers to information given by Berthe Krull herself. For the dating, see Kim Sichel, pp. 33–34. One of the photographs bears a dedication from Germaine to Berthe for her eighteenth birthday.
7 Johannes Faber Gallery, now in a private collection. Shown at Paris Photo in November 2013. Warm thanks to Johannes Faber for this information. Gelatin silver prints, 17.1 x 21.2 cm, mount 34.6 x 25.4 cm, in portfolio, first board covered with paper with red fronds on a black ground, printed label 'G. Krull * Spuk/8 Aufnahmen weiblicher Akte'.
8 Three gelatin silver prints in the same format as *Spuk*, Swann Galleries, auction 2370-II, 11 December 2014, lot 335.
9 Portfolio of the same make and presentation. First board with floral motifs on a black ground, label with same typography and similar title (copy at the Fotomuseum in Stadtmuseum München).
10 This image appeared on an internet sales site in 2014 with the signature 'Krull' at bottom left.
11 Gelatin silver postcards with the indication 'G. Krull (Aus Mappe: Dämmerstunden)'.
12 *Kara-Mappe, Germaine Krull, Körperbildungsgruppen Adolf Koch, Aktkunstmappe1, Burschen und Mädels, 6 Photo-Handabzüge*, Ernst Oldenburg-Verlag, Leipzig, n.d. [1923 or 1924], according to the cover reproduced in the catalogue of the Piasa Sale SVV, Paris, 23 May 2006. My thanks to the expert Yves di Maria for these details. Prints 15 x 19 cm and 16.5 x 22 cm, mount 33.7 x 24.7 cm. There is apparently also an *Aktkunstmappe II* with gelatin silver prints (three were found in the envelope of I). One of the photos is signed on the back by Germaine Krull with the words 'Kara-Kunstdruck-Verlag'.
13 Kim Sichel, plate 3.1 and 3.2, pp. 50–51, text pp. 32–33.

a portfolio of twelve gelatin silver prints,[14] Gretel Hübschmann (Kurt's wife, an associate of Germaine's) and an unknown partner pose together, most of the time on a sofa with a double rest, draped with a big paisley pattern shawl (the same sofa and shawl can be seen in two photos from the *Spuk* series). The two women are seen together in positions suggestive of intimacy, of sensuous entente, suggesting a sexual relation, but no more than that. They are lightly clad in white underwear and slowly undressing. In two of the photographs they are totally nude. The photographic sequence seems to unfold in three phases: on the sofa with a shawl in the middle; away from the sofa, with one of them draped in the shawl; and, again, on the sofa, this time with the shawl to the right. These are moments of allusion to an amorous scene, to a sexual intermezzo, without insistence, with no clear caresses, and almost no contact between the two women. Krull spoke frankly of the matter: 'I would like to do something unexpected, photographs without embarrassment, amorous photos, perhaps. Gretel Hübschmann thinks it's good and we have made a half-nude series, which were not erotic enough and perhaps too much so to be simply handsome nudes. But nothing was to my taste.'[15]

The other ensemble evokes something very different: it is a portfolio with a cover titled 'Friends'[16] and containing eleven prints of two women[17] on the same sofa covered with the paisley shawl on the left, and with a black crocheted shawl on the right. This time, the sexual relation is very explicit. The ensemble seems to be organised in the manner of a short script, starting with two clothed women, with hats and shoes on, holding cigarettes, talking on the couch, then embracing, still dressed, then with one of them sitting on the floor, hiding the groin of the partner lying on the couch, and again, still partially dressed (one with a shirt and tie), lying together and kissing. The two women keep their black stockings on in the other pictures (one of them, however, keeps her high-heeled shoes in the seven photographs in which she is naked). The sexual positions are explicit, because of both the poses and the respective relations of the faces, the hands and the pubises, but the intertwining of the bodies hides anatomical details, as does the slightly blurred focus. In these two lesbian sequences Krull escapes all the conventions of the artistic nude, and at the same time avoids pornography, which has always accounted for a considerable part of the photography scene and has always – if especially in those days – had a sizeable clientele.

But does this series coincide with the affirmation of a personal sexual orientation? Here we can unreservedly refer to the sincerity of Krull's autobiography, where she speaks openly of questions of mores and twice mentions her 'only' experience in this area – a limit that did not exclude fleeting encounters. She mentions this during the evocation of her short-lived return to Berlin in 1925, when her studio was doing fairly good business: 'I had a friend, Elsa ... She was the only woman for whom I had feelings that were more than amicable.'[18] She is more explicit when talking about her move to Paris, where she had Elsa come and live with her for a few weeks: 'I have never loved a woman. With Elsa the joy of feeling at one was so great ... We'd have had a right laugh if anyone had told us we were lesbians.'[19] The closeness of Germaine's evocation of this memory to the closure of the Berlin studio – despite the sometimes confused nature of the chronology – indicates that the two lesbian series, which are extremely rare, reflect both the moral permissiveness of the Berlin artistic milieu and the effort to obtain new income from a photographic innovation (involving her associate Gretel) that might attract a clientele comprising, as it happened, both men and women. Germaine was looking for a degree of financial autonomy. She mentions, for example, that when Lenin died (21 January 1924) the studio took up the idea suggested by Hans Basler, who had been close to the Soviet regime, of 'little books' of photographs about Lenin, which sold well.[20] It would also seem that in Berlin Germaine started accumulating documentation about the spots she frequented (such as the Romanische Café) and city life in general.

14 Collection Dietmar Siegert. Format of the charcoal grey gelatin silver prints, approx. 16 x 22 cm mounted on 24 x 34 cm. Eight horizontals, four verticals. This series is not boarded, unlike the aforementioned portfolios. Only extant copy. My thanks to Dietmar Siegert for kindly giving me access to this series.
15 VMD, p. 106.
16 See Kim Sichel, p. 34, and note 32; plates 3.7–3.10. The portfolio belongs to Susan Ehrens, Berkeley. Isolated prints have been on the market. Reproductions of unknown provenance have been shown on the internet.
17 It is not possible to identify these women with either of the women in the *Akte* portfolio. However one of them, who has a very slender figure, could be her younger sister Berthe.
18 VMD, p. 112.
19 VMD, p. 115. Germaine Krull states that Elsa, who had a husband and a lover, never experienced orgasm with them. 'I was the one who had to make her come. It was all so simple and we were happy to have our own secret.'
20 VMD, p. 105: 'Lenin as a child, Lenin as a student, Lenin in exile ... Basler came back with an order for 300 items' (for Russia).

Was Germaine's personal situation in Berlin, as a woman and photographer, really that surprising or unusual in 1925? We must begin by distinguishing the different photographic trades, from taking photos to retouching them. Without a doubt, ever since the nineteenth century most photographers had been men, while the 'little helpers' doing the retouching were often women. The 1914–18 war gave women access to the more 'noble' functions while the men were away on the front. When studying photography in 1916–17, indeed, Germaine was with only two or three men and twenty women. In spite of her political adventures, she managed to find herself at the head of an 'urban' studio in 1923–24, and she was anything but an isolated example: Suse Byk (1890–1942) had a studio on the Kurfürstendamm in 1911; Erna Lendvai-Dircksen (1883–1962) had a studio in Berlin in 1916, as did Elli Marcus in 1918, Wanda von Debschitz-Kunowski (1870–1935) in 1921 and Yva in 1925.[21] But Germaine was certainly the youngest and least stable of the women in this position. Still, we should note that if we take a wider view of photographic/artistic/media functions (outside the traditional studio), then we see a number of women born, as Krull was (1897), between 1893 and 1900, coming to the fore and playing a role in avant-garde photography after 1925. Some had done specialist studies, others had first been married and had children, and some were self-taught. The list is impressive: Ella Bergman-Michel (born 1895), Irene Bayer (1898), Marianne Brandt (1893), Aenne Biermann (1898), Ilse Bing (1899), Elsbeth Heddenhausen (1897) who worked at the Ullstein agency, Florence Henri (1893), Lotte Jacobi (1896), Alice Lex-Nerlinger (1893), Lucia Moholy (1894), Charlotte Rudolf (1896) and Cami Stone (1892).[22] Krull's life is thus part of this history, which also includes the Bauhaus, where male teachers trained women who would be part of the avant-garde, but where, also, Lucia Schulz-Moholy, who had studied photography in Leipzig (1923–24) stimulated her husband's interest in photography, with results that are well known. In 1925 Laszlo Moholy-Nagy published *Malerei, Fotografie, Film* (Bauhaus Bücher), in which photography was given equal status to painting and cinema as an avant-garde medium. But Krull could have had no sense of this emerging history.

It was when Basler was away that Germaine met the young Joris Ivens. This happened at the home of two of Hübschmann's Dutch friends, the poet Hendrick Marsman (1899–1940) and the writer Arthur Müller-Lehning (1899–2000; he later became editor of the journal *i10*). The son of a Dutch owner of a chain of photography shops, Ivens saw 'a hint of uneasy availability' in her eyes.[23] 'I felt strangely attracted to him,' Germaine wrote. 'His very simple way of looking at things gave me confidence. I told him everything.'[24] For Ivens, Germaine was 'an anarchist, a revolutionary and an artist, acutely sensitive'. She 'was obsessed with death and the idea of suicide. I became her lover, her friend and her companion in life.'[25] At the time, Germaine was alone at the head of Hübschmann's studio. 'Berlin was quite literally on the boil ... Men and ideas were in a state of disequilibrium and freedom which meant that anyone could throw themselves into the adventure of life as they felt like doing.'[26] Ivens also tells us that 'in Berlin drugs were the rage. Every kind of drug.'[27]

This symbolic encounter between the male heir to a big photography business and the somewhat eccentric manager of a modest Berlin studio is symptomatic of the ruptures and antagonisms roiling the resumption of activity after 1918 and leading to the formation of the avant-gardes in around 1925. This was the fruit of new practices, new and lighter cameras, and a set of social and political aspirations that sought to express themselves in photography and its new images (the New Photography). Still, Krull and Ivens were not yet protagonists of all this. Neither cinema nor revolution were in Joris's thoughts, and Germaine made no connection between photography and her – betrayed – ideals. 'Through Joris I entered an unknown world, that of the affluent Dutch bourgeoisie. Through me, he entered that of the workers' struggle.'[28] Their lifelong love and friendship would lead them both to aspirations and goals they had never imagined.

21 All this data is taken from the essential, pioneering study by Ute Eskildsen for the exhibition and catalogue *Fotografieren hiess Teilnehmen: Fotografinnen der Weimarer Republik*, Essen: Museum Folkwang, 1994–1995; Barcelone: Fundació 'La Caixa', 1995; New York: The Jewish Museum, 1995, Düsseldorf: Richter Verlag, 1994, referred to by Kim Sichel, op. cit., pp. 36–37.
22 We could add Else Thalemann (1901) who had a studio in 1926, and Annelise Kretschmer (1903), working in a studio in Essen in 1922.
23 Robert Destanque and Joris Ivens, *Joris Ivens ou la mémoire d'un regard*, Editions BFB, 1982, p. 44 (this is Ivens's autobiography).
24 VMD, p. 108.
25 Destanque and Ivens, op. cit., pp. 44–45.
26 Ibid., p. 38.
27 Ibid., p. 42.
28 VMD, p. 109.

A 'NEW PHOTOGRAPHER'?

Joris Ivens (1898–1989) arrived in Berlin in 1922, having lived in Nijmegen and Rotterdam. Something of a provincial, he found the city disorienting – so much so, indeed, that he went back to his parents, embarked on a retreat, and only returned there again in September 1923. He met Germaine shortly after that. They were soon living together. 'Joris was disorder personified. He piled everything up in a corner and that was that.'[29] Joris said pretty much the same thing of her: 'Germaine was a force, and that force was disorderly.'[30] In August 1924 she was briefly and somewhat reticently invited to stay with Ivens's parents in Nijmegen. When Joris was forced to return home in 1925 to look after the family business in Amsterdam, Germaine decided to 'close down the studio in order to go there' too. At the back of her mind was the thought that, 'Later, I'll be able to go to Paris.'[31] She hung out in sailors' bars but could not speak or understand Dutch. As Ivens later said, Germaine 'was like the ferment that pushed "the young Mr Ivens" into this "Bohemian" life in which they both felt capable of great things'.[32] Joris started filming in a bar frequented by 'tramps and sailors between boats'.[33] Germaine's idle wanderings in a polite and strict society where she felt no affinities and no prospects proved to be a blessing: she escaped into her photography. 'Our greatest joy was walking around the port in Rotterdam. Everything was made of steel. I loved walking along the docks to watch the boats loading and unloading. Seeing how all this worked was a new idea for me. I wanted to see them, to show the strength, I wanted them on my film.'[34] And so she started to find an outlet and personal inspiration in the cranes of Dutch ports.

A Parisian episode brought her a little distraction, and at the same time gave her a few ideas (Paris had been the setting of her happiest childhood moments). Joris offered her a few weeks in the city, so that she could spend time with her Berliner friend Elsa, a lesbian with whom she had a secret relationship – her 'only' female love affair. 'We never expected to find a room in Montmartre [Rue Becquerel] and there we were, happy and in love.'[35] Here she experienced a new way of living: views over the roofs and down into apartments, the freedom of the bistros and cabarets. When Elsa left (they would never meet again), she continued to enjoy herself. She met a man: it was 'as if I was hypnotised'. He was a crook and robbed her. She fell ill and returned to Amsterdam. 'I was still fascinated by all the iron ... I had to proceed as if I saw a part but the whole was there, part of a turning crane, and it is all there.'[36] She could not know that her future as a photographer was being played out in the docks, in front of these cranes, silos and transporter bridges that were all she wanted to photograph. A friend of the Ivens family now agreed to finance a fashion photography studio in Paris, with the condition that Germaine take on a young Italian, Luigi Diaz, as her assistant.[37]

PARISIENNE

And so, Germaine settled in Paris in late 1925: 'Back at last. Images from my childhood: Quai de la Rapée, a villa in a little garden, me climbing trees ... I am greeted by all these memories.'[38] But here she was in an uncomfortable apartment, apparently on Boulevard Malesherbes,[39] taking the kind of photographs she hated ('Neither Luigi nor I thought that the business would work').[40] However, two new acquaintances, Robert and Sonia Delanunay, got this new phase off to a very auspicious start. In 1924 Sonia Delaunay (1885–1979), whose paintings first came to attention during her Fauve period in 1908 (when she married Robert), had opened a shop, Sonia, at 19 Boulevard Malesherbes to sell the clothes, fabrics and accessories she made by printing her colourful abstract motifs on textiles. In mid-1926 Krull and Diaz opened Photos Presse Paris at 11 Avenue Junot. Their partnership appears to have endured until some time the following year. The inventory of the Delaunay archives at the BNF Prints and Photographs department includes twenty-four photographs that can be attributed to Germaine.[41] Some of the negatives are signed

29 VMD, p. 110.
30 Destanque and Ivens, op. cit., p. 76.
31 VMD, p. 113.
32 Destanque and Ivens, pp. 66–67.
33 Idem., p. 70.
34 VMD, p. 114.
35 VMD, p. 114.
36 VMD, p. 117.
37 The account given by Germaine Krull in CEDG (pp. 3–4) differs on this point. There it is Sonia Delaunay who introduces her to Luigi and orients her towards fashion photography.
38 CEDG, p. 1.
39 Germaine Krull gives her address as 'Boulevard Malherbes' (sic) in VMD, p. 118, but it is possible that she was actually nearby at 6 Avenue – or Rue – Daubigny (Paris 17th). That is the address given in the first letterhead used by Krull and Diaz. See Kim Sichel, note 7, p. 316. The Delaunays' apartment was at 19 Boulevard Malesherbes, which was at the opposite, southern end.
40 VMD, p. 118.
41 Cécile Godefroy, 'Images simultanées: les photographies de mode de Germaine Krull commandées par Sonia Delaunay', *Histoire de l'art*, no. 48, June 2001, pp. 99–113. Also, Cécile Godefroy, 'La photographie au service du simultanéisme', *Études photographiques,* 12 November 2002: http://etudesphotographiques.revues.org/322. Fifty-seven photographs are attributed to Photos Presse Paris at 11 Avenue Junot, including the ones by Krull and Diaz. See C. Godefroy, note 21. See also Anne Montfort and Cécile Godefroy, exh. cat., *Sonia Delaunay, Les couleurs de l'abstraction* (Musée d'Art Moderne de la Ville de Paris), Paris: Paris Musées, 2014.

with a rather emphatic 'Krull' in ink. A number of the images seem awkward in their attempt to capture the textile patterns, occasionally with other fabrics in the background, probably in keeping with Sonia's indications and in the environment that she so passionately created for them. These could be described as fashion photos of the kind being produced by others at the time, more artistically or professionally (Steichen and Man Ray, to name but two), views which isolated the garment and highlighted the forms. Germaine was certainly not attracted by the designs, and she loathed the bourgeois, aristocratic milieu of Sonia's clientele.[42] Still, the photos were published in magazines that took an interest in fashion as well as in modern textile production, which was particularly dynamic in Europe in the 1920s.[43] Some of the images are more sophisticated and reveal growing skill in lighting and posing the models, especially when the latter are actresses or dancers, such as Violetta Napierskaand, above all, Lizica Codreano,[44] who both played in *Le P'tit Parigot*, the film by René Le Somptier (1926) for which Sonia Delaunay designed the costumes. Codreano appears twice, fetchingly posed, with her hands carefully placed and wearing special make-up, and in a Delaunay dress. These are not 'fashion' photos but portraits of an artist, designed to reflect her personality, or 'simultaneist' artworks (to borrow Sonia Delaunay's term).[45] The prints, moreover, are excellent. In other photographs of Delaunay models, the attention to posture and, above all, the principle of cast shadow on a bare wall, emerge as Krull's stylistic hallmark. Evidently, she was recalling the insights of her Berlin days and adapting them to a Parisian artistic milieu that was receptive to all kinds of innovations and rapid change. Germaine had plenty of work,[46] but she was bored in 'this Magdalene-like sadness' – 'this conception of photography' that put her 'behind the black cloth' of her camera, 'a great big wooden camera on a tripod'. 'Photography simply could not go on being static like that.'[47] Soon, she would leave the studio to Luigi Diaz.[48]

Robert Delaunay was the other face of Germaine's Parisian good fortune, providing her with some serious photographic prospects when she showed him her 'photos of ironwork' – what she called her *fers* – in Amsterdam and Rotterdam. After the disappointment of presenting her pictures to the very serious, smart and pictorialist Société Française de Photographie, where they were criticised because the camera was 'not in line' with the image, 'Robert threw his arms round me, took my photos and showed them to all his friends there.' He also promised to exhibit them alongside his own works at the coming Salon d'Automne.[49] The co-founder of Simultaneism (based on colour contrasts), Robert Delaunay (1885–1941) represented the same artistic tendencies as Sonia and his artistic development had followed a similar path, but his themes tended more towards the technological, notably aeroplanes, embodying speed and movement (*Homage to Blériot*, 1913–14), and the Eiffel Tower (*Eiffel Tower with Trees*, 1910; *Red Eiffel Tower*, 1911), a subject he returned to in the 1920s with high- and low-angle views of the Tower that were more decorative and larger in format. In 1926 and 1927 he was working on variants inspired by aerial views of the Tower and the gardens around it. Photos by Krull (1926) show him on a ladder on his studio, working on one of these large-format paintings.

Robert Delaunay's encouragement proved decisive for Germaine. He also took her to the home of his Romanian friends, Roma and Arthur Aron, who had a luxurious apartment near the Vert Galant. There she met a 'young man of extraordinary beauty . . . with an ironic smile playing about his lips', 'a Greek profile and brown eyes expressing a goodness that almost hurt'.[50] His name was Eli Lotar, and he was the son of the Romanian poet Tudor Arghezi. Born in Paris, he had just returned from a trip to Bucharest. 'I could not resist him,' wrote Germaine. He would be her companion for two years. They lived in a hotel on Place Émile Goudeau (location of the Bateau-Lavoir painters' studios) in Montmartre. Lotar 'quickly learned the craft of photography'. He was meticulous, patient (much more so than Germaine, she said), and had 'a natural eye for detail'. He also had a passion for laboratory work (development, printing), and could stay

42 'The women she dressed looked a bit like advertising hoardings.' VMD, p. 118.
43 *Bilder Courier, Frankfurter Zeitung* and its supplement *Für die Frau, Die schöne Frau, Textil- Revue, Minerva, Blanco y Negro*, etc. according to Sonia Delaunay's press albums. See C. Godefroy, op. cit.
44 Lizica Codreano had a brief career in the Parisian avant-garde from 1922 to 1926. She danced to the *Gymnopédies* by Erik Satie in Brancusi's studio, with costumes by Brancusi (1922), played in *Cœur à gaz* by Tristan Tzara at the *Soirée du Cœur à barbe*, with costumes by Sonia Delaunay, at the Théâtre Michel (1923). See Doïna Lemny, *Lizica Codreano, une danseuse roumaine dans l'avant-garde parisienne*, Lyon: Fage Éditions, 2011.
45 This is not the costume for *Le P'tit Parigot*, where she dances the role of Pierrot Eclair, a costume with zigzag trousers and a big floppy collar. Fonds Delaunay, BNF, Department of Prints and Photography.
46 Possibly for other companies: a Max fur appears in *Revue de la femme*, February 1928, no. 14, p. 23, 'Symphonie en noir et blanc'. A zebra skin has been placed on the stairs.
47 CEDG, pp. 4–5.
48 Luigi Diaz was still active in 1935, when his work appeared in issue no. 14 of a hairdresser's publication, *Antoine Document*, Paris: Tolmer, 1935
49 VMD, p. 7. There is no documentary evidence that this actually happened. It certainly seems unlikely.
50 CEDG, p. 9, and VMD, p. 121.

51 CEDG, p. 9.
52 Annick Lionel-Marie et al, *Eli Lotar* (Musée National d'Art Moderne, Paris), Paris: Centre Georges Pompidou, 1993. In practical terms, they had two rooms in the same hotel, one of which served as a laboratory. With the money from her fashion photos Krull bought 'a small enlarger and three baths'. CEDG, p. 9.
53 Marriage contract dated 10 March 1927, Amsterdam. Marriage papers, certificate no. 552, town hall of the 18th arrondissement. Passports, recorded at the Préfecture de Police de Paris, 2 May 1927, Archives GKN, Essen. The French papers state, however, that 'there is no prenuptial contract'. The divorce was pronounced at Ivens's request in Chihuahua in August 1941.
54 VMD, p 124.

up whole nights doing it.[51] The combination of their talents was a real strength ('we were very complementary'), and they soon came to form a duo that was free of rivalry, working both in reportage and modernist photography. They published in the same magazines and appeared in the same exhibitions.[52] They remained lifelong friends, as can be seen from the extant correspondence. Gradually, however, Lotar began taking steps towards cinema, which interested him more than photography, doing so under the influence and with the support of none other than Joris Ivens.

It so happened that when Germaine met Eli she was planning to marry Joris, both because of the strength of their relationship (it appears that they took it in turns to travel between Amsterdam and Paris in 1926–27, and no doubt beyond), and because of Germaine's passport needs due to Germany's cession of the region where she was born to Poland in 1919. Despite all the scruples and prevarications on Germaine's part (and not Joris's), the wedding – now considered a 'marriage of convenience' – was held in Paris on 2 April 1927 (a contract allowing for separate possessions and homes had been drawn up in Amsterdam on 10 March 1927), giving Madame Germaine Krull-Ivens a Dutch passport, which she would keep all her life. She was now registered as a journalist.[53] Germaine felt some remorse but deplored the effects of her own 'temperament': 'He had built a life with me, and me, I had no life to build.' Joris told her about his film projects. He and Lotar became friends. Lotar was even hired as cameraman on two Ivens films in 1930 (*Wij Bouwen* [We Are Building] and *Zuyderzee*).

Through Eli, and also because of her improved personal circumstances, Germaine entered another milieu, the world of painters and writers. She frequented the Deux Magots, where she 'discussed the fate of the world' and she also met filmmakers such as René Clair, Alberto Cavalcanti and Luis Bunuel.[54] Photographers, however, 'were not true members of the gang, because they were not artists and not painters'. And yet, 'When I went with my *fers* they all exclaimed and admired.' While we are familiar with Lotar's work from 1927 – this included production stills on films – it is difficult to know what Germaine was doing at this time. 'Dreams and not always enough to eat.' Perhaps, when the opportunity arose, she was getting on with her *fers* in Holland? Joris sent money, Roma Aron gave money, and Eli borrowed.

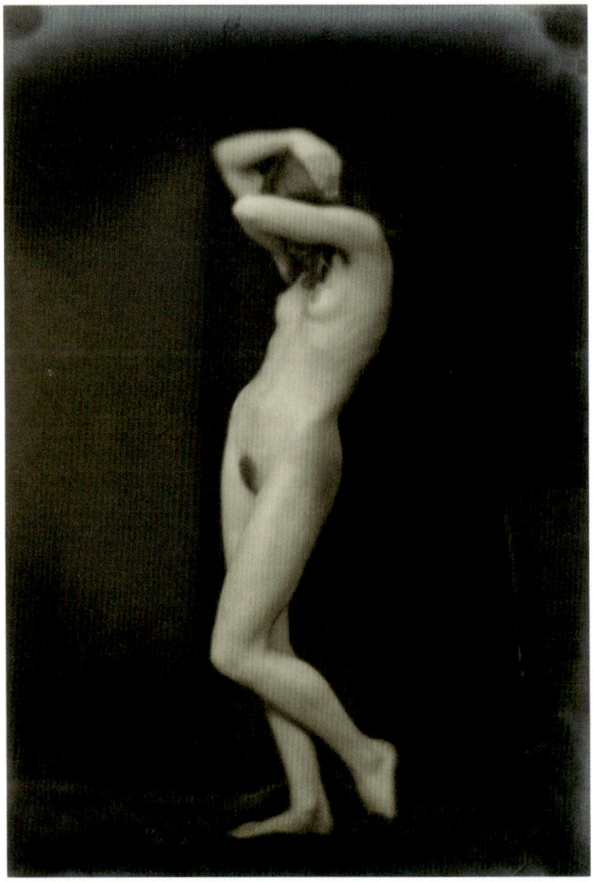

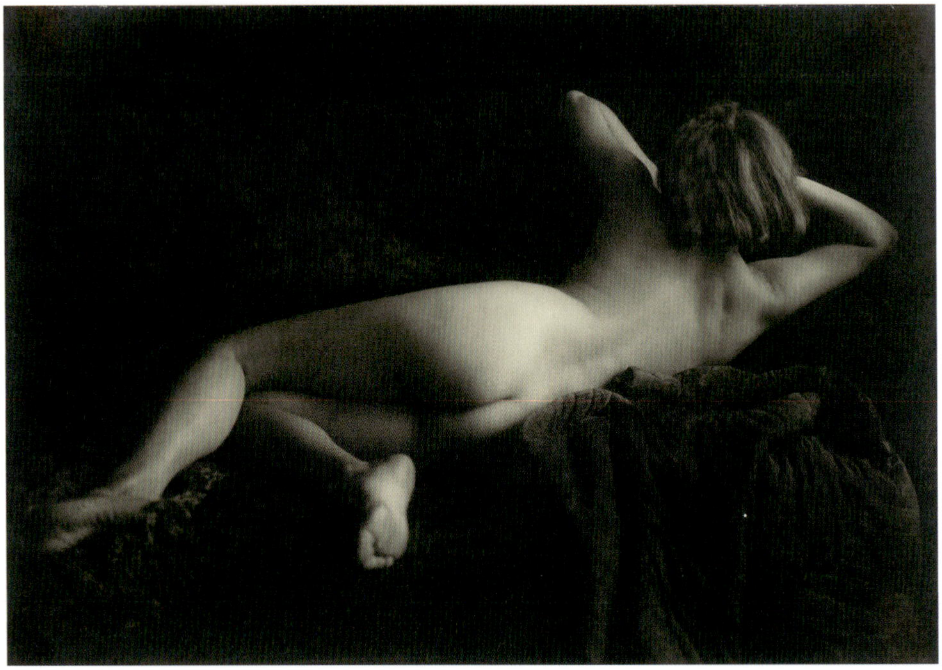

Plates from **Dämmerstunden-6 Aufnahmen weiblicher Akte**, c. 1923

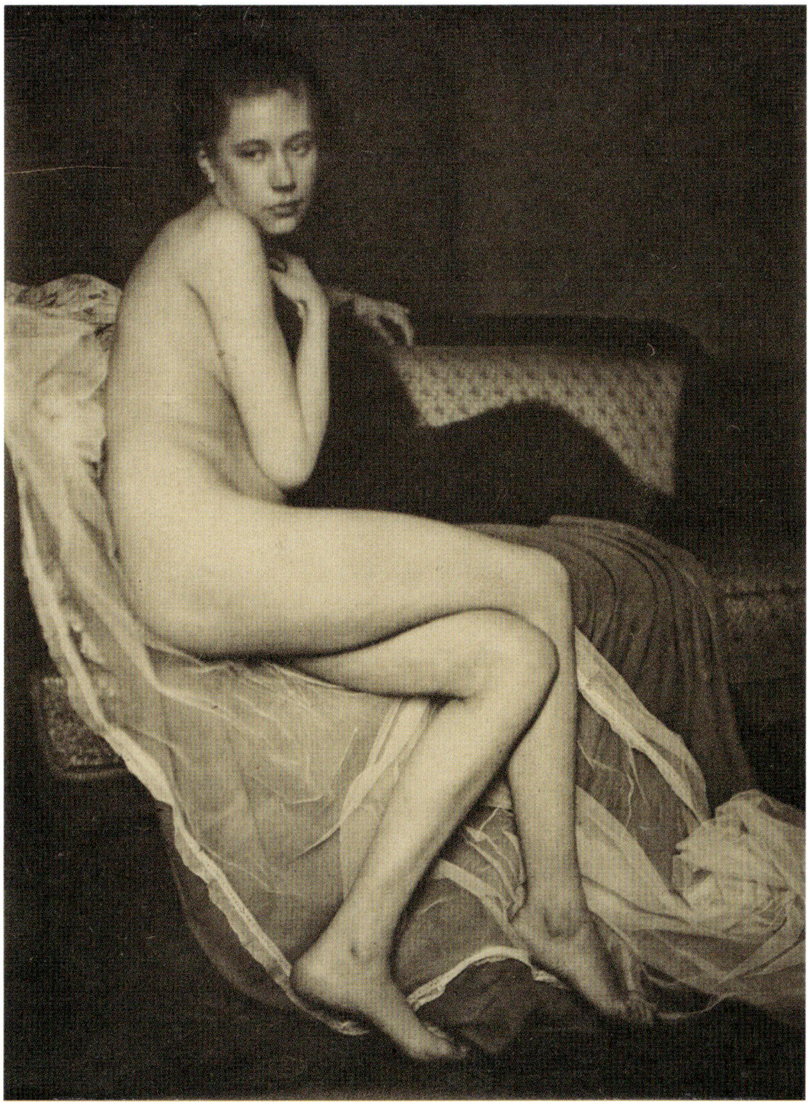

Plate from ***Der Akt, Zwanzig photographische Aufnahmen weiblicher Körper nach der Natur***, 1918

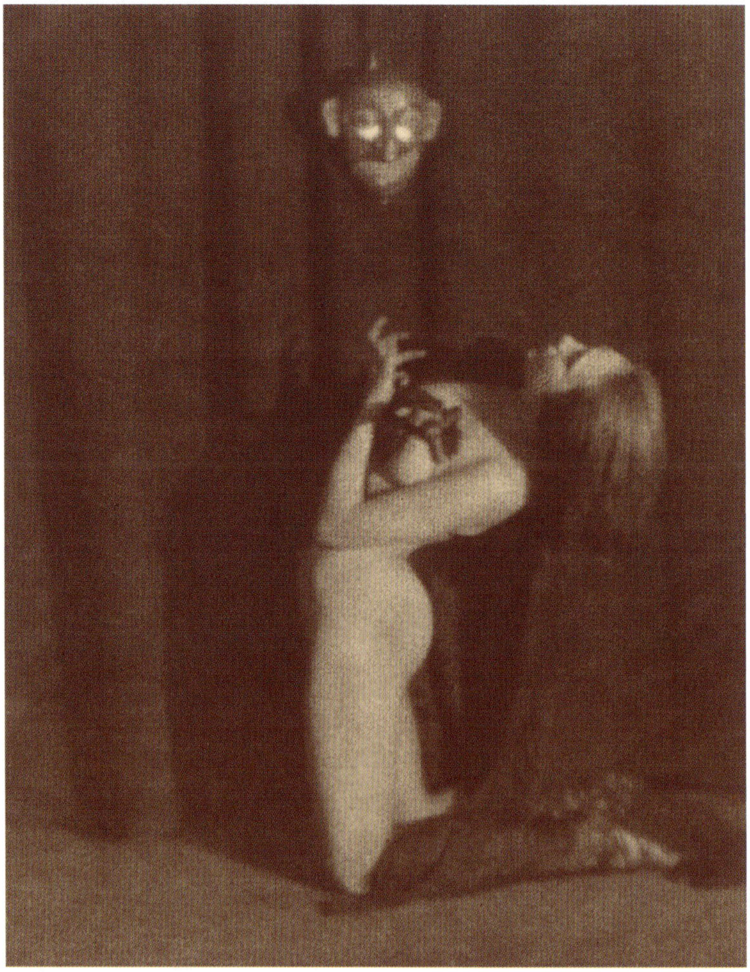

Dance Study with Mask II, in *Spuk*, 1923

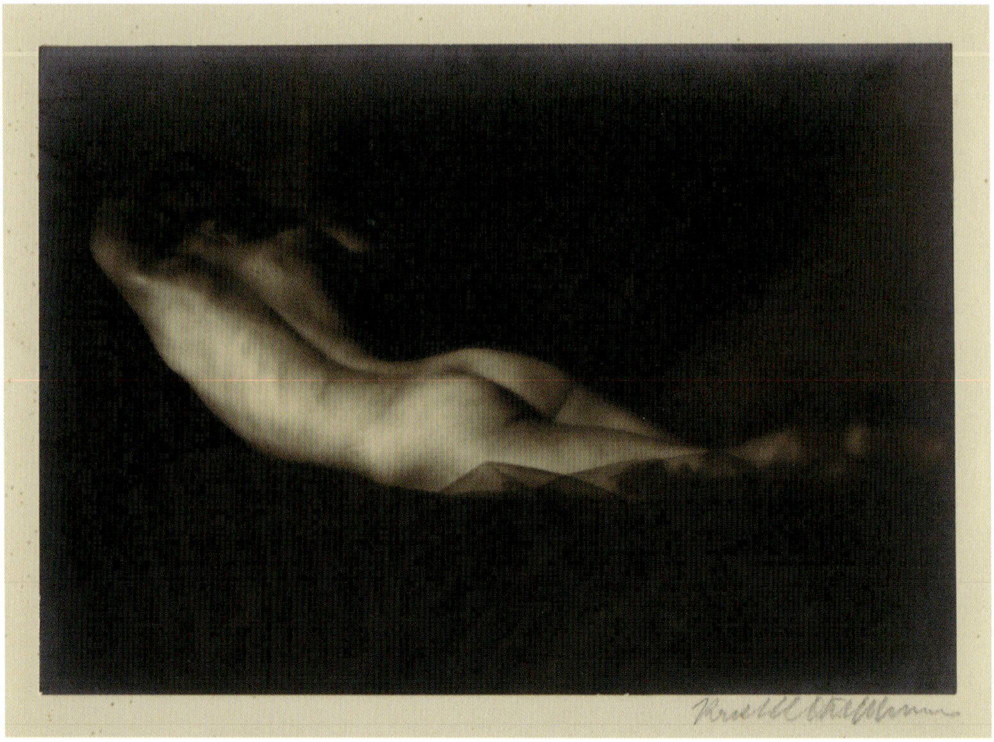

Krull-Hübschmann (attributed to), **Reclining Nude**, 1919

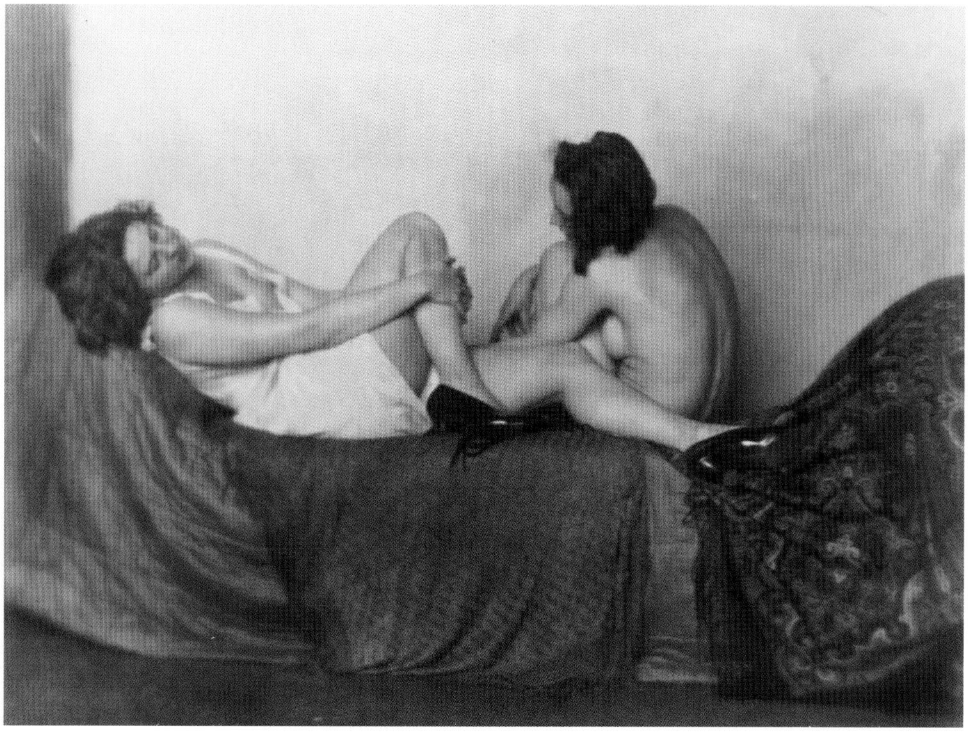

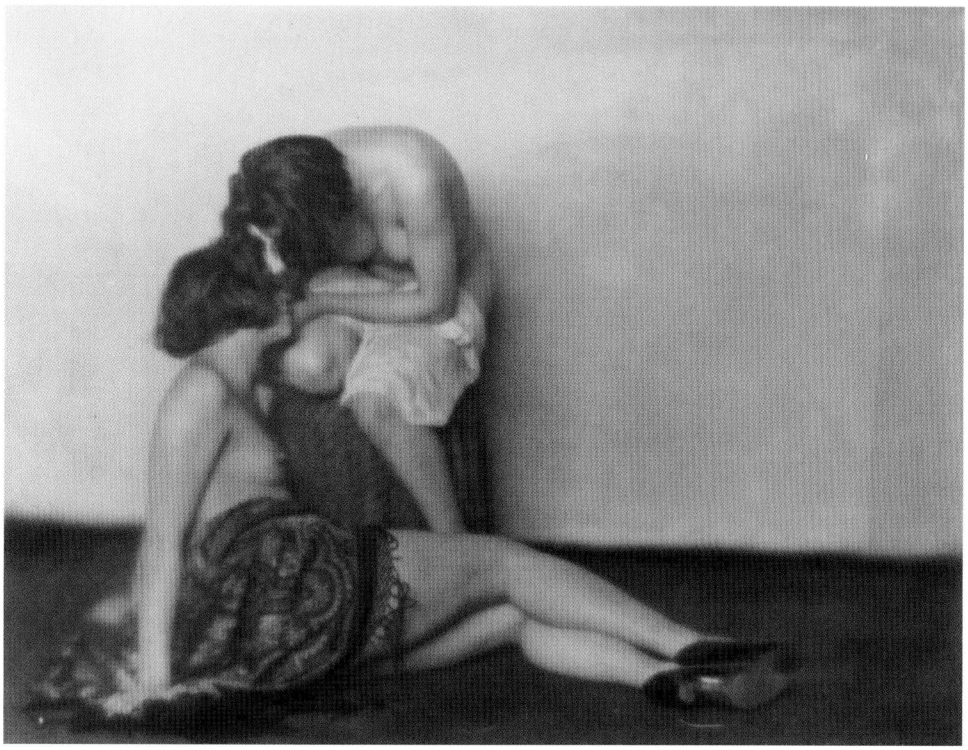

Nudes, 1924

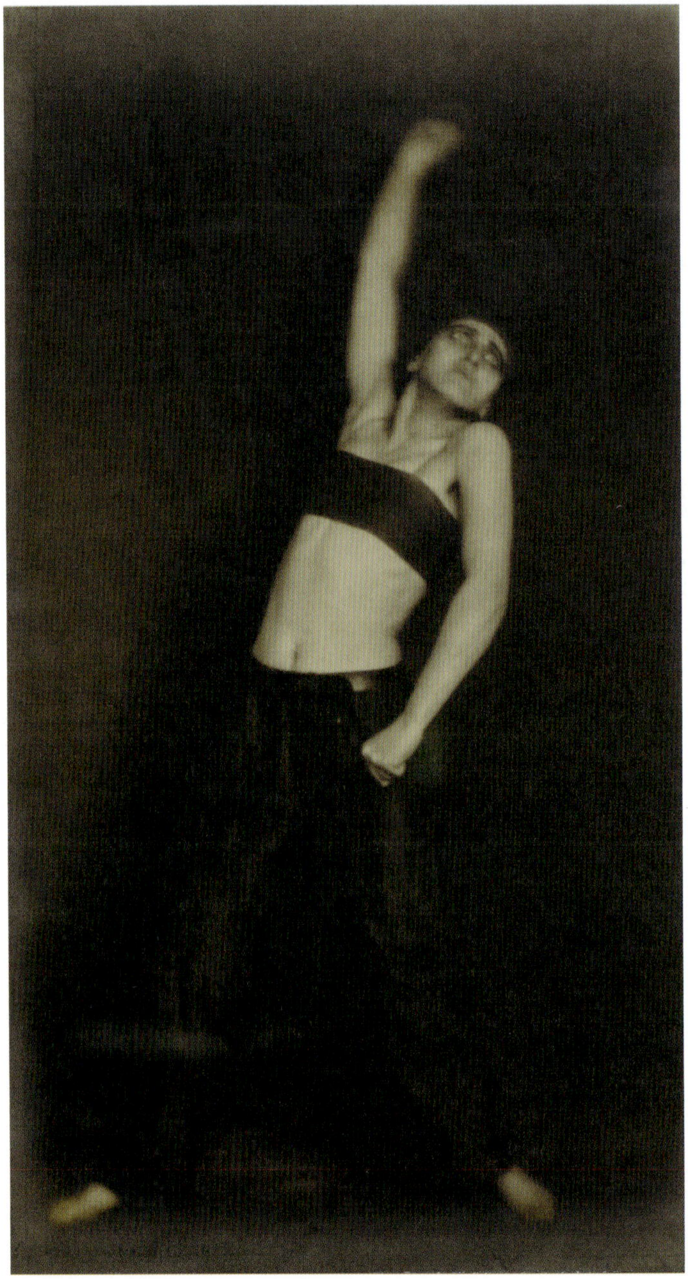

The Dancer Jo Mihaly Dancing 'Revolution', 1925

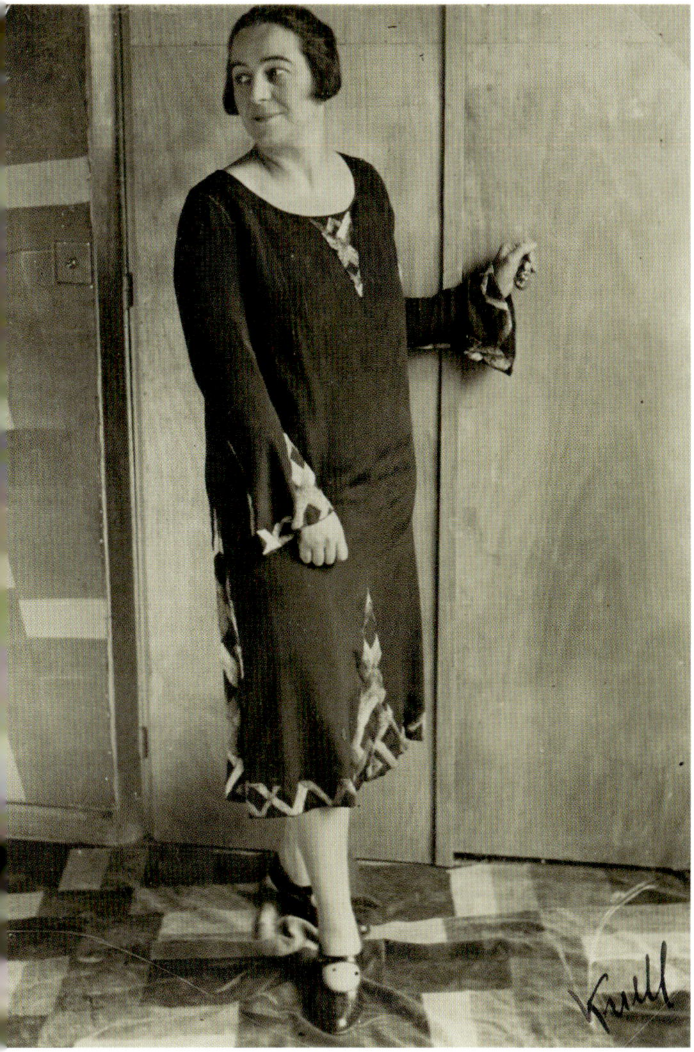

Sonia Delaunay, 1925

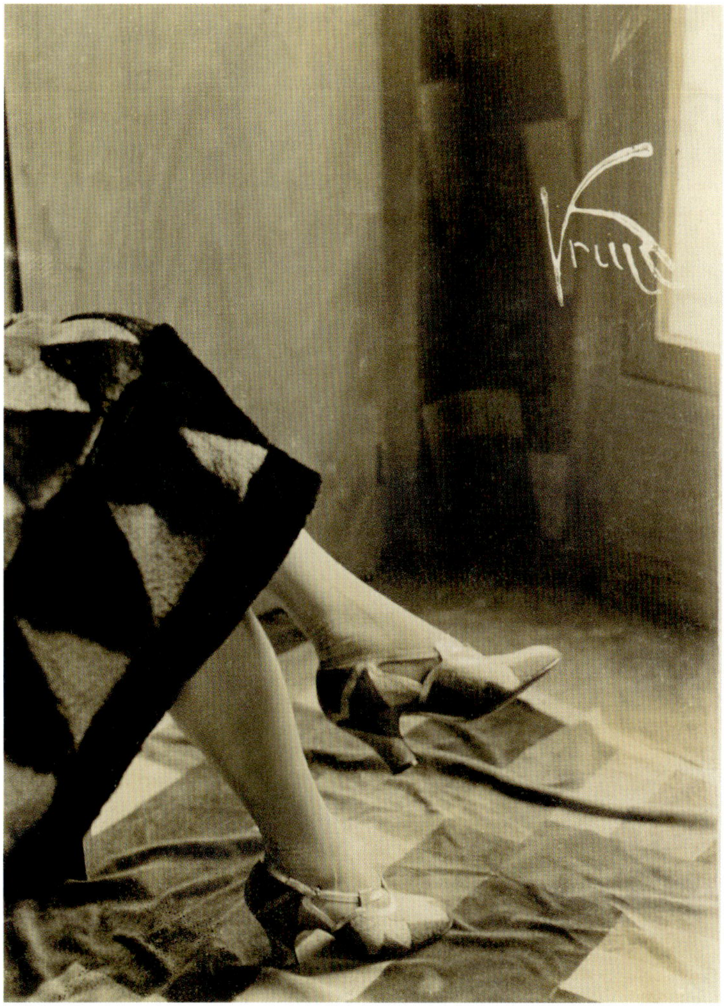

Sonia Delaunay Showing One of Her Dresses, 1925

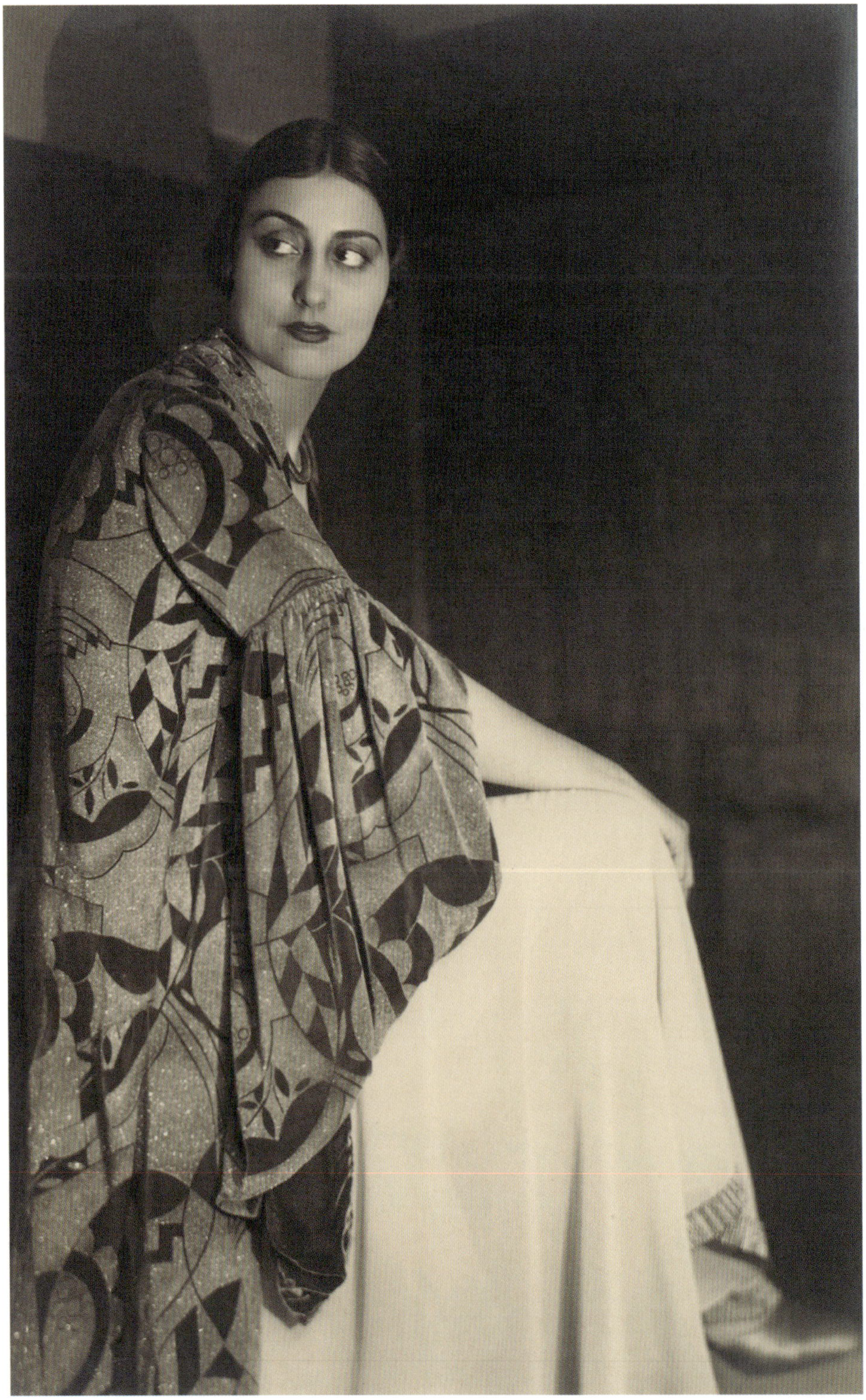

Demaria Wearing a Model by Sonia Delaunay, 1926

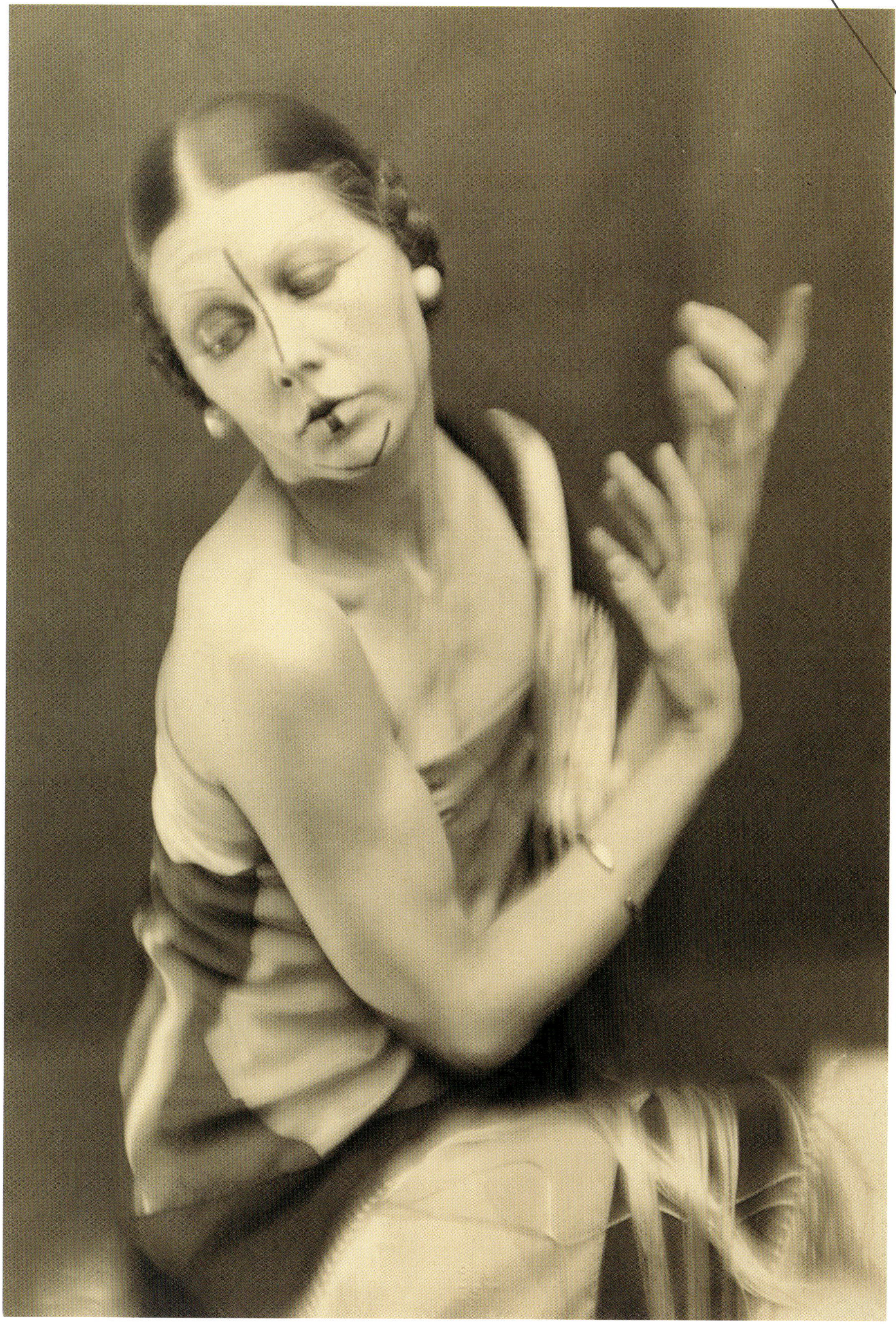

Lizica Codreano in a Dress by Sonia Delaunay, 1926

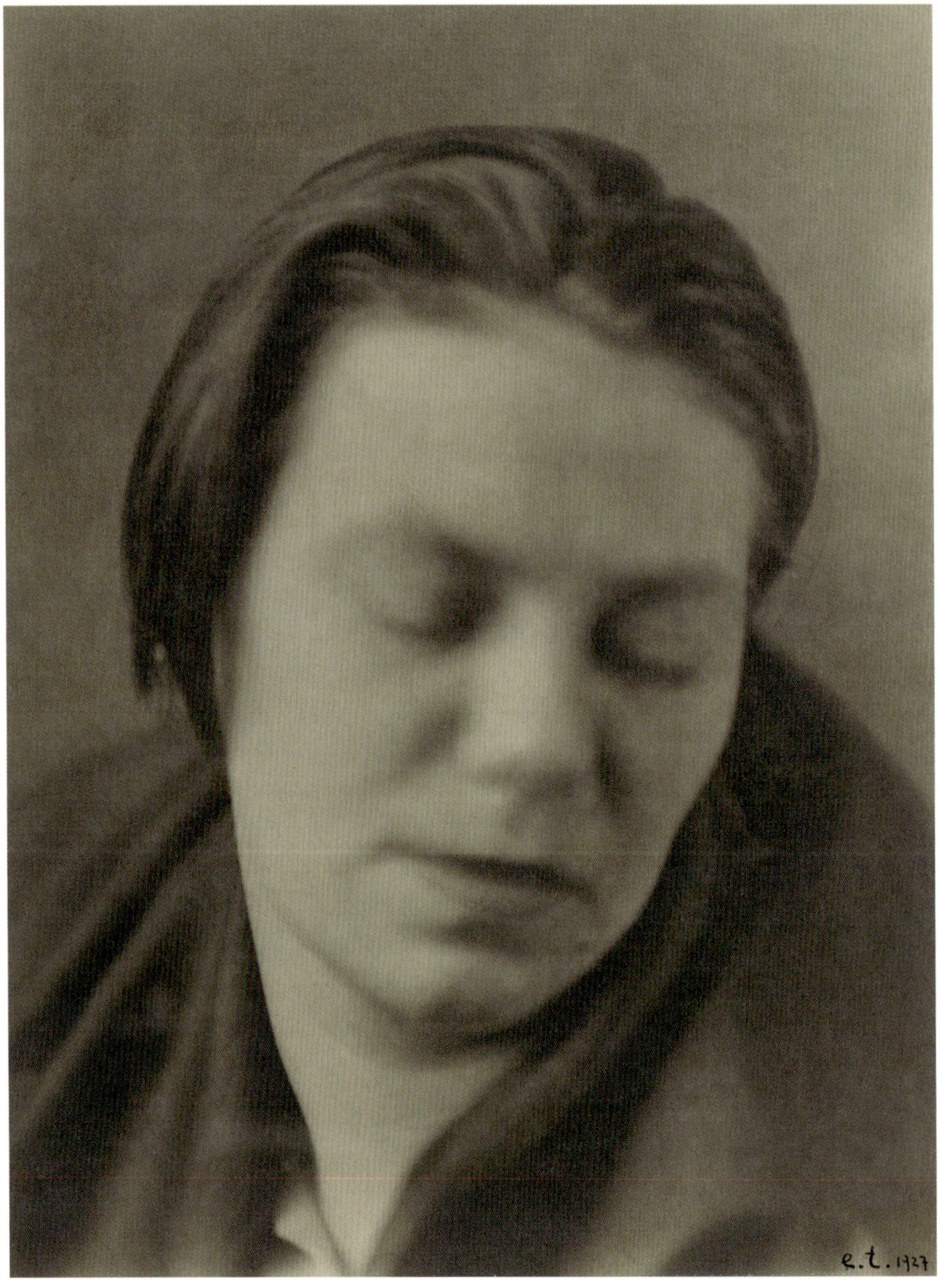

Eli Lotar, **Portrait of Germaine Krull**, Paris, 1927

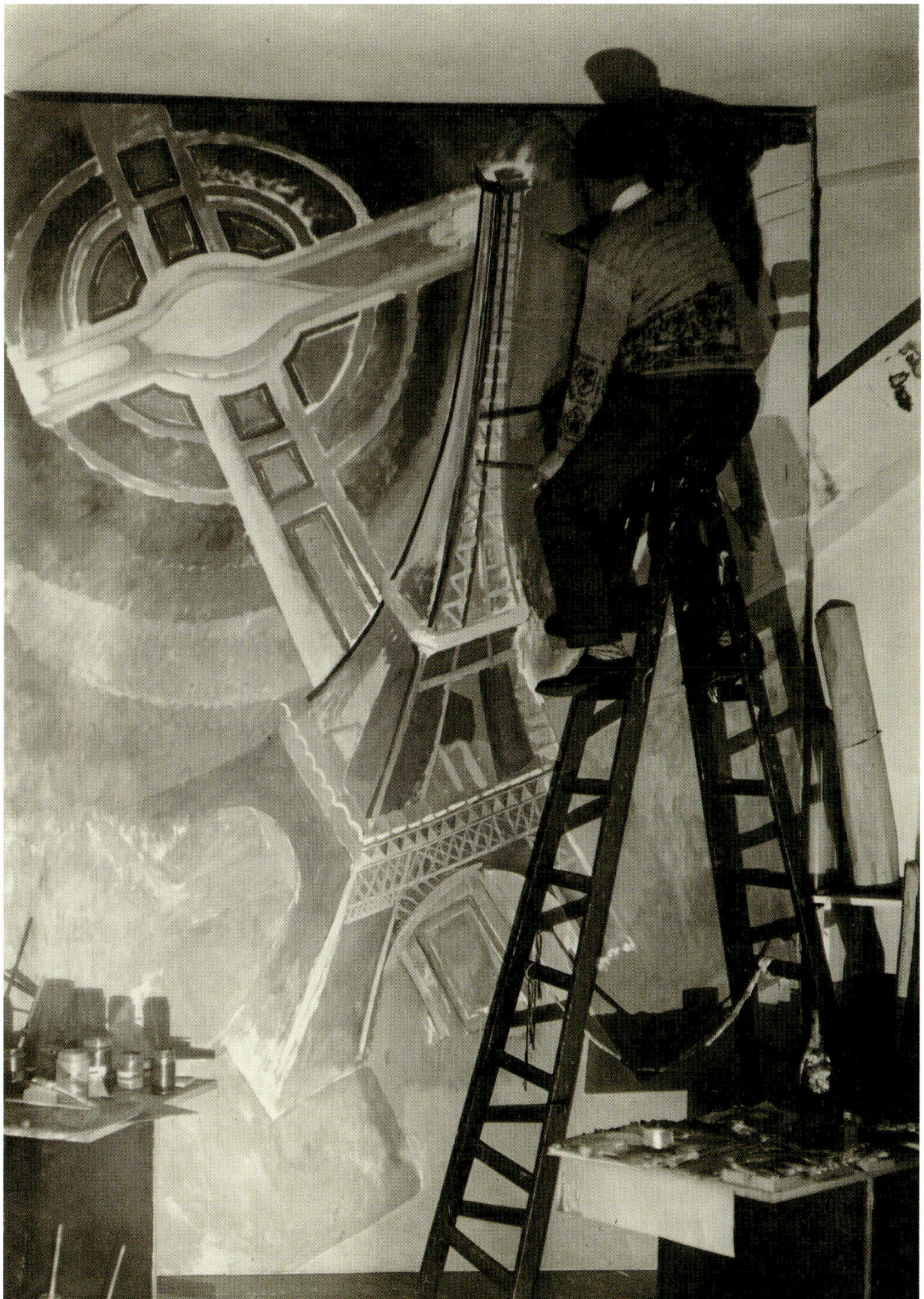

'Interior', Robert Delaunay, 1926

1928: *VU* AND 'MY *FERS*'

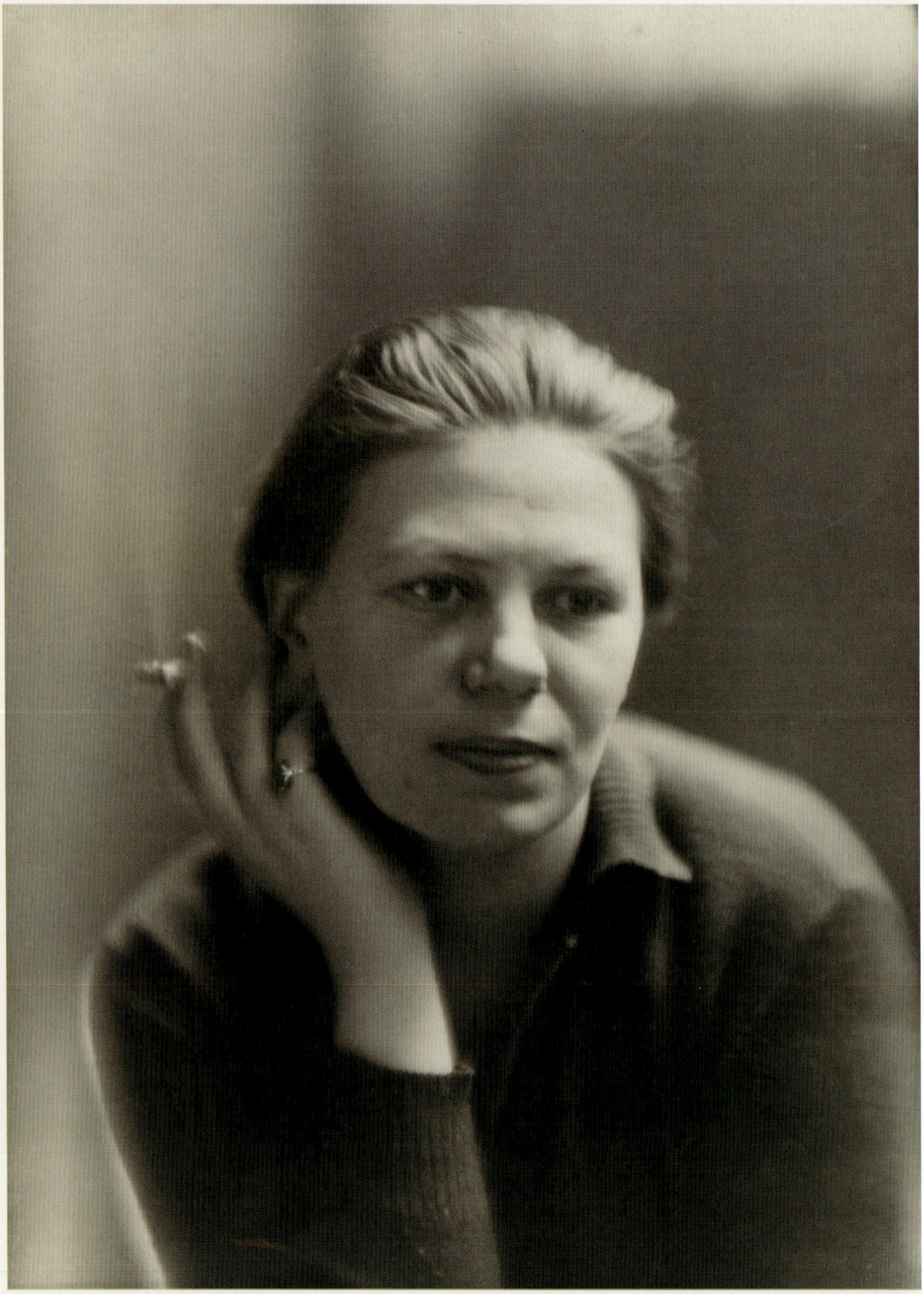

1 CEDG, p. 12. Germaine recalls that it was [Edmond] Gréville who announced the news around a table in a café. Gréville was one of the contributors to *VU*. He wrote the cinema column and made a film for its launch, promoting *VU* as 'a great, modern illustrated newspaper'.
2 VMD, p. 124.
3 CEDG, p. 12.
4 Idem.
5 VMD, p. 125.
6 VMD, p. 125: 'We made the first issue of *VU* together and it was very fine.' CEDG, p. 12. 'Our first issue is ready' (Vogel).
7 *UHU*, December 1927, pp. 106–111. Four photos according to Kim Sichel.
8 Michel Frizot and Cédric de Veigy, *VU, The Story of a Magazine,* New York: Thames and Hudson, 2009.

THE MAGAZINE *VU*

For Germaine Krull, one event in particular promised salvation, like 'a morning cry'. This was the announcement of plans to launch a major magazine illustrated with photographs, *VU*. Lucien Vogel was the 'big man who had decided to produce a big illustrated magazine' – 'and he wanted to do it with lots of photos. It was just what we needed.'[1] Germaine and Eli met this publisher of *Le Jardin des Modes*, elegantly dressed in a light grey suit. 'He was looking for youngsters. He had seen my *fers*.'[2] He wanted the Eiffel Tower done the same way as the '*fers*': at once, for the first issue. Germaine asked for money to take the Métro and go up the tower, because she was 'skint' and a bit reluctant: 'The Tower itself is quite handsome, but nothing special. It doesn't inspire me like the iron structures in Amsterdam . . . that black mass of lifeless iron.'[3]

Certainly, the architectural language of the Eiffel Tower was very different. It did not move and had no mechanical or industrial function. It was an abstract structure, with nothing animal about it. Germaine recalls passing a 'no entry' sign and discovering, with Eli Lotar, the lift machinery, the wheels, the cables, the pistons and the shaky staircases that she captured with her faithful Icarette. 'The tangles of iron, that lacework of little iron pieces that served as decoration, seen against the light, it was like giant spiders . . . The iron was alive.'[4] 'The Tower became beautiful in the laboratory of our little room.' Vogel 'was delighted and kissed me and showed them to everyone. I had arrived! And so had *VU*.'[5] The retrospective enthusiasm of Germaine's memoirs may gloss over the reality at the time,[6] for some of these photographs of the Eiffel Tower were taken before the end of 1927 – they were published in *UHU* in December that year.[7] And, for all their future success, they simply did not appear in the first issue of *VU*. Indeed, it was not until issue no. 11 that the magazine included a full page about the Eiffel Tower, featuring three of her photos.

Nevertheless, the creation of *VU* and her relationship with Lucien Vogel were a real boon for Krull: her work appeared in the first four issues. She was part of the team of dynamic young modernist photographers assembled by Vogel, a punchy trio formed by Germaine Krull, André Kertész and Eli Lotar, with Man Ray as guide and Surrealist sanction, and James Abbé for his experience in photojournalism. The first issue came out on 21 March 1928 (there would be some seven hundred in all, ending in May 1940, including special issues).[8] Its editorial promised 'pages packed with photographs' and a 'new formula: illustrated news from around the world'. What made *VU* so extraordinarily original, and unique in 1928, was this abundance of photographs. They were on every page, which was new for the press. The front page was always photographic (at first with a white margin, then full page as of March 1930) and the magazine organised the news ('Vu cette semaine' – seen this week) into sections: science, history, sport, cinema, theatre. It always contained at least one in-depth report. The unifying principle was to have a selection of surprising and, in terms of tone, highly varied photographs, challenging the reader on every page. *VU* also innovated in the various ways it juxtaposed photographs and text (the text of the article, drawn titles, caption blocks), evoking the movement of film

Self-portrait, Paris, 1927

('lively like a fine film'). The magazine was launched by Edmond Gréville's film *Un grand journal illustré moderne*, shown during Gaumont newsreels. Photography was to chronicle contemporary events and match the 'brisk rhythm of modern life'.[9]

The other novelty, not trumpeted but highly visible nevertheless, was the new printing technique: rotogravure, instead of halftone, with bistre rather than black ink. This technical revolution, which would spread to many other magazines, permitted a subtlety of photographic gradation that did justice to the qualities of the medium. Above all, it introduced new possibilities for layout, with the montage of autonomous elements – photographs, text, titles and captions – which were now available on sheets of transparent celluloid that could be cut up and freely assembled on a double page. The light table used for this montage replaced the typographer's 'stone' used for metal 'plates', making the layout process extremely flexible and dynamic, giving it a narrative potential drawing on the contents of the photographic images. Under the direction of Irène Lidova, the page designs were carefully composed, sometimes in advance. Instead of repetitive, standardised configurations, each double page had its own dynamic, inspired by its contents, and in particular the nature of the photographs and the subject. The great originality of *VU* lay in the free, energetic visual design of the articles, organised around the choice of photos and their montage in the space of the double page (often close to Constructivist photomontage), the distribution of the columns of text, and the inventive graphics of the (drawn) titles.

These new conceptions brought into being a new profession: 'photo-reporter'. This was quite different from the job of the 'press photographer' working for a daily newspaper, which had existed since the turn of the century, and which involved covering political and other news on a daily basis and hurrying to supply the paper with one or two photos. These photographers might also supply images to an agency, which would then distribute them nationally or internationally. Major international agencies, including Keystone, were set up in the late 1920s, some of them in Paris, to cater to the demand generated by the creation of *VU* (which made abundant use of agency photographs). These photographers used view cameras with tripods or relatively unwieldy hand-held cameras with medium-format plates (13 x 18 cm). They would take only one or two pictures of an event in a neutral style, with no latitude for personal viewpoints – indeed, their photographs were not signed.

In contrast, *VU* set out to promote a new kind of reportage, a more lively and dynamic style for illustrated magazines, with series of photographs on a subject chosen in advance by the editors, to be published alongside text from a selected author. Sometimes, the photographer and journalist/reporter went out on the assignment together. This is why Lucien Vogel immediately contacted Kertész, Krull and Lotar, who had no agency links, worked without set formulae and followed a modernist aesthetic using handier, small-format plate or film cameras (4.5 x 6 to 6.5 x 9 cm, small Klapps, folding cameras). New, brighter or more precise cameras of this kind, the Leica and the Ermanox, appeared in the 1920s, and were taken up by all those who wanted to deal directly with the 'modern' subjects of everyday life, and therefore needed speed and flexibility. It would seem that Germaine had acquired her 6 x 9 cm Icarette film camera when in the Netherlands – no doubt through Ivens.[10] It appears in her famous self-portrait 'dated' 1925:[11] 'It was a simple camera, an amateur's camera, which I carried with me for years.'[12] She was therefore well prepared to form, with her two colleagues Kertész and Lotar, the brigade that would pioneer this new reportage based on the forward-looking alliance between editors, art directors, a photographer and an author, to create a new journalistic and photographic style that was set for a glorious future. In her memoires (1981), Krull recalls that with Man Ray and Kertész she formed 'the team that created *VU* and gave photography the appearance it has today'.[13]

9 'Remarques sur un nouveau journal illustré', *VU*, no. 1, pp. 11–12, reproduced in full in Frizot-de Veigy, op. cit., pp. 300–301. Stills from Gréville's film: pp. 298–299.
10 'I was in Berlin and I was in Dresden, with Ica and Ernemann' (on an internship), Ivens in Destanque and Ivens, op. cit., p. 43.
11 It was Germaine Krull who provided this information, but the date remains uncertain.
12 VMD, p. 125. The Icarette came in several sizes (500/1, 501, 502). Since 1919 it had been made by Ica AG Dresden, using lenses by Zeiss. The only one in which all the elements surrounding the lens, as well as the metal viewfinder frame, are exactly the same as one in the self-portrait is the Icarette II, which can be seen on www.kl-riess.dk/goerz.html and http://click-clack.fr/piwigo/picture.php?/444. The former dates it to 'around 1926', the latter to 1926. It is indicated for plates and films 6 x 9, roll 120. Carl Zeiss Jena Tessar lens, 1:4.5, f = 10.5cm. The Icarette II 500/1 dated 1926, film, 6 x 9, has the same frame but not the same lens board or release (www.emtus.ch).
13 VMD, p. 127.

THE *FERS* AND THEIR PUBLICATION

As early as its third issue *VU* demonstrated its interest in industrial architecture with a central double-page spread titled 'Steel'. While it included no photograph by Krull, a text by Florent Fels did herald future developments.[14] Vogel's interest in the Eiffel Tower, and the photographs published in issue number 11, brought Krull's career to a turning point. The layout was itself significant: in keeping with *VU*'s graphic concept, photos were not just simple illustrations, but became elements of a more sophisticated mental understanding. Under the title 'In All Its Strength', the three interlocking images, interpenetrating and forming a single body, guide the eye up towards the summit, propelled by robust wheels. The bottom page, the shadow of the Tower on the ground, invites viewers to imagine themselves up at the top, *where we see from*. The images on this page anticipate Roland Barthes's analysis of the Tower as playing the role of 'pure signifier, i.e., of a form in which men unceasingly put meaning'. For him, 'The Tower ... transgresses this separation, this habitual divorce of *seeing* and *being seen*; it achieves a sovereign circulation between the two functions; it is a complete object which has, if one may say so, both sexes of sight.'[15] Other artists had captured the power of this signifier some time before Krull: Robert Delaunay (1909–11, then 1925–26), Apollinaire with a *calligramme* in 1914, René Clair in *Paris qui dort* (1923), and Moholy-Nagy and Sigfried Giedion, who ascended the tower in 1925 and both took photographs.[16] In 1921 a ballet by The Six, with a libretto by Jean Cocteau, made the tower a romantic, if not for the time being poetic object. Most importantly, it had served as a military transmitter and was later home to the first TSF (radio) broadcasts, with Radio Tour Eiffel in February 1922 followed by Radio Paris in 1924.

If Krull was not yet fully aware of the tower's imaginary and visual resonance, she understood its intuitive visual impact on all who saw it. For all the strangeness of her photos, she saw that it made what she called her *fers* (photos of cranes, port scenes and transporter bridges in the Netherlands) more accessible. The Eiffel Tower helped reveal the qualities of its metal cousins in the Netherlands, as well, soon, as other French relations that were to hand but did not particularly interest photographers or writers. It was now that Krull became the great poet of iron structures, of cranes and, by extension, machines, turbines, steel and, even more generally, 'metal'. In 1927 and 1928 she continued to photograph these 'metal giants' that she first noticed in the docks at Amsterdam because they moved. 'Those steel monsters that moved on their own and unloaded huge crates or bundles onto other monsters' had 'revealed something that made me love photography' and gave her an 'irresistible desire to capture them, to get near them, and perhaps to make them more human'.[17] The many photographs she took of the transporter bridge at Rotterdam in early 1928 came out because of *The Bridge* (*De Brug*), the film that Joris started making there in late 1927 and completed in spring 1928.[18] Krull's metal mania thus found public outlet thanks to the Tower, which itself became an object of contemplation six months before its fortieth birthday (1889–1929).

The great photographic event concomitant with and indirectly linked to the creation of *VU* was the organisation of the first – and, as it turned out, last – Salon Indépendant de la Photographie Moderne, held on the staircase of the Comédie des Champs-Elysées theatre from 24 May to 7 June 1928. The selection committee comprised Lucien Vogel, publisher of *VU*, Florent Fels, editor of the influential modernist magazine *L'Art vivant*, Georges Charensol, an art critic who wrote for the journal, film director René Clair and journalist Jean Prévost. Celebrated in the history of photography as the first gathering and exhibition of modernist photography in France, it lasted two weeks. Although its impact was limited, this Salon de l'Escalier, as it became known, was of interest first of all because of its chosen venue, the Comédie des Champs-Elysées at 15 Avenue Montaigne (and not the adjoining Théâtre, on its left), which had been directed by Louis Jouvet since 1925.[19] It was here that Darius Milhaud's ballet *Le Bœuf sur le toit* had

14 *VU* no. 3, 4 April 1928, pp. 70–71, with five photos by Gutschow and three photos by Weiss. This may be where the idea for the *Métal* portfolio came from, for the text by Fels is a rough version of the *Métal* preface: 'this is how steel can be rehabilitated' (in terms of its social uses).

15 'The Eiffel Tower', Susan Sontag (ed.), *A Barthes Reader*, New York: Hill and Want, 1983, p. 238.

16 I take these examples from David Travis, 'In and of the Eiffel Tower', *Art Institute of Chicago Museum Studies*, 1987, vol. 13, no. 1, pp. 5–23. See also Olivier Lugon in *Le Pont transbordeur de Marseille*, Moholy-Nagy, Institut National d'Histoire de l'Art, Collège International de Philosophie, Éditions Ophrys, 2013.

17 CEDG, p. 6.

18 'In spring 1928 I showed the film to my friends of the Filmliga' (an association founded in September 1927). Ivens, in Destanque and Ivens, op. cit., p. 74.

19 This building by Auguste Perret was inaugurated in 1913. Considered the finest modern theatre of the 1920s, the ensemble comprised the Théâtre, Comédie, and Studio des Champs-Élysées (the Studio was directed by Gaston Baty from 1924 to 1928).

been presented in 1920 and that Jouvet directed *Siegfried* by Jean Giraudoux in 1928. As for the Théâtre, it had witnessed the premiere of *The Rite of Spring* by the Ballets Russes in 1913 and was the home of the Ballets Suédois. The Salon de l'Escalier is of interest also because of its organisers, who made it resonant, and first of all Vogel and Fels (Krull says she had the idea and suggested it to Louis Jouvet).[20] Under the banner of two photographic forefathers, the portraitist Nadar and Eugène Atget, the 'documenter' of Paris (who had died in 1927, and in those days was still misspelt Adget, and of whose work a 'retrospective' had been announced), it presented the new modernist generation, most of them non-French photographers who had recently settled in Paris: Berenice Abbott, André Kertész, d'Ora, George Hoyningen-Huene (Studio Vogue-Paris), Germaine Krull-Ivens, Man Ray, Paul Outerbridge and (a Parisian) Laure Albin Guillot.

The great merit of the Salon de l'Escalier was to have started a movement, based on a non-pictorialist idea of photography that adhered to a strict practice of the medium, without reference to painting and eschewing non silver-based printing techniques, known as pigment printing. In reaction to the soporific Salon International d'Art Photographique put on by the Société Française de Photographie, the custodian of tradition, these photographers rejected velvety, blurred finishes in favour of clarity and exactitude: 'They are all concerned to be exact, clear, precise ... They do not cheat either with the model or with their craft which, if it is to be defined as an art, must have its own laws ... A good photo is above all a good document,' wrote Fels with great alacrity in *L'Art vivant*, which he edited, on 1 June 1928. 'What we really wanted to avoid was "artistic" photography.' The article was accompanied by reproductions of four works from the exhibition: Nadar, Eugène Atget, Kertész and Krull. Her 'Port', a low-angle view of cranes, was the first of her *fers* to be reproduced in France. Fels clearly understood Germaine's energetic temperament. She was 'a sort of Valkyrie of photographic film. She has reportage in the blood. When she goes out to make her photos, nothing can stop her.'[21] Not surprisingly, Germaine Krull-Ivens caused a sensation with her *fers*, exhibiting her Dutch specialities, which were somewhat opaque to Parisian eyes, alongside the very new and more attractive Eiffel Tower pieces. Three of her thirteen images were views of the Eiffel Tower, three showed the docks and bridge at Rotterdam, and one was a view of the harbour at Saint-Malo. On 1 October 1928, *L'Art vivant* put her Eiffel Tower on the cover, like a minimalist arrow, and gave Krull its centre spread, with four perfect gravure reproductions of the same subject (gravure being the *VU* technique), accompanied by a text, 'The Eiffel Tower, Elder Sister of Aeroplanes', by Marcelle Auclair, who was none other than the wife of Jean Prévost (from the Salon de l'Escalier committee). This came as a prelude to the forthcoming publication of a book on 'Eiffel' by Jean Prévost at Rieder Éditions, containing fresh 'original documents'. This book, which seems not to have been published until March 1929, at a time when the now celebrated, quadragenarian Tower[22] was becoming the symbol of the modernist aesthetic, contained six views from 'the Germaine Krull studios', a title that elevated the photographer's modest view camera to the industrious level of the book's other purveyor of images, the Compagnie des Établissements Eiffel.[23] This, indeed, was the only time that Krull's views were captioned in the style of technical documents,[24] illustrating the difficulty of recognising this as 'work of photography', let alone a work of art. The Tower stood at the point of at what, in 1929, was the possible but difficult convergence of an architectural and technological modernity and an artistic modernity already being cultivated by Delaunay. The exceptionally enlightened art critic Pierre Bost recognised Eiffel as 'one of those powerful engineers who no doubt deserve to be honoured as much as great artists'.[25]

Another exhibition now consolidated Germaine's position in the modernist movement emerging in Paris, and provided her with more media exposure. This was held at the Galerie L'Époque in Brussels in October 1928. In this Belgian version of the Salon de l'Escalier, she again showed alongside Atget, Abbott, André Kertész, Man Ray, as well as

20 VMD, p. 128: 'We needed to put on an exhibition' after the publication of the *Métal* portfolio, which 'was a great success.' 'Louis Jouvet took me by the shoulder: "How would you like to exhibit in the theatre foyer?" In fact, the organisation of the Salon, in May, came well before the publication of *Métal*, which was most probably in November/December.

21 Florent Fels, 'Le premier salon indépendant de la photographie', *L'Art vivant* no. 83, 1 June 1928, p. 445; 4 illustrations, p. 444, with one photo by Germaine Krull (with Nadar, Atget, Kertész).

22 In May *VU* sent Kertész to photograph the Tower for its fortieth birthday. He came back with the famous image of the shadow seen from the first floor: no. 63, 29 May 1929, pp. 431–433.

23 Jean Prévost, *Eiffel*, Paris: Les Éditions Rieder, 1929, pl. 43–48, six photos. Part of the *Maîtres de l'art moderne* collection including Cézanne, Manet, Van Gogh, William Blake, Odilon Redon, etc.

24 No. 43: Assemblage of metal framework; no. 44: Between the 1st and 2nd floors. Lift shaft seen from below; no. 46: Upper ceiling seen from below; no. 47: View of the ground through the upper framework; no. 48: A forest of assemblages.

25 Review of *Eiffel* by Jean Prévost, in *Jazz* 8 (July–August 1929), p. 386.

26 Titled 'La Photographie', this was a repeat of the text 'L'Art littéraire d'imagination et la photographie', published in Paris in *Les Nouvelles littéraires*, no. 310, 22 September 1928.
27 Xavier Canonne, 'Paul-Gustave Van Hecke et la photographie', in *L'Animateur d'art Paul-Gustave Van Hecke (1887–1967) et l'avant-garde, Cahiers des Musées royaux des Beaux-Arts de Belgique*, no. 12, March 2012, pp. 110–113.
28 Johan De Smet and Cathérine Verleysen, *Variétés. Spiegel van de dolle jaren*, Museum voor Schone Kunsten Ghent, 2004.
29 Ibid., p. 56.
30 F.L. 'L'exposition de la photographie à la Galerie 'L'Époque', *Variétés* 1, no. 7 (15 November 1928), pp. 400–401.
31 *Métal*, Librairie des Arts Décoratifs, Paris: A. Calavas Éditeur, n.d., insert of four pages with text by Florent Fels, 64 plates.
32 Fels's involvement both in the Salon de l'Escalier and in *Métal* would have provoked other reactions if the events had been concomitant. The legal deposit at the BNF gives 1929 as the publication date.
33 The artistic name of Louis Bonin, also called Lou Bonin-Tchimoukoff, or Lou Bonin, who was a poster designer, graphic designer, actor and filmmaker, a member of the Octobre group (1932), costume designer for *Drôle de drame* (1937), and actor in *L'Atalante* (1934). He was also known for his photograms of plants, thought to be used for designing his fabrics. The name he used varied with the activity concerned.

Eli Lotar, Moholy-Nagy, Aenne Biermann, and Robertson from Berlin, and the Belgians Robert Desmet, E. Gobert and E. L. T. Mesens. She showed two Eiffel Towers, a *fers* image, pictures of Marseille including the loading of coal, the docks, the transporter bridge and two street photos, plus the hands of the painter Mariette Lydis and a portrait of Walter Benjamin. The preface was by Pierre Mac Orlan.[26] At this event, which was less Paris-centred than the Salon de l'Escalier and also looked towards Germany, the exhibitors were all in their early thirties (except Man Ray, who was thirty-eight). The figure of Moholy-Nagy (1895–1946), a painter and teacher at the Bauhaus and author of the *Malerei, Fotografie, Film* manifesto, who showed five photograms, three photomontages (*Photoplastik*) and a negative, set a more international, avant-garde tone which was echoed by the five rayographs by Man Ray and the ten photos by Eli Lotar, most of them details and close-ups, with concrete subjects similar to Krull's ('Cables', 'Anchor', 'Mast', 'Unloading Coal'). It was pointed out that 'the photos in the exhibition are for sale'. Lotar even specified the number of limited prints available for each photo (between seven and fifteen), and one could on request be shown 'a considerable number of photos by the same artists'.

L'Époque, which opened in October 1927, was the most modernist gallery in Belgium. In 1927 and 1928 it exhibited Magritte, de Chirico, Kandinsky, Klee and Hans Arp. Its dynamic founder, P. G. van Hecke (1887–1967), a Fleming from Ghent, was active in the theatre, publishing and contemporary art. He chose E. L. T. Mesens as gallery director. L'Époque represented Expressionism and Surrealism (both French and Belgian), but also stood out for its commitment to photography and folk art. A collector and friend of many artists, Van Hecke was very interested in modern photography.[27] He was the founder (among other publishing initiatives) of the journal *Variétés, revue mensuelle illustrée de l'esprit contemporain* (May 1928), which aimed to embody a 'new approach' to 'intellectual activity' and be a 'mirror of the modern era'.[28] An extraordinary hub of artistic activism, *Variétés* was active for two years (to April 1930), exciting curiosity with twenty-five issues full of surprising and novel articles on film, photography, literature, music, theatre, folklore, ethnic art, fashion, cars and sport.[29] The original presentation alternated the texts of articles, studies, poems and essays with eight-page illustrated sections showing two photos per page. *Variétés* played a central role in Krull's short career. Its review of the L'Époque show referred explicitly to 'the tendency represented by Germaine Krull, Eli Lotar and André Kertész. They aim, essentially, to suggest power, peace or mystery by emphasising the essential fragment that is the photo. The two "Eiffel Towers" by Germaine Krull, the "Masts", and "Rails, Speed" by Eli Lotar poetically exalt the modern picturesque.' This aesthetic that 'sweeps away a few houses of cards' was one of the journal's great inspirations.[30] Krull's first appearance in the illustrated section of *Variétés* came in September 1928 (1, no. 5), with an Eiffel Tower and an image of Delaunay painting – also – a *Tower*. Other *fers* were published subsequently, but before that, in July 1928, the journal run by Robert Desmet (or De Smet) in Brussels had published 'grain pumps' and 'elevators in the port at Antwerp' that were stylistically very close to Krull (issue no. 3).

THE *MÉTAL* PORTFOLIO

The greatest event of this breakthrough year for Krull was the publication of a portfolio of sixty-four plates, simply titled *Métal*, with a three-page preface by Florent Fels.[31] There is still uncertainty about the actual date of publication. It cannot have been 1927, as often been suggested, but must have been late 1928, because the reviews did not appear until early 1929.[32] This was a completely new kind of object, made up autonomous plates, numbered but without captions, in a black canvas portfolio with a cropped photo of Eiffel Tower lift machinery on the front board. The design, by Tchimoukoff,[33] showed the name 'Krull' in reserve against the vertical, geometric graphics. The object was difficult to place. The printing was fairly muted, in keeping with common publishing practice for the documentation of architecture and furniture, or nude models for artists – especially in the work of this publisher.[34] But *Métal* asserted its status as a personal work, and an avant-garde one to boot, something quite new and without concessions. That status may also have been uncertain – an advertisement published in *Variétés* announced: 'Germaine Krull: *Métal*. Dance of Naked Metals'.[35] Such a prospect probably didn't attract many customers (they were always few and far between).[36] However, *Métal* did have an immediate impact in the art world, and on the 'New Photographers', the apostles of the New Vision, which was making a place for itself in art magazines, Surrealist publications, and advertising. René Zuber, a former student of Moholy-Nagy's, indicated the moment when Krull 'pointed her camera at the sky and photographed the Eiffel Tower, from bottom to top' as an epiphany: 'Since that day', he argued, 'photographs have set out to discover the world.'[37] For, as Christian Bouqueret notes, it was precisely the disarticulation of this Vision, which put the emphasis on high- and low-angle shots, close-ups and surprising framing, creating non-referential form, that gave *Métal* as an ensemble its power, its homogeneity and coherence, maintaining an element of invention and surprise – and also perplexity – on sites whose only aesthetic particularity lies in the fact that they are wholly metallic. According to a note by Krull reproduced after the preface, the portfolio contains (no other details are given), images of the Eiffel Tower (eleven), the cranes and transporter brides of Amsterdam, Rotterdam (twenty-five), Marseille and Saint-Malo, the Conservatoire des Arts et Métiers (seven), the power station at Saint-Ouen (eleven), and the Citroën factories.[38] Two of them involved overprinting. The lift bridge (railway bridge) in Rotterdam is shown some ten times and has a particular status because Krull was there at the same time as Ivens, who was filming it.[39] Most of the images share the aesthetic particularity of showing fragments that give absolutely no idea of the overall form of the structure itself. This is especially true for the bridge in Rotterdam and the Eiffel Tower, whose (admittedly well-known) outlines we never glimpse, as if the point was to show an anonymous and unknown – or at least never-seen – structure.[40] For the Eiffel Tower, we cannot even get our spatial bearings from the direction of the shot, be it high- or low-angle or horizontal. Sometimes it is impossible to tell which way an image should be looked at.

Critics struggled to describe these impressive but rather cold oddities, which were clearly machinist and seemed to derive from the most radical German constructivism, which banished all human allusions (we will see below that *Métal* remained unique in Krull's work). The work has the impact of an aesthetic exploit. The shots are constantly acrobatic, but they do not seem to embody a credo. (Compare this with *Die Welt ist schön* by Albert Renger-Patzsch, the emblematic book of the New Objectivity, published in the same year, which is extremely varied in its subjects but constant in its compositional rigour.) The preface by Florent Fels, who was unpartisan in his aesthetics and generally favourable to the Montparnassian modernity of the Roaring Twenties, was far from combative, and even seemed to admit to a degree confusion: 'The industrial activity of our times puts before our eyes spectacles to which they are still unaccustomed. We are struck and frightened by their novelty, as by great natural phenomena.' In these 'fine photographs, representative of a new romanticism' he found only evocations of 'orchids' or 'disturbing insects'. Not long ago, he wrote, the Tower was still an 'incongruous monstrosity' cajoled by the 'mane of stars' constituted by the lights of its Citroën advertisement from 1925 to 1936. *Métal* could at least be seen as a promise that bad memories might soon be soothed: 'Ten years after the war, steel may at last be serving a noble cause, and so, steel may at last be rehabilitated.'

Critic Pierre Bost admitted his reticence: 'If we are not yet perfectly prepared to understand this modern beauty, we are already starting to feel it very intensely, and Mme Krull's book will be one of the best guides to this new aesthetic.'[41] This was written in the second issue of *Jazz*, subtitled *L'Actualité intellectuelle* (Intellectual News), a new magazine edited by

34 The three portfolios by Antoine Roche, *Paris 1928*; *Paris 1929*; *Paris 1930*, published in the same format as *Métal*, were anthologies of the most modern examples of design and decorative arts from the year in question. Roche would become one of Krull's faithful friends.
35 *Variétés* 2, no. 2 (15 June 1929), p. 128.
36 A facsimile reprint was published in an edition of fifty by Ann and Jürgen Wilde, Cologne: Zülpich, 2002.
37 Unpublished text quoted in Bouqueret, *Paris. les livres de photographie*, op. cit., p. 20.
38 The numbers given here are my own estimate.
39 See above.
40 The overly 'objective' image showing the shadow of the Eiffel Tower on the ground did not appear in *Métal*.
41 Pierre Bost, review of *Métal* in *Jazz* 2 (January 1929), p. 92.

42 Christian Bouqueret interviewed by Carlo Rim, in Bouqueret, *Livres...*, op. cit., p. 33.
43 15 January 1929, pp. 76–80.
44 *VU* no. 38 (5 December 1928), pp. 834–835.
45 Text pp. 508–509, photograph p. 488.
46 The caption for this in fact says Saint-Malo.
47 *Variétés* 2, no. 9, (15 January 1930), p. 670.
48 *L'Art vivant* no. 105 (1 June 1929), pp. 368–369, text p. 365.

the journalist Titaÿna, but above all by the editor-in-chief Carlo Rim, who wanted to exploit 'the Surrealist side of photography', with images 'escaping the common definition of what are known as news photos'[42] supplied by the new Parisian generation represented by Tabard, Krull, Landau, Kertész, Lotar, Man Ray, Parry, Dréville. This programme echoed the credo of *VU*, focusing on intellectual and artistic objectives (Carlo Rim would later become editor of *VU*, in spring 1930).

Nearly all the issues of *Jazz* have a 'modern' photograph on the cover, an image that is slightly difficult to read. Given that the publication of *Jazz* (December 1928) coincided with that of *Métal*, and in view of their shared radicalism, Krull was naturally the star of the first edition, with one of her photographs illustrating an article by Pierre Mac Orlan about the London docks (although these were not from *Métal*), and another four of her photographs (three of them from *Métal*) reproduced in an article by Jean Prévost titled 'Is the Eiffel Tower in Danger?' Her photographs of cranes also appeared in planned articles about the docks of Amsterdam, again by Florent Fels (no. 2, 15 January 1029, pp. 55–58, with seven photos), Hamburg, by Pierre Mac Orlan (no. 4, 15 March 1929, pp. 151–156, with two photos), and Toulon, by André Salmon (no. 8, July–August 1929, pp. 343–346, three photos, and another three by Lotar). As early as the second issue, Pierre Scize's film column featured a review of *Steel Bridge* (*De Brug*), Joris Ivens's film about the port of Rotterdam, which was a good pretext for showing three fine photos by Krull,[43] and a little later an article on 'Steel' by Florent Fels explored the theme over three pages of issue no. 5 (15 April 1929, five photos by Krull). This affirmation of the machine aesthetic was the finest homage yet received by *Métal*, with five of the strangest photos from the portfolio, the kind of thing that readers had 'never seen before', things that were almost 'unidentifiable', accompanying the text by Fels who, if a champion of the New Photography, was also manifestly reticent when it came to unconditionally enthusing over the industrial or mechanical. In December 1928, for an article on the docks at Antwerp, *VU*, which made abundant use of Krull's other photographic qualities, featured two strange shots taken behind the cathedral clock, spread over a double page.[44] However, the disorienting viewpoints and incongruous details that would become the hallmark of *VU* over the coming years were still a minority taste.

Variétés, too, did its bit. It published a review of *Métal* quoting Fels's text in its ninth issue (January 1929), with a reproduction of a photograph, a very severe composition of geometrical lines.[45] The 'metal masts' of Amsterdam (in fact, they were cranes) were published in April 1929 and in May, an issue whose main subject was ports, the photographs from *Métal* were a natural fit. Eight images showing the ports of Antwerp, Hamburg,[46] London and Rotterdam (titled 'Geographies'), plus the clock at Antwerp (under the title 'Port Panoramas') and novel views of life on board a cruiser ('On Board a Cruiser', 'Washing', 'Chores') formed a kind of personal mini-portfolio. But this effervescence was short-lived. The *fers* were not documentary material, and what magazines wanted was illustration, while art journals wanted unusual and poetic evocations. Fortunately, Krull, who was the favoured photographer at *Variétés*, could provide other, more evocative material. In January 1930 Van Hecke, the editor of *Variétés*, published an 'Ode to the Machine Aesthetic', in which, as if regretfully, he skewered 'those prima donnas who believed in a ridiculous mission: inaugurating a new era by announcing the age of steel, metal, iron'.[47]

As for Fels's journal, *L'Art vivant*, it continued its campaign in favour of the New Photography (as represented by the Salon de l'Escalier) by focusing on industrial photography. On 1 June 1929 an article by Charles Saunier on 'Metal, Inspiration of Art' was accompanied by an impressive central spread, blue-grey gravure prints of six photographs by Krull.[48] The text, in praise of *Métal*, enthused over the 'possibility of beautiful formal poems', over 'a sequence of superhuman visions that grip the mind . . . a dizziness that disorients like skyfall in a deep well . . . a drunkenness of space, a desire to fly into the ether.' When Krull was promoted in a series by Jean Gallotti titled 'Is Photography an Art', she was once again given a splendid spread with two grandiose images of pipes (a power station) and a metal framework (the pit-head of a mine), across which her name was majestically displayed. The Germanic surname and very French given name were far from neutral in a context of industrial growth driven by iron and steel in an age that, as Fels wrote, had 'rehabilitated steel' after the cataclysm of artillery and barbed wire. Metal became an appreciated ingredient of furniture and decoration: we should not forget that Laszlo Moholy-Nagy had been head of the 'metal' workshop at the Bauhaus since 1923 (and not the photography one – which, in fact, didn't exist).

The publication of *Métal* was followed by other commissions for power stations. 'My first clients were Electricité de Paris,' Krull recalled. 'I photographed all the factories and all the infrastructure. For many years they were my best clients.'[49] She had no doubt forgotten that she had already included the power station at Saint-Ouen in *Métal*. After that, no doubt, came the one at Issy-les-Moulineaux, photographed for the Compagnie Parisenne de Distribution d'Électricité, which included in its own publication (June 1929) seven of Krull's pictures which, although documentary, were infinitely more spectacular than the other illustrations. *Variétés* reproduced six of the Issy-les-Moulineaux pictures in an issue all about iron and steel, and more generally, as its title put it, about 'The Life of Machines' (15 January 1930), with two more of her 'industrial' photographs, probably of a Citroën factory (close-ups of machines). The same issue also included a long review of Jean Prévost's book on Eiffel, mentioning 'a few fine photographs by Mme Germaine Krull, part of her poem of iron [Métal]'.[50]

Up until 1930 the *fers*, the Eiffel Tower, *Métal*, the factories and machines, plus the commissions from Citroën and Peugeot, constituted Krull's personal territory and artistic hallmark. These artefacts gave her an aesthetic identity, while for readers they were highly recognisable as subjects of 'modern photography', or of the new 'art of photography'. Krull tried to extend this stylistic identity in her advertising photography (Ahetze shirts, Shell, etc.), but also undertook other bold innovations.

49 VMD, p. 128.
50 *Variétés* 2, no. 9 (15 January 1930), p. 632 a, c, d, h. Some of the prints held in the AMSAB collection have captions on the back for a section on 'Mysteries of the Factory'. Text on Jean Prévost, p. 647.

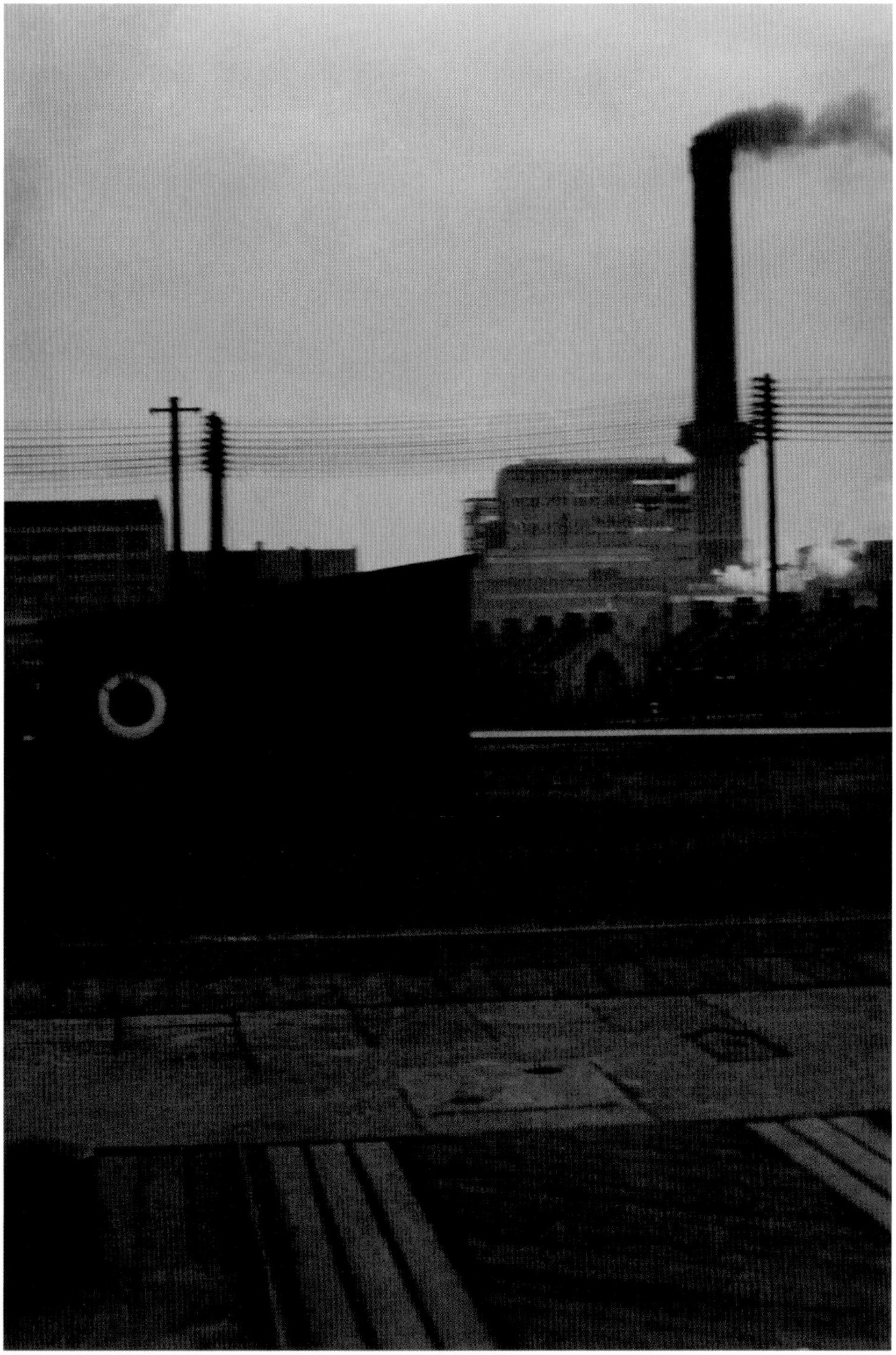

'London', 1927

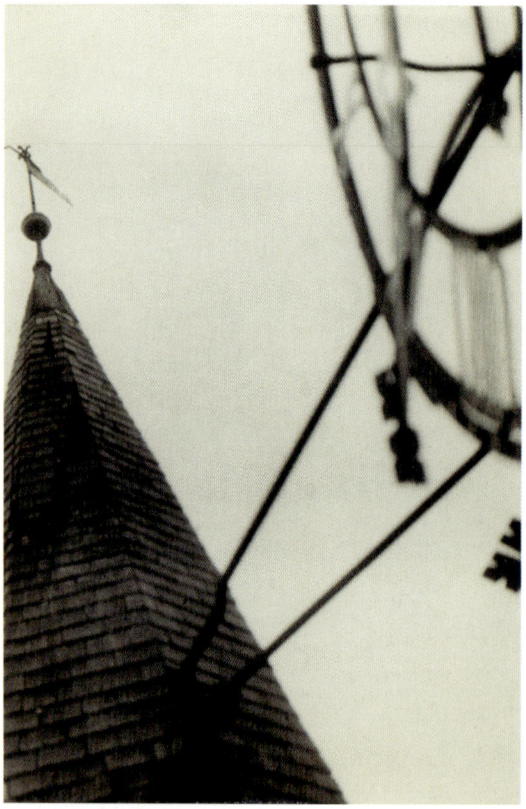

Belfry, c. 1928

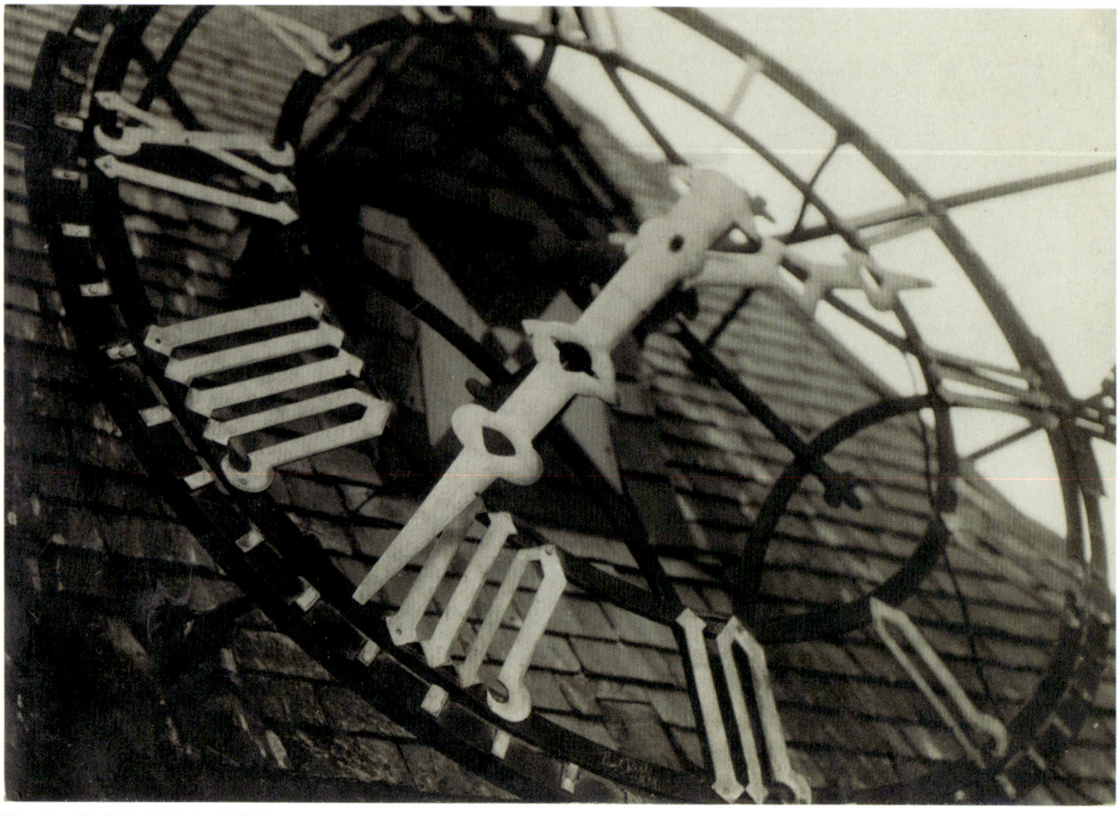

'Flanders: the Belfry Clock', c. 1927

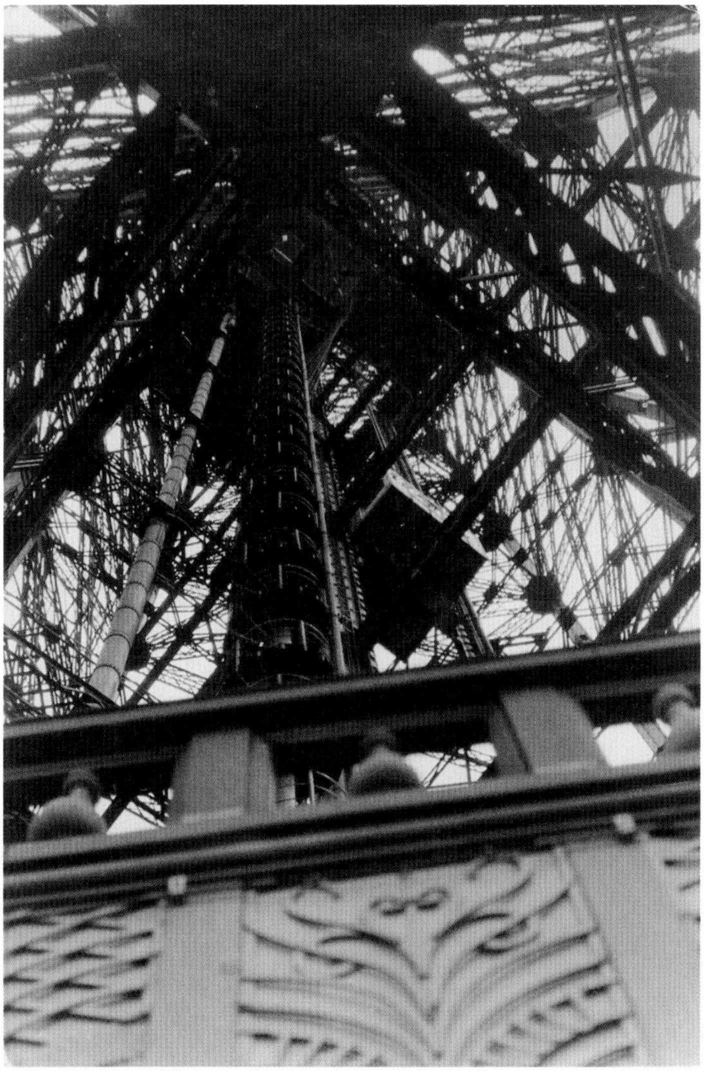

Eiffel Tower, c. 1928

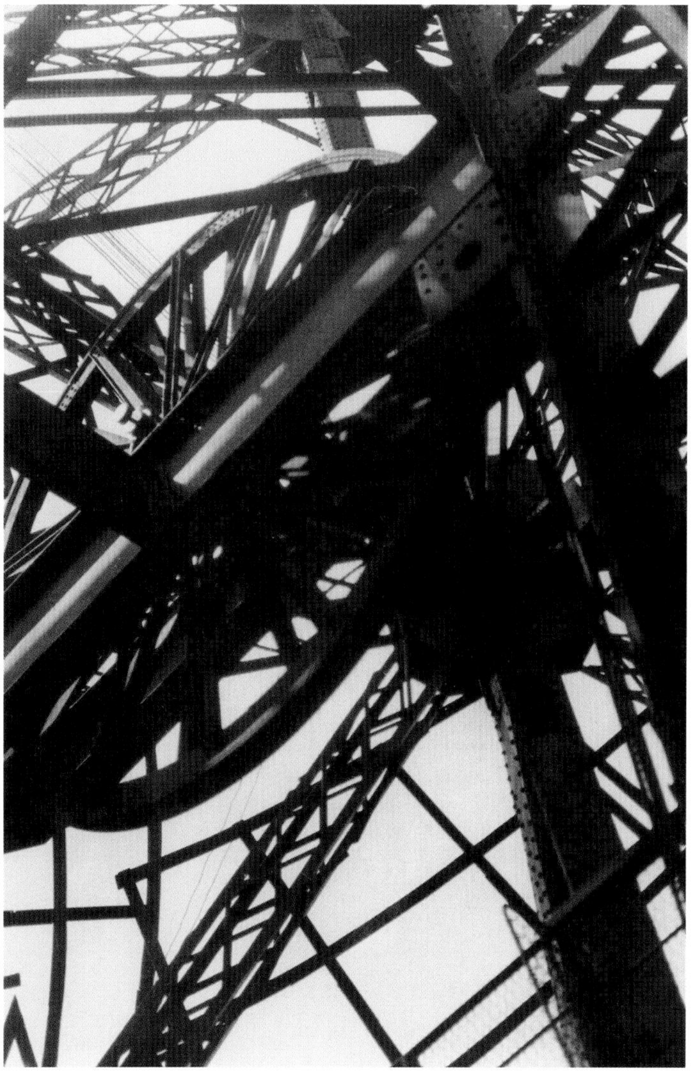

Eiffel Tower, 1927

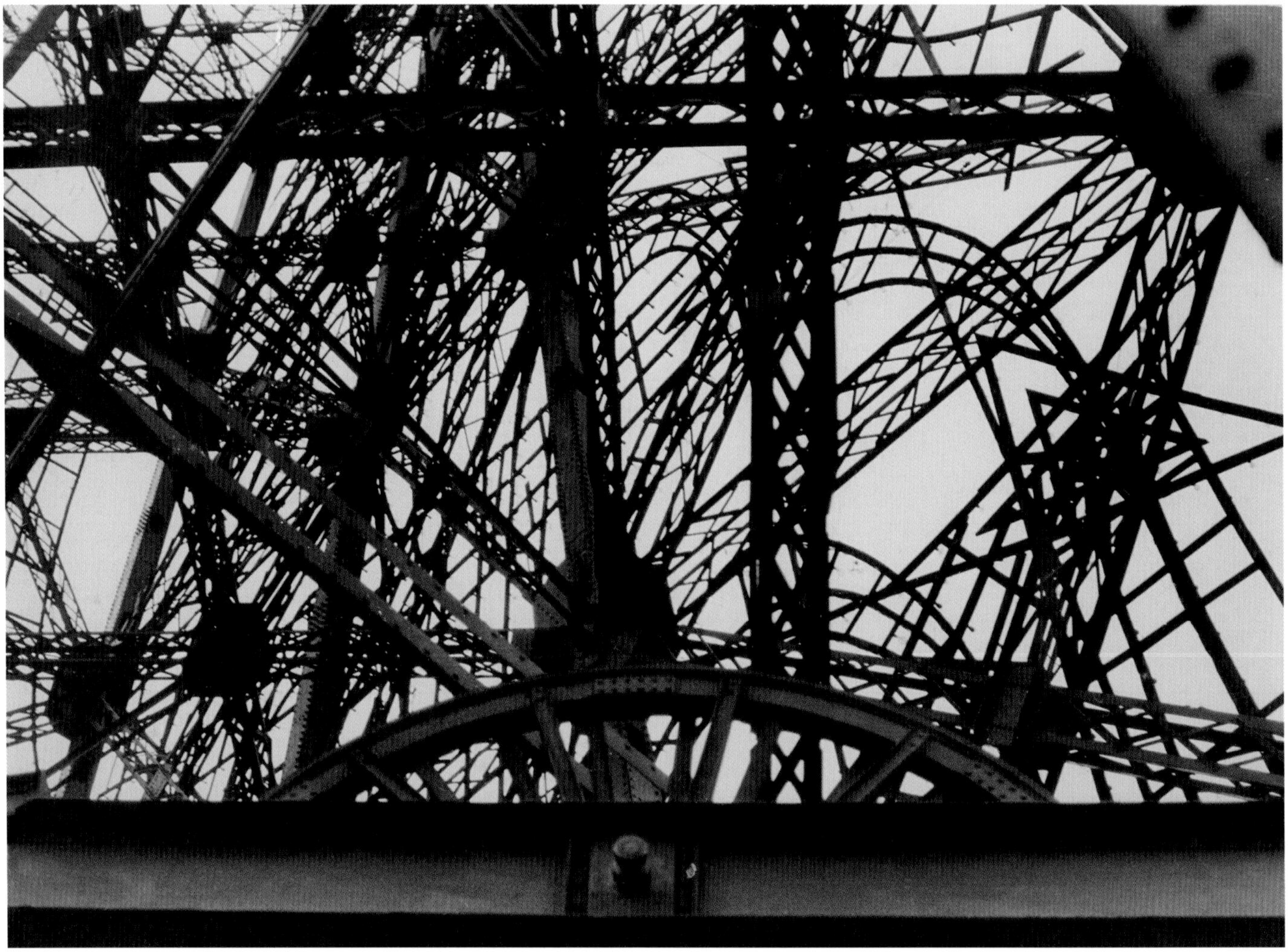

Eiffel Tower, Paris, c. 1928

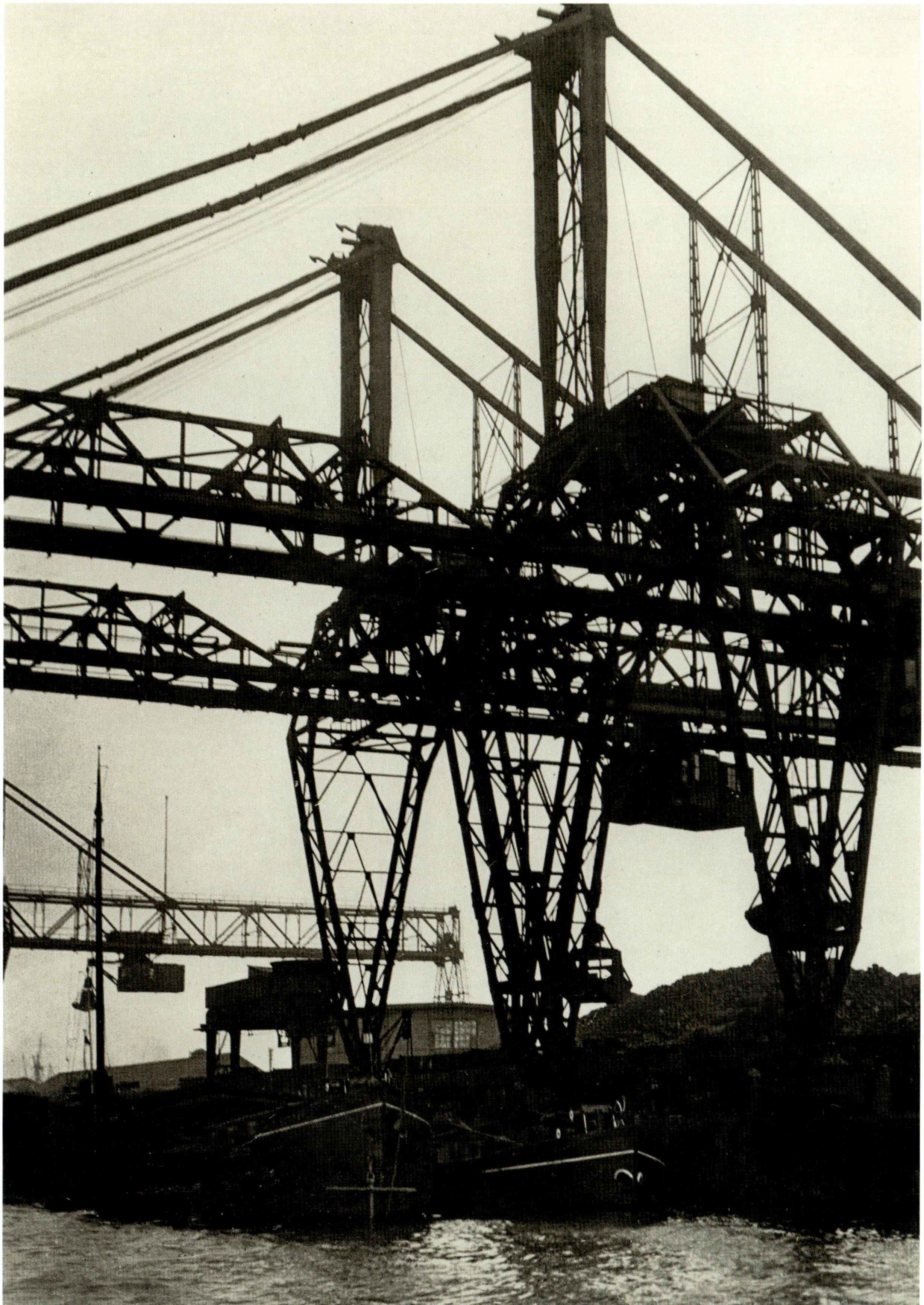

Bridge Crane, Rotterdam, c. 1926

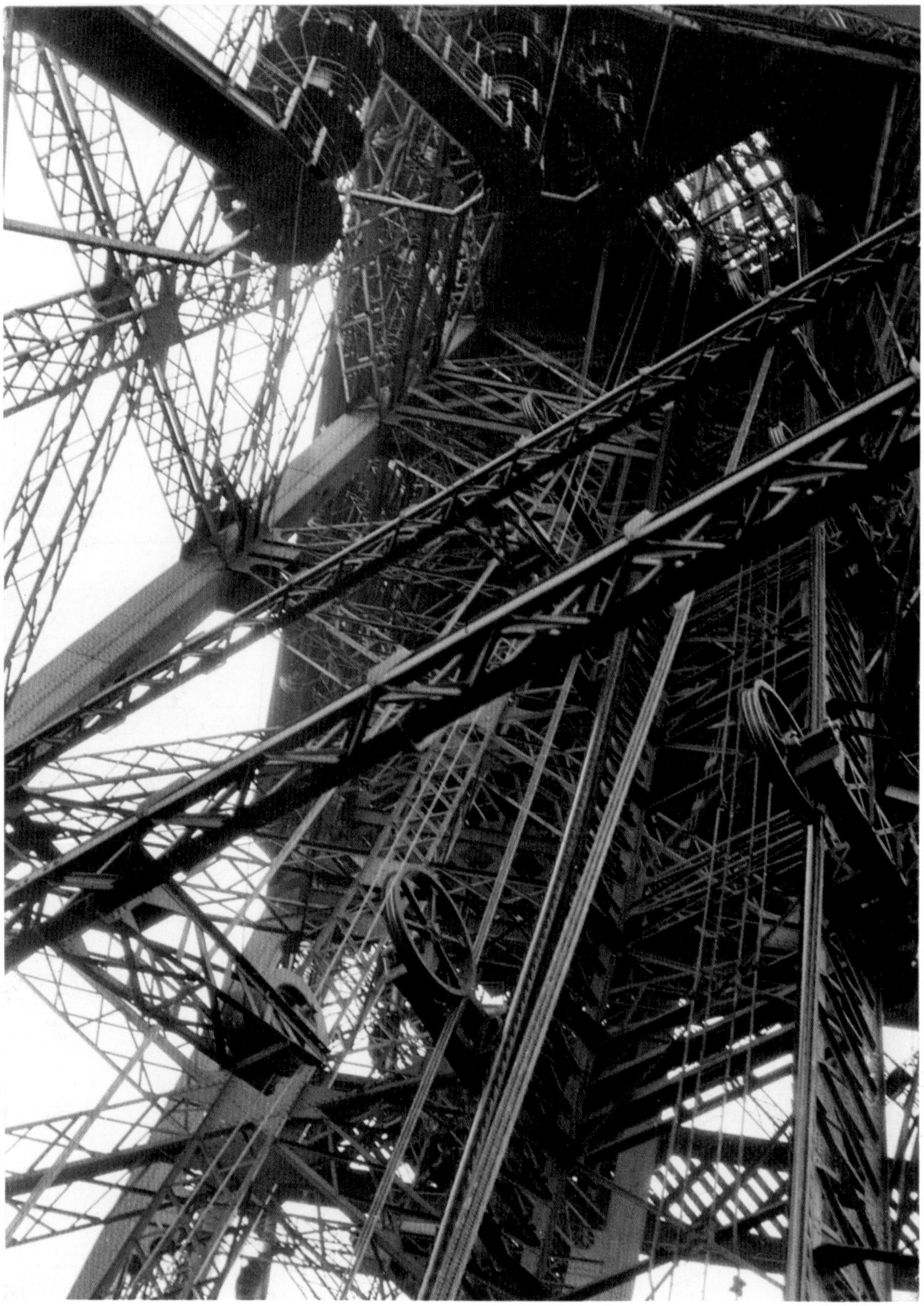

'Eiffel Tower', c. 1927
'With All Its Strength', by Florent Fels, *VU* no. 11, 30 May 1928, p. 284 (facing page)

Dans toute sa force

PHOTOS
GERMAINE
KRULL

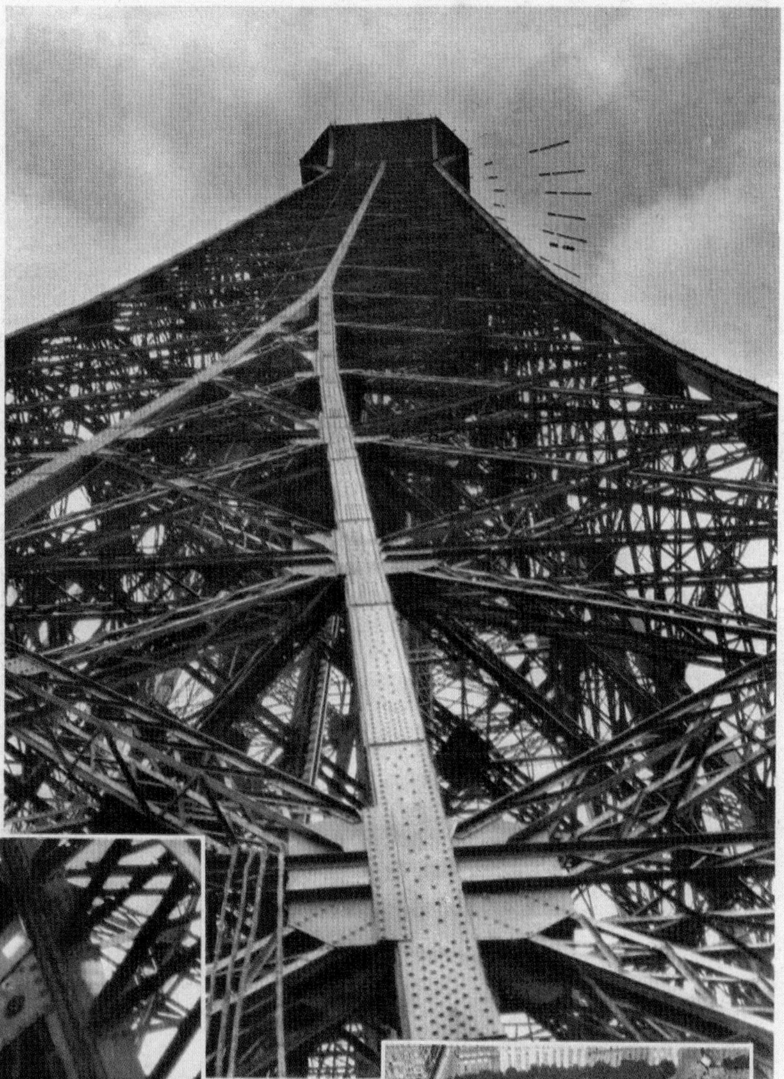

La Tour. Clocher des ondes. Sa monstruosité incongrue a surpris et irrité. Maintenant, à trois cents mètres du sol, les amoureux y donnent des rendez-vous aux oiseaux. Et les poètes, du douanier Rousseau à Jean Cocteau, prétendent que les beaux soirs de printemps, des fées jouent au toboggan sur ses élytres. La Tour demeure l'ultime symbole des temps nouveaux. En quittant New-York et ses palais couronnés de fumées, c'est la Tour Eiffel, balise aérienne, que Lindberhg visait, pour atteindre Paris, au cœur sentimental du monde.

Elle a les pieds dans la Seine qui, jusqu'à Rouen, traîne derrière les remorqueurs la France calculée en tonnes. Il manquait à cette géante une chevelure d'étoiles : on la lui a donnée. L'industrie inscrit maintenant son progrès lumineux sur l'échine nocturne de la Tour. FLORENT FELS.

Poutres, poutrelles, rivets sont ici comme le vers, les mots et la rime. On ne pense plus à la merveille mécanique, au labeur, à la forge, à la mine. On oublie l'ingénieur, l'ouvrier, le manœuvre, pour ne songer qu'au poète inouï, incomparable : EIFFEL.

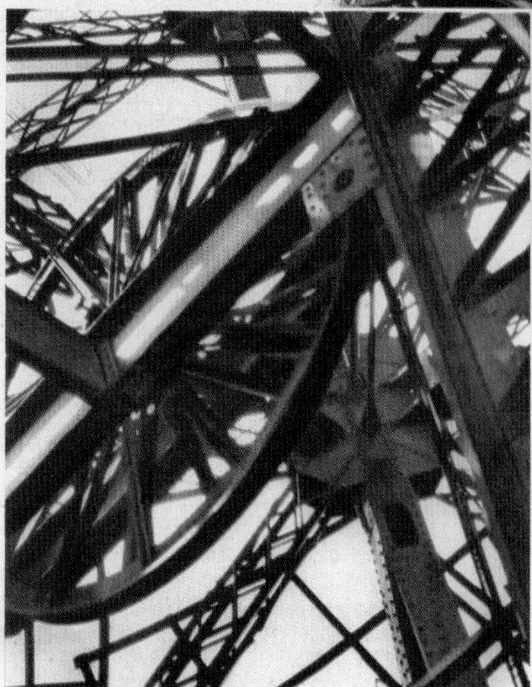

L'ascenseur, la roue qui entraîne quelques humains jusqu'au royaume des oiseaux, change soudain jusqu'à notre naturel élément. (A gauche.)

En haut, il semble que l'on se détache un peu des contingences terrestres. On glisse en pensée tout le long, le long de la Tour, jusqu'à la pointe de sa sœur d'ombre, qui gît comme l'aiguille d'un cadran solaire. (A droite.)

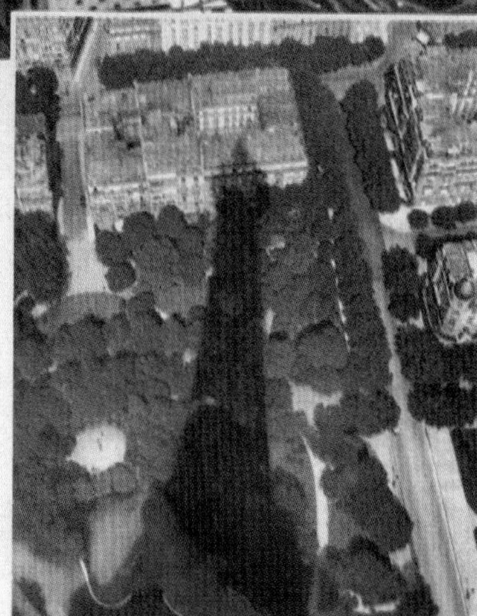

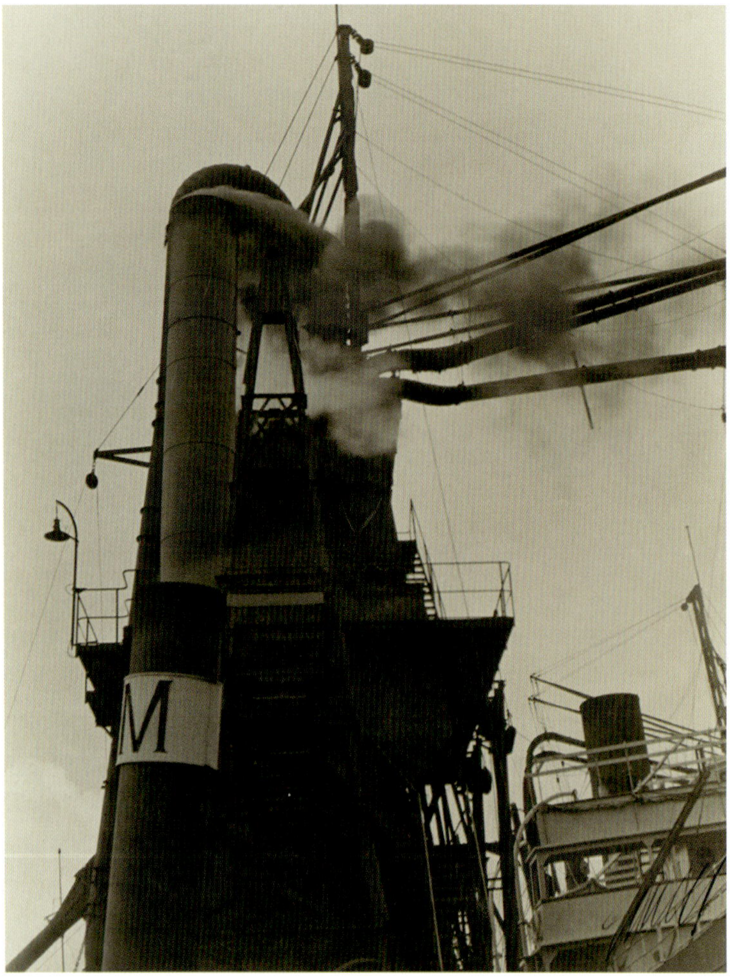

Grain silo, Rotterdam, c. 1924

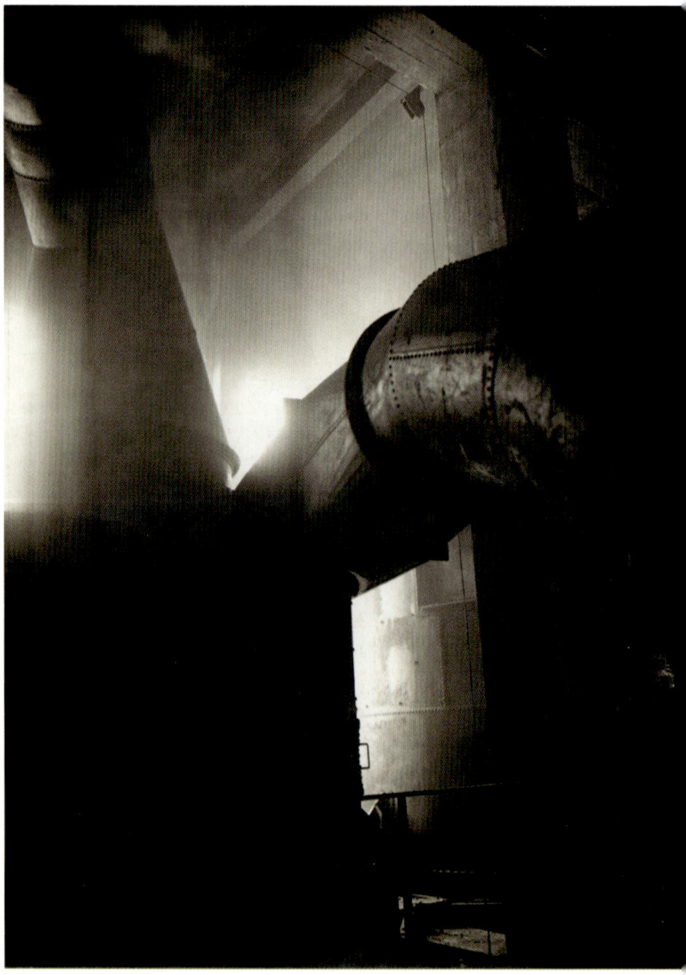

Electricity Plant, Issy-les-Moulineaux, 1928

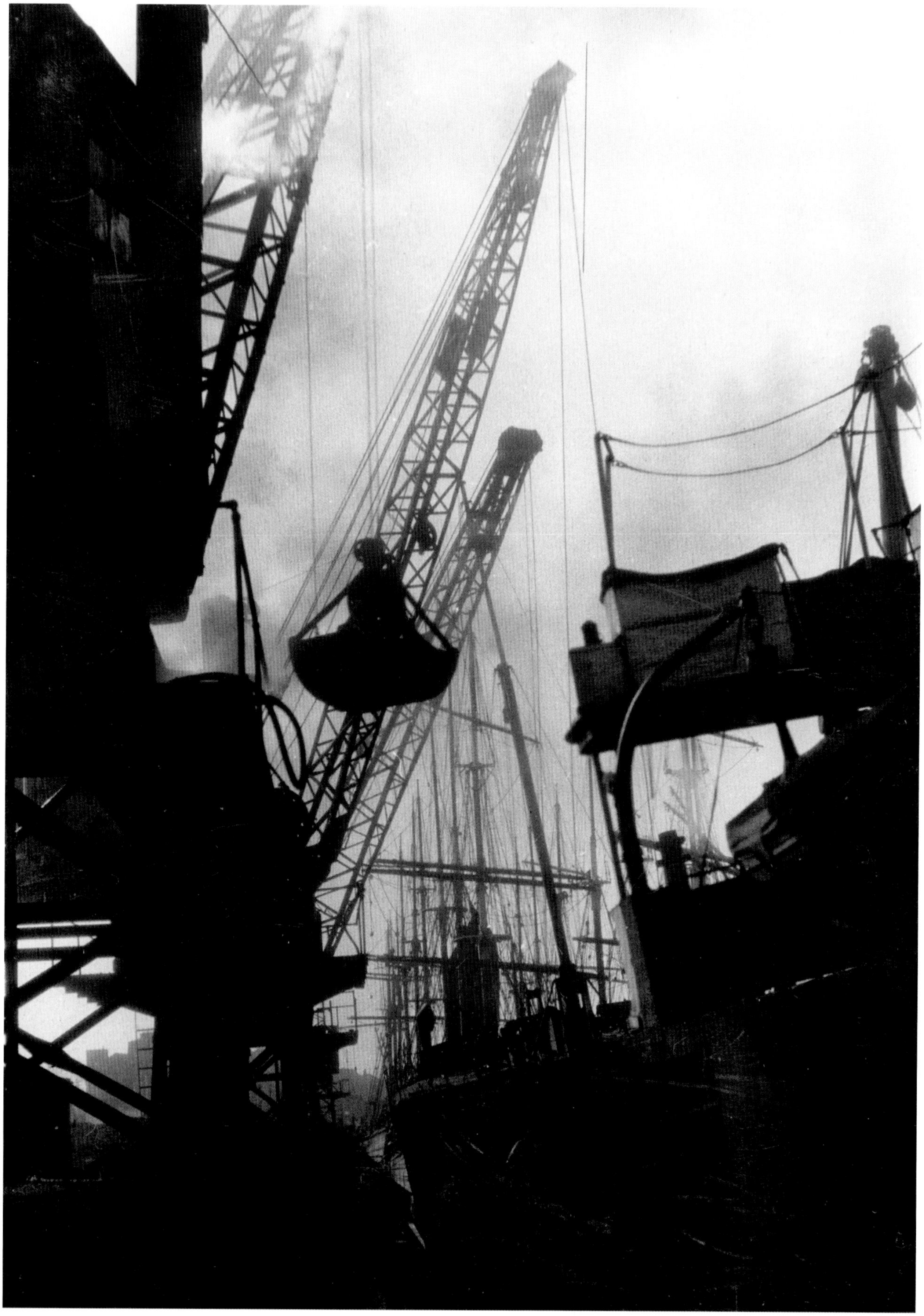

'Port St Malo', 1928

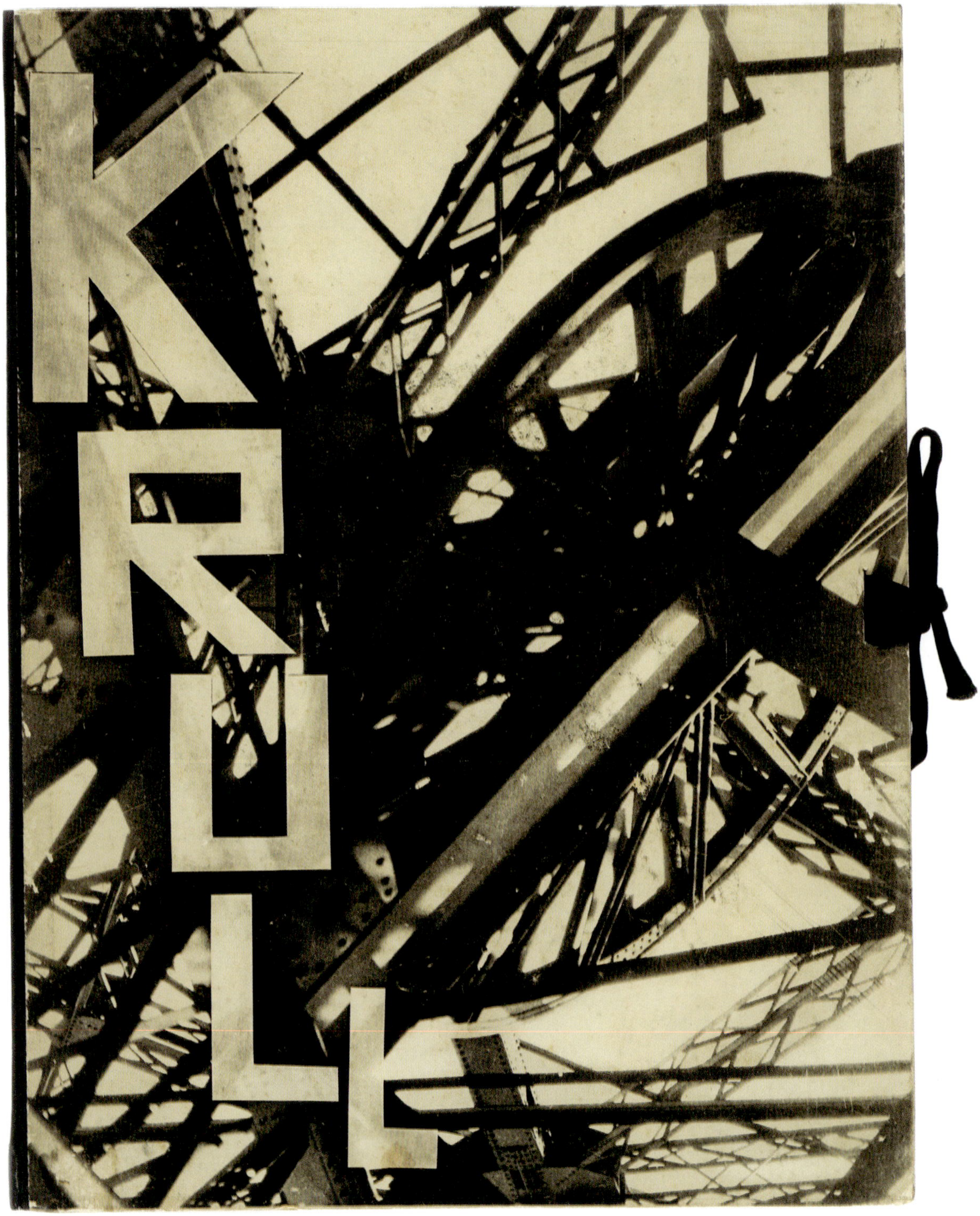

Métal, Paris, A. Calavas, 1928 (and facing page)

KRULL, MÉTAL 44

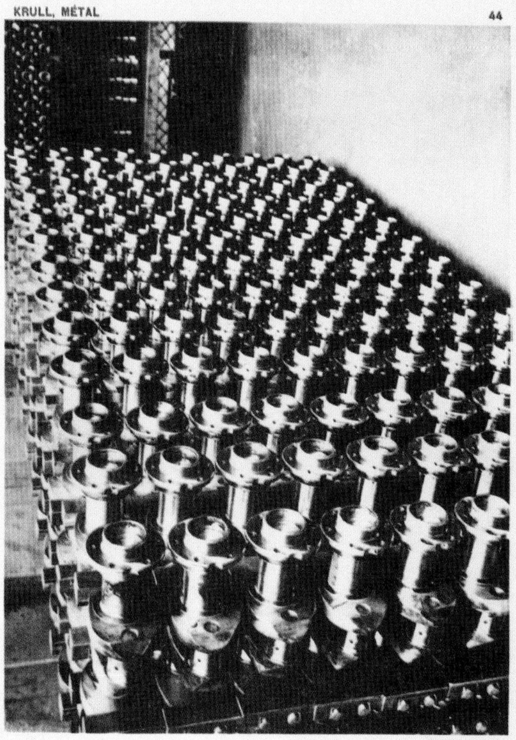

A. CALAVAS, PARIS

KRULL, MÉTAL 25

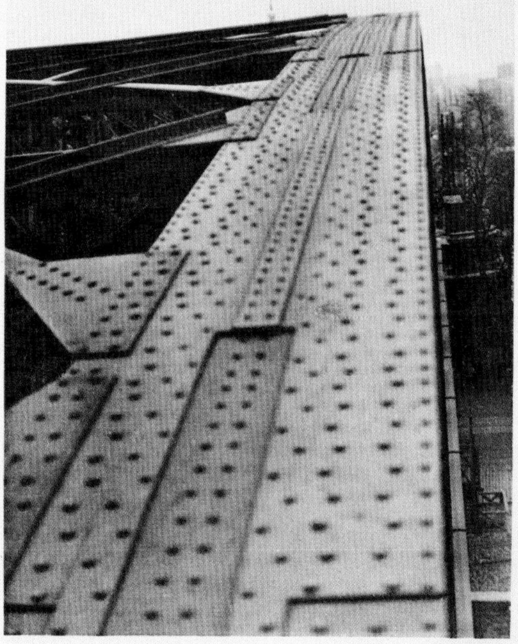

A. CALAVAS, PARIS

KRULL, MÉTAL 22

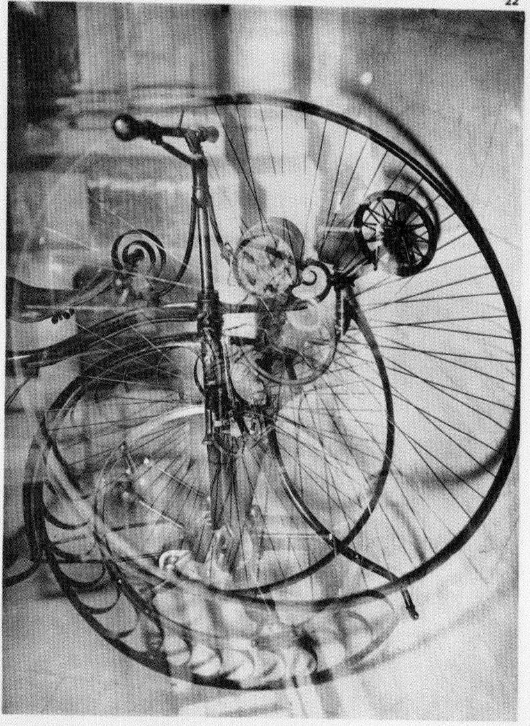

A. CALAVAS, PARIS

KRULL, MÉTAL 49

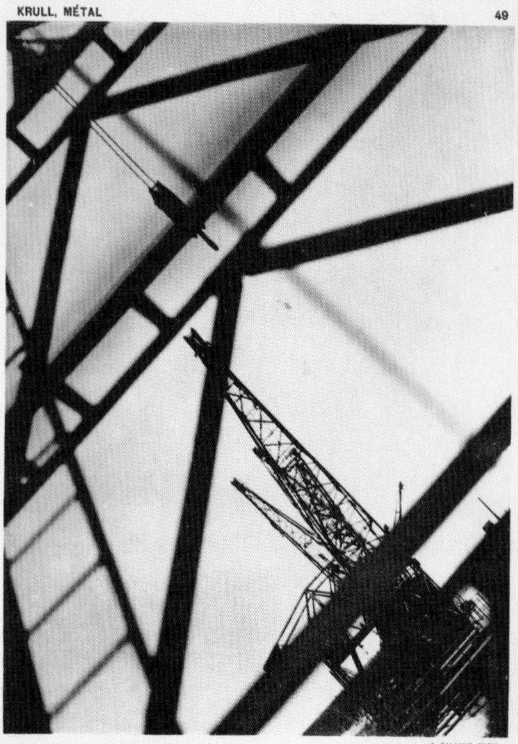

A. CALAVAS, PARIS

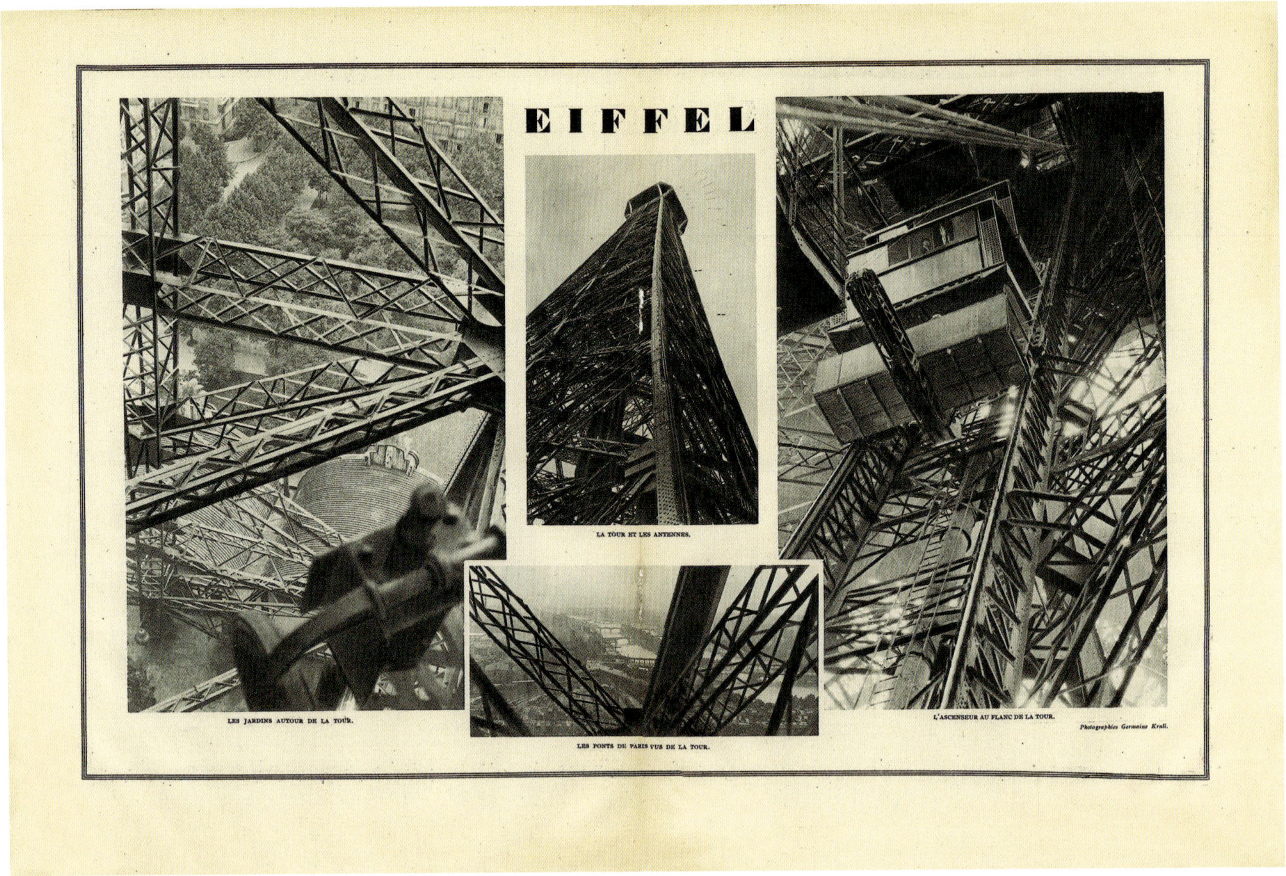

EIFFEL

LA TOUR ET LES ANTENNES.

LES JARDINS AUTOUR DE LA TOUR.

LES PONTS DE PARIS VUS DE LA TOUR.

L'ASCENSEUR AU FLANC DE LA TOUR.

Photographies Germaine Krull.

'Eiffel', *L'Art vivant*, no. 91, 1 October 1928, pp. 75–77

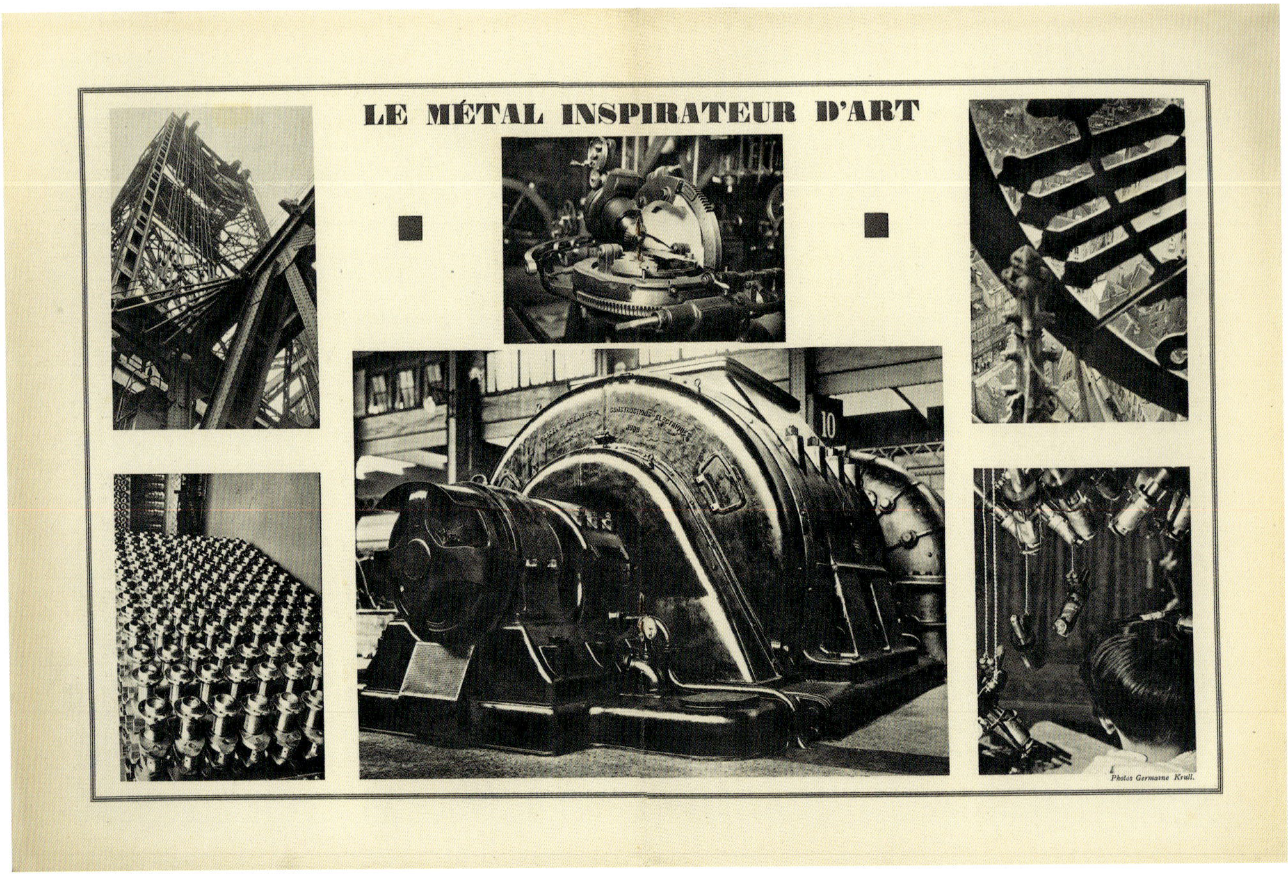

LE MÉTAL INSPIRATEUR D'ART

Photos Germaine Krull.

'Metal, Inspiration of Art', *L'Art vivant*, no. 105, 1 May 1930, pp. 368–369

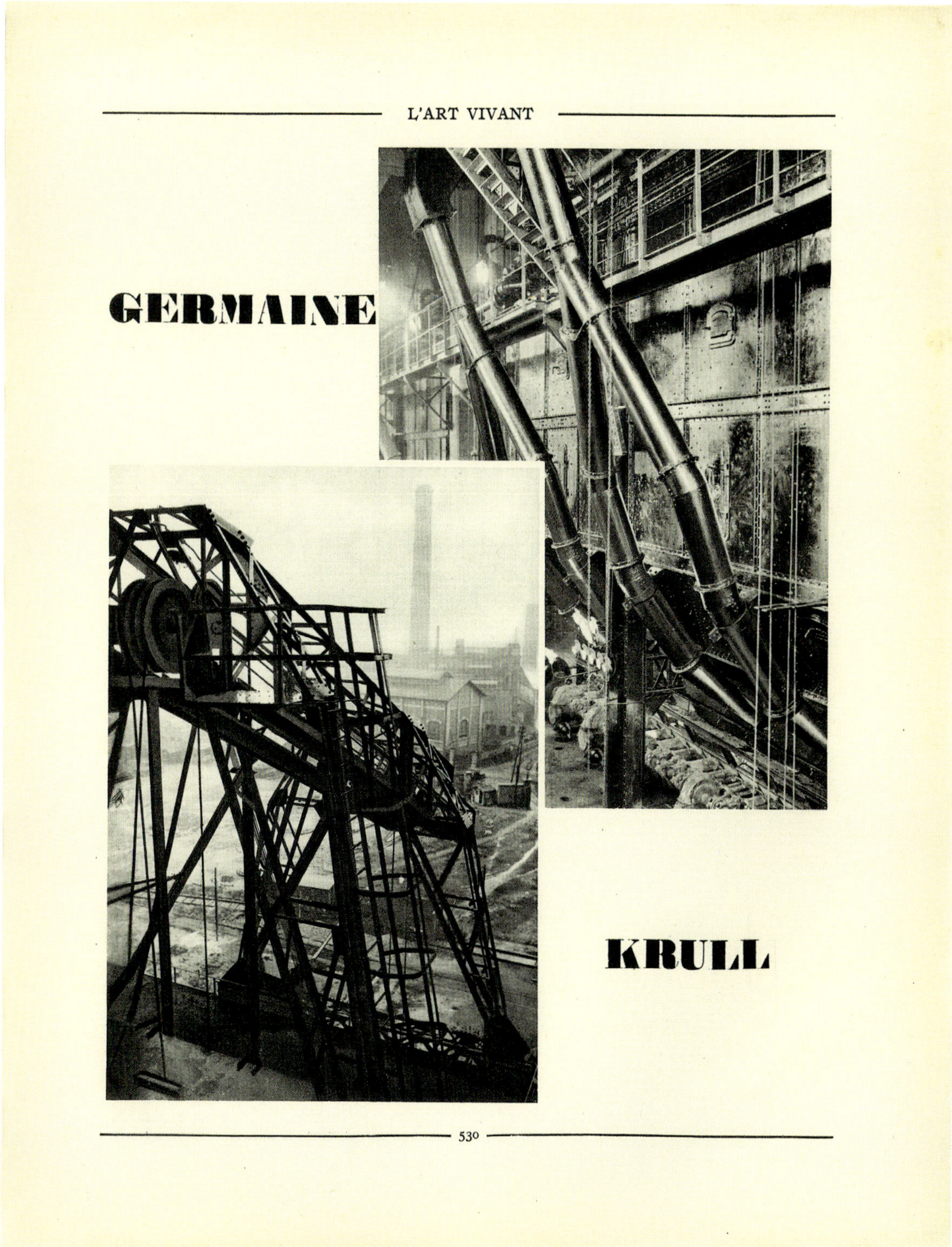
L'ART VIVANT

GERMAINE

KRULL

530

Germaine Krull, *L'Art vivant*, no. 109, 1 July 1930, p. 530

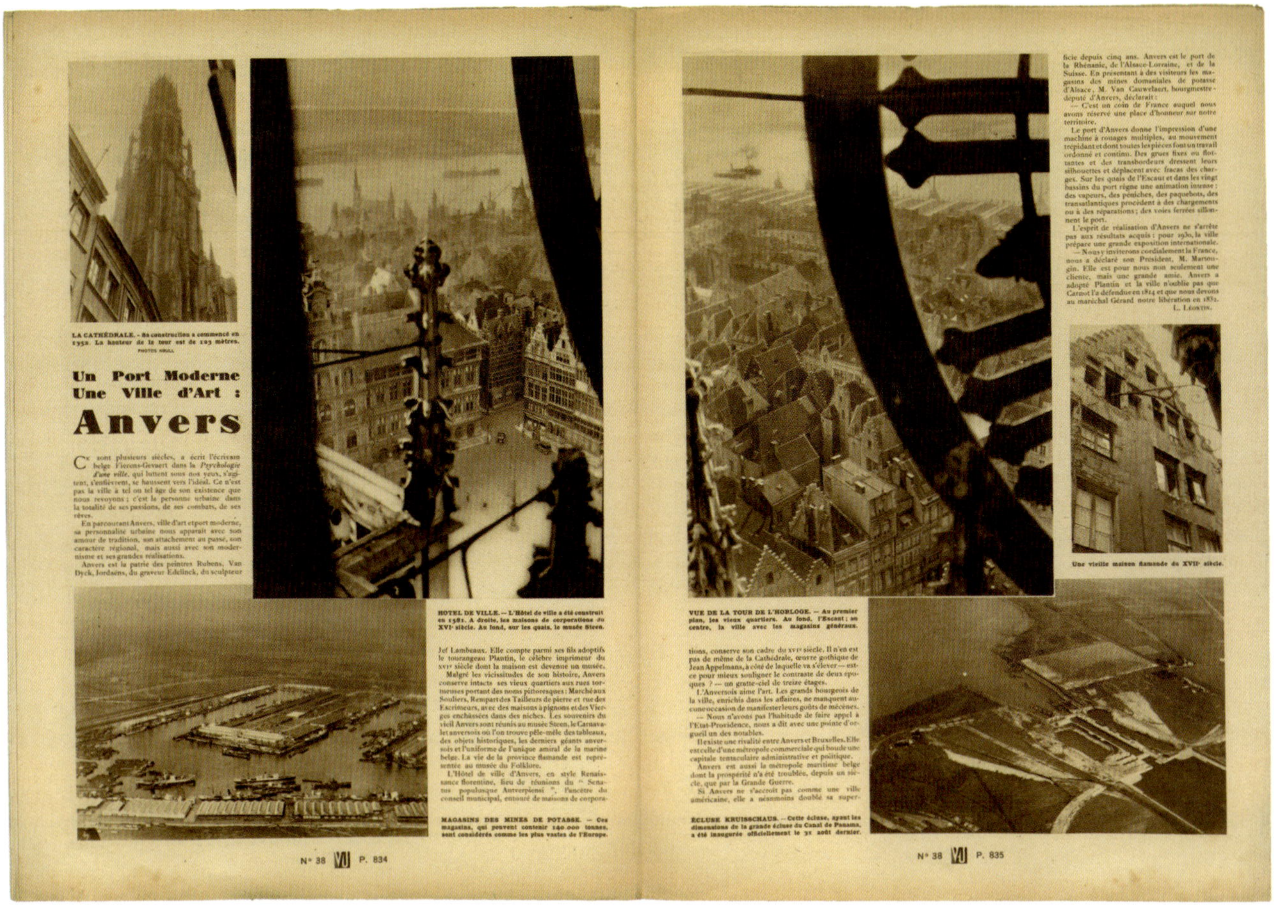

LA CATHÉDRALE. – Sa construction a commencé en 1352. La hauteur de la tour est de 123 mètres.
PHOTOS KRULL

Un Port Moderne Une Ville d'Art : Anvers

Ce sont plusieurs siècles, a écrit l'écrivain belge Fierens-Gevaert dans la *Psychologie d'une ville*, qui luttent sous nos yeux, s'agitent, s'enfièvrent, se haussent vers l'idéal. Ce n'est pas la ville à tel ou tel âge de son existence que nous revoyons ; c'est la personne urbaine dans la totalité de ses passions, de ses combats, de ses rêves.

En parcourant Anvers, ville d'art et port moderne, sa personnalité urbaine nous apparaît avec son amour de tradition, son attachement au passé, son caractère régional, mais aussi avec son modernisme et ses grandes réalisations.

Anvers est la patrie des peintres Rubens, Van Dyck, Jordaens, du graveur Edelinck, du sculpteur Jef Lambeaux. Elle compte parmi ses fils adoptifs le tourangeau Plantin, le célèbre imprimeur du XVIe siècle dont la maison est devenue un musée.

Malgré les vicissitudes de son histoire, Anvers conserve intacts ses vieux quartiers aux rues tortueuses portant des noms pittoresques : Marché aux Souliers, Rempart des Tailleurs de pierre et rue des Escrimeurs, avec des maisons à pignons et des Vierges enchâssées dans des niches. Les souvenirs du vieil Anvers sont réunis au musée Steen, le Carnavalet anversois où l'on trouve pêle-mêle des tableaux, des objets historiques, les derniers géants anversois et l'uniforme de l'unique amiral de la marine belge. La vie de la province flamande est représentée au musée du Folklore.

L'Hôtel de ville d'Anvers, en style Renaissance florentine, lieu de réunions du " Senatus populusque Antverpiensi ", l'ancêtre du conseil municipal, entouré de maisons de corporations, conserve son cadre du XVIe siècle. Il n'en est pas de même de la Cathédrale, œuvre gothique de Jean Appelmans, à côté de laquelle va s'élever — est-ce pour mieux souligner le contraste de deux époques ? — un gratte-ciel de treize étages.

L'Anversois aime l'art. Les grands bourgeois de la ville, enrichis dans les affaires, ne manquent aucune occasion de manifester leurs goûts de mécènes.

— Nous n'avons pas l'habitude de faire appel à l'Etat-Providence, nous a dit avec une pointe d'orgueil un des notables.

Il existe une rivalité entre Anvers et Bruxelles. Elle est celle d'une métropole commerciale qui boude une capitale tentaculaire administrative et politique.

Anvers est aussi la métropole maritime belge dont la prospérité n'a été troublée, depuis un siècle, que par la Grande Guerre.

Si Anvers ne s'accroît pas comme une ville américaine, elle a néanmoins doublé sa superficie depuis cinq ans. Anvers est le port de la Rhénanie, de l'Alsace-Lorraine, et de la Suisse. En présentant à des visiteurs les magasins des mines domaniales de potasse d'Alsace, M. Van Cauwelaert, bourgmestre-député d'Anvers, déclarait :

— C'est un coin de France auquel nous avons réservé une place d'honneur sur notre territoire.

Le port d'Anvers donne l'impression d'une machine à rouages multiples, au mouvement trépidant et dont toutes les pièces font un travail ordonné et continu. Des grues fixes ou flottantes et des transbordeurs dressent leurs silhouettes et déplacent avec fracas des charges. Sur les quais de l'Escaut et dans les vingt bassins du port règne une animation intense : des vapeurs, des péniches, des paquebots, des transatlantiques procèdent à des chargements ou à des réparations ; des voies ferrées sillonnent le port.

L'esprit de réalisation d'Anvers ne s'arrête pas aux résultats acquis : pour 1930, la ville prépare une grande exposition internationale.

— Nous y inviterons cordialement la France, nous a déclaré son Président, M. Martougin. Elle est pour nous non seulement une cliente, mais une grande amie. Anvers a adopté Plantin et la ville n'oublie pas que Carnot l'a défendue en 1814 et que nous devons au maréchal Gérard notre libération en 1832.

L. LÉONTIN.

HOTEL DE VILLE. — L'Hôtel de ville a été construit en 1581. A droite, les maisons de corporations du XVIe siècle. Au fond, sur les quais, le musée Steen.

MAGASINS DES MINES DE POTASSE. — Ces magasins, qui peuvent contenir 140 000 tonnes, sont considérés comme les plus vastes de l'Europe.

VUE DE LA TOUR DE L'HORLOGE. — Au premier plan, les vieux quartiers. Au fond, l'Escaut ; au centre, la ville avec les magasins généraux.

Une vieille maison flamande du XVIIe siècle.

ÉCLUSE KRUISSCHANS. — Cette écluse, ayant les dimensions de la grande écluse du Canal de Panama, a été inaugurée officiellement le 31 août dernier.

N° 38 VU P. 834

N° 38 VU P. 835

'A Modern Port, a Heritage City: Antwerp', *VU*, no. 38, 5 December 1928, pp. 834-835

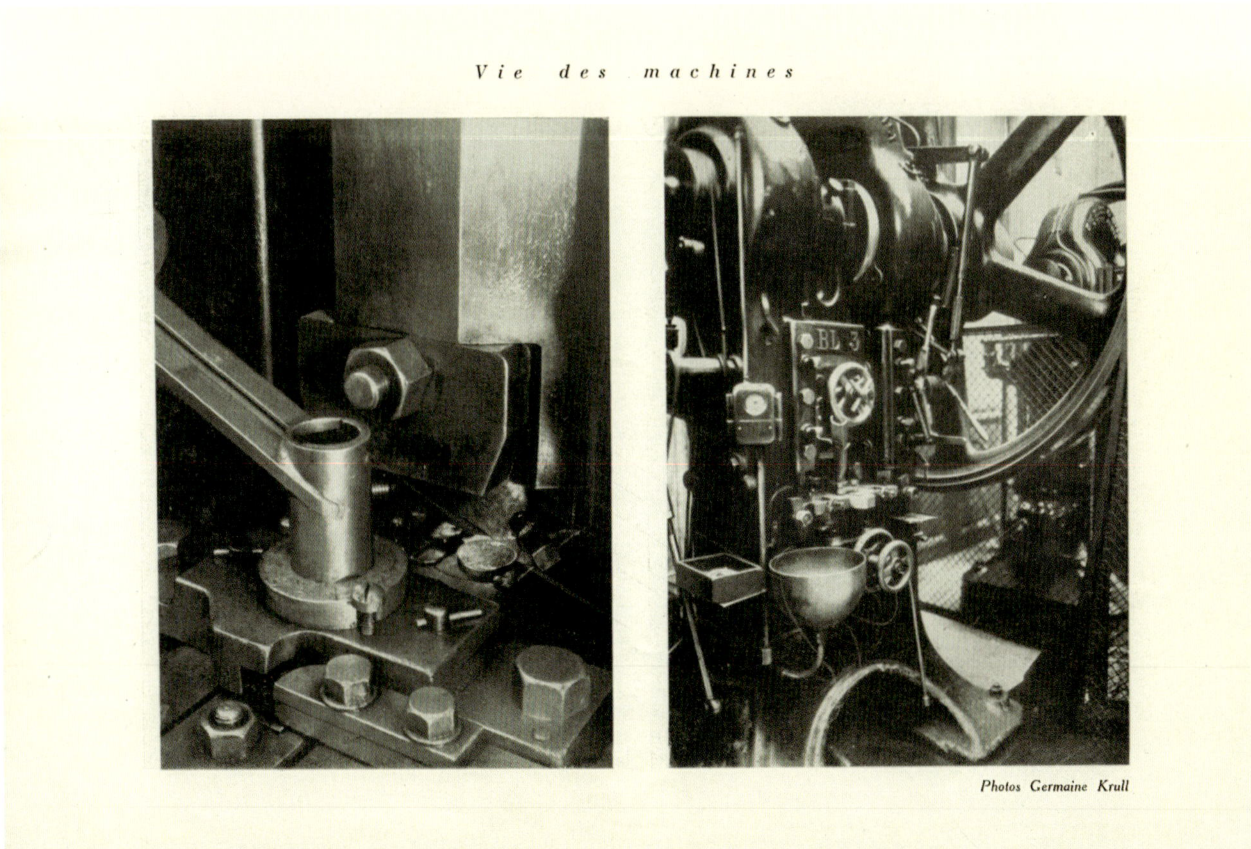

Vie des machines

Photos Germaine Krull

'Life of Machines', *Variétés*, 1st year, no. 9, 15 January 1930, p. 632a

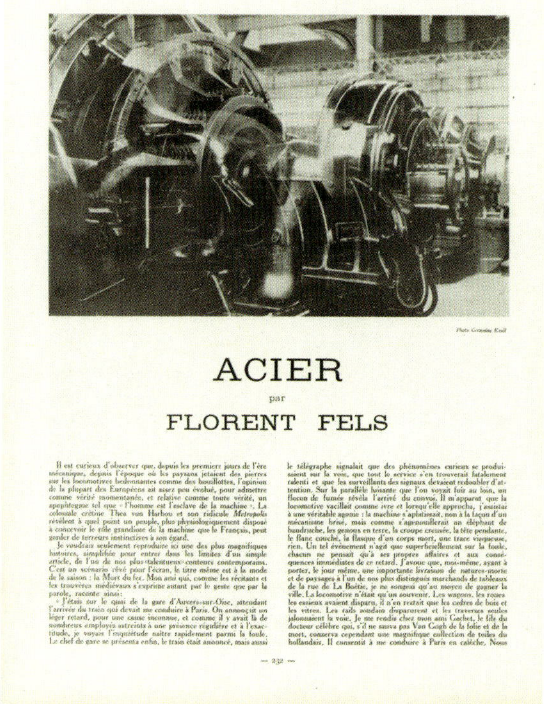

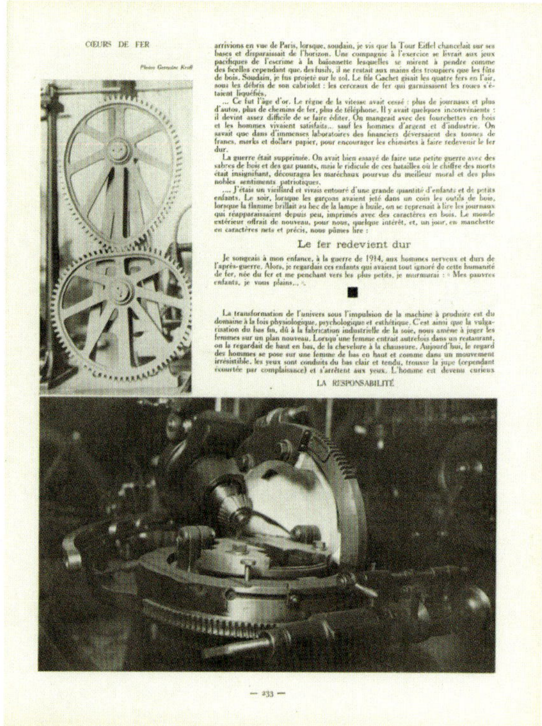

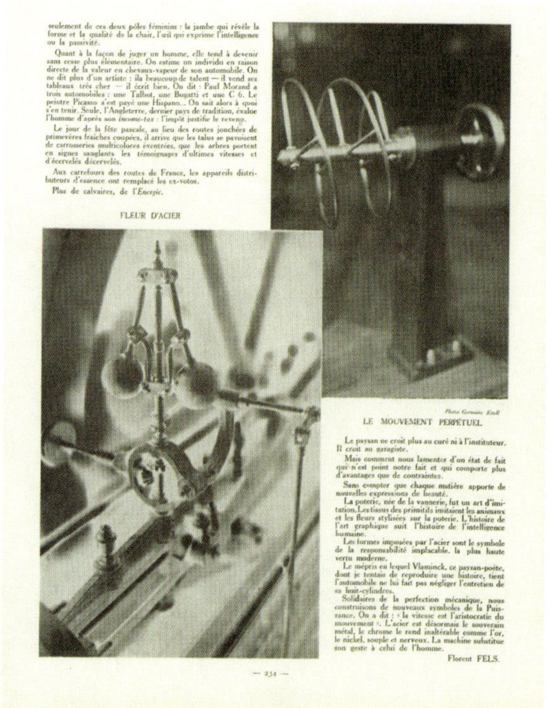

'**Steel**', *Jazz*, no. 5, 15 April 1929, by Florent Fels, pp. 232–234 (top and above)

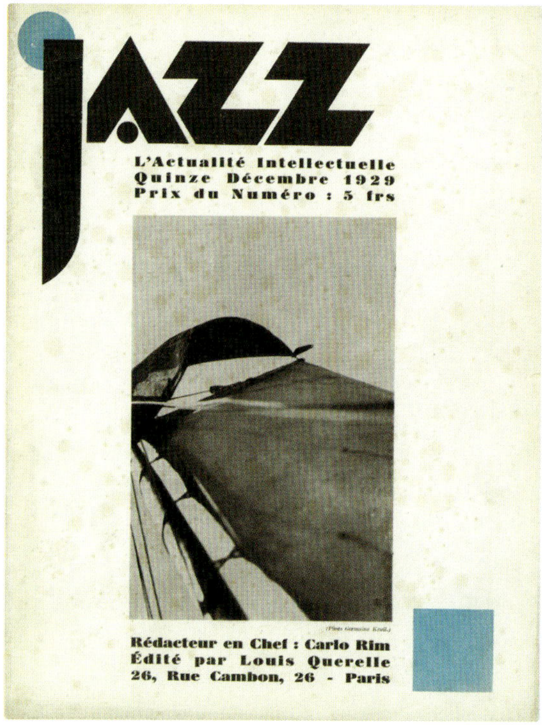

Cover of *Jazz*, no. 12, 15 December 1929

REPORTAGE AND MAGAZINES

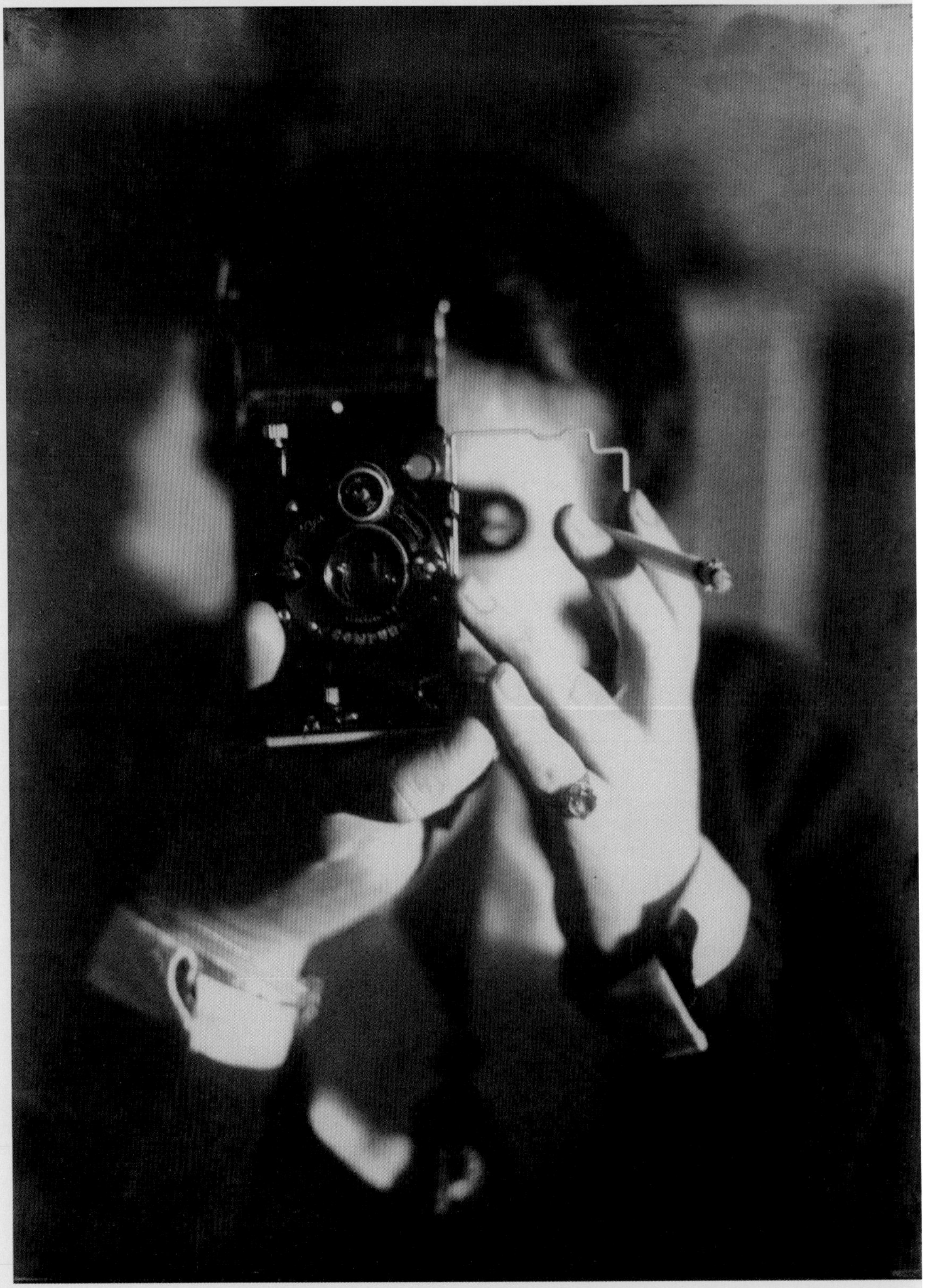

THE WATERSHED IN KRULL'S CAREER – the same one that triggered the Salon de l'Escalier and probably the publication of *Métal* – occurred when she joined the team at *VU* in March 1928. There she carried out reportage in 'a new manner', that is to say on carefully coordinated subjects, an approach that seemed to appeal to her temperament as well as to her convictions. Krull clearly found herself under pressure, because her boss's 'dynamism didn't stop at the girders of the Eiffel Tower. He wanted to *see* everything. He flung me into the streets, to fun fairs, to the Tuileries Gardens with their children, into car traffic, to the boats on the Saint Martin canal, the banks of the Seine, everywhere. Usually Lucien Vogel asked a well-known reporter to write the story, and I'd go along "to see".'[1] For the remainder of 1928, Krull was torn between a desire to benefit from the popularity of the 'iron aesthetic' of her *fers* by participating in exhibitions with her own distinct identity and the need to pursue new avenue of reportage. The latter soon captivated her, because *VU*'s media profile corresponded to her own social and political leanings. She could also count on her friendship with Eli Lotar, who soon turned out to be another photojournalist skilled in the 'new manner'.

VU, NEW-STYLE REPORTAGE

Suddenly Krull had to churn out a great number of pictures, because this type of photojournalism often involved 'treating' a subject by returning to it several times, in different places, at different moments. In practice, it was more like careful documentation than news reporting, which focused on fleeting events and required only a swift response. A magazine spread called for consistency and for an editorial line, which was initially supplied by the commissioning magazine yet allowed the photographer to come up with a personal angle, to take a position with respect to the subject, and perhaps to pursue it independently. '*VU* was a great hit! You had to come up with something every week.'[2] Here again, working in tandem with Lotar proved decisive, because they effected a kind of division of labour based on affinities or on the editors' wishes, or else sometimes – perhaps often, at first – they worked jointly, for example on a story on the Newfoundland-bound ships (Terre-Neuvas) that sailed from Saint-Malo. The Lotar-Krull couple moved to 61 Rue Damrémont and set up a new 'studio corner' where they perfected their techniques and material. They also found an assistant, Marcel from North Africa, who was an 'excellent retoucher' and who continued to work with Krull until she left Paris,[3] ultimately replacing Lotar 'in [her] life'. Since she 'increasingly had to go to artists' homes', that is to say, take indoor photos, she bought an 18 x 24 view camera that Marcel would carry (he also retouched negatives). 'With an advance from Vogel' Krull furthermore bought the latest thing, 'a small camera with extremely fast lens that should make it possible to take photos with little or no lighting'[4] – perhaps an Ermanox – so that she could work in theatres and cabarets. She said that the press wanted 'glossy, that is to say, shiny', pictures, an effect she obtained through the tricky process of drying the photos slowly on glass. She developed an entire craft of special practices and techniques in order to match demand.[5] Later (1929?), she bought 'a glazing machine that did the job in five minutes'.[6]

1 CEDG, pp. 12–23.
2 VMD, p. 126.
3 'My devoted factotum until I left Paris' (CEDG, p. 27).
4 CEDG, p. 19.
5 The idea that *VU* was based on the *Berliner Illustrierte Zeitung* and the *Münchner Illustrierte Presse* – repeated in many articles without verification, and developed by Kim Sichel – does not hold water. The German weeklies published photographs on only a few pages, and were printed in offset rather than higher-quality photogravure. The idea sprang from Tim Gidal's *Modern Photojournalism: Origin and Evolution 1910–1933*, New York: Macmillan, 1973, which drew on German sources and lent credence to this bias. See Frizot and De Veigy, op. cit.
6 VMD, p. 134.

Self-portrait with Icarette, '1925', c. 1928

One restriction on the 'craft skills' that Krull notably acquired leaps to the eye upon opening magazines such as *VU* and *L'Art vivant*: illustrative pictures were not handled like exhibition photographs, because they might be reframed, recropped – even cut out – or overlap one another. Contrary to standard press practice, however, *VU* did insist on publishing copyright credit for every photo printed, granting its reporters the status of artists. Another aspect of *VU* appealed to photographers: the magazine's general interest in photos was accompanied by attentive selection, layout and narrative sequencing, all under the artistic direction – in the early years – of Irène Lidova, then by Alexandre Liberman.

Photoreportage quickly yielded a stock of pictures on subjects that needed to be specified, accurately described and subsequently fleshed out with other shots, then archived or offered for sale to other magazines. The question of the property of the photographs then arose: for stories commissioned by *VU*, the photos that were published appear to have belonged to the magazine, while those not published were theoretically available for other publications; then there were pictures taken at the photographer's own initiative, which might be offered to *VU* and other magazines or even placed with an agency. For Krull and her colleagues, this represented unprecedented income. The issue was crucial, triggering an inevitable discussion between the Krull-Lotar-Kertész 'group' – who identified themselves as 'three independent avant-garde photographers' – and Vogel in December 1928. At stake were the conditions for foreign sales (to Germany, in fact), conditions on use of their photos in France (free right to exploit unpublished pictures), and the sharing of royalties.[7] Krull retained copyright for Germany and placed many photos with two German agencies, Mauritius (founded in Berlin in 1928) and Schostal (Vienna, Paris, Milan).[8] Over the months, the 'photojournalists' began specifying potential subjects that might suit a given photo, perhaps indirectly: a picturesque shot of a market stall, say, might represent a given city, or a trade, tradition, type of food, social context or immigrant population. On the backs of two pictures of the Eiffel Tower taken by Krull in 1928 are two lists, in Lotar's hand, of potential photographic subjects, clearly shared with Krull. Like a catalogue of ideas to be handled, they provide a broad outline of their targets: fashion, shops, shopping galleries, diamond merchants, mid-Lent celebrations, the Palais de la Femme, pearls, Amsterdam, the bridges of Paris, Saint-Malo sailboats, flea markets, department store, Rotterdam, London (markets), London (docks), Arab cafés, Paris streets, Paris by night, Paris advertising, flowers, nudes.[9]

Successive issues of *VU* – which commissioned the subject, hired a journalist to write the text, and handled the selection and evocative layout of pictures – document Krull's constitution of a stock of photographs devoted primarily to Paris. It was *VU* that established the framework, at least during the first year, for her new photographic activity. As Krull put it, Vogel 'sent [her] into the street' – the streets of Paris that seemed so wonderfully picturesque to foreign photographers and poets such as Kertész, Krull and Lotar. 'People wanted to see Paris the way they'd never seen it before, to discover things they hadn't known.'[10] The trio was obviously skilled at finding what 'people' didn't see, putting it right under their noses in a magazine that was nothing if not 'lively'. Their vision of old, traditional Paris hiding in disquieting little alleys was of course haunted by the ghost of Atget, whose work these photographers and other journalists discovered at the Salon de l'Escalier.

PARIS STREET LIFE

As early as issue four *VU* published a spread on FunFairs with photos exclusively by Krull and a text by Edmond Gréville, who was also a film-maker. Krull benefited from a dynamically balanced double-page layout highly typical of *VU*'s brilliant approach. It was arranged into cinema-like

7 Joint letter of 11 December 1928 to Lucien Vogel, signed by Germaine Krull, André Kertész and Eli Lotar. They agreed to lend for forty-eight hours, under the magazine's responsibility and for a specified number of copies, 'the photographs that you have accepted for *VU* . . . This excludes all other photographs taken by us as part of a reportage for your magazine.' They wanted to receive 50% of the sale of reproduction rights and asked for monthly statements of sales. Clause 7 sought to make mention of the photographer's name mandatory, lest 'the agents with whom you deal replace the photographer's name by that of their agency, which happens frequently'. Kertész archive, Médiathèque de l'Architecture et du Patrimoine, French Ministry of Culture. See Michel Frizot and Annie-Laure Wanaverbecq, *André Kertész*, Paris: Jeu de Paume/Hazan, 2010, p. 187.
8 The founder of the Mauritius agency, Ernst Mayer, also started the Black Star agency in New York in 1936. The fact that Schostal had a Paris branch must have made things easier for Krull.
9 One, numbered 1, is in the Folkwang Museum (NR 250/89); the other is the Thomas Walther Collection, Museum of Modern Art, New York (1750.2001), numbered 2, handwritten list in pencil. The only photo by Krull published in issue 1 of *VU* is a photo of mid-Lent, with another by Lotar on the same subject. An allusion to 'Cardinal Dubois' refers to a spread by Lotar published in issue 11 of *VU* (30 May 1928); 'Election (night)' refers to another story for *VU* by Lotar, 'Comment on fabrique l'opinion: Une visite de nuit aux usines politiques' (no. 7, 2 May 1928). The rather unexpected subject of pearls yielded a three-page spread in *VU* no. 33 (31 October 1928), including three photos by Lotar and one by Krull. 'Palais de la Femme' was a Salvation Army building that became the object of a reportage by Krull and Lotar for *VU* no. 44 (16 January 1929).
10 VMD, p. 126.

11 VMD, p. 126.
12 *VU* no. 12 (6 June 1928), pp. 306–307.
13 *L'Art vivant* no. 104 (15 April 1929), p. 341, following an article by Léo Larguier on 'Tableaux – Bric-à-Brac – Curiosités', p. 340.
14 Charles Fedgal, 'Vieux coins, vieilles boutiques', p. 313, illustrated on page 312 by a montage of five photos from Berenice Abbott's collection, thereby also echoing the Salon de l'Escalier.

'shots' that signposted aspects of the fair: the 'scenic railway' (roller coaster), the parade clown, the 'fairground freak', the crowd seen from above, the old merry-go-round and the Ferris wheel all shrewdly impart visual motion, sending the eye (like a camera) looping back-and-forth in a strikingly successful way. In a shot of a slide, Krull and the editors even indulged in spectacular superimposition, certainly deliberate rather than accidental. This unusual avant-garde effect was obviously related to photomontage and the idiom of experimental cinema, yet was highly original in a magazine for the general public in 1928, and it created a fine sense of movement. This slide was not spectacular like the one at Luna Park and the Rabier slide at the Foire du Trône on the Cours de Vincennes, but was a smaller ride with a single drop, probably also present at the Foire du Trône, of which an overall shot by Krull survives.

The FunFairs were followed by the 'Titaÿna' story. A somewhat scandalous female journalist and adventurer named Titaÿna, the same age as Krull, who was anything but fainthearted, recounted to readers of *VU* (in issue no. 6 of 25 April 1928) 'how [she] stole the head of a Buddha from Angkor' – which she now wanted to return! Krull took one photo of the head held by Titaÿna pictured as a wild kid not unlike herself, and another of it placed on the railings of the obelisk at Place de la Concorde, temporarily on hold. Titaÿna shortly afterward became the editor of *Jazz*, where Krull was very well treated.

But for Vogel (and Florent Fels) 'in the street' meant first of all working-class streets, including not only the boulevards with their motor traffic (which Krull would also handle), but also alleys with their strolling vendors. 'I'd walk the streets. I loved the hawkers – the sellers of fruit, vegetables, fish. Everything happened at the doorstep, on the vendors' little carts.'[11] Yet 'the street' also meant the outskirts, the wastelands ringing Paris – dubbed *la Zone* – with its marginal characters. A feature on 'the mysteries of the flea market' by Fels, published in June 1928,[12] was accompanied by seven photos, all taken by Krull, which lent homogeneity to the spread. They showed striking heaps of bric-a-brac and the people who rummaged among it (including Fels himself and American women 'wandering in search of the Old World'). The Paris-born Fels, a fan of the School of Paris painters, wrote that he even 'acquired a taste for rustic statues', a taste that he defended by citing a few 'modernist' figures such as Tristan Tzara, André Lhote and Jean Lurçat. Krull's pictures were bold and unexpected, evoking a reality in movement (just as *VU* wished), in direct contact with human activity and the tools of that activity. They were diametrically opposed to what was expected of the photographer of *fers* – they were new and somehow casual in a way that lent them an almost anti-professional look. When Fels covered the same subject for *L'Art vivant,* with a full page devoted to a scrap-iron market on Boulevard Richard-Lenoir, he published two photos by Krull (of the flea market at Saint-Ouen!) and three of his own, which are much less appealing wide-angle shots.[13] Another sign of the new photography's affinity for working-class culture was a feature in the same issue on 'old shops, old street corners', which resuscitated and honoured Atget through five photos of shop windows and stalls.[14]

Seeking in her memoirs to describe the impact of her involvement with *VU,* Krull immediately mentioned the down-and-outs. In a highly descriptive passage on her commitment to the new style of photojournalism, she wrote, 'There were also the "tramps" – they were the lords of the beggars, and themselves weren't even beggars. They had a particular view of liberty and wanted to organise their lives in accordance with their own ideas. I did a story on them with my friend Henri Danjou, a highly intelligent journalist who, like me, enjoyed street life. We went down along the embankment of the Seine, on Quai Montebello, opposite Notre-Dame. There the lords of the beggars were right at home. I arrived in the morning and left at night. They didn't exactly welcome us with a smile, but little by little they got used to our presence. My camera bothered them a good deal, but once again they wound up accepting it. They wanted to be free, free of laws and free of men. They asked nothing more from life than a litre of wine and a hunk of bread. They would work for a few hours early in the morning at Les Halles, hauling vegetables, meat and so on. Then they would settle along the banks of the Seine with a supply of wine and bread. In winter, or when they unfortunately failed to find work, they would head to the Salvation Army where they were given hot soup ... I had a great deal of difficulty taking pictures, but I managed even so. They're good, my photos of the tramps. I enjoyed the company of those men, and sometimes I felt I understood them – maybe they're not so crazy as all that.'[15]

This feature on 'tramps on the underside of Paris' was published in October 1928, during *VU*'s meteoric rise.[16] It included ten photos by Krull and was a model of artistic layout, opening with a double page that included two fine figures of tramps – one described as 'the philosopher of Place Maubert' and the other 'full of merriment' – placed above the reality of the 'underside', conveyed below in a 'falling' series of images (dormitory, bench, stairs leading down to the embankment). The spread continued on a third page, where the gazes of people looking at the Seine pass over the curled-up, sleeping figures. This story was a model of journalistic reporting and collaboration, thanks to the article by Danjou (1898–1954), who earlier that year had published *Place Maubert. Dans les bas-fonds de Paris*.[17] He described a stroll in the company of a tramp somewhat shrewder than the others. Danjou showed little interest in the tramps' way of life, and even less in their difficulties – he focused more on their personal 'stories', on the circumstances behind their apparent fall, and on their unconventional ideas (which the pictures do not evoke).[18] Three pages, ten photos by an artist, an article by a real author: that is what put this story at the top of a poll of *VU* readers carried out in late 1928 under the title 'Which Ones Deserve a Prize?'[19] It beat out a story on '*VU* in Russia' by James Abbé, published in the first issue, and was joined, in order of preference, by one on culturing pearls (photos by Lotar and Krull), another on a 'house of gloom' (Lotar) and the one on the theft of a head of Buddha (Krull). It is nevertheless worth noting that the journalists were credited as the 'authors', while the photographers were not taken into consideration; furthermore, a story by Kertész on the Trappist monastery at Soligny, although done in the autumn, was not in competition because it had not yet been published.

Krull's highly popular photos of tramps were reused in the special Christmas 1932 issue of *Le Sourire* for an article by Jim Tully.[20] One picture of a tramp and two of the soup line were printed in Jean Lasserre's *Paris misère* in 1935,[21] although by that time it was clear that Krull's photos were no longer innovatory, but were encountering competition from Wide World Photos. The lower classes were crowding certain quarters of Paris day and night, notably the central market at Les Halles where 'the market gardeners' large vans brought fruit and vegetables to be skilfully displayed in stacks or mounds' in the 'pale light of a weakly glowing gas lamp'.[22]

Through her work at *VU*, the Parisian lower classes of whom Krull was fond became one of her own photographic subjects, enabling her to make a living and at the same time pursue her oeuvre, given that she still viewed herself as part of the 'avant-garde' (as she wrote to Vogel, and as invitations to international exhibitions would demonstrate). With hindsight, however, Krull also acknowledged the important influence of writers (who were also journalists). 'Francis Carco's *Jésus la Caille*[23] was a revelation to us all concerning the Paris ruffians who were terrorising the bourgeoisie. Thanks to Mac Orlan, Cendrars and others, the underworld became "mobsters". Their laws, their women, even their crimes, took on a human face.'[24] She described her strolls with Danjou in the former fortified zone ringing Paris: 'Huts made of corrugated tin,

15 VMD, p. 126.
16 'Les clochards dans les bas-fonds Paris', *VU* no. 31 (17 October 1928), pp. 688–690.
17 Paris: Albin Michel, 1928, legal deposit 31 May.
18 For that matter, Danjou wrote about the tramps on Place Maubert whereas Krull focused on those at Les Halles and the embankment near Notre-Dame.
19 'Quels sont ceux que vous récompenseriez?', results announced in *VU* no. 44 (16 January 1929), p. 33. The poll/contest was launched in issues 34, 35, and 36. The first prize for readers was a portable wireless in a travelling case.
20 Jim Tully, 'Le monteur d'étoiles', *Le Sourire de Noël* (1932), unpaginated.
21 Jean Lasserre, *Paris misère*, Grenoble: Artaud, 1935.
22 CEDG, p. 13.
23 Carco's famous 1914 novel took its title, *Jésus la Caille*, from the name of its homosexual protagonist.
24 CEDG, p. 16.

25 'Le dernier interview de la Goulue: Un million à retrouver?', *VU* no. 47 (6 February 1929), pp. 84–85, with two photos by Krull.
26 Charles Fegdal, 'Les "Mannousch" de Bagnolet', *L'Art vivant* no. 125 (1 March 1930), p. 201. On pages 204–204 *Manousch* is spelled *manousch;* Fegdal claimed that 'the *romanichels* are French *Manousch*, the *gypsies* come from Great Britain, the *zingaries* from Italy, and the *tziganes* are from central Europe.'
27 CEDG, p. 24.
28 VMD, p. 134.
29 *Jazz* (January 1929), pp. 51–53.
30 *Jazz* (July–August 1929), pp. 347–350.

cardboard, and straw sheltered an entire little world. Hatless women and dirty children lived there.' The *fortifs,* also known as *la zone* even though it had no real boundaries, was the site of the fortified rampart built by Adolphe Thiers in the nineteenth century and demolished in the 1920s; it became a wasteland occupied by the poor and immigrants, plus rag-and-bone men to the north (the Saint-Ouen flea market), and 'gypsies' to the east (Bagnolet) and south (Porte de Vanves). There Danjou and Krull also met La Goulue, the famous dancer immortalised by Toulouse-Lautrec, by then 'a poor old woman who still made up her face with powdered pigment . . . Her feet were swollen, toes peeking out of torn shoes, her hands misshapen.' Krull took pictures of what would become one of her 'most moving' spreads to accompany the article by Danjou.[25]

Charles Fegdal, another Krull friend who wrote a column for *L'Art vivant,* went in search of the gypsies (*manouche*) at Bagnolet in March 1930. His article was masterfully illustrated by a central two-page spread of four pictures by Krull and two by Atget, who had also photographed 'the zoners' and rag-pickers in 1920–21. In order to reach the *manouche*, one first had to cross *la Zone*, 'a refuge of wretched, pitiful poverty, alas. It is an inextricable jumble of the ragged, the shabby and vagabond, the threadbare and barefoot, the unfortunate and the self-defeated.' Beyond this zone lived the gypsies of Bagnolet, 'a tough race, brutal yet jaunty'. Fegdal viewed them as *gitanos* who had come from Spain, 'indifferent to their hypothetical homeland', who for the moment sang and danced while living 'in tents with multiple poles, sketching the lines of an Arab camp halted at the edge of an oasis.' Ultimately, the reader begins to sense *L'Art vivant*'s broader goal of promoting 'diversity' in passages such as, 'They respond to their artistic souls. Artists from where, of what, for whom? It matters not!'[26] The illustrations, however, make no distinction, turning human beings into objects to be looked at, which is indeed the natural bias of photography and the illustrated press. And yet the sincerity and compassion of both writer and photographer are unquestionable.

For literary reasons, Krull also mentioned her closeness to writers when exploring the 'mob world'. 'My other stories with [brothers Georges and Joseph Kessel] took Lotar and me to the dance halls on Rue de Lappe, in the heart of the mob.' Georges Kessel, with backing from Gallimard publishers, had founded *Détective* (1 November 1928), a new magazine inspired by *VU* but specialising in crime and court-room stories. He was probably counting on contributions from Krull, which turned out to be minimal because she was too committed to *VU.* In fact, Krull was perfectly familiar with many bars, cabarets and dance halls since she often went dancing. 'There was no club in Montmartre, big or small, where Eli and I hadn't spent hours dancing . . . Little by little, waltzes, tangos and blues were replaced by the one-step and two-step, and later by the charleston and foxtrot.'[27] 'I learned to dance the *java* waltz with them, but only after asking Eli's permission.'[28] According to Krull, 'Only Eli knew where to find the good bistrots.' Her pictures of bars, bistrots and dance halls remain a model of spontaneity in which the beholder senses that the photographer knew the scene and was a regular there, while customers behave as though they hadn't noticed the camera, as though it had been placed incognito on the bar. Three striking photos of head-on faces appeared in *Jazz* in January 1929, introducing Jacques Dyssord's article on 'Rue de Lappe'.[29] That same issue of *Jazz* included an article on FunFairs by Henry Thétard (a specialist on the circus) with a photo by Krull, echoing the earlier one in *VU.* An article by Dyssord on the disappearance of traditional cafés, 'Here Lies the Café', was illustrated by three 'bar' shots by Krull for the July–August 1929 issue of *Jazz.*[30] A story by Danjou for the September 1929 issue of *Détective,* titled 'To the Sound of the Accordion', included a double-page spread of medium shots of 'authentic types' wearing their 'traditional caps, scarves and jumpers' while drinking with prostitutes. This type of forbidden image, 'shot by lamplight', was not normally found in the press, or else only in the form of drawings.[31] Thanks to photography, the reader is drawn into this shady world 'where so many unfortunates come to purchase, for five sous, an outlaw's happiness', where 'pimps reward their girls for work well done before dark by taking them to the dance hall' (Danjou). The reader has the impression of witnessing scenes so realistically conveyed: '[A woman] exchanged a few words with a kind of dwarf in an olive-green jacket who was trying to even up, thanks to the mirror behind the bar, the two ends of his necktie' (Dyssord).

VARIÉTÉS

Clearly, the choice of potential photos for a reportage would vary considerably depending on the overall tone of the article, the policy of a given magazine and the readership it targeted. Also to be taken into account was the news magazines' systematic cropping, combining and overlapping of photos, which thereby lost their original status. That is why a magazine such as *Variétés,* an illustrated monthly with a contemporary approach to 'modern' art, sought to respect the status of a photograph as a work of art like painting or poetry.

The magazine's use of inset plates (text was never set with photos, only drawings) in successive four- or eight-page sections reflected an editorial line that respected the original format of the photograph and the work of the photographer, accompanying the picture with a very straightforward caption that sought no contradiction between word and image, as did other magazines of surrealist tendency (*Bifur, La Révolution surréaliste, Documents*). Also carefully studied was the juxtaposition of two pictures on each page, as witnessed by the backs of the surviving prints.[32] It was a veritable laboratory of photographic montage in which, as in film montage, different images are juxtaposed to produce meaning through 'the poetic collision of two more or less remote realities'.[33] Its December 1928 issue, which coincided with Krull's heyday, was largely devoted to Paris, at least in terms of illustration. It hinged on two articles, 'Dawn' by Pierre Mac Orlan and 'Venus and the Dummies' by Paul Fierens (a Belgian art critic living in Paris). In fact, the issue opened with an article on Eugène Atget by screenwriter and director Albert Valentin:[34] 'As recorded by [Atget's] lens, these outlying neighbourhoods and remote dead-end alleys constitute a natural stage for melodrama and violent death.'[35] Each of the four pages, with two photos per page, was headed 'photographic works by Atget'. There were four pictures of shop windows, two of prostitutes, one of a street hawker and another of a circus entrance. The subsequent four-page gathering of eight illustrations included six photos by Krull – two of department stores, one of the scrap-iron section of the flea market, and three of market stalls at Les Halles – and ended with 'two fragments of Georges Lacomb's film, *La Zone*'. The next four-page section of eight photos in this issue is particularly remarkable and most homogeneous, with each page headed 'Tramps by Germaine Krull' as though it were an article, a poem or artwork. The pictures are indeed medium shots of 'tramp figures' in action, like a shot from a film. Mac Orlan's text, titled 'Dawn', offered a lucid analysis: 'The frightfully picturesque tragedy begins with the intellectual decline of these grey ghosts in the half-light ... In such circumstances, it becomes easy to assume they have few stories to tell.' Photography probably told their story better than they could themselves. Then Fierens' article, 'Streets and Intersections: Venus and the Dummies, or from "Autumn" to "Spring"', discussed shop windows and the novelty of Siégal window dummies. The next section featured Krull's pictures of a printshop and of a dance hall on Rue de Lappe.

A similar subject resurfaced in the July 1929 issue of *Variétés,*[36] given the social and 'surrealist' interest shown in a 'World Congress of Vagabonds' held in Stuttgart in June 1929 (at the same time as the *Film und Foto* exhibit!), organised by Gregor Gog. The problem was

31 Henri Danjou, 'Au son de l'accordéon', *Détective* no. 47 (19 September 1929), pp. 12–13, five photos variously credited to Krull and *Détective*.
32 In the AMSAB archives, published photographs are systematically linked to the photo with which they were laid out, including legend and the wording, 'place on the page with...' What is more, the notes specify '13 cm base' or '9 cm base', which leaves the other dimension somewhat variable (there are never any crop marks).
33 Jacques Brunius, preface to *125 collages et objets d'E.L.T. Mesens*, Knokke-le-Zout, 1963, quoted in Anne Reverseau, 'E.L.T. Mesens en pieces détachées: une poétique de l'assemblage', *Textyles* no. 43, 2013, pp. 63–72; http://textyles.revues.org/2355.
34 Albert Valentin serialised *Aux soleils de minuit* in twelve issues of *Variétés,* wrote for *La Révolution surréaliste,* served as assistant director to René Clair, and worked with Charles Spaak.
35 *Variétés* 1, no. 8 (15 December 1928), pp. 403–407.
36 *Variétés* 2, no. 3 (15 July 1929), photos by Krull, pp. 160–161.

37 See 'Women', below.
38 'Magie Noire au Moulin Rouge', *VU* no. 70 (17 July 1929), p. 574. *Blackbirds of 1928* was a Lew Leslie production that ran on Broadway before playing Paris in 1929.
39 *Variétés* 2, no. 4 (15 August 1929), p. 256c (256b for Lotar).
40 Photos of the building actually credited to Krull are very rare. One of her pictures was published in André Warnod, *Visages de Paris*, while another (of the façade) appeared in a programme of March 1930 (neither figured in the brochure), yet another in Adolf Hallman's *Paris*. Two photos of the Théâtre Pigalle following the picture of Earl Tucker in *Variétés* 2, no. 4 are unattributed. This author is certain that the ones in *L'Art vivant* (15 July 1929) and *VU* no. 68 are all by Tabard, but these are not the ones in the Draeger-Carlu brochure, either. It would seem there was a problem of copyright over some of the photos of the theatre, which might nevertheless be by Krull but the object of a special contract.
41 Michel Georges-Michel, 'Tabarin', *VU* no. 94 (1 January 1930), pp. 10–11, four photos of eleven.
42 VMD, p. 141.
43 CEDG, p. 42.
44 The AMSAB archive has four photos of Baty rehearsals of *Le Simoun*, a play by H. R. Lenormand performed at the Théâtre Pigalle in 1930.

addressed in articles by Nico Rest ('The Congress of Vagabonds') and Mac Orlan ('The Signs And Slogans Of Vagabonds', and again in his 'Nocturne' column). It seemed natural that Krull's pictures appear here in a magnificent eight-page section of sixteen photos, even if the vaguely defined vagabonds extended to tramps, gypsies and itinerant pedlars: subjects included 'Fried fish on a windy day', 'the refuge' and 'gypsies', along with Atget's lampshade vendor, all pure examples of Krull's 1928–29 style.

These issues of *Variétés* were exemplary of the evolution of a photojournalist whose still undefined status was beginning to emerge – and would evolve quickly, for that matter, as magazines were founded and editorial lines developed. 'Taking photos' also meant thinking about their immediate future as well as their potential use for other projects – all the while remaining in tune with oneself.

Other subjects in *VU* included 'unknown religions' in January 1929, and a May 1929 spread on a beauty parlour that probably spurred Krull's interest in female labour and would later lead to the series of Paris working women in 1932.[37]

Paris reportage also covered theatrical shows, where Krull was a regular, and could lead to special features outside the 'entertainment' section, which relied on other, more available photographers. Krull thus published a four-photo page on Earl Tucker, aka Snakehips, a fascinating Black dancer who headlined the *Blackbirds* revue that opened at the Moulin Rouge for a three-month run on 7 June 1929. The unsigned article on 'Black Magic at the Moulin Rouge: Earl Tucker Bewitches Paris' referred to a 'dark, double-jointed puppet' who mimed an 'extraordinary scene of anguish and sorrow' as 'shivers ran up his body from the tip of his toes to his clenched throat'.[38] Krull – like Kertész – also photographed Clayton 'Peg Leg' Bates, a hoofer with a wooden leg who was also in the show, and dancer Mary Clemens. *Variétés* immediately scooped them up and put Earl Tucker on the same page as Krull's shot of Clemens, plus two other pictures by Lotar of Black dancers in their dressing room.[39] In the same issue, Fierens published an article on 'a real theatre', namely the Théâtre Pigalle built for Philippe de Rothschild, which opened on 20 June 1929. It was conceived as the most modern theatre in the world in terms of architecture, lighting, stage machinery and illuminated ceiling. Gaston Baty was appointed to run it. Krull photographed it inside and out, as witnessed by a plate in *Paris 1929* (published by Calavas), an album whose inclusion of Krull demonstrates the interest taken in her work. Meanwhile, the eight photographs in a stunning brochure on the theatre published by Draeger, with layout and cover by Jean Carlu, are often attributed to Krull, but proof is lacking.[40] The theatre was already hosting a branch of Louis Moyses's cabaret Le Bœuf sur le Toit when Krull did a small reportage on Moyses's Enfants Terribles cabaret as soon as it opened. In the same Pigalle neighbourhood, Krull was a regular at the Tabarin dance hall, home to the French cancan ever since the Tabarin had hosted Moulin Rouge shows after the latter burnt down in 1915; it was given a good presentation on a double-page spread laid out like a gaudy spectacle – which was *VU's* credo. Other pictures from that reportage would appear in a small publication devoted to the French cancan in August 1930, in which the dynamism of Krull's seventeen photos contrasts with the facile quality of other pictures by the Marcello studio.[41] A photo of two dancers also appeared in the July 1929 issue *Bifur* with the offbeat caption of 'Landscape'.

Krull went to the theatre often, and was a friend of Louis Jouvet and Jean Cocteau. 'At that time I was at the theatre a lot myself, with Jouvet and Jean Cocteau. It was a joy to see those two great men work together.'[42] She followed the career of Gaston Baty, 'who amazed people as an extraordinary director, putting on works by young German writers',[43] and she certainly took many photos of stagings and rehearsals, but apparently those pictures were never published.[44]

BEYOND PARIS

'The Rebirth of the French Navy', published in July 1928, was Krull's first reportage as *VU*'s 'special correspondent' (a title indicated beneath each photo). The occasion was a naval review by French president Gaston Doumergue at Le Havre. It also yielded Krull's first cover photo, a fine shot of a seated sailor looking straight at the reader ('On the eve of review').[45]

A trip to Menez-Hom in Brittany (probably the first, in August 1928) for a conference on Breton autonomy enabled Krull to address a tricky socio-political subject, which *VU* cautiously presented as an 'open forum' (penned by Louis Martin-Chauffier). Krull recorded the event in ten pictures of protagonists and situations (the planting and confiscation of a Breton flag, a bard at the Chapelle Sainte-Marie). To a certain extent it was Krull's 'baptism by ideology', for she would return to issues of beliefs, opinions and ideas with a noteworthy reportage on 'unknown religions' in Paris (January 1929), which took her from an Antoinist church to the theosophical temple via the Society of Friends (Quakers), Liberal Catholic Church, Sufi headquarters and Divinist cult in Montmartre, all in the loyal company of Danjou.[46] At the same time she and Lotar headed to the evangelical Salvation Army.[47] A little later, *VU* published her complete feature on a day spent with the editor of the newspaper *L'Intransigeant* (September 1929).[48] Clearly such questions interested her when they allowed her to show individuals acting out their beliefs or opinions. In July 1928 she was dispatched as a 'special correspondent' to Carcassonne to cover that city's bimillenary celebrations.[49] She was also 'pushed onto a train' for Saint-Malo to attend a religious festival for the Terre-Neuvas ships (once again as 'special correspondent', and apparently accompanied by Lotar). The feature, including six photos, was published in the February 1929 issue of *VU*. The tall sailing ships appealed to her, and she learned to spot good poses (for example, sailors at work). These trips enabled Krull to experience French provinces, sites and cultural traditions unfamiliar to her. Yet she dealt with them in a straightforward, uninhibited way. Probably a second trip to Brittany was required for a story in Locronan, Finistère, again as 'special correspondent' accompanied by journalist Marc Daubrive. There a religious procession held every six years, La Grande Troménie, allowed her to get close to 'local people' while avoiding quaint folklore, by showing the same consideration and even respect she displayed towards Paris tramps and crooks. She also contributed four pictures[50] to illustrate an essentially 'photographic' subject, the depiction of popular superstitious habits, which yielded some original imagery.[51] Probably thanks to the influence of André Malraux, she covered a 'major artistic discovery' concerning the dating of Christian and Oriental religious statues,[52] as well as, somewhat later, an exhibition of Gothic-Buddhist art that Malraux organised at the gallery of the Nouvelle Revue Française.[53] A writers' conference held at the abbey of Pontigny, to which she went unenthusiastically, immersed her in a world of disparate individuals – Gide, Mauriac, Martin du Gard, Malraux – whose ideas she did not always appreciate; although 'extremely polite to [her]', these literary stars only tolerated the presence of the female photographer once Vogel showed up. She had to sleep in the village and was authorised to take pictures 'of these gentlemen only when they were strolling on the grounds', whereas she had wanted to photograph them during their debates.[54] Yet the reportage became 'the finest and simultaneously most difficult' of her photo stories.[55]

The consequence of doing photo spreads for *VU* was that Krull – like her colleagues Kertész and Lotar – wound up travelling across France. Brittany was followed by trips to the south, beginning with Marseille, which she very much liked and where she often returned. A Danjou story on 'Marseille, Gateway to the World', was accompanied by her photos of narrow streets and little shops.[56] Shortly afterwards (July), she found herself in Saint-Tropez for the

45 Jean Fayard, 'La renaissance de la marine française', *VU* no. 17 (11 July 1928), pp. 402–403.
46 Henri Danjou, 'Religions inconnues', *VU* no. 42 (2 January 1929), pp. 909–910, eight photos of eight. The subject was taken up in Maurice Magre, 'Religions multiples / Course à la vérité', *VU* no. 419 (28 March 1936), pp. 44–46, two photos of nine.
47 'Les sauvetages de l'Armée du salut', *VU* no. 44 (16 January 1929), pp. 38–39, two photos of ten.
48 'Les maîtres de l'opinion', *VU* no. 74 (11 September 1929), pp. 720–722, six photos of six.
49 'A Carcassonne, le mirage des fêtes du bimillenaire', *VU* no. 19 (25 July 1928), pp. 449–451, seven photos of nine.
50 See 'Free Spirit' below.
51 Sylviac, 'Superstitions', *VU* no. 143 (10 December 1930), pp. 1343–1345.
52 'Une grande découverte artistique', *VU* no. 50 (27 February 1929), pp. 147–148.
53 André Malraux, 'Une exposition d'art gothico-bouddhique', *VU* no. 151 (4 February 1931), pp. 161–162.
54 CEDG, p. 51.
55 '10 jours chez Socrate ou les entretiens de Pontigny', *VU* no. 78 (2 October 1929), pp. 720–722, ten photos of ten.
56 Henri Danjou, 'La porte du monde: Marseille', *VU* no. 56 (10 April 1929), pp. 276–278, five photos of ten.

holidays, and later (September) in Maillane, again for local celebrations, this time related to the poet Mistral.[57] She most likely took the opportunity to take other pictures for her own collection and for possible supply to other magazines in the present or the future, for that was indeed the goal of a photojournalist: 'Foreign journals asked me for photos. I began to have a large collection of travel and street views in stock.'[58] At the time, one picture of Marseille appeared in *Bifur* (May 1929, on the gypsy quarter) and three others in *Jazz*.[59] Her Brittany pictures took the same path through the media by appearing in *Bifur* (3 September 1929, two photos of 'picturesque Brittany')[60] and *Jazz* (three photos accompanying a Mac Orlan text on 'Brittany young and old'), the latter focusing on Ouessant, 'an island where women wore their hair loose – strange, mystical "daughters of the rain", of spindrift and fog, of mariners' tales.'[61] Ouessant, which constituted a reportage in itself, later resurfaced in *Variétés* (February 1930) with shots of 'a windmill' and 'the inland' (a farmer burning kelp and a woman with a cow), accompanied by photos of 'Pointe du Raz', 'a fisherman', 'the market at Quimper', and 'the market at Douarnenez'.[62] After an interval appropriate to a magazine devoted not to topical news but to 'cultural heritage' such as *Art et Médecine* (published by the Debat pharmaceutical firm for a readership of doctors),[63] in February 1932 seven of Krull's photos accompanied a story on 'Brittany and the Bretons', printed in the impeccable brown photogravure technique characteristic of that magazine.[64] They included a windmill, the port of Douarnenez, little girls in the Grande Troménie religious procession and three other photos of Locronan.

Art et Médecine, a lavish magazine that must have paid well, provided a good outlet for photos by Krull and Kertész in 1931 and 1932, a time when the more intellectual publications were folding. In four issues over the period July 1931 to March 1932, it published thirty-seven of her photographs. A July 1931 article on Roman vestiges in Provence, for example, included ten photos that eschewed the traditional frontal view of monuments, taken in Nîmes, Uzès and Aigues-Mortes.[65]

The March 1932 issue was entirely devoted to Provence, and three major articles included pictures by Krull. 'Provence' featured Fréjus, Toulon, Le Cap Brun, Arles and Ramatuelle, demonstrating that Krull had been there. 'Three Great Mediterranean Beauties' focused on Marseille – the six Krull photos (of the port plus one shot from the transporter bridge) reflected the poetry evoked in the text: 'Marseille with its crowds, its local and cosmopolitan crowds, lives the life of a great seafaring and merchant city. Life in Marseille is a spectacle all on its own. Its poetry is one of power – its ports, its docks are a world unto themselves.' Finally, a text by Colette included a Krull photo of an olive grove and a high-angle shot of the abbey of Thoronet.[66]

Krull's stock enabled her to place pictures with foreign as well as French magazines, and with agencies such as Schostal and Mauritius. That, however, was one of the pitfalls of this new profession, because it required the management of negatives, the printing of prints, the return of said prints and payment, all of which was difficult for a single person who had to concentrate on taking photographs. And such a stock was not always profitable. A given style might become unfashionable within a year, and prints were soon flooding the market given the number of new photographers from 1930 onwards: the boom in illustrated magazines created a demand that spurred new, younger people to join the field, more likely to fulfil less demanding but swifter and more standardised requirements. Krull's most successful period in the media lasted from June 1928 to July 1930, prolonged into 1931 and 1932 thanks to *Art et Médecine.*

Her last innovative, attention-getting spreads in *VU* focused on the common people, on social classes like the Paris tramps of her early days. First came a story on female labourers in Paris, penned by Emmanuel Berl, that began at year's end and continued over six issues –

57 Philippe Lamaur (it must be Philippe Lamour, in fact), 'La fête des Espagnols à Saint-Tropez', *VU* no. 121 (9 July 1930), pp. 672–673, seven photos of seven. Jean-Jacques Brousson, 'Les Fêtes de Mistral à Maillane', *VU* no. 131 (7 September 1930), pp. 918–919, three photos of eleven.
58 VMD, p. 138.
59 Charles Arno-Brun, 'Marseille', *Jazz* no. 7 (15 June 1929), pp. 313–316, three photos.
60 *Bifur* no. 3, September 1929, p. 24.
61 *Jazz* no. 12 (15 December 1929), pp. 515–516. The cover photo of a sail was taken by Krull.
62 *Variétés* 2, no. 15 (February 1930), pp. 698–699. The AMSAB archives in Ghent have three photos of windmills on Ouessant.
63 *Art et Médecine, revue mensuelle réservée au corps médical* was published by Laboratoires du Dr. Debat, Garches, and printed by Kapp in Vanves. Founded in October 1929 under the title *Revue du médecin,* the magazine became *Art et Médecine* in October 1930, then *Revue du médecin* in September 1936, and finally *Art et Médecine* again from October 1938 to 1939.
64 *Art et Médecine* strove for photographic quality, and sought out the young generation at *VU,* beginning with Kertész and Krull, later Zuber, Caillaud and Régis-Lebrun for advertising. Charles Le Goffic, 'La Bretagne et les bretons', *Art et Médecine* (February 1932), pp. 12–25, seven photos of nineteen.
65 Jean-Jacques Brousson, 'Rome en France', *Art et Médecine* (July 1931), pp. 24–29, ten photos.
66 Gabriel Hanotaux, 'Provence', pp. 9–19, five photos of fourteen. Louis Bertrand, 'Les trois grandes beautés de la Méditerranée', pp. 20–25, six photos of eight. Colette, 'Midi sévère', pp. 26–29, two photos of five. *Art et Médecine* (March 1932).

numbers 247 (7 December 1932) to 252 (11 January 1933) – covering four pages in each issue. These photographs represent the high point of Krull's focus on individuals, on the activities and struggles of small craft trades, and on the fate of women.[67]

Her contributions to *VU* virtually came to an end in 1934, in a special 'holiday' issue dated 18 July. First came a two-page spread for which she alone supplied six photos, showing Sunday leisure activities on the banks of the Marne River. It was a predictable, seasonal subject, yet now takes on special meaning given the events of two years later, when the Popular Front government decreed 'paid holidays' for the first time in 1936. Krull's photos showed people splashing in the water, sleeping on the grass. The accompanying article by Louis Cheronnet, 'Suburban Eden', referred to 'stepping over nameless bodies bled by six days of labour. The men snore. The women daydream immodestly, underarms open to the sky.'[68]

In the same issue, Jean Gallotti – a colleague of Vogel, Krull and Fels in the days of *VU* and *L'Art vivant* – explored 'the continuity of lower-class characters' based on seventeenth-century paintings by the Le Nain brothers.[69] Five photographs of details from the paintings were compared to 'lower-class characters' drawn from Krull's archives, with particular emphasis on facial expressions, poses and similarities of social class. This exercise in noting expressions and poses was conducted by Gallotti following the exhibition that first 'rediscovered' the Le Nain brothers, held at the Petit Palais in Paris in 1934. He emphasised the paintings' 'view of human suffering', which constituted 'a great ledger of the people's distinguished dignity in life'. He wrote that Louis Le Nain 'was interested only in characters and, within those characters, in their faces and poses which reflected their thoughts and the effect their entire lives had on them.' A peasant woman in front of the wheel of a cart, a blacksmith's assistant, a woman spinning, a melancholic boy, a woman seated in an interior (viewed as though in cinematic close-up, essentially presenting her gaze as her expressive core): 'Something indescribably and profoundly sad, which never leaves their eyes even during these moments of relaxation, suffices to reveal the dark secrets of their souls to us.' Gallotti felt there was 'not only an underlying agreement, but an agreement in detail' between these 'realist', humanistic paintings of people's everyday condition and Krull's well-chosen photographs. The juxtaposition with these powerful paintings, with the bold layout encouraging comparison, brings out the compassionate nature of her photos.

This, however, was the last publication of Krull's photos, and they were probably acquired through an agency thanks to the stock she had built up. Her presence in the press was already declining by 1931, the year she placed more emphasis on publishing books and making forays into the cinema.[70] The commotion created by Krull's appearance on the scene lasted just three years. The same was true, in fact, for others who experienced the founding of *VU* as the veritable birth of a new kind of photojournalism: her friend Lotar, who moved into film, and Kertész, who experienced the same decline. Krull left Paris in 1935, Kertész in 1936. In 1928 Krull, Kertész and Lotar had been the only three independent photographers without a studio, amidst many agency and anonymous photographers. But there soon emerged younger photographers who viewed the profession from a different angle – Tabard (February 1929), Kitrosser (late 1929), Ichac (May 1929), Hug Block (April 1931), Schall (June 1931) and Gaston Paris (December 1931) – who would occupy centre stage.

In the end, the great photographic reportages – traces of which can found in the Schostal agency and other archives as well as in publications – ranged over the FunFairs, the tramps, the dance halls, Paris markets including Les Halles, the various women's trades (typists, cigar rollers, feather makers),[71] Marseille and southern France, sailors, the French cancan, Paris by night and studies of hands.[72] Some of these stories were offered to foreign agencies

67 See 'Women' below.
68 Louis Cheronnet, 'Eden de banlieue', *VU* no. 331 (18 July 1934), pp. 902–903, six photos of six. Louis Cheronnet (1899–1950) was the author of *Extra-Muros*, Paris: Louis Bellenand, 1929, and *Découverte du monde: A Paris...vers 1900*, Paris: Chroniques du Jour, 1932. After 1945 he published books of historic photographs: *Paris Imprévu* (Tel, 1946), *Petit Musée de la Curiosité Photographique* (Tel, 1945), and *Paris tel qu'il Fut* (1951).
69 Jean Gallotti, 'Permanence du type populaire: Les modèles des frères Le Nain', *VU* no. 331 (18 July 1934), pp. 912–914, six photos of six.
70 See below.
71 See 'Women' below.
72 See 'Play of Hands' below.

73 Christian Bouqueret – Eric Rémy Collection. My thanks to Éric Rémy for making this material available to me.
74 Foreword, *Études de nu par Germaine Krull*, Paris: Calavas, 1930, reprinted in an appendix to this volume.

(Schostal and Mauritius) as organised sequences of pictures, sometimes accompanied by an explanatory typewritten text or captions (as was done with press photos during the interwar period). One such text concerned a spread on the signing of the Briand–Kellogg Pact in August 1928 (partially published in *VU*); it was written in German and referred to thirteen photos (far more than are known today).[73] Numbers written on the back of prints now in archives certainly relate to captions in the typescript.

For two or three years *VU*-style photojournalism had been Krull's main affair. In her 1930 preface to her studies of nudes she clearly analysed her total commitment to the role of photojournalist, marking a break with her brief *fers* period and *Métal*. It is true that with the Icarette she had discovered a sensitive tool that accorded with her impulsive, direct, empathic temperament. Elaborate framing was not her strong suit, and this camera was not suited to it anyway because of its crude viewfinder. 'The camera does not have to invent, concoct, or contrive. / It is not painting, nor imagination. / The photographer is a witness. / A witness of his times. / The true photographer is an everyday witness, a reporter. / It's normal that he not always keep his eye a metre and a half above the ground. / But he must always be aware of that ground, the ground today, this very morning, this Thursday morning, this day so beautiful one forgets to ask the name it happens to have been given. / The world. / The world of our times.'[74]

PERSONAL CONNECTIONS

Germaine Krull's swift career in Paris was first of all linked to four people: Lucien Vogel (1886–1954), Florent Fels (1891–1977), Pierre Mac Orlan (1882–1970) and André Malraux (1901–1976). We do not know which initial contact led to the others, but these men knew and appreciated one another. Vogel claimed to have been the first to contact Krull, before *VU* was launched. There is a certain logic to that, because *VU*'s need for illustrations called for the hiring of a new type of photographer. Vogel might have led to Fels, who had edited the magazine *L'Action* and was then editor of *L'Art vivant*. *L'Action* had published Mac Orlan and Malraux, the former having backed the latter. Malraux was friendly with Fels, in whose home he met his future wife, Clara. Such connections were reinforced by links to publishers: Gallimard became Mac Orlan's publisher in 1921, notably publishing his best-selling *Quai des Brumes* in 1927; that was when Malraux joined Gallimard's reading panel, which decided to publish a little book on Krull with a text by Mac Orlan in its 'NRF New Photographers' series. Mac Orlan, who had published a ground-breaking article on photography in *Les Annales* in 1928, became a keen promoter of avant-garde photographers, notably Krull and Kertész, and cited the example of their forerunner Atget, who died in 1927 and was honoured by photographic exhibitions from 1928 to 1932; Mac Orlan penned the foreword to the retrospective volume on Atget in 1930.

Fels, who wrote the foreword to *Métal* in 1928, was also a supporter of new photography via *L'Art vivant*, which launched a feigned investigation into the question, 'Is photography an art?', beginning with Atget. Fels also had links to the publisher Firmin-Didot, for whom he headed the Images du Monde imprint. This led to Krull's introduction to Jacques Haumant, who soon founded his own publishing house, with Krull serving as its photographer-muse until it went bankrupt. Titaÿna, the journalist Krull met in 1928 through *VU*, founded the modernist magazine *Jazz*, whose art director, Carlo Rim, favoured the new-style photography, and Krull in particular – he went on to become editor-in-chief of *VU* in 1930. Krull met Colette when Vogel dispatched her to do a portrait at the writer's home, which led to contact with Renaud de Jouvenel, followed by Jouvenel's friend Philippe Lamour, concerning a short-lived magazine, *Grand' Route*. Jouvenel's mother, Isa de Comminges, was also a great friend, whom

Krull joined in the South of France in 1935. Eugène Merle, editor of *Le Merle* and *Le Courrier littéraire,* made a fleeting appearance in Jouvenel's wake in 1930.

At an early date Krull met Louis Jouvet and Jean Cocteau at the Théâtre des Champs-Elysées, followed by Gaston Baty at the Théâtre Pigalle. Through Jouvet she met one of his secretaries, Yves Gladine, who became a loyal friend and wrote three screenplays for her. It is possible that Mac Orlan was the link to Paul van Hecke, who published the Brussels magazine *Variétés*, steeped in the spirit of Belgian surrealism and expressionism, and who was a sturdy supporter of Krull's unusual images.

Krull's most steadfast contact was Malraux: they met up again in free France in 1944–45 alongside De Gaulle. Then, when she moved to Asia, Krull stayed in contact with the entire Malraux family – when André became France's Minister of Culture he backed the Germaine Krull exhibition at the Cinémathèque Française in 1967, leading the way to rediscovery of her work. She herself had awarded Malraux's 1930 novel *La Voix royal* with the Interallié Prize, having apparently been a founding member of the first jury.

EXHIBITIONS

Krull's early career was more or less based on her inclusion in the 1928 Salon de l'Escalier alongside other young modernist photographers, followed by a similar event in Belgium at the Galerie L'Époque. Logically enough, she was also selected for the major international avant-garde event, 'Film und Foto' (FIFO), held in Stuttgart in May–June 1929 under the aegis of Laszlo Moholy-Nagy. This film and photo fair forged an international style and permanently established the characteristics of modernist photography in both Europe and the United States. There Krull found herself in the company of Berenice Abbott, the Bauhaus, Herbert Bayer, Imogen Cunningham, Florence Henri, George Hoyningen-Huene, André Kertész, Eli Lotar, Man Ray, Albert Renger-Patzsch, Kurt Schwitters, Edward Steichen, Maurice Tabard, Umbo and the Soviet contingent led by El Lissitzky. Presence could be measured by the number of photos on show: if Stone had sixty-eight, Umbo thirty-nine, and Finsler thirty-seven, then Krull was doing fairly well with twenty photos, whose content shows that the *Métal* effect was still present but no longer preponderant, there being just one Eiffel Tower, one hydraulic ramp in Rotterdam, one *fer* picture (*Eisen*), one electric power plant and two warships (Le Havre?). The rest were largely drawn from her photojournalistic repertoire: four tramps, one gypsy cabin outside Paris, one *manouche* (gypsy), shots of 'scrap iron' (flea market) and sailors. Lotar's twelve photos were probably closer to the 'new vision' trend, and he also exhibited a portrait of Krull. Man Ray showed only twenty-two 'rayographs', which had already been exhibited at the Époque event in Brussels.

Krull was also included in the 1930 Salon de l'Araignée, a show normally devoted to illustrators, at which *Jazz* editor Carlo Rim decided to hang photography in the Manuel brothers' gallery. Unsurprisingly, Krull was joined by Atget, Lotar, Moholy-Nagy, Parry, Sougez and Tabard. The salons of 1931 were also held in art galleries. Krull was included in a show on 'advertising through photography' hosted by the Galerie d'Art Contemporain (135 Boulevard Raspail in Paris) alongside Boiffard, Forence Henri, Kertész, Landau, Lotar, Man Ray, Parry, Sougez, Tabard, Vigneau, Zuber and others. At the end of the year she found herself at the Galerie de la Plume d'Or with Kertész, Parry, Florence Henri and Man Ray. In 1932, at the Studio Saint-Jacques, Krull, Kertész and Tabard participated in an exhibition organised by the Société des Artistes Photographes at the instigation of Laure Albin Guillot, herself often excluded from these group shows because her work appeared more academic.

75 Photographs of the Paris Commune of 1871 were also exhibited (Kertész had an album of such photos).
76 Louis Aragon, 'Un "salon" photographique', *Commune* no. 22 (June 1935), pp. 1189–1192. *Commune* was published by the AEAR.
77 This information is drawn from Christian Bouqueret, *Des années folles aux années noires*, éditions Marval, 1997.
78 See below.

In the somewhat less specialised context of an international photography show in Brussels in 1932, Krull's four photos reflected photojournalism (cabaret, dance hall and two female labourers), while Man Ray's twenty-two pictures made him out to be mainly a portraitist, whereas previously he had been famous as an inventive surrealist. Krull took part in the same event the following year, 1933. But from that moment onwards exhibitions did not really have an impact on career recognition, due to so much new competition. Only the Galerie de la Pléïade (73 Boulevard Saint-Michel), run by Jacques Schiffrin and incorporated into the Gallimard publishing house in 1933, could be considered an intellectually appealing, left-leaning venue – in late 1934 the gallery hosted a show that included Krull, Kertész, Lotar, Florence Henri and Ilse Bing, all members of the avant-garde. But the most striking event was that same gallery's June 1935 show titled 'Documenting Society', organised by the Association des Écrivains and Artistes Révolutionnaires (AEAR). The Communist-inspired AEAR was founded in 1932 and Lotar, having become a film-maker, organised its photography section. The theme shifted significantly away from 'new vision' criteria to embrace the implications of what Louis Aragon called 'the social content of photography'. Krull and Kertész were both included.[75] Her work was even singled out by Aragon – for criticism. 'Germaine Krull is indisputably one of the best photographers of the day, but her contribution to this show is disappointing, despite the terrible grimness of a worker's canteen that creates so little desire to eat. Several shots of women at work, in factories, next to machines, express little more than the photographer's lack of enthusiasm.' Although Aragon's expectations of AEAR's 'revolutionary realism' was limited to 'portraits of old women, of fisherman pulling nets, of peasants in the field, of brats playing in the street',[76] it was indeed Krull's interest in 'the labour of men, lower-class kids, the petty trades and blokes in the street, factory or fields' that she had brought to *VU*. But what looked 'social' in 1928 did not seem revolutionary in 1935, and Krull's 1932 workers were not always the exploited labour of large industries – instead of expressing their suffering on the job, some women displayed attentiveness and attachment to their craft. Aragon seems to criticise these pictures for not being photojournalism because they did not 'express anything', unlike the things expressed by 'shots of the February [1934] demonstrations in Paris, the uprisings in Cuba, the exploitation of the Chinese proletariat' and by Henri Cartier-Bresson's 'two unemployed men before a meal on a table'. In 1935 Krull, about to leave for Monte-Carlo, had virtually no new attention-grabbing pictures.

MAGAZINES

There is no doubt that around 1930 magazines represented the new photographers' bread-and-butter, apart from the portraiture that sustained some of them, either because they had a studio (which was the case with Ergy Landau, who had set up in an affluent neighbourhood) or because magazine commissions for celebrity portraits had brought in a private clientele. That is exactly what happened to Kertész, who arrived in Paris in 1925 and by 1926 had begun a career in portraiture, notably of Hungarian artists and individuals living in Paris.

If we look at Krull's situation vis-à-vis the magazines in late 1930, after three very successful years, it is clear that *VU* was her main backer, and that it brought in other clients. Krull published 281 photos in seventy-one issues of *VU*. In 1928, however, outlets were limited: only *L'Art vivant* and *Variétés* offered the possibility of any income. *Variétés* published 119 of her pictures in sixteen different issues, but the magazine folded in April 1930. Meanwhile, *Jazz* (December 1928–May 1930), which encouraged Krull (seventy-seven photos in thirteen issues), apparently did not pay photographers, arguing that it provided a promotional showcase.[77] *Bifur* and *Grand' Route,* art reviews with very limited circulations, probably provided very little income.[78]

Voilà and *Paris Magazine,* which ran few Krull photos,[79] only entered the picture in 1931, as did *Art et Médecine,* which published fifty-five Krull pictures over fourteen issues (although thirty-six of those were concentrated in five issues). Publication in *Le Sourire, Le Figaro illustré* (1932 and 1933), and German magazines such as *Das Leben* and *Der Querschnitt* was very occasional. In 1931 *Les Annales* was notable for taking an entire reportage. Only *L'Image,* a small magazine founded in March 1932, and which printed in fine photogravure, offered greater possibilities in Krull's personal register (it also published Mac Orlan). The number of photographs by Krull published in French and foreign magazines – excluding books – can currently be estimated at over 600 (although some of them were published several times).

In the spring of 1930 *Le Courrier littéraire*[80] was noteworthy for its fleeting existence, its rarity and its impressive layout. It published twenty-three of Krull's finest photographs.

The substantial *Arts et Métiers graphiques* magazine, launched in September 1927 by the Deberny & Peignot type foundry (with Lucien Vogel on its editorial board), ran a Krull advertising page for the Rees Radio Company in its thirteenth issue. But the magazine remained unimportant until March 1930, when it devoted issue number 16 to photography. Titled *Photographie 1930,* this special album had a very 'modern' and 'graphic' metal-spiral binding, and it took up the cause of the 'new photography' in the wake of the 1929 'Film und Foto' show. Waldemar George's introductory article on 'Photography, a Vision of the World' was very clear on this point, featuring illustrations of the type found in Moholy-Nagy's *Painting, Photography, Film.* Some 130 photographs from all over the world (fourteen of which had been shown at FIFO) were printed full page, along with many advertising photos (Deberny & Peignot had set up an advertising photo studio). Two Krull *fer*-type photos were included (without remuneration): the top of a warship and pipes in a factory. The special photography issue became an annual affair in the same format, and in 1931 Krull had another two pictures. In 1932 she had only one photo, perhaps an advertising shot, and only one in 1933–1934.[81]

NOVEL ILLUSTRATION

For any other photographer of the time it would be incongruous to talk about illustrations for novels, but it now appears that this field, rarely associated with the avant-garde, is particularly pertinent to Krull's work, although she herself hardly mentioned it. She produced a first series of images in 1930 to illustrate thirteen instalments of a 'new crime novel' by Pierre Mac Orlan, *Ombres de Paris*, in *Détective*,[82] featuring on one page in each issue, with two pictures per page. Each image was devised to illustrate a situation in the text, with models for each character, and was accompanied by an inset sentence, such as 'he took her gloved hand' or 'Marie recognises the voice of her husband'.[83] The important stage of the 'novel' that consists solely of photos with no text, discussed further on in 'Women',[84] and about which Krull spoke in her memoirs,[85] can be dated to this same period, early in 1930. It was followed by the creation of the first 'photo-texte' (a novel illustrated with photographs), *La Folle d'Itteville* by Simenon (August 1931), which would be a failure due to defective printing. A second novel, *L'Affaire des 7'* (meaning *L'Affaire des sept minutes*), by Simenon, was announced by Haumont, but they never published it, even though the photographs had probably already been taken. Instead, it appeared as a serial in three issues of Marianne in early 1933 under the title *La Nuit des sept minutes*, each page being illustrated with three photographs.[86] The final submission contained the first part of another novel illustrated by Germaine Krull, *La Chatte*, 'an unpublished novel by Colette', which would be spread across nine issues.[87] In response to this event, Germaine Krull said 'When Marianne got me to illustrate Colette's "la chatte" I was over the moon.'[88] For this assignment, she demonstrated her customary

79 *Paris Magazine* published just five (issues 5, 17, 37, and 40) even though it was largely devoted to nudes, bars, dance halls and music halls.
80 See below.
81 1930, pl. 74 and pl. 89, *Electric power plant*; 1931, pl. 8, *A portrait [Mrs. Hubbell]*, and pl. 116, *Hands in front of a face*; 1932, pl. 66, *A chemical vessel*; 1933–1934, pl. 90, *Ships in the port of Marseille*.
82 *Ombres de Paris, new crime novel by Pierre Mac Orlan*, in *Détective*, no. 69, 20 February 1930, to no. 81, 15 May 1930, p. 7, photos by Krull, in general two per page.
83 The models were certainly friends, perhaps including Renaud de Jouvenel and Carlo Rim.
84 See below, 'Women'.
85 CEDG, p. 36.
86 Georges Simenon, *La Nuit des sept minutes,* new novel, in *Marianne*, nos. 23 to 25, 29 March, 7 April, 12 April 1933, p. 5, with nine photos by Krull, and the credit 'illustrations by Germaine Krull'.
97 Colette, *La Chatte,* new novel, in *Marianne*, no. 25, 12 April 1933; no. 26, 19 April 1933; no. 27, 26 April 1933; no. 28, 3 May 1933; no. 29, 10 May 1933; no. 30, 17 May 1933; no. 31, 24 May 1933; no. 32, 31 May 1933; no. 33, 7 June 1933, p. 7, photos by Krull, in general three per page.
88 VMD, p. 143.

originality: 'I did the illustrations with my cat, partially with Colette's Persian cat. I was given complete freedom of interpretation. It was amusing; the theme was basically the break up of a couple because of a cat's life, which gave scope for considerable photographic imagination.'[89] Indeed, as in many of her assignments, Krull responded imaginatively and sensitively. And she was quick to devise the best solutions for these forms of illustration in which she felt free to make personal suggestions.

89 CEDG, p. 68. Krull erroneously says this was published in the last issue of *Marianne*, and declares that 'to her great relief, the printing of Marianne was good and the photos were successful'. No edition of the novel with photos by Krull was ever published.
90 *Le Crapouillot* (March 1929), pp. 32–33.
91 Christian Bouqueret described Krull as 'the leader of photographic publishing in the early 1930s'. See Bouqueret, *Des Années folles aux années noires: La nouvelle vision photographique en France, 1920–1940*, Paris: Marval, 1997, p. 175.

A BOLD APPROACH TO BOOKS

Krull was clearly able to survive on publications in magazines in the years 1928 to 1931, spread over commissioned reportages, prints placed with agencies, occasional fashion photography, some commissioned portraits, advertising and perhaps nudes. Yet in addition to her founding role in the field of photojournalism (alongside several other bold colleagues), she made a decisively pioneering contribution to the realm of publishing books of photographs. It was something to which she remained attached all her life. Of all the photographers who began their careers around 1925, she was certainly the one who published the greatest number of photography books. And they were truly 'books of photographs', with little text, rather than books illustrated by photos. Indeed, the novelty lay in the fact that the body of the book was composed of plates, or more precisely of pages occupied by just one photo, with or without a caption; and the dust jacket itself might feature photographs. Such books found willing readers – it was Mac Orlan once again who grasped the phenomenon: 'People who buy albums of photographic visions these days are driven by a very pure need to feel moved, with no hope of ever getting their money back.'[90]

The innovation of reproducing high-quality photographs in large format on each page – in black or brown tint – was the result of the introduction of rotogravure, also used on dust jackets. This process made inroads in the press thanks to *VU,* at a time when dailies continued to use offset. But the imitators of *VU*'s success, such as *Détective, Voilà* and *Regards,* also adopted rotogravure in order to have better photographic 'reproductions' with a wider range of greys. The same was true of the annual photo issue of *Arts et Métiers graphiques*. 'Photography books' were thus naturally inclined to use the rotogravure process in order to obtain the required quality.

Krull's calling in the field was probably encouraged by two circumstances. One was the publication of *Métal*, which was not a book properly speaking yet stemmed from a similar approach. It is not known which of her friends of 1928 pointed her in the direction of the Calavas publishing house – Fels, Vogel, Pierre Bost or Antoine Roche? – but that album did a great deal for Krull's reputation. The other decisive factor was her familiarity with the German publishing world, and the experiments notably carried out at the Bauhaus and by the 'new photography' movement epitomised by Karl Blossfeldt's *Urformen der Kunst* and Alber Regner-Pattzsch's *Die Welt ist schön* of 1928. Following the German publication of Mario von Bucovich's *Paris* in 1928, another Berlin publisher, Verlag der Reihe, issued Krull's *100 × Paris* with captions in three languages in 1929. From that point onwards, Krull would follow one book with another, each having a noteworthy impact on the publishing scene of the day.[91] The stages of the various publications will be more fully discussed later in this study, but a simple chronological list (with number of photos) for the Paris period already gives an idea of the general scope: *Métal* (portfolio, 1928, 65 photos), *100 × Paris* (1929, 100 photos), *Etudes de Nu* (portfolio, 1930, 24 photos), *La Route Paris-Biarritz* (87 photos), *Le Valois* (1930, 47 photos), *La Folle d'Itteville* (1931, 104 photos) and *Marseille* (1935, 49 photos), plus her contributions to *Route de Paris à la Méditerranée* (1931, 38 photos), *Paris* by von Bucovich (1928, 23 photos), *Visages de Paris* by André Warnod (1930, 46 photos) and *Paris under 4 Årstider* by Adolf Hallman (1930, 41 photos). That amounts to over 600 photographic reproductions. For Krull, the years 1928 to 1931 were clearly busier than for any other photographer of that time – Kertész managed to publish just two books in 1933 and 1934 (*Enfants* and *Paris*). No other photographer of the interwar period demonstrated such enthusiasm, over so little time, for books of photographs, then in their infancy. Comparison is tricky, but all of the other major books – August Sander's *Antlitz der Zeit* in 1929, Roger Parry's *Banalité* in 1930 (Gallimard) and Brassaï's *Paris de Nuit* in 1933 – were one-offs. True enough, Krull largely owed this dynamism to her relationships with the Firmin-Didot publishing house and Fels, as well as one of Fels' colleagues, Jacques Haumont, who became an independent publisher. The publication of books of photographs nevertheless remains a Krull speciality, which she pursued all her life, from Monte-Carlo (*Les Ballets de Monte-Carlo*, 1937) to Rio de Janeiro (*Ouro Preto,* 1943) and also to Asia. She always cultivated a desire to continue this activity, which she viewed as an integral part of the photojournalistic calling she discovered in Paris.

ADVERTISING COMMISSIONS

Krull's advertising work is harder to pin down, because such commissions often went unsigned, and even when signed their publication history occasionally requires tracking down. It appears that her first commission came from the local electricity company (Compagnie Parisienne de Distribution d'Électricité) for its Saint-Ouen power plant – in the 1928 *Métal* – followed by the Issy-les-Moulineaux power plant in 1929. Krull also went to the Citroën factory on the Seine in Paris, as depicted in *Métal*. At the time, however, Krull was still following her *fers* line, rather than photographing objects in a studio (which she was still unequipped to do). Then Peugeot called on her: 'More and more people are beating a path to my door . . . the advertising manager for Peugeot factories would like me to do their next catalogue.'[92] It is also possible that, following her work for Sonia Delaunay in 1926, she was contacted by other fashion designers such as Worth, whose shop window was included in von Bucovich's *Paris* in 1928.

The first advertising work Krull shot in a studio seems to have been a commission from the gentlemen's shirtmaker, J. C. d'Ahetze, 'the most fashionable shop on the Champs-Elysées'.[93] They supplied her with shirts and pyjamas 'in delicate colours' for an 'advertising project'. She carried out several tests, wondering if she 'could superimpose a motorcar wheel or engine piston over a photo of a shirt. [She] tried, and the results were amazing. After that first attempt, everything was simple.'[94] It was May 1930 (according to the date marked on extant prints),[95] and motorcar fever was in full swing. Her friend Jouvenel, the founder of *Grand'Route* and a Bugatti owner, represented a 'warehouse of props for ad photos' with 'all the paraphernalia – spare automobile parts, gears, petrol and oil cans, a steering wheel'. These items can indeed be seen on the J.C. d'Adhetze proposals, superimposed or not. Other, simpler shots, of detachable collars in half-light, or in shadow, sometimes featured on the back cover of *Grand'Route*.[96]

This first effort apparently led to other advertising photos that employed superimposition, such as a proposal for Shell motor oil that was similar in intent but probably never used.[97] Likewise, a proposal for fashion designer Paul Poiret, which employed 'avant-garde' superimposition of a masked face in a precise and refined manner, may have followed, but we are uncertain of the date[98] and unsure it was ever used. She also did photographs for the designer-furrier Heim in 1931,[99] and received commissions from Columbia for Damia, Marie Dubat and Cocteau's *La Voix humaine*.[100] An important commission for Mercier Frères furniture filled an entire page – showing furnished interiors – in seven issues of *VU*.[101]

92 CEDG, p. 27.
93 12, Arcades des Champs-Élysées.
94 CEDG, pp. 38–39.
95 Notably those in the A. & J. Wilde Foundation, Munich.
96 *Grand'Route* 3 (May 1930) and 5 (July 1930).
97 See her 'poster proposal' (1930) in *Photographes Nouveaux*, Paris: NRF, 1931, p. 60.
98 It is assigned the date of 1926 in *Voici Paris: Modernités Photographiques, 1920–1950*, Paris: Pompidou Centre, 2012, p. 93, but that is most implausible.
99 Advertising insert (two women walking in a forest); see also *Heim* 4 (1932), five photos by Krull.
100 See 'Women' below.
101 *VU* no. 196 (16 December 1931), p. 2755; no. 197 (23 December 1931), p. 2869; no. 201 (20 January 1932), p. 14; no. 207 (2 March 1932), p. 280; no. 212 (6 April 1932), p. 444; no. 220 (1 June 1932), p. 922; and no. 263 (29 March 1933), p. 452.

One enigma over Krull's activity concerns a commission for a foundry at Pont-à-Mousson. 'One of my finest and most exciting photo spreads was certainly the one for the Fonderies de Pont-à-Mousson. In a pleasant, if somewhat grey landscape in Lorraine. The factories occupied a vast area ... they made only tubes and pipes, but of every size and width ... The Pont-à-Mousson visitors' book was a hit with them and a joy for me.' And yet this book cannot be found. The only known example of this type of publication is *Confort,* whose extraordinary photos have been ascribed to Krull.[102] However, that book has nothing to do with Pont-à-Mousson, but with foundries at Saulnes and Hussigny owned by the Société Générale de Fonderie. Thirty photographic plates, featuring shots of the blast furnaces, the smelting of iron, collections of identical items (such as Chappée coal buckets), photomontages, high-angle close-ups, shadow effects and night-time shots of the installation, all accord with Krull's style and habits. It is therefore unthinkable to attribute this veritable book of photographs, printed in black photogravure, to any other photographer, at least at that date.[103] The fact that Mac Orlan penned the text is another factor in Krull's favour.[104]

In contrast, the 'photographs by G. Krull and Helce' credit on a lavish promotional brochure for the Debat pharmaceutical firm – the publisher of *Art et Médecine* magazine, which ran Krull's pictures – makes it possible to attribute to her the large plates of photomontages and views of factories.[105] Not only are they of very high quality, but they are similar to those in *Confort.*

It was precisely to the year 1931 that she dated her annoyance regarding advertising and photomontage. 'Advertising projects and photomontages had become a kind of routine that began to weary me somewhat. On top of which came my disappointment concerning plans with Jacques Haumont's publishing firm.'[106] In a fast-changing context, only *La France à table* commissioned work from Krull in 1934, for ads promoting O'Connor silverware, Amora mustard, L'Héritier-Guyot blackcurrent liqueur and Pougues Saint-Léger mineral water.[107] The reproductions are once again impeccable photogravures.

ATGET AS MODEL

Following his posthumous show at the Salon de l'Escalier in 1928, the name of Eugène Atget and his essentially Parisian oeuvre became ubiquitous. Man Ray had been Atget's neighbour on Rue Campagne-Première, and had bought prints from him; upon Atget's death, Berenice Abbott acquired a large quantity of negatives and prints on behalf of Julien Levy. The contents of Man Ray's collection are well known – prostitutes, shop dummies, display windows, two petty tradesmen, six photos of *la Zone* (Porte d'Asnières, Porte de Montreuil, Poterne des Peupliers) and six of FunFairs (rides).[108] Atget had also photographed tramps around 1899. In the summer of 1928, such subjects may have given Vogel – who was a member of the salon organising committee as well as editor of *VU* – some ideas for photo-features. In November 1928, Mac Orlan illustrated his innovatory article in *Les Annales* on 'social weirdness in photography' with a picture by Atget, and he mentioned Krull.[109] It was again Atget who was featured at the launch of a famous series of articles asking 'Is photography an art?' in *L'Art vivant* on 1 January 1929; this series, which promoted the 'new photography' under the auspices of Atget, also featured Kertész, Krull, Lotar and, later on, Alban and Tabard. But the comparison was the most telling with Krull. In 1929 she made photographic reproductions of old pictures belonging to the Société Française de Photographie, which turned out to be early photographs by Hippolyte Bayard. Krull certainly became aware of the existence and relevance of these great forerunners of depicters of Parisian life, as stressed by the accompanying article by Charles Fegdal, 'Retrospective Images of Paris'.

102 *Confort,* published by the Société Générale de Fonderie, Paris, 1931, with texts by G. Lenôtre, Paul Reboux, Marcel Prévost and Pierre Mac Orlan. The photographs are 'attributed to Germaine Krull' by Christian Bouqueret, *Les Livres de photographie*, Paris: Gründ, 2012, p. 94.

103 The book was printed on 30 November 1931. The contract may have stipulated that the photos belonged to the company, and would bear no signature. No extant prints have surfaced. With regard to Peugeot, Krull complained that she had to relinquish the negatives to the firm.

104 In fact, the portfolio of photographs, titled *Confort, 1931, Pierre Mac Orlan,* is preceded by a not very interesting history of 'comfort'. Mac Orlan's text, which was incorporated into the photographic layout, developed his ideas on the modernity of the phonograph, photography, cinema and cars.

105 *La Leçon de travail dans un parc*, Paris, Office d'Éditions, n.d. [c. 1931]. Eight large photogravure plates plus cover photo, mostly photomontages.

106 CEDG, p. 71.

107 *La France à table* (May 1934, Savoie), O'Connor, back cover; (July 1934, Burgundy), Amora, inside back cover, L'Héritier-Guyot, back cover; (September 1934, Lyon), wines and cheeses, back cover; (January 1935, Provence), Pougues Saint-Léger, back cover.

108 Thomas-Michael Gunther, 'Les photographies d'Atget achetées par Man Ray', Atget symposium, special issue of *Photographies* (March 1986), pp. 70–72.

109 *Les Annales* (1 November 1928), p. 413.

The comparison then changed direction – the young were perceived as determined successors. Regarding Krull's *100 × Paris* in 1929, Paul Fierens wrote, 'The Atget tradition survives in a [shot of a] grocer, several views of Les Halles, and in a portrait of a bench on which five tramps are sitting.'[110] In a context where there were few books of photographs, attention focused upon Atget with the publication of *Atget, photographe de Paris* in 1930. Mac Orlan contributed a long foreword, in which he mentioned Krull and even alluded to her photographs by referring to 'the tin hovels of rag-pickers on the outskirts [of Paris], beyond the dance halls around La Bastille'. Mac Orlan stressed the originality of his protégé, just like Atget's. 'Paris is not a city which immediately gives herself to the whim of a photographer, however lyrical.' It required a feel for poetry. Reciprocally, Mac Orlan invoked Atget when discussing Krull's pictures in the 'NRF New Photographer' series: 'In 1894, [expressionist photographic art] was already associated with contrivance, perhaps more visual than poetic but at any rate clearly literary. Those were the days of Atget, who was no innocent but a man who loved his craft and performed it masterfully.' Still regarding Atget, Mac Orlan argued that, 'this set of photographic records has given birth to a lofty poetry that we are only just beginning to grasp.'[111] Finally, Walter Benjamin based his original definition of 'aura' on Atget's oeuvre: 'He seeks the forgotten and the forsaken, and hence such pictures are directed against the exotic, ostentatious, romantic sound of city names; they suck the aura out of reality like water from a sinking ship. What is aura? A peculiar web of time and space: the unique manifestation of a distance, however near it may be.'[112] When he wrote this 'Short History of Photography' in 1931, Benjamin had already been a friend of Krull's for several years, and he illustrated his text not only with Atget but with two pictures of shop windows by Krull,[113] prints that belonged to him.

110 *Variétés* 2, no. 7 (15 November 1929), p. 508.
111 Mac Orlan, 'Visages', *Art et Médecine* (October 1931), p. 47.
112 Walter Benjamin, 'A Short History of Photography,' trans. Stanley Mitchell, *Screen* 13, 1 (September 1972), pp. 20ff. Originally 'Kleine Geschichte der Photographie', serialised in *Literarische Welt* 7: 38, 39 40 (18 September, 25 September, 2 October 1931).
113 In the original edition, *Literarische Welt*, 2nd installment, no. 39, 25 September 1931, pp. 3–4. Reproduction of the page in Gunthert, op. cit., p. 16.
114 CEDG, p. 14.

CINEMA AS MODEL

While Krull's photographic vision was shaped by silent film in Berlin, Amsterdam and Paris, it is possible she wasn't fully aware of it, any more than were numerous photographers in the late 1920s whose work was characterised by uncommon combinations of images, techniques and explorations, as symbolised by the title of the 'Film und Foto' show to which Krull contributed in Stuttgart in 1929. When, in her memoirs, Krull reflected on the 'unexpected and unknown' novelty of her vision of iron girders and cranes 'that moved', she related it to her 'lens-eye' yet also employed the metaphor of 'crank': 'I think that showing this new way of seeing things as my lens-eye had discovered it was like the turn of a crank, which triggered a whole series of new ways of seeing, looking, making. The same thing went for photo-reportages of street life . . . A new wind was blowing, a different gaze was needed.'[114] In hindsight, she spoke of it like shooting a film.

It should be pointed out that Krull viewed the cinema through – and sometimes against – the figure of Joris Ivens. When she met Ivens in Berlin he was selling photo equipment, but when they were together in Amsterdam in 1925–26 he took an interest in the cinema and became a film-maker while Krull took photos of the port's travelling cranes. Maybe that was already a kind of division of labour (cinema versus photography) alongside shared artistic interests and an underlying harmony. They linked up again in late 1927–early 1928 for Ivens' first film experiment, *The Bridge*, on the Rotterdam drawbridge, even as Krull took photographs that she would use in *Métal*. The storyboard drawings prepared by Ivens do not differ much from a 'montage' of photos. But the sharing was also educational, that is to say they learned together by looking at films, especially once Ivens founded a film club to that end, the Filmliga. That is where he (and she?) saw Walter Ruttmann's *Berlin, Symphony of a Great City* in 1927. Ruttmann's film was the prototype of the city symphony, and a model for Ivens. 'I remembered the films

115 Destanque and Ivens, op. cit., p. 72.
116 Such is the opinion of André Stufkens, *Passages. Joris Ivens en de kunst van deze eeuw* Nijmegen: Museum Het Valkof, 1999, p. 88.
117 Destanque and Ivens, op. cit., p. 79.
118 Ibid., p. 91.
119 VMD, p. 129.
120 In January 1929, *Variétés* 1, no. 9 reported that, following the screening of his own film, *La Tour*, René Clair projected Lacombe's *Zone*, 'a poem of everyday filth, rubble and detritus', pp. 510–511.
121 In each of these films, there are sequences focusing on hands, a dancer and a pianist, respectively.

I saw at the Filmliga – Ruttmann pointed the way.'[115] Ruttman's film also included many shots that would later be echoed in Krull's views of Paris: rooftops, clocks, shop windows, cranes, chimneys, warehouses, offices, secretaries, cars in the street, restaurants, printing machinery, a roller-coaster scene with an on-board camera, lighted signs at night, music halls, cancan and dancers' legs, bars and dance halls, fireworks. It was an entire programme to be variously developed through multiple photographs.

Ivens' second short film was *Études de mouvements à Paris* (3½ minutes), shot in Paris at the end of 1927 and beginning of 1928. Krull never mentioned it, even though it opened with a view of rooftops probably shot from her apartment on Montmartre. The movements of the title are exclusively those of Paris traffic, the camera being variously placed in the middle of the street, in a car, among pedestrians, sometimes flat on the ground. Given the similarity of imagery, it is possible that some of Krull's photos were taken at the same time.[116] When Ivens summed up the period of his evolution into an avant-garde film-maker, he said, 'Germaine's influence on that transformation was undeniable.'[117] When Sergei Eisenstein came to Paris in early 1930 for *The General Line* he was accompanied by Ivens, and Krull not only photographed Eisenstein but accompanied them 'from Montparnasse to Montmartre and from the Louvre to the flea market at Saint-Ouen'.[118]

Krull also had contact with Paris film-makers through Lotar, who 'was drawn more to cinema than photography'.[119] In the company of Lotar she hung out with a group at the Deux-Magots that included René Clair and Alberto Cavalcanti. Cavalcanti's 1926 film *Rien que les heures* (38 minutes) was a dream-like trip through Paris in the space of twenty-four hours, employing movement, reflections and soft-focus to record chimneys, shop dummies, no fewer than seven tramps sleeping on the ground, a party and dancers, ultimately ending with nocturnal images of the uneasy streets. In 1928 René Clair filmed *La Tour* (14 minutes) on the Eiffel Tower that included travelling shots in the lift, on the girders and among the machinery, similar in every respect to Krull's pictures. Clair's assistant on *La Tour* was Georges Lacombe, who in 1928 released *La Zone: Au Pays des chiffonniers* (36 minutes) on the rag-pickers and the flea market at Saint-Ouen, including a shot of La Goulue in front of her caravan.[120] Krull was therefore in direct contact with the people producing these images, whose themes she would adopt a few months later. Although she does not mention it, she must have known Germaine Dulac, a friend of (*Thème et variations*, 1928; *Disque 957*, 1928–1929)[121] defended by *Jazz*. Inevitably, Krull must have frequented Studio 28, an avant-garde film-making place opened in Montmartre early in 1928, which screened Ivens's *De Brug (The Bridge)* in 1929. She might also have seen André Sauvage's *Études sur Paris* (1928, 75 minutes), with its quayside, car traffic, port and street scenes featuring numerous high-angle shots; or Boris Kaufman's *Les Halles Centrales* (1927, 20 minutes) on the market at night, with all the unloading of meat and vegetables, and the surrounding bistrots. Then there was Eugène Deslaw's *Nuits électriques* (1930, 9½ minutes), which plays exclusively on the neon signs, lights and illuminations in Berlin and Paris, with strollers moving by shop windows at night. Had Krull seen Henri Chomette's *Jeux des reflets de de la vitesse* (1925, 7½ minutes), she would have been impressed by the shots of tracks of the Métro by a camera affixed to the front of the train. She was certainly a reader of the *Revue du cinéma,* published in 1929–30 by Gallimard, with whom she had links through Mac Orlan. All this simply means that, for a period of a few years, the quest to reveal and elucidate the city, its 'social weirdness', was shared by these film-makers and this photographer. Krull was perfectly in tune with the modern spirit that combined Eiffel Tower and tramps, electrical magic and the latest motorcar. Each to his or her own medium, at the risk of overlap. And Krull had her reasons for remaining a photographer: 'I felt that individual creativity wasn't possible in the cinema. One was dependent on too many things, not just the camera but also the cameraman, the actors ... I like to watch films, but not make a profession of them.' Taking photos was a little like making a film, except that she could do it alone, on her own terms, as sole master on board. 'When I look at a photo, I can imagine a bunch of things and I can look at it from all sides and I know it's my own creation. Which isn't possible in the cinema.'[122] In 1928 films were still silent and hence retained certain photographic qualities. But within two or three years the dreamy, imagination-triggering effect of 'pictures that moved' would be history.

The cinema was certainly an omnipresent model for Krull, as it was for others, both as a pole of attraction and something to imitate, but also as a force of resistance.[123] The diversity of her photographic subjects reflects a type of scenario derived from silent film of the 1920s, from which she adopted high-angle and low-angle shots, oblique shots, close-ups of avant-garde photo-cinema, whose milieu she frequented (Dziga Vertov, who she does not mention). As it happens, her work illustrating novels (Mac Orlan, Simenon, Colette) and novel-reportage (Berl) from 1930 to 1933, sticking closely to the text, corresponded to talkies, which required a new kind of image from 1930. When she was asked in 1931 about her links to cinema, she attacked it for being a 'vulgar copy of theatre', and said of Cocteau's *Sang d'un poète*, which she had seen privately, 'Now that's cinema.'[124]

122 VMD, p. 129.
123 Michel Frizot, 'D'un imaginaire-cinéma de la photographie (1928–1930), in Guido Laurent and Olivier Lugon (eds.), *Fixe-Animé. Croisements de la photographie et du cinéma au* xx*e siècle*, Lausanne: L'Âge d'homme, 2010, pp. 203–224; for Henri Cartier-Bresson, see Michel Frizot, *Henri Cartier-Bresson, Scrapbook, Photographies 1932–1946*, Göttingen: Steidl, 2006.
124 Jean Laurent, 'Germaine Krull', *La Rampe*, 15 April–1 May 1931, p. 54.
125 VMD, p. 141. According to www.cinema-francais.fr, from 1929 to 1959 Yves Gladine (1902–1964) acted in a number of films by the likes of Raymond Rouleau, Abel Gance, and Robert Siodmak. Krull spelled his name Gladyne.

THE FILMS OF GERMAINE KRULL

Krull paradoxically turned somewhat suddenly to cinema even though she was not convinced of either her talent or her personal interest in the medium. In *Click entre deux guerres* she wrote that by 1931 she was weary of photo-studio routine. 'I wanted something different. With Loup we decided to make a little film.' It turns out that 'Loup' was Yves Gladine, an actor friend who wrote screenplays, and 'handled correspondence and speeches for Jouvet',[125] with whom Krull was friends till the end of his life. Gladine was patently the Georges H. Patin who wrote the screenplays for her two extant films. Krull went on: 'The first, *Six pour dix francs*, was a charming little photo documentary but lacked the very basics of a film. We chose a ravishing village in the greater Paris area.' A local photographer carrying a large camera on a tripod prepares to take photographs of 'a silly bride and bridegroom'. A sign in front of his studio says 'Six for ten francs – likeness guaranteed'. Still according to Krull: 'The action: the couple is dragged through the streets of the village and photographed at the six prettiest spots. I had a little portable camera.' It starts with preparations for the wedding in a restaurant, then the couple scour the village in search of an interesting backdrop, but they are constantly disturbed by some incident or misunderstanding. The style is slapstick: the bridegroom tears her gown; at one picturesque setting a coffin passes into view; the bride loses veil and wig; an artificial set collapses. The photographer finally snaps the picture and displays the six prints, of which only one is satisfactory. Thus went the nine-minute *Six pour dix francs*, 'a fictionalised documentary by Germaine Krull and Georges H. Patin'. The comic effects are somewhat overdone, and the are scenes too long if perfectly clear, yet there are a few interesting shots (of the photo equipment and the shadows) that reveal Krull's participation.

'We made a second, longer [film] that was supposed to show the Seine. Two kids play truant and walk along the river from the wine merchants' docks as far as the bridge at Suresnes. It wasn't bad, the Seine is always lovely and this little effort was screened as a documentary in a cinema on the left bank.' Referred to several times in Krull's memoirs as *La Seine*, the eleven-minute film survives with the title *Il partit pour un long voyage*,

126 CEDG, p. 72.
127 CEDG, p. 73.
128 Both films were produced by the Office Française d'Information Cinématographique (OFIC) and are available for consultation at the branch of the Centre National du Cinéma (CNC) in the Bibliothèque Nationale de France.

credited to Germaine Krull and Georges H. Patin. The first scenes were shot on the docks in the Bercy quarter of Paris (Halle aux vins) – a kid climbs onto a barge in the hope of getting to America. The lad, scolded by his father, is intelligent but absent-minded, and is interested only in geography. He daydreams in his bedroom while looking at compass and maps. He returns to the barge. His friend walks along the quayside, in search of him – hoists, stacks of wine vats, travelling cranes, piles of coal. Near Notre-Dame we see tramps, an artist with an easel, a carder of mattress flock. The promenade is intercut with shots of the boy stowed away on the barge. The film is clearly the work of a photographer carefully arranging each shot, and reflects the entire typology of Krull's photos: shots of objects, cranes in movement, high-angle and low-angle views, hands holding things.

Yet Krull 'took no satisfaction from the cinema even though [she] was wielding the camera'.[126] She nevertheless decided, once again with Gladine, 'to make a film that had no screenplay, just a conceptual framework: a very old car with plenty of defects' would be driven 'by a young actor friend wearing a boater.' Three cars set off: the star of the film, another packed with luggage and Krull's own car, all driven 'by people without a driving licence ... Every incident en route was filmed.' Krull was 'concerned only with camera angle, feeling that everything else was of minor interest'. The saga ended with a very real breakdown of the car in Nice. Krull made a stab at editing the film with Gladine, then sent the cans of film to the person who commissioned it, a family friend of Gladine. It was supposed to bear the title *La Route Paris–Nice*, reflecting the theme of two of Krull's books of 1931. 'I realised that as far as I was concerned, cinema wasn't an art, nor even a craft.'[127]

Two other films credit Germaine Krull as 'technical advisor', both shot during World War Two in French equatorial Africa, where Krull was working with the Free French authorities. One was *Autour de Brazzaville* (1943), directed by François Villiers, the other was *L'Amitié noire* (1943–46), also directed by François Villiers, with a commentary by Jean Cocteau.[128]

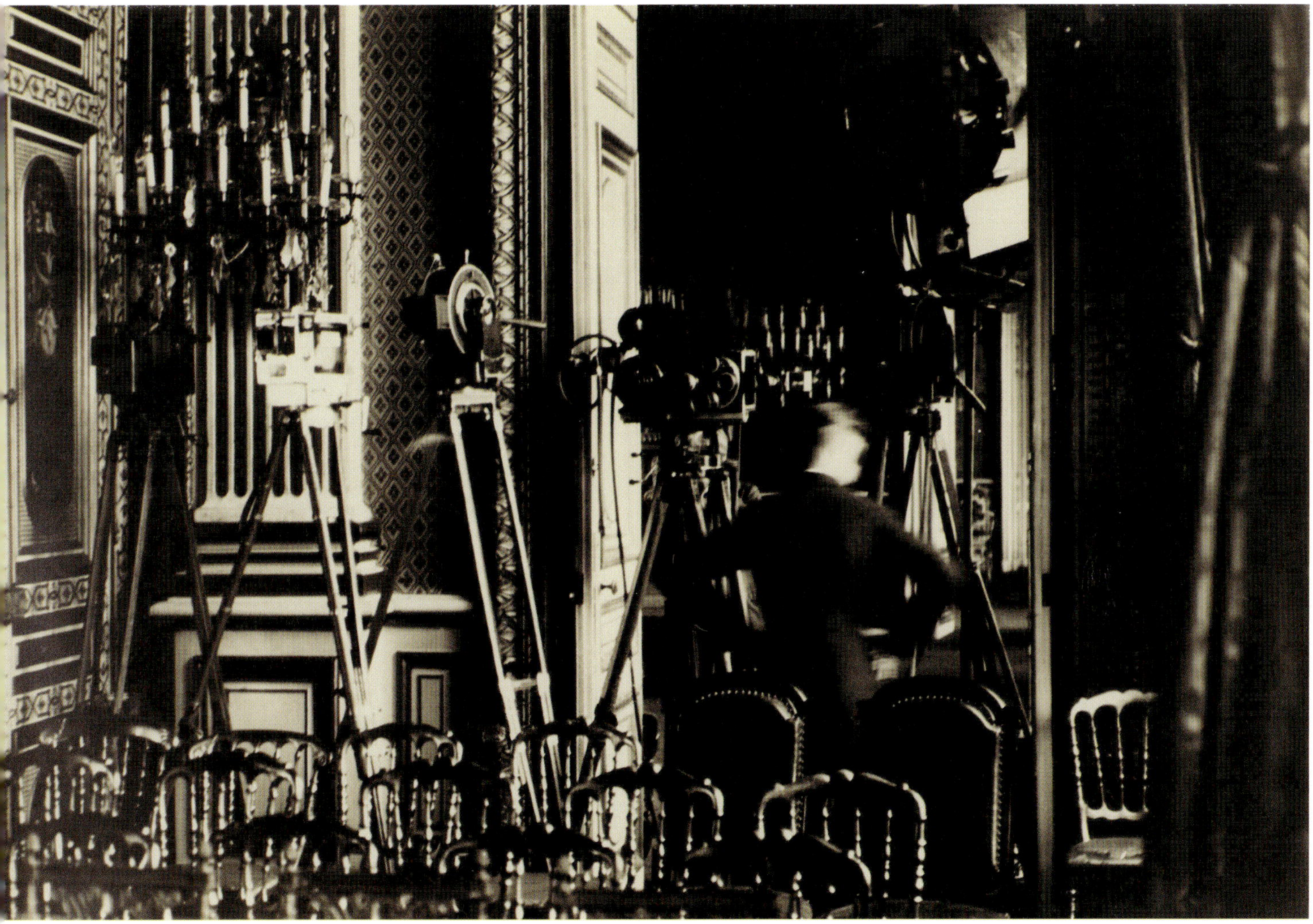

ehind the Scenes at the Signature of the Briand-Kellogg Pact, 1928

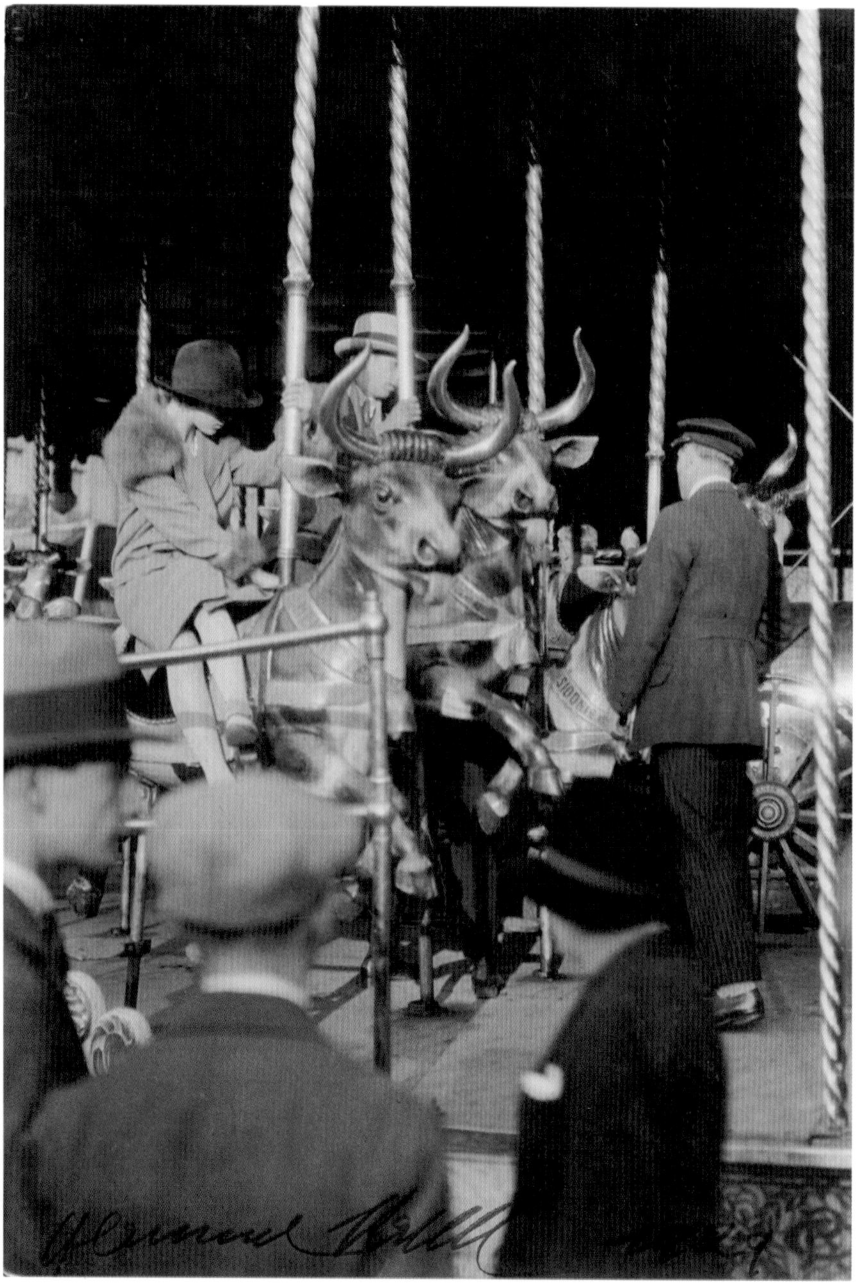

Fair, Paris, 1928

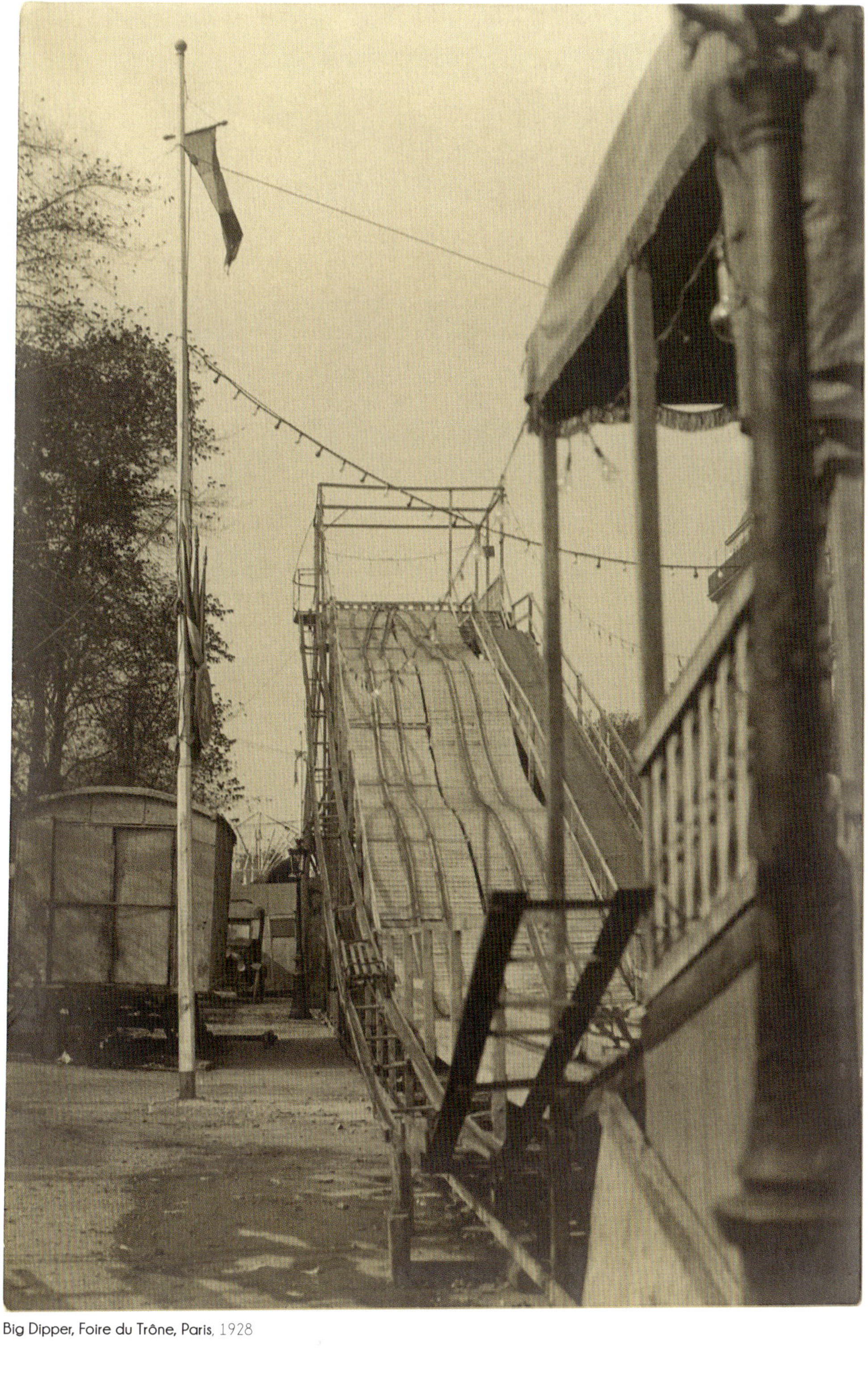

Big Dipper, Foire du Trône, Paris, 1928

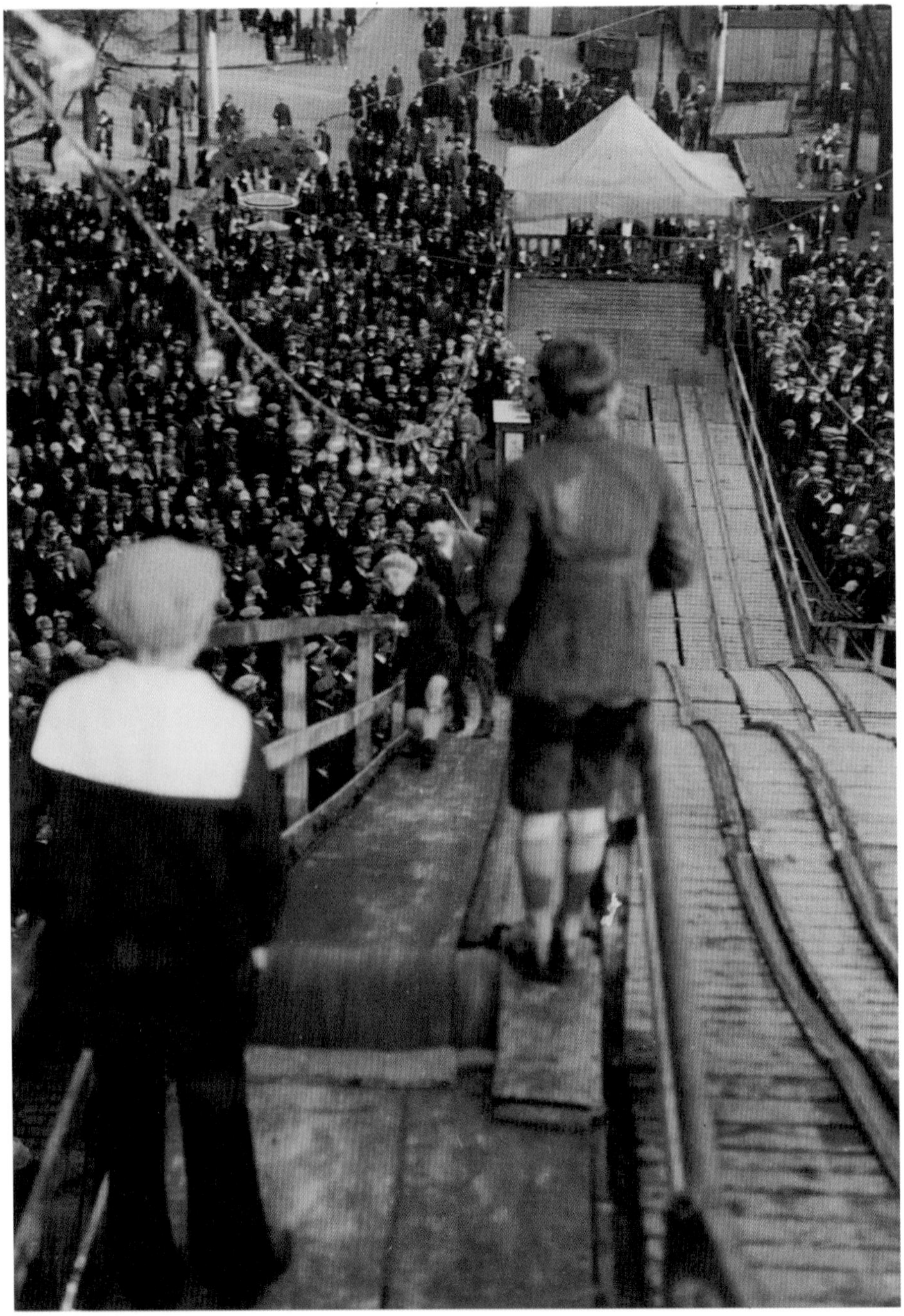

Big Dipper, Foire du Trône, Paris, 1928

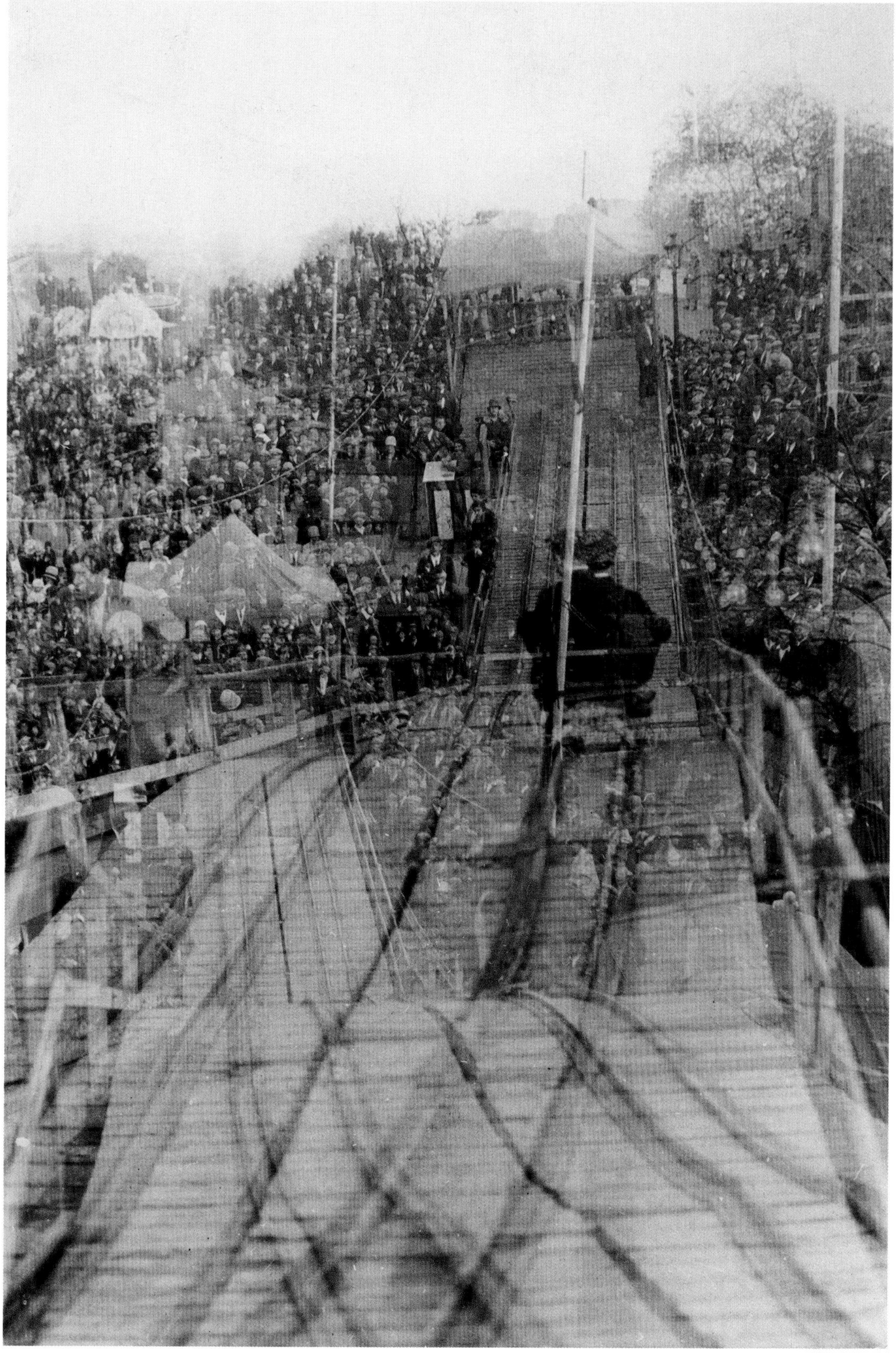
Big Dipper, Foire du Trône, Paris, 1928

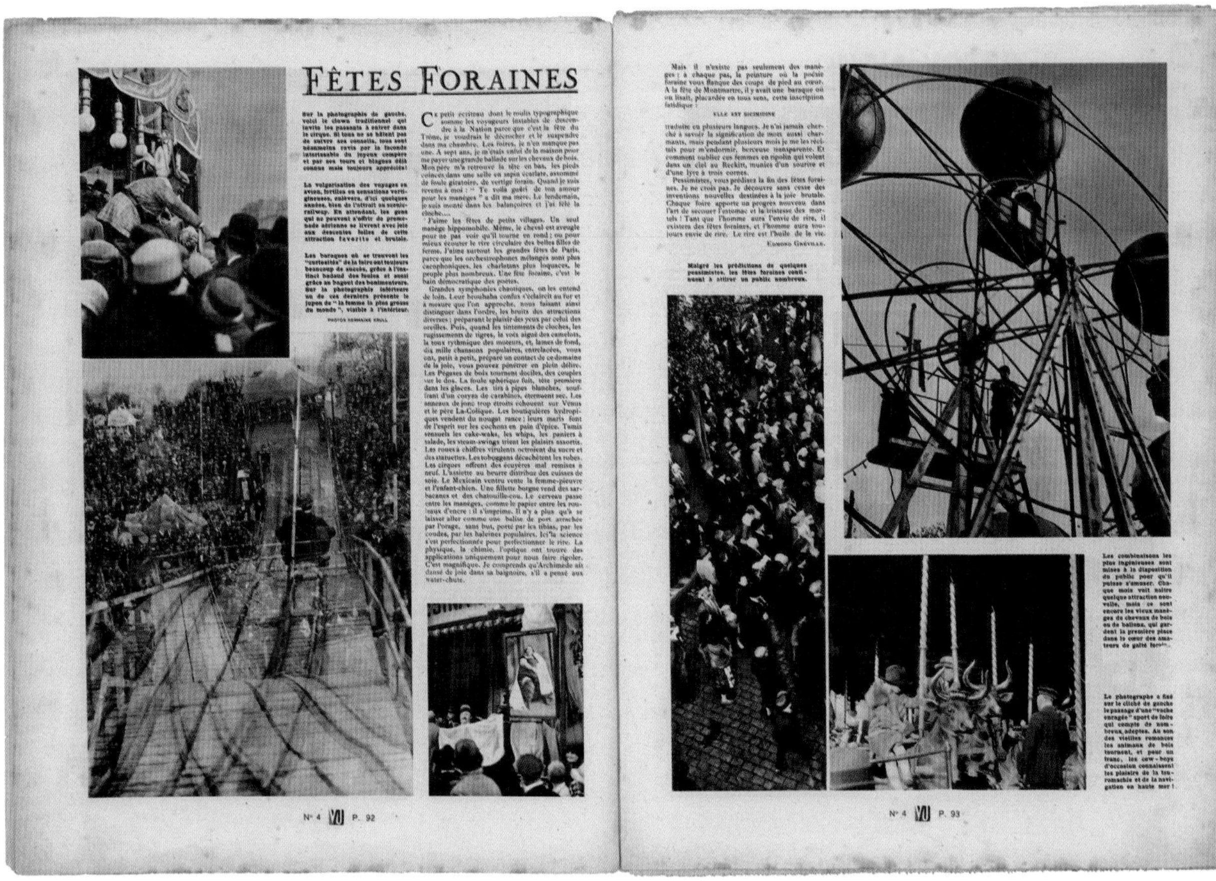

'Fairs', *VU*, no. 4, 11 April 1928, pp. 92–93

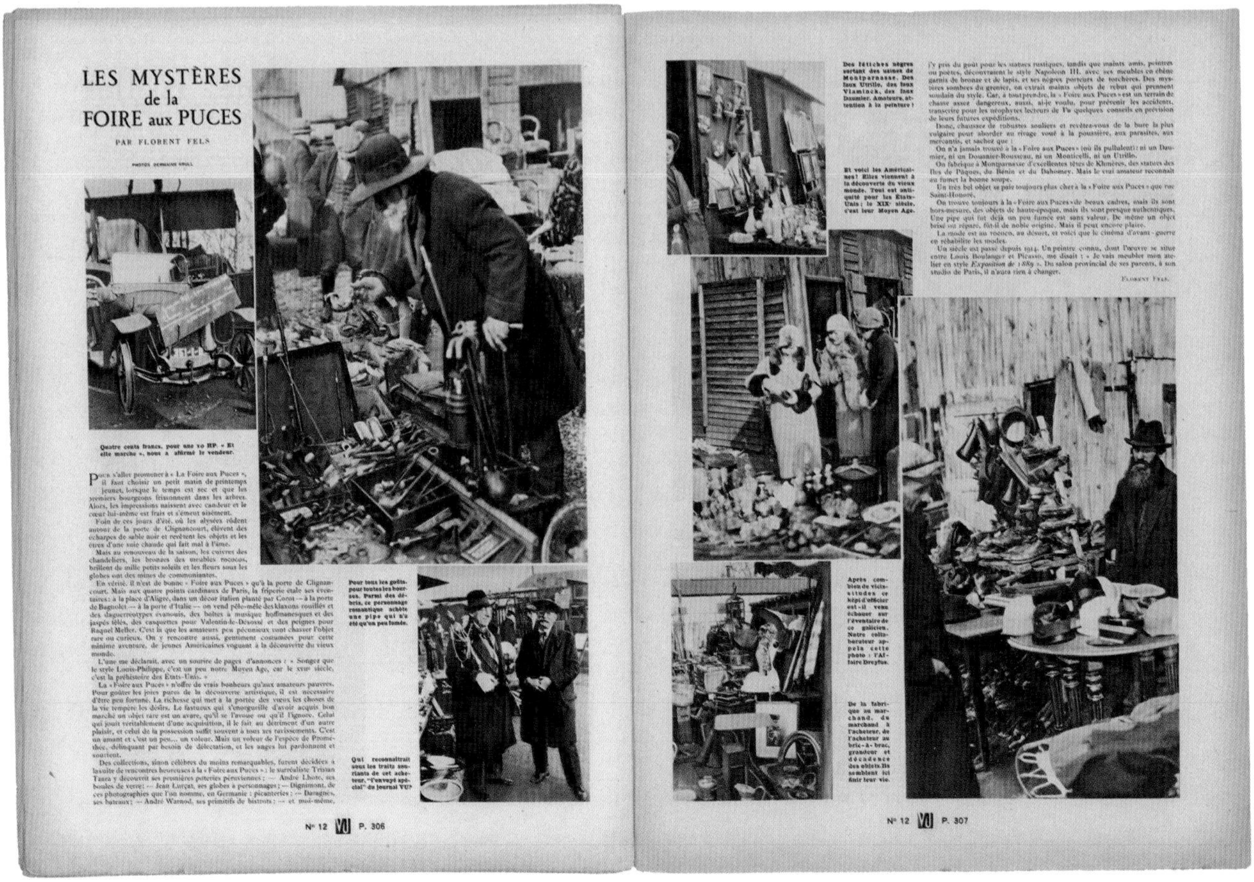

'Mysteries of the Flea Fair', *VU*, no. 12, 6 June 1928, pp. 306–307

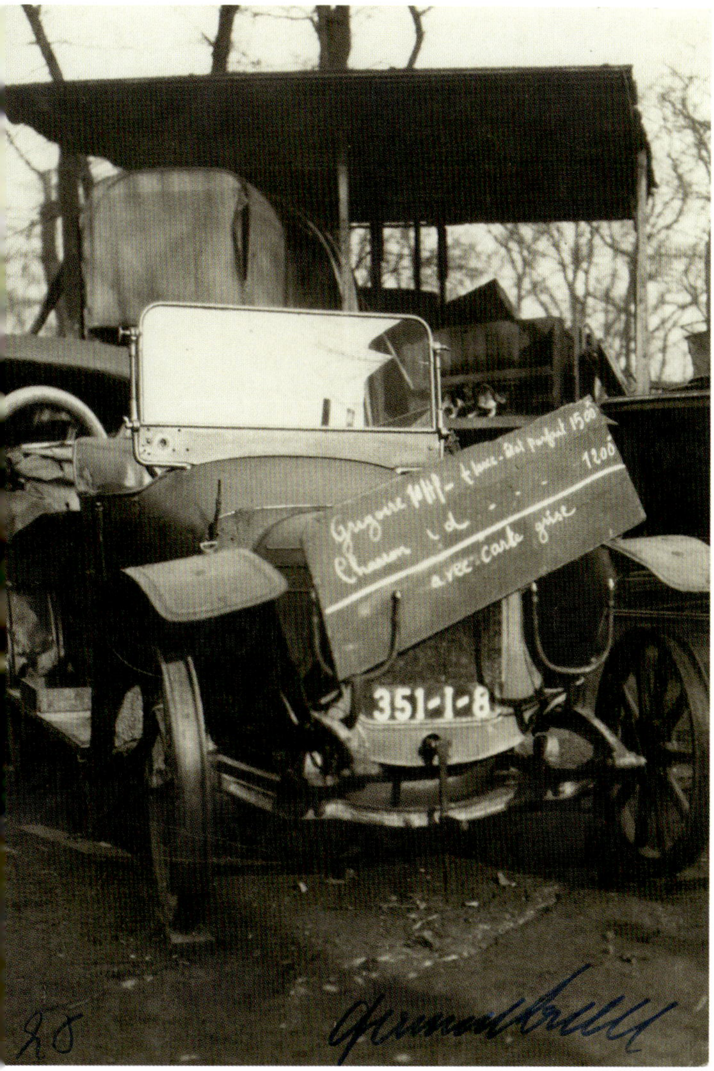

n a Courtyard, Rue des Rosiers', Flea Market, Paris, 1928

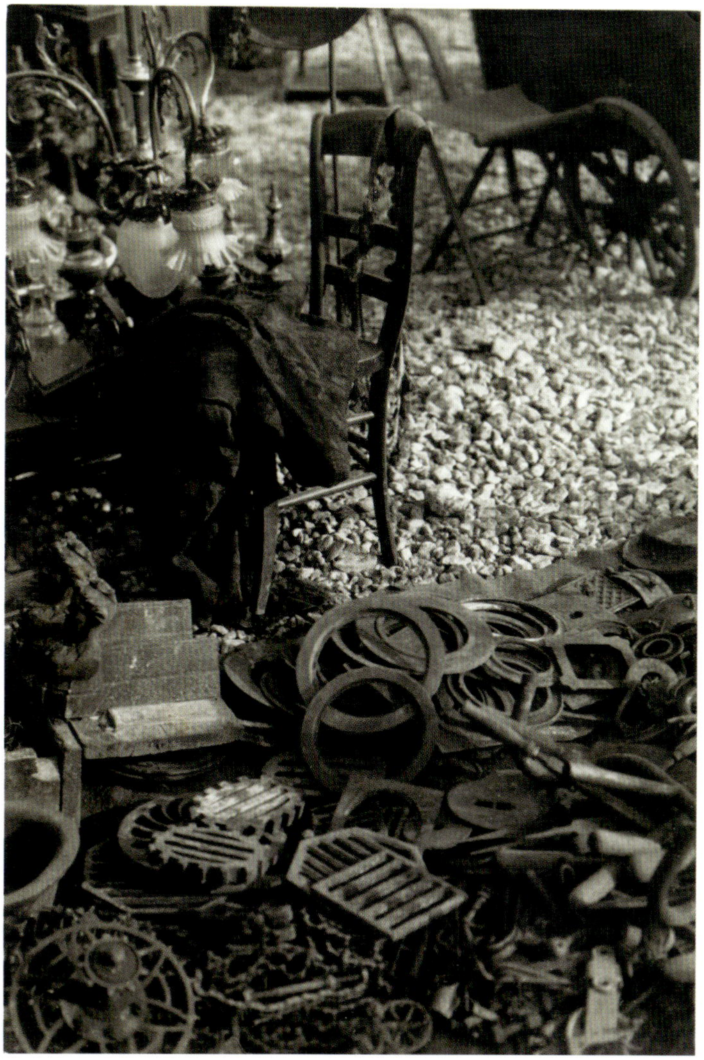

Flea Market in Paris, Old Iron, 1928

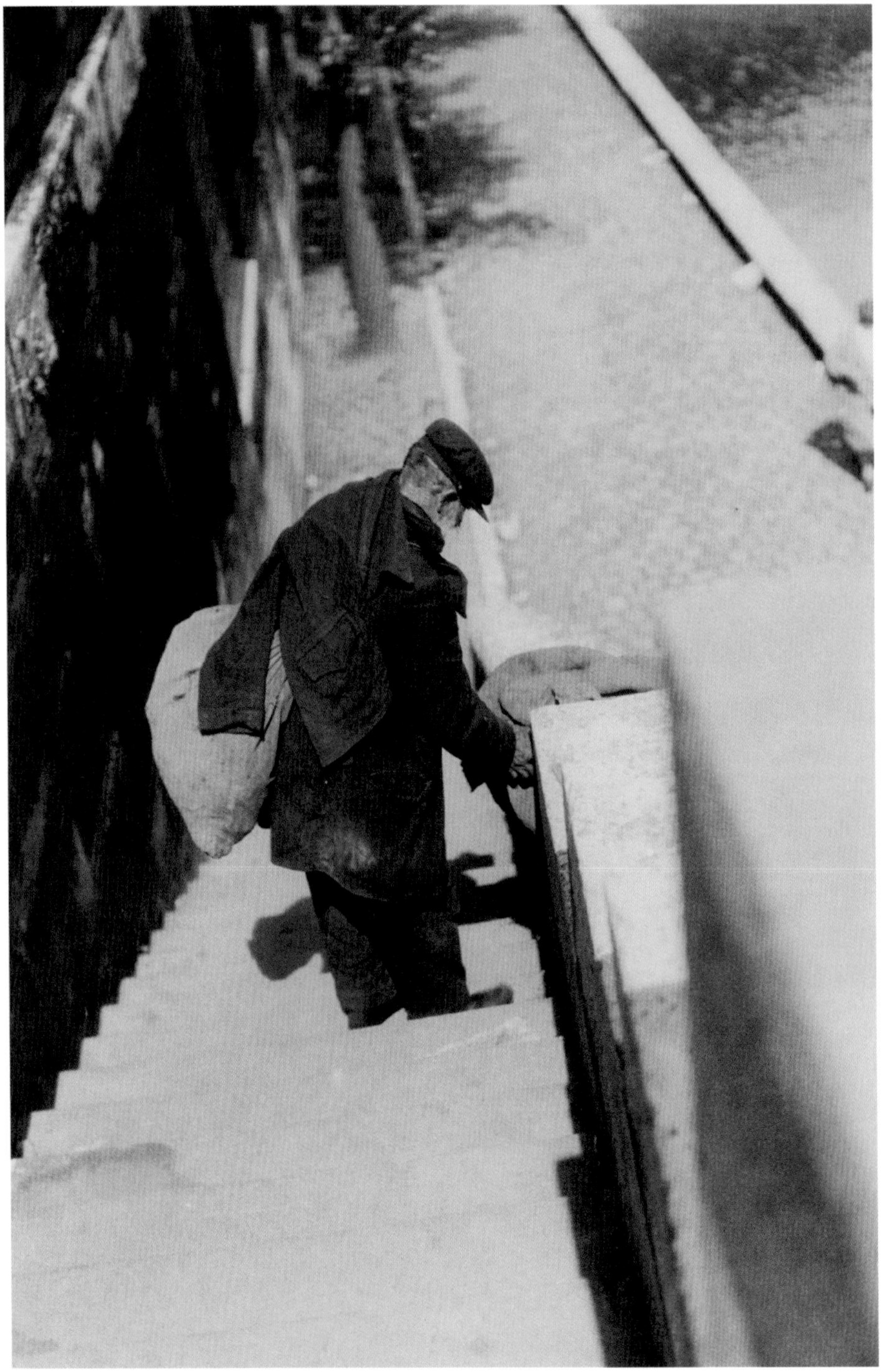

'Tramp', 1928

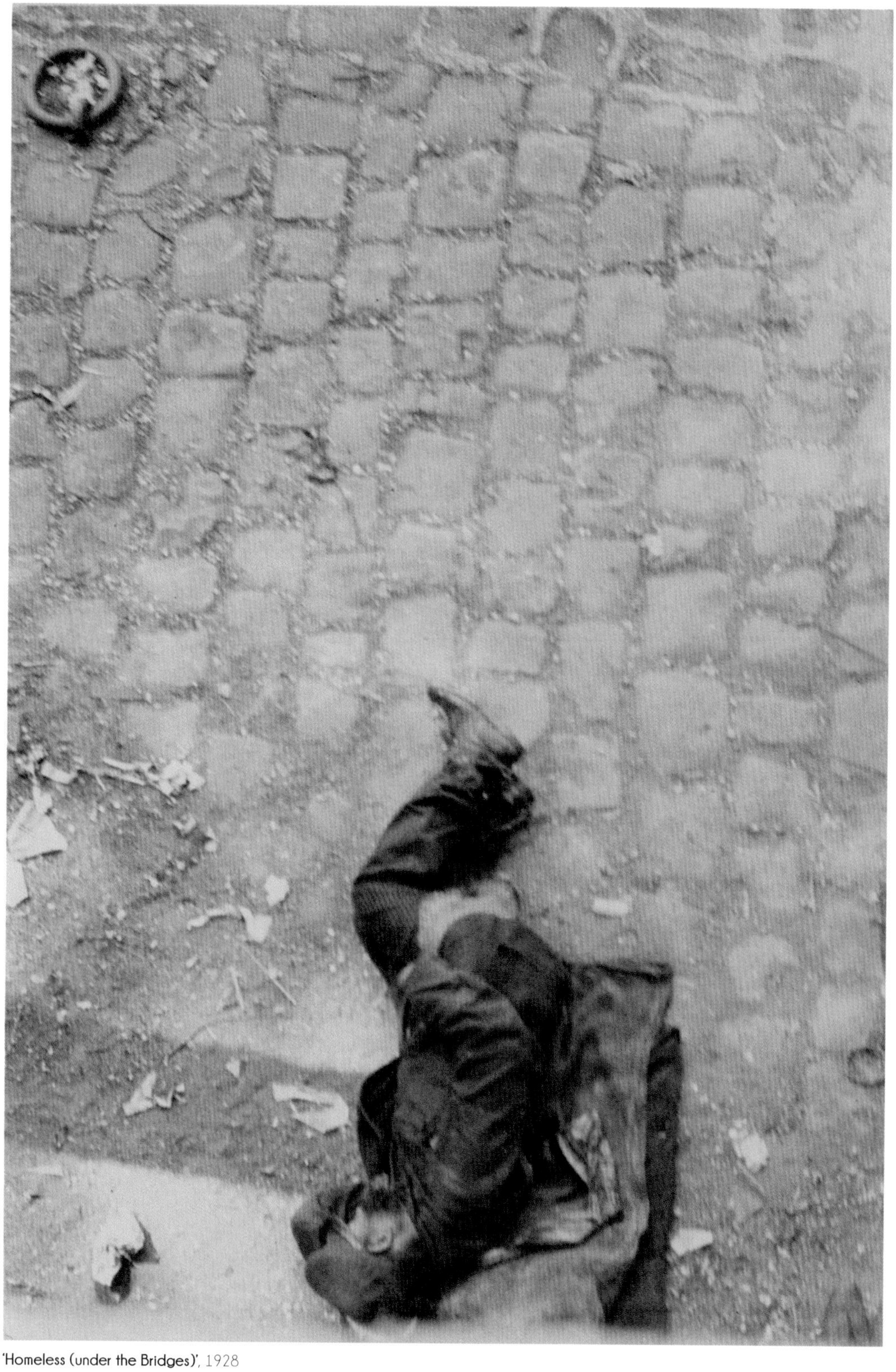

'Homeless (under the Bridges)', 1928

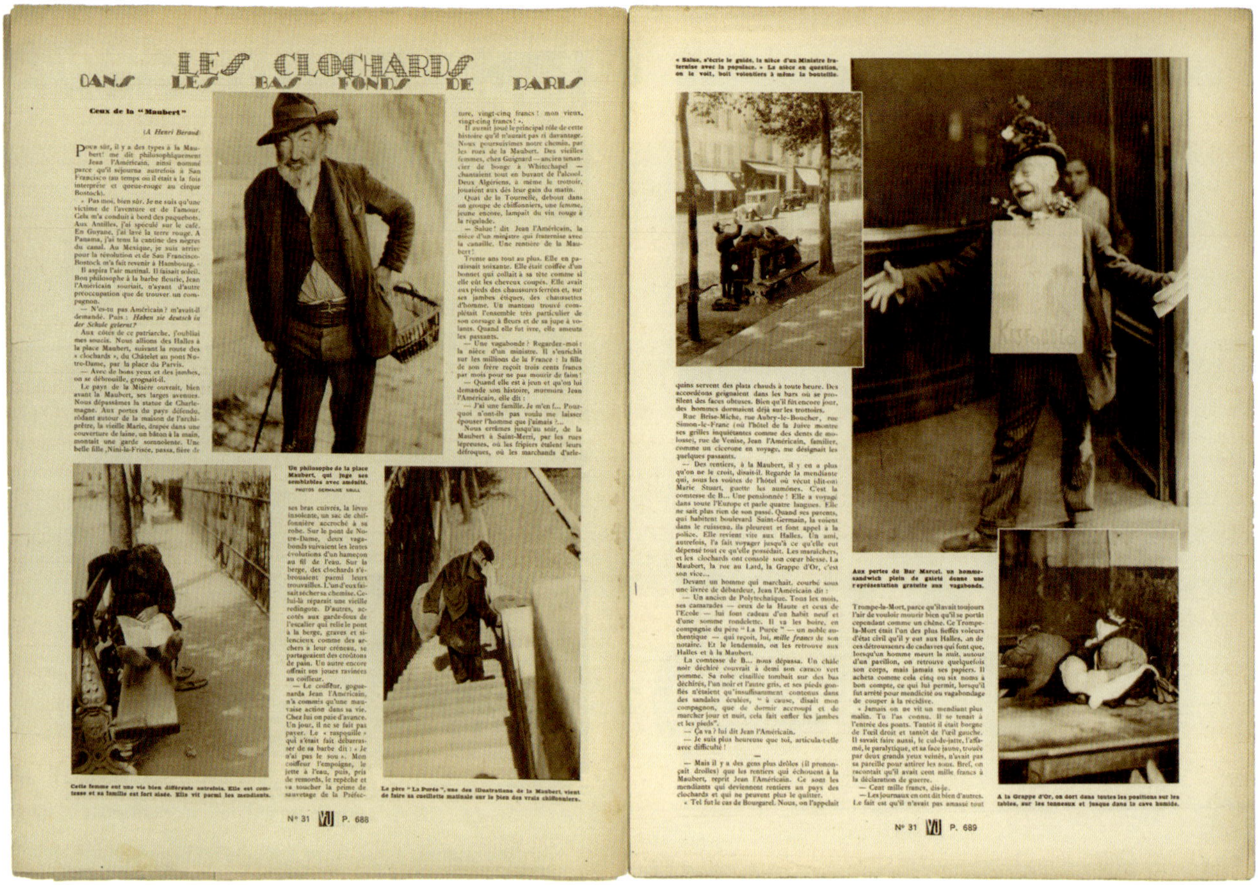

'Tramps in the Lower Depths of Paris', *VU*, no. 31, 17 October 1928, pp. 688–690

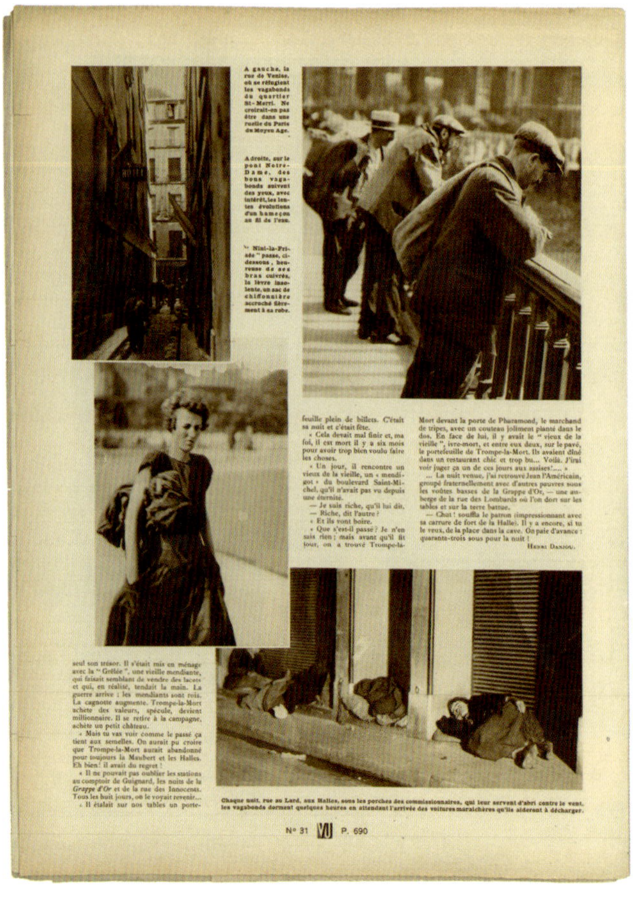

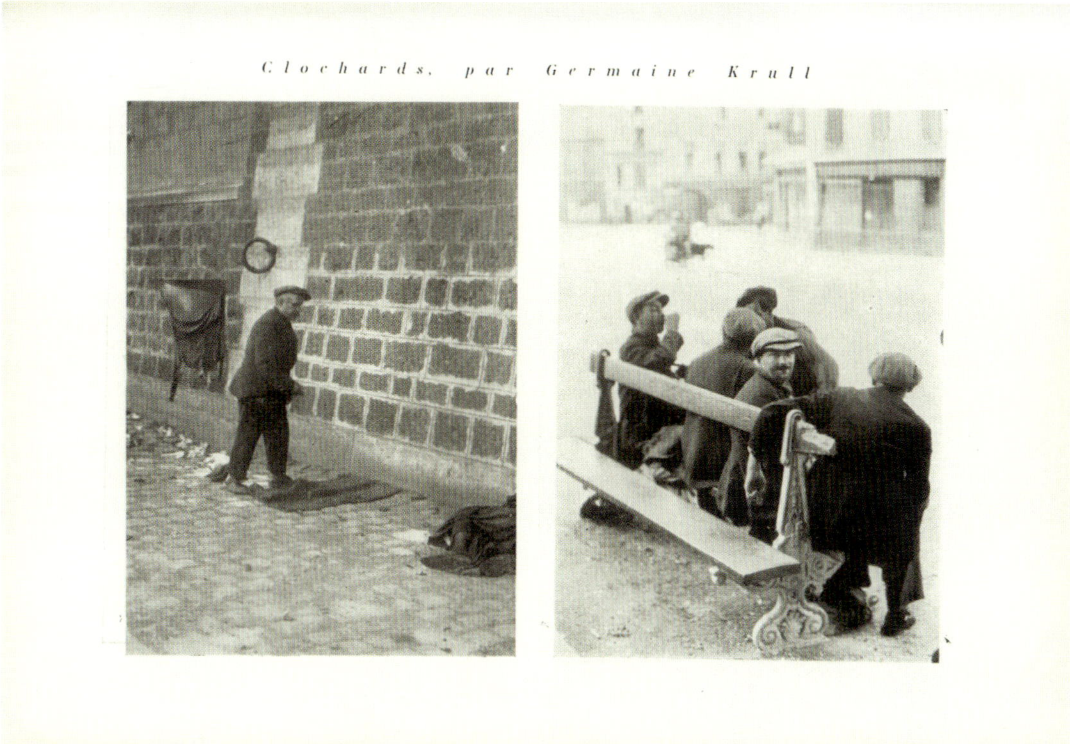
Clochards, par Germaine Krull

'Tramps', *Variétés*, 1 st year, no. 8, 15 December 1928, p. 422c

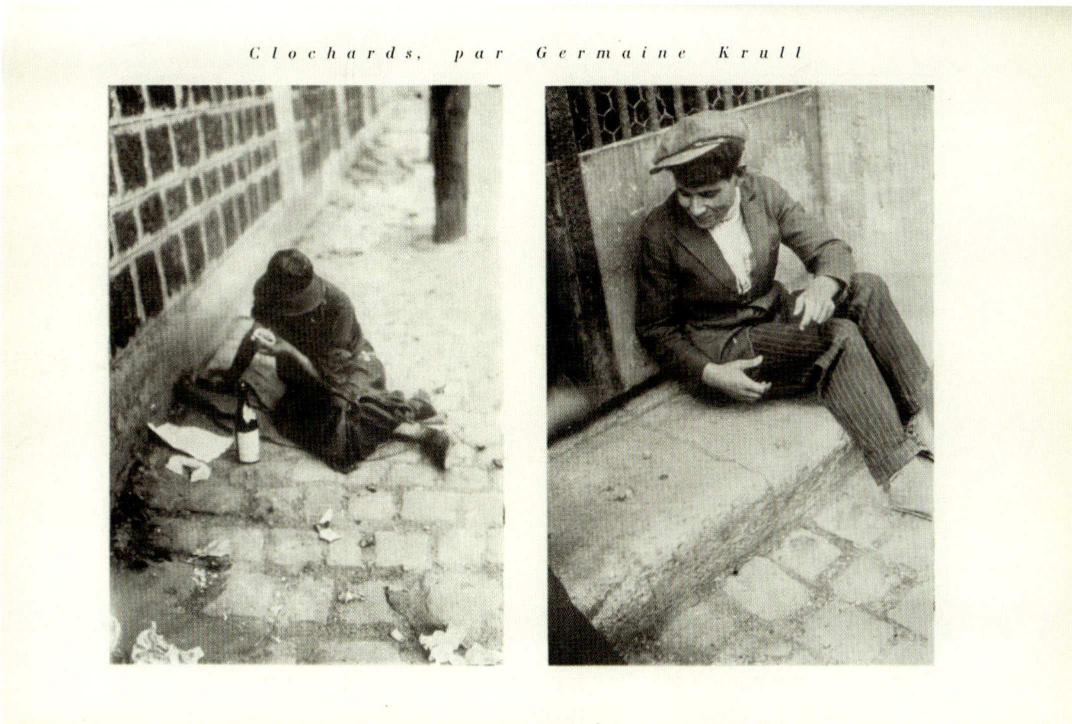
Clochards, par Germaine Krull

'Tramps', *Variétés*, 1st year, no. 8, 15 December 1928, p. 422a

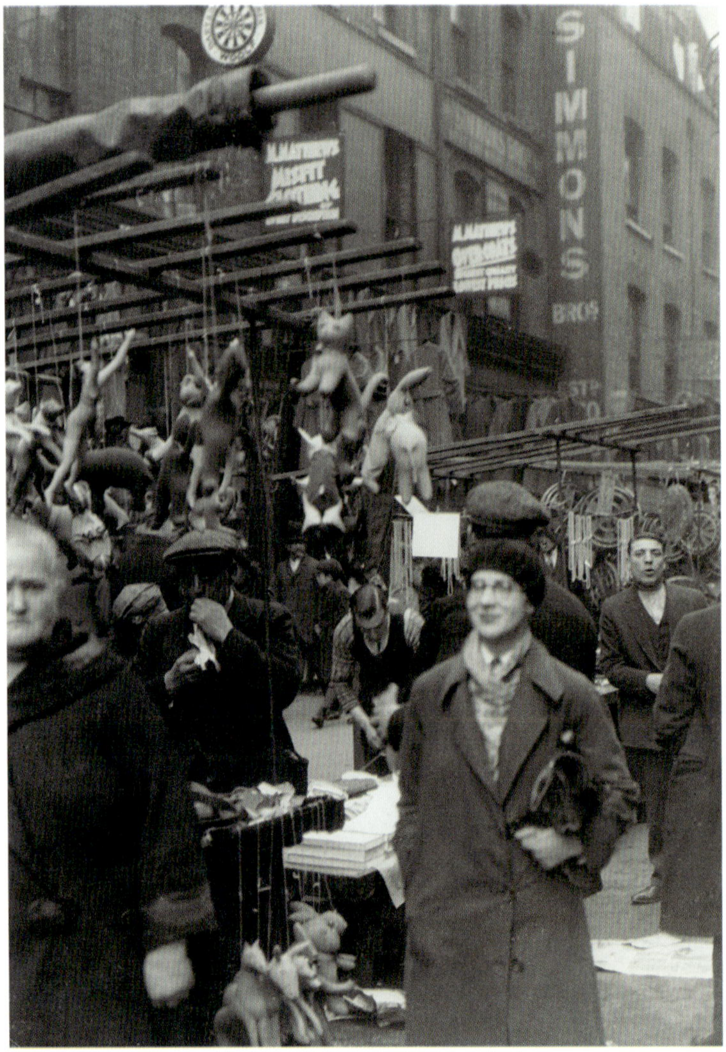

London, c. 1927

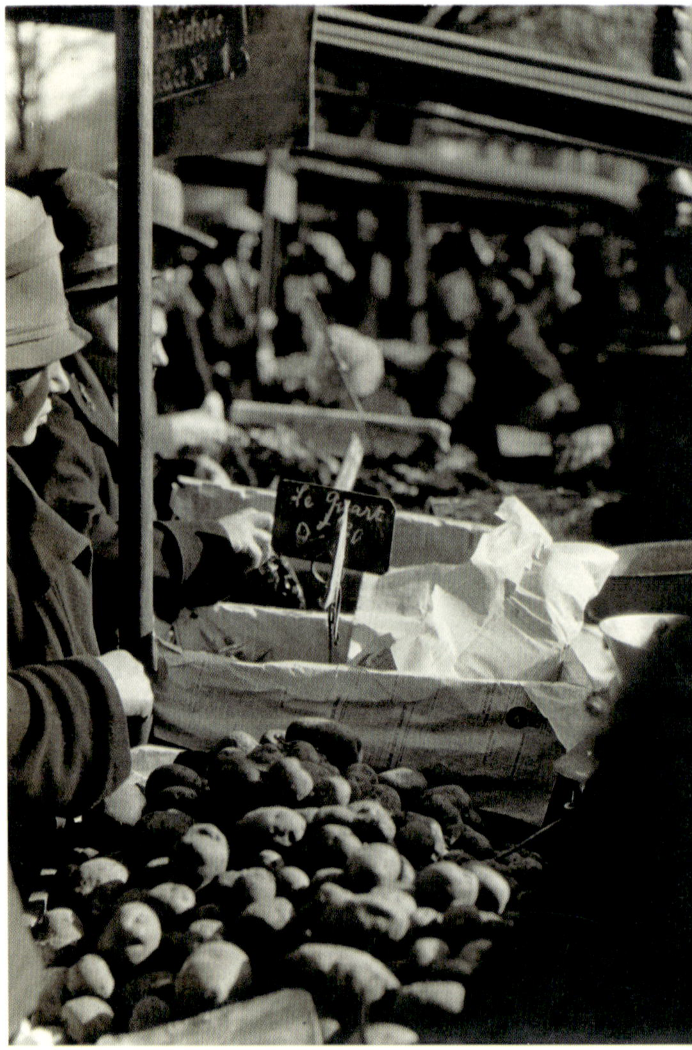

Market Scene, c. 1928

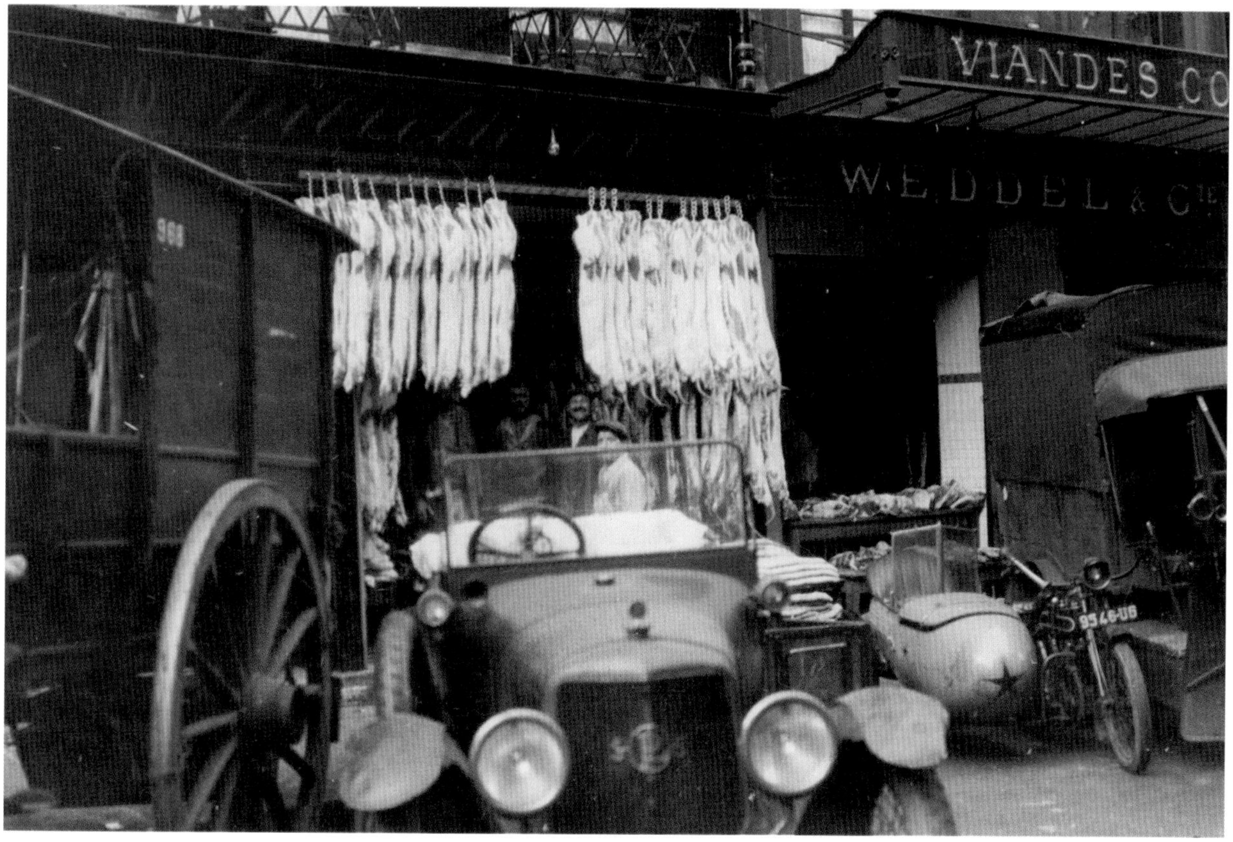

Les Halles, Meats, Villette et Cie, Paris, c. 1928

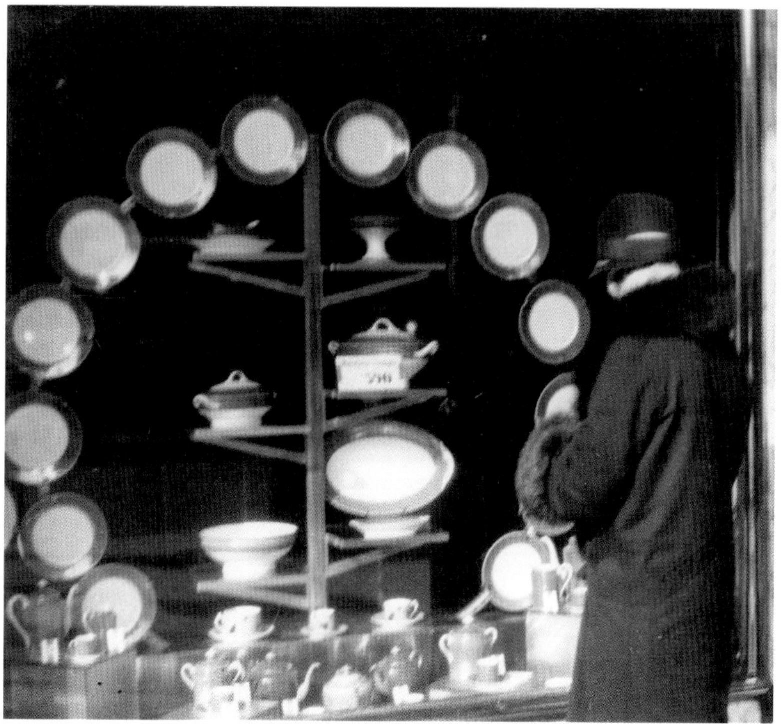

Porcelain Window, c. 1928

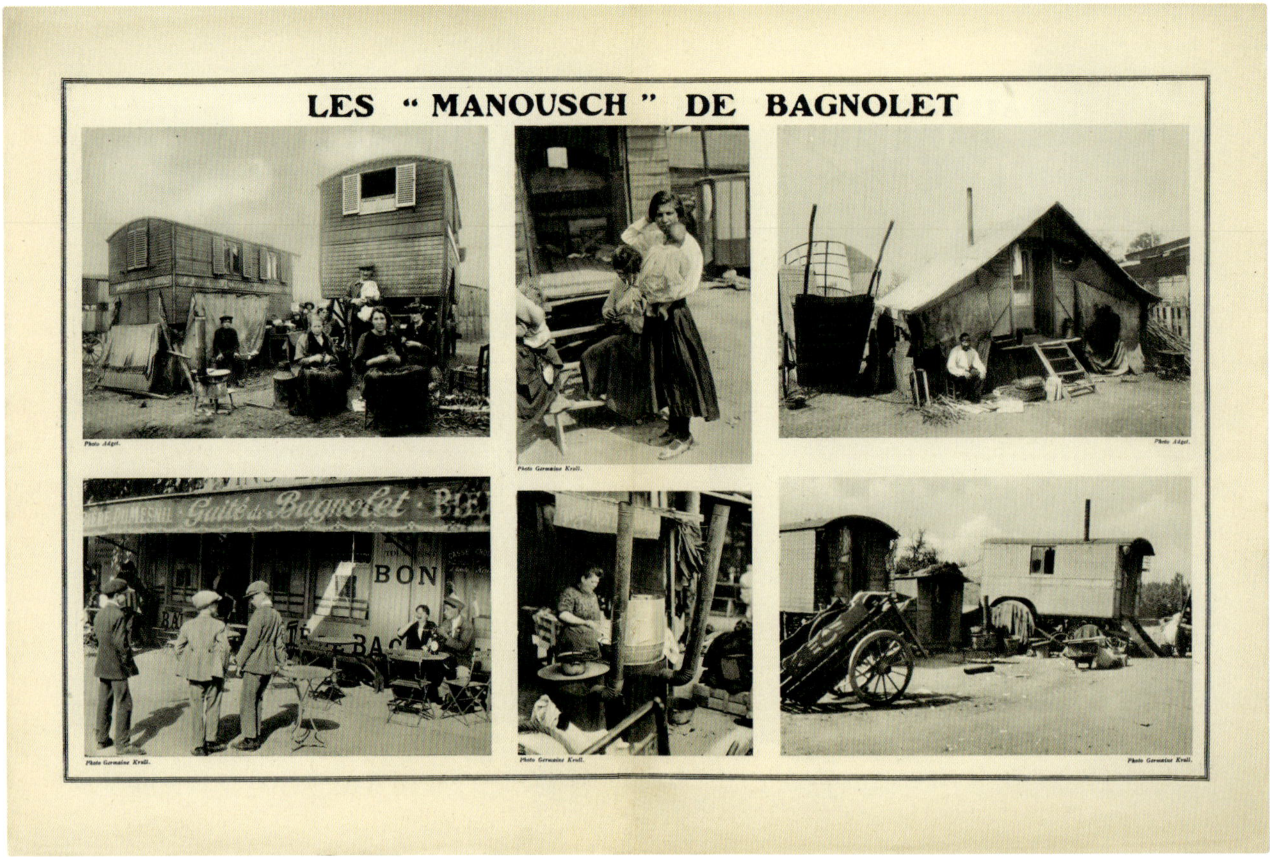

LES “ MANOUSCH ” DE BAGNOLET

'The "Manouch" of Bagnolet', *L'Art vivant*, no. 125, 1 March 1930

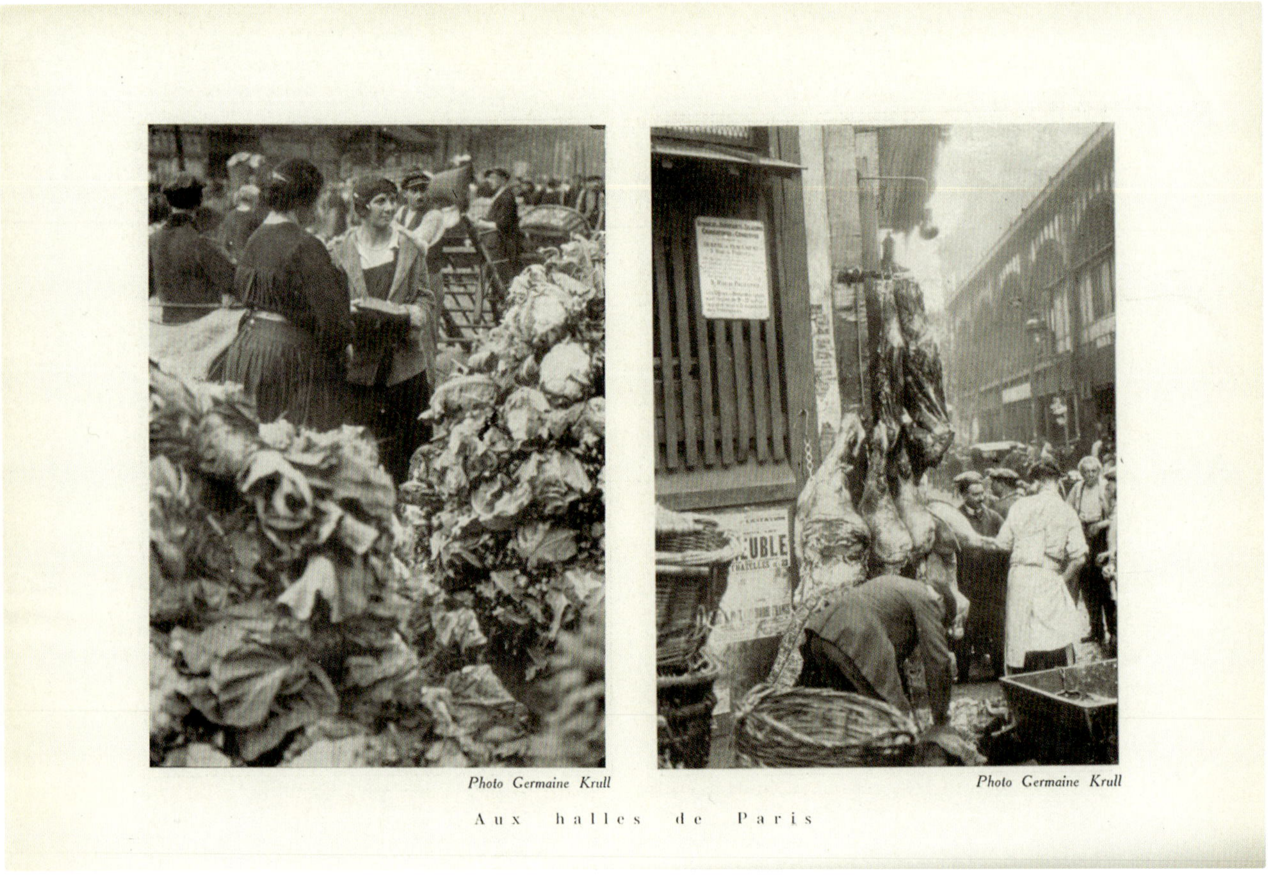

Photo Germaine Krull

Photo Germaine Krull

Aux halles de Paris

'At Les Halles in Paris', *Variétés*, 1st year, no. 8, 15 December 1928, pp. 414f

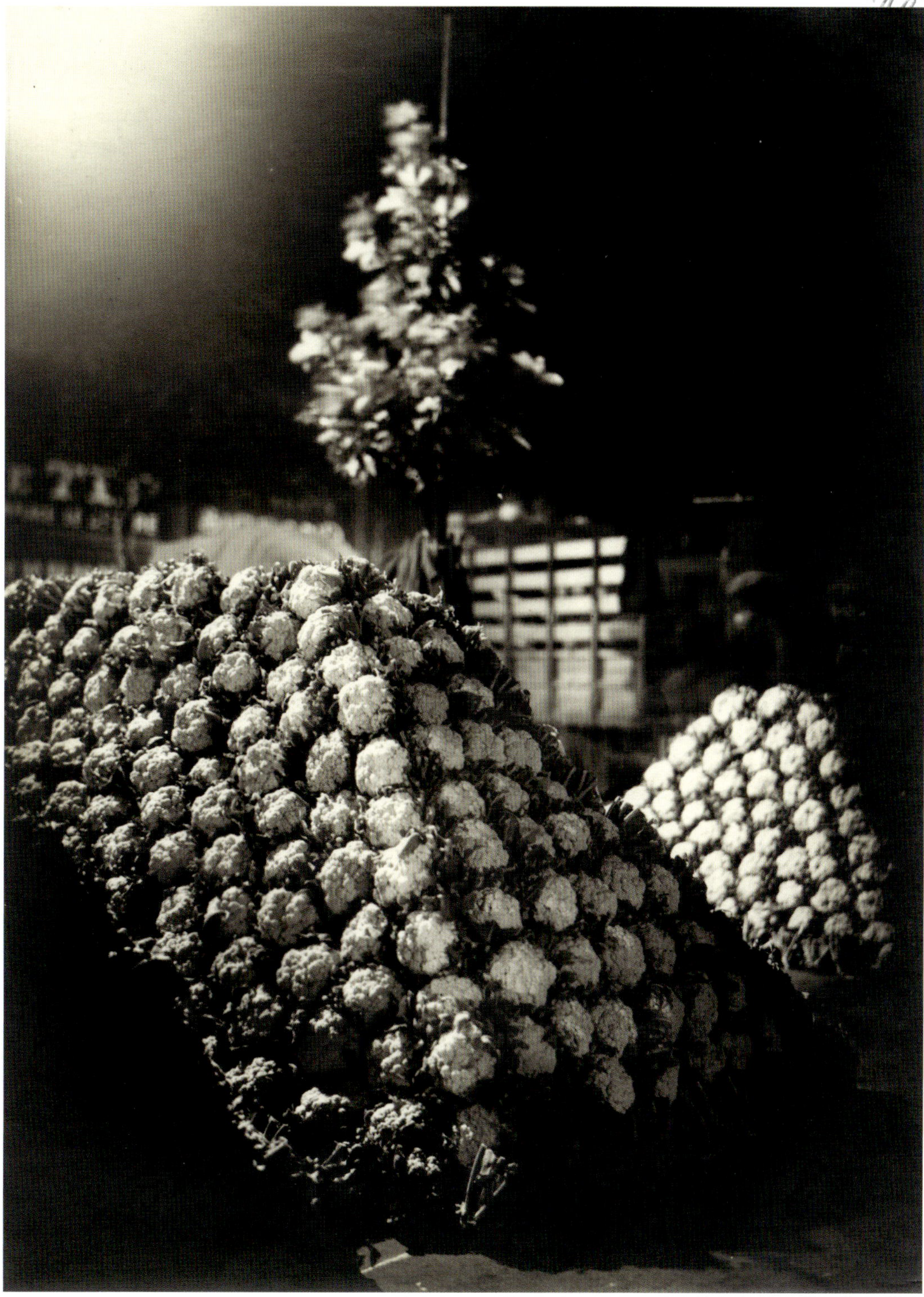

Les Halles at Night (with Van Ecke), c.1928

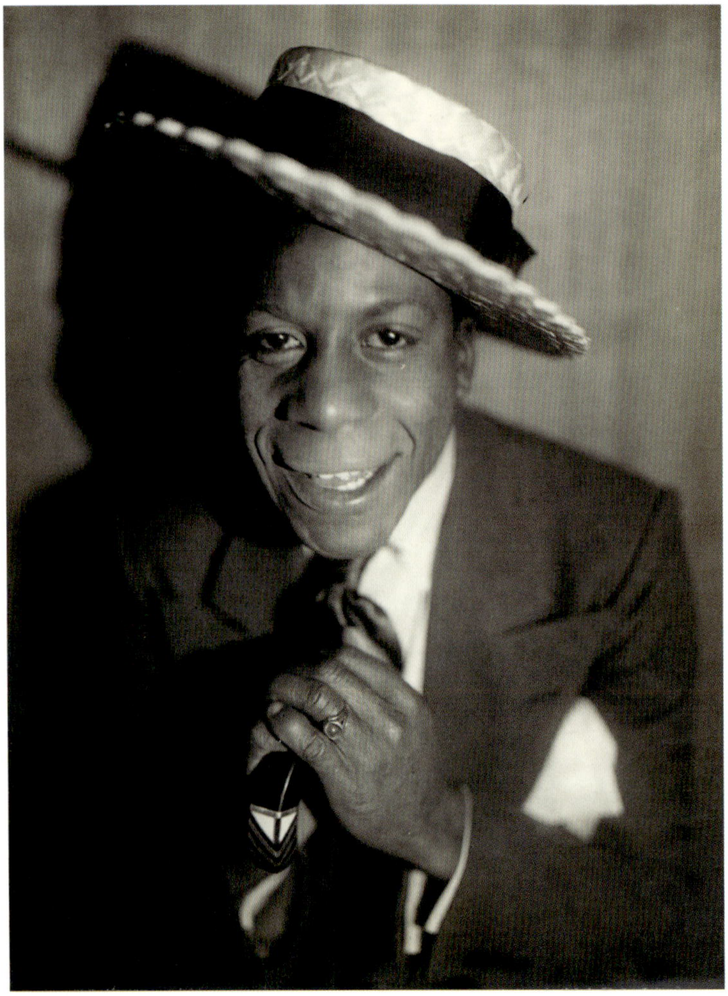

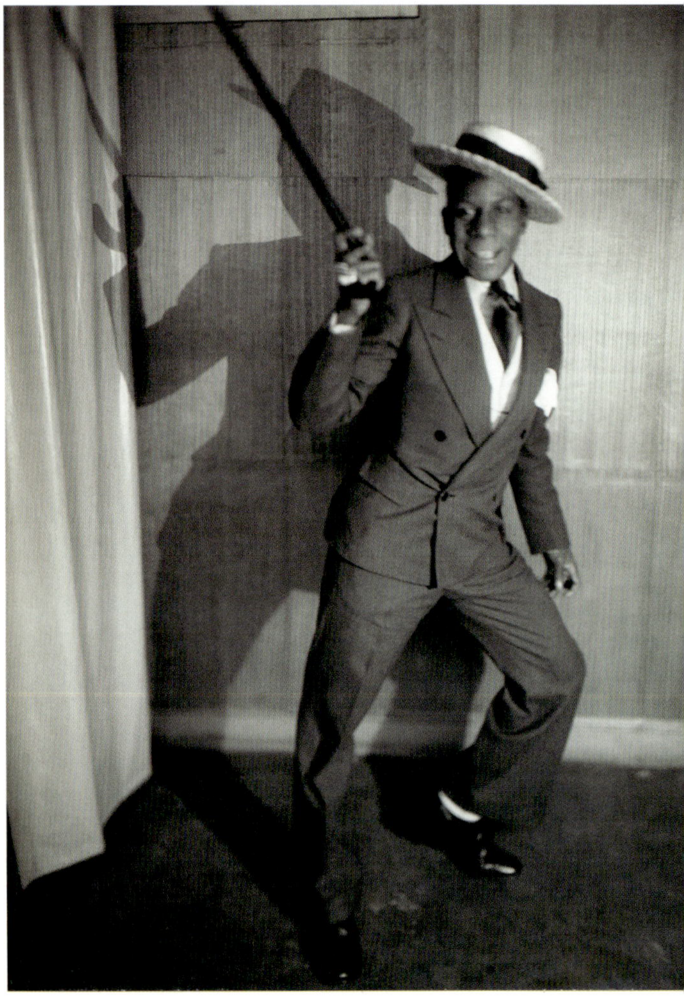

The Dancer Earl Tucker, Blackbirds Revue at the Moulin Rouge, 1929 (above and right)
'Black Magic', *VU*, no. 70, 17 July 1929, p. 574 (facing page)

MAGIE NOIRE

AU MOULIN ROUGE

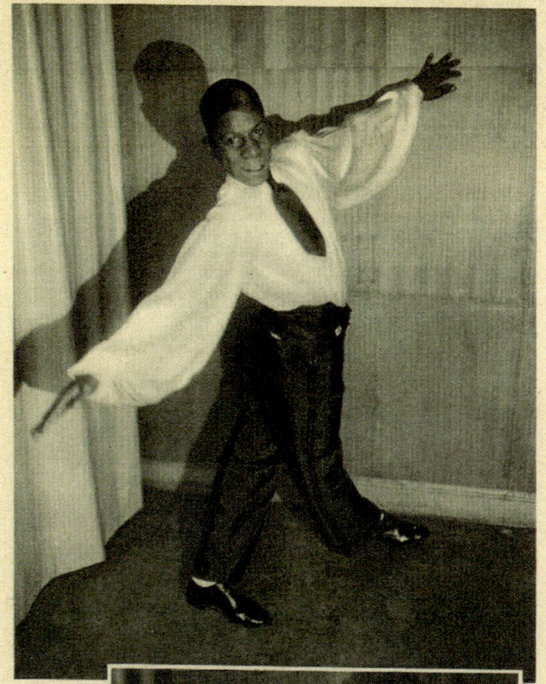

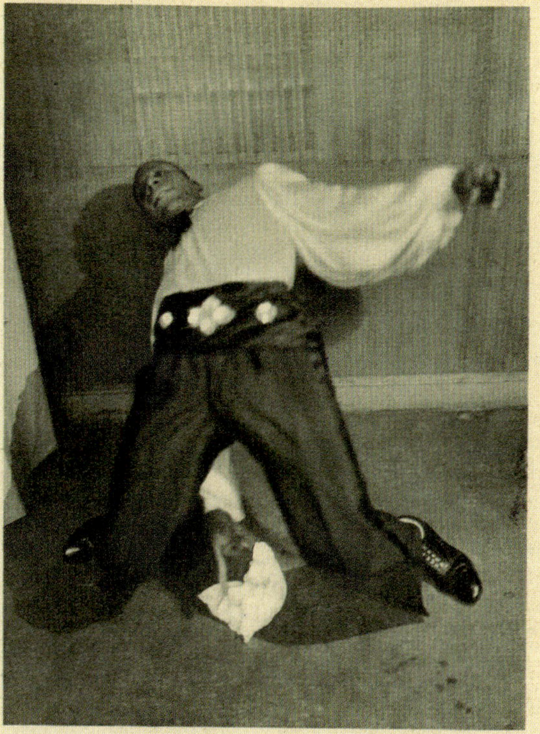

EARL TUCKER

sombre pantin disloqué, magicien des formes, des sons et de la lumière

ENSORCELLE PARIS

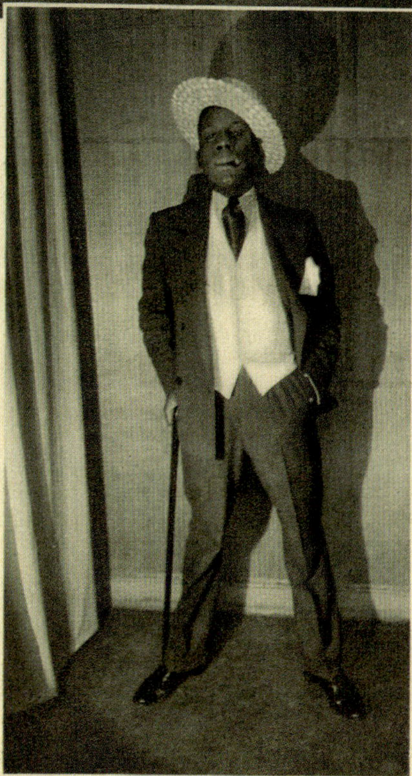

PHOTOS GERMAINE KRULL

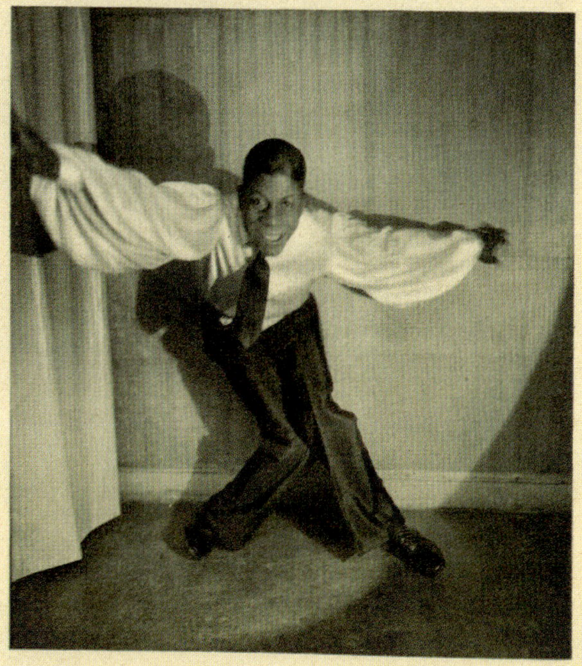

UN RYTHME ENRAGÉ, une agilité presque acrobatique, un cynisme drolatique, analogues aux autres danses nègres. Tel est Earl Tucker qui se distingue pourtant nettement des autres danseurs noirs. Ses danses sont parfois d'une dignité grave et même d'un lyrisme poignant. C'est une scène extraordinaire d'angoisse et de douleur qu'il mime, lorsque de la pointe des pieds, le long du corps et jusqu'à sa gorge contractée, des frissons le parcourent et que sa peau, qu'on dirait détachée des os, frémit pouce par pouce comme si chaque parcelle était indépendante des autres. C'est d'une telle perfection que devant ce spectacle inattendu et effarant on oublie même de s'étonner.

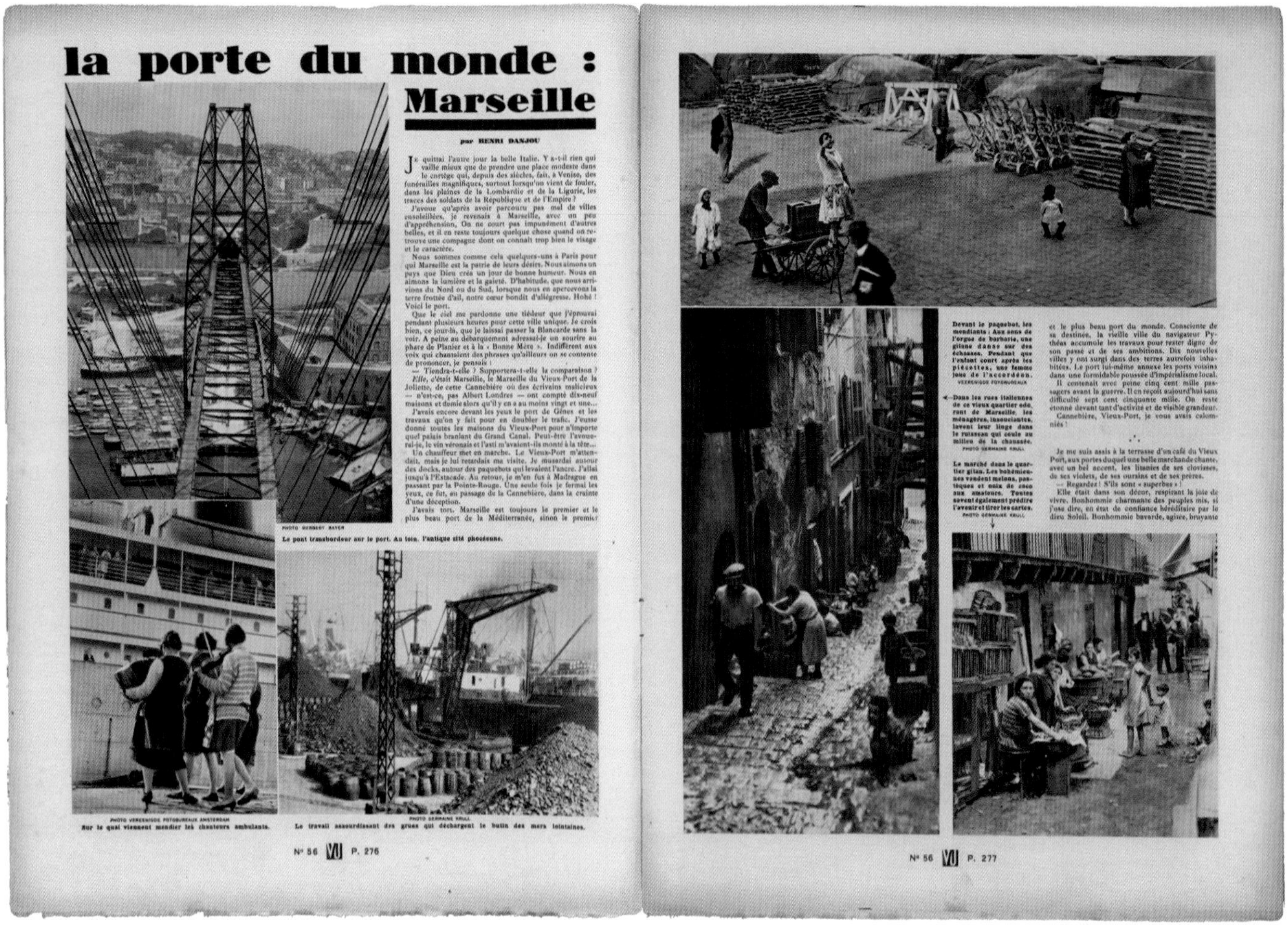

'Gateway to the World: Marseille', *VU*, no. 56, 10 April 1929, pp. 276–277

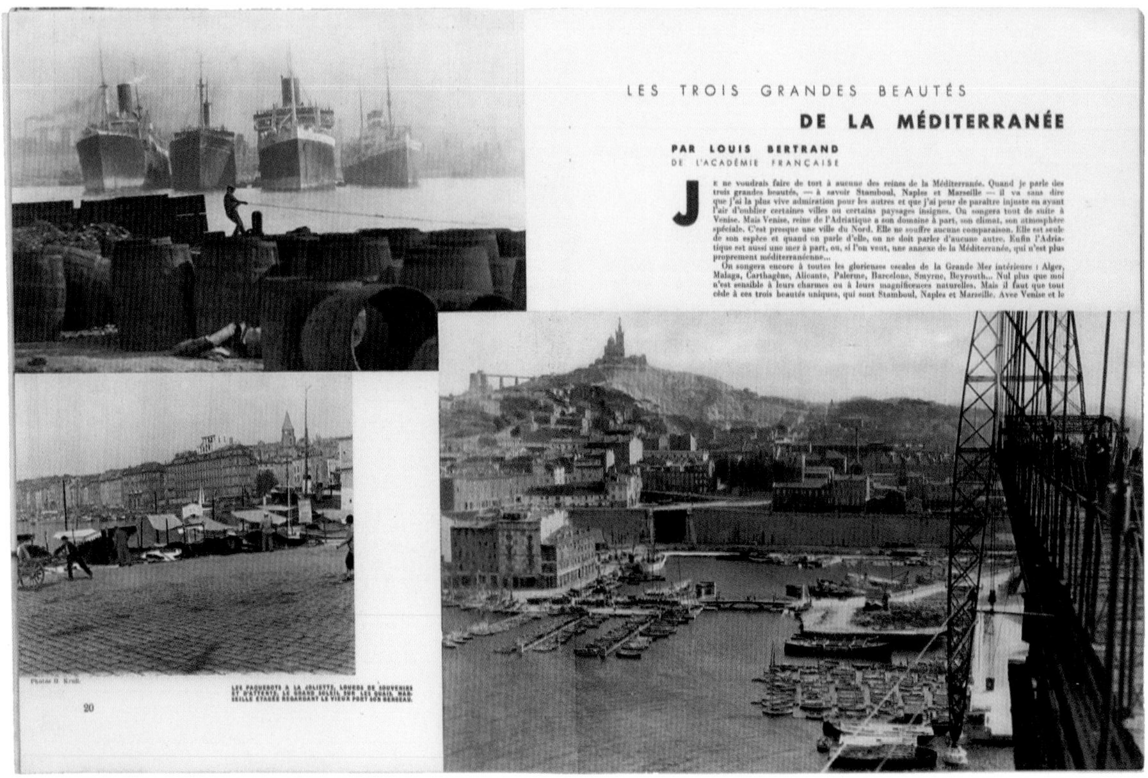

'The Three Great Beauties of the Mediterranean', *Art et Médecine*, March 1932, pp. 20–21

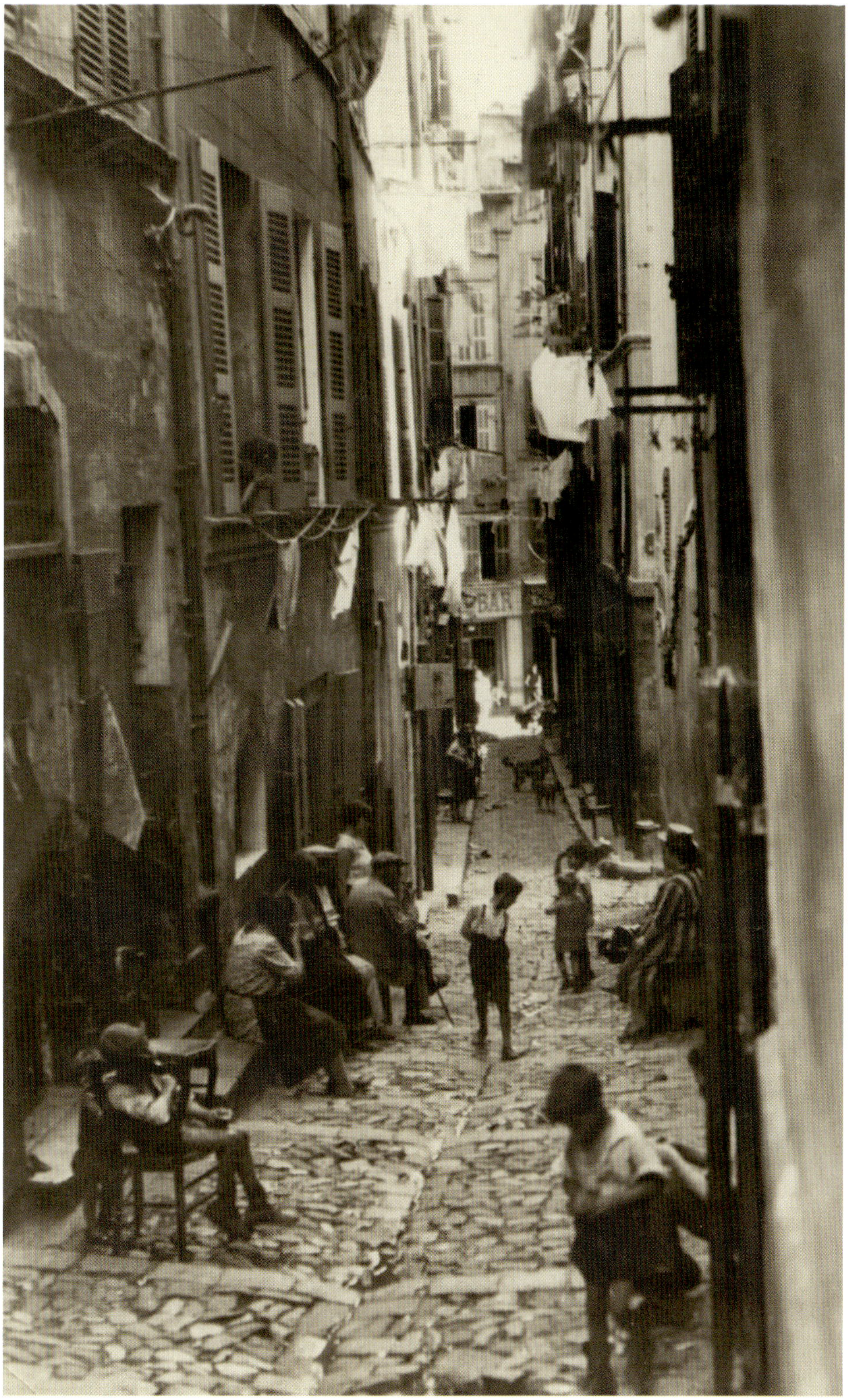

Marseille, c. 1929

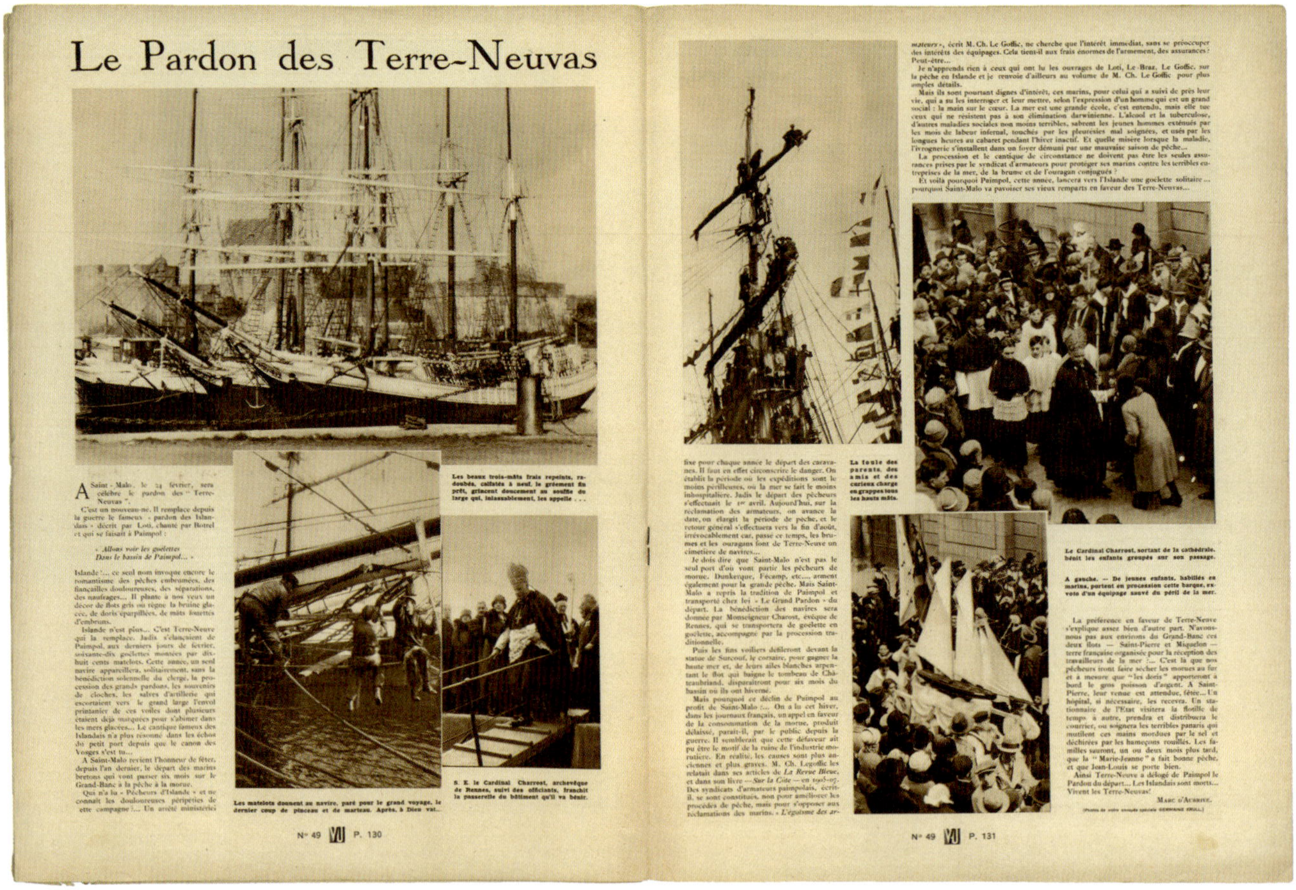

Le Pardon des Terre-Neuvas

Les beaux trois-mâts frais repeints, radoubés, calfatés à neuf, le gréement fin prêt, grincent doucement au souffle du large qui, inlassablement, les appelle . . .

Les matelots donnent au navire, paré pour le grand voyage, le dernier coup de pinceau et de marteau. Après, à Dieu vat...

S. E. le Cardinal Charrost, archevêque de Rennes, suivi des officiants, franchit la passerelle du bâtiment qu'il va bénir.

N° 49 VU P. 130

La foule des parents, des amis et des curieux charge en grappes tous les hauts mâts.

Le Cardinal Charrost, sortant de la cathédrale, bénit les enfants groupés sur son passage.

A gauche. — De jeunes enfants, habillés en marins, portent en procession cette barque, ex-voto d'un équipage sauvé du péril de la mer.

N° 49 VU P. 131

'The Terre-Neuvas Pilgrimage', *VU*, no. 49, 20 February 1929, pp. 130–131

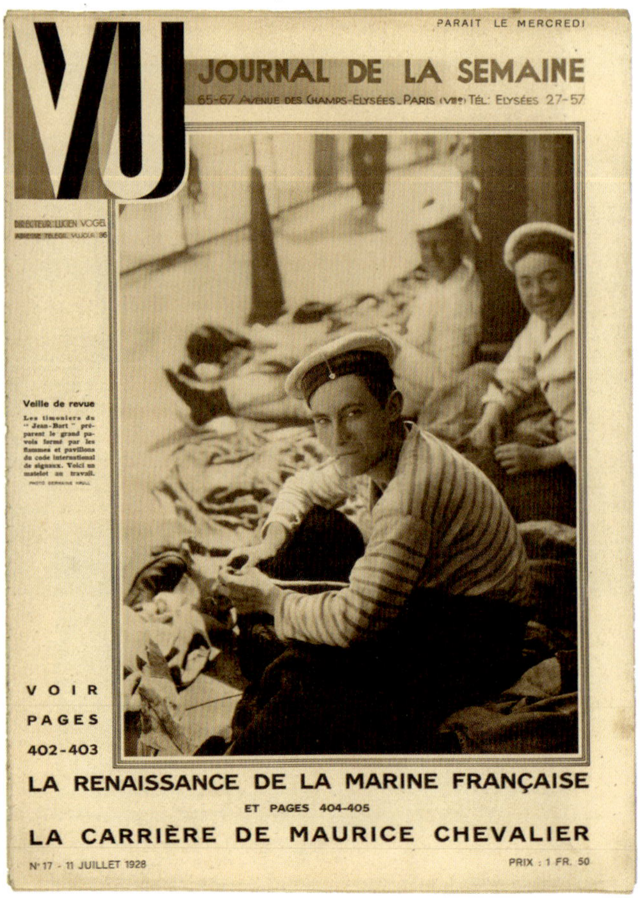

PARAIT LE MERCREDI

VU

JOURNAL DE LA SEMAINE

65-67 AVENUE DES CHAMPS-ELYSÉES_PARIS (VIIIe) TÉL: ELYSÉES 27-57

Veille de revue

Les timoniers du "Jean-Bart" préparent le grand pavois formé par les flammes et pavillons du code international de signaux. Voici un matelot au travail.

VOIR PAGES 402-403

LA RENAISSANCE DE LA MARINE FRANÇAISE

ET PAGES 404-405

LA CARRIÈRE DE MAURICE CHEVALIER

N° 17 - 11 JUILLET 1928

PRIX : 1 FR. 50

'The day before the review', *VU*, no. 17, 11 July 1928, pp. 402–403

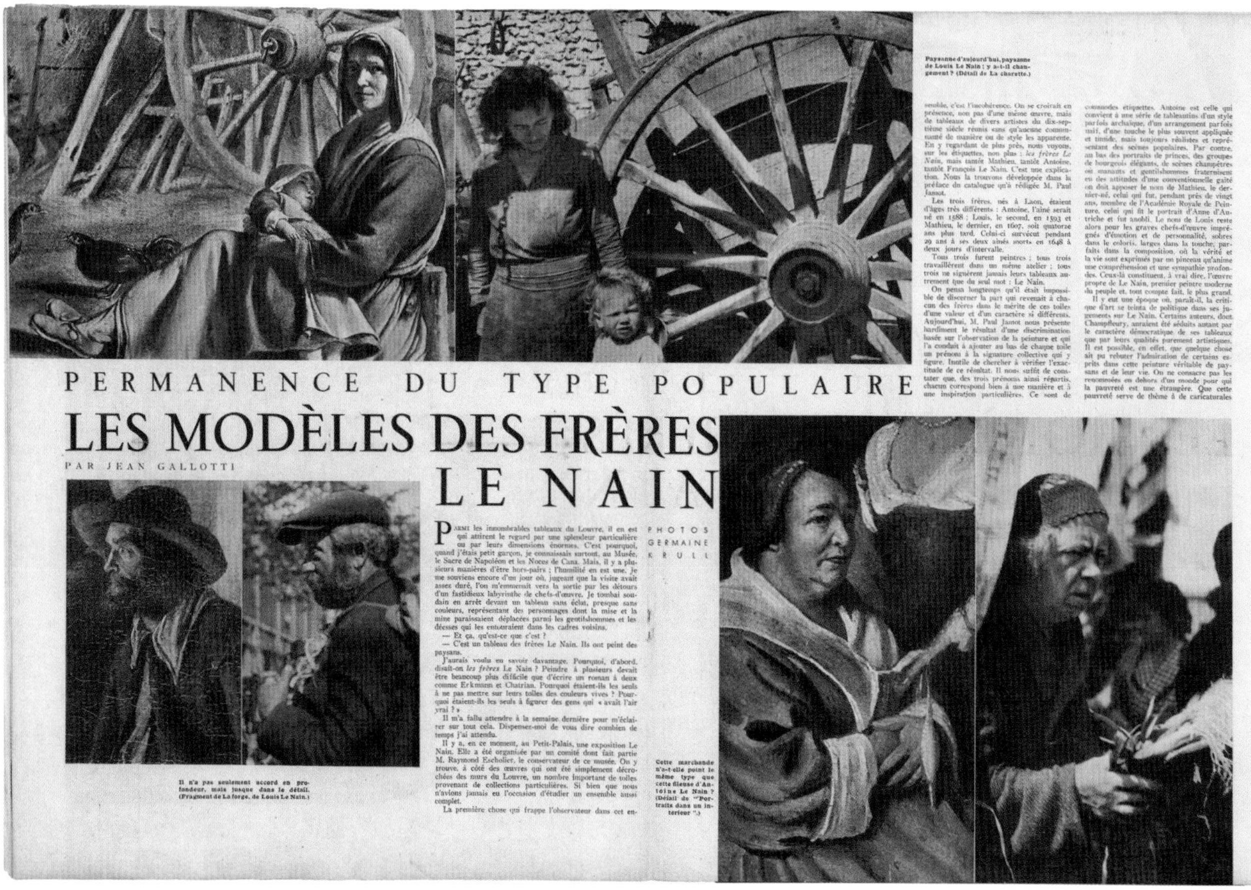

'Enduring Popular Types: the Models of the Le Nain Brothers', *VU*, no. 331, 18 July 1934, pp. 912–913

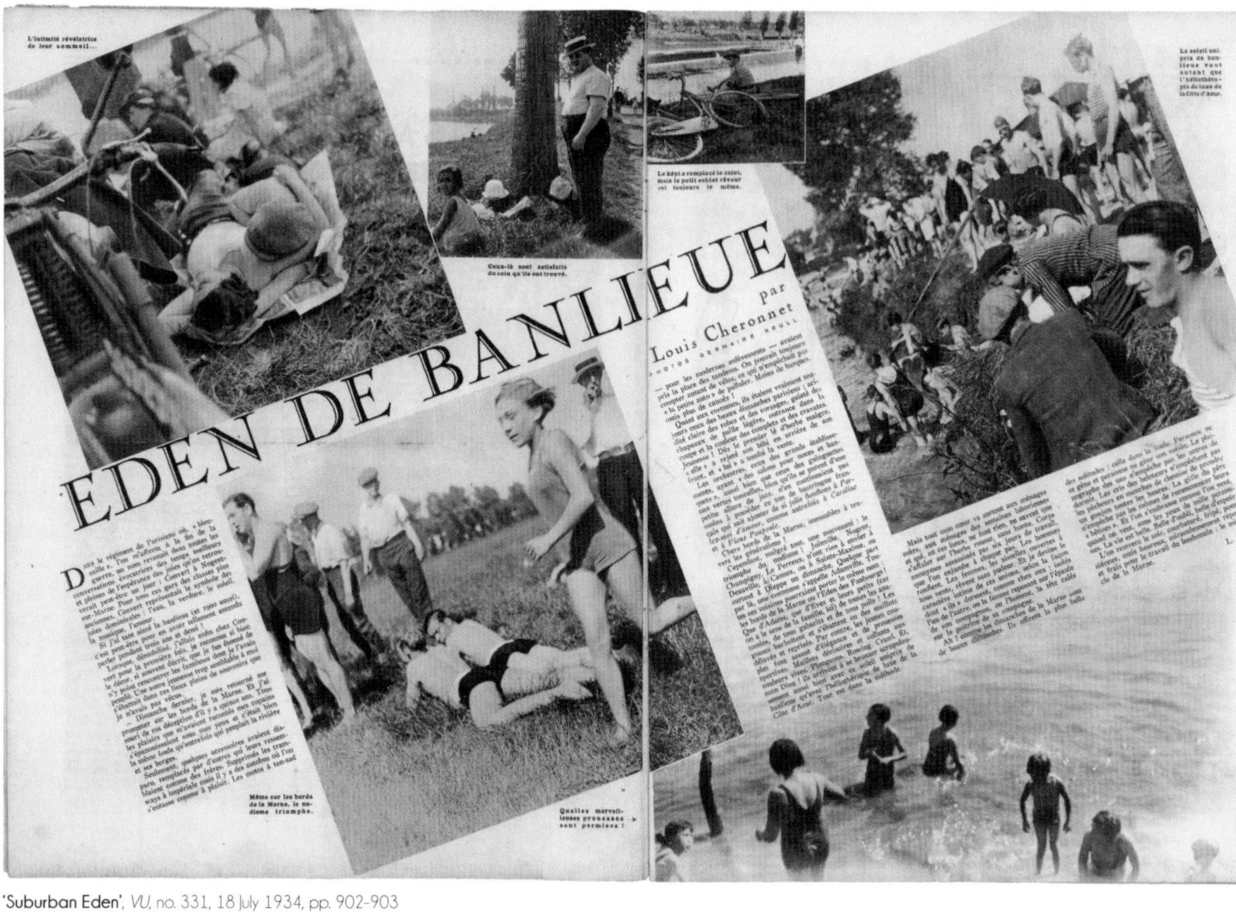

'Suburban Eden', *VU*, no. 331, 18 July 1934, pp. 902–903

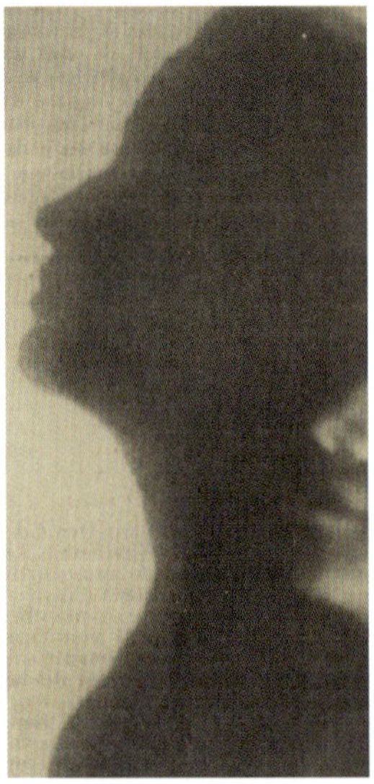

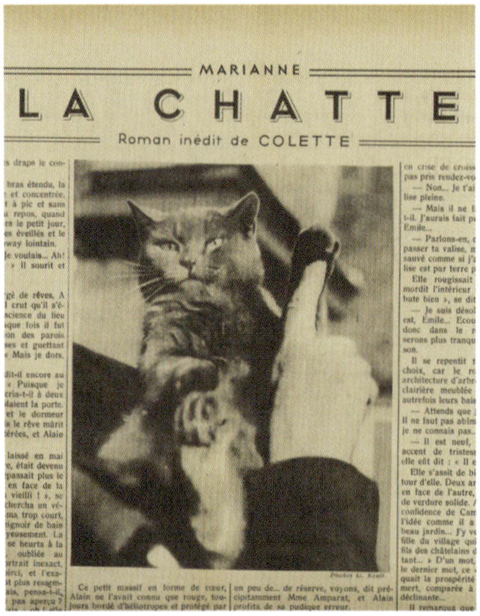

MARIANNE

LA CHATTE

Roman inédit de COLETTE

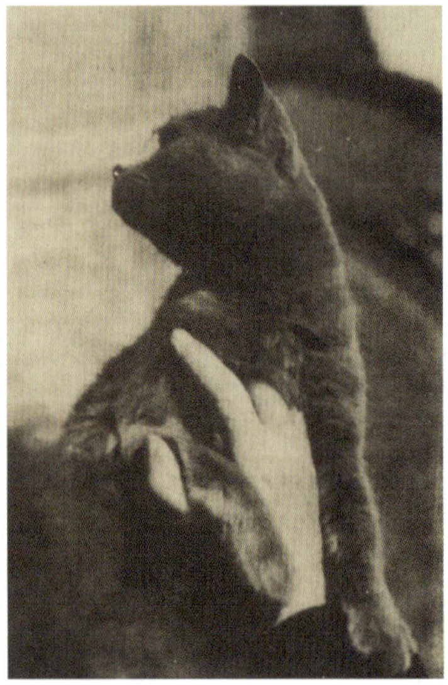

'La Chatte', unpublished novel by Colette, *Marianne*, no. 28, 3 May 1933, p. 7; no. 26, 19 April 1933, p. 7; no. 33, 7 June 1933, p. 7

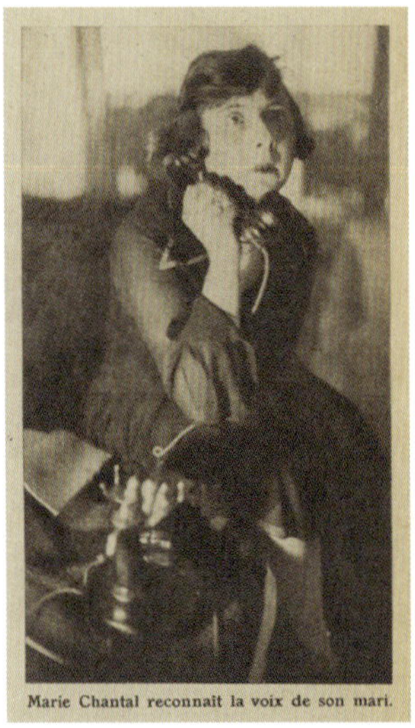

Marie Chantal reconnaît la voix de son mari.

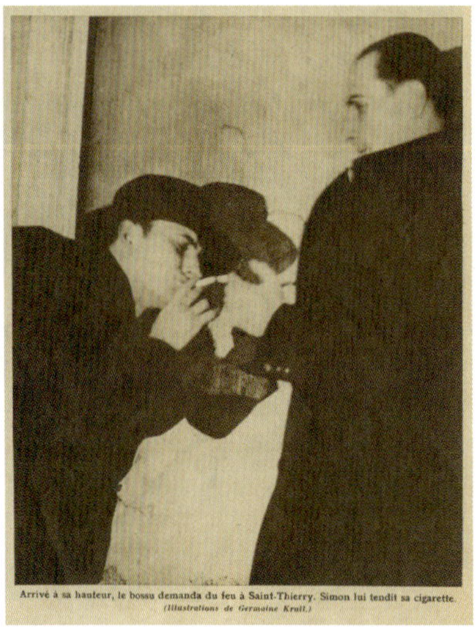

Arrivé à sa hauteur, le bossu demanda du feu à Saint-Thierry. Simon lui tendit sa cigarette. (Illustrations de Germaine Krull.)

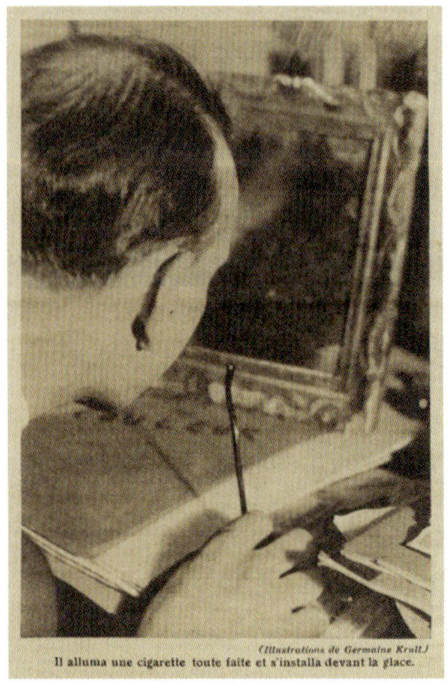

(Illustrations de Germaine Krull.) Il alluma une cigarette toute faite et s'installa devant la glace.

'Shadows of Paris', detective story by Pierre Mac Orlan serialised in *Détective*: no. 74, 27 March 1930, p. 7; no. 78, 24 April 1930, p. 7; no. 75, 3 April 1930, p. 7

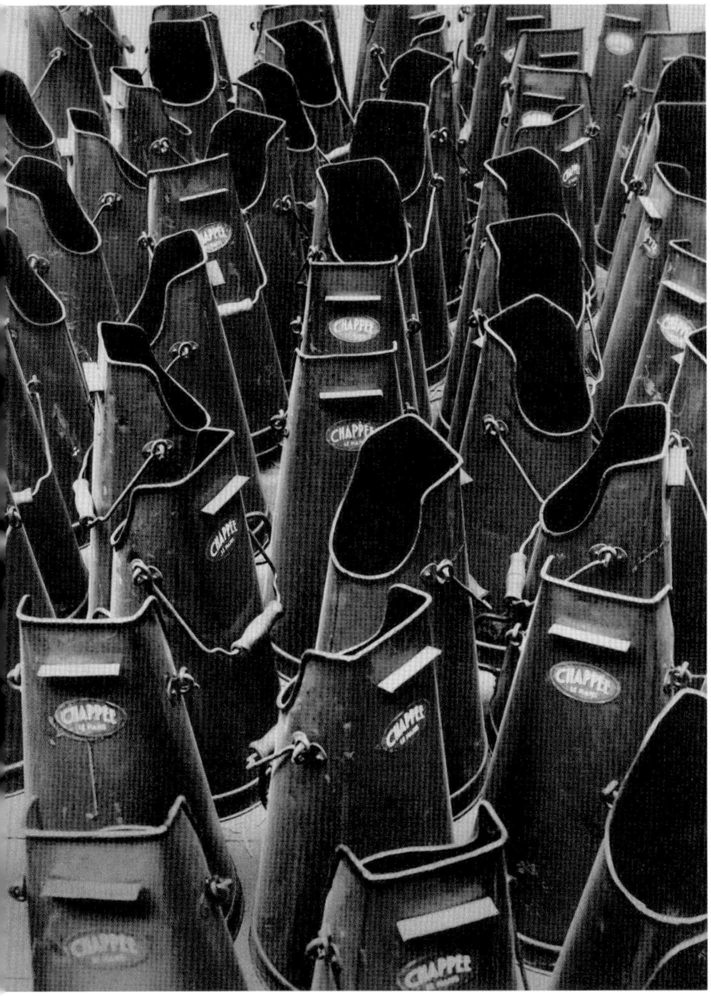

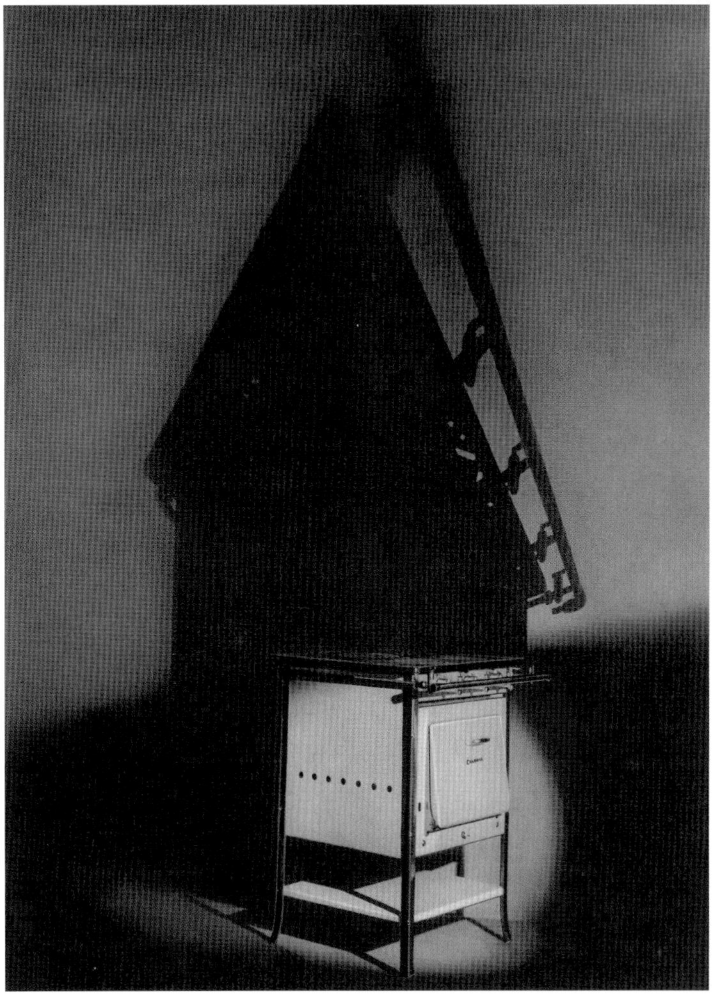

omfort, Société Générale de Fonderie, 1931 (above and right)

PARIS, PARIS

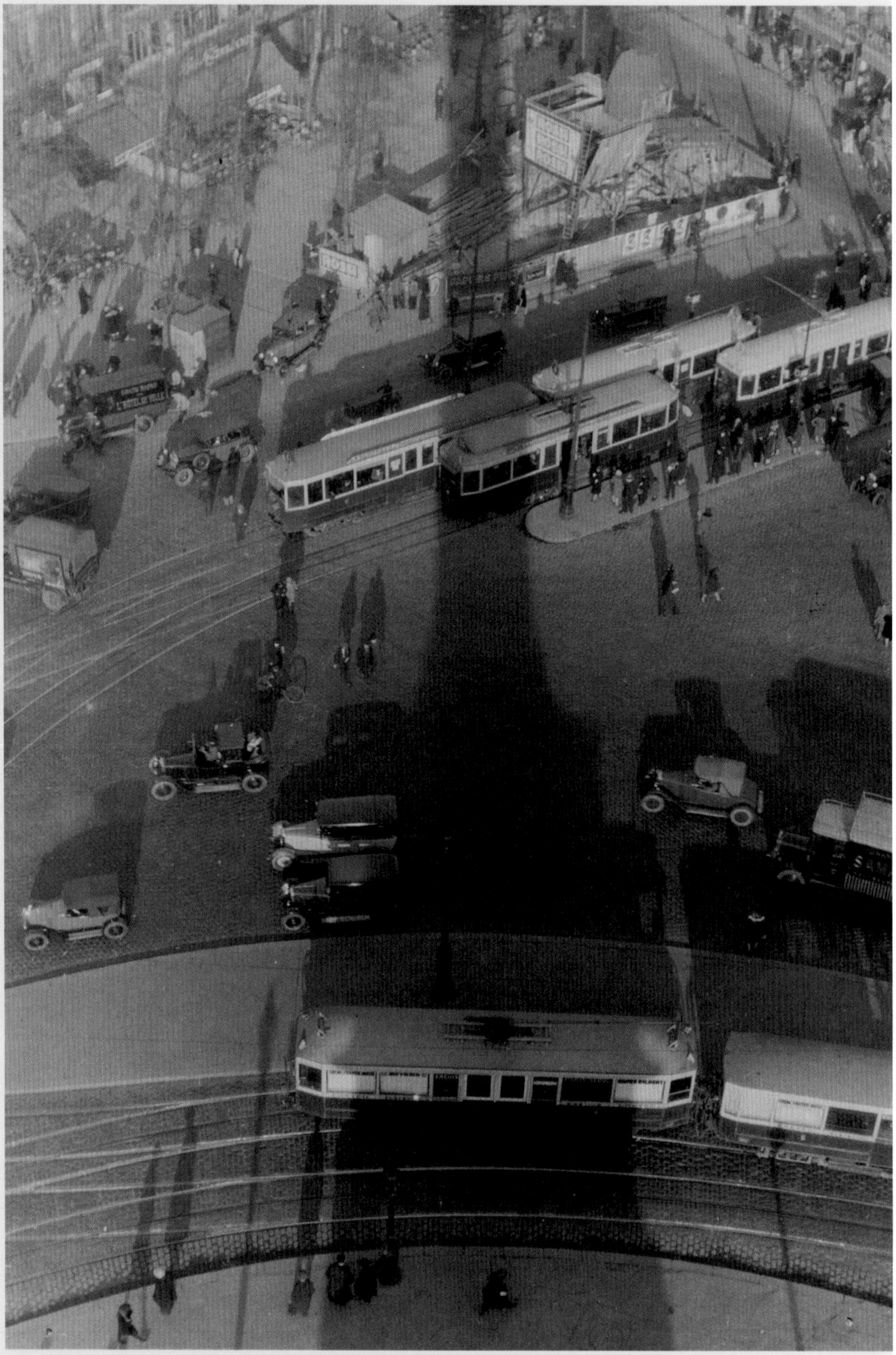

ILLUSTRATING PANAME[1]

The first issue of *VU* opened, not with a Krull view of the Eiffel Tower, but with the shoot of *Paname n'est pas Paris*, a Nikolaï Malikoff film based on Francis Carco's novel *Paname* (1927),[2] with five photos of Paris at night (the shoot)[3] by Eli Lotar. In fact, these are very similar to Krull's (especially in early 1928). She made nocturnal Paris one of her great specialities, even if it was Kertész who really pioneered this theme in 1925, and helped advise and steer his friend Brassaï towards a similar approach. Paris at night meant bars and nightclubs: 'All these Parisian nights, like the days in this city, so different, I explored them in the first weeks of my work for Vogel and also later, either alone or with Eli Lotar.'[4] Krull tried to capture the lights on the boulevards, the advertising neons, the illuminations of the shops and attractions. She loved this kind of challenge and the strange effects it afforded – witness the photo of a carrousel on Place Pigalle. Magazines were eager to publish these surprising views, in which the distortions due to light and movement confuse direct, objective vision. The shops' Christmas illuminations were a popular attraction and a popular subject for photographs. *L'Art vivant* published a selection of them under the title 'Nocturne 1930', with the text gushingly describing Citroën's illuminations on the Eiffel Tower as 'a gigantic torch, a beacon to the glory of the new religions'.[5]

VU was also interested in these new manifestations of photographic art, and especially the ones that afforded a 'different' vision of the world. In 1929 it published a central spread on 'The Bright Nights of Paris', with images that would have astonished readers at the time. Three of the photos were by Krull. In its July–August issue of same year, *Jazz* echoed the theme with 'Paris by Night'[6] and another three photos showing *Rue Pigalle*, *Les Halles* and *Commercial Lighting on Boulevard Haussmann*.[7] Krull took many photos of Les Halles, both at night and at various times in the early morning – always noting the hour on the back – when the market was closing.[8] She did the cover for the third issue of *Détective*, titled 'Paris at Night'. Credited to Germaine Krühl, it showed a typical nocturnal view of a stairway, the possible scene of the crime to be described by Joseph Kessel's 'unbelievable account' in the magazine, which was illustrated by three more of her photos and one by Lotar.

As a photographer, Krull was so steeped in Parisian life that Mac Orlan coined the expression 'Paris-Krull' for what, he wrote, 'is sometimes Carco's Paris, because on occasion it expands into the tenderness of regrets, but also the Paris of ghosts, of crimes and other events, and of the androids of prostitution. It is a powerful and truly tragic commentary, for it contains an element of irresponsibility.'[9] This 'Krull Paris' that can be mapped onto Carco's Paris is the place of society's lower depths, of bars and cafés and above all of the street and of night-time, a place already described by Carco in 1914 in *Jésus-la-Caille* with a vision that remained vivid. But the Carco Paris of the 1920s was the one depicted in *Scènes de la vie de Montmartre* (1919), *Promenades pittoresques à Montmartre* (1922), *Pigalle* (1927) and *La Rue* (1930), whose locations all coincided very precisely with the places frequented by Krull.[10]

When *Art et Médecine* published a special issue on Paris in October 1931, Krull, naturally, was included (even if she had to face stiff competition from Kertész and Man Ray),

1 Paname, a popular name for Paris, began to be used at the turn of the century. Synonymous with notions of scale and a rather tainted big-city wealth, it may have originated with the financial scandals surrounding the Panama Canal and the fashion for panama hats.–*Trans.*
2 *Paname n'est pas Paris*, by Nikolaï Malikoff, supervising producer Marcel L'Herbier, released 17 February 1928, after the novel *Paname* by Francis Carco (1927, Henri Jonquières et Cie, illustrations by Jean Oberlé; text only: 1934).
3 Four night-time photos in Paris, with lighting from the shoot, including *Place Blanche*, *Fairground Stand*, and a photograph of equipment from the shoot, *Montmartre at Night*, a 'somewhat fantastical vision', *VU* no. 1 (21 March 1928), p. 21, with an article by Edmond Gréville.
4 CEDG, p. 13.
5 Louis Cheronnet, *L'Art vivant* no. 121 (1 January 1930), p. 17, with four photos of Christmas lighting.
6 Original title in English.–*Trans.*
7 *Jazz*, July–August 1929, pp. 371–373.
8 Amsab Collection, Ghent.
9 *Germaine Krull par Pierre Mac Orlan*, Paris: NRF Gallimard, 1931.
10 Carco also wrote the screenplay of the film *Paris la nuit* by Henri Diamant-Berger (1930), about Parisian lowlife.

Place de la Bastille with the Shadow of the July Column, 1928

thanks to the cooperation of two of her favourite authors: Francis Carco and Pierre Mac Orlan. The former wrote about louche aspects of Paname, about 'The slimy cobblestones, the wretched glow from a street-side bar, the closed shutters of a brothel, the furnished flats near the stations, the fences round the waste grounds and the seamy, sticky, foul entrances of certain nocturnal refuges that take in their load of wrecks when night falls, have always exerted such a pull on me that I can't go without them.' Then there was the Paname of the Parisian pedestrian: 'Wherever you go in Paname you feel as lonely as if you were in a complicated Baroque city extended by another city with its grey houses and lights, its naïve stalls, its shops, its tobacconists, its picture palaces, its creameries, its greasy spoons and, from time to time, its dance halls.'[11] For his part, Mac Orlan dwelt on the 'Popular Aspects and Scenes of Paris' in a text that reads like a summary of Krull's Parisian photos: 'the poetry of little streets with medieval names continues alongside the incessant comings and goings of the cars.' He celebrated the cries of the street, the ambulant fruit and vegetable sellers, ruffians, policemen, the bal-musettes.[12] He aspired to a film 'full of humour and melancholy, something like a perfectly Parisian *Threepenny Opera*'.[13] Krull was also to be seen in *L'Art vivant*, with her picturesque, flâneur's views of the banks of the Seine, including a few high-angle views.[14]

For *VU*, she continued her exploration of Parisian themes in 1929 with the department stores, the new shops whose windows had been given a makeover by the 'first window dressers': 'the big *maisons* who always used to fill their windows with all kinds of different goods, were now beginning to replace these crammed displays with one or two carefully presented objects.'[15] The new mannequins created by Siégel under the direction of André Vigenau for the 1925 Exposition Internationale des Arts Décoratifs were Brancusiesque sculptures, part physiology and part artwork. These humanoids particularly appealed to the Surrealists with their strangeness, their air of hopeless, silent solitude. Here too, as we shall see, Krull achieved some fine results. For many provincial and foreign visitors to the city, what really summed up Paris-Paname was its department stores. Le Printemps was both the oldest of these (1865) and, in around 1930, the most dynamic. Krull did several assignments, one on *La Semaine du blanc* (low prices for household linen), and another with some very constructivist high-angle views of the interior, both published in *Variétés* in December 1928,[16] as part of a special Paris section that also featured a polish seller in Les Halles. Krull also illustrated an article in this issue about the Siégel mannequins in the Printemps windows, titled 'Venus and the Mannequins'.[17] Published in October 1930 by Gallimard, Pierre Mac Orlan's little book *Le Printemps*[18] was a colourful description of the department store by a cultivated visitor beguiled by the modernity and strangeness of its goods. Although not credited, the twenty-three photographs illustrating the text on separate pages were certainly by Krull, or at least some of them – the high-angle shots of the empty store, the decorated windows, night views of the displays, a huddle of mannequins in a window: these bold perspectives were her hallmark. What is more, evoking the poetry of these accumulations of objects, Mac Orlan praised 'the photographs by Germaine Krull, Berenice Abbott, Tabard and Kertész [which] could bestow a literary look on this exhibition' and 'can become the great intermediaries of the poetry of the city and of the department stores'.[19]

In the summer of 1931, *Les Annales littéraires et politiques*, a magazine well disposed towards Krull,[20] in which Mac Orlan published his analysis of photography and the social fantastic, and which had a special eight-page section for photogravure prints of photographs, published a series of six issues of 'grand reportage' – not its usual genre – titled 'Department Stores: Report by Louis Roubaud and Francis Ambrière'. Devoted mainly to Le Printemps, this intelligent piece of advertorial extended over forty-three pages, with thirty-four photos

11 Francis Carco, 'Paname', *Art et Médecine*, October 1931, p. 44.
12 A form of popular dance to hurdy-gurdy or accordion music.– *Trans.*
13 Pierre Mac Orlan, 'Visages et paysages populaires de Paris', *Art et Médecine*, October 1931, pp. 46–49.
14 Centre spread, with five photos by Krull, *L'Art vivant* no. 121 (1 January 1930), pp. 20–21, and the article 'Spicilège des quais de Seine' by Charles Fegdal, p. 23.
15 CEDG, p. 21.
16 This 'semaine du blanc' was held in January 1928. The photo was published in *L'Excelsior* on 18 January 1928.
17 Paul Fierens, 'Vénus et les mannequins ou de l'"automne" au "printemps"', *Variétés* 1, no. 8 (15 December 1928), pp. 433–435.
18 Pierre Mac Orlan, *Le Printemps*, Paris: Gallimard, 1930.
19 Ibid., pp. 86 and 155.
20 Her friends Henri Bidou, Pierre Bost, Pierre Mac Orlan, Hervé Lauwick and André Warnod were all regular contributors to the magazine.

21 'Grands magasins. Enquête de Louis Roubaud et Francis Ambrière', *Les Annales politiques et littéraires* no. 2385 (1 July 1930), pp. 17–24, three photos by Krull; no. 2386 (15 July 1930), pp. 73–80, nine photos by Krull; no. 2387 (1 August 1930), pp. 113–120, eleven photos by Krull; no. 2388 (15 August 1930), pp. 163–170, seven photos by Krull; no. 2389 (1 September 1930), pp. 201–207, four photos by Krull; no. 2389 (15 September 1930), pp. 245–248, no photo.

22 See the chapter 'Women'.

23 An American edition was published by Random House in 1930.

24 Mario von Bucovich emigrated to the United States and from there went to Mexico. Paul Morand also prefaced *Paris de nuit* by Brassaï in 1933. The jacket of the German edition shows two policemen in their capes.

25 Germaine Krull, *100 × Paris*, preface by Florent Fels, Berlin-Westend: Verlag der Reihe, 1929.

by Krull reproduced in fairly large format (she was the only photographer).[21] The subjects of the photos were matched with the text and reflected her interests: interiors and exteriors, internal workings, machinery, shop windows and presentations, the life of the staff, the goods and the clientele (these images would also go into her series on 'Women Workers of Paris').[22] Forced to take her photographs mainly inside, Krull used night-time to heighten the contrasts. As in Les Halles with the tramps, she avoided the kind of conventional poses epitomised by fashion and advertising photography, but looked instead for closeness, natural poses and the mysterious atmospheres and unusual situations that defined Mac Orlan's 'social fantastic', whose poetry only photography could hope to capture.

PARIS, BOOKS

Paris by Mario von Bucovich

It was probably thanks to her German contacts that Krull was asked to contribute to Mario von Bucovich's *Paris*, a book published in Berlin by Albertus-Verlag as part of its 'Das Gesicht der Städte' ('Faces of Cities') series, in which the *Berlin* volume (1928) boasted a preface by Alfred Döblin. The French edition (printed in Germany) was published by Henri Jonquières[23] with a preface by Paul Morand and very concise captions in four languages: Germany, English, French and Spanish. Both the format and the black photogravure printing made for a fairly luxurious volume. Bucovich (1884–1947),[24] who had a studio in Berlin in the 1920s and, for a shorter spell, in Paris, took most of the 255 photographs, but twenty-three of them were by Krull. If the Eiffel Tower was to be expected in such a context, it was more surprising to see the streets already full of cars, big advertising posters on a building (this was a short series that she did not repeat) and a window of Worth fashions. The brand new Rue Mallet-Stevens (from 1927), with the Martel townhouse, was a particularly modernist theme. Place Pigalle and the Moulin-Rouge, both seen at night, were unusual visions, as was the close-up of the 'Apéritif' bar, located on the pavement facing La Samaritaine and, even more so, the photo looking down onto the Métro rails. These views by Krull evince an original approach to the city that contrasts with the neutrality of Bucovich's images.

100 × Paris

A few months later Krull had accumulated enough images to publish a book of a hundred photographs, curiously titled *100 × Paris*, with Verlag der Reihe, with an introduction in three languages: German, English and French.[25] This was clearly Krull's own initiative, since the preface is by her friend Florent Fels, her foremost supporter in 1929. But this is a long way from the experiment that was *Métal*. *100 × Paris* is a real book of images, in small format, with a soft cover, easy in the hand, meticulously printed in brown-red photogravure (like *VU*). It came with four different jackets, one of them clearly designed for German readers, two others that were more graphic and one showing two photographs.

In his text Fels, who was always uncomfortable with modernity, talks about Les Halles, the florists on Place de la Madeleine, the neighbourhood theatres, the cabarets of Montmartre, the dances in Rue de Lappe and the prostitutes of Pigalle, and praises 'the intelligent lens of this image-hunter, Germaine Krull, who, in coming to understand her [Paris], succeeds in making us love her'. Unjustly viewed as banal (for twenty-first-century eyes), *100 × Paris* was in fact highly innovative, and no equivalent publication we know of places such emphasis on photography – on the photographic 'oeuvre', insofar as this is more than simple illustration. Although a few famous monuments are shown frontally and centrally, the viewpoints offered by the photographs are constantly changing – high-angle, oblique, from the side, at different heights (from the Arc de Triomphe, from the Bastille column, from a bridge, from a river bank), as if they were reproducing the walker's perspective from wherever he is standing or looking. This stroller is no longer a standard visitor presented with standard views already seen elsewhere. Here, if admittedly in a more measured way, Krull is continuing with her work of ocular destabilisation by offering photographic 'viewpoints' that were unusual in 1929. There is an emphasis on the car traffic (some of the views are taken from cars) and the easy picturesque is dismissed in favour of a visual impact that we also find in the reportage for *VU*. The influence of cinema is of course felt in the diversity and differing directions of the shots, and in the ruptures between many of the facing photographs. Films about cities evidently are not far away, starting with Ruttmann's one about Berlin, which Krull knew well, or the *Studies in Movement in Paris* made by Joris Ivens in 1927–1928. It is indeed likely that some of Krull's photographs were of the same vintage.

The review in *Variétés* saw the book as a personal statement: 'Germaine Krull ... has devoted an album to a hundred aspects of Paris. We write "aspects", but "attitudes" would be a more appropriate word, for not only are they all the expression of the same body, but they obey the photographer's deliberate choice, a secondary personality that was imposed on them. This intelligent and sensitive little atlas tells us both about the Paris it reveals to us and about the person revealing it – of whom it can be said that she is the leading photographer of our time.'[26] In the November 1929 issue of *Variétés* Paul Fierens dedicated his 'Monthly Chronicle' to *100 × Paris*, in which, he wrote, photography allows another vision of the city, one that is 'powerful, complete, complex and true'. 'To learn to see, nothing beats looking at photographs.' He saw the book's (cinematic) layout as a manifestation of 'Cubism and Surrealism': 'There is Cubism when the intervention of will is manifested in the ordering, the breakdown, the division or the synthesis of the subject.'

Visages de Paris by André Warnod

In 1930 André Warnod published *Visages de Paris* (Firmin-Didot),[27] an illustrated book that set out to 'recreate the atmosphere of Paris as it used to be, based on period documents, prints and drawings, all reproduced in photogravure (and therefore from photographs) in a handsome, warm shade of Prussian blue, and preferring photographic documents to all others. For us, a photograph is a document of the first order because the lens is a cruelly impassible and impartial eye.' It was, as Mac Orlan concluded, 'an important work in the sense that it uses, for the first time, all the anecdotal resources of photography'. Talking up the role of photography in this innovative book, he noted that after the old photographs from the Société Française de Photographie, and from agencies founded at the turn of the century (Branger, Rol, Delius and Harlingue), 'the end of our book is illustrated by the finest photographs by Germaine Krull.' The author's position was eminently human: 'We have kept with the people in the street.' A friend of Florent Fels (Firmin-Didot), Warnod (1885–1960) was a great connoisseur of Montmartre, of the School of Paris and of the life of the city's working people. As the author of *Bals, cafés et cabarets* (1913), *La Brocante et les petits marchés de Paris* (1914), *Les Plaisirs de la rue* (1920), *Les Bals de Paris* (1922), *Les Fortifs. Promenades sur les anciennes fortifications et la zone* (1926), he could hardly fail to agree with Krull, who herself sought to achieve the right distance and maintain a direct relation to her subjects. The frontispiece of his book was a photograph of the shadow of the Eiffel Tower cast over gardens. Of the total of 502 illustrations, forty-six were by Krull – in other words, the bulk of the 'modern' photographs. The subjects were ones she was already famous for, such as fairgrounds, bars and, above all, tramps (no less than seven photos), presented as illustrating the 'pre-war' years when in fact they dated from 1928. Krull

26 *Variétés* 2, no. 2 (15 June 1929), pp. 142–143, signed M. B.
27 André Warnod, *Visages de Paris*, preface by Jean de Castellane, Paris: Firmin-Didot & Cie, 1930.

28 A *midinette* was a young woman or worker in the fashion industry, synonymous with slightly foolish, naive and sentimental tastes.– *Trans.*
29 Ibid., pp. 267–275.
30 Nico Rost, *Variétés* 2, no. 7 (15 November 1929), pp. 518–519.
31 Chas Laborde also illustrated Colette and *Rues et visages de Paris* by Valery Larbaud, Paris: Éditions de la Roseraie, 1926.

is also present and just as effective in the final chapter, 'Charms of Paris 1930', which evokes midinettes,[28] Paris at night, the avenues and car traffic, and the banks of the Seine. The book offers fine descriptions of a rather dark, murky Paris which the images back up: 'Everything is dead. But, over there, a shadow is moving. A tramp with a limp, an uncertain gait, heading for a familiar place.' In the *zone* the 'humanity swarming in the filth seems to be one with it. Dressed in rags, unkempt women rummage doggedly through the pile of waste, sorting wood from iron, wool from silk, bones from paper.'[29] But a few unexpected jewels are also scattered through this particularly attractive book: 'Japanese flowers', the interior of the Théâtre Pigalle, the 'impromptu juxtapositions' of the flea markets, a fairground stall, Rue Rambuteau at night. Neither a history book nor a book of photographs in the recent sense of the term, *Visages de Paris* is a work of photographic reportage, which, in 1930, was still a novelty. In a commentary published in *Variétés* on Kurt Tucholsky's *Deutschland, Deutschland über alles!*, a new publication abundantly illustrated with photographs by John Heartfield, we read that 'there is already an abundance' of books 'in Russia drawing on purely photographic illustration', featuring 'direct photos, montage, overprinting, collage, etc.'.[30]

Paris by Adolf Hallman

Much less known, if not positively unknown, *Paris under 4 Årstider* ('Paris through the Seasons'), a fine book about working-class life in the city published in Stockholm in 1930 (and in Swedish), offers an even more striking demonstration of Krull's talent and her taste for Parisian oddities. Its author, Adolf Hallman (1893–1968), was a Swedish illustrator with anarchist sympathies who lived in Paris in the 1920s, and his book is illustrated by his artist friends Jules Pascin and Chas Laborde. Laborde had also illustrated books by Francis Carco and Pierre Mac Orlan.[31] The role played by Krull's photographs, which takes us into an almost imaginary Paris that is rarely seen, is almost as important as that of the drawings, if not more so. Forty-one of them are distributed throughout the volume, but twenty-six are shown full-page as part of an inner portfolio that is exclusively photographic and focuses on her vision of the city. There are six Eiffel Towers, plus tramps and bars, coupled with a number of very unusual images, some of them never shown outside this book: the rhinoceros at Trocadero, the Maldoror restaurant, a reader beside the Seine, stairs in Montmartre, a wooden hut and a lottery stand. Here, Krull is evidently close to the poetic spirit of her friend Kertész.

Accumulated between 1928 and 1930, Krull's numerous photos offer a determined yet spontaneous vision of an often ignored but very real and even prosaic Paris. Coming after her *fers*, the photos of iron structures, they represent a significant part of her output. They were reproduced not only in books about Paris but also in magazines. The fact was that Paris, with its day-time and night-time life, its cosmopolitan population packed into a relatively small area, its distinctively atmospheric old and modern quarters, its mixture of the dissolute and the innocent, of intellectualism and vileness, was one of the great subjects of the 1920s (as indeed was Berlin), whether in literature, cinema, illustration, caricature, urban research or painting. Although – or perhaps *because* – they were foreigners, both Krull and Kertész (who published his photographic book *Paris vu par André Kertész* en 1934) found themselves at the forefront of this adventure, along with the painters of the School of Paris (the name, École de Paris, was thought up by André Warnod in 1925).

The 'social fantastic'

Here, of course, we need to consider the literary and poetic concepts underpinning Krull's photographs from 1928 to 1930. In his review of *Visages de Paris* (1930), Mac Orlan spoke of 'photographs chosen with the keenest sense of the social romanticism appropriate for each change of scene' and offered one of his many definitions of the social and literary impact of the new photography: 'Social mystery loves to disguise its finery. Photography puts man back in his place in the scene. This place is not that of a creator god, but of a melancholy god who is the victim of his own creations.'[32] His words are accompanied by two of Krull's photographs. With experience as a reporter in Germany in 1918–19, and already the author of a considerable body of literary work including the celebrated *Quai des Brumes* (1927), Mac Orlan was the first French commentator to analyse the new role of photography with such acuity. This lover of technologies, advertising, the phonograph, jazz, department stores and cinema (he co-wrote the screenplay for Marcel L'Herbier's *L'Inhumaine* in 1924) put forward his innovative ideas about the New Photography in 1928, shortly after the Salon de l'Escalier, in two articles published in two well-known literary magazines, 'The Literary Art of Imagination and Photography', and 'Photography and the Social Fantastic'.[33] This last term was the name he gave to the new alliance between literary imagination and photography, an ill-defined concept somewhere between Expressionism and Surrealism (to which Mac Orlan did not adhere), manifested especially in modern big cities and revealed by reportage: 'One must see humanity in magazines of photojournalism' (this interpolation, made in September 1928, was addressed directly to *VU* and Krull). He was more precise when he wrote that 'certain literary reviews such as *Querschnitt*, *Variétés* and *VU* have understood all the secret things that photography can reveal, in a face, in a posture, in an attitude, in a city, a street, a simple geometrical form, a shadow on a wall.'[34] Himself a journalist and reporter, Mac Orlan saw this kind of photography not only as offering snapshots of society, but also as a support for the imagination, and means of introspection, offering the possibility of 'contemplating these records of the social activity of our time and extending one's own ideas to their extreme limit in order to seek out … the traces of one's own end, that is to say, one's own disquiet.'[35]

Resulting from the contradictions between modernity, the imaginaries of the past and their continuation in a changing society, the social fantastic is embodied in persons, objects and evidence that photography excels at revealing and raising to a poetical level: 'Photographic vision attaches itself with great dexterity to the secret loves of things. It often exaggerates their tragic and fantastical aspect and makes sentimental investigations in the realm of shadow relatively easy,' writes Mac Orlan in his introduction to *Atget photographe de Paris*, a retrospective volume published in 1930. Clément Chéroux, who emphasises the imprecision of the notion of the 'social fantastic', lists its signs as follows: 'The characteristic figures: the adventurer, the vagabond, the demobbed soldier, the deserter, the murderer, the prostitute … the favoured places, such as port cities, sailors' bars, stations and dark backstreets. Certain objects, such as masks, fetishes, mannequins or rag dolls … specific atmospheres: in the early morning or the middle of the night, in the cold light of streetlamps and advertising lights.'[36]

Krull's photographs, which span both the New Photography and the New Reportage introduced by *VU* in 1928, are without a doubt authentic representations of the 'social fantastic'. Mac Orlan, who is implicitly referring to Krull when he evokes the powers of photography, also mentions her frequently in his theoretical writings,[37] and a number of his texts are illustrated with her work. Krull had a privileged artistic relationship with Mac Orlan, something no other photographer obtained with a writer.

Mac Orlan also looked to Germany, to Moholy-Nagy and Renger Patzsch, and above all their respective books (*Malerei, Fotografie, Film*, 1927, and *Die Welt ist schön*, 1928). He saw these 'two books with an undeniable penetrative power' in March 1929.[38] The apostle of the social fantastic was thus, also, an admirer of photomontage, of *Photoplastik* and the

32 Pierre Mac Orlan, 'Visages de Paris', *Les Annales politiques et littéraires* 2370 (15 November 1930, pp. 454–457), repr. in Pierre Mac Orlan, *Écrits sur la photographie*, texts edited with an introduction by Clément Chéroux, Paris: Textuel, 2011, pp. 97–101.
33 Pierre Mac Orlan, 'L'art littéraire d'imagination et la photographie', *Les Nouvelles littéraires, artistiques et scientifiques* 310 (22 September 1928), p. 1, illustrated by a rayograph by Man Ray; idem, 'La photographie et le fantastique social', *Les Annales politiques et littéraires* no. 2321 (1 November 1928), pp. 413–414.
34 Ibid., p. 414.
35 Pierre Mac Orlan, 'L'art littéraire d'imagination et la photographie', loc. cit., p. 1, quoted in Chéroux, op. cit., p. 19.
36 Chéroux, op. cit., in his introduction: 'Pourtant Mac Orlan. La photographie et le fantastique social', p. 13.
37 In 'Photographie. Éléments de fantastique social' in January 1929; in 'Graphismes', *Arts et métiers graphiques* in May 1929; in his preface to Atget in 1930; in *L'Art vivant* regarding Atget in March 1939; and in the *Mercure de France* in 1953!
38 *Le Crapouillot*, March 1929, in Chéroux, op. cit., p. 72.

39 CEDG, p. 54.
40 *L'Art vivant* no. 127 (1 April 1930), pp. 289 and 293.
41 *L'Art vivant* no. 135 (1 August 1930).
42 *Variétés* 2, no. 2 (15 June 1929), p. 110. 'La symphonie d'une grande ville', pp. 114–116.

German New Vision. 'The work of Moholy-Nagy is poetic, typical of the social poetry of recent years.' Encouraged by her lover, Eli Lotar, who himself was closer to the Surrealists, Krull could have been tempted to go in the same direction. 'For *L'Intransigeant* I made one of my first photomontages when I had to illustrate the city traffic or the street trades of Paris. Even if photomontage was amusing and new, it didn't bring anything new to the daily, which was equipped for big print runs and not for printing this kind of thing.'[39] She made a few attempts at photomontage in the form of fantastical urban visions. We know of one of these original photomontages (perhaps the one she mentions in relation to *L'Intransigeant*), and three of them appear under the title 'Anticipations parisiennes' in *L'Art vivant* in 1930,[40] signed 'G. Krull and Eli Lotar' and accompanied by a text by Charles Fegdal. Another one appears on the cover of *L'Art vivant* in August the same year, under the title 'Curiosités photographiques'.[41] 'The eyes of artists look at Paris . . . the urban landscape unburdens itself of the profuse dross of reality, most finely copied.' Photomontages, those 'joys of the dilettante and voluntary hallucinator' were a novelty for habitués of modern painting, but they spoke the language of art and poetry: 'Dominating present reality, subjecting it to our dreams, or even our nightmares – is there not some surreal logic in all this?' Fegdal, who was more at ease with the relics of the past, looked to the contemporary arts for support: 'Fantasies? Perhaps. The surreal can become the real and take over the city, like Cubism . . . Façades, displays, posters, lighting: Cubism.' According to her memoirs, Krull produced other photomontages that were 'a great success in the field of theatre and dance'. Did she also use the term to mean double exposures, a few examples of which we will see here? In a section showing 'New Images of Paris', *Variétés* reproduced, along with high-angle views of Place de l'Étoile and the shadow of the July Column on Place de la Bastille, an astonishing double exposure by Krull (a photomontage, therefore) of two street views, with traffic and a walker, titled 'Traversée de Paris'. These photographs should also be viewed in the light of an article by Paul Fierens, 'La symphonie d'une grande ville', which, by echoing the title of the Walter Ruttmann film *Berlin, die Sinfonie der Grosstadt* (Symphony of a Great City, 1927), encourages us to see them as overprinted shots from a film.[42]

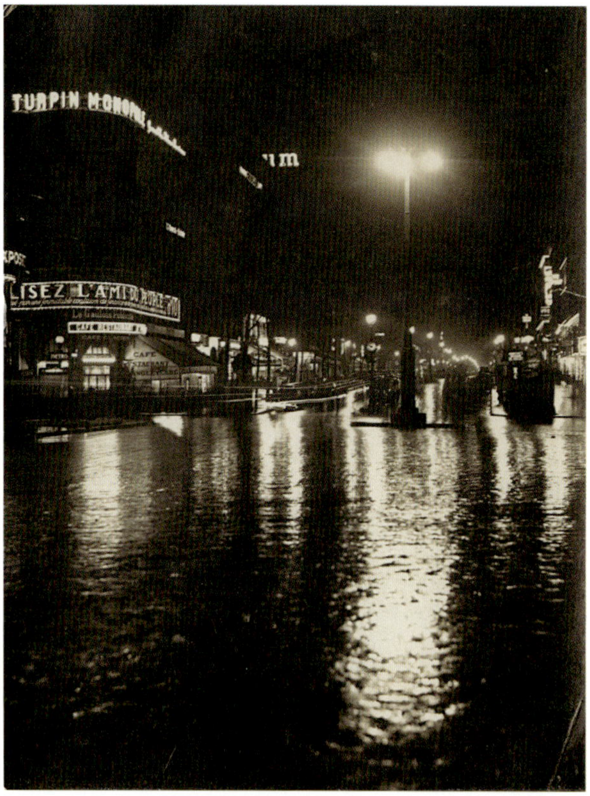

The Grands Boulevards at the Haussmann Crossroads, Evening, Paris, 1928

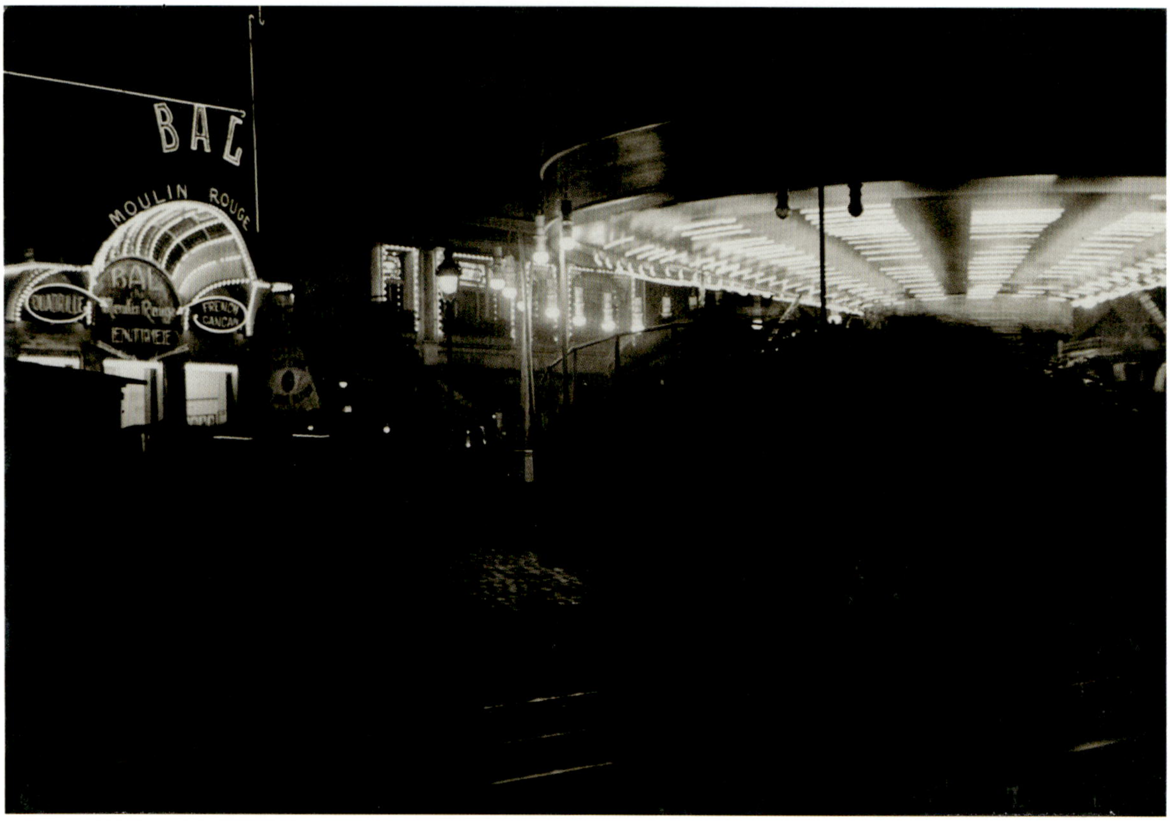

'The Montmartre Fair at Night', 1928

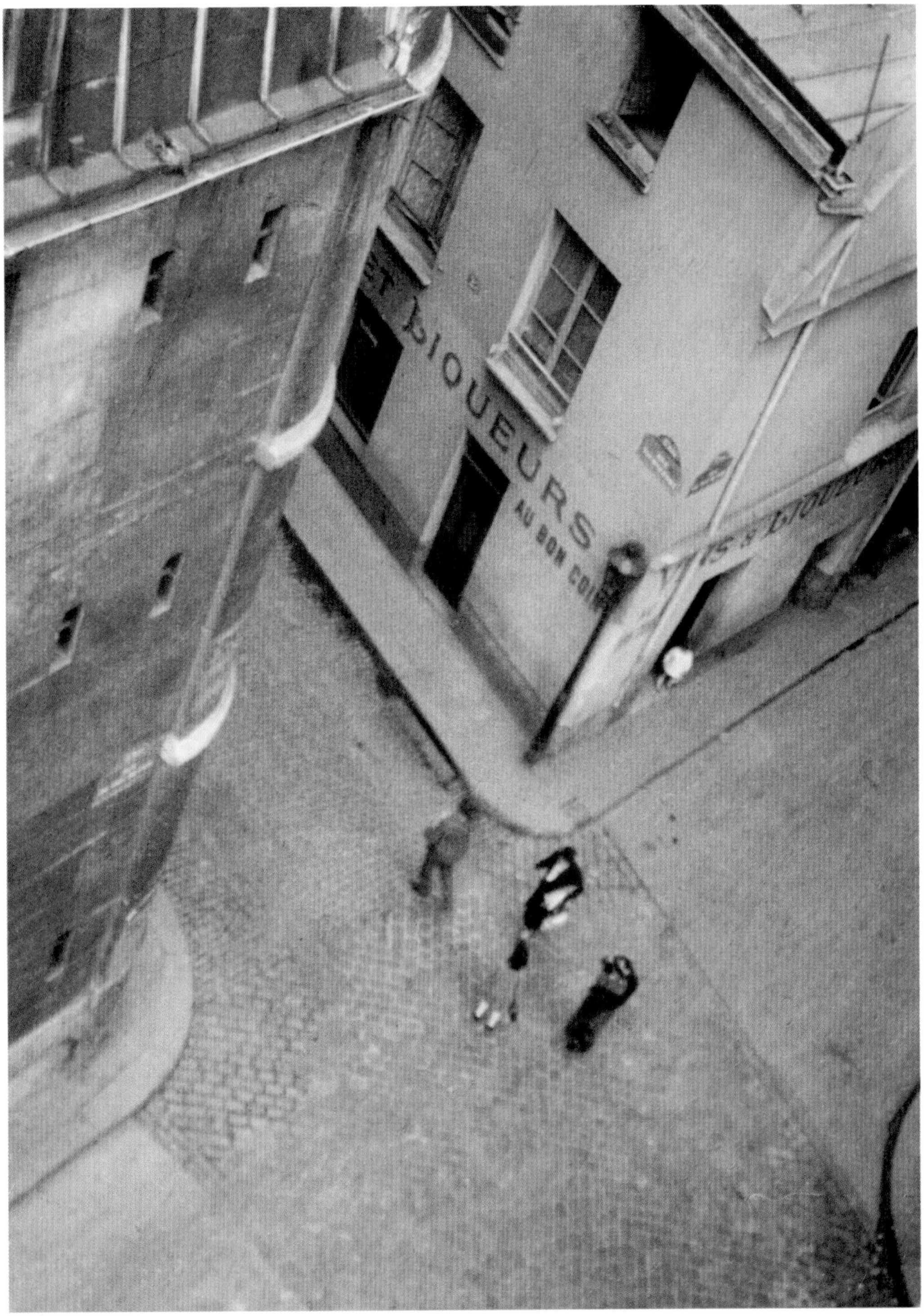

Au Bon Coin, Paris, 1929

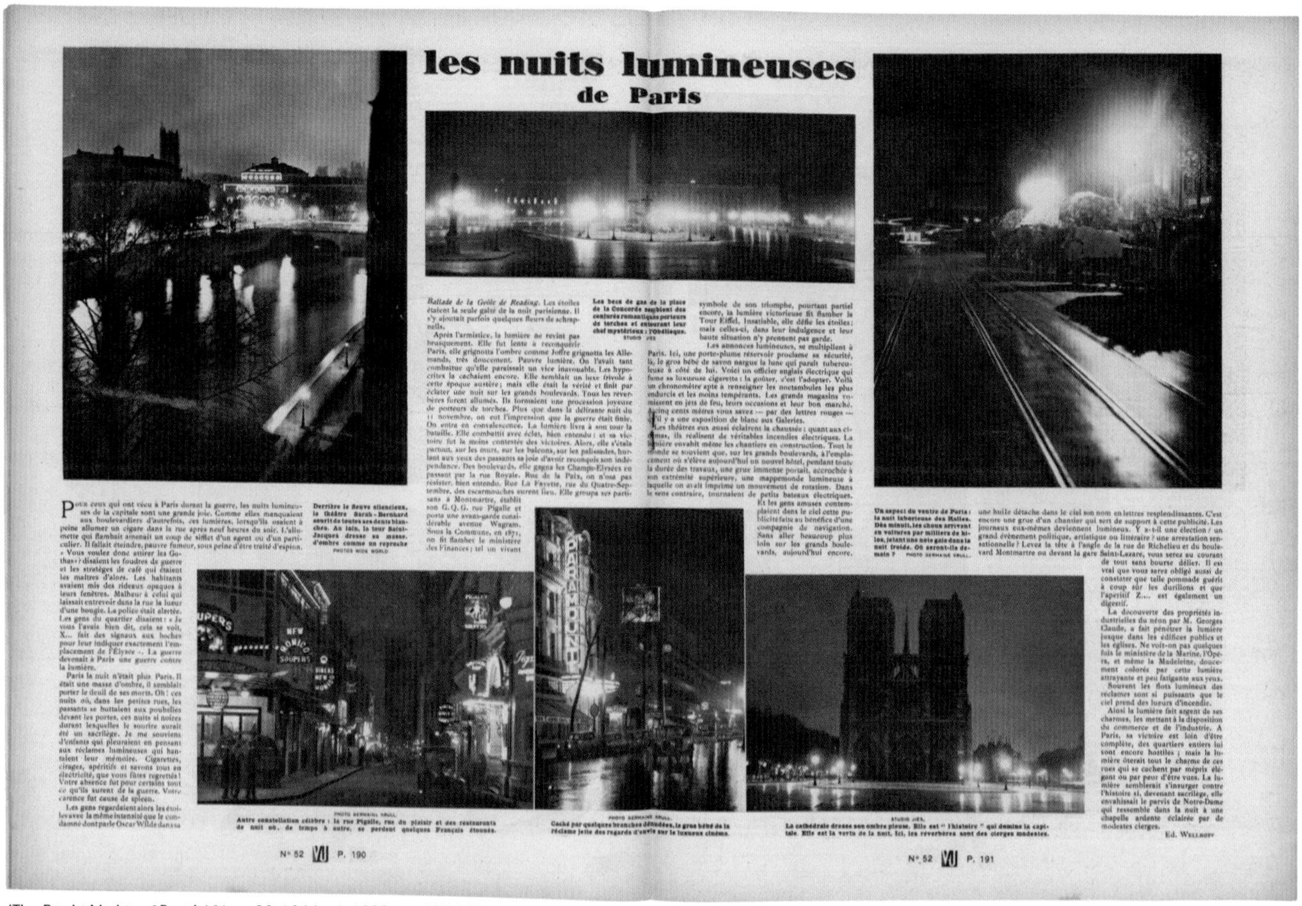

'The Bright Nights of Paris', *VU*, no. 52, 13 March 1929, pp. 190–191

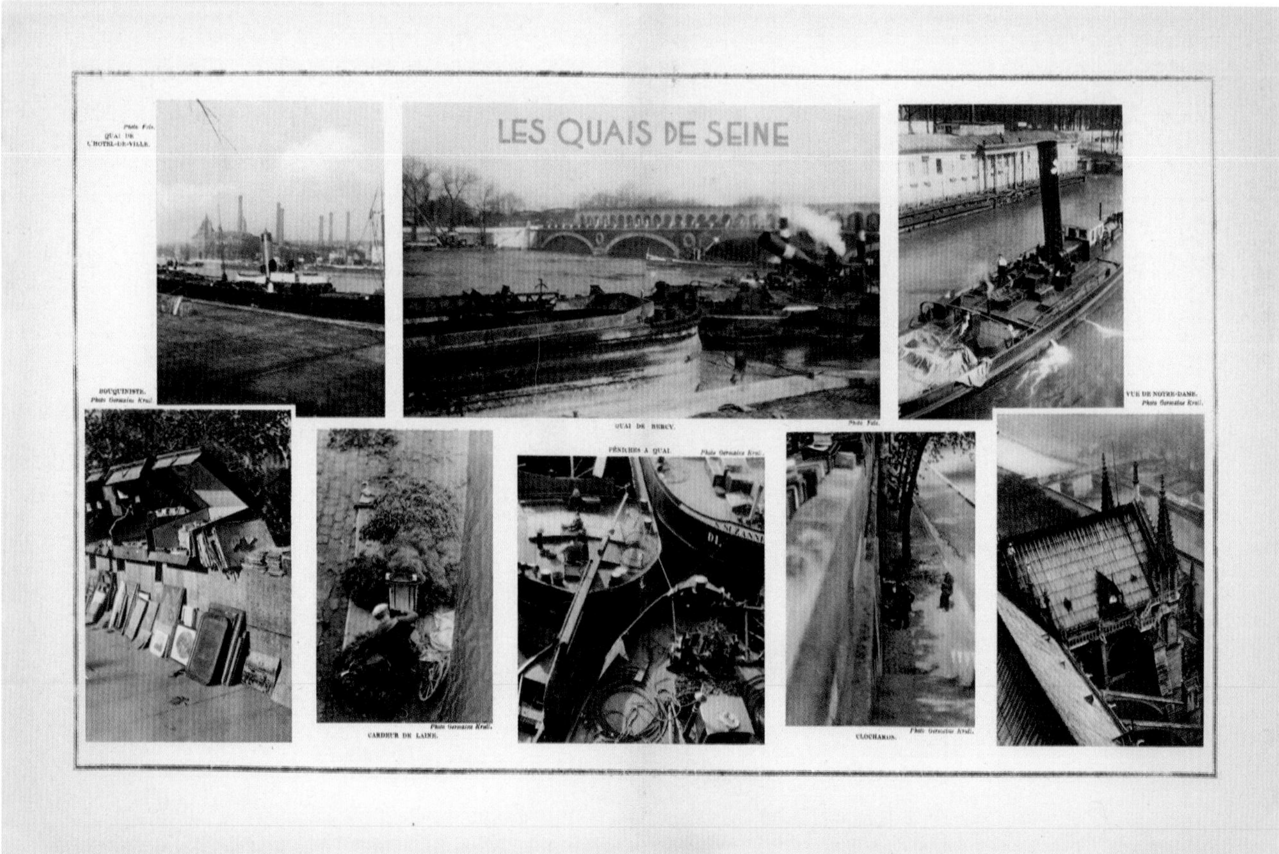

'The Banks of the Seine', *L'Art vivant*, no. 121, 1 January 1930, pp. 20, 21

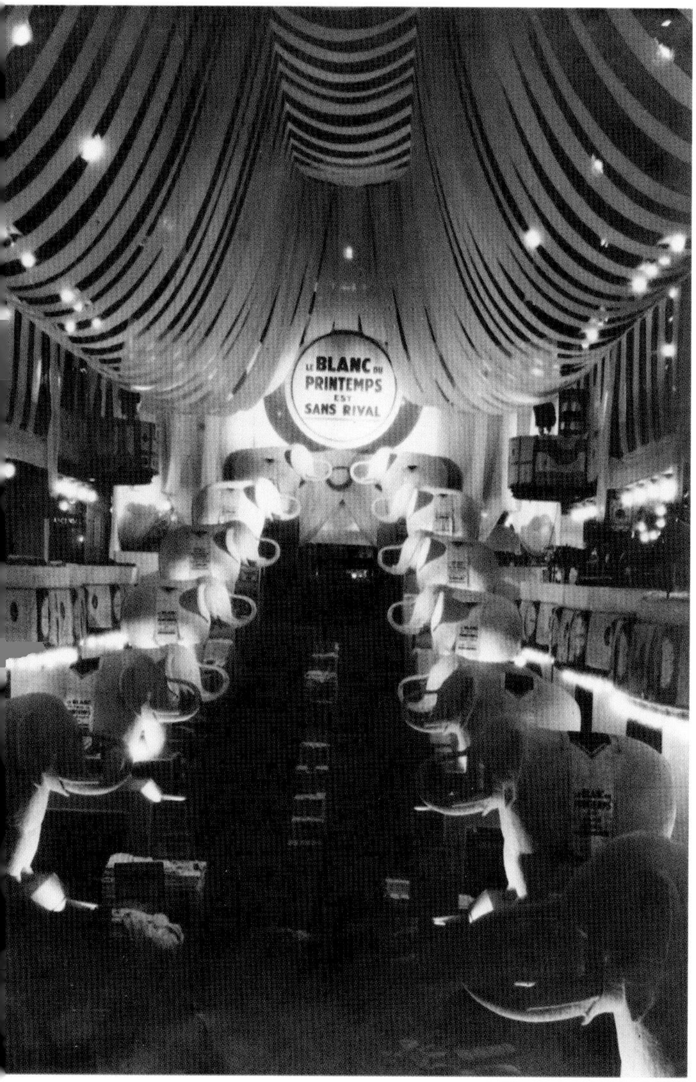

en Week in a Department Store, Le Printemps, Paris, 1928

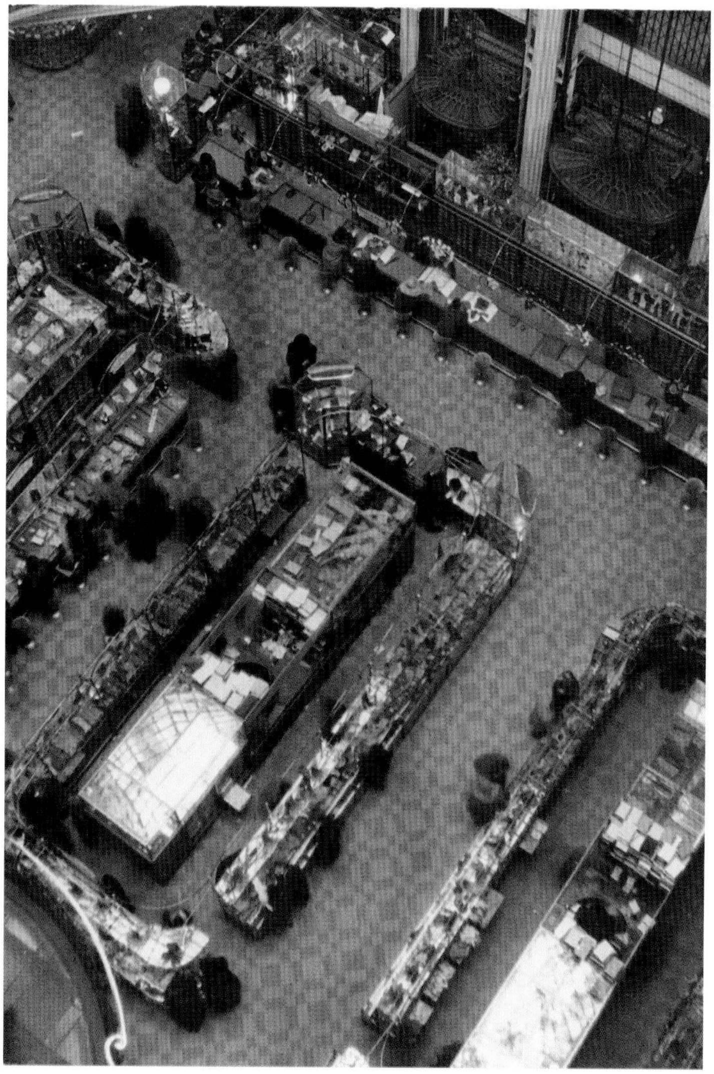

A Department Store, Le Printemps, Paris, 1928

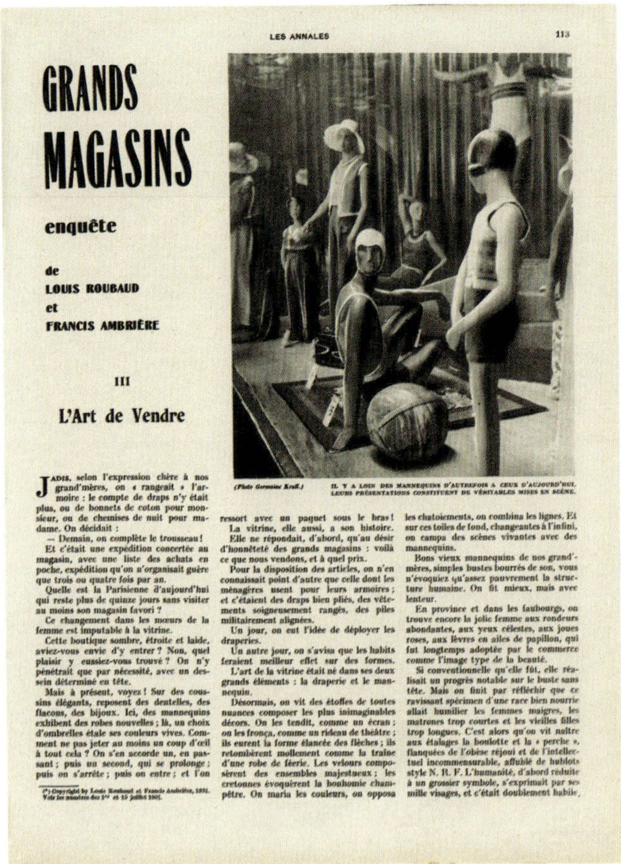

LES ANNALES 113

GRANDS MAGASINS

enquête

de LOUIS ROUBAUD et FRANCIS AMBRIÈRE

III

L'Art de Vendre

(Photo Germaine Krull.) IL Y A LOIN DES MANNEQUINS D'AUTREFOIS À CEUX D'AUJOURD'HUI. LEURS PRÉSENTATIONS CONSTITUENT DE VÉRITABLES MISES EN SCÈNE.

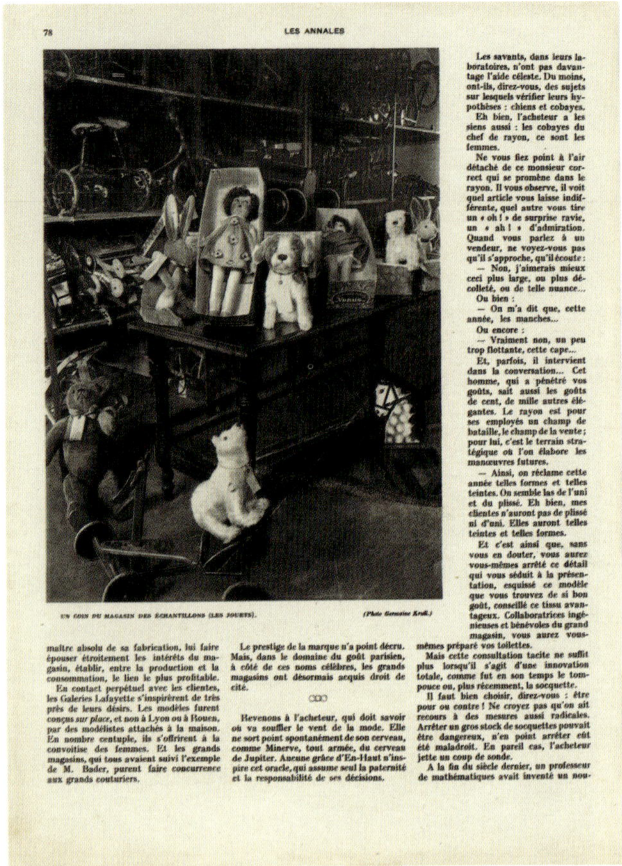

78 LES ANNALES

UN COIN DU MAGASIN DES ÉCHANTILLONS (LES JOUETS). (Photo Germaine Krull.)

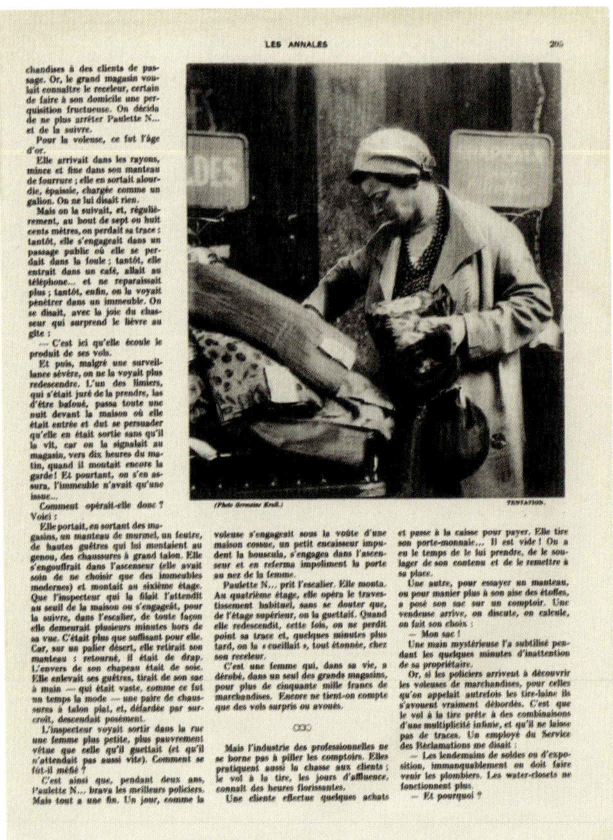

LES ANNALES 205

(Photo Germaine Krull.) TENTATION.

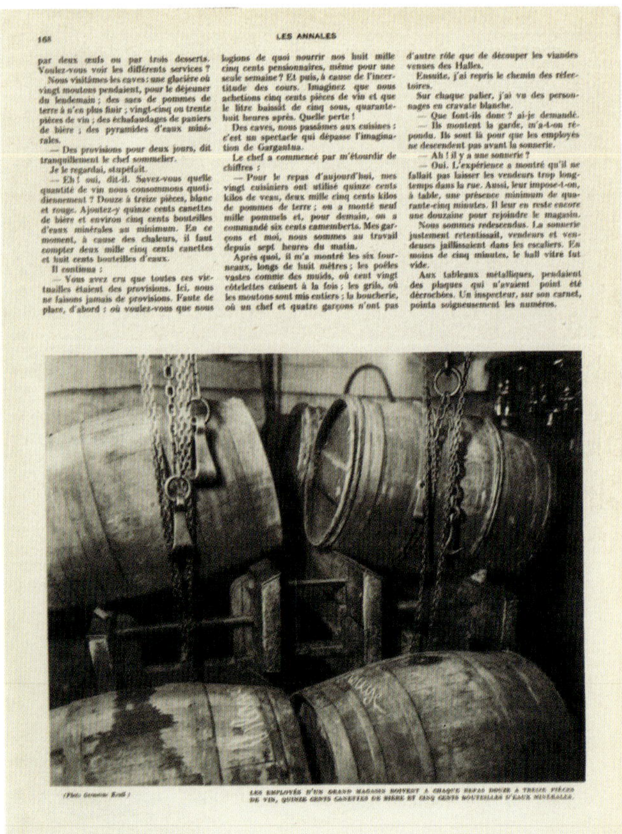

168 LES ANNALES

(Photo Germaine Krull.) LES EMPLOYÉS D'UN GRAND MAGASIN BOIVENT À CHAQUE REPAS DOUZE À TREIZE PIÈCES DE VIN, QUINZE CENTS CANETTES DE BIÈRE ET CINQ CENTS BOUTEILLES D'EAUX MINÉRALES.

'Department Stores', *Les Annales*, 1 August 1931 p. 113, 15 July 1930 p. 78, 1 September 1930, p. 205, 15 August 1930, p. 168

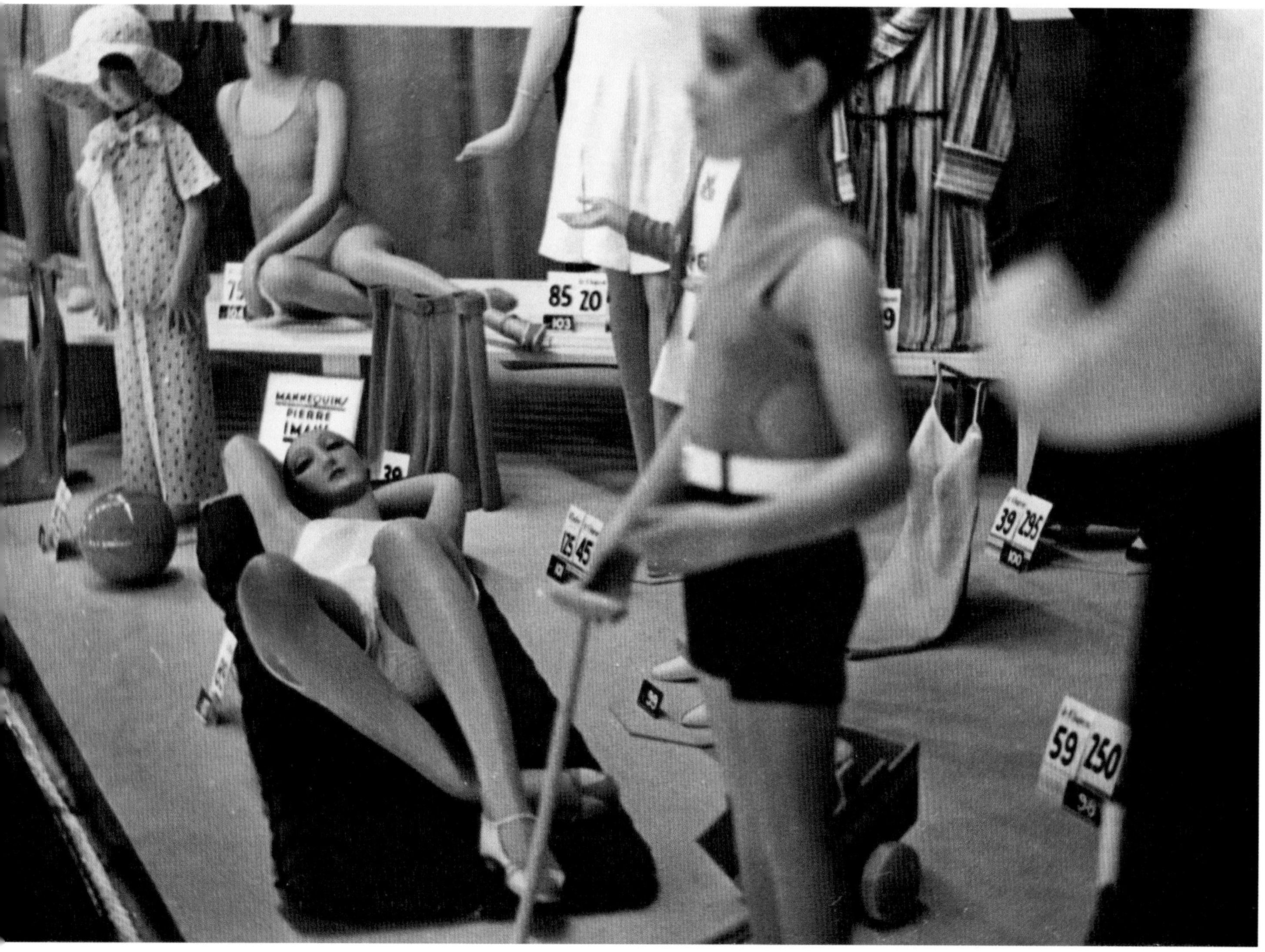

nnequins in a Shop Window, 1930

12

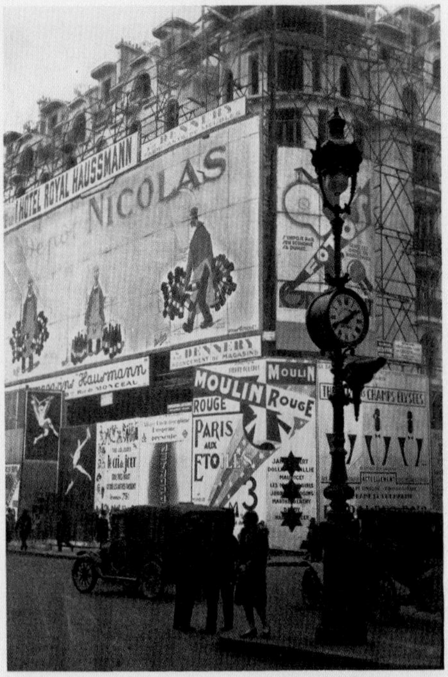

Reklame

13

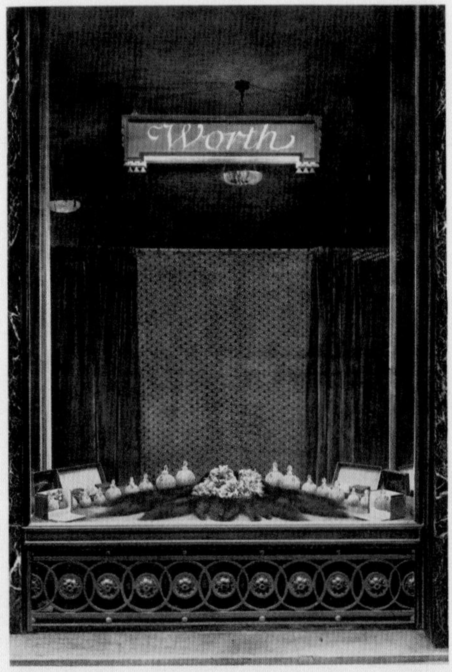

Auslage | Etalage
Shop Stalls | Puestos de venta en la calle

183

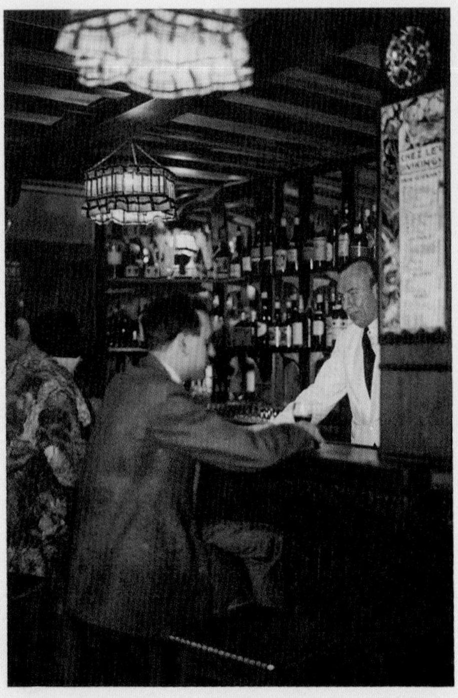

»Apéritif«

254

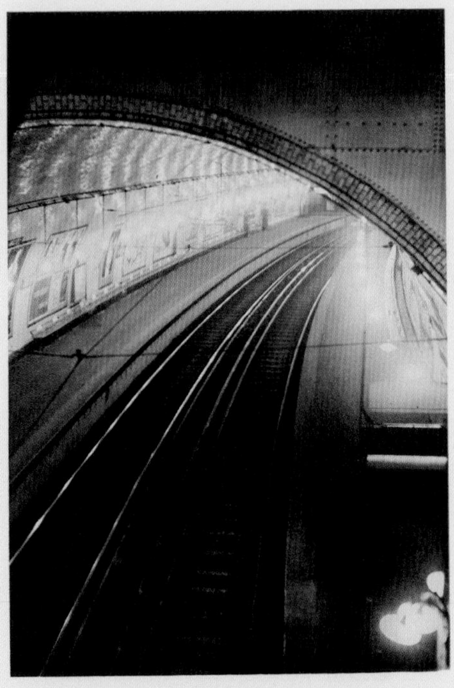

Métro, Station

Mario von Bucovich, ***Paris***, Albertus-Verlag, Berlin, 1928, pp. 12, 13, 183, 254

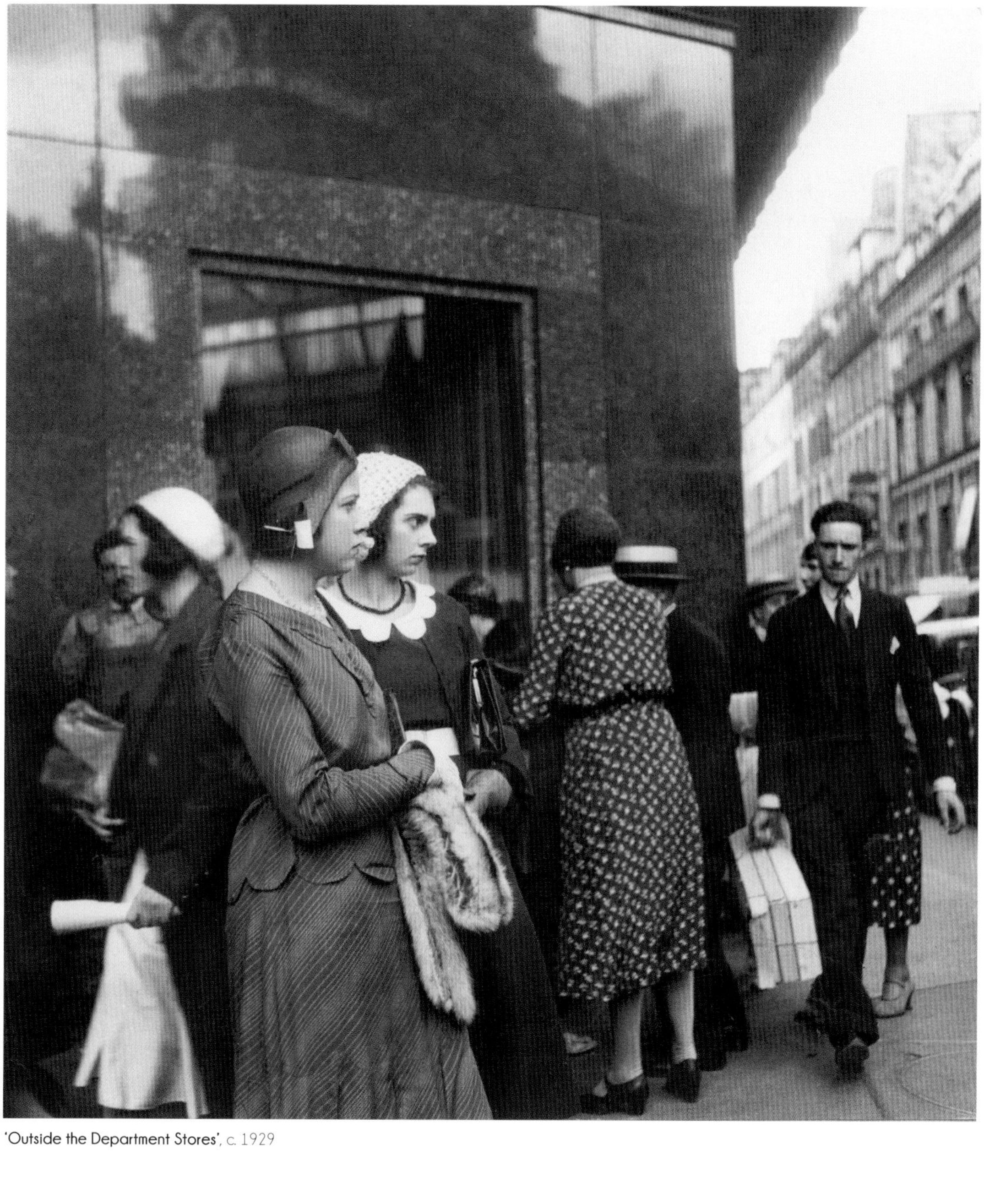

'Outside the Department Stores', c. 1929

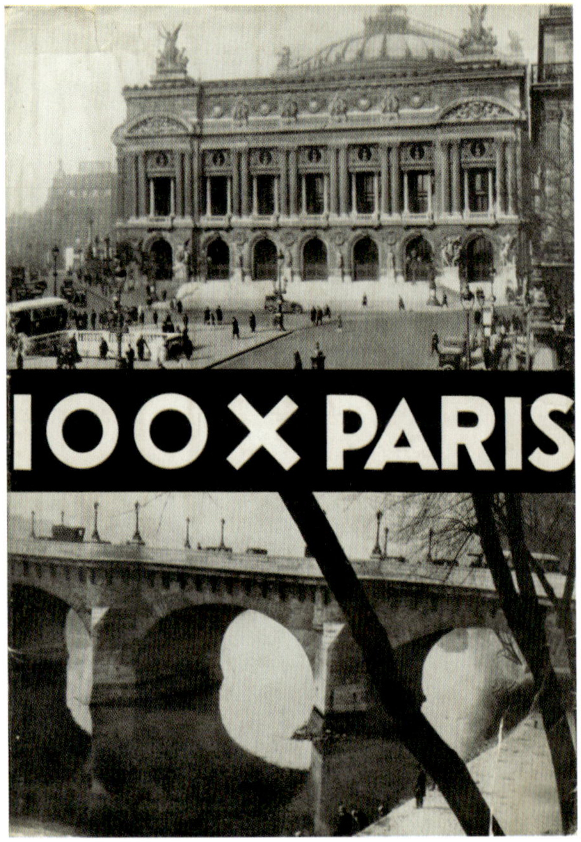

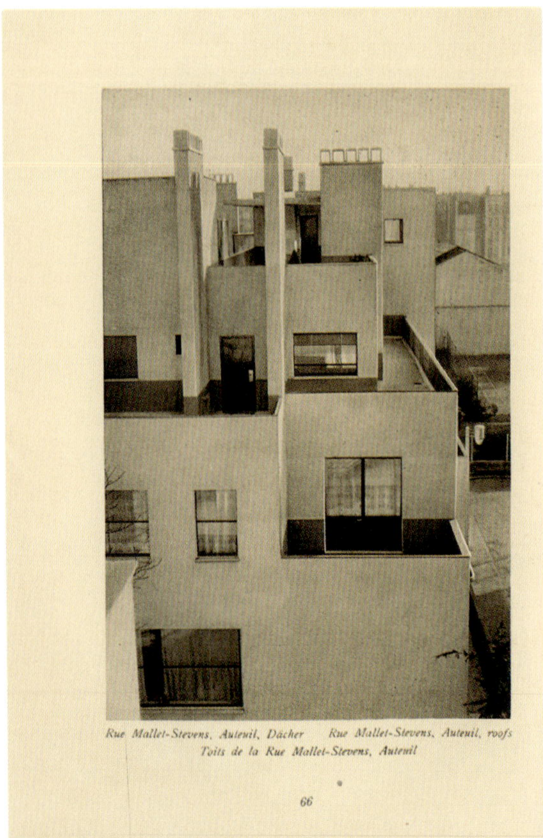

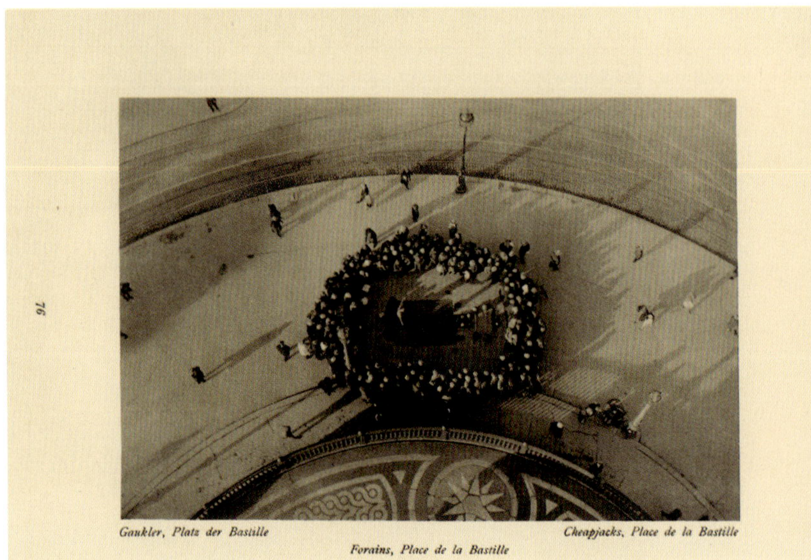

Germaine Krull, ***100 × Paris***, Verlag der Reihe, Berlin-Westend, 1929, cover, pp. 66, 76, 94-95, 80-81 (above and facing page)

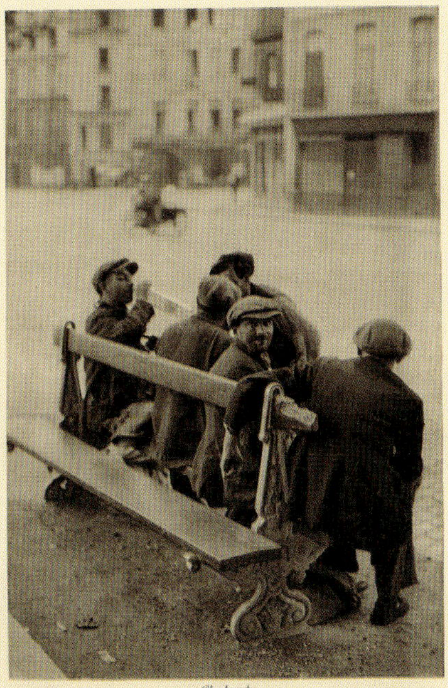

»Clochards«

94

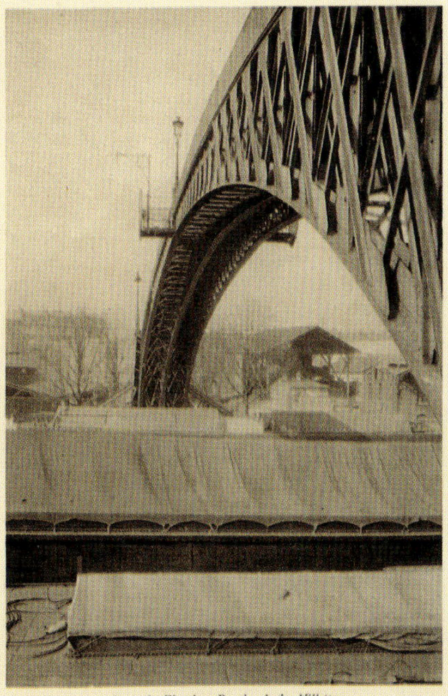

Pont de Flandre, Bassin de la Villette

95

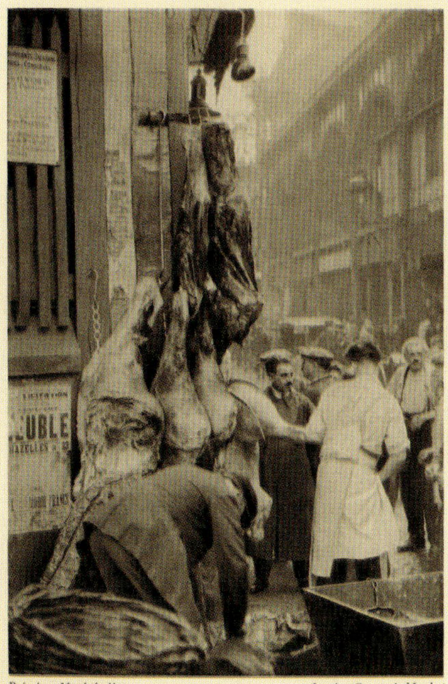

Bei den Markthallen — Aux Halles — In the Covered Market

80

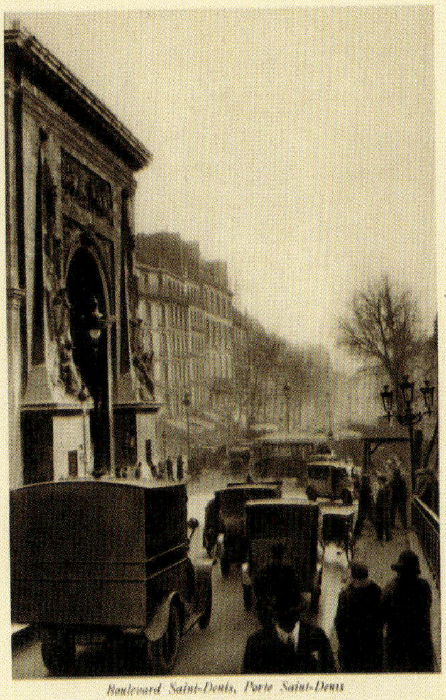

Boulevard Saint-Denis, Porte Saint-Denis

81

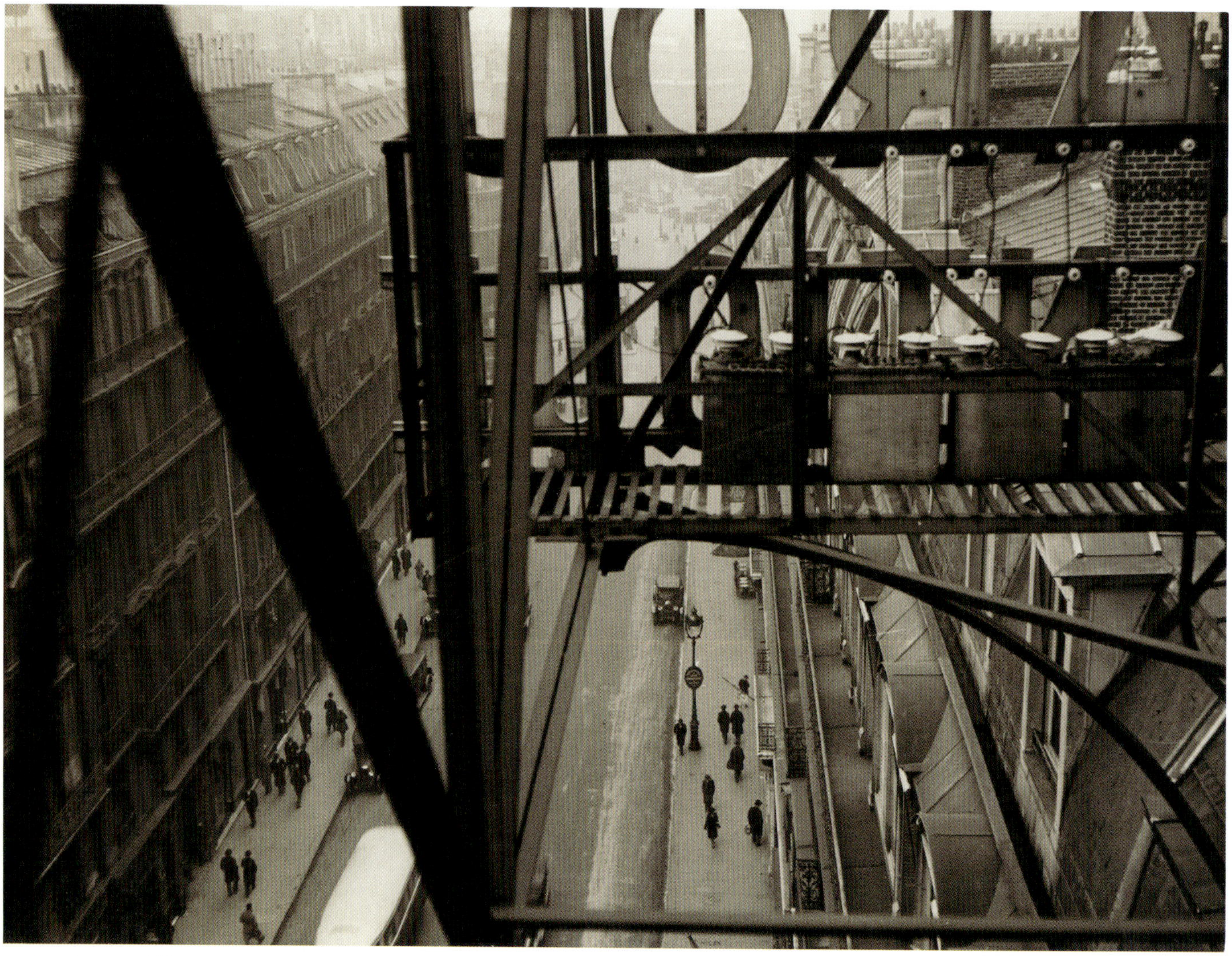

Rue Auber in Paris, c. 1928

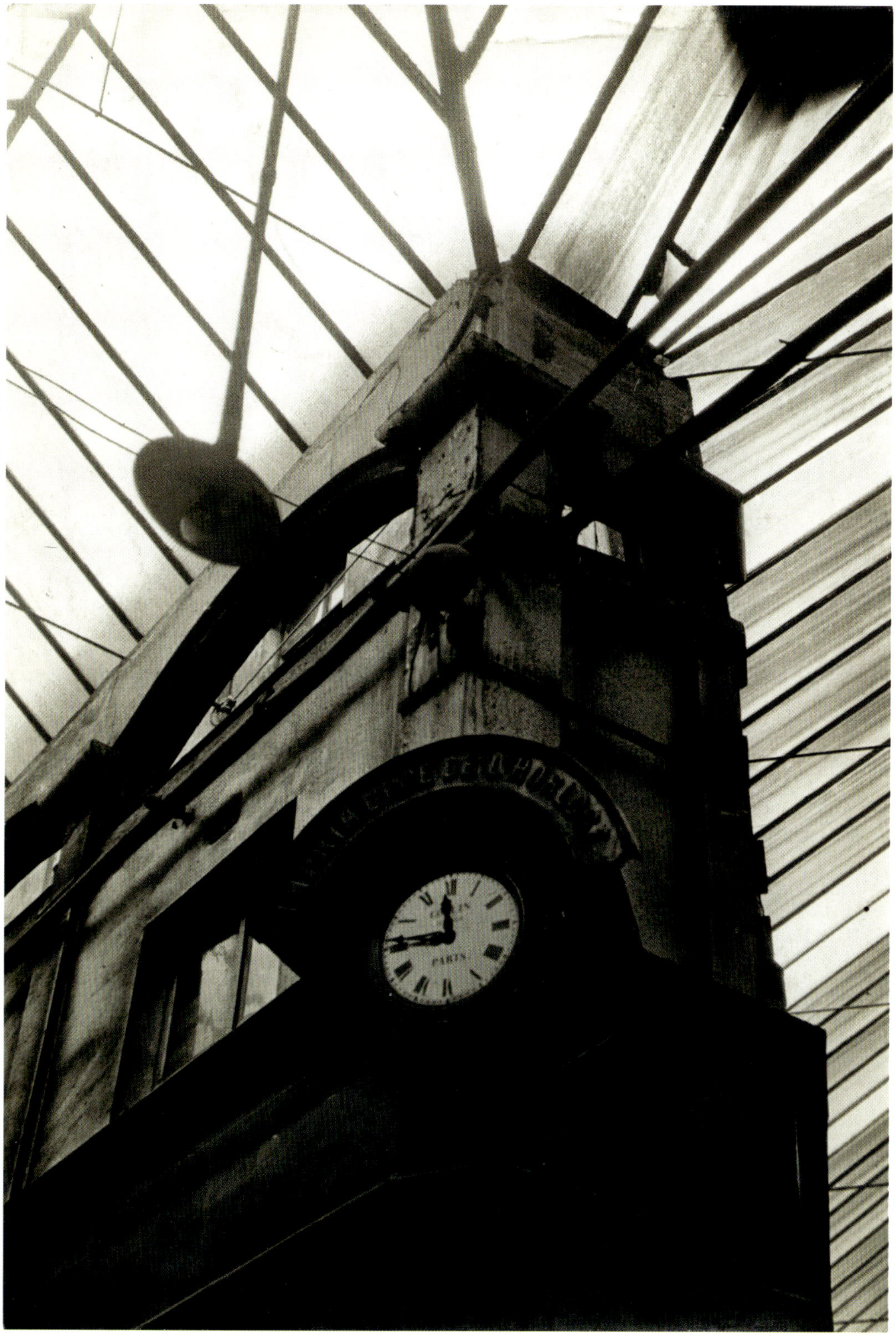

Old Architecture: L'Horloge Print Works, 1928

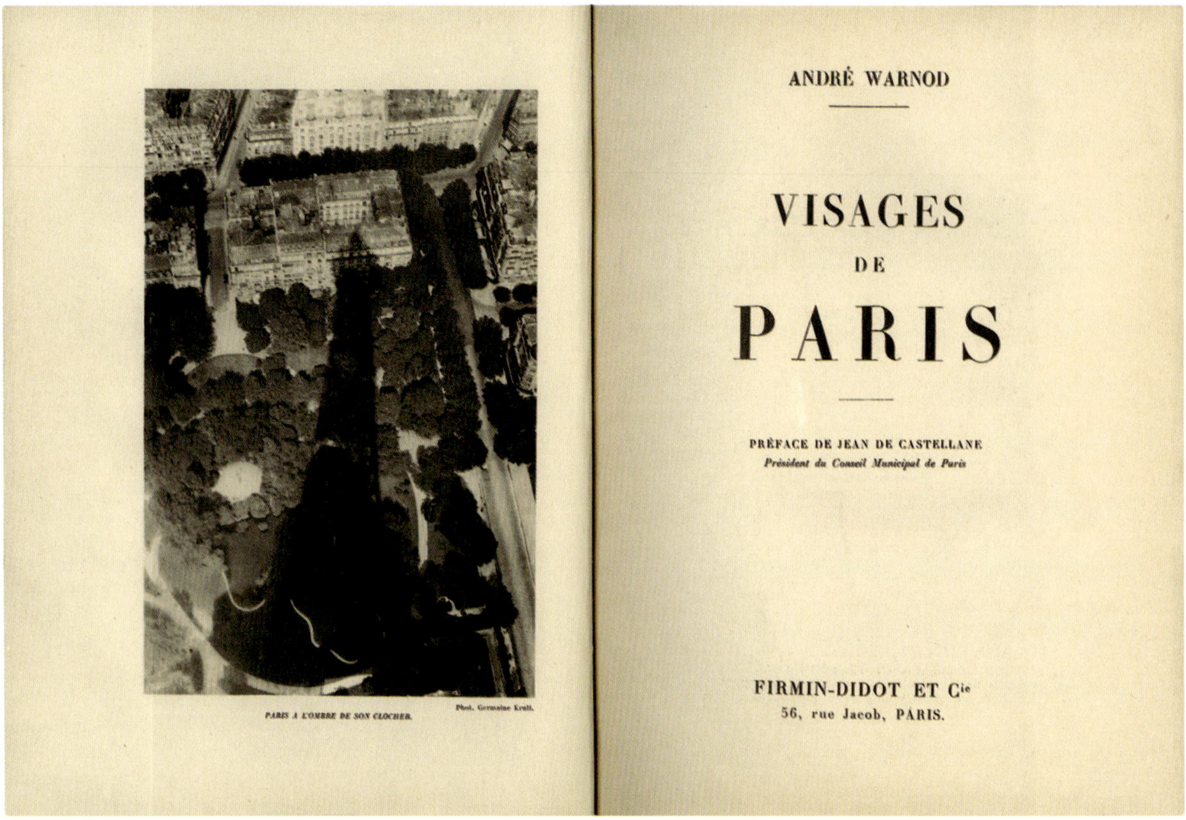

PARIS A L'OMBRE DE SON CLOCHER.

Phot. Germaine Krull.

ANDRÉ WARNOD

VISAGES

DE

PARIS

PRÉFACE DE JEAN DE CASTELLANE

Président du Conseil Municipal de Paris

FIRMIN-DIDOT ET Cie

56, rue Jacob, PARIS.

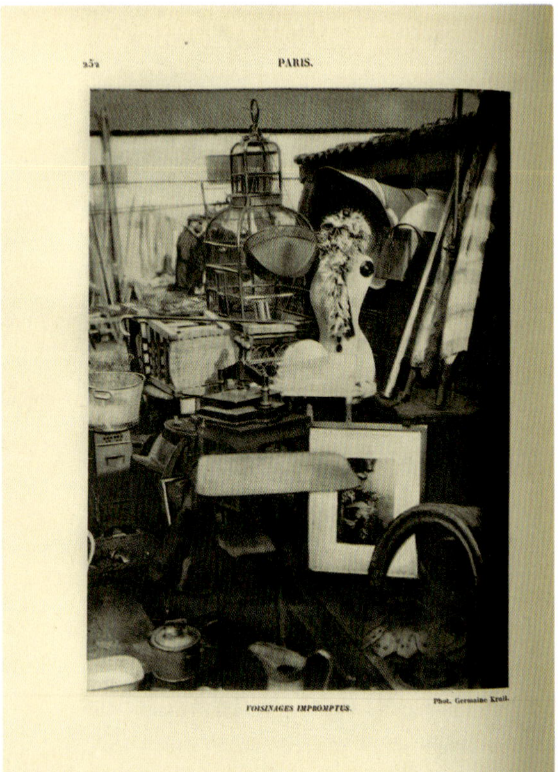

252 PARIS.

VOISINAGES IMPROMPTUS.

Phot. Germaine Krull.

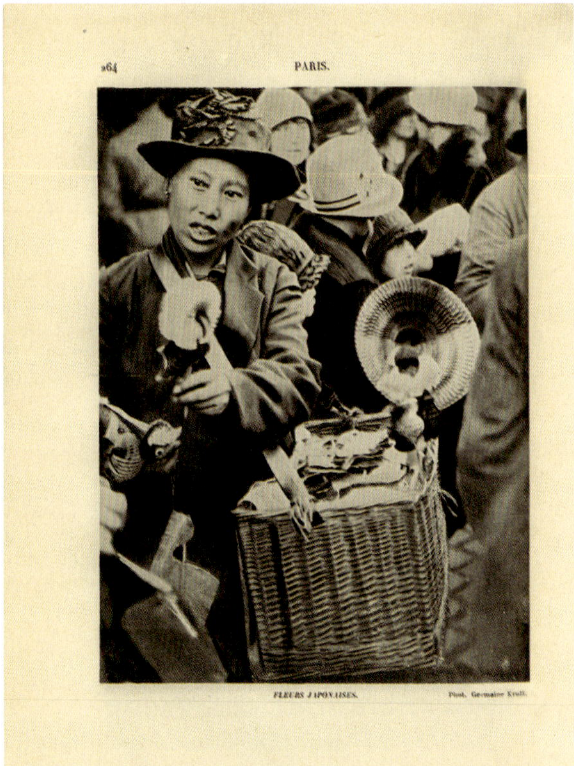

264 PARIS.

FLEURS JAPONAISES.

Phot. Germaine Krull.

André Warnod, ***Visages de Paris***, Firmin-Didot, Paris, 1930, pp. 5-6, 252, 264, 266-267, 274-275 (above and facing page)

266 PARIS.

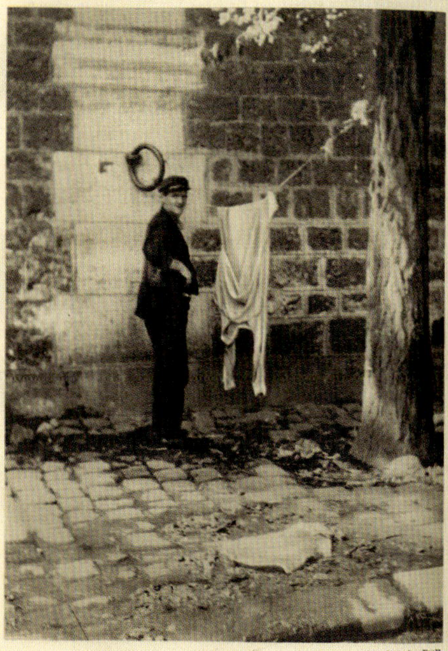

CHASSE AUX POUX. Phot. Germaine Krull.

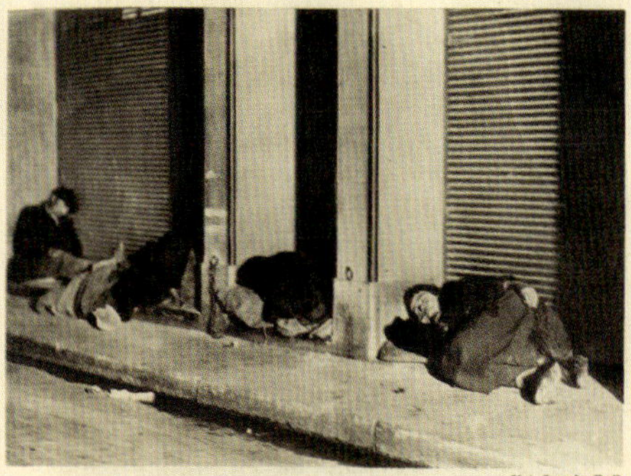

Phot. Germaine Krull.

LES CLOCHARDS.

La nuit pèse lourdement sur le quartier de la place Maubert, les rues étroites s'enchevêtrent, bordées de maisons anciennes dont la vieillesse est crapuleuse. Le mur des églises monte plus haut et se perd dans le noir. Les pas résonnent dans le silence, sur le pavé de la nuit provinciale, qu déchire de distance en distance la lumière d'un bec de gaz.

Un chat aux yeux phosphorescents se glisse, furtif, d'un mur à l'autre, ou bien un rat qui disparaît aussi vite qu'il est apparu...

Tout est mort. Cependant, là-bas bouge une ombre. C'est un clochard à la démarche molle et mal assurée, qui s'en va vers un endroit qu'il connaît et où il pourra, nocturne juif errant, s'arrêt r pour un instant.

Les asiles de nuit sont des endroits épouvantables, mais le tragique de certains bars, près de la *place Maub'* est peut-être encore plus poignant.

L'odeur doucereuse et écœurante des asiles de nuit, la pénombre où mijotent des déchets d'humanité, n'est pas pire que la brutalité de certains cafés-bars qui n'ont rien de particulier, avec leur comptoir en zinc et leurs bouteilles alignées, sous la lumière crue des lampes électriques.

Cette lumière impitoyable inonde de clarté tous les clients et c'est ce qu'il y a d'épouvantable. Ils dorment. Ils dorment partout, la tête sur le bras, écroulés sur un guéridon, mal assis sur des chaises ou des tabourets.

274 PARIS.

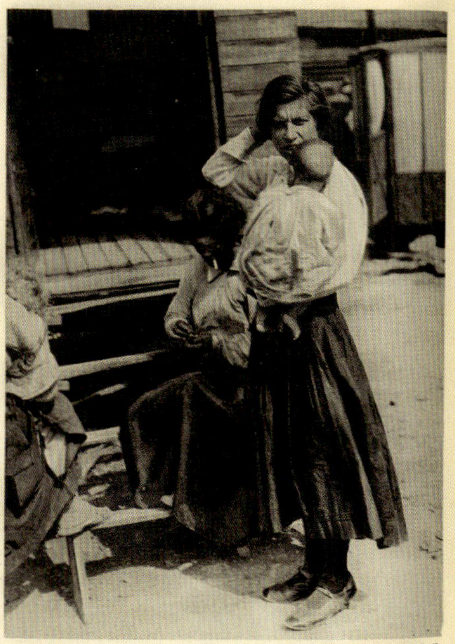

GITANES. Phot. Germaine Krull.

L'AVANT-GUERRE. 275

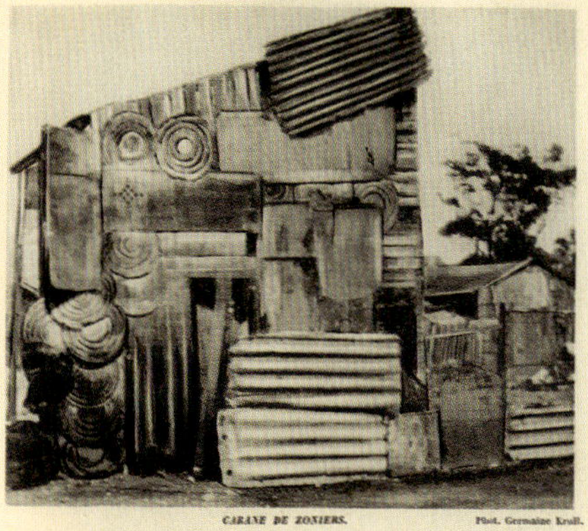

CABANE DE ZONIERS. Phot. Germaine Krull.

petits, transportent sur leurs ailes et sur leurs pattes un peu de l'ignoble poussière et mêlent toutes les pourritures.

Les détritus et les ordures envahissent tout. Ici, c'est un tas de carcasses de poulets, plus loin un amoncellement de vieilles boîtes de camembert, ailleurs un petit monticule fait de chiffons; la même crasse recouvre les murs, les pavés de la rue, et tout ce qui vit dans cet empire. L'humanité qui grouille dans l'ordure semble faire corps avec elle. Vêtues de loques, des femmes mal peignées fouillent avec acharnement les tas de déchets pour séparer le bois du fer, la laine de la soie, les os du papier. Leurs bras souvent couverts de plaies mal enveloppées de linges crasseux, leurs yeux rouges et pleurards disent les dangers de triturer ainsi cette pourriture; d aucuns ont un œil crevé, accident du travail ou fruit de batailles. Ce qui est inimaginable, c'est la crasse qui couvre leur peau, une crasse noire qui balafre les visages, noircit les joues et fait paraître blanc le tour des yeux et de la bouche. Les vieilles sont ignobles : sorcières étiques échappées de quelque sabbat, ou, ce qui est pire, d'une obésité triomphante. Les appâts trop abondants tendent les jupes et les corsages déteints. Parfois, fraîche fleur de printemps poussant sur le fumier, une belle fille bien en chair dont la peau apparaît par les trous de ses loques, s'épanouit dans cette boue, ou bien c'est le clair sourire d'un petit enfant tout nu, vautré sur un tas d'immondices.

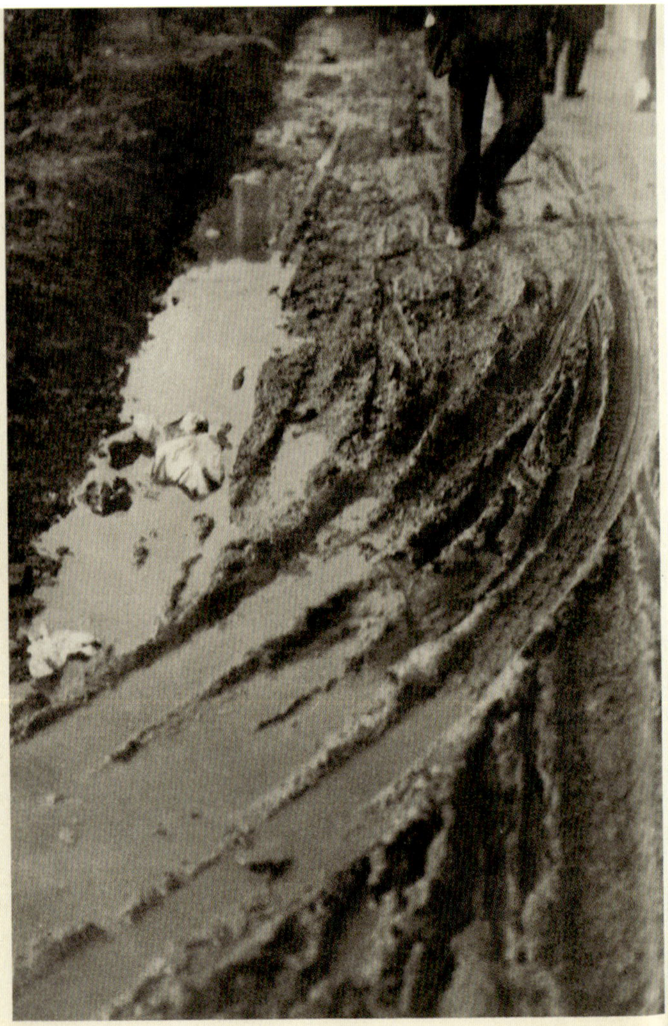

"La Zone."

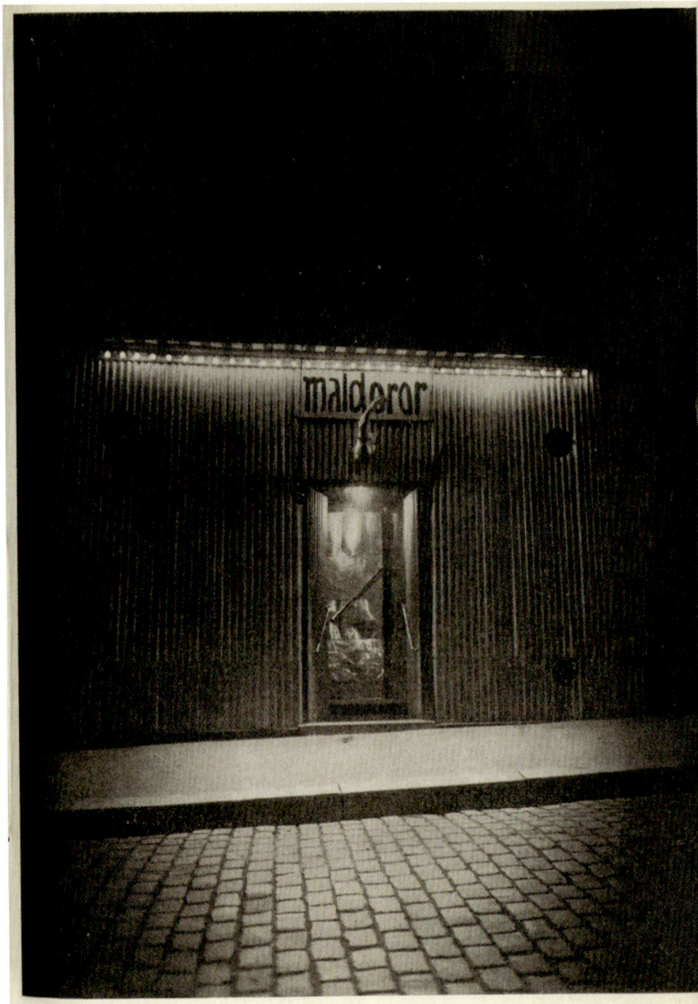

Parisrestaurangen 1930.

Adolf Hallman, ***Paris under 4 Årstider***, Albert Bonniers Forlag, Stockholm, 1930, pp. 118, 121, 125, 135 (above and facing page)

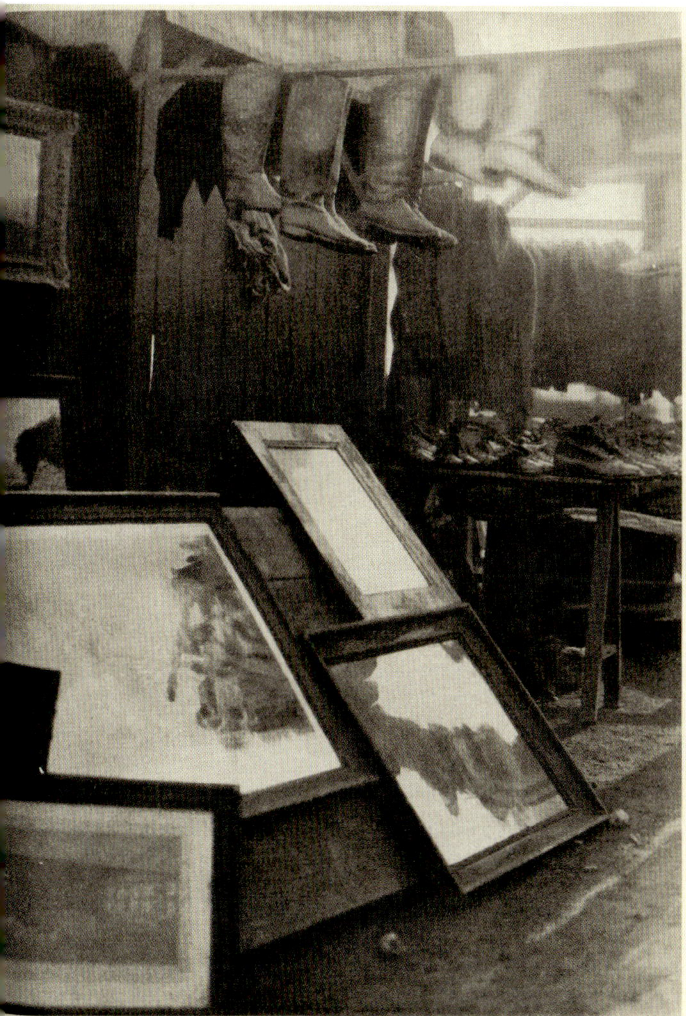

...ån "Loppmarknaden".

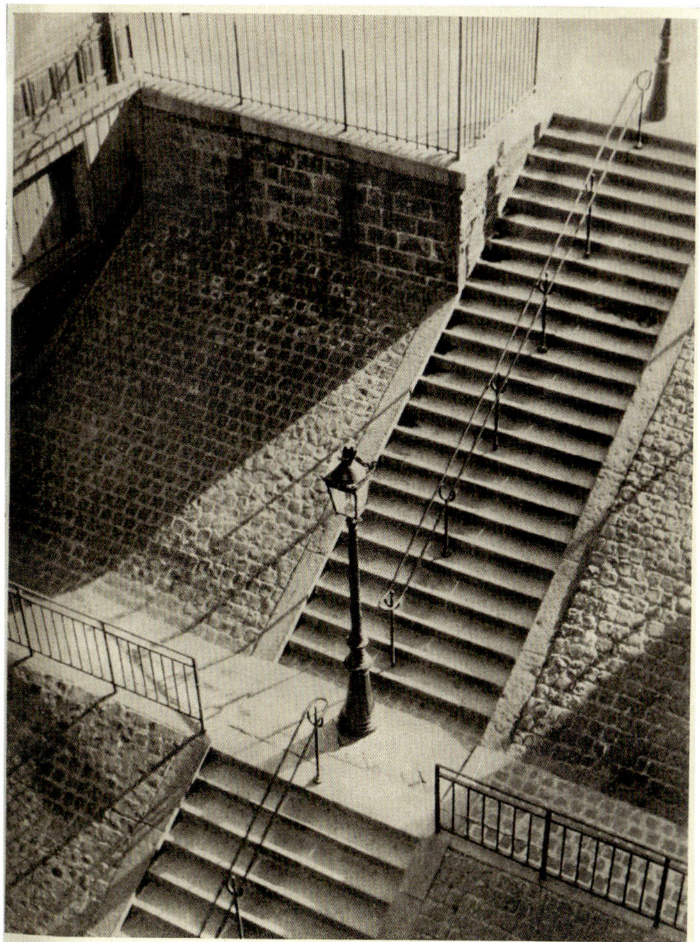

Trappgata i Montmartre.

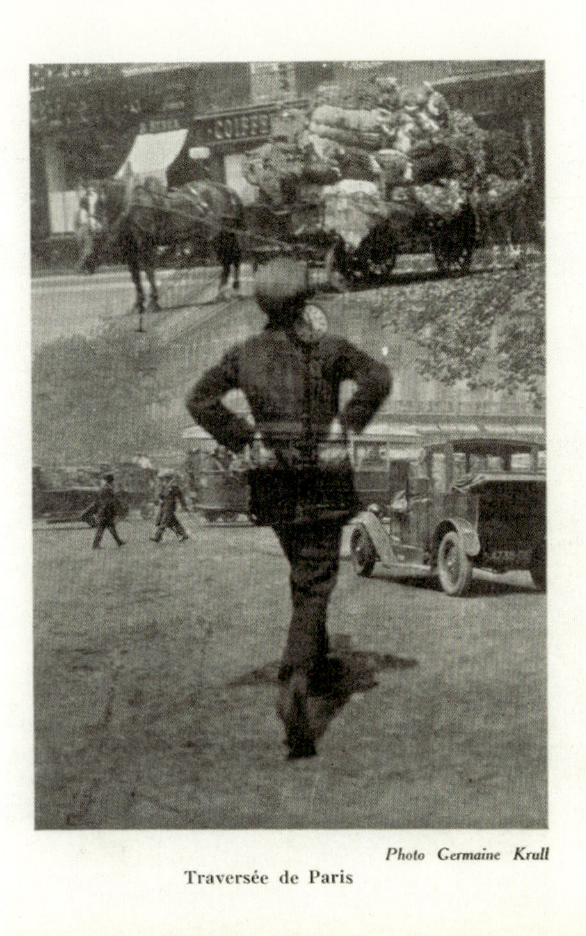

Photo Germaine Krull

Traversée de Paris

'New Images of Paris: Around Paris', *Variétés*, 2nd year, no. 2, 15 June 1929, p. 110c

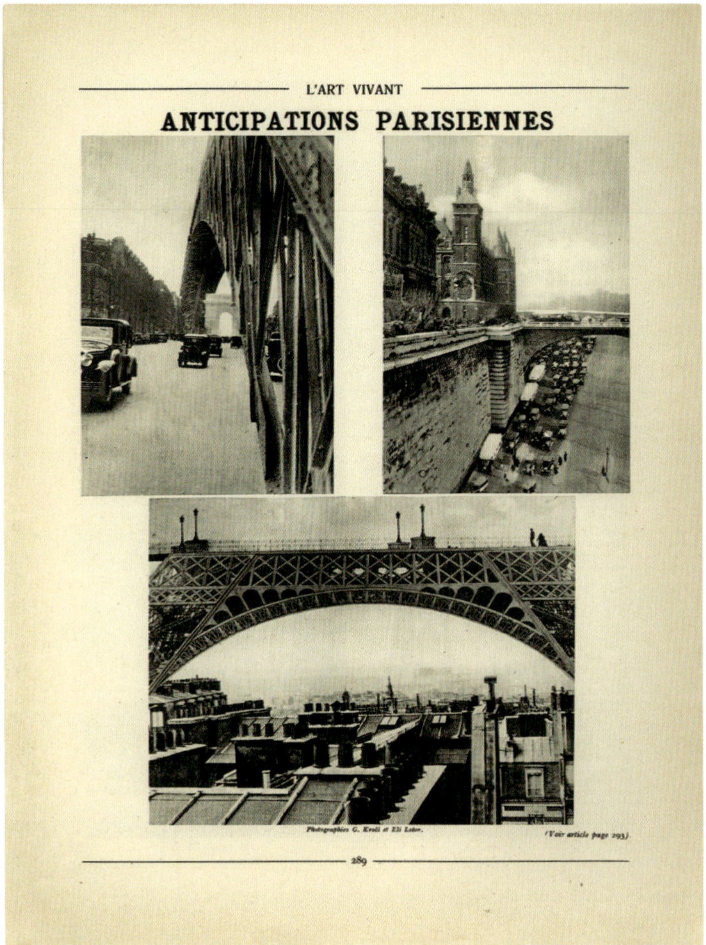

L'ART VIVANT

ANTICIPATIONS PARISIENNES

289

'Tomorrow's Paris', *L'Art vivant*, no. 127, 1 April 1930, p. 289

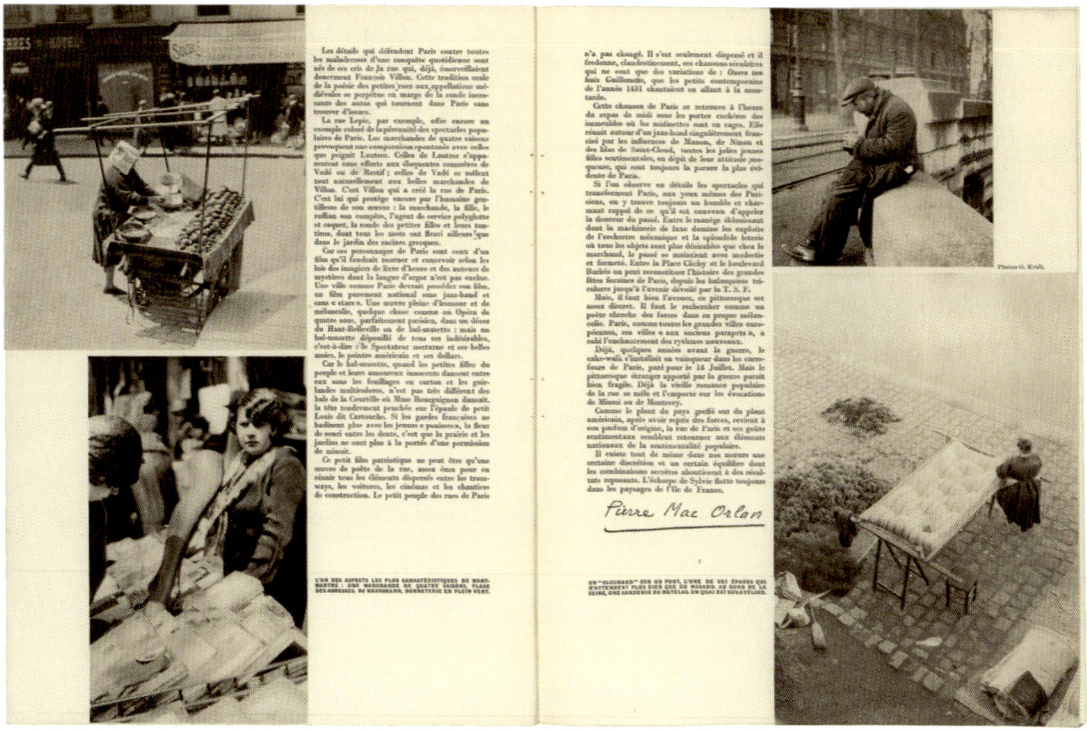

Pierre Mac Orlan

'Faces and Scenes of People's Paris', *Art et Médecine*, October 1931, pp. 48–49

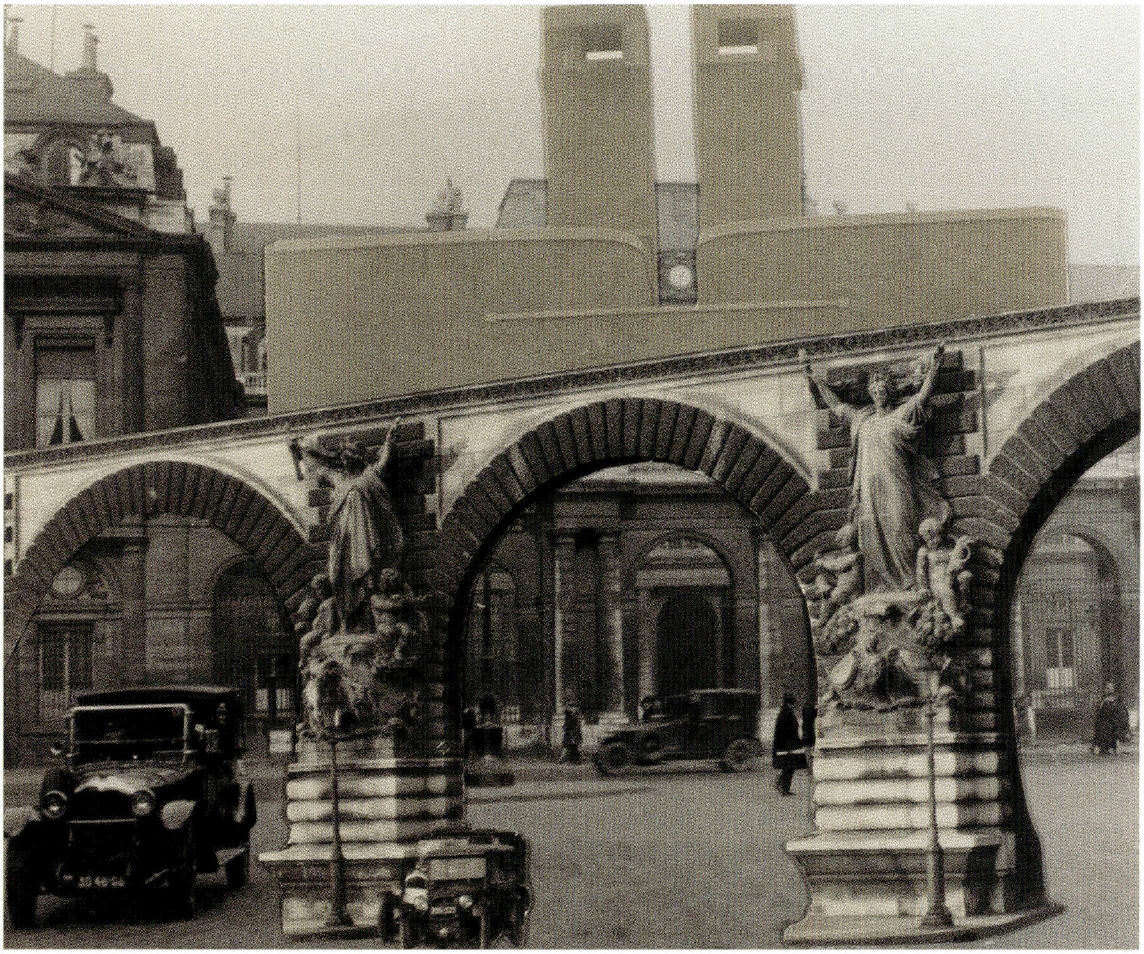

Untitled, photomontage, 1930

AUTOMOBILES, ON THE ROAD

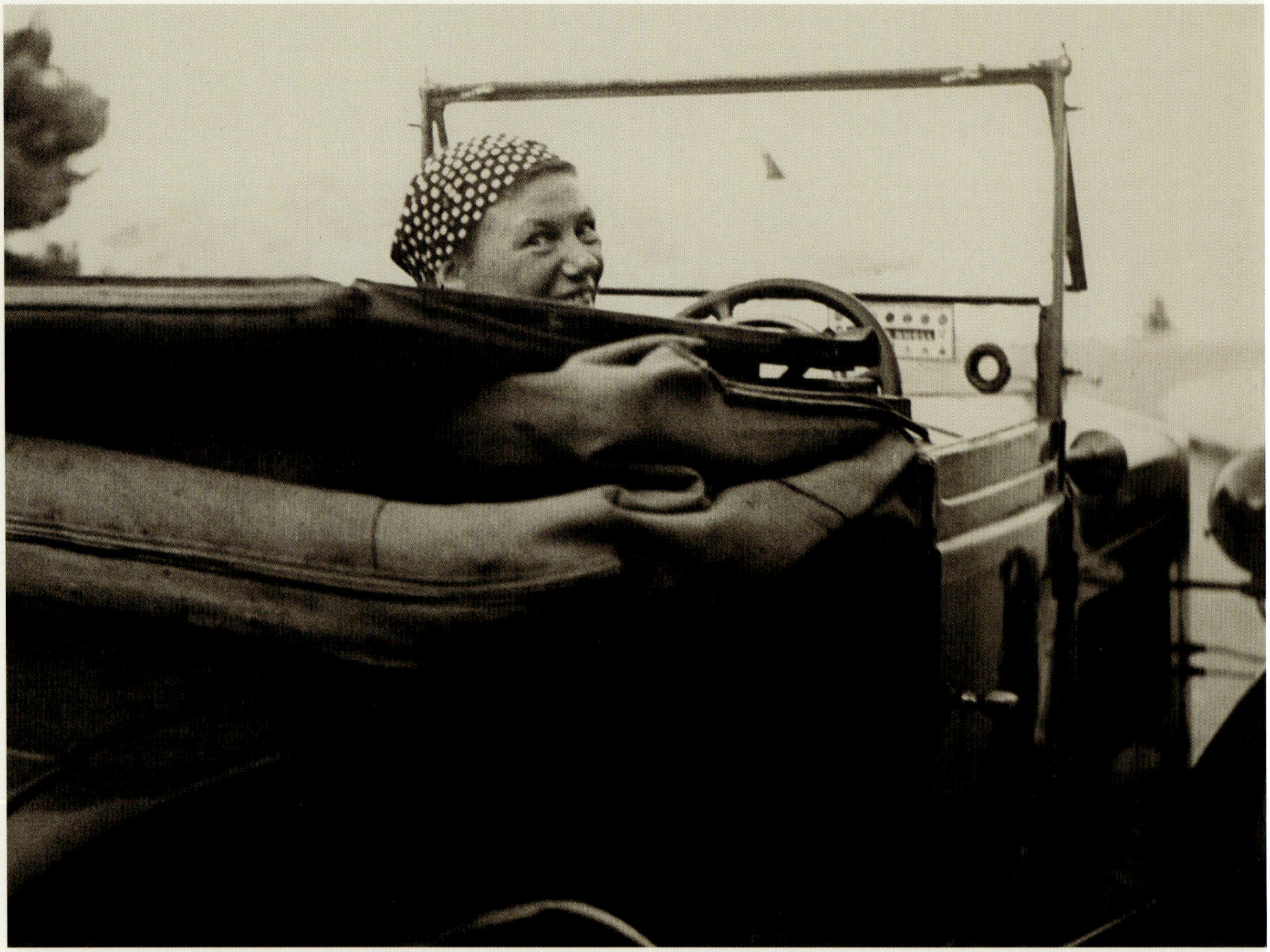

1 *L'Art vivant* no. 117 (1 November 1929), p. 843.
2 VMD, p. 130.
3 *VU* no. 81, special 'Salon de l'Automobile' issue (2 October 1929), pp. 781–783. The inside cover is on p. 778.
4 CEDG, pp. 28–29.

THE MOTOR CAR WAS THE GREAT PHENOMENON of the 1920s, and this mechanical fact had a tremendous social and cultural impact. In simple practical terms, it transformed modes of transport. Central Paris was affected, too. Already, in the 1938 film of Eugène Dabit's story *Hôtel du Nord* (1929) we see the new truck drivers arriving in the early morning at Les Halles, replacing the old horse-drawn wagons. In *L'Art vivant*, Charles Fegdal noted with surprise that 'Speed is in control. The motor car is invading the streets and overpowering our thoughts. We live under the sign of engines and garages.'[1]

MY PEUGEOT

If Krull's memoirs are to be believed, it all began with Peugeot, in 1929: 'A lot of different people walked up the stairs to the studio. One morning, the director of advertising for Peugeot came along. He wanted me to do the [Peugeot] factories in Sochaux [near Belfort], and their new cars. I had to pack my things, my cameras, etc., and then off we went, with Marcel. We did two days of hard work. I had to do mainly cars, which for me were just like any other cars! That left no time for the factory and I was very disappointed.'[2] Krull was confused because she assumed that the commission was a result of her work at the Citroën factories, as featured in *Métal*, but 'they wanted me to take photos [of cars] for their catalogue, and no one else.'

The series, done with a view camera in prepared settings, was not entirely successful. Not realising that the cars had 'to be shown in their entirety', Germaine cut out the wheels. She redid some of the shots 'on the road with my Icarette'. The first leaflet containing her photos was 'the hit of the season'. Some of them were used in advertisements in 1929. Three were used in a pull-out 'handbill' for the 201 at the 1929 Salon de l'Automobile. The same images were used for a full page ad in a special Salon de l'Automobile issue of *VU*, shown on the inside front cover, but with no reference to the photographer. An article, 'Ligne, Force, confort, 1930', was illustrated by eleven photos, only one of which was by Krull (probably one of the ones with 'cut-off wheels').[3] Clearly many other photographers (Tabard, who produced a superb cover, and Marcel Ichac) had been asked to produce car photos, and were more sophisticated in their approach (Tabard worked for the Deberny-Peignot advertising studio). The issue of *VU* published for the 1930 Salon contained many photographs of cars: none were by Krull, many were by Tabard.

With real chutzpah, she asked to be paid with the car she had just photographed, the new Peugeot 201, presented at the 1929 Salon. And so, 'My first car, my bright grey little Peugeot 5 cv with a licence plate in my name stood proudly in the studio courtyard.' She still had to obtain a driving licence and had to take the test three times because the examiners had 'agreed amongst themselves to fail all women at least twice'.[4] She enlisted the help of her friend Titaÿna, the publisher of *Jazz*, who was also involved in the advertisement for the new Peugeot 201, published in *Femina* . It shows her face, frontally, with the caption: 'I couldn't stop thinking about it, so I bought it. Titaÿna.'

Unidentified photographer, **Monte-Carlo, Germaine Krull in Her Car**, 1937

Krull made no secret of her enthusiasm as a new driver: 'The history of my little Gisette [as she called her car] was not very glorious. She crashed into just about everything she could: bridges, walls, trees, but she was a great joy for me, a sign of total freedom.' 'In my 5 cv I showed Joris and Eisenstein the Ile de France.' There are photographs of these two filmmakers in a car in Montmartre.[5] A very fine print captioned 'Germaine Krull in her Peugeot in Fontainebleau' shows the car under the trees, decorated with leaves, with Germaine smiling broadly inside.[6]

Being both driver and photographer, Germaine sometimes took her photographs from the car with her Icarette. An attentive look at *100 × Paris* shows that at least ten of the shots are designed to highlight the motorised traffic and its shiny coachwork, rather than this or that building. And these photographs, which also feature in the other books, are noteworthy because they were taken from within the traffic, right close to the vehicle, and not from a distance. Krull loved to photograph cars in her distinct way, askew, in detail, like a machine or a *fer*, an aesthetic object: steering wheel, bumper, headlights, bonnet, dashboard – all these distinct elements whose forms were highly graphic in the cars of the period. They were part of the 'automobiles' section published in a November 1929 issue of *Variétés*, not far from an article on Krull's *100 × Paris*, and just after the pages on the Salon de l'Automobile in Paris.[7]

The association of the car and 'the road' seems obvious, but it was also a new idea, in that cars 'revived' the use of roads that were conceived for horses. The density of France's road network determined other meanings: traveling on the road (by car) and the state and practicability of the roads became concerns, which could be presented in the form of photographic illustrations, especially in *VU*. In the issue on the 1929 Salon de l'Automobile, *VU* set the tone by publishing an article on the 'Resurrection of the Road' richly illustrated with photographs: 'the roads were dying of boredom' [then along came] 'the first car! From that day on, the road came back to life.'[8] There was also an article about 'Things Seen from the Wheel of a Racer' (two photos by Tabard), and 'Traversée de Paris en Automobile'.[9] This articulates practices and experiences for which Krull already had a penchant.

In spite of the numerous details given by Krull in her memoirs, but also because of its chronological deficiencies, it is hard to grasp the sequence of the events involving three men: Renaud de Jouvenel (1907–1982), Philippe Lamour (1903–1992) and Jacques Haumont (1899–1974), who each played a role in her 'automobile' adventures and in the resulting photographs. It all began with Colette, to whom Lucien Vogel apparently sent Krull for her 'first report' on a writer. 'When I left her, she said with a laugh, "You should take some photos of my daughter, Colette, who lives with her father in Jouvenel's *palais* somewhere on the Left Bank. She is young but she has lots of ideas like yours. I also think that with her brother Renaud de Jouvenel, they are starting up an avant-garde journal, I'm sure they'll like your machines."'[10] To explain the context, since 1912 Colette had been married to Henri de Jouvenel, with whom she had a daughter, Colette-Renée, and who himself had a son from his first marriage, Bertrand de Jouvenel. Colette's amorous relationship with Bertrand, which lasted five years, was the subject of *Le Blé en herbe* (1923). Her half-brother Renaud de Jouvenel (1907–1982) was the adulterine son of Henri and his mistress, Isabelle de Comminges, who was also married, and who would become Germaine's friend. 'A few days later, indeed, I saw Renaud drive up outside my studio in a bright Bugatti sports car. A boy of my age[11] . . . he had come to explain the purpose of the journal he was going to create, about which nothing was known, not even the name. "You must come with us, it will be very different from *VU* which is made for the general public of concierges. We are the avant-garde of the young."' At Renaud's place she met 'everyone who had ideas. People recited German Dadaist poems, they talked about André Breton, Klee, Max Ernst, Mondrian.'[12]

5 *Rondon Joris Ivens werelcineast, Het begin, 1898–1934*, Nijmegen: Wereldvenster, 1988, pp. 92–93.
6 Ann und Jürgen Wilde Foundation, Munich, AJW 585.
7 The front of a Bugatti (still), the dashboard of a Peugeot, the wheel of a taxi, a bumper, *Variétés* 2, no. 7 (15 November 1929), pp. 526–527.
8 *VU* no. 81, special 'Salon de l'Automobile' issue (2 October 1929), pp. 798–800.
9 Idem., pp. 795–796 and 787.
10 CEDG, p. 31.
11 He was, in fact, ten years younger.
12 CEDG, p. 32.

13 CEDG, p. 33.
14 Here I am drawing on 'Machines Primitives: Philippe Lamour, Germaine Krull and the Fascist Cult of Youth', *Qui Parle*, 10/1/2001, vol. 13, no. 1, pp. 57–102, reprinted in Mark Antliff (ed.), *Avant-Garde Fascism: The Mobilization of Myth, Art and Culture in France, 1909–1939*, Durham and London: Duke University Press, 2007, and on the original texts of *Grand'Route* in French.
15 'La ligne générale', *Plans* no. 1 (January 1931), p. 9. The title was of course taken from Eisenstein's *The General Line*.
16 Jean-Robert Pitte, *Philippe Lamour: Père de l'aménagement du territoire en France (1903–1992)*, Paris: Fayard, 2002.

GRAND'ROUTE

Renaud de Jouvenel became publisher of this journal, which was eventually called *Grand'Route*, while the editorial committee was made up of André Cayatte, Philippe Lamour and Eric B. Hurel. But for all its lofty ambitions and sterling content, *Grand'Route* did not become the journal of avant-garde youth that Jouvenel was hoping for. Only five issues were published, from March to July 1930. No doubt, the financial crisis of 1929 was not very favourable to this kind of publication, which aimed at sophisticated intellectual debate, combined politics, sociology and the arts (cinema, photography) and, by including 'avant-garde' photography on tipped-in plates, came up against technical difficulties but also problems of understanding. Only the first three issues had full-bleed photographic covers that were signed (in the strict sense, on the negative) 'Germaine Krull'. These were extremely disorienting, apart from the fact of their reference to the road: on the first issue, a view apparently taken through a car window, showing a hazy landscape with difficult, barely legible trees; for the second, a curving railway or Métro line; and for the third a night view of the front of a car with the road lit up by its headlights. Krull was the journal's one and only photographer-illustrator. The photogravure printing is very dense. A photograph of a detail of a car engine (the inscription 'carburateur Zenith Lyon' is visible) accompanying a text on 'Mechanical Art' by Philippe Lamour (no. 1), the 'machinery of the Théâtre Pigalle, composition by Germaine Krull', which in fact is a double exposure (no doubt done when printing), and a very close-up portrait of Eisenstein (cropped more tighty than the known original) all appear in the third issue. 'The Human Hand', showing a metal turner in close-up, appears in the fifth issue. Some of the issues also have uncredited back covers by Krull: a detachable collar and its shadow, advertising the shirtmaker Ahetze, and '12, Arcades des Champs-Elysées'. Eight photographs in all, which are among Krull's most mysterious and impressive images, striking in their appropriateness for the subject of the text (the road, railways, cars, mechanics, cinema editing) and by their almost extravagant approach, based on a very narrow angle of vision. The only obvious comparison, in terms of audacity, is with photographs by Boiffard from 1929–1930 (toenails, hands).

But the central character of *Grand'Route* is Philippe Lamour: 'In Renaud's gang there was also a brilliant young lawyer . . . He dreamed of great things, of changing the world, of reorganising justice, of making people happy. He was a fascinating person, Philippe Lamour one of the most virulent companions in our group, who at the same time was also becoming part of my life.'[13] A lawyer and journalist, Lamour (1903–1992) was anything but insipid: he had been a supporter of fascist ideas (the Italian model) within the Faisceau, then in 1928, of the Parti Fasciste Révolutionnaire. He was drawn both to Lenin and Mussolini, but even more than that he upheld the ideas of the Marxist Georges Sorel and opposed nationalism. Between 1928 and 1930, the ideas he developed in *Grand'Route*, which would have reciprocal links with the work of Germaine Krull, revolved around the cult of youth and praise for 'producers', and were based on the machine aesthetic, as Mark Antliff demonstrated in his study 'Machine Primitives: Philippe Lamour, Germaine Krull and the Fascist Cult of Youth'[14] (the term fascism should be understood in its 1928 context, with no Nazi connotations). Lamour renounced his ideas after a journey to Germany in 1931 (according to Antliff) and became an anti-fascist in 1933. In January 1931 he founded *Plans* (1931–1933), a journal specialising mainly in architecture, with Jeanne Walter as editor and contributors including Le Corbusier and Fernand Léger. In it he observed the 'unsuitabilty of institutions and morals with regard to economic realities and mores'.[15] He would later help to shape development policy in France.[16]

His 'fascist project' of 1928–1930 took a 'Sorellian myth' of youth (Antliff) as the foundation of a machine aesthetic, first articulated in *Entretiens sous la tour Eiffel* (1929), which also contains a chapter on 'Lenin and Mussolini'. In September 1929 he also praised 'the photographic art' of Man Ray and Germaine Krull in the journal of none other than Henri de Jouvenel.[17] Most important, in the first issue of *Grand'Route* he published a manifesto titled 'Mechanical Art. Birth of a Collective Art',[18] promoting mechanical arts such as cinema, photography, serial architecture and car design. This believer in Sorel's vision of the industrial revolution saw the car as the most aesthetic manifestation of a 'republic of producers': 'Mechanical art is a collective art. It is not the result of one individual but of the collaboration between constuctor-individuals and user-individuals'; 'The Salon ... is the Salon de l'Auto'. He shared many things with Krull: the Eiffel Tower, first of all, the industrial aesthetic, avant-garde photography, cars of course (Germaine's Peugeot),[19] cinema and an amorous relationship. When Eisenstein was visiting Paris with Joris Ivens'[20] it was Krull who introduced him to Philippe Lamour and Renaud de Jouvenel, leading to the French publication of his text on montage, 'The Fourth Dimension in Cinema', in *Grand'Route*, illustrated by a portrait by Krull.[21]

We can also observe the deep connection between these ideological developments and Krull's photographic commitments and, more specifically, the photographs published in *Grand'Route*, which are primarily iconographic manifestos and, more than her other work, embody the effects of montage by 'shocks' described by Eisenstein. *Grand'Route* also contains the finest paean to the photographer, written by the poet Eric B. Hurel: 'Let us cast our eyes, and also cast the eye of the lens, oh Germaine Krull! On these iron roads: the rail, from these threads suspended all along; in this secret domain of waves. Let us raise our eyes to our tower, the Eiffel Tower, a new constructive Babel, young clarity of languages, Esperanto of iron, of bridges in woven trelliswork, of trapezoids.'[22]

THE ROAD: BOOKS

'Mechanical art is a dyanmic art'; 'Mechanical art has created new pleasures: speed, productive rhythm, statistical drunkenness': reading these words by Philippe Lamour in *Grand'Route*, we imagine that Germaine and Philippe came together in their fascination with speed, the photography of movement and driving cars – combined (why not?) with poetry. 'It was he (Lamour), driving my little Peugeot as badly as me, who introduced me to the poetry, beauty and charm of the Ile de France, that land sung by Gérard de Nerval ... The discovery of a landscape of such mildness contrasted with my pieces of iron and fascinated me.'[23] These outings no doubt enabled Lamour to round out his conception of the dynamic automobile aesthetic: 'The aesthetic sensation given by the automobile artwork will vary in accordance with the way it is driven.'[24]

But other circumstances (and another affair of the heart) brought about another photographic event. Germaine describes it well: 'The house of Firmin-Didot [for which Florent Fels worked] had a young partner who seemed to have new ideas. He felt the need to bring the outfit up to speed. I can still see myself sitting facing Jacques Haumont and listening as he said he wanted to do a book with photographs and a text by Paul Morand ... the book would contain only photos ... It was exactly my kind of programme ... Since I had a car, I could take it on.'[25] The book would be called *Route de Paris à la Méditerranée* and would describe photographically what one can see on the way from Paris to the Côte d'Azur: 'It was also with Philippe that one day I set off with Gizette [her Peugeot] to explore the South of France. The Paris–Mediterranean route gave us both our first view of France.'[26] This must have been in spring 1930. Her passion for Philippe was linked to the fascination with the new car and the exultant enthusiasm for a New Photography that was more direct, free and wild: '[Philippe] could still feel his peasant's shirt under the cap of the Parisian lawyer. Life was beautiful, with a car, with a beloved lover and money. The whole thing was not to take more than two weeks. It was a programme made for us; Philippe drove the little banger at breakneck speed and I sat on the open hood and took photos

17 'La pensée des jeunes. Sur une prétendue crise de l'esprit', *La Revue des vivants*, September 1929, pp. 150–154 (quoted by Antliff, op. cit.). The journal was edited by Henri de Jouvenel, Renaud's father.
18 Philippe Lamour, 'L'art mécanique. Naissance d'un art collectif', *Grand'Route* no. 1 (March 1930), pp. 37–40 (followed by a photograph of an engine by Krull).
19 I noticed an advertisement (a drawing) for the Peugeot 201 in *Plans* no. 1.
20 Related in S. M. Eisenstein, *Beyond the Stars. Memoirs of S. M. Eisenstein*, Calcutta: Seagull Books, 1995, pp. 205–213. Mentioned by Antliff, op. cit.
21 'La quatrième dimension au cinéma', *Grand'Route* no. 3 (May 1930, pp. 19–26. This seminal essay defining montage in *The General Line* was published in Russia in 1929 and in English in 1930 (*Close-Up*, March-April issue).
22 Eric B. Hurel, 'La confusion des arts', *Grand'Route* no. 3 (May 1930), p. 73.
23 CEDG, p. 33.
24 'L'art mécanique', op. cit., p. 39.
25 VMD, p. 132.
26 CEDG, p. 33.

27 VMD, pp. 132–133.
28 'Mer, marines, marins', 1930, text by Paul Valéry: 'Races', documents with commentary by Jean Bruhnes, 1930; 'Bêtes', text by Jean Giraudoux, 1931.
29 An advertisement with a fine photo of the road was published in *L'Art vivant* no. 145 (February 1931).
30 Since the 202 was from 1938, the 201 could be the 1931 model, as seen in the advertising insert in *L'Illustration* no. 4 (October 1930), with an uncredited photo by Krull, the original being in the MNAM collection.
31 These are the words of Renaud de Jouvenel, no great admirer of Philippe Lamour, see VMD, p. 135.
32 VMD, p. 132.
33 VMD, p. 139.
34 Ibid.
35 VMD, p. 140.
36 These themes are announced at the end of the first volume with a photograph by Lebondidier for 'Femmes', and one by Kertész (reflections in headlights) for 'L'Automobile'. Only the first volume would be published.
37 VMD, p. 141.

as we drove. I thought it was more original! It was madness. Not one clear photo came out of it. None of them could be used, but that's how felt, and that was that.'[27]

Indeed, this book with its very original design, the fourth in the 'Images du Monde' collection initiated by Florent Fels, did not correspond to any predictable theme, unlike the previous offerings in this series conceived as an 'encyclopaedia of modern life'.[28] With a montage of five photos by Krull on the cover evoking the view of a road, carefully executed photogravure printing in dark black, it exploited photographic visuality, the ability of the camera to direct the gaze to what would unusually be neither seen nor looked at. In this sense, the book had been adapted to Krull's manner: thirty-eight of the ninety-six pictures in all were by her (compared to only ten for André Kertész). At least ten of these purported to do no more than show the road itself, and seven seemed to have been taken from inside the car (the bonnet is sometimes visible). Throughout we find the off-centre, high- or low-angle views and blurred close-ups that are the signature of Krull's refusal to conform to the classicism of the book's other illustrators, namely, Blanc and Demilly, or the Touring Club de France.[29]

Krull's line in motor car photography was going well. 'Business was good ... The Peugeot factories asked me to do a catalogue that got me a nice little 202, a new model. That car did 100,000 kilometres with me and never had one accident. Unlike the little Peugeot that ended up with Philippe Lamour in a train accident in Brittany. Fortunately for him he lived to tell the tale.'[30]

Meeting Jacques Haumont for *Paris Méditerannée*, however, she was also troubled by the man, especially since Philippe Lamour had by now 'found his life' in the person of 'a rich heiress':[31] 'Had I found the man who would make my dreams come true?'[32] 'The dream of illustrated books was also growing, and Haumont too was very enthusiastic.'[33] And when the publishers Firmin-Didot failed to share his ideas, he decided to set up his own publishing house. 'I don't know what happened. It seems that he was excited by my ideas, and perhaps, too, by his love for me ... All he could think about was my ideas and nothing else.'[34] Encouraged by Lucien Vogel, she moved to Boulevard Saint Michel. Another resident in the building was Antoine Roche, a personal friend of Jean Cocteau and opium addict, who produced the Calavas portfolio *Paris 1928*, *Paris 1929*. The work – installing a darkroom and a bathroom – was paid for by Jacques Haumont. 'I became the neighbour of Malraux, who lived in Rue du Bac.' One day he turned up with a little black cat whose 'father is Morand's cat and whose mother is Berl's cat ... and she is brought to you by me. You couldn't be more literary if you tried.'[35] She was called Mitsou and her kitten would be called Noiraud.

Haumont's idea was to make a series of small books of photographs titled *Voir. Documents de photographie et d'art*. The first would be about 'The Paris–Biarritz seen and photographed by Germaine Krull', the second, 'Women of France', third, 'the Automobile'.[36] All of which of course reflects Germaine's editorial and photographic inclinations. 'So when I went with Jacques Haumont to do the first book, "La Route Paris–Biarritz", I did the road in Jacques' s big car, a Talbot. There was something sad about the photos. They were like me. Jacques really wasn't my type and as a lover he was dreadful.'

Sentimental misunderstandings notwithstanding, she wanted to see the adventure through to the end. Jacques loved fine publishing, she trusted him, even though she knew him to be a 'dreamer of the beautiful and the impossible'. 'The book was at the printer's. In a few weeks [Jacques] will have new capital to do "The Rivers of France".' Roads, rivers – the idea meant something to her. A new offset machine was on its way, but in Germaine's view 'For photography only photogravure will do.'[37] She capitulated and took refuge in the theatre with Cocteau and Jouvet. 'When "La Route Paris–Biarritz" came out, it was a disaster, it wasn't as good as the Firmin-Didot books, and I was so sorry.'

Looking closely at the book today, it is hard to see why Germaine was disappointed: the format is pleasing, the paper well chosen, the photogravure printing, by Lang-Archereau, is a good black, and many of the photographs are highly attractive, even the *fers*. It is possible that she had confused this printing with the one of 'La Folle d'Itteville', another production by Haumont from 1931 which was indeed disastrous.[38] Starting with a view of the Champs-Élysées taken from the wheel of a car, 'La Route Paris–Biarritz' offers a very precise description, with captions for each image, of a drive, complete with stops in villages to look at the views, visit a famous monument of little charge, see a riverside, a petrol station or to photograph a flock of sheep or a caravan of donkey drivers who are blocking the road, or an assembly of Basques. The book ends with two masterly photographs of cars at night, and on the 'circles of light from the headlights'. Many of the views are astonishing, including the ones of monuments, many of the photos of roads and paths. This was the first manifestation of the emerging 'culture' of car travel. In the 1930 Salon de l'Automobile issue of *VU*, a long (ten-page) article titled 'La Route' about the circumstances and accessories of car driving, and about roads, opens with a road photograph by Germaine Krull.[39] Her photos of the road taken from her car continued to be popular: in a special issue of *VU* from 1933, there are two of her images in this style showing the bonnet and the windscreen.[40]

Krull's allusion to Nerval when talking about her promenades with Lamour connects with her book *Le Valois par Gérard de Nerval illustré par Germaine Krull*, published by Firmin-Didot in 1930. This luxury edition, worthy of Haumont's ambitions, with finely executed large-format photogravure prints of forty-seven original photographs, is a fine early flowering of the photography book, and another achievement for Krull. The photographs, many of them views of roads and country lanes, dominate the fairly short text by Nerval. In all, three books of photographs came out of her amorous relations with Lamour and Haumont.

'Jacques's affairs were going very badly, but that didn't really matter to me. I was trying to get out of this relationship which was weighing on me.'[41] She threw herself into a short film about the Seine, and then another, about '"the Paris–Nice route" with an old car and actor'. A friend and secretary of Jouvet's, Yves Gladine, was to write the script: a young man, a bank employee, is fed up with his life and buys an old car, like the clapped-out taxis of the Marne, and 'drives off with it for the sun'. Krull found a backer 'with the help of my name', neglected the script, and hired Gisol as an actor. 'We did Paris–Nice and it was very joyful.' But just when she was working towards an 'ending' in the old streets of Nice, the car 'got out of control on a slope.... We had been working for months and months to get kilometres of film in the can which we handed over to the backer. I don't know what he did with them.'[42]

END OF THE ROAD: MARSEILLE

Was it a lack of interest in the cinema? Fleeting depression? Germaine Krull lived off her 'stock of photographs'. Someone had stolen her Icarette. She replaced it with a Contact and a Rolleiflex, but it wasn't the same thing. It is clear that in 1931 people had stopped asking her for reportage. Other photographers did it, and did it differently. She left for Provence, for 'the olive trees are always a kind of consolation'. She realised that she had lost 'my time and my ideas'. She was about to break with Haumont when he told her he had gone bankrupt.[43] She couldn't leave him anymore. 'And when my car was seized, along with his, I made a terrible scene. My car came back to me, but it was awful.'[44] What follows in her story are a few photographic episodes, like the beginning of the publication of the weekly *Marianne* by Gallimard, directed by Malraux and Emmanuel Berl, in October 1932, which gained Krull the illustration of Colette's *La Chatte*, published in serial form.[45]

38 See below., 'Women'.
39 *VU* no. 185, special 'Salon de l'Automobile' issue (September 1931), p. 2279. This issue also contained an article on 'L'ennui des routes' (The Boredom of the Road), with text and photos by Marcel Ichac, pp. 2290–2291.
40 *VU*, n.n., (289b, 1 October 1933), p. 40, in 'D'abord, rester sur la route' by E. H. Weiss, and p. 56.
41 VMD, p. 141.
42 VMD, p. 142.
43 Éditions Jacques Haumont went through several addresses in 1931: 12 Avenue Pasteur (on the cover of *Paris–Biarritz*), 7 Rue Méchain (on the title page) and 42 Rue Eugène Carrière (for *La Folle d'Itteville*).
44 VMD, p. 143.

Eli Lotar, who came back into the picture 'from time to time' but hated Haumont, advised her to safely store her photos and glass plates at his place to prevent them from being seized. Germaine made prints of her best photos of France, 'about eighty photos, some of the finest', that she kept 'as evidence of my work'.[46] She also tried to sell 'the hundreds of film shots representing all my collections of French landscapes' to an agency, but 'nobody wanted to buy them'. Again, there was a car-shaped consolation: in the meantime, she had swapped her Peugeot for an 'astonishing Citroën with wooden coachwork, a bit flashy and rather large. I was happy.' She left the apartment on Boulevard Saint Michel, where Jacques had not finished paying for the bathroom, and took refuge with wealthy Argentinean friends in Monfort-l'Amaury, with her cats, in a small independent house (this chapter of her memoirs is titled 'Flight'). She had chosen 'the worst solution'.[47] Eli Lotar was living with Lala, her mother and her young daughter. Joris had come back from China and wanted her to join him in Spain. She set out but, on reaching Marseille, decided to say and join Isa de Comminges, Renaud de Jouvenel's mother, in Saint-Tropez, where she witnessed the reconciliation between Colette and Isa, the two rivals.

Krull settled in Cannes, where she found a studio. She got to know Germaine and Francis Picabia. The publishers Plon wanted her to do a 'Marseille' book. She returned to Paris, became aware of Hitler's atrocities and realised that 'war was at the door'.[48] She wanted to work out a divorce with Joris.

As it turned out, Plon did produce 'a very fine book, "Marseille", which gave me a bit of dough.' It may even be Krull's most satisfying photography book, crowning her published work. Part of the same series as the 1934 *Paris vu par André Kertész*, and produced just a little later, in February 1935, the book had the same design – we can assume that it was inspired by the Kertész[49] – and enjoyed all kinds of graphic advantages: a very balanced, almost constructivist layout, spreads, bluish-black photogravure and discreetly placed texts by André Suarès harmoniously positioned on the page.[50] The contents, taken from previous reportage work, notably from 1929, included views of the transporter bridge, or from the apron of the bridge where a restaurant had been installed, at a height of fifty metres,[51] which have been considered Krull's most representative work ever since, plus views of the docks with the cranes and boats, and of their narrow streets with their markets, tramps, cafés and street vendors. There was only one view of the 'tumult of the Canebière', possibly taken from a bus. This, Krull's most accomplished book, appeared just when she could see no future for her activity as a photographer, rivalled as she now was by the many 'youngsters' who were more in tune with the fast-moving developments of the medium in the 1930s. Only four years after the creation of *VU*, Krull was already disconnected from this dynamism and the excitement surrounding it. Kertész, Lotar and others were in the same situation, forced to find a more stable but not independent form of work, for press or advertising agencies or publishers.

END OF THE DREAM: MONTE-CARLO

In summer 1935 Germaine Krull moved to Monte-Carlo. In November she was living at 4 Rue des Violettes, which was the address on the rubber stamp she now used. She was first taken on by the casino in Monte-Carlo as a photographer for its weekly magazine. Like the adjoining opera house, it was built in around 1880 by Charles Garnier. Germaine may well have felt ill at ease in such a powerful structure and with its high society clientele, but at least it was work: 'I have found a job at the casino in Monte-Carlo,' which 'consists in photographing the well-known figures who come to lose their money here', and also the theatre and ballet seasons. The Ballets Russes of Monte-Carlo performed at the opera, directed by René Blum (brother of the future French president Léon), whom Germaine photographed. Although she lost her job in 1937, she still

45 See the chapter 'Reportage and Magazines'.
46 VMD, p. 144. In CEDG, p. 74, she says that she left the negatives with the parents of Lotar's girlfriend: 'large plates, 18 x 24, about two hundred boxes'.
47 VMD, p. 145.
48 VMD, p. 146.
49 As André Kertész designed the layout of *Death in the Making* by Robert Capa in New York in 1936, it is very possible that he inspired or executed this layout, which in fact derives from the presentation of his postcards in 1927–1930.
50 *Marseille par Germaine Krull*, text by André Suarès, Paris: Éditions d'Histoire et d'Art, Librairie Plon, 1935. Jeanne Laffitte's 'reprint' was not at all in keeping with the original.
51 *Le Pont transbordeur et la vision moderniste*, (Musée Cantini, Marseille), Marseille and Paris: Musées de Marseille, Réunion des Musées Nationaux, 1991; Bon, Lugon and Simay, op. cit.

published one more book, on the Monte-Carlo Ballet. The halftone printing was faulty, but the cover at least featured a drawing by Matisse.[52]

She now tried to set up an independent 'applied photography' business with a view to doing press and fashion photography, industrial photos, portraits and books, and even giving photography lessons.[53] She was, in fact, becoming an independent and 'local' press photographer. We can judge Krull's work at this time from a set of 283 photos from her Monte-Carlo period, curated and exhibited recently in Montreal by Kim Sichel,[54] and from a number of the photographs in the Christian Bouqueret collection, now at the Musée National d'Art Moderne. The subjects in the first ensemble represent the standard material of a photographer covering local events: 'sports, motor racing, gambling, ballet, figures from the arts, film stars, musicians, everyday life',[55] receptions, the Ballets Russes (Serge Lifar in *L'Après-midi d'un faune*), the Monaco Grand Prix – back to the motor car, once again. Although a member of the Black Star agency in New York, she found few outlets.[56] She turned to her friends Max (Horkheimer) and Fritz (Pollock), no doubt to ask for financial help. Max sent her monthly payments. As for Walter Benjamin, who was in Paris, we know from the letters she wrote to him in 1937–38 that she asked him to approach one Gaston Cohen with a view to publishing a 'very long novel' she had written, 'that in fact is my life' – this was *Chien fou* – and that had already been turned down by Gallimard (Malraux), Le Sagittaire and Grasset.[57]

We know that 'for the Monte-Carlo pavilion' at the 1937 Exposition Universelle in Paris she produced 'big photomontages 5 to 6 metres long' about the regattas of Monte-Carlo, the Monaco Grand Prix and another about tennis. 'This was the last piece of work I did before the war.' After the declaration of hostilities, she lived at the home of her friend Maurice Privat (1889–1949), 'one of the first speakers on the news from the Eiffel Tower. I met him at *VU* where he explained to Vogel, and to us all, the importance and reality of astrology.'[58] Privat was the author of *L'Astrologie scientifique à la portée de tous* (1936), but in 1939 he gave a very sizeable hostage to fortune with a book of predictions describing 1940 as 'the Year of French Grandeur'. Germaine gave his son, Jean, photography lessons and 'learned to do astrology', which interested here greatly. Soon, she said, she was able 'to do the themes for a given year'.[59]

52 Germaine Krull, *Ballets de Monte-Carlo*, cover by Matisse, Nice: Marcel Roche, 1937.
53 'Projet de Germaine Krull pour la réalisation d'une affaire commerciale', typescript, Archives Folkwang Museum, Essen.
54 Kim Sichel, *Germaine Krull à Monte-Carlo, The Monte Carlo Years* (Montreal Museum of Fine Arts, 2006–2007), Montreal: Montreal Museum of Fine Arts, 2006.
55 Ibid., p. 10.
56 Publicity material indicates that she was a France Presse correspondent for *L'Intransigeant* and *Le Petit Niçois* (ibid., p. 13).
57 Nathalie Raoux, 'Walter Benjamin, Gisèle Freund, Germaine Krull et Hélène Léger. Deutschland-Frankreich; Mann-Weib. Eine Folge von Briefen', *Revue germanique internationale*, 5, 1996, http://rgi.revues.org/570
58 CEDG, p. 77. 'Interpretations of the horoscope were generally done by his wife, Loulou Privat.'
59 VMD, p. 147.

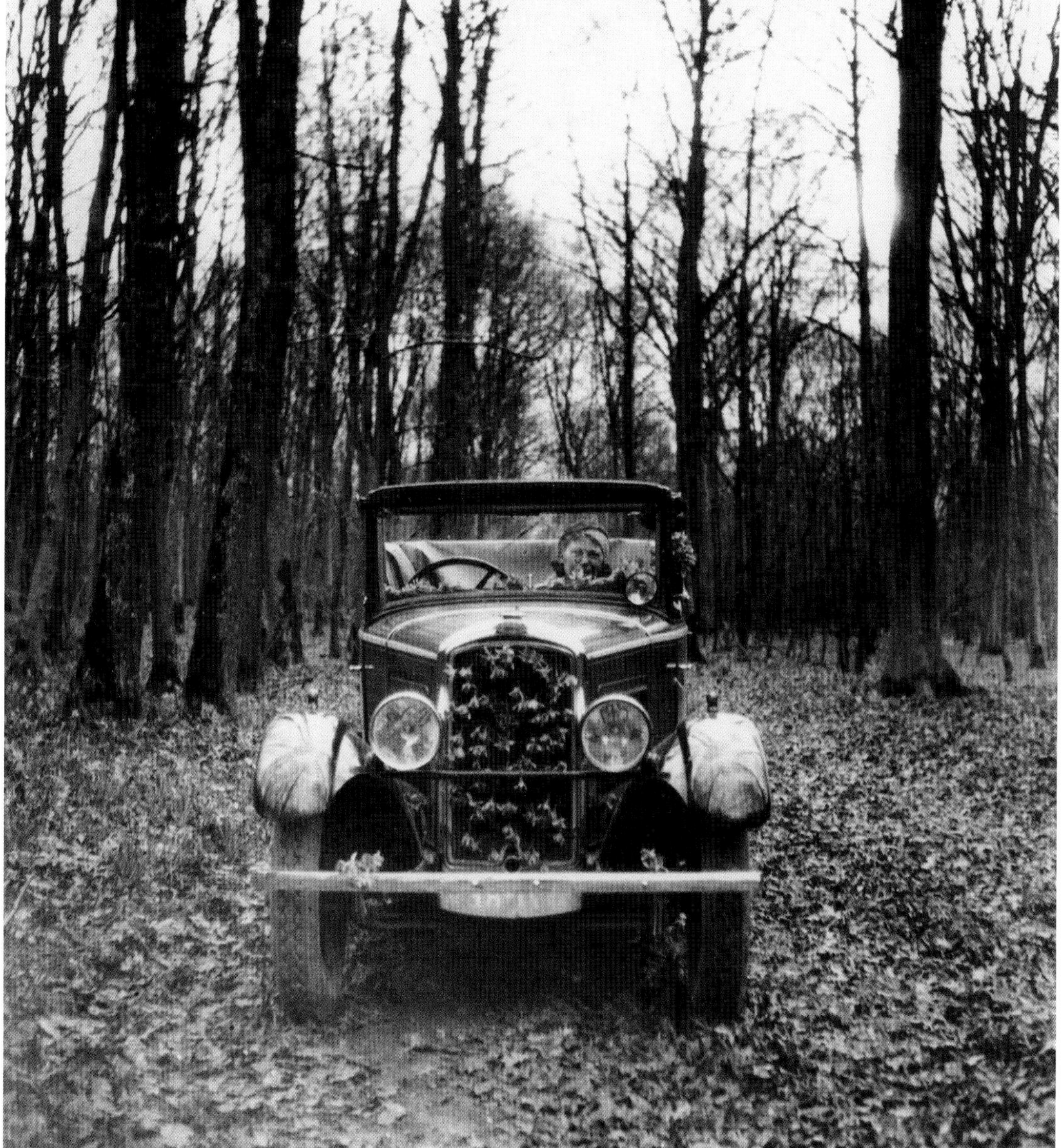

Germaine Krull in Her Peugeot at Fontainebleau, c. 1929

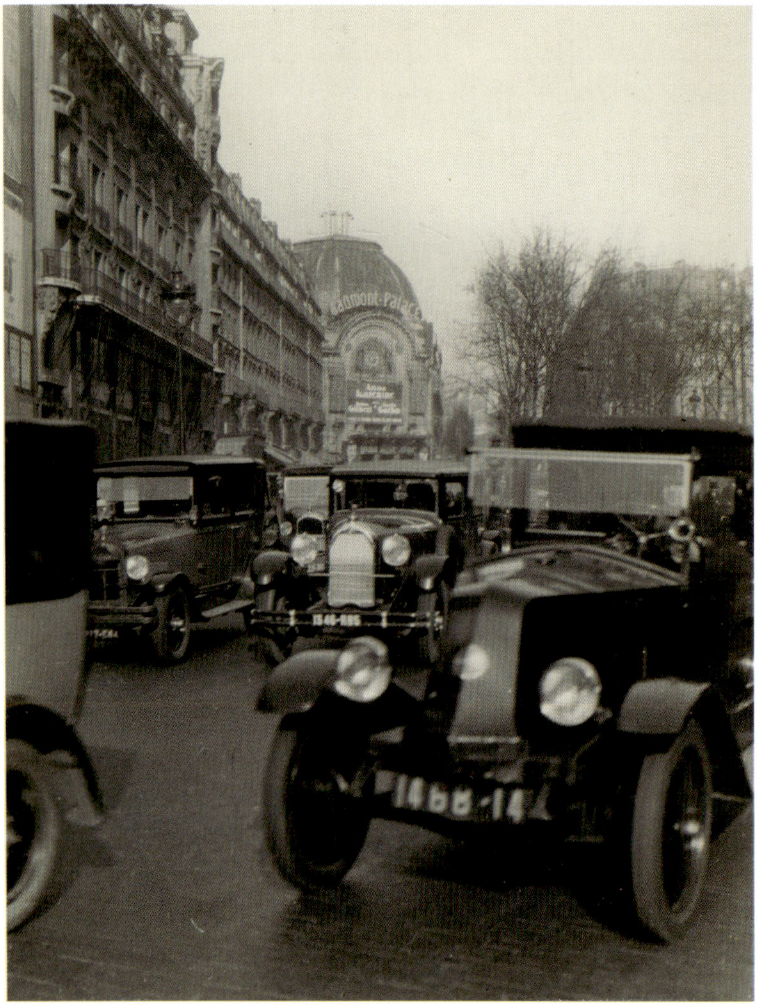

Place Clichy, 1928

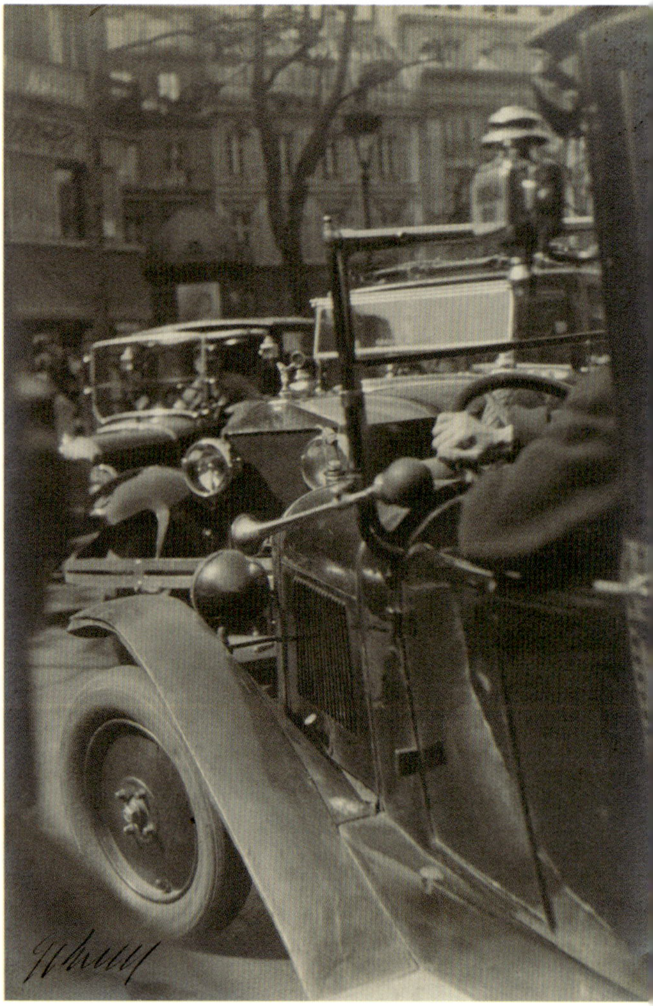

'Traffic in Paris', 1926

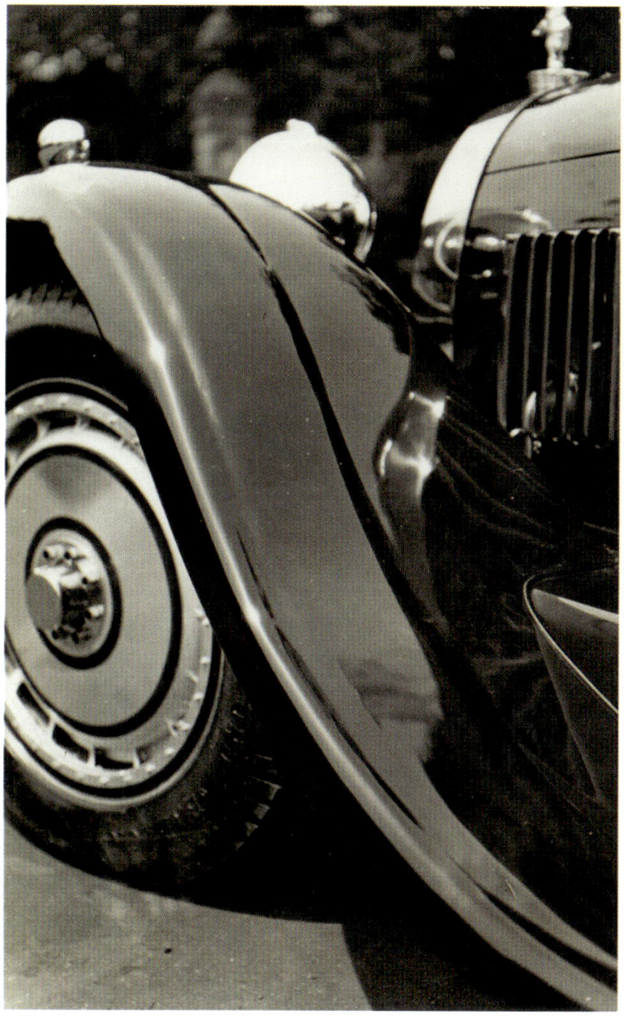

'Bugatti', c. 1928

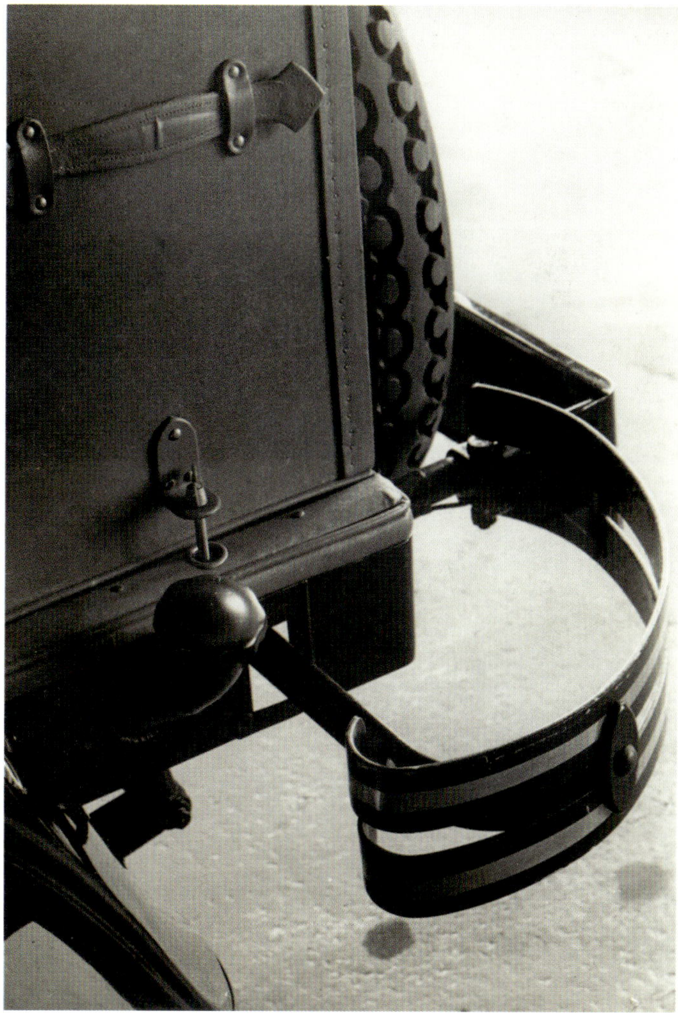

The Bumper, c. 1928

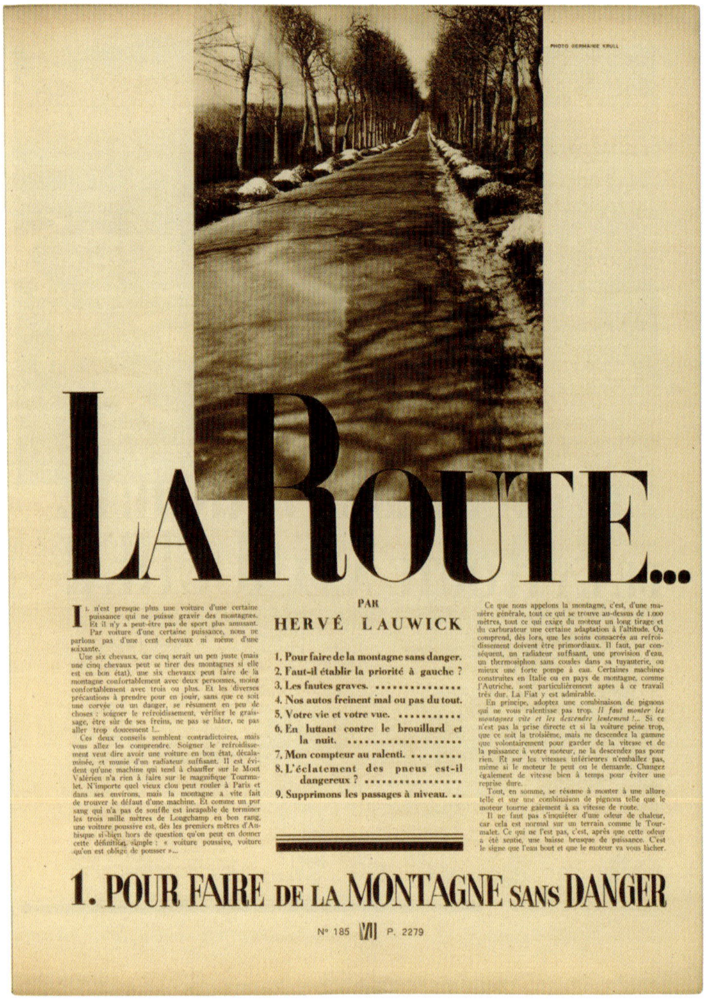

PHOTO GERMAINE KRULL

LA ROUTE...

PAR

HERVÉ LAUWICK

Il n'est presque plus une voiture d'une certaine puissance qui ne puisse gravir des montagnes. Et il n'y a peut-être pas de sport plus amusant.

Par voiture d'une certaine puissance, nous ne parlons pas d'une cent chevaux ni même d'une soixante.

Une six chevaux, car cinq serait un peu juste (mais une cinq chevaux peut se tirer des montagnes si elle est en bon état), une six chevaux peut faire de la montagne confortablement avec deux personnes, moins confortablement avec trois ou plus. Et les diverses précautions à prendre pour en jouir, sans que ce soit une corvée ou un danger, se résument en peu de choses : soigner le refroidissement, vérifier le graissage, être sûr de ses freins, ne pas se hâter, ne pas aller trop doucement !...

Ces deux conseils semblent contradictoires, mais vous allez les comprendre. Soigner le refroidissement veut dire avoir une voiture en bon état, décalaminée, et munie d'un radiateur suffisant. Il est évident qu'une machine qui tend à chauffer sur le Mont Valérien n'a rien à faire sur le magnifique Tourmalet. N'importe quel vieux clou peut rouler à Paris et dans ses environs, mais la montagne a vite fait de trouver le défaut d'une machine. Et comme un pur sang qui n'a pas de souffle est incapable de terminer les trois mille mètres de Longchamp en bon rang, une voiture poussive est, dès les premiers mètres d'Aubisque si bien hors de question qu'on peut en donner cette définition simple : « voiture poussive, voiture qu'on est obligé de pousser »...

1. Pour faire de la montagne sans danger.
2. Faut-il établir la priorité à gauche ?
3. Les fautes graves. ....
4. Nos autos freinent mal ou pas du tout.
5. Votre vie et votre vue. ....
6. En luttant contre le brouillard et la nuit. ....
7. Mon compteur au ralenti. ....
8. L'éclatement des pneus est-il dangereux ? ....
9. Supprimons les passages à niveau. ..

Ce que nous appelons la montagne, c'est, d'une manière générale, tout ce qui se trouve au-dessus de 1.000 mètres, tout ce qui exige du moteur un long tirage et du carburateur une certaine adaptation à l'altitude. On comprend, dès lors, que les soins consacrés au refroidissement doivent être primordiaux. Il faut, par conséquent, un radiateur suffisant, une provision d'eau, un thermosiphon sans coudes dans sa tuyauterie, ou mieux une forte pompe à eau. Certaines machines construites en Italie ou en pays de montagne, comme l'Autriche, sont particulièrement aptes à ce travail très dur. La Fiat y est admirable.

En principe, adoptez une combinaison de pignons qui ne vous ralentisse pas trop. *Il faut monter les montagnes vite et les descendre lentement !*... Si ce n'est pas la prise directe et si la voiture peine trop, que ce soit la troisième, mais ne descendez la gamme que volontairement pour garder de la vitesse et de la puissance à votre moteur, ne la descendez pas pour rien. Et sur les vitesses inférieures n'emballez pas, même si le moteur le peut ou le demande. Changez également de vitesse bien à temps pour éviter une reprise dure.

Tout, en somme, se résume à monter à une allure telle et sur une combinaison de pignons telle que le moteur tourne gaîment à sa vitesse de route.

Il ne faut pas s'inquiéter d'une odeur de chaleur, car cela est normal sur un terrain comme le Tourmalet. Ce qui ne l'est pas, c'est, après que cette odeur a été sentie, une baisse brusque de puissance. C'est le signe que l'eau bout et que le moteur va vous lâcher.

1. POUR FAIRE DE LA MONTAGNE SANS DANGER

Nº 185 VU P. 2279

'The Road . . .', *VU*, no. 185, 30 September 1931, p. 2279

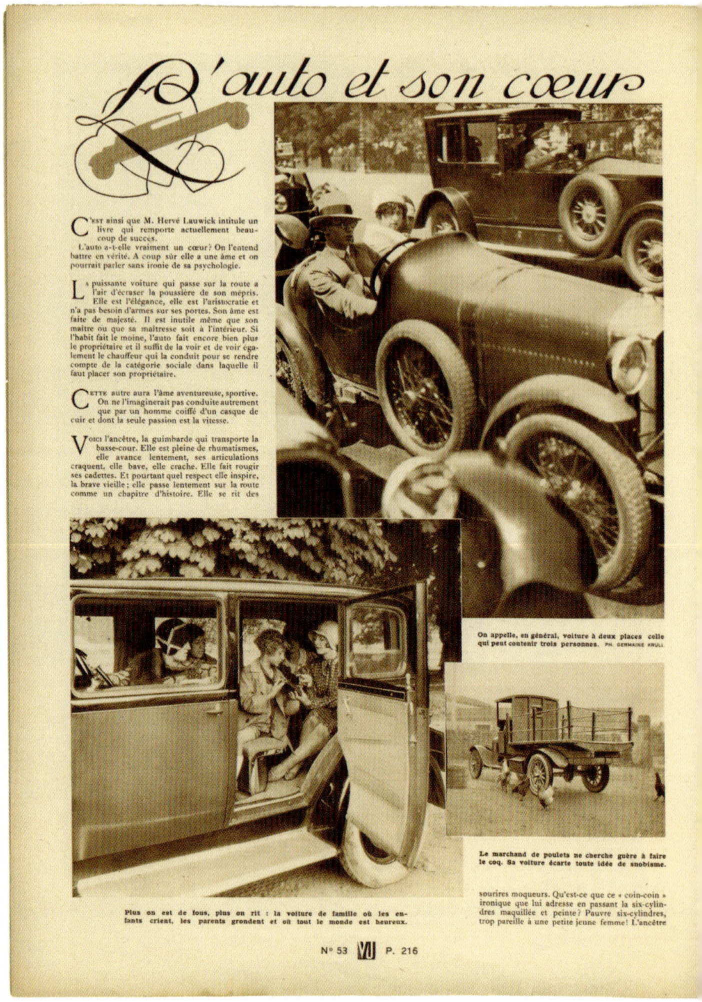

L'auto et son cœur

C'est ainsi que M. Hervé Lauwick intitule un livre qui remporte actuellement beaucoup de succès.

L'auto a-t-elle vraiment un cœur? On l'entend battre en vérité. A coup sûr elle a une âme et on pourrait parler sans ironie de sa psychologie.

La puissante voiture qui passe sur la route a l'air d'écraser la poussière de son mépris. Elle est l'élégance, elle est l'aristocratie et n'a pas besoin d'armes sur ses portes. Son âme est faite de majesté. Il est inutile même que son maître ou que sa maîtresse soit à l'intérieur. Si l'habit fait le moine, l'auto fait encore bien plus le propriétaire et il suffit de la voir et de voir également le chauffeur qui la conduit pour se rendre compte de la catégorie sociale dans laquelle il faut placer son propriétaire.

Cette autre aura l'âme aventureuse, sportive. On ne l'imaginerait pas conduite autrement que par un homme coiffé d'un casque de cuir et dont la seule passion est la vitesse.

Voici l'ancêtre, la guimbarde qui transporte la basse-cour. Elle est pleine de rhumatismes, elle avance lentement, ses articulations craquent, elle bave, elle crache. Elle fait rougir ses cadettes. Et pourtant quel respect elle inspire, la brave vieille ; elle passe lentement sur la route comme un chapitre d'histoire. Elle se rit des sourires moqueurs. Qu'est-ce que ce « coin-coin » ironique que lui adresse en passant la six-cylindres maquillée et peinte? Pauvre six-cylindres, trop pareille à une petite jeune femme! L'ancêtre

On appelle, en général, voiture à deux places celle qui peut contenir trois personnes. PH. GERMAINE KRULL

Le marchand de poulets ne cherche guère à faire le coq. Sa voiture écarte toute idée de snobisme.

Plus on est de fous, plus on rit : la voiture de famille où les enfants crient, les parents grondent et où tout le monde est heureux.

Nº 53 VU P. 216

'The Car at Heart', *VU*, no. 53, 20 March 1929,
Peugeot advertising pull-out, **'La 201'**, 1929 (facing page)

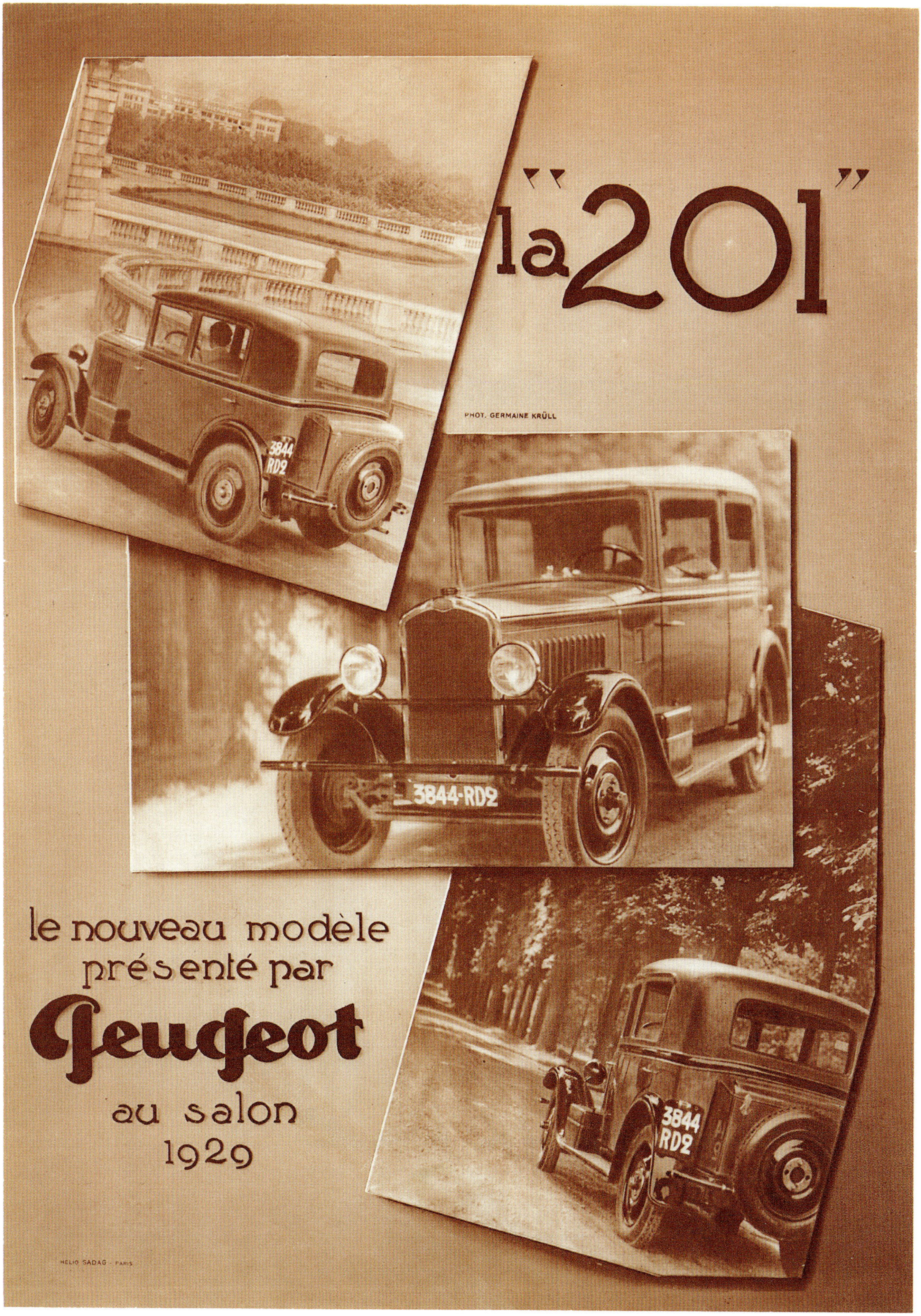
"la 201"
PHOT. GERMAINE KRÜLL
3844 RD2
3844-RD2
3844 RD2
le nouveau modèle
présenté par
Peugeot
au salon
1929
HELIO SADAG - PARIS

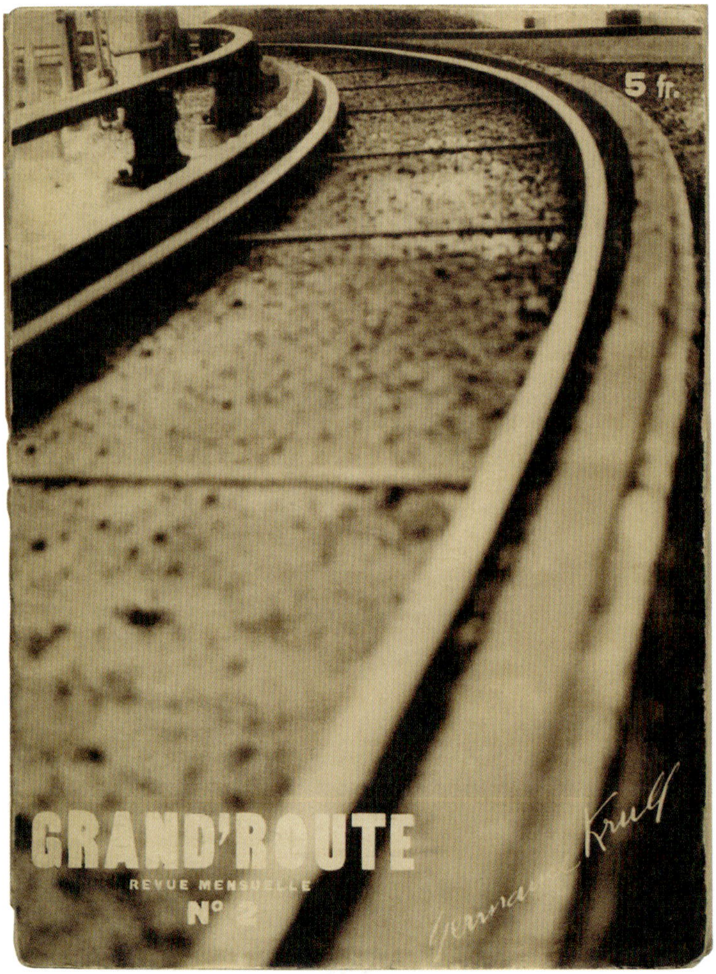

Grand'Route, no. 2, April 1930, cover

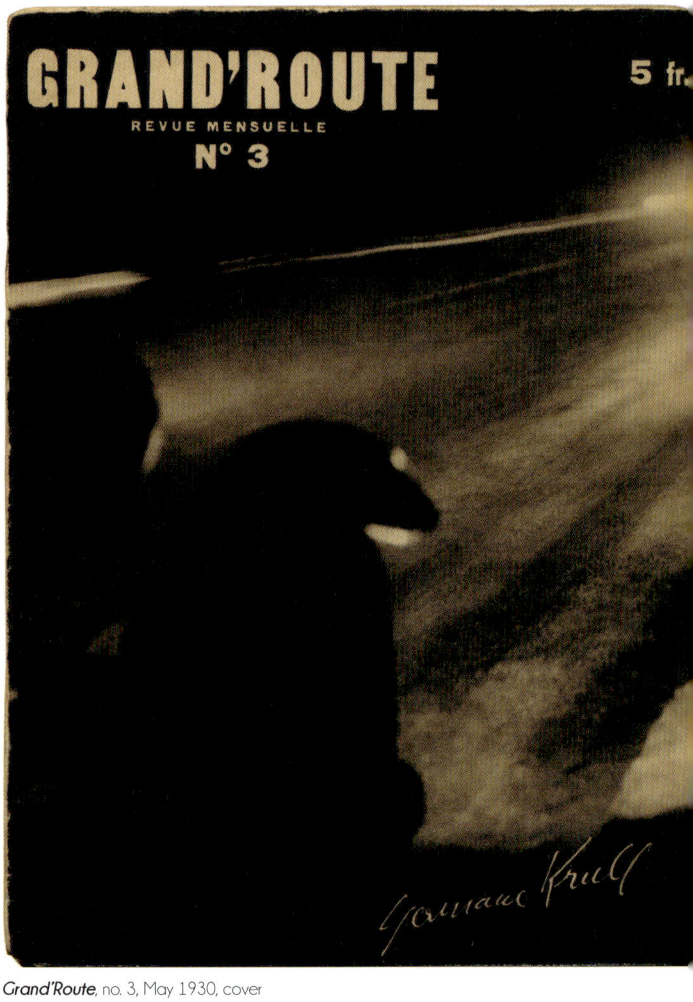

Grand'Route, no. 3, May 1930, cover

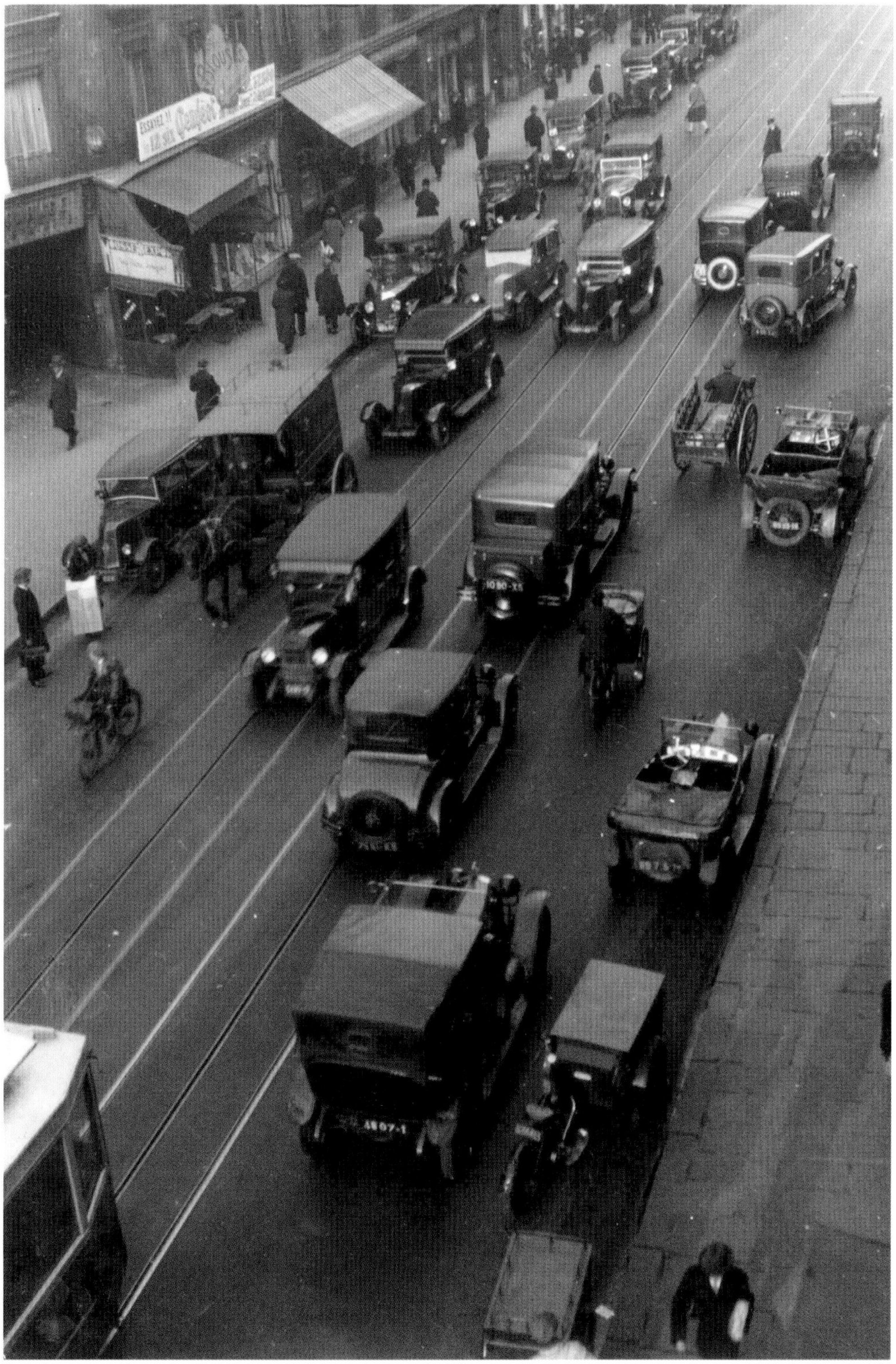

Paris, Street Seen from Above, 1928

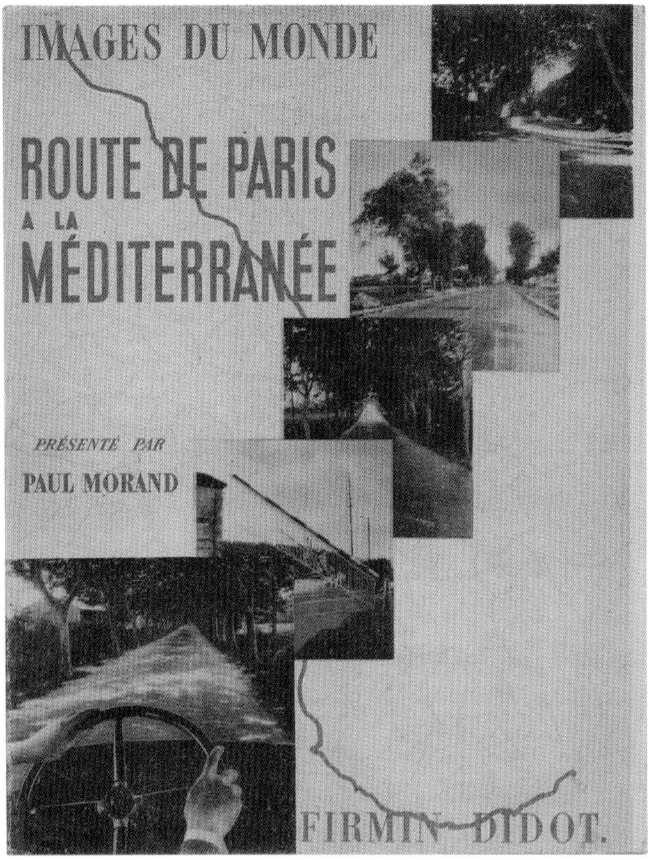

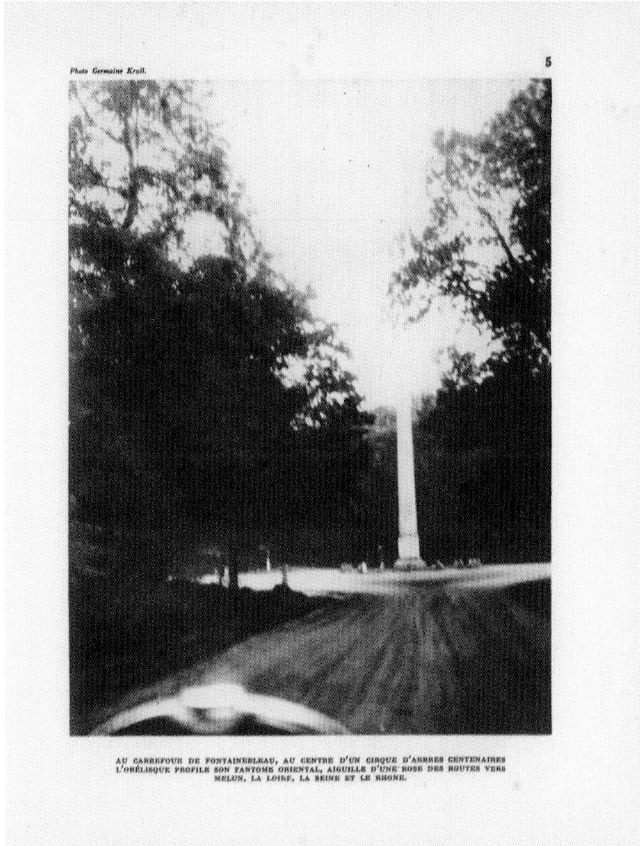
Photo Germaine Krull. 5

AU CARREFOUR DE FONTAINEBLEAU, AU CENTRE D'UN CIRQUE D'ARBRES CENTENAIRES L'OBÉLISQUE PROFILE SON FANTOME ORIENTAL, AIGUILLE D'UNE ROSE DES ROUTES VERS MELUN, LA LOIRE, LA SEINE ET LE RHONE.

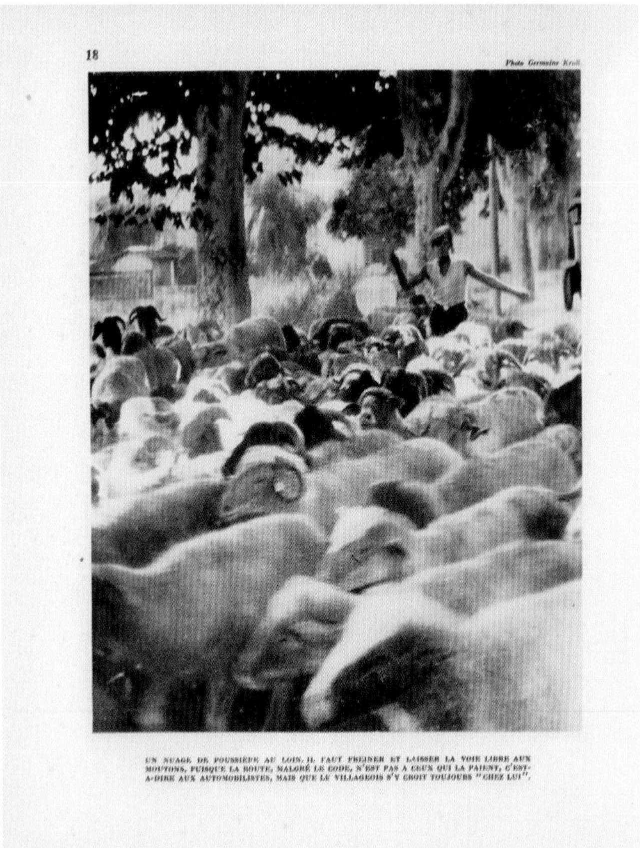
18 Photo Germaine Krull.

UN NUAGE DE POUSSIÈRE AU LOIN. IL FAUT FREINER ET LAISSER LA VOIE LIBRE AUX MOUTONS, PUISQUE LA ROUTE, MALGRÉ LE CODE, N'EST PAS A CEUX QUI LA PAIENT, C'EST-A-DIRE AUX AUTOMOBILISTES, MAIS QUE LE VILLAGEOIS S'Y CROIT TOUJOURS "CHEZ LUI".

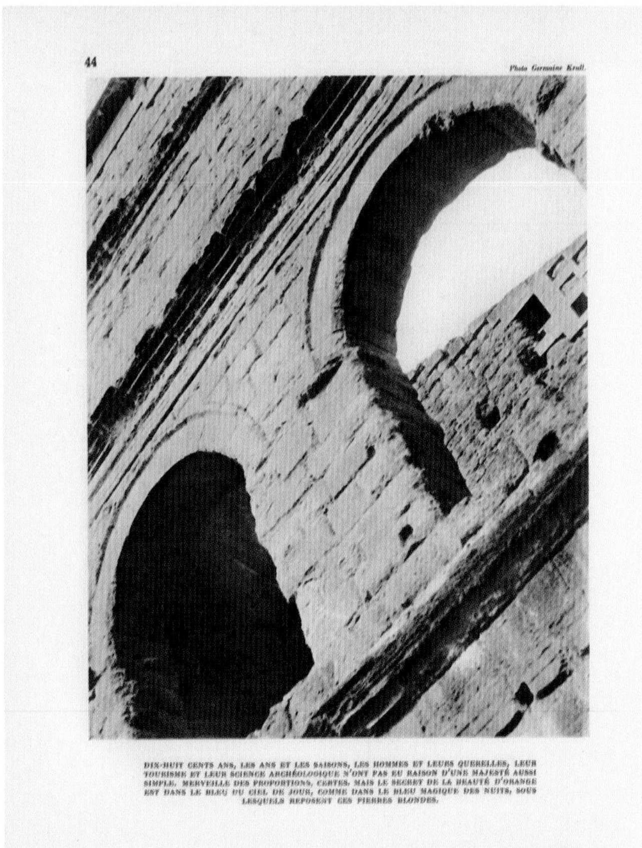
44 Photo Germaine Krull.

DIX-HUIT CENTS ANS, LES ANS ET LES SAISONS, LES HOMMES ET LEURS QUERELLES, LEUR TOURISME ET LEUR SCIENCE ARCHÉOLOGIQUE N'ONT PAS EU RAISON D'UNE MAJESTÉ AUSSI SIMPLE. MERVEILLE DES PROPORTIONS, CERTES, MAIS LE SECRET DE LA BEAUTÉ D'ORANGE EST DANS LE BLEU DU CIEL DE JOUR, COMME DANS LE BLEU MAGIQUE DES NUITS, SOUS LESQUELS REPOSENT CES PIERRES BLONDES.

Route de Paris à la Méditerranée, Paris, Firmin-Didot et Cie, 1931, cover, p. 5, 18, 44

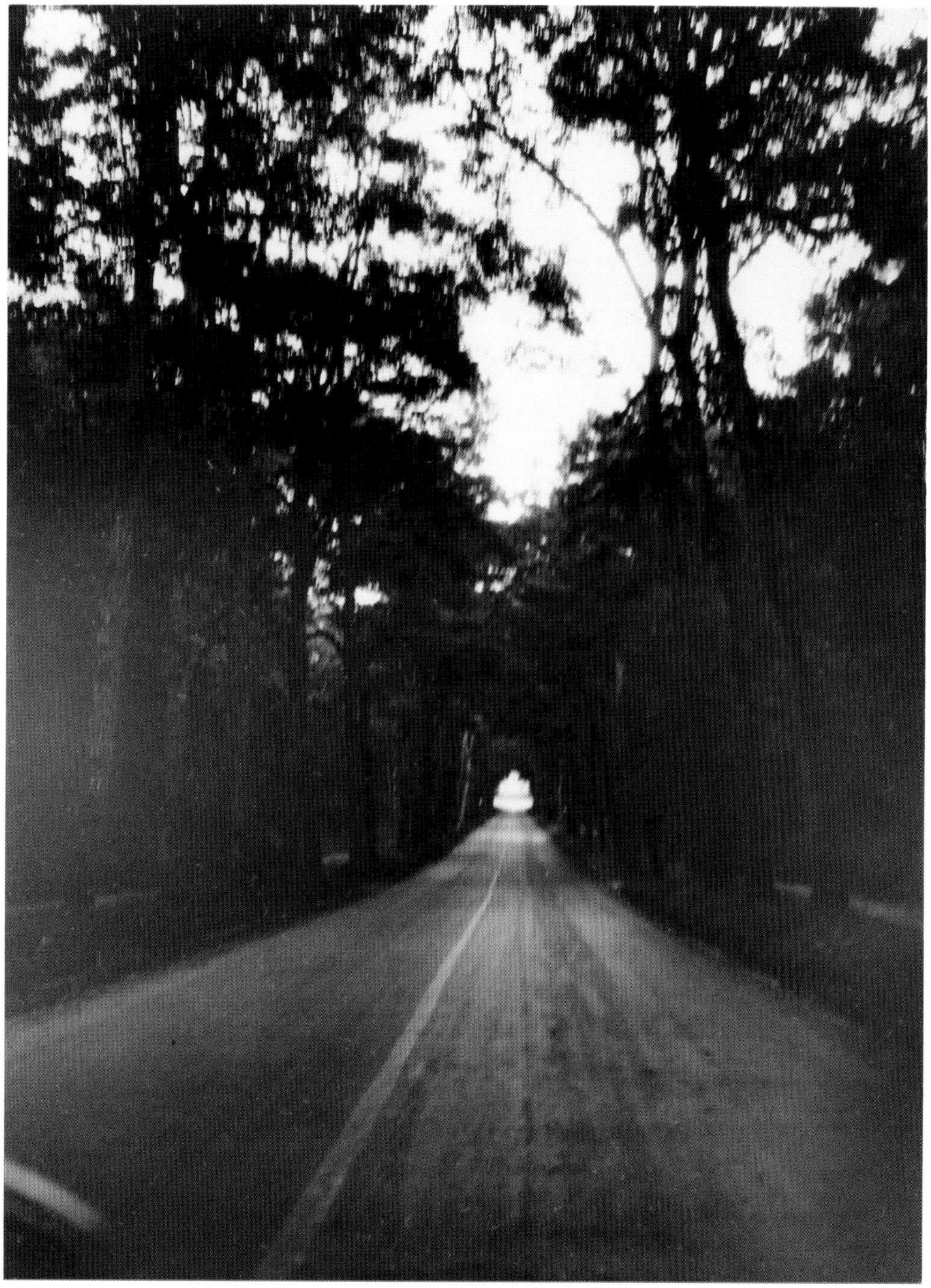

Road, c. 1930

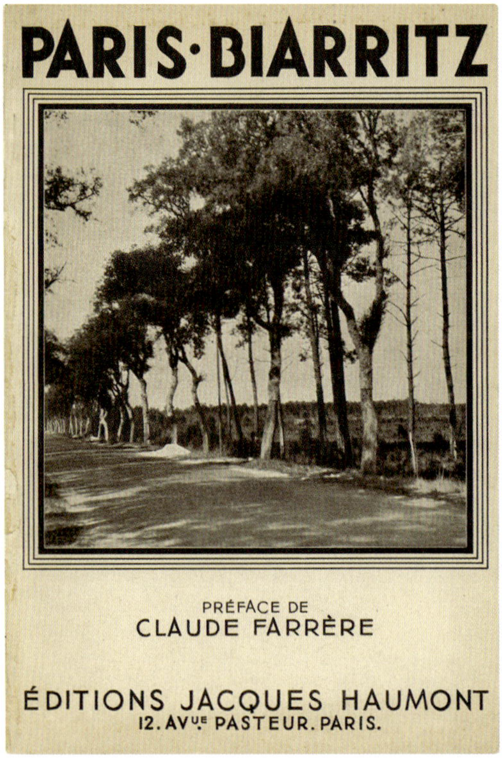
PARIS·BIARRITZ

PRÉFACE DE
CLAUDE FARRÈRE

ÉDITIONS JACQUES HAUMONT
12. AV^UE PASTEUR. PARIS.

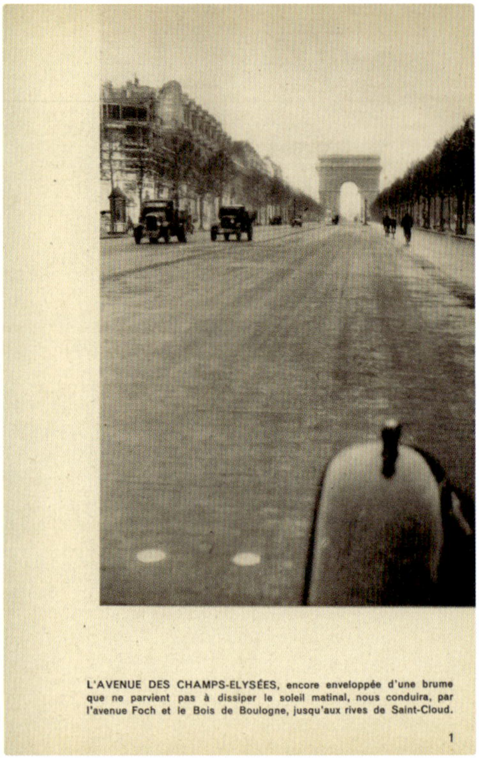
L'AVENUE DES CHAMPS-ELYSÉES, encore enveloppée d'une brume que ne parvient pas à dissiper le soleil matinal, nous conduira, par l'avenue Foch et le Bois de Boulogne, jusqu'aux rives de Saint-Cloud.

1

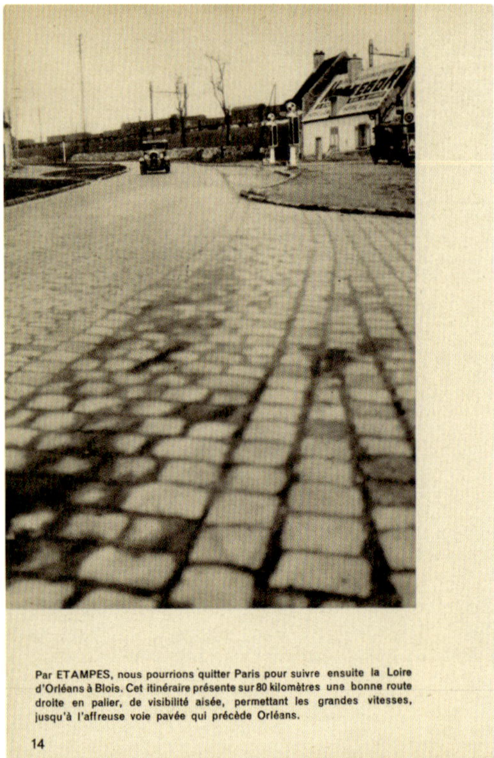
Par ETAMPES, nous pourrions quitter Paris pour suivre ensuite la Loire d'Orléans à Blois. Cet itinéraire présente sur 80 kilomètres une bonne route droite en palier, de visibilité aisée, permettant les grandes vitesses, jusqu'à l'affreuse voie pavée qui précède Orléans.

14

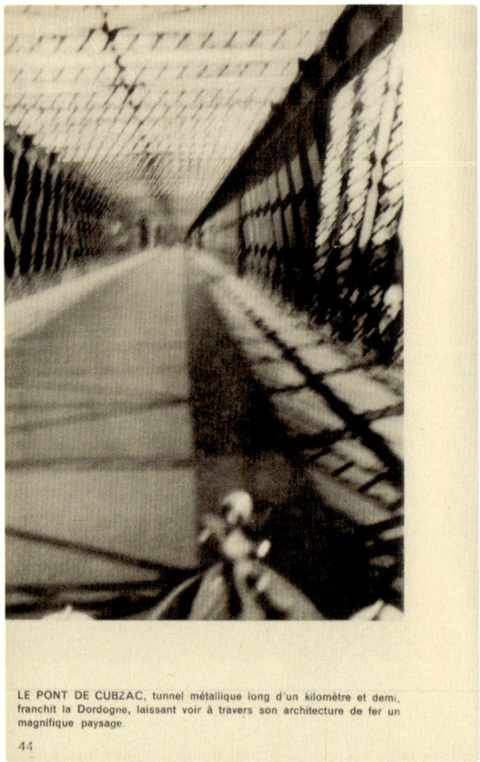
LE PONT DE CUBZAC, tunnel métallique long d'un kilomètre et demi, franchit la Dordogne, laissant voir à travers son architecture de fer un magnifique paysage.

44

La Route Paris–Biarritz, Éditions Jacques Haumont, Paris, 1931,
cover, pl. 1, pl. 14, pl. 44, pl. 22–23, pl. 86–87 (above and facing page)

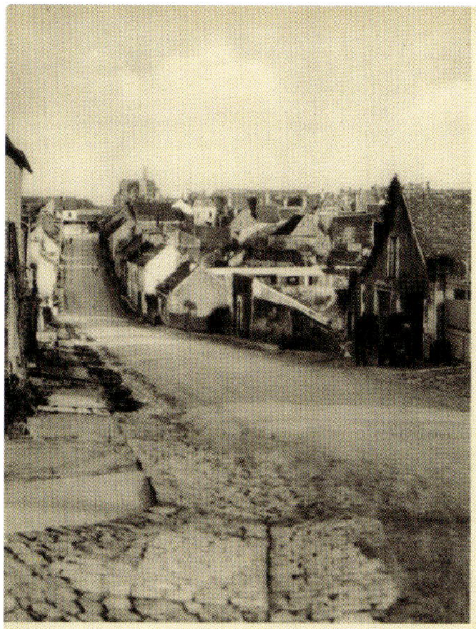

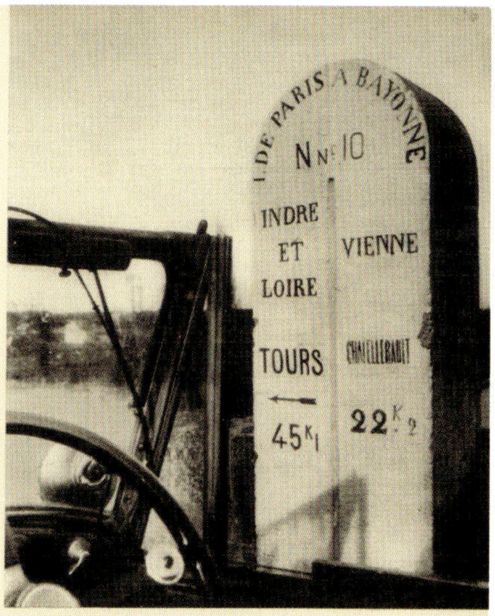

SAINTE-MAURE. Nombreuses sont les ressources archéologiques de cette région, où les sanctuaires romans et du gothique angevin se rencontrent partout. Le long même de la route, il existe des monuments mégalithiques, dolmens et menhirs. On trouve aussi dans ces parages des villages accrochés aux collines et des habitations troglodytes.

22

La route franchit la Creuse qui forme limite entre les départements d'Indre-et-Loire et de la Vienne.

23

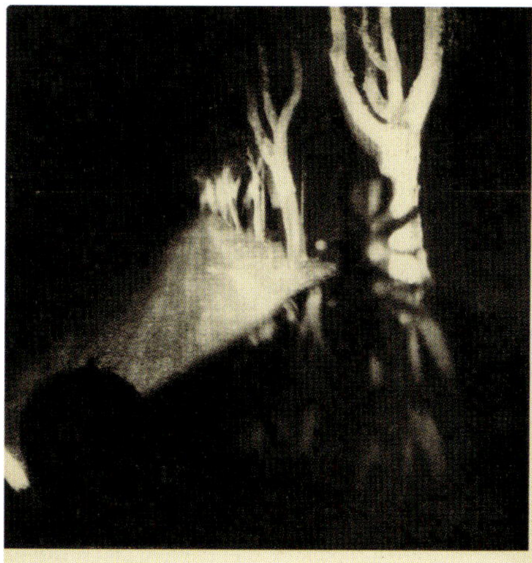

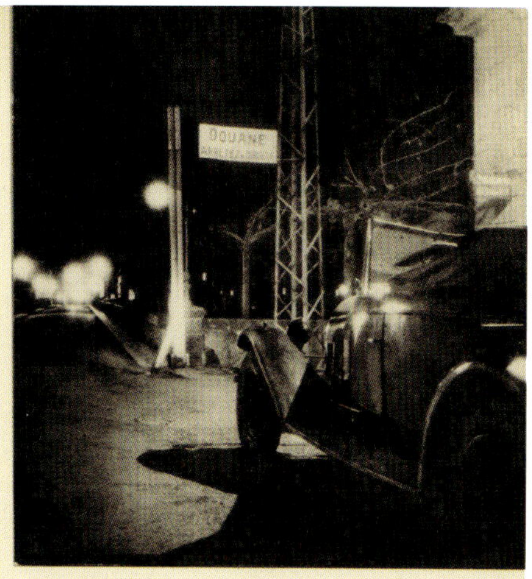

Dans le cercle de lumière des phares, les silhouettes des arbres ouvrent leurs bras devant nous, puis les referment après notre passage.

86

Voici le terme de notre voyage, et la halte pour la douane française de Béhobie. Devant nous, le Pont International sur la Bidassoa. Et, de l'autre côté, Irun et l'Espagne.

87

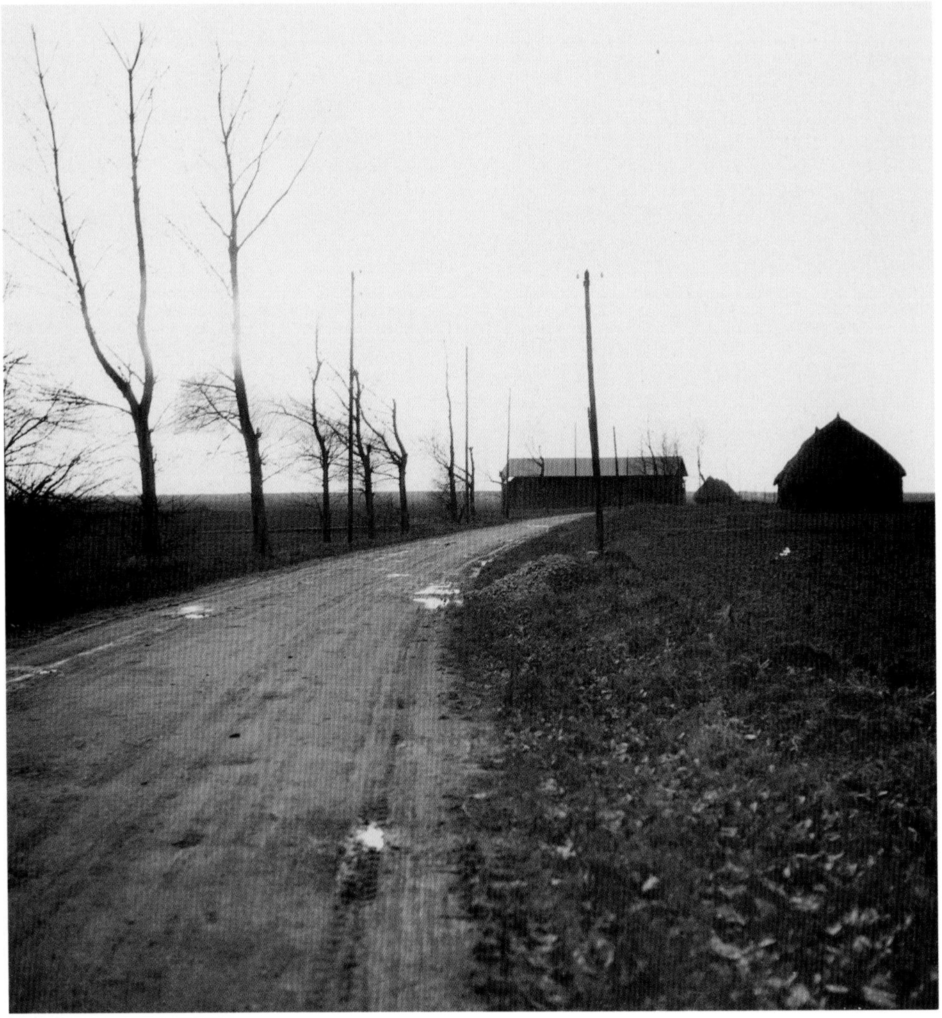

A Country Road, c. 1931

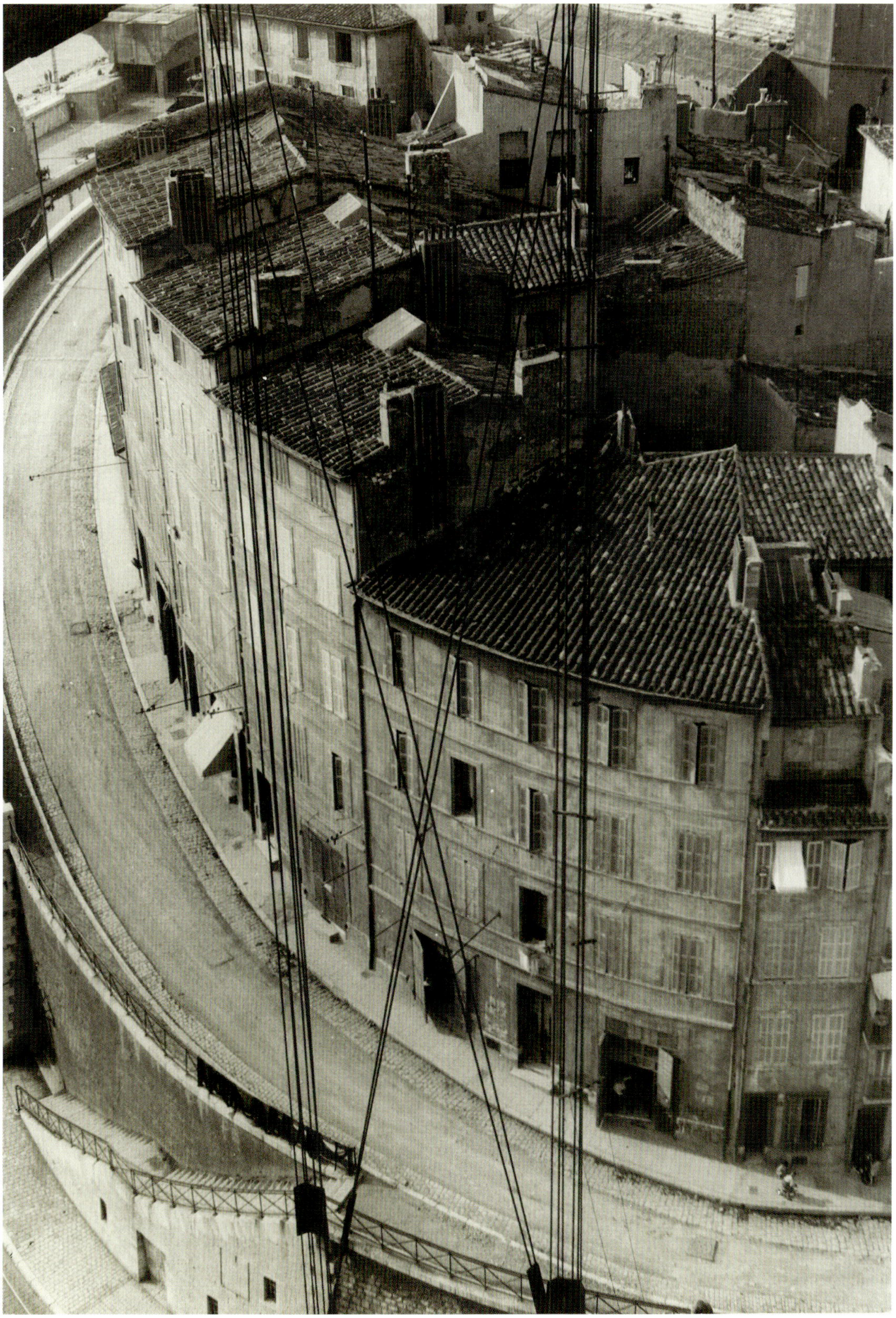

Marseille, June 1930

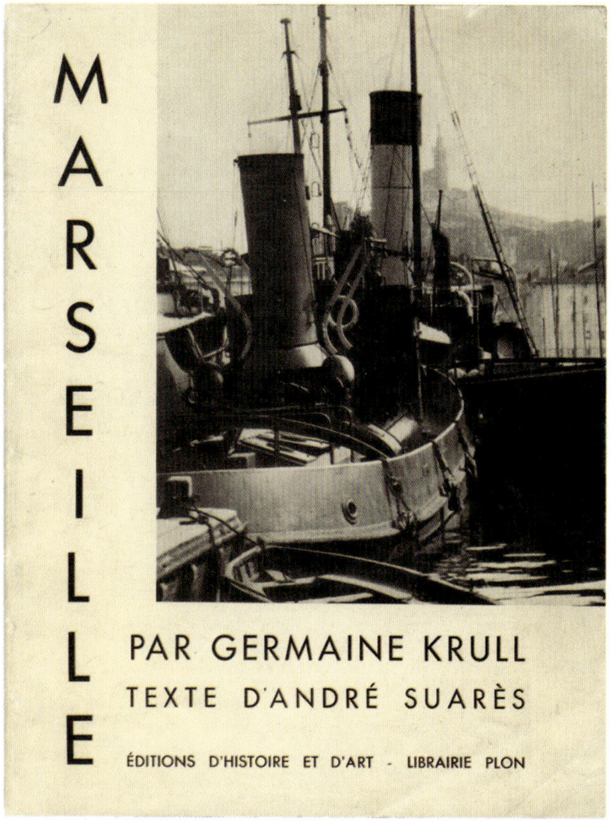

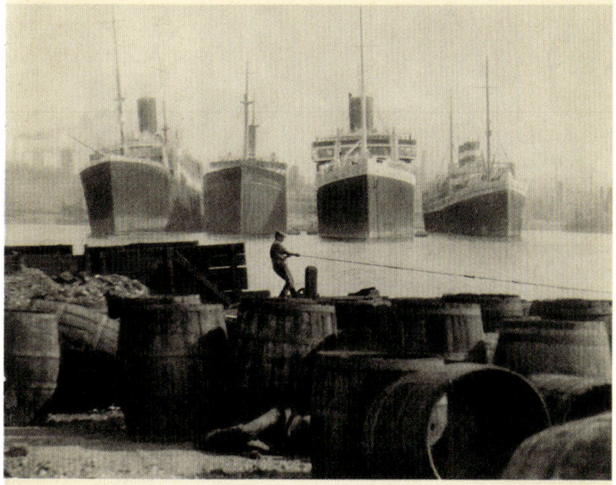

Sans emphase et sans clameur, le grand navire est l'abrégé de toute la science. Et tous les voyageurs le prennent pour une diligence.

Je rêve de partir et d'être ailleurs. Je suis femme, je suis homme. Je dis adieu.

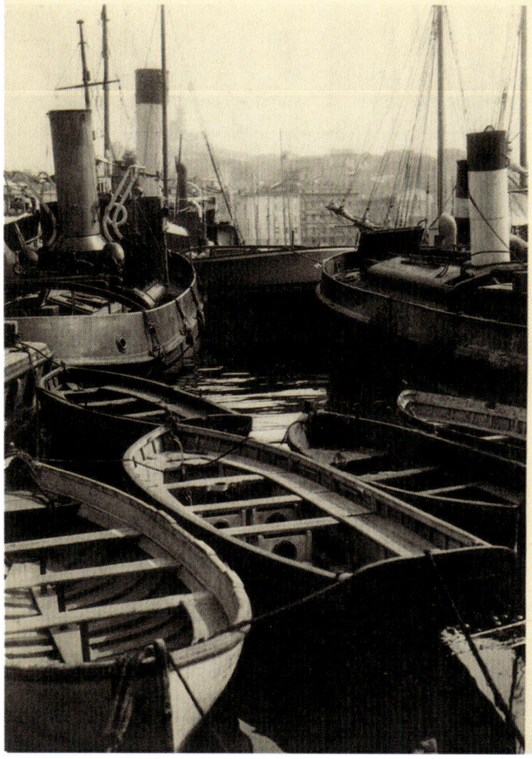

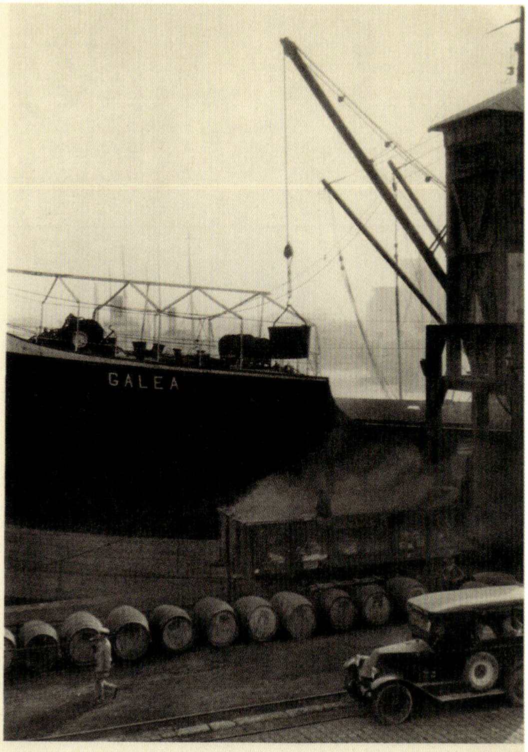

Les grues happent tout ce qu'elles touchent et l'enlèvent d'un coup; mais jamais elles ne peuvent l'avaler. Désespoir des Harpyes : elles regrettent l'Enfer.

Marseille par Germaine Krull, Éditions d'histoire et d'art, Librairie Plon, Paris, 1935, n. p. (above and facing page)

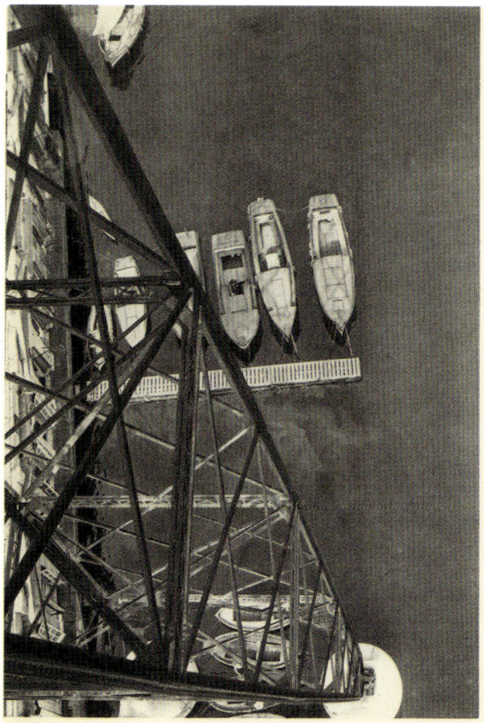

Marseille et Venise, même climat. Quand il neige à Saint-Marc, il neige sur la Bonne Mère. Ha! s'ils avaient eu, le long du Vieux Port, ces vrais Grecs, les Doges!

Voyage, rêve des imaginations lentes.
Rêve, voyage des imaginations ardentes.

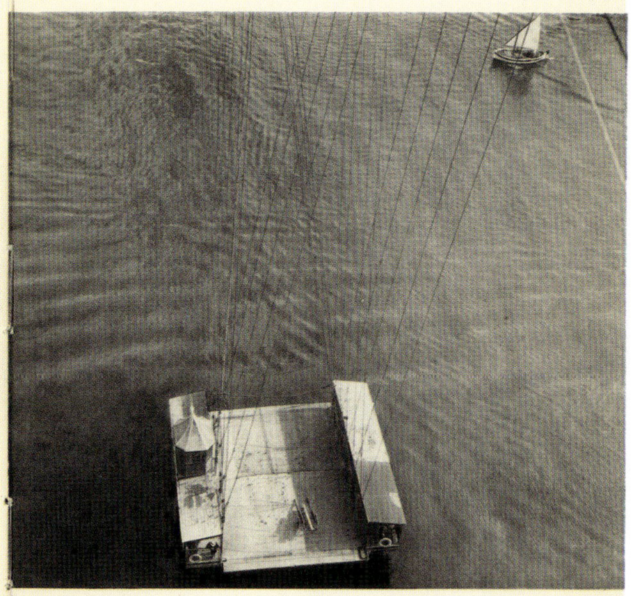

Le Berbère ou l'homme de Palma?
L'Ibère, à demi Carthaginois, des Baléares, vend tous les fruits à Marseille. Berger des oranges et pasteur des melons.

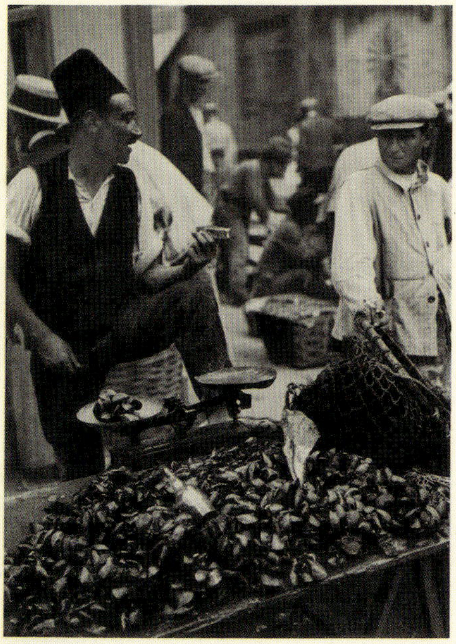

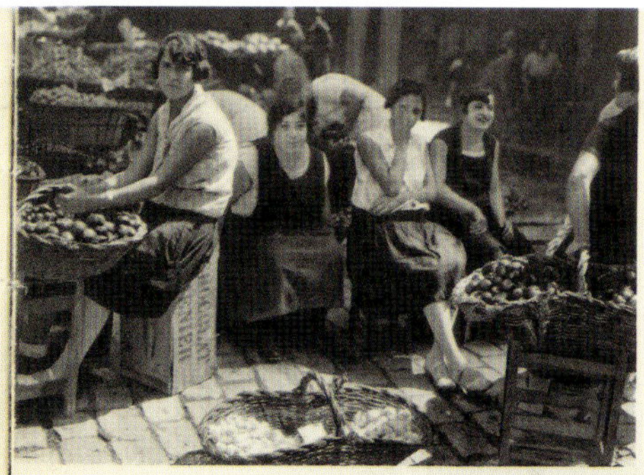

L'étal, tout fleuri de fruits rouges, luit dans l'ombre violette.

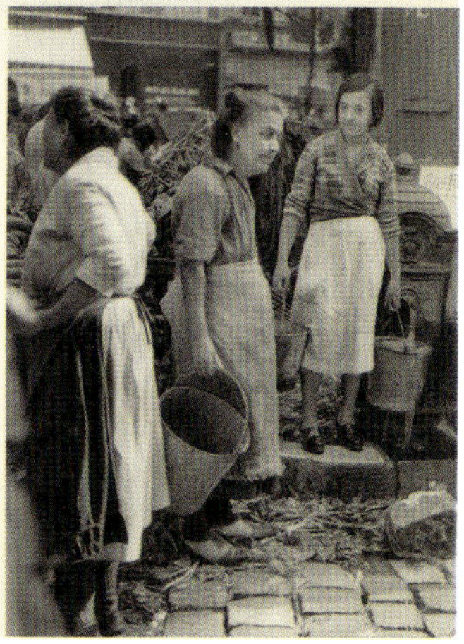

WOMEN

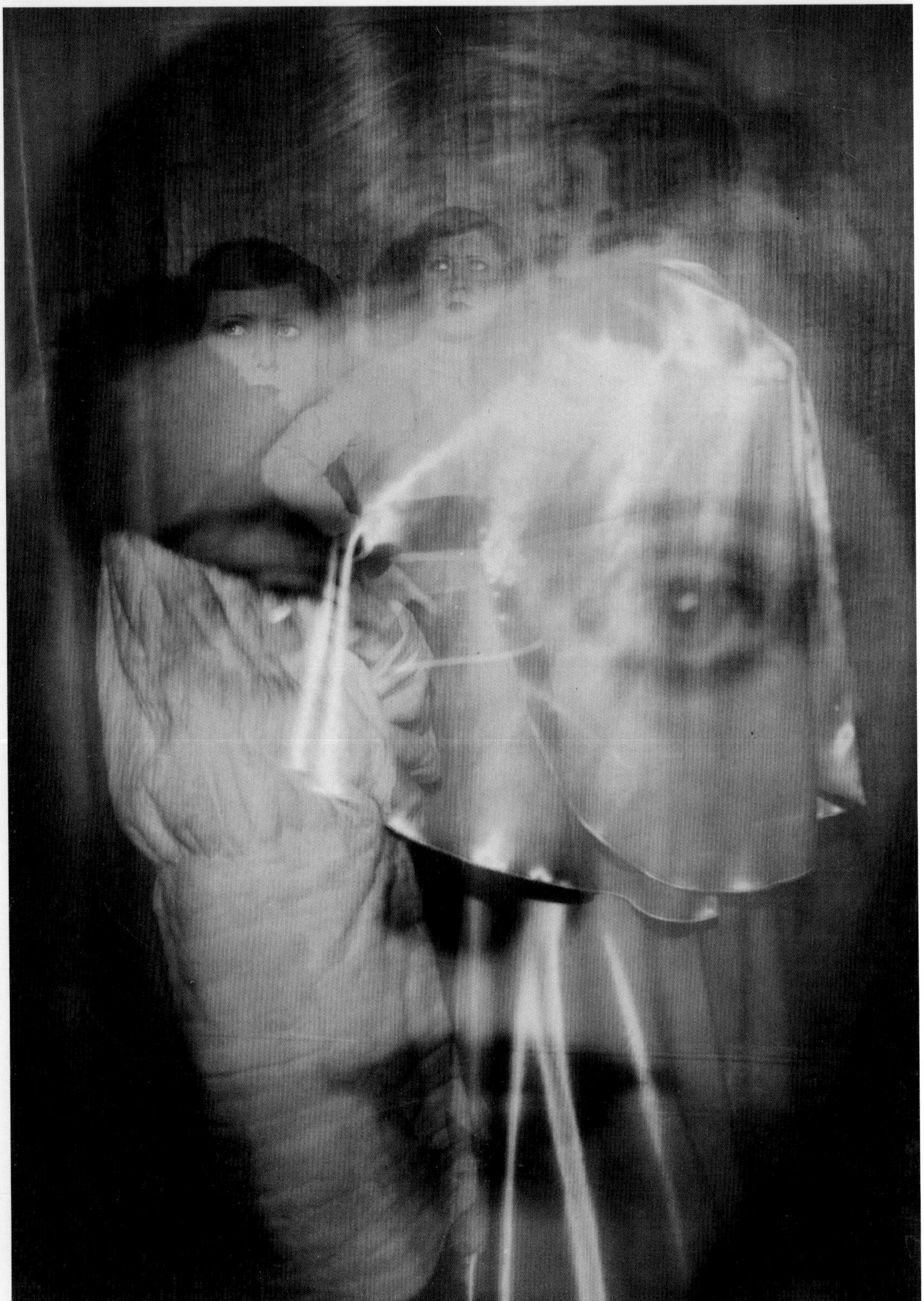

1 *Germaine Krull par Pierre Mac Orlan* with new photographs, Paris: NRF, Librairie Gallimard, 1931.
2 In addition to paintings, two of his rayographs were reproduced, 1924.

ALTHOUGH SHE IS STILL KNOWN as one of the 'women photographers' to have emerged in France and Germany in the 1920s, Germaine Krull remains a figure of mystery, an example of refusal to copy a model, such as that of the artist-photographer. One could, for example, enumerate the ways in which she differed from Florence Henri, Lucia Moholy, Aenne Biermann or Ilse Bing. For in Paris Krull was engaged in all kinds of photographic actions that seemed to be a response to her desire for emancipation (or simply autonomy) through photography. Whether her subject was Titaÿna or La Goulue, a tramp or Colette, she always had her own personal approach to 'woman', or 'women'. Few photographers are capable of such constancy and proximity, while remaining what Krull always claimed to be, a reporter. This was, of course, a long way from the work on the self and on the image undertaken by Claude Cahun at the same time. Krull remained within the register of her 'profession', which one could define as photographer and woman, and that was where she wanted to be. This certainly put her in a particular position, but at *VU*, for example, she never seemed to be overshadowed by her male colleagues (Kertész and Lotar, particularly), even though she was the only woman to publish so many photographs in this very open magazine.

WOMAN AND PHOTOGRAPHER

In early 1928, when she emerged onto the Parisian art scene, Krull was only just thirty. Evoking the comparison with Balzac's novel about *The Woman of Thirty*, Yvonne Sarcey wrote in *Annales politiques et littéraires* that 'The woman of thirty is the modern masterpiece.' Three years later, Krull had produced a good part of her 'modern work', and nearly everything worth keeping from 'a figure of the photographic avant-garde', given that the avant-garde is not made to last. But she was not aware of having reached the moment for a first assessment.

In 1931 there occurred a small editorial event that was of great importance to Krull: the publication, in an NRF collection of inexpensive small-format monographs on contemporary artists created in 1924, of a volume on *Germaine Krull par Pierre Mac Orlan*.[1] To this popular collection ('at least one volume per month'), which already included forty-four titles on 'new painters' and eleven titles on 'new sculptors', a 'new photographers' series was now added, the first beneficiary of which was a woman photographer. This was an event for photography, but also for the cause of women – bear in mind that the 'painters' series included only Marie Laurencin and Suzanne Valadon, and the 'sculptors' Chana Orloff and (a recent addition) Renée Sintenis. In fact, this would be the only publication in the 'photographers' series. Man Ray appeared in the collection as a painter.[2] This, as Krull tells it, was an initiative by Malraux, who came 'to find out how I made my *fers*' and decided to ask Mac Orlan for a text. 'He liked my photos and thought, as I did, that photography was not yet "grown up".' She speaks of a delay (it had probably been ready for publication since 1930, or even 1929) 'because of changes in the photos. We couldn't decide which ones we should use.'

Advertisement design for Paul Poiret, 1926

She had trouble seeing this publication, not 'by Krull' but 'about Krull', as a summing-up. 'Even today, I feel that it isn't really me.'[3] The small tome was nevertheless well put together, with a little photograph of a 'Mannousch' on the cover (in photogravure, the inside being in halftone) and an interesting introduction by Pierre Mac Orlan, illustrated by a very oblique shot of Avenue du Bois taken from the car door, followed by three hands of artists and artisans, then Krull's 'thoughts on art' (her preface to *Études de nu*). It reproduced a total of thirty-three photographs, which work better in this small format than any painting. The Eiffel Tower, still life, a warship, 'gypsies', a tramp, a factory chimney, the hands of Cocteau, images from her reportages in Ouessant and Marseille, nude studies, advertisements, the transporter bridge in Marseille (dated 1930), a portrait of Eisenstein and a landscape in the Valois – all give an idea of Krull's artistic ambition, her reportage itself being singular and modernist. 'Among the works of all those who have been the lyrical and meticulous witnesses of the social picturesque since 1918, I particularly like those of Mme Germaine Krull, no doubt because we all have more or less the same reactions to certain visions which are plastic only by necessity,' wrote Mac Orlan, relating the photographer's strong 'personality' to her conception of the 'social fantastic': 'This adroit and self-confident artist, who is a great reporter and a poet of everyday life, closely associates her personality with all the elements of steel and flesh that form and later serve to formulate the picturesque and the social fantastic of the contemporary period.' Mac Orlan, who had written copiously about Krull's photos and was undeniably her best and most essential literary support, had at the same time to legitimise photography as an 'art' and a photographer as woman and artist. And he did so with words that were very appropriate: 'Her art strikes the intelligence. It is a loud shock and all kinds of unacknowledged thoughts, even the most intimate ones, arise at the sly call of the secret elements on the plate. When Krull transposes a machine landscape into a kind of stupefying symphony . . . she does not create easy anecdotes, but she makes visible the secret details that people do not always see, but that the light of her lens flushes out from its hiding place.' He presents her in a very concrete way as a modern woman, in contact with the street: 'I like to imagine Krull in her studio, a cigarette between her lips, with a bit of smoke in her eyes. She knows that the street, which is the most securely closed domain of human thought, will reveal to her the shadow of its carriage entrances.'

NUDES

In 1929–1930, Krull felt fully at home in her profession as photographer, as she had learnt it and as she had practised it, on the one hand, and, on the other, in the Parisian milieu she moved in, the intellectual and artistic but also media world (magazine and book publishing, with her friends and lovers). This harmony was experienced in the context of the rising fortune of photography in Europe during the late 1920s, symbolised in 1929 by 'Film und Foto' and *VU*. It is logical that at this moment of personal fame and when the medium was being promoted in new forms, the publisher Calavas (Librairie des Arts Décoratifs), who had already produced *Métal*, should have repeated the experience with the 'New Photographer' Krull by proposing a new portfolio, in a somewhat smaller format, with twenty-four gravure plates on a subject that was much less arid than *Métal*, more accessible and more likely to reach a broad public: this was *Études de nu* by Germaine Krull, in 1930.[4]

In 1924 Calavas had already published *Nus. Cent photographies originales de Laryew* and in 1929 he brought out *Les nus de Drtikol* (thirty plates).[5] Pierre Bost, the spokesman of the photographic avant-garde, had also just published a portfolio of *Photographies modernes* with Calavas, in which he championed young photographers such as Eli Lotar, André Kertész,

3 VMD, p. 135. In this passage as in others, the dates given by Krull are erroneous.
4 Germaine Krull, *Études de nu*, Paris: Librairie des Arts Décoratifs, A. Calavas, 1930, 22.5 × 16 cm, portfolio with label on the first orange board.
5 In a larger format than *Études de nus*, 29.5 × 39 cm.

Roger Parry, Maurice Tabard, Joris Ivens, André Vigneau and Germaine Krull. For Krull, all this was very natural. As we have seen, she had already published portfolios of nudes in her Berlin period, and the 'book of nudes' was accepted by the mores of naturist culture, a culture of the body, sport and the open air best exemplified by the publications of one of Krull's mentors, Adolf Koch (the *Körperbildung* series, 1927–1931). In a similar vein, or under the same pretext, the *Akt-Kunstbücher* series by Ernst Schertel was published in Leipzig between 1927 and 1931. In 1925 Krull contributed to *Natur und Kultur, das Weib*, by Peter Landow, which benefited from excellent printing. In a more erotic and suggestive vein, in 1928 Heinz von Perckhammer published *Edle Nackteit in China*. For her publisher, therefore, Germaine Krull had the same legitimacy as the Prague artist Drtikol. And, to clarify the chronological framework, it should be pointed out that *Études de nu* preceded the editorial vogue that began to emerge in 1931 with *Paris Magazine* (in which Krull actually published very little) and a number of ambitious books or portfolios such as *Images d'une femme* by Maurice Pillard-Verneuil, Denoël and Steele, 1931; *Nus. La beauté de la femme* by Daniel Masclet, 1933; and *Femmes*, by Sasha Stone (Arts et Métiers), 1933. We may also note that these titles were a lot more enticing than *Études de nu*, implying a very different conception of the subject.

Krull herself was simply getting back to what she had done so well in her early days. More surprising is the original way in which she treated the subject, especially if we compare it to her Berlin period. Faithful to the method that she adopted for her fashion photographs, and then transposed for her portraits, she created somewhat abrupt lighting with her 'lamp', making the shadows of the body highly present, creating strong contrasts while giving the impression that the model is captured in a private room at night, and not in the more artificial situation of a specialised studio. The ensemble thus gains in intimacy, especially since the poses are very natural: sitting casually on the edge of a bed with her back to us, with the blanket askew, or simply lying on a couch, but seen from above, or squatting, balancing on the floor thanks to the natural support of the hand. Some poses are more languorous, with the bust thrown back, arms raised, hair falling, or with an arm bent over the face, in line with the bust. Krull preferred to play on the effect of a lighted surface rather than on the complete line of the body. The framing of many of the poses in this portfolio is surprising and bold (they were probably cropped), so that the corporeal form appears to be constructed by the frame. The most innovative images are tight close-ups on parts of the body that do not evoke a naked body or any connection with a whole, but are restricted to detail, to the partial line of a foot or a bust, seen as being just as sensual as the whole body. Krull, for example, isolates the upper part of the back and nape of the neck, the chest and abdomen, the feet and part of the legs dangling from a bedside, a forearm beside a foot. At once human and geometrical, these forms bring to mind a Brancusi sculpture or a white relief by Hans Arp. Two of the plates in which we see the whole body are double exposures, which clearly show that Krull meant to subvert the 'nude genre'. 'Photographers have discovered that the human face and body should be represented like still lifes,' argued Pierre Bost in *Photographies modernes* (1930, from the same publisher). The visual register here, certainly, is no longer that of the 'nude', but that of the new photography, which invented forms on the basis of a present, enlightened, living and not imaginary subject. The term 'Études' (studies) is particularly apt in this sense, because it references the pictorial tradition, and even the painter's profession.

Krull did not limit herself to these visual innovations, which nevertheless represent a number of significant steps in this particular field of the nude. She also wrote her own preface to her portfolio and stated her position as a photographer and woman (these being female nudes), starting in these terms: 'Taking photographs is a profession. An artisan's profession. A profession that one can learn, that one does with varying degrees of proficiency, like any other profession.'[6] This short preface of no more than thirty lines, which, in order to fill three pages, had to be specially laid out with double borders and boldface, capital letters, is above all a manifesto, the only text Krull wrote about photography at this time, the only one that was 'written' in the literary sense, in order to serve as a preface. We can sense that in this concentrated text Krull was trying to say as exactly as she could things that were essential to her about the foundations of the photographic act. It mattered that they should be said by a photographer and not a writer, and especially a woman photographer writing about female nudes: 'The first science of the photographer is to know how to look ... With one snap of the shutter, the lens registers the world from the outside, and the photographer from the inside.' These are simple statements of the kind we do not hear from writers who, if more profuse, are further from photographic realities, objects and conceptions. Rather than comment on an image that is already there and what it suggests or evokes, she observes that a photograph can and must first be imagined, and calmly asks the question, 'How is a photograph conceived?' In 1930, the only people to raise these questions were Waldemar Georges ('Photographie, vision du monde', in *Arts et Métiers graphiques*) and, above all, Pierre Bost (in *Photographies modernes*), but they were not photographers (and they were men). When we read that 'Every new angle multiplies the world in itself,' we look differently at the photograph showing details of a woman's legs. 'The lens is an eye that is better made than the eye,' Krull affirms. And, again: 'The camera cannot invent, combine or trick. It is neither painting nor imagination. The photographer is a witness' – albeit, in this instance, one working within the classically pictorial theme of the nude. She concludes: 'The true photographer is the witness of each day's events, a reporter.' This preface to *Études de nu* is above all a statement about the craft of the photographer in 1930, about the new prospects then being opened up, covering or juxtaposing different creative fields (illustration, advertising, literature, poetry, etc.). She concludes by sidestepping the issue of the nude, which is not reportage and which belongs to a genre whose legitimacy is uncertain because it is personal and private, based on a personal idea explored using personal methods. 'So why do nudes? Because they have always been beautiful, and because one summer morning they just appealed to me.'

Études de nu does not have the modesty of its title. It is an overt statement, self-affirmation, a manifestation of her presence in a world of men who look at nude photos and present their aesthetic quality as an excuse. She makes her point with text, photography and 'the' woman's body—her woman's body, which is not without significance. Meaning, function and gender are interwoven, if only in a rather weak echo of Cahun's *Aveux non avenus*, published that same year, but then this outburst and manifesto are the work of a *photographer* who is not a writer.

6 See the full text in the appendices.

WOMEN ARTISTS

Unlike Man Ray and Berenice Abbott, Krull did not have a studio/workshop, a place where artists and intellectuals came to be photographed, usually for the purpose of promoting an artistic event, book or play. Portraits of artists were very common in the 1930s, and many women photographers took them, including Rogi André, Ergy Landau, Mme d'Ora and Laure Albin Guillot. If one had access to prominent figures from the arts, there was an assured income to be had from selling the photos to specialist magazines (the daily papers, in contrast, had their own structure or used agencies).

7 Three recent prints from original negatives are kept at the BNF, Paris. One shows her with a cigarette in her hand, the other holding her Prix Renaudot, *Piège*, with her shadow behind her.
8 CEDG, p. 37.
9 CEDG, p. 37. At the time Germaine was in the middle of her rather short-lived romance with Philippe Lamour.
10 'La Voix humaine', *VU* no. 102 (26 February 1930), pp. 170–171, six photos by Georges Marant.

It was at the request of Lucien Vogel that Krull went to photograph Colette, who 'hated photographers'. She took a view camera with tripod, a lamp and her assistant Marcel, whose manner Colette found frightening. What broke the ice was Colette's grey cat, which sat on Germaine's lap. 'I managed to take some photos that she really liked.' They became friends. 'She was full of stories and loved beautiful girls.' The photo, from the waist, shows Colette reclining on a couch, resting her head on her arm. Unusual for a writer, this pose is also seen in André Kertész's photograph of Colette, taken at her home no doubt at around the same time. But with Kertész Colette is looking into the lens, and projects something of her status, underscored by a handsome bouquet of flowers, Krull's 'Colette' is simply a pensive young woman, her eyes lost and distant and her hair blurred, lit by a lamp below her – another deviation from standard practice – that casts a huge shadow onto the wall behind. Her light, rough-textured cardigan contrasts with the smooth face and the line of the eyes.

We know that Colette was a friend and faithful champion of the novelist and journalist Germaine Beaumont (1890–1983). Krull's photograph was no doubt taken when she won the Renaudot prize with her novel *Piège* in 1930. She later chaired the jury for the Fémina prize.[7] 'L'éclat emprunté', an article about hand and face care that she published in a spring 1934 issue of *Miroir du monde* ('A woman who knows what she owes to her face will continue to please longer than another,' pp. 15–16) was illustrated by four photos of Krull's, showing manicure, facial massages and the eyelashes. The known 'portrait' of Beaumont is a severely cropped version representing about a quarter of the original negative, showing the writer from the waist upwards. Here we see only the right side of the face, without the hair, in a style characteristic of the avant-garde at the end of the 1920s (*Lotte* by Burchartz, reprised by Kertész for his portrait of his wife Elisabeth).

The actor and member of the Comédie-Française Berthe Bovy (1887–1977) was already famous when, in that company's temple of classicism, she performed Cocteau's very disturbing play *La Voix humaine* in early 1930. Krull described it thus: 'The set: a woman's boudoir. Berthe Bovy sitting by the telephone in a lace negligée. She is waiting. Eventually, the telephone rings. Then come fifteen minutes of conversation. A break-up ... The man is leaving her. The expressive power of the face and the hands turn a simple phone conversation into a tragedy. It was an unprecedented success and a superb performance.'[8] The challenge – and Cocteau's unparalleled success – was due not only to the fact of having a single actor alone on stage throughout the play, and to silences that punctuate the monologue, but also to the tension arising from what is not heard (the implicit male presence, and what it formulates), to the need to imagine this. Above all, there was the personality of Berthe Bovy, the way she physically inhabited the role, raising the drama to the level of existential tragedy by her physical performance and the expressiveness of her face and hands.

Krull was asked to report on the performance by photographing Berthe Bovy at her home. In doing so she made great use of lighting effects, while also making a personal transposition. Her account lets us in on one or two secrets of the job: 'When I turned up at Berthe Bovy's place with Marcel carrying the big camera, and she acted for me, freezing her expressions for the camera, I came away from the session with a broken heart, as if my own lover had just left me. The photos, which were published in *VU*, brought Jean Cocteau my way.'[9] Contrary to what Germaine believed, however, the photos that appeared in *VU* were not by her but by Georges Marant, and featured wide views of the set by Christian Bérard (a table, with lamp and lampshade, the telephone on its stand, an armchair covered by a white dressing gown, gloves), and the actress on stage, with lighting that was much more even, capturing the play more than the individual tragedy.[10] The actress appears as, 'by turns sensitive, touching, in pain, and always infinitely moving'. The captions written by Cocteau clearly describe the stages of betrayal and despair: 'She learns that he is not at home, he is standing to talk, in a phone room'; 'She tries to make him admit his lies'; 'She listens as he tells his lies, in the silence'; 'She is numbed by the voice.'

Judging by the seven seldom-published poses known to us, Krull's photos must have been too striking, too expressive and too disturbing.[11] They are almost expressionist: tightly framed, their intense, single light source places the woman's face in a worrying darkness as it is contorted by tension, frowns and rictuses. The gaze is hypnotised, devastated, drained. The carriage of the head, the eyebrows and the tension of the lines all contribute to the expressiveness. And so, as always with Krull, do the hands. In each image the actress appears as 'voiceless', simply hanging on to that unusual object that is the phone receiver and its cord.

These poses in the apartment transcribe in photography what André Levinson saw in *La Voix humaine* for *L'Art vivant*: a 'duel at a distance, this combat between a panting woman and the shadow of a voice – for her, life and death hang by a thread:[12] "Don't hang up!"... On the actress's distressed or tense face we can read each of her torturer's presumed lines.' Posing for Krull, Berthe Bovy is left with only her own resources, outside the theatre, off the stage. A photograph of her shadow on the wall resonates fully with this notation: 'This confined soul is struggling against mortal solitude.'[13] When he received the prints of Bovy and at the same time his own portraits, Cocteau immediately wrote her a letter, which was published:[14] 'I am hastening to thank you ... Berthe Bovy: R. de Saint-Jean wrote to me: "Do you have Krull's prints? The shadow of Bovy on the telephone? It is like a suffering machine."... Your prints of Bovy in *La Voix humaine* are masterpieces. The actress is ageless. She has that age of silence, moonlight, Decembers, car crashes that, a second after they occurred, acquire the grandeur of an Egyptian ruin. These tears, these locks of hair, this mouth/wound, bring back a memory from 1927... I heard a loudspeaker, a terrible voice, an Oedipal voice (invisible because blind) declaiming stock exchange prices. The effect was poignant, theatrical, utterly new. Do not believe that I am turning away from your work. I am turning to see it. I am trying to communicate to you what I feel when faced with these documentaries about a ravaged woman, a statue undergoing torture.' This letter, never before published in its totality,[15] is a poetic paean to Krull: 'Few artists were born under the sign of the camera, under the rainbow of the object glass, under the star of the lens. You belong to that little troupe that Man Ray once set in train.' It ends with these words: 'You are a deforming mirror. You and the camera obtain a new world, a world that has crossed machines with a soul.'[16]

The singer Damia, 'the Great Damia, singer of the people', as Krull described her, whose songs always had 'that pathetic note, either of the sailor at sea, or of the prisoner in his cell', would also pose. 'The big record company Columbia was one of the first to ask me for a series of Damia to make a luxury brochure to sell her records. I like Damia a lot. She was a simple girl, a daughter of the people, and it was friendship, the stories told by her first lover who had narrowly escaped jail, that inspired her first songs. She herself made up the songs, by describing them to composers. Damia crossed the sky of Paris like a meteor and disappeared very quickly.'[17] For the brochure in question, with fine black photogravure printing, Damia is given a treatment similar to that of Berthe Bovy as far as the artificial lighting is concerned, but quite different in expressive terms: in chiaroscuro, against a black ground, in a black dress so that all we can see are the singer's bare arms and face, and her handsome profile. Distress and solitude are evoked here too, but Damia's methods are less theatrical: 'There, before you, was her face suffused with ardour and grief.' 'This great-hearted woman wrests tears from

11 Six of the vintage prints are signed, including the five at the Maison Jean Cocteau in Milly-la-Forêt. One of them was used to promote a phonographic recording of *La Voix humaine*, with the Columbia logo and a title card (1930, two 78 rpm records). Another one was published, cropped differently, in *Variétés* 2, no. 12 (15 April 1930), p. 872, next to the clown Dario. Four would be reused in the booklet of *Berthe Bovy interprète la Voix humaine de Jean Cocteau*, Pathé Marconi box set, 1958.

12 In French, the word *fil* is used both for thread and a phone cord.– *Trans.*

13 André Levinson, 'Du plateau à l'écran. Le monodrame de Jean Cocteau et le superfilm de Fritz Lang', *L'Art vivant* no. 125 (1 March 1930), pp. 195–196.

14 'Germaine Krull', *Le Courrier littéraire* (April-May-June 1930), pp. 65–81. A page from the manuscript is reproduced on p. 81. This letter is reproduced in full in the appendix here.

15 See the appendices.

16 Krull herself transcribed the term inaccurately as 'miroir *réformant*' in the preface to *Études de nu*.

17 CEDG, p. 56.

18 Photographic print, 30 x 23 cm, with the Columbia logo inlaid.
19 CEDG, p. 56.
20 'Au revoir Blackbirds', *VU* no. 77 (4 September 1929), cover.
21 *French Cancan*, texts by Paul Perret, *Les Images de Paris* 2, Éditions de Paris, August 1930 (nineteen photos by Krull, the second part is illustrated by photos from Studio Marcello).
22 'Tabarin' by Michel Georges-Michel, *VU* no. 94 (1 January 1930), pp. 10–11, four photos out of eleven.
23 CEDG, p. 68.
24 Krull also has a photo of a side street in Marseille illustrating *Sing-Sing ou La maison des trois marches*, by Georges Simenon, *VU* no. 158 (25 March 1931), p. 409.

the least sensitive people,' wrote commentator Henri Béraud. Other known images show her with an expression that is less mild and more fraught than in this brochure (nine photos), the layout of which is equally remarkable. There is also a close-up portrait by Krull, a print used for promotional purposes by Columbia.[18]

'It was also Columbia that asked me to make the first photographic poster which was pasted on the Morris columns of Paris.' It was a big poster one metre by one metre fifty, with Marie-Dubas dressed in black and white, a cap on her head, eyes wide open, arm raised in joy singing 'The Hussars of the Guard'. Krull repeated her device of shadow on a wall, just behind the subject, echoing the form of the body. Using the same formula (subject erect, raising their arms, and cast shadow in the background), she also photographed the duo Gilles and Julien, who were from the theatre, whom she confuses with the Compagnons de la Chanson in her memoirs.[19]

Without a doubt, Krull had a preference for women in her portraits of artists – or perhaps her clients knew she was more at ease with them. In 1929, obliged to photograph the male star of the Blackbirds at the Moulin Rouge, she nevertheless produced a fine portrait of Adelaide Hall, one of the stars of the troupe, wearing a boater, which appeared on the cover of *VU* in September 1929, at the time of the group's departure.[20] At the Bal Tabarin, Krull also photographed the French cancan and its profusion of dancers, no doubt emboldened by the various possibilities of the costumes. The result was a little book, 'French Cancan',[21] printed in photogravure in two colours, with nineteen of her photographs. These are much more inventive and dynamic than the ones in the second part, which are by another photographer. Some of them appeared on a double page of *VU* about the Tabarin.[22]

LA FOLLE D'ITTEVILLE [THE MADWOMAN OF ITTEVILLE]

In 1931 Krull was still living her 'publishing dreams' with Jacques Haumont, with whom she was able to drive from Paris to Biarritz. Together they had an innovative project. The conclusions she draws in her memoirs are very lucid: 'I was supposed to be doing my first illustrated book with Georges Simenon: "The Madwoman of Itteville". This was a short detective story in which, for the first time, when it came to describing things or places, the camera would replace text. For example, when the inspector broke down a door, then "instead of the text", the image showed what he saw. At the time [1931], this was quite a bold thing to do. But it required perfect printing of the images. Jacques Haumont, with the weakness that made him take promises and reassurances at face value, had failed to have an eye kept on the printing and I found myself looking at a book that was so badly printed that on some pages you couldn't even recognise the images. This not only dashed my hopes, but also sank Éditions Jacques Haumont. For me, the dream was over, and despite Haumont's assurances and the efforts he made to redress his business, and to return to the books about the great rivers of France [another project for an illustrated series], I had to resign myself to stop thinking about it.'[23] This 'bold', if flawed, effort effectively marked the end of a period of intense activity. There were a number of structural reasons for this, but the primary cause was the printing: the choice of newsprint and perhaps of process (photogravure by Georges Lang, despite the fact that he was a specialist), which made the images smudgy and illegible, especially the numerous night-time pictures with their strong contrasts. The actual idea was original and excellent, but it was let down by the book's unattractive finish. Krull's photographs were a very inventive response to Simenon's story, and technically they were surely of very fine quality.[24]

It was, then, a detective story, illustrated exclusively by photographs on almost every page (104 photographs for 128 pages), a booklet in novel format, with a fairly short text expanded to go with the images.[25] This was the first time this formula (a detective story with photographic illustrations) had been used. The publisher dubbed it 'Phototexte' (the photo-novel had yet to be invented). A second title was already planned, another Simenon: *L'Affaire des 7' [sept minutes]*, which in the end was never published. ('Voir' [See] was the title of another series that the publisher discontinued.) Simenon's story, written on his barge at Morsang-sur-Seine (not far from the village of Itteville) in May 1931, and originally titled 'Two Corpses', is built around the personality of a 'strange person', a young blond-haired woman, 'very pretty and very elegant – who lives all alone and whom people almost never see', whom we see at the beginning of the story in the middle of the countryside, at night, near her house in Itteville, prostrate and distraught beside the 'corpse' of a man.[26] Then, an hour later, when the first passer-by has been to fetch the gendarmes, she is still there, but the identity of the corpse has changed. During the course of the investigation we find out that she has been cared for in the specialist clinic of Doctor Canut, where he carries out 'head operations', for 'she was afraid of going mad', and the doctor paid her frequent visits. The second [stabbed] corpse, which was taken to the clinic, has disappeared. The narrative takes us through a kind of trap imagined by Inspector G7 in order to trick the offender, or at least the main protagonists, into revealing themselves. In the end, the doctor admits his guilty association with the young woman (Marthe, in fact Wanda), the motives behind the affair and the murder of a blackmailer who was using Wanda for his swindles. The key to the plot is that Wanda killed her procurer/swindler in order to save the doctor.

The essence of the visual argument lies in the contrast between the beauty of the young woman and her mental weakness, between the 'woman's body' and her 'young girl's mentality'. Wanda, who is responsible for these circumstances but totally innocent, the central figure to whom we keep returning, attracts the lens by her allure, her elegance, her hair, her uncanniness, which comes out in the nonchalance and mental absence, and above all in the gaze, which expresses that 'fundamental inability to put ideas together'. The general motif of the short story is mental illness and 'clinical swindling'. It even contains this appraisal by the (fooled) doctor: 'As often happens in psychoanalysis, Wanda was overcome with an exclusive affection for me.' And it turns out that Wanda had previously been in treatment with 'a psychiatrist in Vienna' (this was 1931).

The illustration culminates over two consecutive spreads in which Wanda's face is seen frontally in close-up, in combination with the text: 'Clear eyes, as if washed by tears, watching us calmly. The enchantment began!' Then: 'She looked at the three of us, then answered like a lesson learned by rote.' The photography's power of emotional evocation and psychic suggestion is as intense as the medium can achieve. There can be no doubt that some of Krull's illustrations here would, if decently reproduced, be considered remarkable. She closely follows the text, distinctly describing the places and evoking ambience mainly by her lighting, and placing the figures clearly and intelligibly. But she also excels at conveying feelings, expressions and even mental attitudes, and at stimulating the reader's sense of anticipation with regard to the main characters. Krull was very much at home photographing night and shadows, a suitable outlet for her rebellious, imaginative spirit. Most of the scenes take place either 'outdoors at night', at dawn, or sometimes indoors, which means that Krull nearly always used lamps, taking advantage of the contrasts between darkness and local lighting, and that the images copiously exploit the effects of shadows on walls.

Krull also chose her models, first of all from among her friends, notably Jacques Haumont and perhaps Renaud de Jouvenel. The choice of the heroine, Wanda, was essential.

25 *La Folle d'Itteville* by Georges Simenon and Germaine Krull, 'Phototexte', Paris: Éditions Jacques Haumont, 1931 (printed in August 1931).
26 The site http://www.association-jacques-riviere-alain-fournier.com/ provides a lot of information, including a plot summary.

27 Another portrait of Mrs Hubbell by Krull came up for auction in 1998.
28 In *Voilà* no. 1 (28 March 1931). See *Roger Parry, photographies, dessins, mises en pages* (Paris, Jeu de Paume, Hôtel de Sully, 2007), Paris: Gallimard/ Jeu de Paume, 2007.
29 CEDG, p. 36. Germaine Krull dates this event to 1929, which is unlikely.
30 Christies sale, London, 'Rare Photobooks', 18 May 2006, lot 113. Format of photos 17.2 x 11.5 cm. Five photos, and the cover, were reproduced in the sale booklet. They are reproduced in David Campany, *Photography and Cinema*, London: Reaktion Books, 2008, p. 85, where I belatedly came across this information.
31 See the chapter 'Free Spirit'.

Krull decided on Mrs Hubbell, whose renowned beauty had led her to be photographed by ten of the best-known photographers of the day, including Germaine Krull (and Alban, Laure Albin Guillot, Hoyningen-Huene, Kertész, Lorelle, Man Ray, Lee Miller, Maurice Tabard, André Vigneau). Krull's image is one of the most striking, with Hubbell's head in profile, thrown back with the hair hanging down, and with that signature shadow of the profile on the wall.[27] The two original prints corresponding to the frontal portraits of Wanda weeping in *La Folle d'Itteville*, now held at the Museum of Modern Art in New York and at the Musée National d'Art Moderne in Paris, are among Krull's most sensitive photographs and, taken on their own, are far from any notion of illustration. They typify the kind of close-up, frontal portraits being produced in France and Germany in around 1930. Mrs Hubbell's gaze and the 'colour' of her eyes have a great deal to do with this.

Photography, which for the first time here offers a complement to a text saturated with hypotheses, impressions and imaginings, acts indeed as an objectification, a welcome means of capturing the reader's attention and orienting them towards certain ideas, like the forensic evidence collected in an investigation. Régis Messac, who in 1929 (the date bears emphasis) was the first academic to publish a thesis on the detective novel, saw it as 'reasoning founded on the observation of a specific fact, leading to another specific fact'. Photography (Krull's photography) certainly lends itself to this function for it is conceived within a highly objective relation to the subject, which also anticipates the image that follows. In other words, the images are produced with a view to their future cinematic montage, and we know how potent this principle is in Krull's work from at least 1927 onwards, even in the reportage and books.

Were it not for this failure, which had nothing to do with her work, Krull might well have found a new impetus in illustration work, getting away from what was now almost the routine work of reportage, just as, in early 1931, Roger Parry found new resources in doing photographic illustrations for the covers and imaginative promotional material for novels.[28] This seems all the more plausible in that Krull herself spoke of a precedent that, in spite of her chronological uncertainties, we can date to 1930, before the Simenon project (which perhaps it triggered). Krull fully espoused this fruitful, if unrealised idea: 'I thought we should do a book with just photographs. A kind of novel without words. With the collaboration of Renaud de Jouvenel and one of his friends, plus a pretty girl, my neighbour, I took about fifty photos. A little photo-novel. Not a word of text. The theme was a bit difficult: two boys fighting over a girl, one of them "intellectual" and the other "sporty", in which the sporty one's Bugatti wins against the poet. There is only one copy of this experiment. Even then I was obsessed with the idea that photos should illustrate a text, and even replace it. That one should be able to read, "He opened the door, then . . .", and that a photo should show what he saw.'[29]

As it happens, this original mock-up reappeared briefly in 2006. It is titled *Roman*, contains forty-two photographs, and is credited to Germaine Krull and Henriette Marquetty. The motor car and the road seem to play a dominant role here, and some of the pictures appear to be photomontages.[30] Manifestly, the idea that Krull put into practice in this experiment went much further than simple illustration of a text, because photography on its own is given the role of constructing a narrative and a plot – no doubt by means of photomontage. One can imagine Krull's ideas here coming out of the narrative solutions found in reportage and cinema, and in magazine layout, something we should bear in mind in connection with all of Germaine Krull's slightly 'strange' photography.[31]

At around the same time (February–March 1930), Krull had another experience that may well have stimulated her new aspiration. This was when she illustrated the serialisation of a 'new detective novel by Pierre Mac Orlan', *Ombres de Paris*, in over ten issues of *Détective* (a magazine recently created by the Kessel brothers). Each instalment filled a double page, and featured two or three photographs per page.[32]

THE WOMEN WORKERS OF PARIS

The street, as Mac Orlan observed, was Krull's favourite territory, the place where she could probe the 'human thought' of the humble, of the workers and indigents who inhabited Jacques Lasserre's *Paris misère* (1935). As we have seen from her preface to *Études de nu*, for her 'the true photographer is the witness of each day's events, a reporter.' In her reportage for *VU* she never neglected the role of women – on the contrary, she singled them out and took their side. These might be tramps, *manouches* or *romanichelles* (gypsies), or La Goulue in the steep decline of her old age. If there was one assignment that really fulfilled her vocation and allowed her to express her concern for women's issues, it was when *VU* asked her to report on women workers in Paris. This is certainly her most comprehensive piece of reportage, to judge by the extant prints. She produced a large number of photos in a homogenous, unified style for the piece, whereas she could easily have used earlier work. This report for *VU* was an exceptional event in terms of editorial policy, in that it extended over six issues, from 7 December 1932 (no. 247) to 11 January 1933 (252).[33] It was a kind of end-of-year gift to readers, and also a promotional initiative, designed perhaps to win back readers. The very long text was written by Emmanuel Berl, who at the time was editor of *Marianne*, a pacifist pro-Front Populaire weekly founded with the support of Malraux at Gallimard. Krull's twenty-five published photographs were used mainly in the first two instalments (eleven and nine, respectively), and clearly credited: 'Reportage photographique Germaine Krull'. This information disappeared from the next issues. Krull was not credited in the third (but then the photos do not appear to be by her), while credits reappear for each image in the last three issues (three and two photos by Krull).

Berl's reportage is highly structured, a first-hand account treated like an investigation starting around the factories 'on the periphery of Paris'. Berl goes into a factory where they make insulation material and are pouring 'burning-hot materials into moulds', then continues with a car factory, probably Citroën on Quai de Javel, where women are working on hydraulic presses and metal casting, and using paint guns. It was man's work, but 'the men are not more skilled than we are,' say the women workers he speaks to. The tinplate workers are proud of their work and their factory. Next he visits a producer of envelopes and writing paper, then makers of glassware and fancy boxes. For these old-fashioned artisans who had never changed their ways, threatened by 'mechanical progress' that would replace manual work (folding the paper), profit came from 'the entrepreneur's exploitation of the labour force'. The next issue featured bead-makers, florists and feather dressers. The bead-makers were the worst treated, exposed to the suffocating vapours used to treat the beads. 'You couldn't spend more than three minutes in there without choking. The boss was choking, just like me. He coughed. I coughed.' The work was paid for by the piece, and very badly. They were 'free' to stop from time to time. Berl 'regrets the workshop rules of the big factories'. The women were young, twenty or less. '"You know", one of them told me, artists are never very well paid.' When asked, 'What do you do on Sunday?' one replies that she does the washing. The striking thing about the twenty photographs by Krull illustrating the first two parts is her closeness to her 'subject', mirroring the precision of Berl's report. Krull shows women in close-up, and above all in relation to their tools or their sometimes monstrous machines, or to the object they make, in a relationship of necessity that requires active hands and a keen eye. Krull captures these eyes

32 *Détective*, nos. 69 (6 March 1930) to 81 (8 May 1930); situated on page 7.

33 Emmanuel Berl, *VU* no. 247 (7 December 1932), 'Les Ouvrières de Paris', by Emmanuel Berl, pp. 1925–1928, eleven photos out of twelve; no. 248 (14 December 1932), pp. 2011–2014, nine photos out of ten; no. 249 (21 December 1932), pp. 2047–2051; no. 250 (28 December 1932), pp. 2079–2082, three photos out of six; no. 251 (4 January 1933), pp. 43–47; no. 252 (11 January 1933), pp. 43–47, two photos out of eleven.

34 There may have been disagreement over the choices or over royalties. This cannot have been an 'oversight' on the part of *VU*, where from 1928 onwards nearly all the reproduced photographs were systematically credited to the author or the agency.
35 *Ouvrières et midinettes au travail et au plaisir*, original manuscript by Emmanuel Berl, eighty-one pages, thirty-one original photographs by Germaine Krull, stuck with adhesive, November 1931 to May 1932. Warmest thanks to Sylvie Aubenas and Dominique Versavel, director and curator of the Département des Estampes et de la Photographie for informing me about, and giving me access to, this remarkable document.
36 No photograph has been removed. The blank left-hand pages are in their original state.
37 'Beauté mon/cher souci' by Jeanne Fernandez, *VU* no. 62 (22 May 1929), pp. 411–414, seven photos out of eleven.

when their expression is more serene and cheerful, on the first page that opens the series ('She likes the factory'), and at the end of the second part, when the women are leaving their drudgery, 'grave and discreet, hurrying towards the Métro, the tram or the bus'. There are also a few close-ups of objects, and the hands are in principle always the scopic focus. The layout varies the perspectives, the direction of the gazes and the distances with the *VU* art directors' usual skill. In the third set, published just before Christmas and all about corset makers, telephone workers, and seamstresses and models in the fashion and couture business, the tone is more amiable. Eleven photographs are not credited but they could be by Krull, especially since one of them shows her friend Damia.[34] The next issue focuses on sales girls in department stores, hairdressers and manicurists (themes Krull had already treated in the past), as well as typists (one photo by Krull). The latter had acquired a distinctive status in the companies where they worked: 'The typist is a modern figure ... Many important men and important organisations end up really depending on a secretary who earns only two thousand francs a month.' The fifth set looked at 'living conditions' both at work (hygiene, meals in the canteen or around the worktable) and at home ('working women are always excessive in the way they go about housekeeping'). There is an element of sociological analysis here: 'Women's salaries are viewed as extra income by the employer. It is implicitly understood that the worker is married, or that she lives with her family.' The series ends with leisure activities on 'Sundays and public holidays': outings, cinema, dances, country trips. Here we find Krull's past images of funfairs and popular dances. The layout constantly varies the 'shots' in such a way as to draw the reader/viewer into the setting, with a communicative visual power that is in effect reminiscent of cinema.

Emmanuel Berl's autograph manuscript, 'Ouvrières et midinettes au travail et au plaisir', which, by coincidence, was discovered recently, offers an exceptional insight into the reportage.[35] Dated November 1931–May 1932, it shows that the research began at least a year before publication. In a notebook with eighty-one pages, Berl's text occupies the right-hand page, with barely any corrections and just a few crossings-out, while some of Krull's original prints punctuate the account on the left, in relation to the text facing them. There are thirty-one photos in all, which she expected to use in the article.[36] As it happened, however, only two of these photographs were taken to illustrate *VU* (a florist and a typist), while a third was a variant of the smiling young woman worker who opens the first article. Where factory work is concerned, the photographs used in the manuscript are harsher, more austere and more realistic than the ones published in the magazine. Much of the original text was reworked, as if the manuscript was a preparatory phase, or constructed around unused prints.

The longest piece of reportage published in *VU*, and a high point of magazine photography, 'Les Ouvrières de Paris' exhibits the interests (working conditions for women, the actions of the workplace, the expressiveness of the hands) and qualities that made Krull a success during a time of innovation.

CARE OF THE SELF

When Krull illustrated an article by Jeanne Fernandez in *Le Jardin des modes* (published by Lucien Vogel), 'Beauté mon cher souci',[37] with seven photographs, the title was surely not to her liking. Indeed, her photos, taken in a beauty parlour, show that her main interest was not in the purported 'female concern' with beauty and ageing well, but in women's bodies, and no doubt her own body, about which she talks at such length in her memoirs when discussing her youthful suffering. What we see at first are women with women, attending to women, hands tending bodies (hands and actions are always important in Krull). And postures that are natural, that are not posed, and speak the truth about a profession (being a photographer is also a profession) rather than offering a photographic anecdote. The spatial positioning is always carefully chosen for all the professions she depicts. Three photographs were reproduced in *Le Jardin de la beauté* (published by *Le Jardin des modes*)[38] in 1931: treating wrinkles, light therapy and massages.

When Krull contributed to *Le Sourire* (the magazine that commissioned Kertész's nude *Distortions*), it was with a sheet of five photos of 'steam baths' to illustrate a 'Visit to the Steam Baths'. Care of the self, care of the body: these women's bodies are not models for artists but women who go to the baths. In the same magazine, 'Dans l'intimité de Vénus (Jambes)', two photographs show only legs (women who are dressed, wearing stockings, sitting on stools or chairs).[39] The two women were in fact photographed in a bar: the full image, with the women smoking, was one of Krull's front covers for the magazine *L'Image* (1932).[40] The others showed, respectively, a good-looking woman with a fan, and once again a cast shadow, and a mother and child (with the shadow). On the cover of *Le Sourire*, a smiling, triumphant woman who could be Mrs Hubbell is driving a car. She is Germaine's alter ego.

In another piece of reportage for *VU,* the article asked how, as the first woman to become a Commander of the Légion d'Honneur, Anna de Noailles would wear her decoration. The question was certainly very silly, and the treatment was slightly slapstick. Anyway, Krull was asked to take the photos, and the model played along.[41]

Advertising led Krull to the model Assia, a young blonde who was the muse of many photographers in the early 1930s, as was Mrs Hubbell, the only difference being that she did nude photographs and advertisements.[42] With Assia, Krull took advertising photographs for Gibbs face and body creams and beauty powder. Assia pretending to powder herself, turning away, her image slightly blurred, is irresistible in these poses, which are so ingenuous that the ideas of other photographers look stiff in comparison. We know of some ten photographs in this series. In the full-page advertisements published in *L'Illustration* in 1930 we see only the hand (or two hands) holding a pot of cream and the shadow of the face and arm projected onto the wall.[43] Krull kept her independence in all circumstances, and also her inventiveness: an unknown, but highly seductive pose, by a model in a negligée with fur lining dozing on a chair appeared under the title 'Vénus 1934, la voluptueuse' in a popular 'discovery' magazine, *Miroir du monde*.[44]

38 Jeanne Fernandez, *Le Jardin de la beauté. Conseils à toutes les femmes*, Paris: S. A. Le Jardin des modes, 1931, pp. 78, 81 and 89.
39 A. P. Barancy, 'Visite aux bains de vapeur', *Le Sourire* no. 839 (1 June 1933), p. 7; plate 'Bains de vapeur par Germaine Krull', p. 8, five photos. 'Dans l'intimité de Vénus (Jambes)' by Renée Dunan, *Le Sourire* no. 892 (7 June 1934), cover and three photos.
40 *L'Image* no. 15, 1932.
41 'Comment la portera-t-elle ?', *VU* no. 150 (28 January 1931), p. 119, five photos out of five.
42 Christian Bouqueret, *Assia, sublime modèle*, Paris: Marval, 2006. Schall's photographs were published in *Paris Magazine* in 1934.
43 Three different photographs along similar lines, *L'Illustration*, 18 January 1930, 8 February 1930, 28 February 1930.
44 *Miroir du monde*, special 'Sourire de printemps' issue, 1934, p. 8.

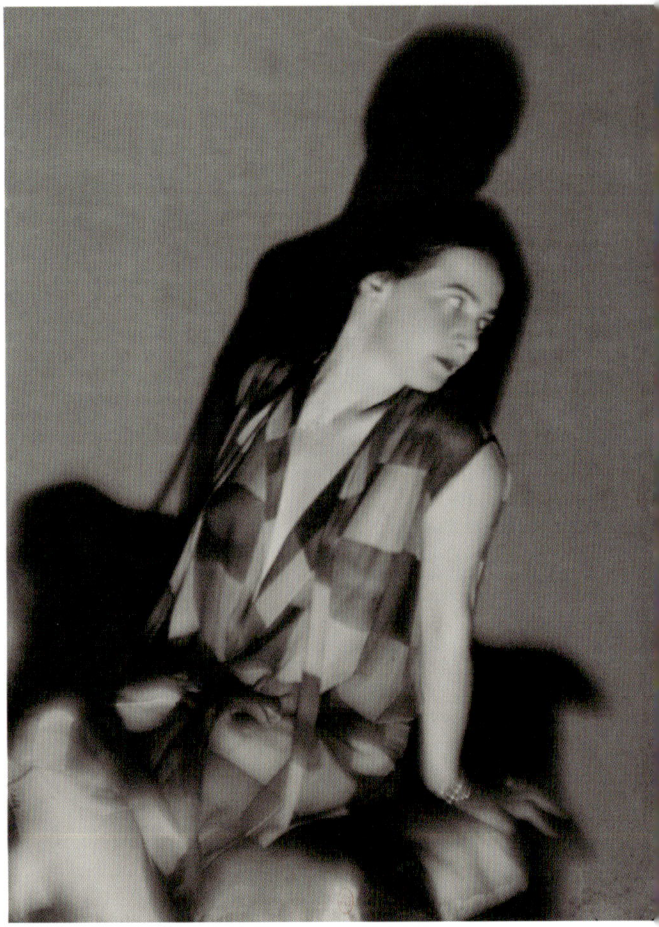

Model by Sonia Delaunay, c. 1926

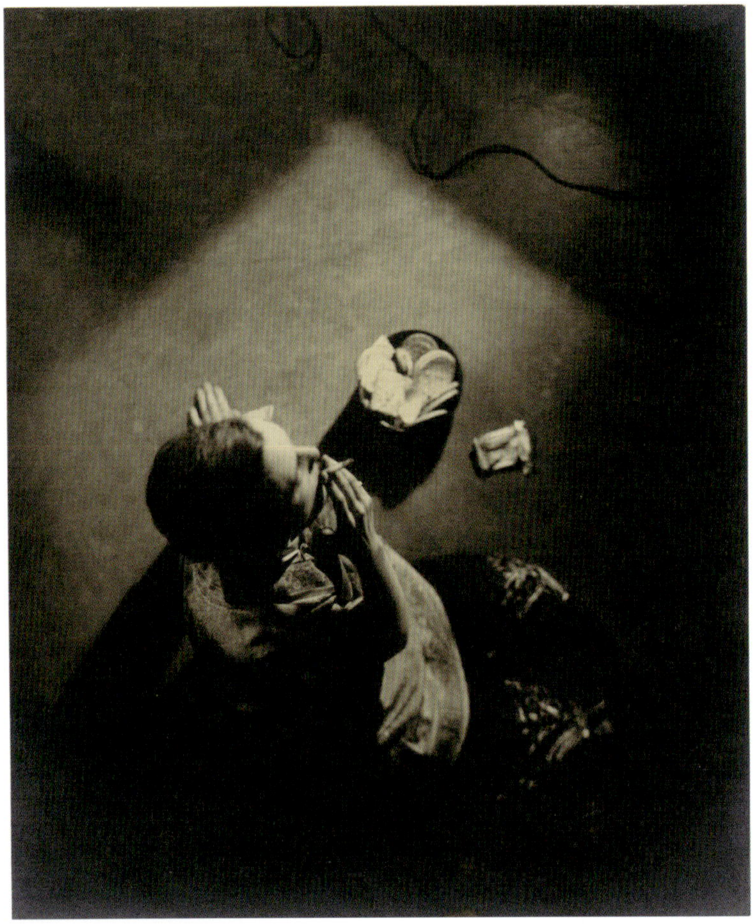

Untitled, c. 1926

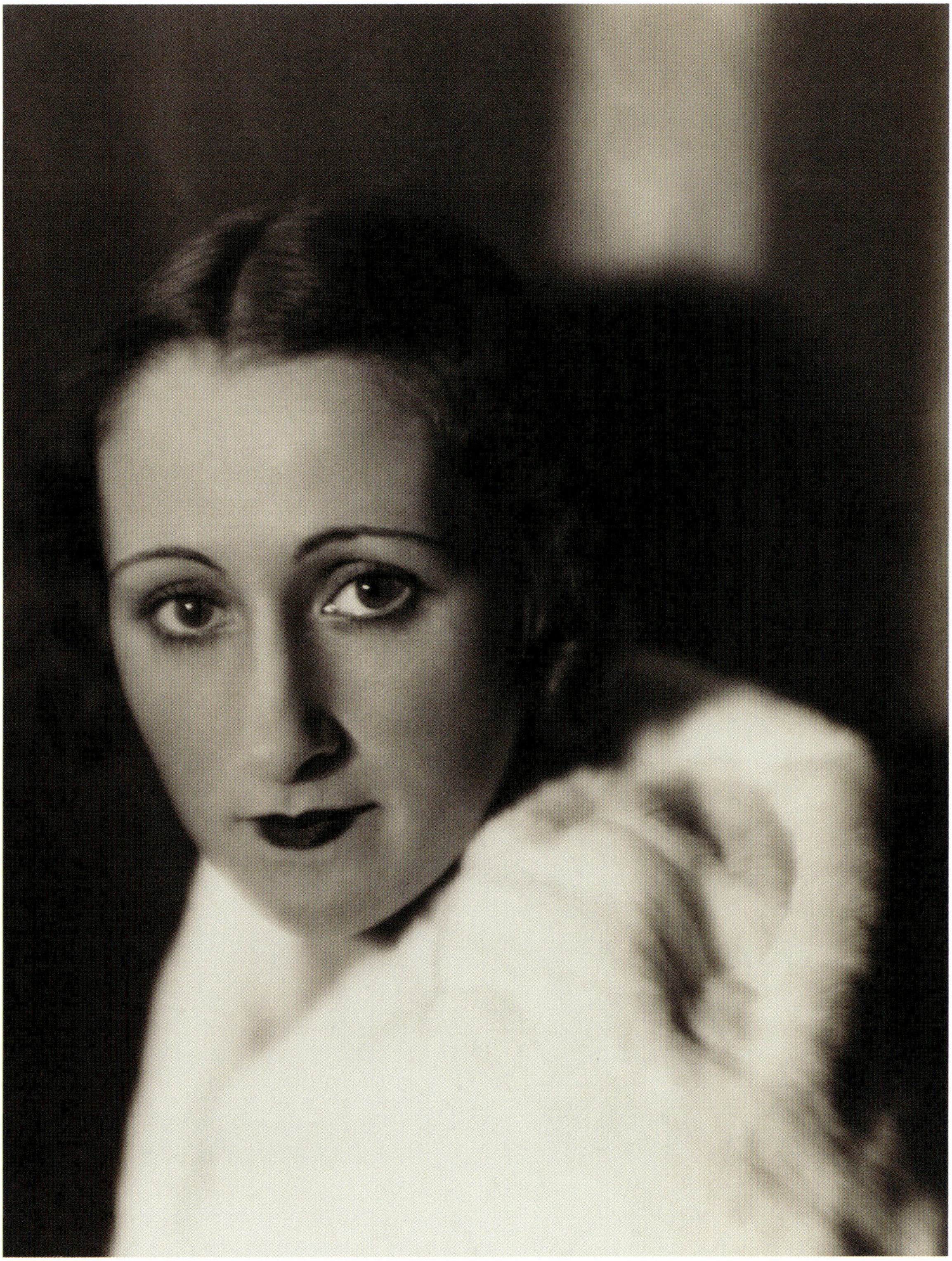

Mme Jacques Heim, c. 1928

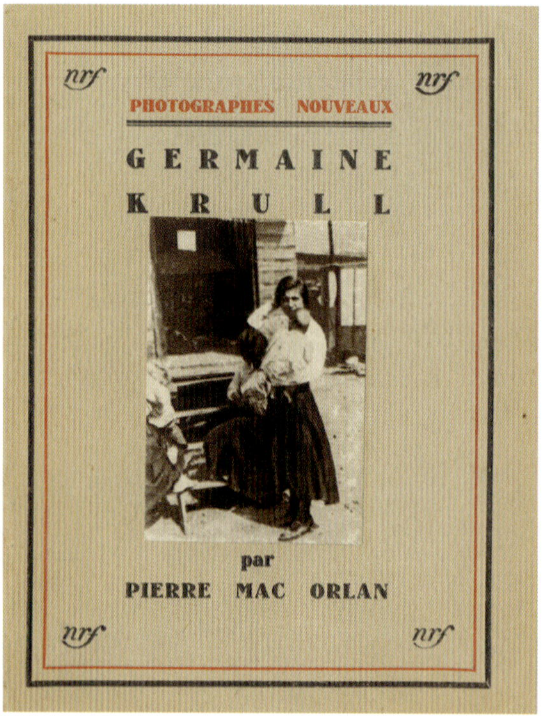

nrf nrf

PHOTOGRAPHES NOUVEAUX

GERMAINE
KRULL

par
PIERRE MAC ORLAN

nrf nrf

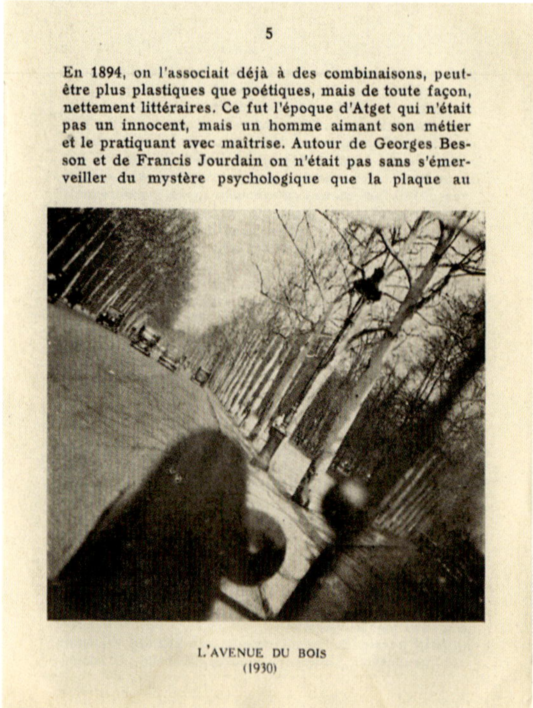

5

En 1894, on l'associait déjà à des combinaisons, peut-être plus plastiques que poétiques, mais de toute façon, nettement littéraires. Ce fut l'époque d'Atget qui n'était pas un innocent, mais un homme aimant son métier et le pratiquant avec maîtrise. Autour de Georges Besson et de Francis Jourdain on n'était pas sans s'émerveiller du mystère psychologique que la plaque au

L'AVENUE DU BOIS
(1930)

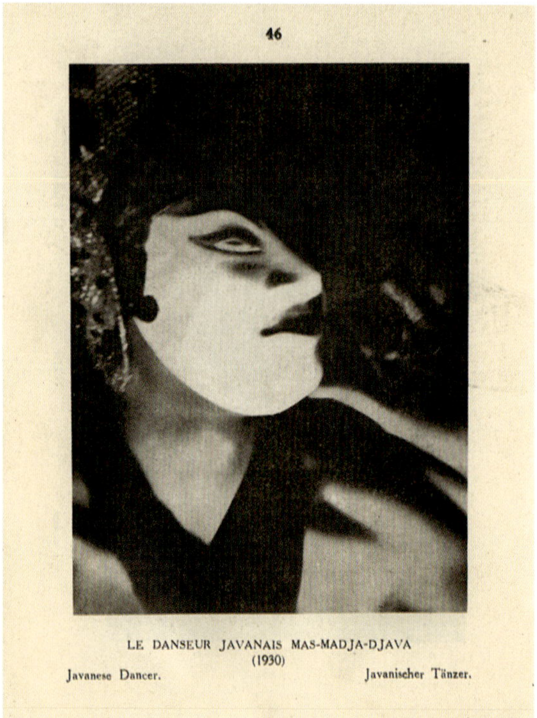

46

LE DANSEUR JAVANAIS MAS-MADJA-DJAVA
(1930)
Javanese Dancer. Javanischer Tänzer.

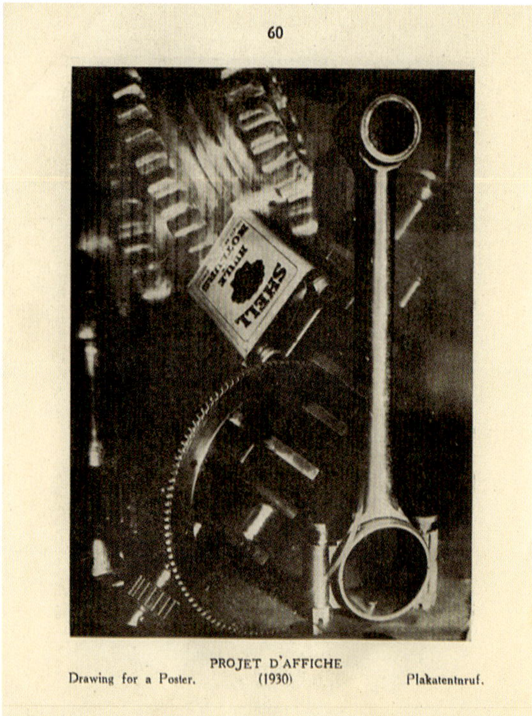

60

PROJET D'AFFICHE
Drawing for a Poster. (1930) Plakatentnruf.

Germaine Krull, by Pierre Mac Orlan, 'Photographes nouveaux' series, NRF, Gallimard, 1931, cover, pp. 5, 46, 60.

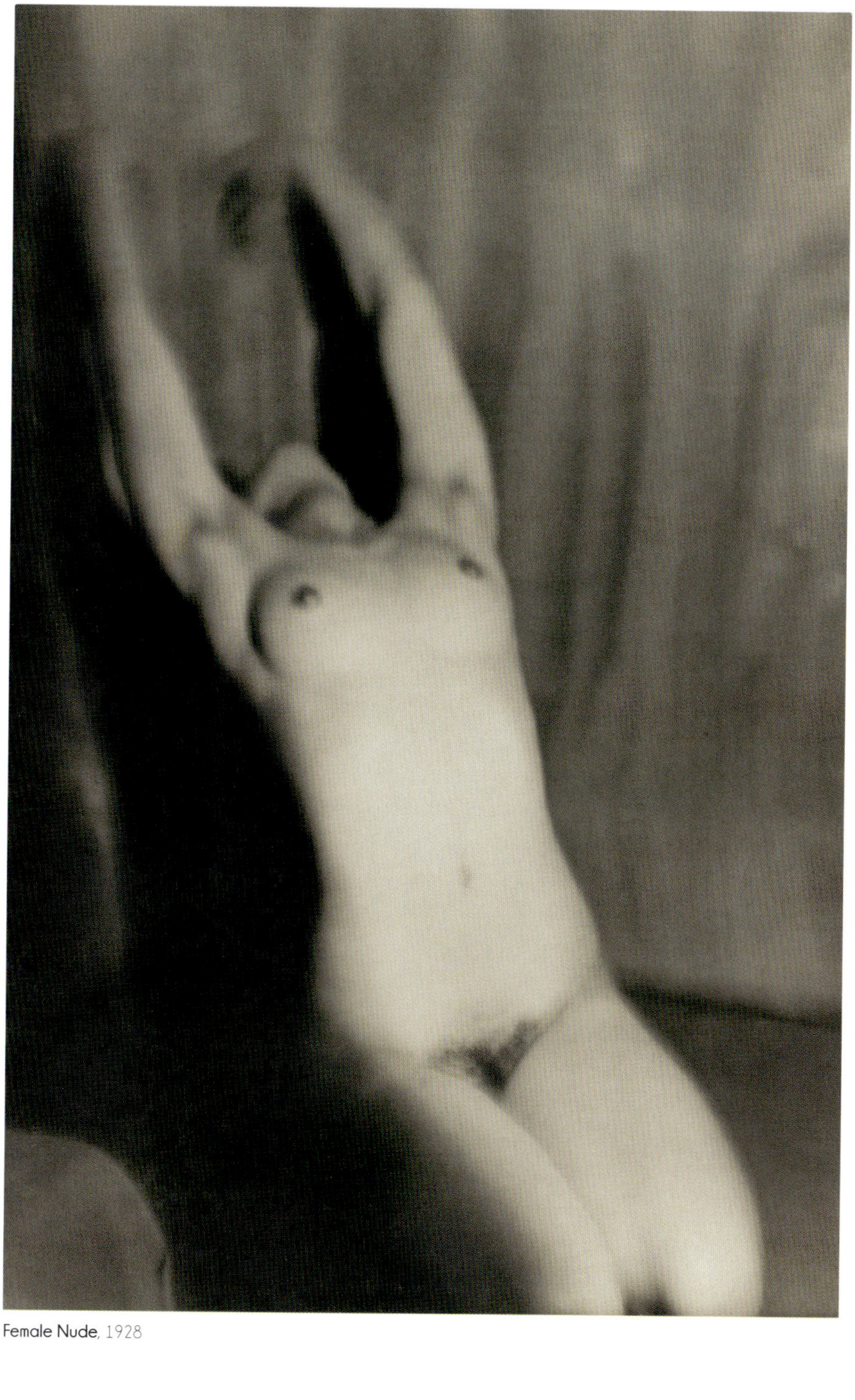

Female Nude, 1928

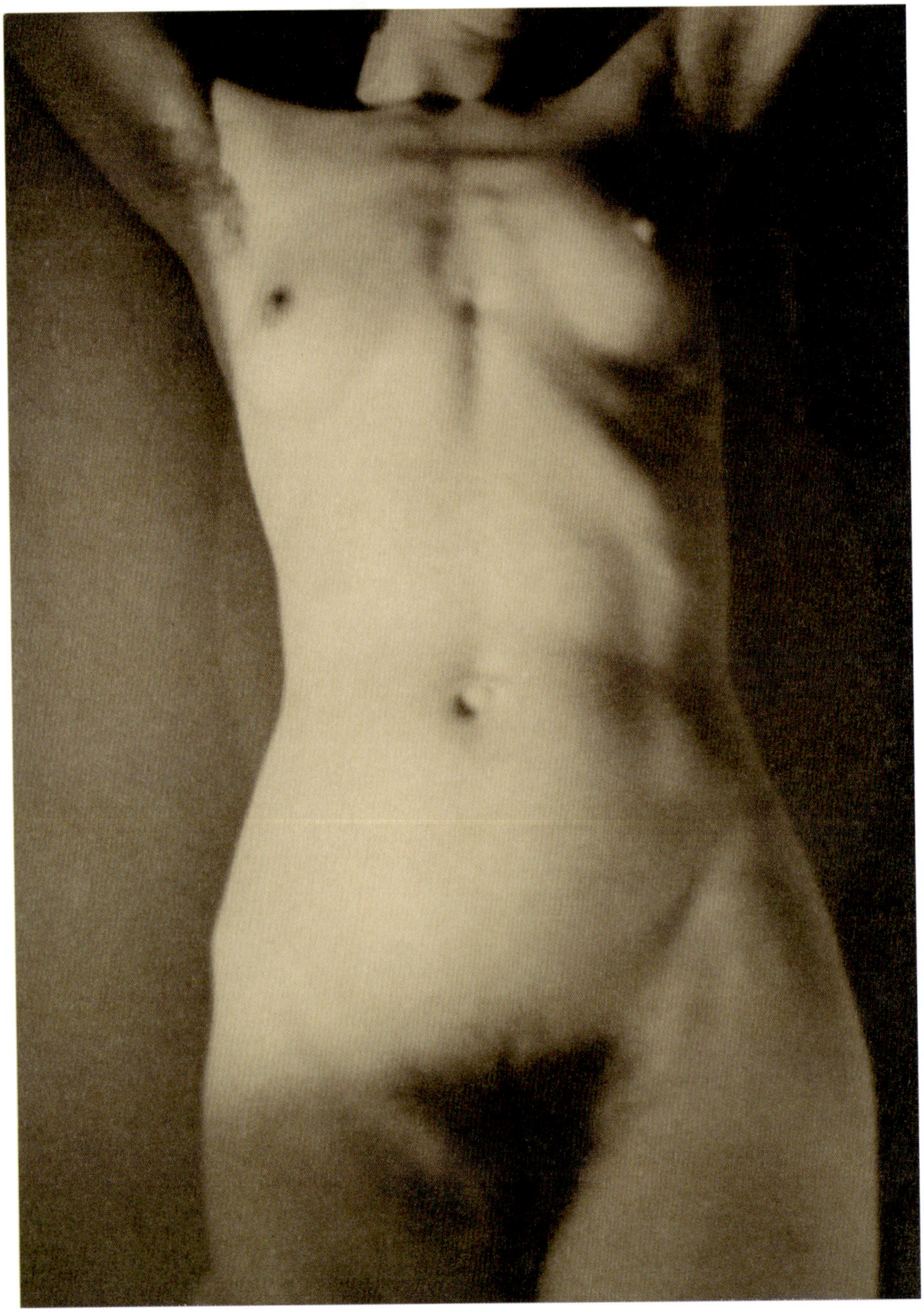

Nude, 1928

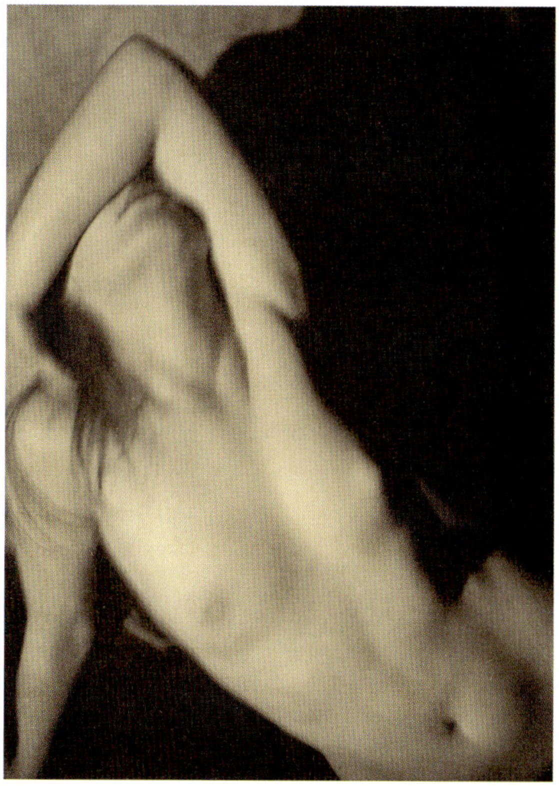

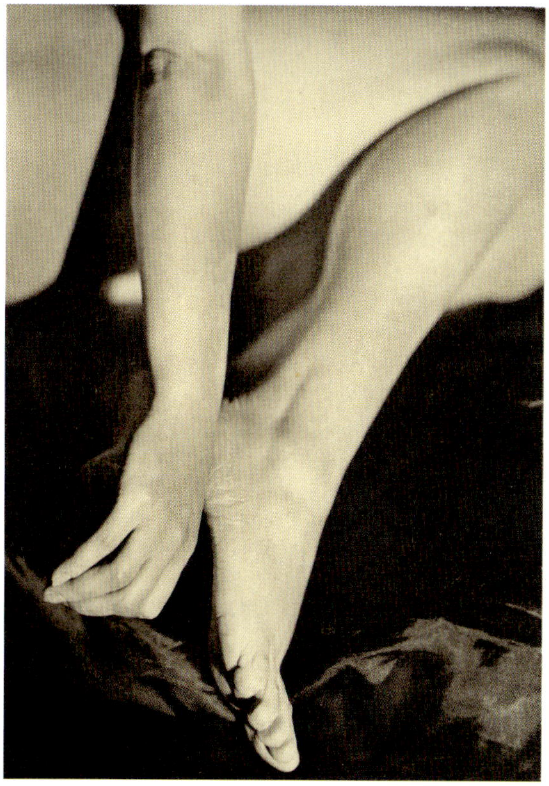

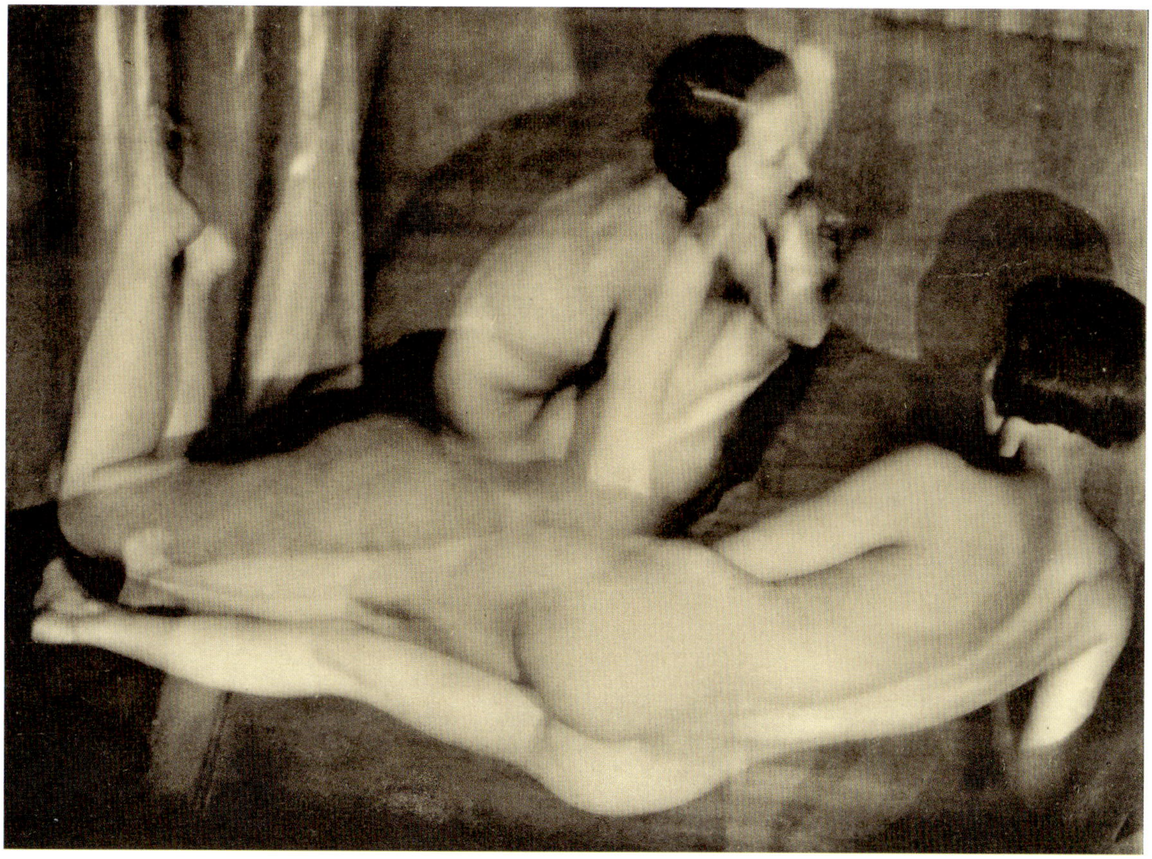

Nude Studies, A. Calavas, Paris, 1930

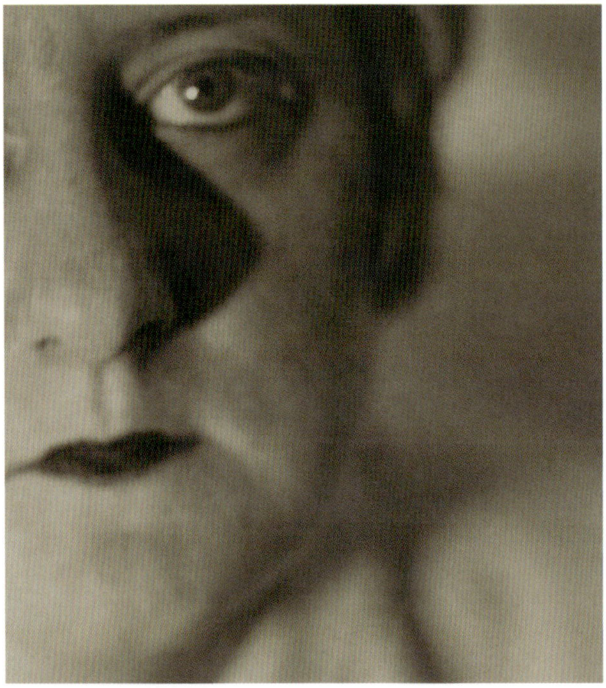

Germaine Beaumont, 1930

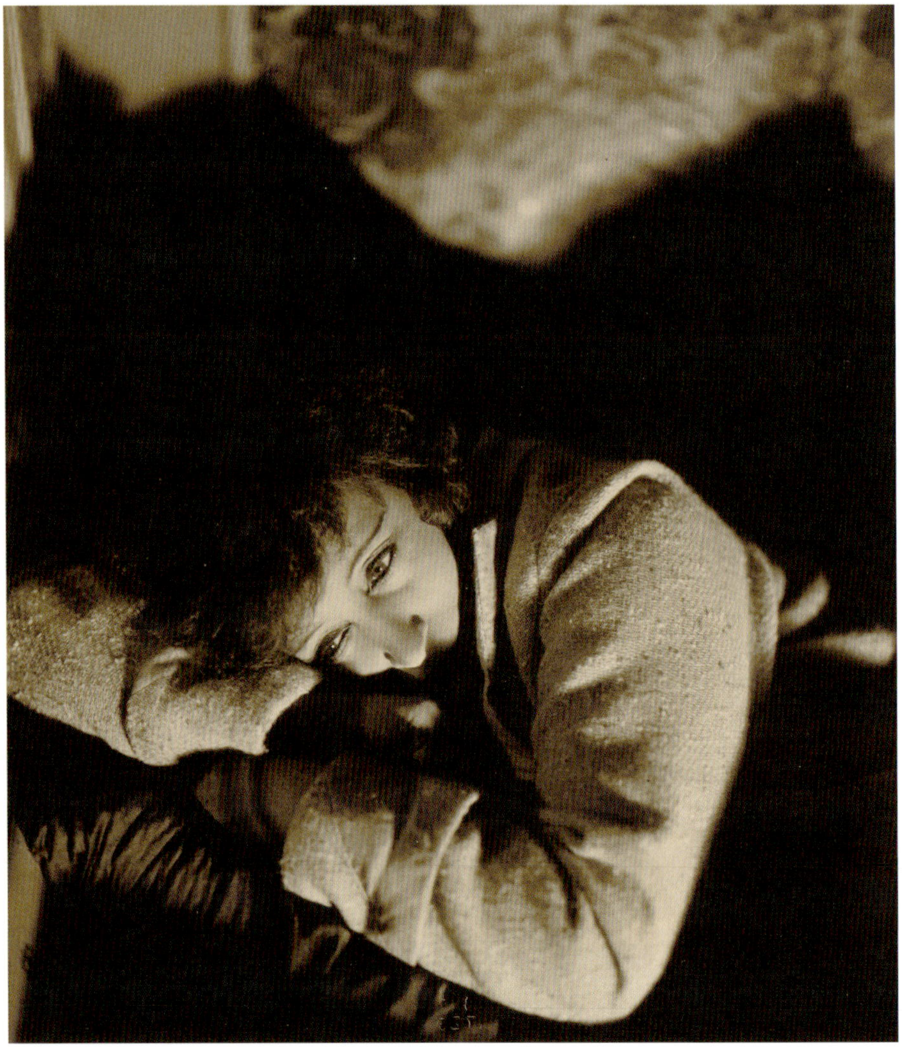

Colette, c. 1929

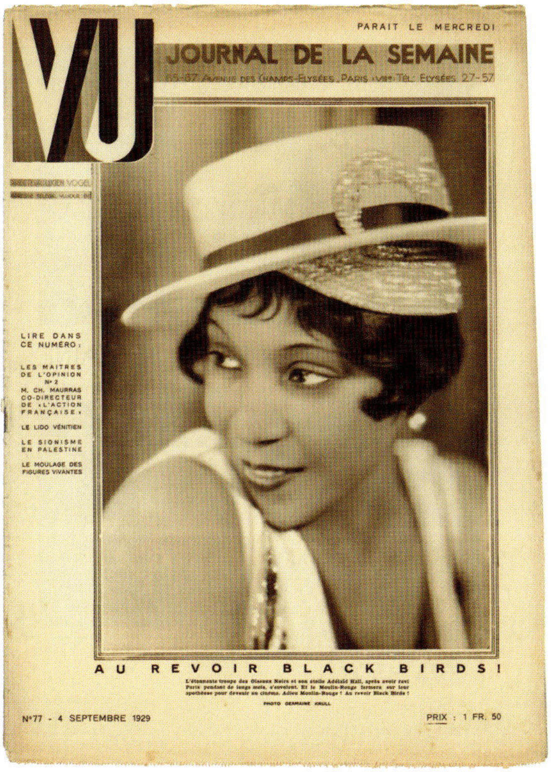

PARAIT LE MERCREDI

VU

JOURNAL DE LA SEMAINE

65-67 AVENUE DES CHAMPS-ELYSÉES, PARIS (VIIIe) TÉL: ELYSÉES 27-57

LIRE DANS CE NUMÉRO :

LES MAITRES DE L'OPINION N° 2 M. CH. MAURRAS CO-DIRECTEUR DE «L'ACTION FRANÇAISE»

LE LIDO VÉNITIEN

LE SIONISME EN PALESTINE

LE MOULAGE DES FIGURES VIVANTES

AU REVOIR BLACK BIRDS!

L'étonnante troupe des Oiseaux Noirs et son étoile Adélaïd Hall, après avoir ravi Paris pendant de longs mois, s'envolent. Et le Moulin-Rouge fermera sur leur apothéose pour devenir un cinéma. Adieu Moulin-Rouge ! Au revoir Black Birds !

PHOTO GERMAINE KRULL

N°77 - 4 SEPTEMBRE 1929

PRIX : 1 FR. 50

'Au revoir Black Birds!', *VU*, no. 77, 4 September 1929, cover

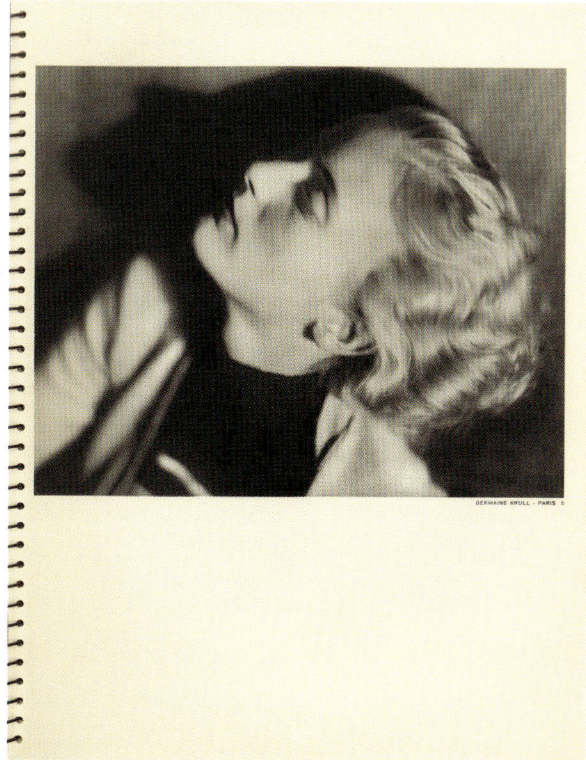

Photo 1931, Paris, Arts et Métiers graphiques, 1931, pl. 5

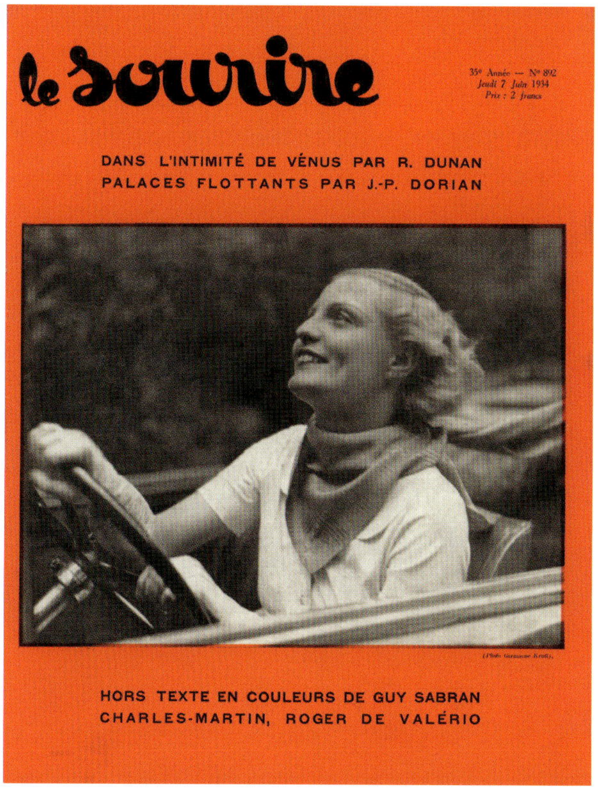

le Sourire

35e Année — N° 892
Jeudi 7 Juin 1934
Prix : 2 francs

DANS L'INTIMITÉ DE VÉNUS PAR R. DUNAN
PALACES FLOTTANTS PAR J.-P. DORIAN

HORS TEXTE EN COULEURS DE GUY SABRAN
CHARLES-MARTIN, ROGER DE VALÉRIO

Le Sourire, no. 892, 7 June 1934, cover

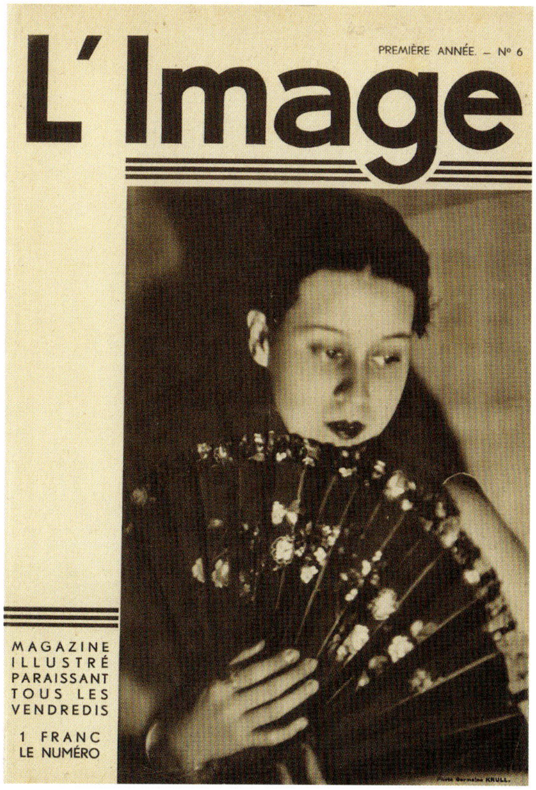

PREMIÈRE ANNÉE. — N° 6

L'Image

MAGAZINE ILLUSTRÉ PARAISSANT TOUS LES VENDREDIS

1 FRANC LE NUMÉRO

Photo Germaine KRULL.

L'Image, 1st year, no. 6, 1932, cover

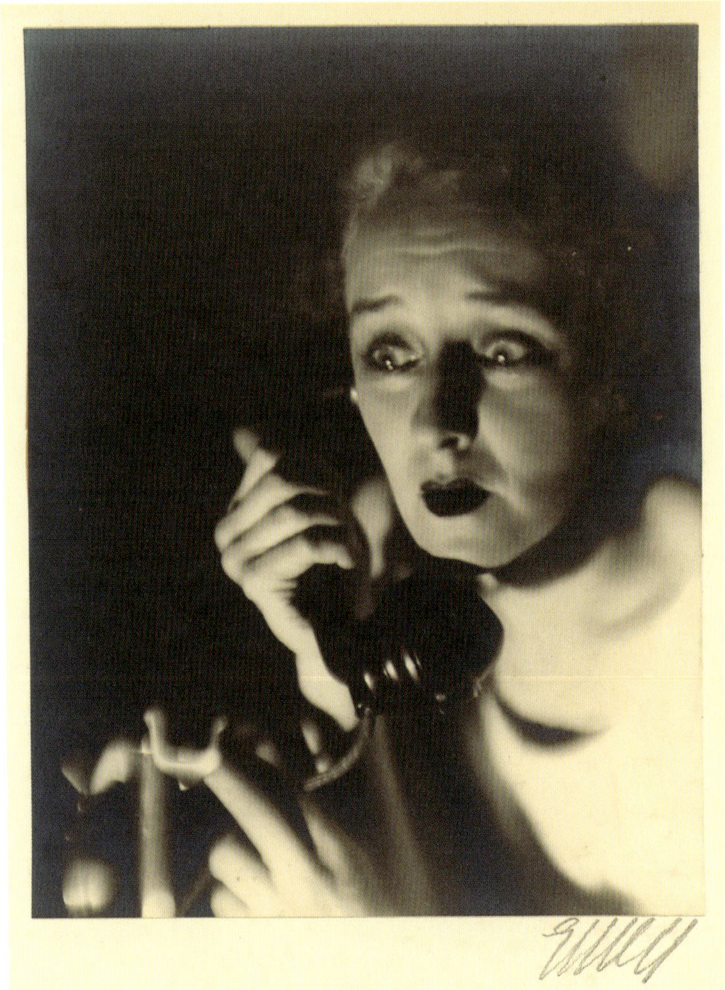

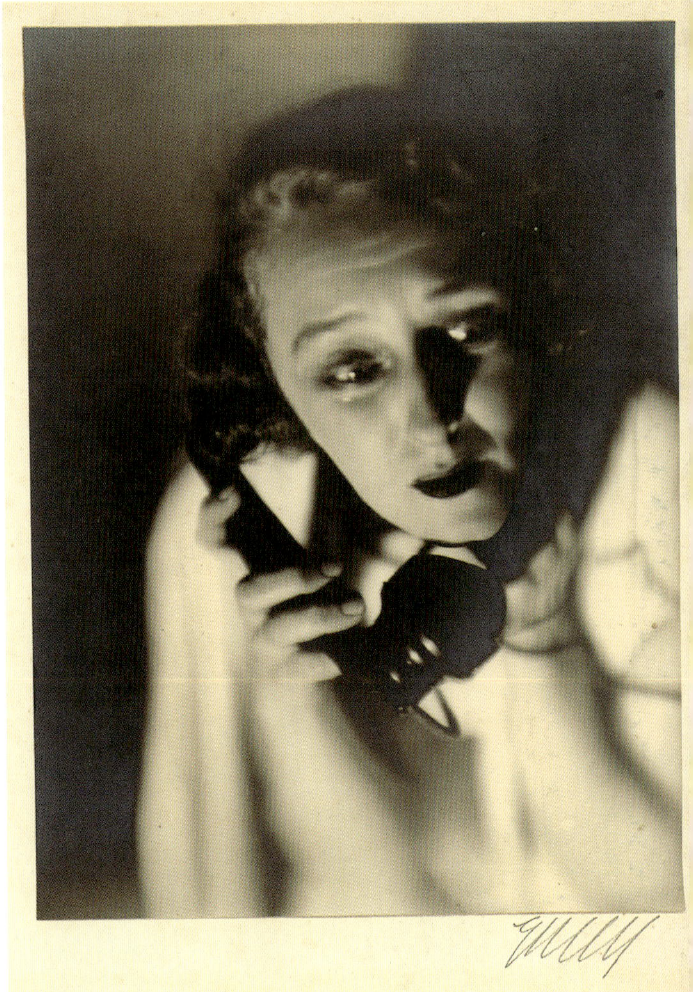

Berthe Bovy in 'La Voix humaine', 1930 (and facing page)

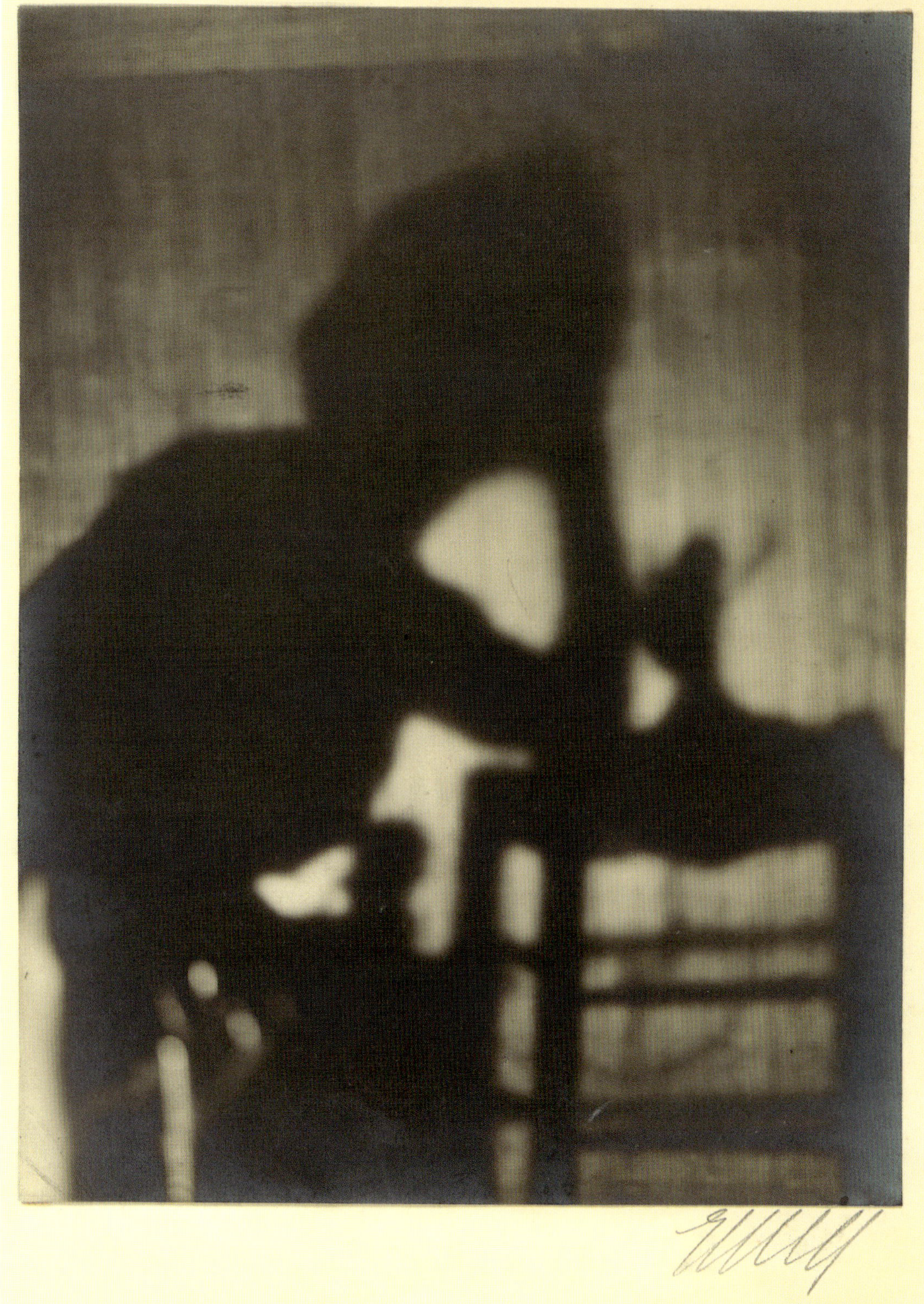

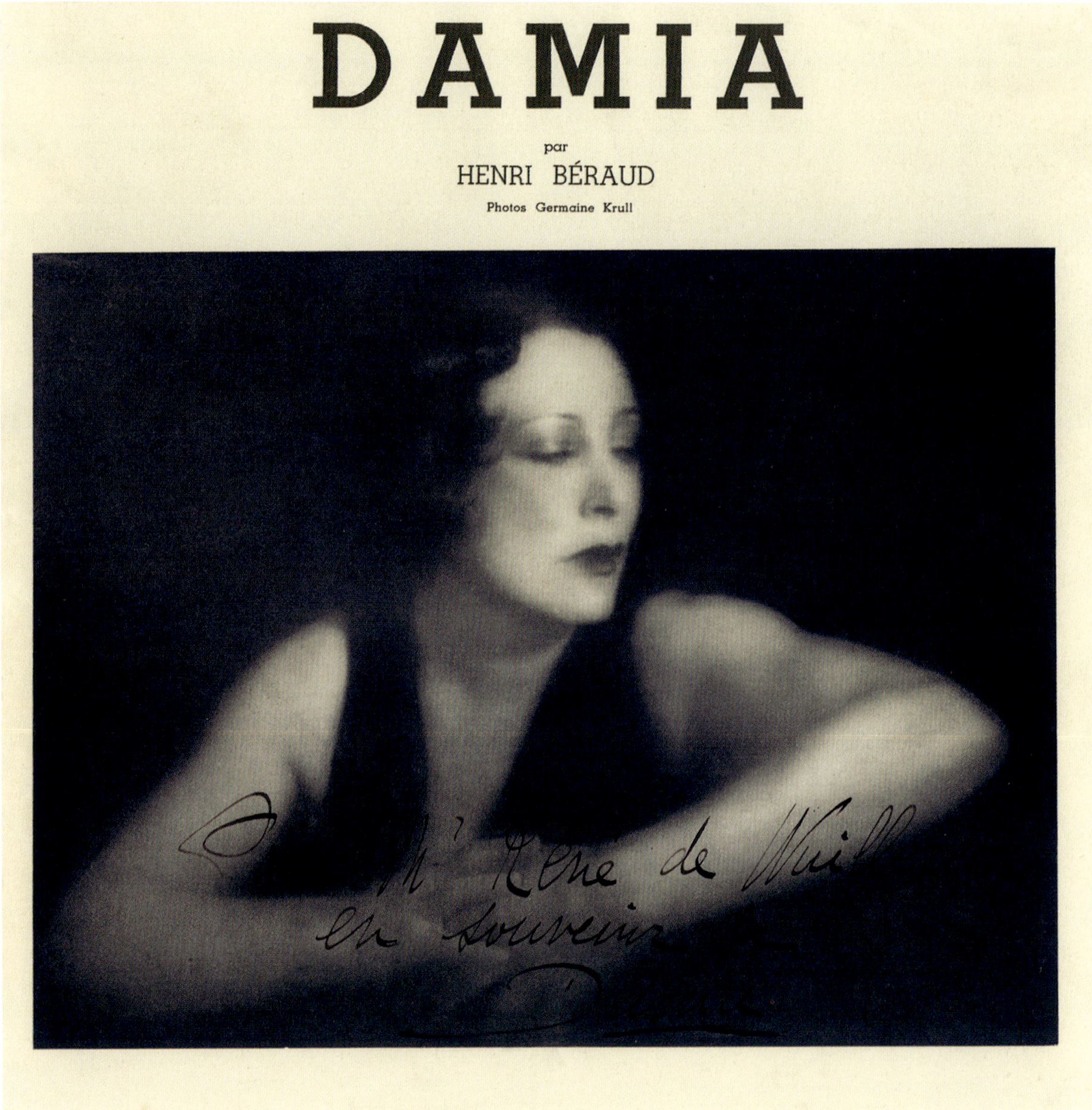

DAMIA

par

HENRI BÉRAUD

Photos Germaine Krull

Damia, by Henri Béraud, for Columbia, Antoine Girard, Paris, c. 1930 (above and facing page)

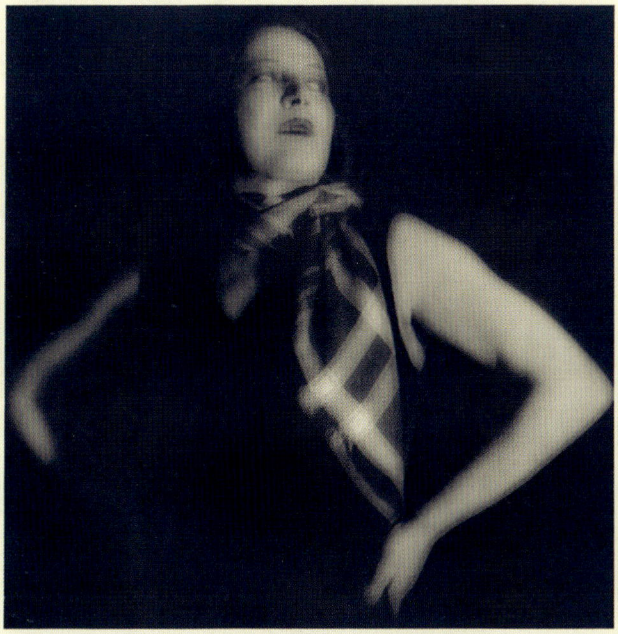

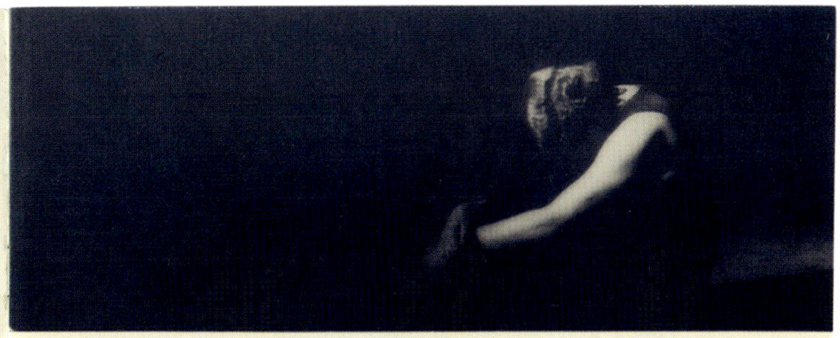

DAMIA

Un soir, j'étais au café-concert. Dans l'obscurité d'une loge voisine, un jeune couple jouissait du spectacle avec élégance, c'est-à-dire en gens que rien ne saurait étonner. On venait d'applaudir une tumultueuse attraction. En guise de prélude au numéro suivant, l'orchestre fit alors entendre une ritournelle de carrefour qui, dans sa langueur banale, évoquait à la fois le bal, le bar et la prison. Ma voisine se pencha sur son programme et d'un ton narquois :

— Voilà Damia, dit-elle, on va pleurer.

Elle ne croyait pas si bien dire. Un peu plus tard, en effet, dans l'ombre d'une loge occupée par un ménage très affranchi, la batiste épongeait le rimmel de deux jolis yeux...

Miracle qu'il serait vain de commenter et, s'il se peut, plus ridicule encore de découvrir ; miracle chaque soir renouvelé : Damia

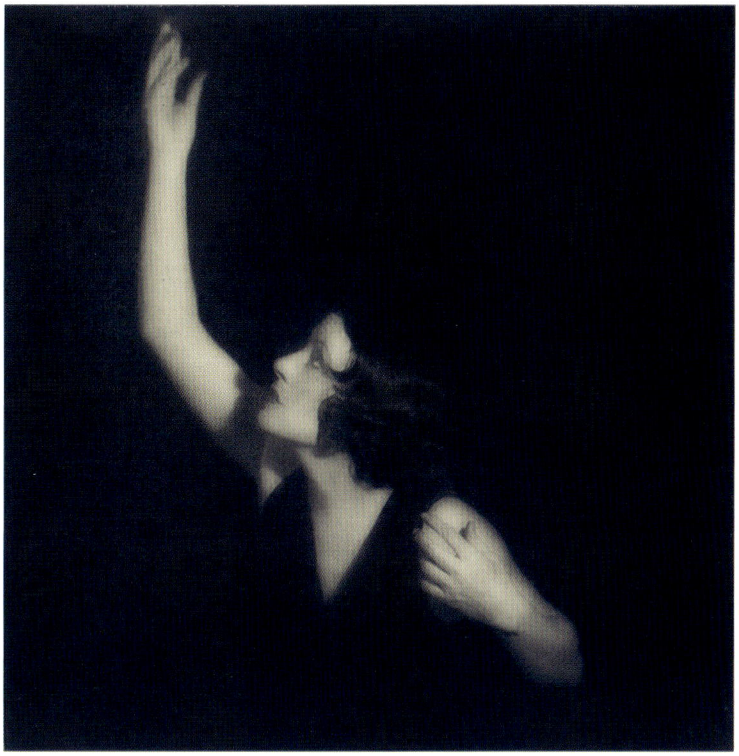

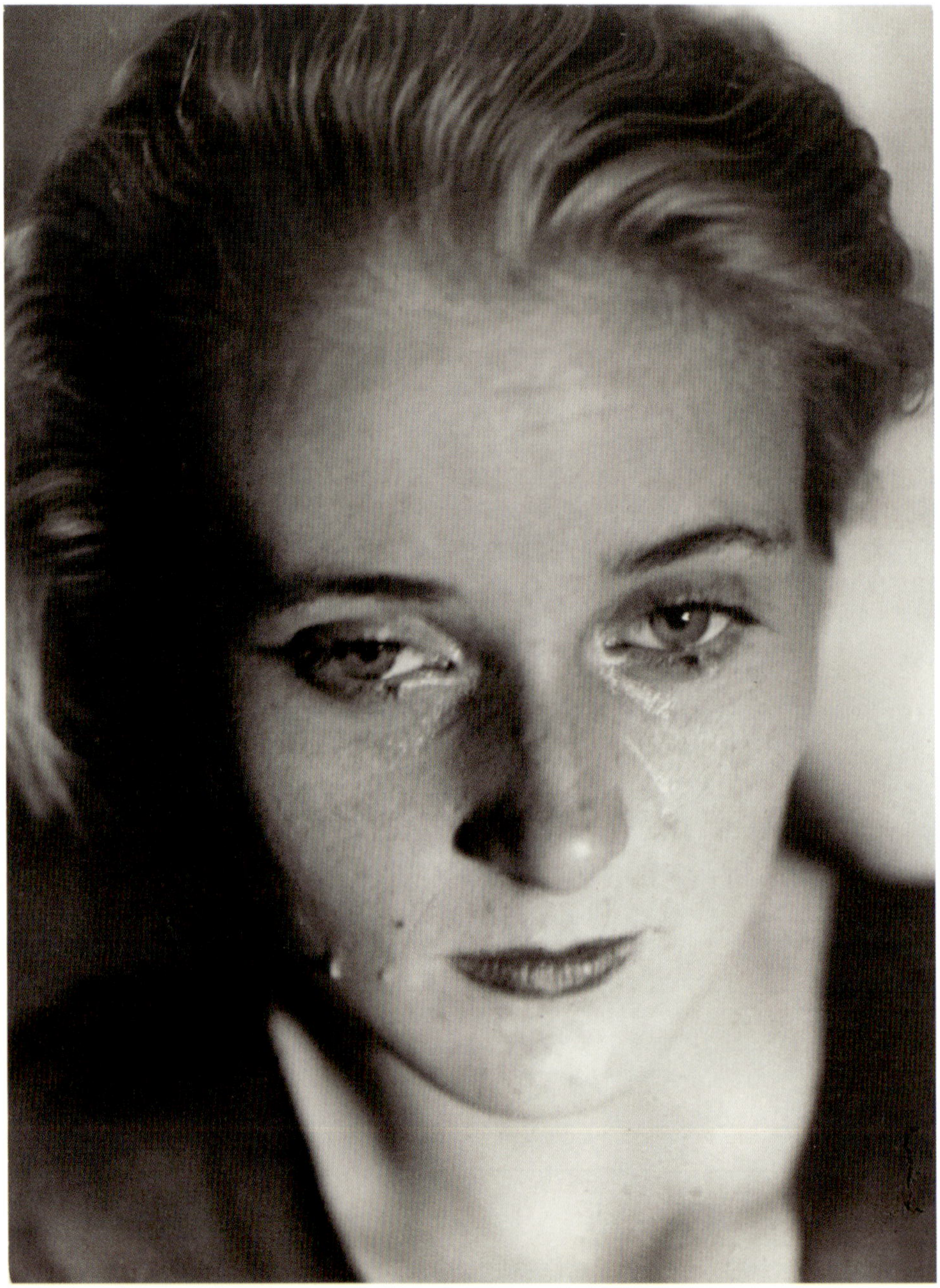

Study for *La Folle d'Itteville*, 1931

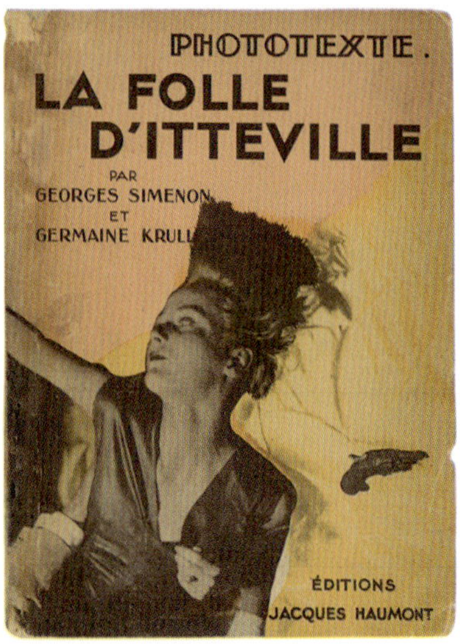

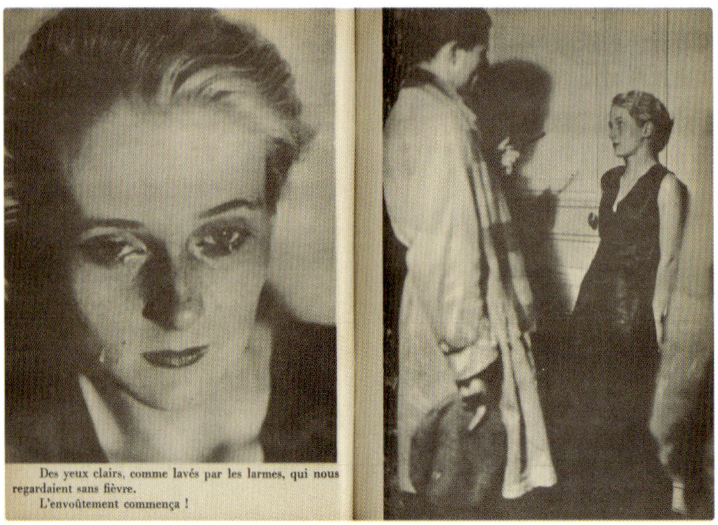

La Folle d'Itteville by Georges Simenon and Germaine Krull, 'Phototexte', Éditions Jacques Haumont, Paris, 1931 (and facing page, bottom)

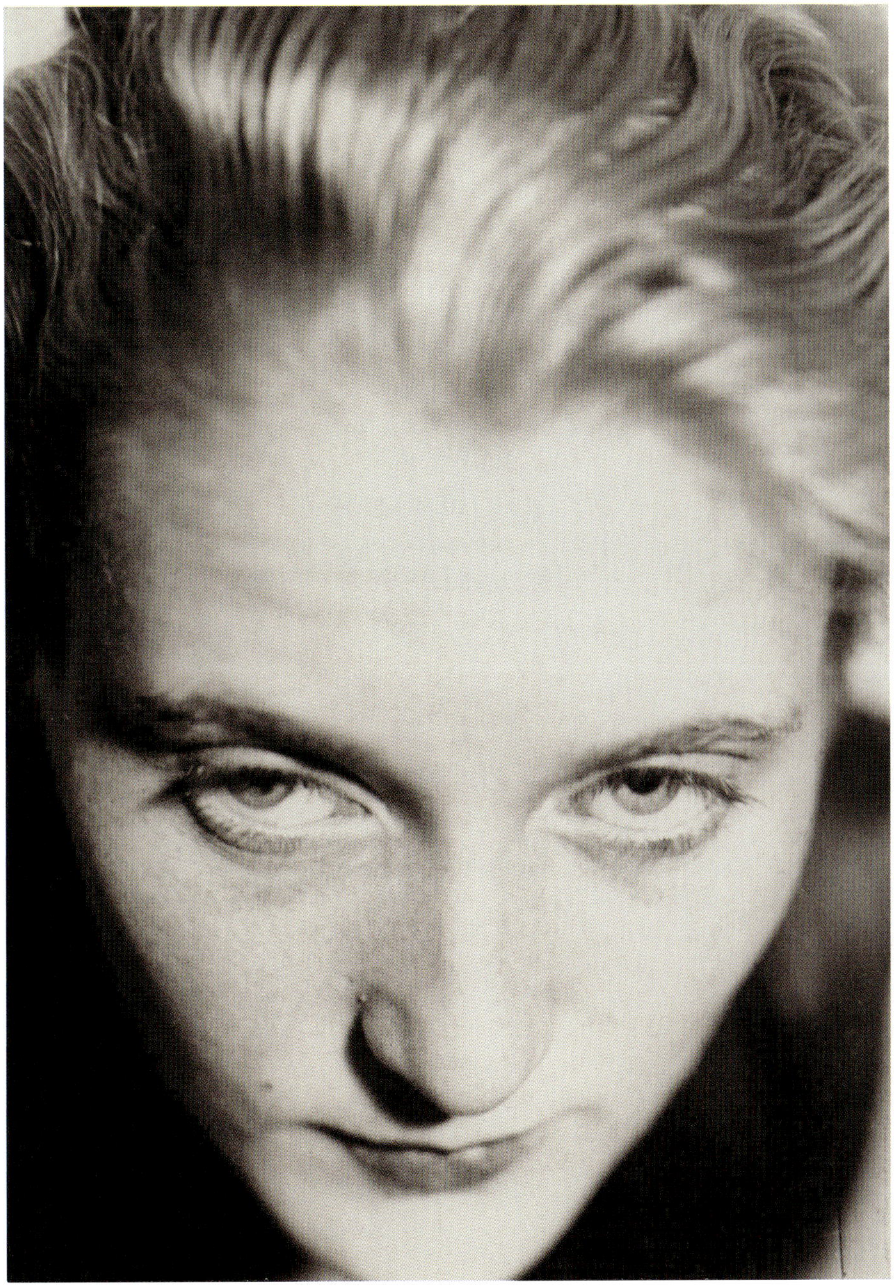

Study for *La Folle d'Itteville*, 1931

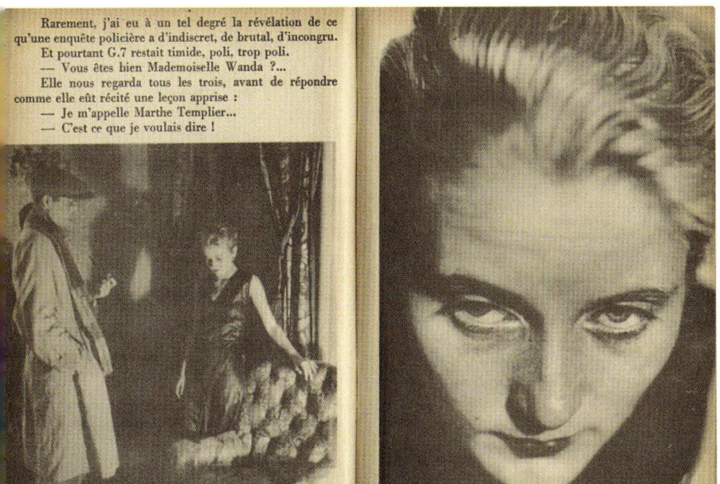

Rarement, j'ai eu à un tel degré la révélation de ce qu'une enquête policière a d'indiscret, de brutal, d'incongru.

Et pourtant G.7 restait timide, poli, trop poli.

— Vous êtes bien Mademoiselle Wanda ?...

Elle nous regarda tous les trois, avant de répondre comme elle eût récité une leçon apprise :

— Je m'appelle Marthe Templier...

— C'est ce que je voulais dire !

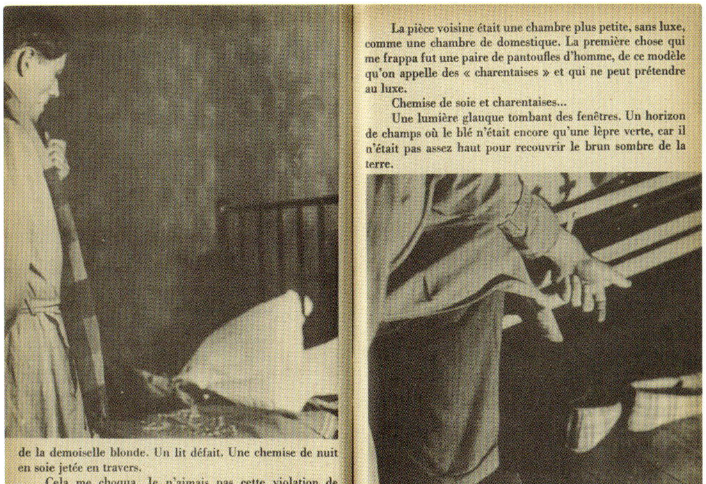

de la demoiselle blonde. Un lit défait. Une chemise de nuit en soie jetée en travers.

Cela me choqua. Je n'aimais pas cette violation de l'intimité d'une jeune fille.

La pièce voisine était une chambre plus petite, sans luxe, comme une chambre de domestique. La première chose qui me frappa fut une paire de pantoufles d'homme, de ce modèle qu'on appelle des « charentaises » et qui ne peut prétendre au luxe.

Chemise de soie et charentaises...

Une lumière glauque tombant des fenêtres. Un horizon de champs où le blé n'était encore qu'une lèpre verte, car il n'était pas assez haut pour recouvrir le brun sombre de la terre.

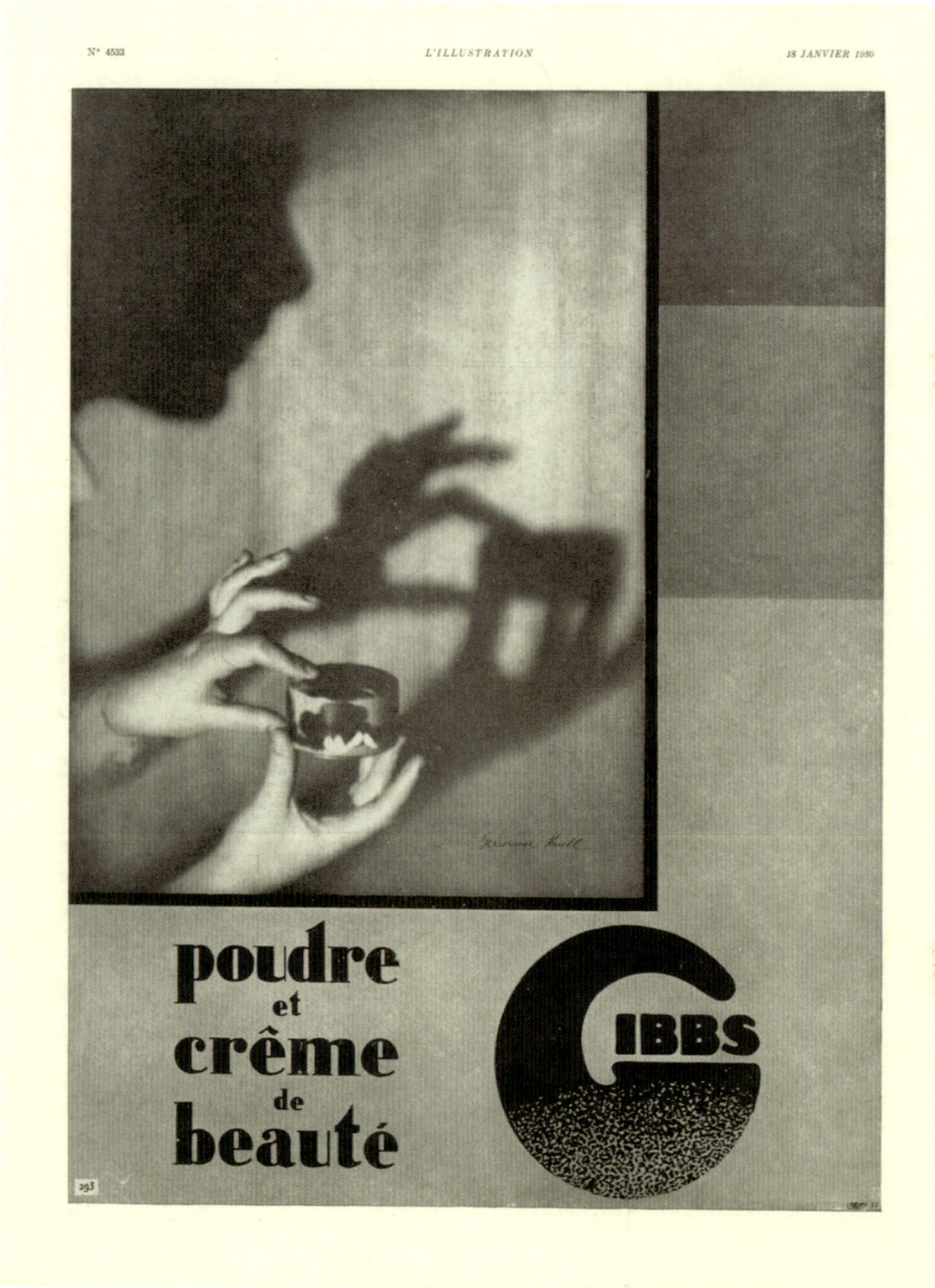

Gibbs advertisement, *L'Illustration*, no. 4533, 18 January 1930

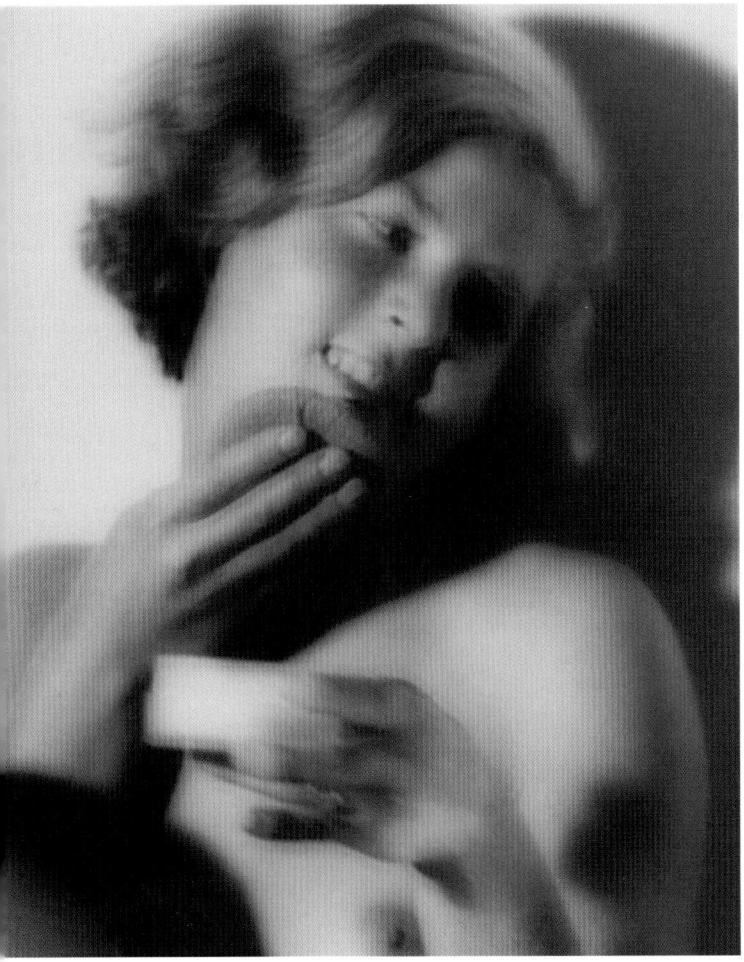

Assia Holding a Pot of Powder, 1930

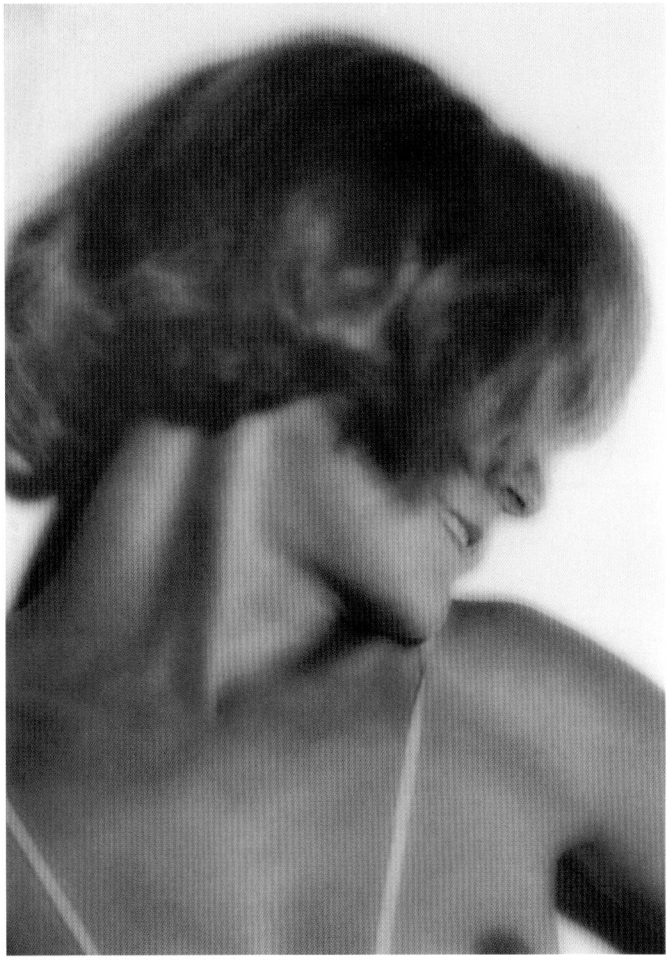

Assia in Profile, 1930

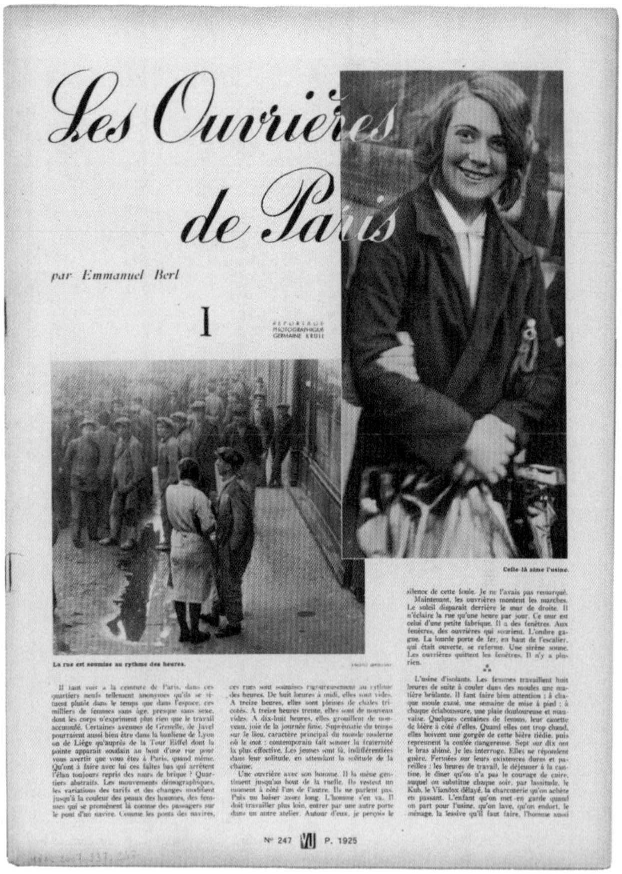

Les Ouvrières de Paris

par Emmanuel Berl

I

Nº 247 VU P. 1925

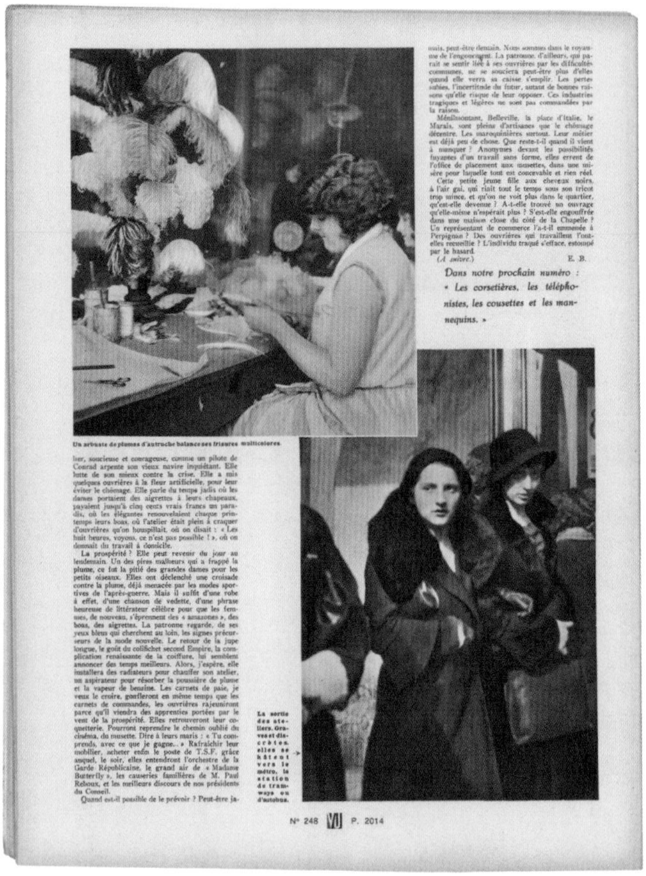

Nº 248 VU P. 2014

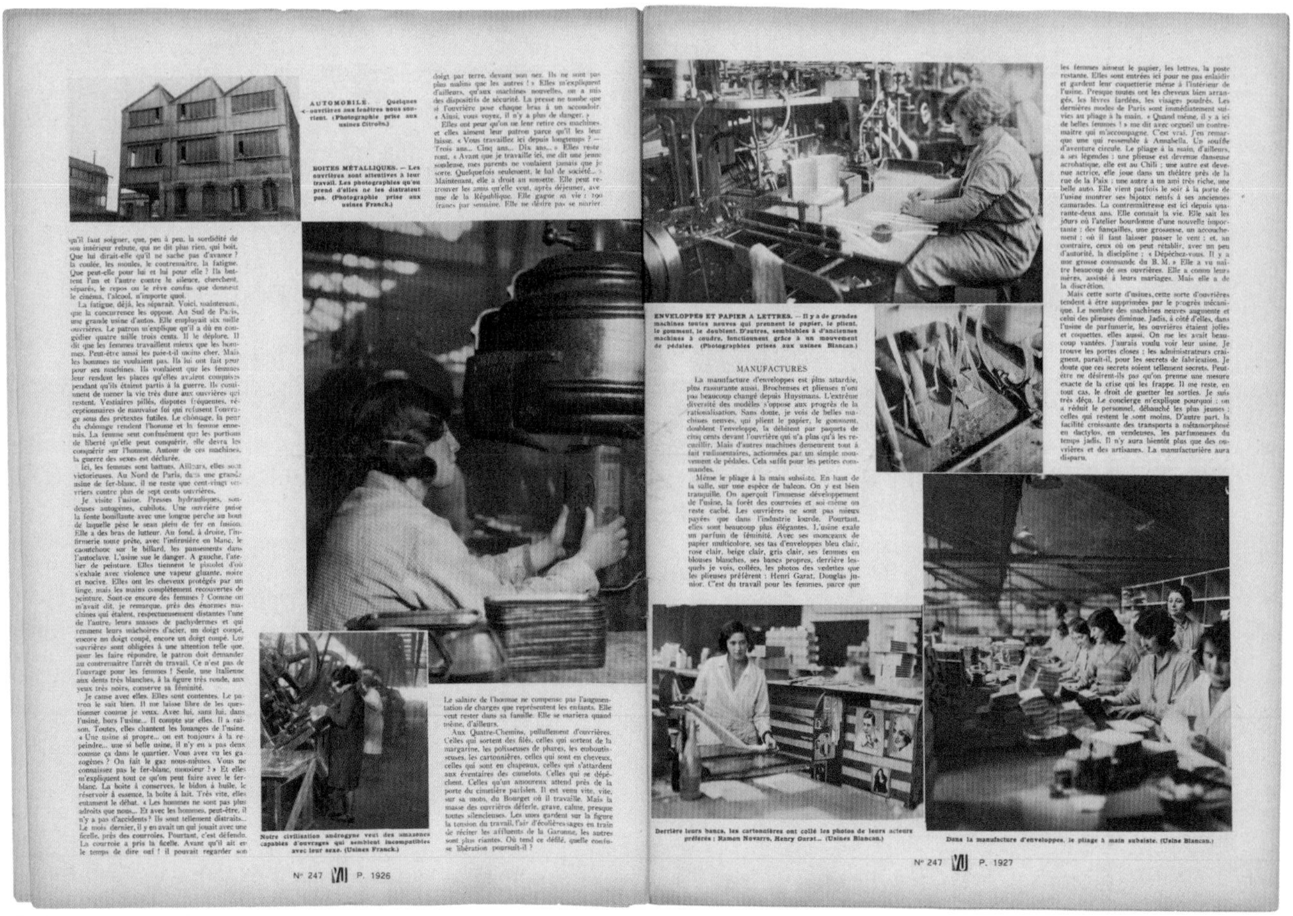

Nº 247 VU P. 1926

Nº 247 VU P. 1927

'The Women Workers of Paris', by Emmanuel Berl, *VU*, no. 247, 7 December 1932, pp. 1925, 1926, 1927 (above left and bottom); no. 248, 14 December 1932, pp. 2014 and 2012–2013 (above right and facing page)

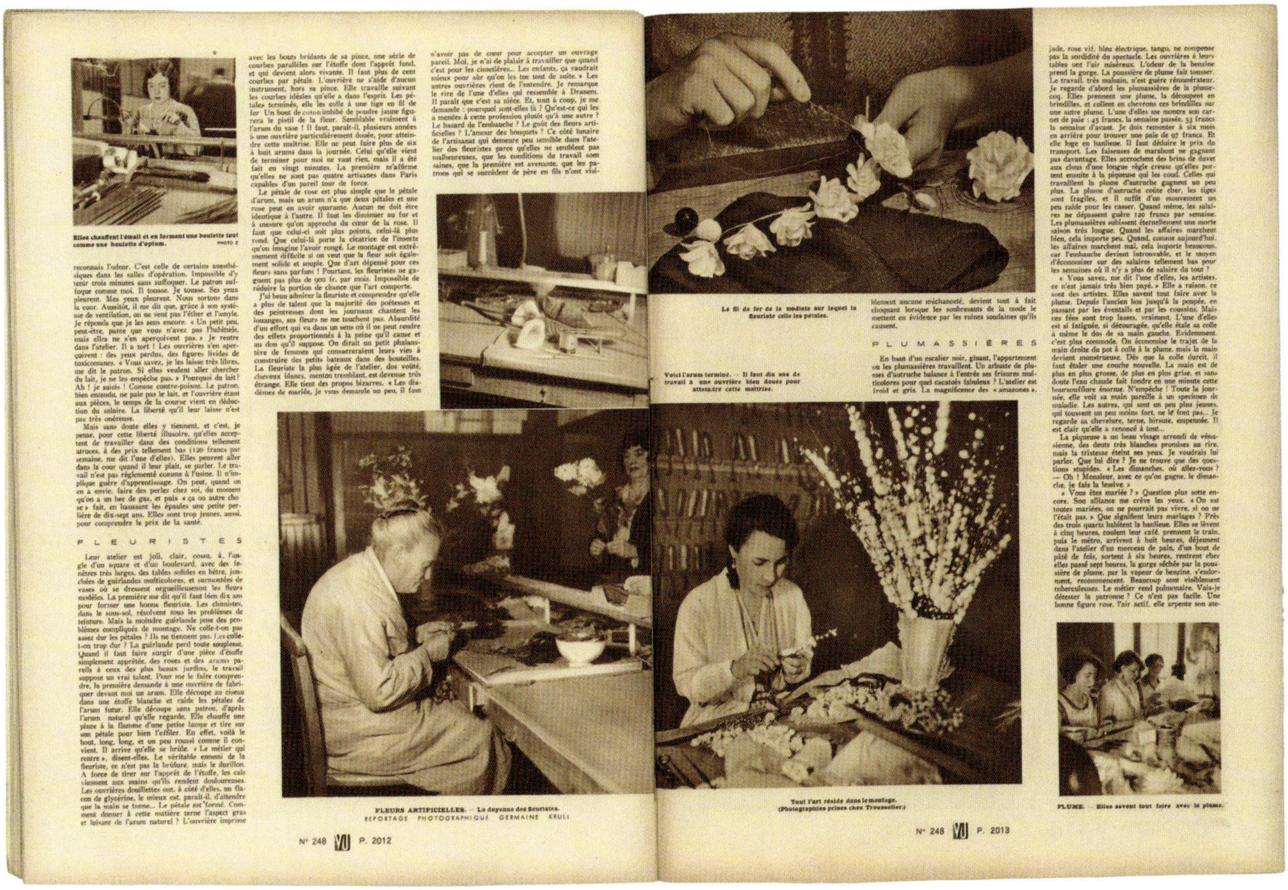

Elles chauffent l'émail et en forment une boulette tout comme une boulette d'opium.

reconnais l'odeur. C'est celle de certains anesthésiques dans les salles d'opération. Impossible d'y tenir trois minutes sans suffoquer. Le patron suffoque comme moi. Il tousse. Je tousse. Ses yeux pleurent. Mes yeux pleurent. Nous sortons dans la cour. Aussitôt, il me dit que, grâce à son système de ventilation, on ne sent pas l'éther et l'amyle. Je réponds que je les sens encore. « Un petit peu, peut-être, parce que vous n'avez pas l'habitude, mais elles ne s'en aperçoivent pas. » Je rentre dans l'atelier. Il a tort ! Les ouvrières s'en aperçoivent : des yeux perdus, des figures livides de toxicomanes. « Vous savez, je les laisse très libres, me dit le patron. Si elles veulent aller chercher du lait, je ne les empêche pas. » Pourquoi du lait? Ah ! je saisis ! Comme contre-poison. Le patron, bien entendu, ne paie pas le lait, et l'ouvrière étant aux pièces, le temps de la course vient en déduction du salaire. La liberté qu'il leur laisse n'est pas très onéreuse.

Mais sans doute elles y tiennent, et c'est, je pense, pour cette liberté illusoire, qu'elles acceptent de travailler dans des conditions tellement atroces, à des prix tellement bas (120 francs par semaine, me dit l'une d'elles). Elles peuvent aller dans la cour quand il leur plaît, se parler. Le travail n'est pas réglementé comme à l'usine. Il n'implique guère d'apprentissage. On peut, quand on en a envie, faire des perles chez soi, du moment qu'on a un bec de gaz, et puis « ça ou autre chose » fait, en haussant les épaules une petite perlière de dix-sept ans. Elles sont trop jeunes, aussi, pour comprendre le prix de la santé.

F L E U R I S T E S

Leur atelier est joli, clair, cossu, à l'angle d'un square et d'un boulevard, avec des fenêtres très larges, des tables solides en hêtre, jonchées de guirlandes multicolores, et surmontées de vases où se dressent orgueilleusement les fleurs modèles. La première me dit qu'il faut bien dix ans pour former une bonne fleuriste. Les chimistes, dans le sous-sol, résolvent tous les problèmes de teinture. Mais la moindre guirlande pose des problèmes compliqués de montage. Ne colle-t-on pas assez dur les pétales ? Ils ne tiennent pas. Les colle-t-on trop dur ? La guirlande perd toute souplesse. Quand il faut faire surgir d'une pièce d'étoffe simplement apprêtée, des roses et des arums pareils à ceux des plus beaux jardins, le travail suppose un vrai talent. Pour me le faire comprendre, la première demande à une ouvrière de fabriquer devant moi un arum. Elle découpe au ciseau dans une étoffe blanche et raide les pétales de l'arum futur. Elle découpe sans patron, d'après l'arum naturel qu'elle regarde. Elle chauffe une pince à la flamme d'une petite lampe et tire sur son pétale pour bien l'effiler. En effet, voilà le bout, long, long, et un peu roussi comme il convient. Il arrive qu'elle se brûle. « Le métier qui rentre », disent-elles. Le véritable ennemi de la fleuriste, ce n'est pas la brûlure, mais le durillon. A force de tirer sur l'apprêt de l'étoffe, les cals viennent aux mains qu'ils rendent douloureuses. Les ouvrières douillettes ont, à côté d'elles, un flacon de glycérine, le mieux est, paraît-il, d'attendre que la main se tanne... Le pétale est formé. Comment donner à cette matière terne l'aspect gras et luisant de l'arum naturel ? L'ouvrière imprime avec les bouts brûlants de sa pince, une série de courbes parallèles sur l'étoffe dont l'apprêt fond, et qui devient alors vivante. Il faut plus de cent courbes par pétale. L'ouvrière ne s'aide d'aucun instrument, hors sa pince. Elle travaille suivant les courbes idéales qu'elle a dans l'esprit. Les pétales terminés, elle les colle à une tige en fil de fer. Un bout de coton imbibé de poudre jaune figurera le pistil de la fleur. Semblable vraiment à l'arum du vase ! Il faut, paraît-il, plusieurs années à une ouvrière particulièrement douée, pour atteindre cette maîtrise. Elle ne peut faire plus de six à huit arums dans la journée. Celui qu'elle vient de terminer pour moi ne vaut rien, mais il a été fait en vingt minutes. La première m'affirme qu'elles ne sont pas quatre artisanes dans Paris capables d'un pareil tour de force.

Le pétale de rose est plus simple que le pétale d'arum, mais un arum n'a que deux pétales et une rose peut en avoir quarante. Aucun ne doit être identique à l'autre. Il faut les diminuer au fur et à mesure qu'on approche du cœur de la rose. Il faut que celui-ci soit plus pointu, celui-là plus rond. Que celui-là porte la cicatrice de l'insecte qu'on imagine l'avoir rongé. Le montage est extrêmement difficile si on veut que la fleur soit également solide et souple. Que d'art dépensé pour ces fleurs sans parfum ! Pourtant, les fleuristes ne gagnent pas plus de 900 fr. par mois. Impossible de réduire la portion de chance que l'art comporte.

J'ai beau admirer la fleuriste et comprendre qu'elle a plus de talent que la majorité des poétesses et des peintresses dont les journaux chantent les louanges, ses fleurs ne me touchent pas. Absurdité d'un effort qui va dans un sens où il ne peut rendre des effets proportionnés à la peine qu'il cause et au don qu'il suppose. On dirait un petit phalanstère de femmes qui consacreraient leurs vies à construire des petits bateaux dans des bouteilles. La fleuriste la plus âgée de l'atelier, dos voûté, cheveux blancs, menton tremblant, est devenue très étrange. Elle tient des propos bizarres. « Les diadèmes de mariée, je vous demande un peu, il faut n'avoir pas de cœur pour accepter un ouvrage pareil. Moi, je n'ai de plaisir à travailler que quand c'est pour les cimetières... Les enfants, ça vaudrait mieux pour sûr qu'on les tue tout de suite. » Les autres ouvrières rient de l'entendre. Je remarque le rire de l'une d'elles qui ressemble à Dranem. Il paraît que c'est sa nièce. Et, tout à coup, je me demande : pourquoi sont-elles là ? Qu'est-ce qui les a menées à cette profession plutôt qu'à une autre ? Le hasard de l'embauche ? Le goût des fleurs artificielles ? L'amour des bouquets ? Ce côté lunaire de l'artisanat qui demeure peu sensible dans l'atelier des fleuristes parce qu'elles ne semblent pas malheureuses, que les conditions du travail sont saines, que la première est avenante, que les patrons qui se succèdent de père en fils n'ont visiblement aucune méchanceté, devient tout à fait choquant lorsque les soubresauts de la mode le mettent en évidence par les ruines soudaines qu'ils causent.

Voici l'arum terminé. — Il faut dix ans de travail à une ouvrière bien douée pour atteindre cette maîtrise.

Le fil de fer de la modiste sur lequel la fleuriste colle les pétales.

P L U M A S S I È R E S

En haut d'un escalier noir, gluant, l'appartement où les plumassières travaillent. Un arbuste de plumes d'autruche balance à l'entrée ses frisures multicolores pour quel cacatoès fabuleux ? L'atelier est froid et gris. La magnificence des « amazones », jade, rose vif, bleu électrique, tango, ne compense pas la sordidité du spectacle. Les ouvrières à leurs tables ont l'air miséreux. L'odeur de la benzine prend la gorge. La poussière de plume fait tousser. Le travail, très malsain, n'est guère rémunérateur. Je regarde d'abord les plumassières de la plume-coq. Elles prennent une plume, la découpent en brindilles, et collent en chevrons ces brindilles sur une autre plume. L'une d'elles me montre son carnet de paie : 45 francs, la semaine passée, 53 francs la semaine d'avant. Je dois remonter à six mois en arrière pour trouver une paie de 97 francs. Et elle loge en banlieue. Il faut déduire le prix du transport. Les faiseuses de marabout ne gagnent pas davantage. Elles accrochent des brins de duvet aux clous d'une longue règle creuse qu'elles portent ensuite à la piqueuse qui les coud. Celles qui travaillent la plume d'autruche gagnent un peu plus. La plume d'autruche coûte cher, les tiges sont fragiles, et il suffit d'un mouvement un peu raide pour les casser. Quand même, les salaires ne dépassent guère 120 francs par semaine. Les plumassières subissent éternellement une morte saison très longue. Quand les affaires marchent bien, cela importe peu. Quand, comme aujourd'hui, les affaires marchent mal, cela importe beaucoup, car l'embauche devient introuvable, et le moyen d'économiser sur des salaires tellement bas pour les semaines où il n'y a plus de salaire du tout ?

« Vous savez, me dit l'une d'elles, les artistes, ce n'est jamais très bien payé. » Elle a raison, ce sont des artistes. Elles savent tout faire avec la plume. Depuis l'ancien boa jusqu'à la poupée, en passant par les éventails et par les coussins. Mais ces fées sont trop lasses, vraiment. L'une d'elles est si fatiguée, si découragée, qu'elle étale sa colle à même le dos de sa main gauche. Evidemment, c'est plus commode. On économise le trajet de la main droite du pot à colle à la plume, mais la main devient monstrueuse. Dès que la colle durcit, il faut étaler une couche nouvelle. La main est de plus en plus grosse, de plus en plus grise, et sans doute l'eau chaude fait fondre en une minute cette boursouflure énorme. N'empêche ! Toute la journée, elle voit sa main pareille à un specimen de maladie. Les autres, qui sont un peu plus jeunes, qui toussent un peu moins fort, ne le font pas... Je regarde sa chevelure, terne, hirsute, empennée. Il est clair qu'elle a renoncé à tout...

La piqueuse a un beau visage arrondi de vénusienne, des dents très blanches promises au rire, mais la tristesse éteint ses yeux. Je voudrais lui parler. Que lui dire ? Je ne trouve que des questions stupides. « Les dimanches, où allez-vous ? — Oh ! Monsieur, avec ce qu'on gagne, le dimanche, je fais la lessive. »

« Vous êtes mariée ? » Question plus sotte encore. Son alliance me crève les yeux. « On est toutes mariées, on ne pourrait pas vivre, si on ne l'était pas. » Que signifient leurs mariages ? Près des trois quarts habitent la banlieue. Elles se lèvent à cinq heures, coulent leur café, prennent le train, puis le métro, arrivent à huit heures, déjeunent dans l'atelier d'un morceau de pain, d'un bout de pâté de foie, sortent à six heures, rentrent chez elles passé sept heures, la gorge séchée par la poussière de plume, par la vapeur de benzine, s'endorment, recommencent. Beaucoup sont visiblement tuberculeuses. Le métier rend pulmonaire. Vais-je détester la patronne ? Ce n'est pas facile. Une bonne figure rose, l'air actif, elle arpente son ate-

FLEURS ARTIFICIELLES. — La doyenne des fleuristes.
REPORTAGE PHOTOGRAPHIQUE GERMAINE KRULL

Tout l'art réside dans le montage.
(Photographies prises chez Trousselier.)

PLUME. — Elles savent tout faire avec la plume.

N° 248 VU P. 2012

N° 248 VU P. 2013

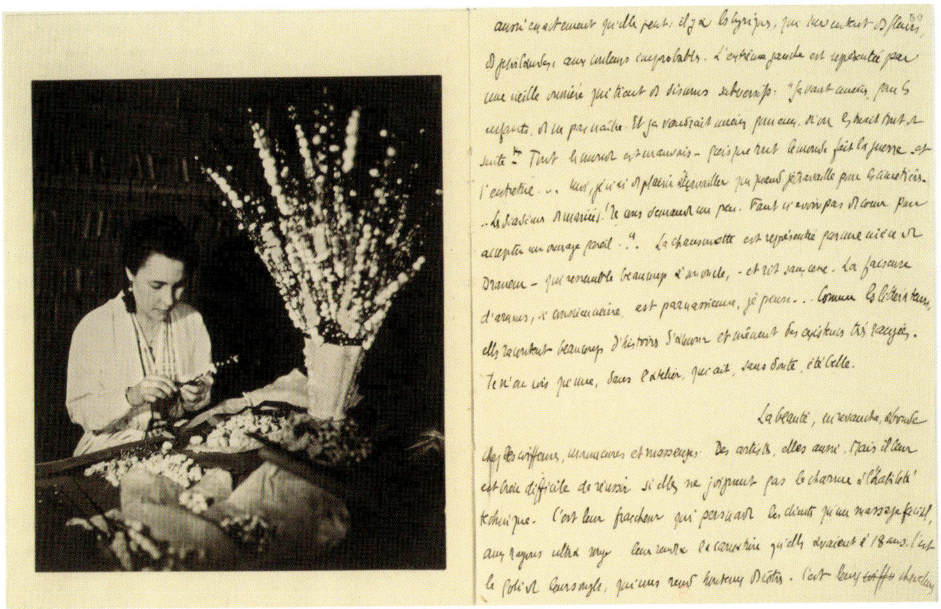

'Workers and Midinettes at Work and Play', original manuscript by Emmanuel Berl (photograph by Germaine Krull), 1931–1932

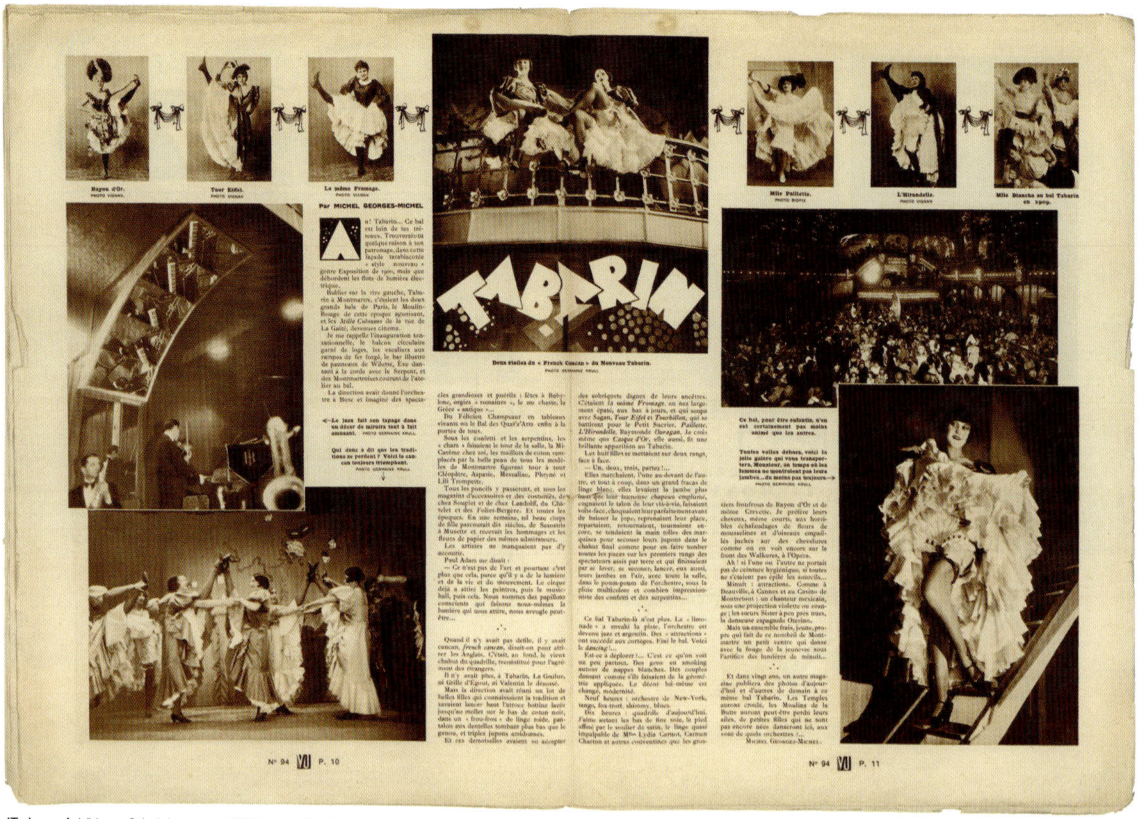

'Tabarin', *VU*, no. 94, 1 January 1930, pp. 10–11

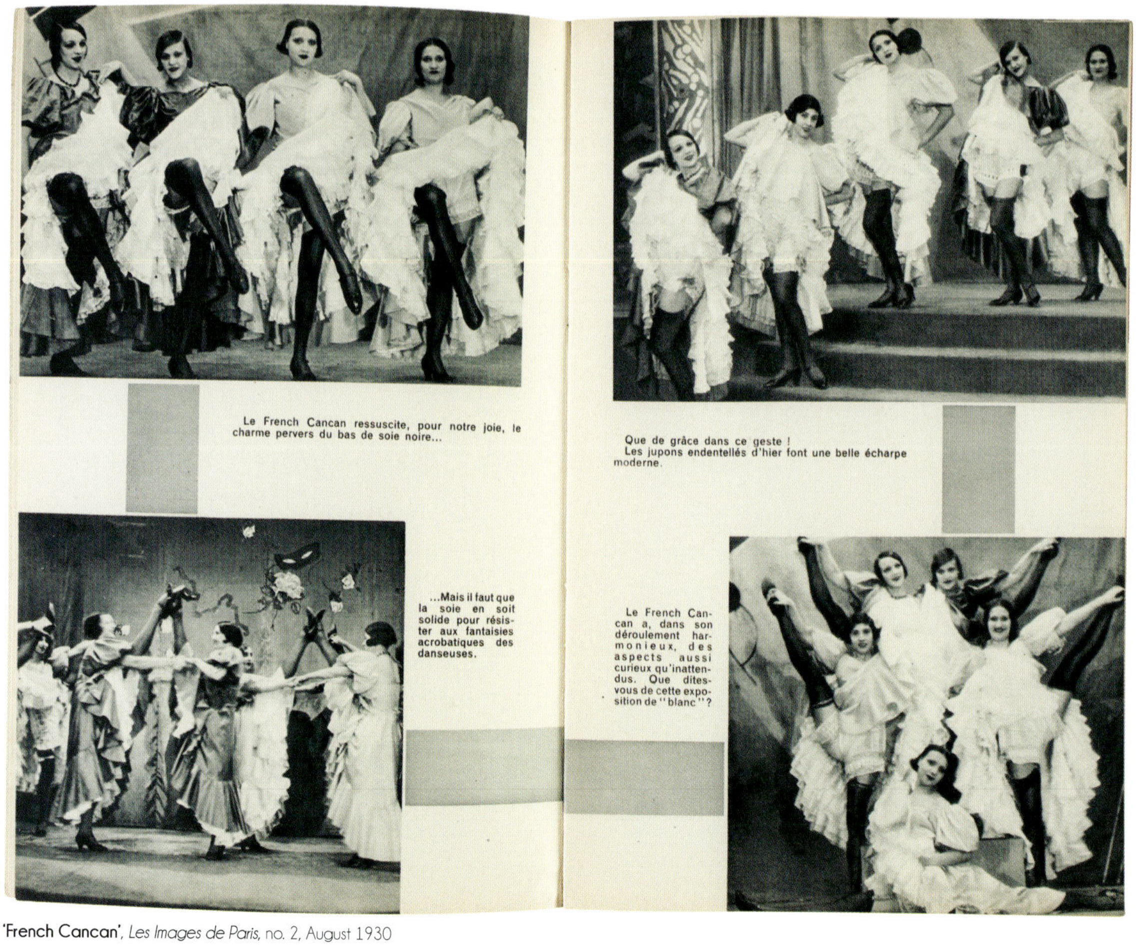

'French Cancan', *Les Images de Paris*, no. 2, August 1930

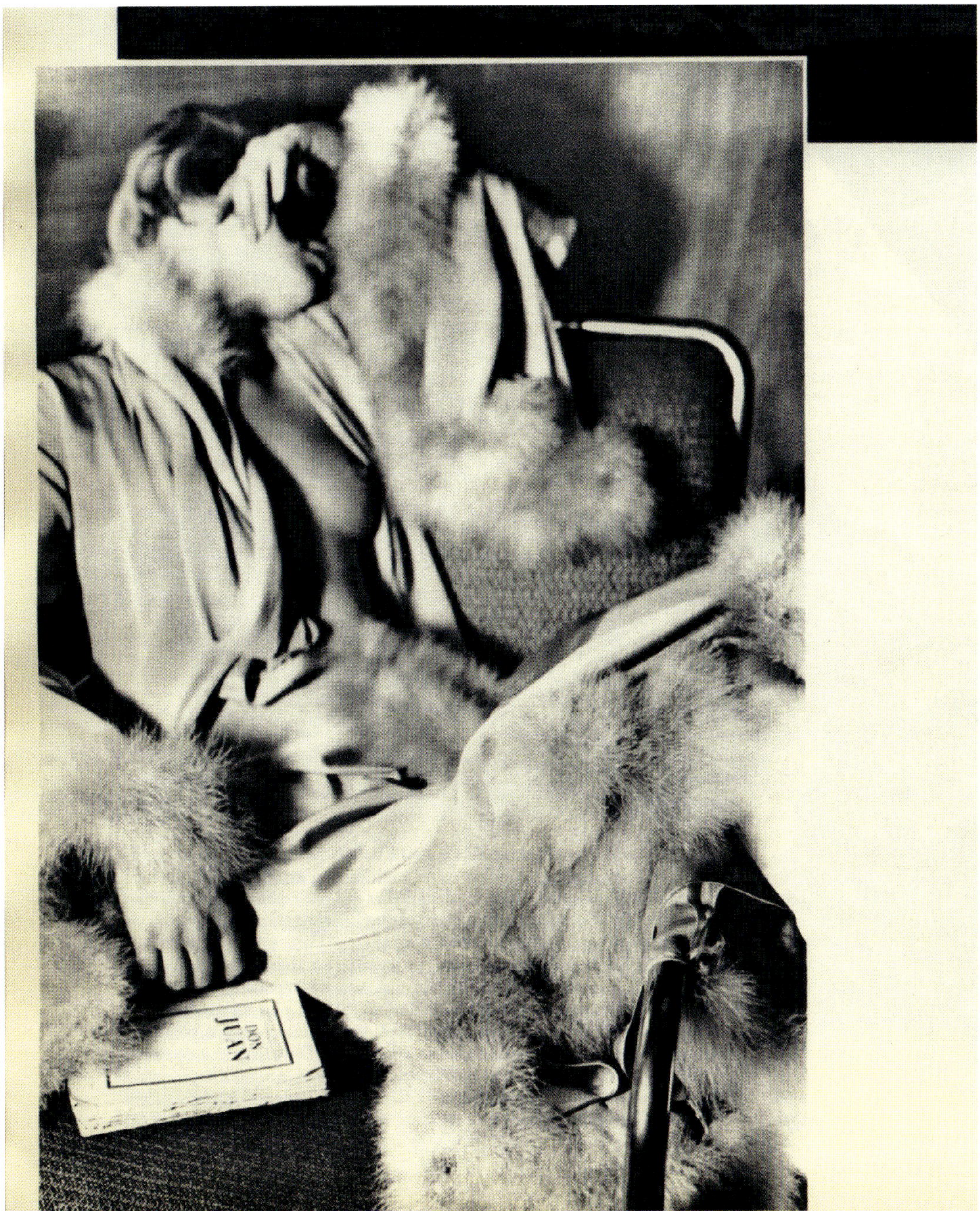

'Venus 1934, the Voluptuous', *Miroir du monde*, special 'Spring Smiles' issue, 1934

‘MY COLLECTION OF HANDS’

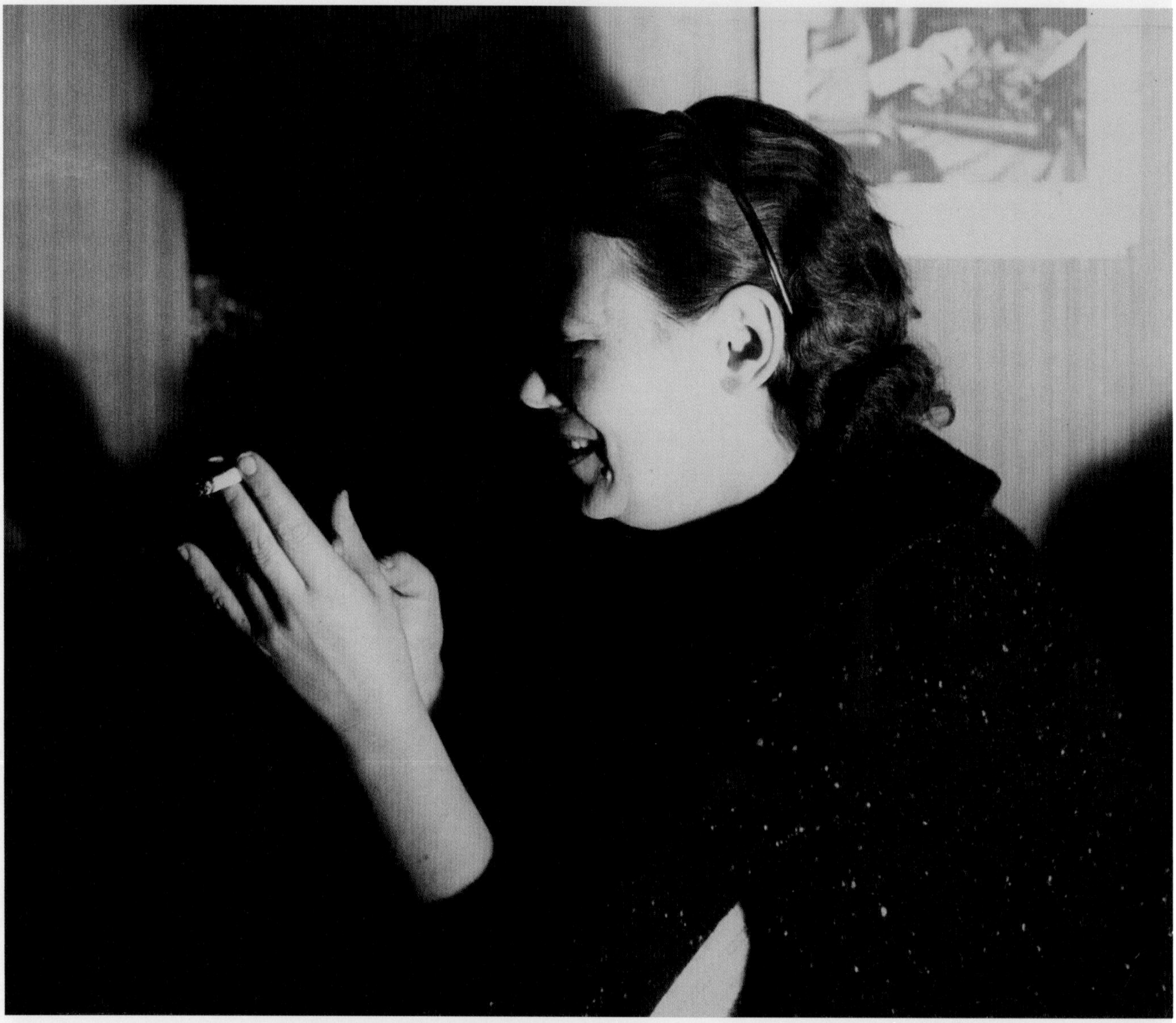

1 CF, p. 147.
2 CEDG, p. 30.
3 VMD, p. 136.
4 VMD, p. 137.
5 *Le Courrier littéraire*, April-May-June 1930, pp. 66–80, letter reproduced in the appendices to this volume.
6 See below *Le Courrier littéraire*.
7 CEDG, p. 46.

IN *CHIEN FOU,* her not entirely factual autobiography, Germaine Krull replaces the photography school in Munich where she actually trained with an art school where she had to produce sculptures for the exams. 'Mad Dog' comes before the jury with a statue of a miner holding a pick. When asked about the piece, she replies: 'When I saw the men at work, I didn't look at the tool. I don't think so. It's the movement I looked at, and above all the hands.'[1] In her commentaries on the people she met, Krull frequently spoke of the hands, seen as a characterisation of their talents, intentions and moods, even without their knowing it. When photographing Colette for the first time, she notes, 'I asked if I could take a photo of her hands, because I had started up a collection of hands, the most amazing part of a human being.'[2] 'Colette's were small, podgy. They wanted to pick things up. They always seemed to attract objects to themselves. Colette didn't understand what I was looking for when I photographed hands.' The writer responded with a lesson on observation: 'Hands change with time, the ears are quite different. Look closely at the ears and you can tell whether the person has a good character … You can come and see me, you have good ears.'[3] With Gide, likewise, she spoke of the writer's reluctance to take up a natural pose: 'I was the young little photographer that an illustrated journal had sent to him.' In the end, however, an opportunity arose: 'After he had posed, he put his knees very close to his face, with his hands in front. That was the best photo. Gide's hands, secret and firm. He almost never opens them.'[4]

It was with Cocteau, who came to her place to be photographed, that she had the greatest success and obtained the greatest recognition, by making him aware of an undiscovered part of himself: 'He could have been any age, just as likely twenty as fifty. He was constantly making expressions and faces … a smiling mouth always expressing a little bitterness … his hands were like seaweed, they lived their own life, they moved, they twisted and they were alive. I have never seen hands like that before.' Cocteau reciprocated her enthusiasm with regal largesse in a letter written upon receiving the photographs of his hands along with the photos of Berthe Bovy in *La Voix humaine*: '"First the hands", as Heurtebise says. I must confess that I did not recognise these hands (my hands). I reacted in the opposite way to my friend's Pekinese. The Pekinese loves my friend's hands – the left hand especially – and hates her face, her legs, etc. When she puts her left hand up to her face, it imagines that her face is approaching the hand to bite it, and it barks. I found it hard to identify these long, nervous things. Then I saw that these beasts, these dead plants, were emerging from a sleeve, from one of my suits, and I understood that they looked more like me than a face.'[5] Four versions of these hands are known: both hands on the knees, both on the shoulders, one hand over the eyes, and one on the month (which appeared in *Jazz* no. 8). Two of them were published in *Le Courrier littéraire* in 1930. And even when we see Cocteau from the waist up, his hands have as much presence as his face.[6]

About Malraux (her portrait shows him holding a cigarette) Krull wrote: 'I liked his hands. They were more virile and tougher than Jean Cocteau's, more the hands of a man of action.'[7] And of her friend, Isa de Comminges, mother of Renaud de Jouvenel: 'Isa had the most beautiful hands I have seen, long and thin like fronds of seaweed, they were the high

Jean Privat, **Portrait of Germaine Krull**, c. 1939

point of my collection.'[8] And then there was the hand supporting her friend Walter Benjamin's chin, also holding a cigarette.

The idea of a fantasy collection is undeniable when one considers both the preserved prints and Krull's published photos. There is a remarkable photomontage showing the humorous draughtsman Pol Rab (creator of the 'philosopher dogs' Ric and Rac, and of 'the newspaper of the same name') set amidst a cloud of hands. The 'Échos photographiques' in the 17 December 1930 issue of *VU* show 'the witty humourist Pol Rab, father of the glorious dogs Ric and Rac', holding in his hand his new creature, Numiphar, in a photo by Krull.[9] A montage of seven of Krull's hand photos was published in *Jazz*[10] under the title 'Coiffeur pour dames' and with the caption 'Hand games by M. Pol Rab'. Another montage with six of her studies of body details, including two photos of hands, forms a page in an issue of *Jazz* on nudism.[11] We also know of *The Hands of Mariette Lydis*, *The Hands of Arthur Honnegger*,[12] a *Hand with Figurine*, *The Hands of Joris Ivens*, *The Hands of Titaÿna*. The Schostal agency distributed at least sixteen photographs of hands, five of them with Pol Rab.

A study of three hands in front of a lowered face was reproduced in *Photographie 1931* by Arts et Métiers graphiques.[13] Another face looking into the camera with the hands before the mouth is held at the Bibliothèque Nationale de France, which has two other fine studies of hands. The Musée National d'Art Moderne has others, including a bust of a naked woman in black gauntlet gloves, which could be part of a series about Mrs Seabrook. A photo attributed to Lotar and Krull and two others by Man Ray, *The Fantasies of Mr Seabrook,*[14] with its SM imagery, show this same woman wearing black leather gauntlets and a black dress and boots. This is presumably Mrs Seabrook, whom Krull knew well.[15] She reappears in a racy magazine, *Allo Paris*,[16] under the title 'Frivolities by Germaine Krull', where she is naked, wearing black gauntlets and holding lace. This is an unusual image for Krull's published work, and takes us back to her daring erotic scenes in Berlin (*Friends*).

The only 'Photographes nouveaux' booklet of 1931 devoted to Krull, features six photographs of hands: *The Sculptor Jean Havermans*, *The Hand of Eli Lotar*, *Worker's Hand*, *Jean Cocteau*, *Mask and Hands of Pol Rab*, *The Hands of André Malraux*. The January 1929 issue of *Variétés* features a four-page 'Hands' section with eight photos, four of them by Krull.[17] On 15 November 1929, she had two photographs of fashion artisans, women's hands cutting fabric and drawing a dress, in a piece titled 'Couture, les grandes mains' (the women who work in fashion are usually called *petites mains* – 'little hands').[18] An advertisement for the Michelin Green Guide shows a hand resting on the guide, and Krull photographed the hands of pianist Walter Rummel when he was passing through Paris.[19] The latter reappear in *Das Leben*, with three other photos of musicians' hands, in a spread titled 'Hands'.[20] *Paris 1929*, a portfolio published by Antoine Roche with Calavas, contains a plate showing two Krull photographs of hands with their shadows, chosen as representative of artistic modernity in 1929. In *Art et Médecine*, the books section opens with hands holding a book, while the recorded music column ('Discophilie') shows hands holding a phonograph arm.[21] And in the serialised publication of Colette's *La Chatte* in *Marianne*, Emmanuel Berl's weekly, illustrated by Krull, there are several close-ups of hands holding a cat.[22] In Monte-Carlo, Krull photographed the hands of the pianist Brailowsky and of her astrologer friend Maurice Privat. And many other photographs are organised around hands, like the illustration for *Du feu pour trois* (one match for three cigarettes).

Of course, all these hands are very much of their time, and Krull was not the first person to deal with the theme. Before her, Kertész photographed *Paul Arma's Hands and Shadows* in 1928. At the turn of the new decade, hands were everywhere in the New Photography.[23] But Krull was particularly constant in her approach, and specifically photographed 'the hands

8 CEDG, p. 59.
9 *VU* no. 144 (17 December 1930), p. 1380.
10 *Jazz* no. 5 (15 April 1929), p. 231.
11 *Jazz*, special 'Nudisme' issue, April 1930, p. 26.
12 *Modern Photography*, 'The Special Autumn Number' of *The Studio*, London, 1931, p. 97.
13 Plate 118.
14 Lotar and Krull, *Gloved Hands in front of the Face*, in *La Subversion des images* (Paris, Centre Pompidou, 2009–10), Paris: Centre Pompidou, 2009, p. 290; sale at Binoche and Giquello, 13 December 2012, lot 461.
15 CEDG, p. 61. She talks about William B. Seabrook, whose publication on voodoo was 'the first book brought out by Éditions Jacques Haumont' (William B. Seabrook, *Secrets de la jungle*, Paris: Jacques Haumont, 1931). 'I took a lot of photographs of him ... I also did the portrait of his girlfriend,' p. 62. See also about the photographies of Mr. W. B. Seabrook, Clément Chéroux and Damarice Amao, *Jacques André Boiffard, la parenthèse surréaliste*, Études du Centre Pompidou / Éditions Xavier Barral, Paris: 2014, p. 84–85.
16 'Frivolités par Germaine Krull', *Allo Paris* no. 10 (March 1934), unpaginated [p. 4].
17 *La Lettre*, two *Mains de femme*, *Aveugles*, in *Variétés* 1, no. 9 (15 January 1929), p. 464.
18 *Variétés* 2, no. 7, (15 November, 1929), p. 534.
19 Another photo of Rummel was on the cover of *Jazz*, on 15 June 1929. Another appeared on p. 339.
20 *Das Leben*, 7. Jahrg., no. 10 (April 1930), 'Musik in Bildern', hands of a pianist, accordionist, violinist and harpist. Five photos by Germaine Krull.
21 *Art et Médecine*, February 1931, p. 39; May 1932, p. 44.
22 Colette, *La Chatte*, in *Marianne*, from no. 25 (12 April 1933) to no. 33 (7 June 1933), p. 7 (except no. 25, p. 1).
23 *Hands*, a photograph by Sougez containing twelve hands, was published in *Jazz* no. 11 (15 November 1929), p. 503. See the very fine hands, in positive and negative, by Aurel Bauh, 1929, in the Bouqueret collection, *Voici Paris. Modernités photographiques, 1920–1950* (Paris, Centre Pompidou, 2012), Paris: Centre Pompidou, 2012, p. 107.

of' a given sitter with the same attention as she would for the face, while in more impersonal photos on the subject she explored her interest in gesture, this interest in making things and handling objects and tools that was at the heart of her practice as a photojournalist. Many of her images show trades and professions (notably, the women workers of Paris), with a particular focus on the action of the hands. Her lover Philippe Lamour formulated the theory behind this in *Grand'Route*, where a fine plate showed Krull's *Man's Hand* as a manifesto in relation to the machine: 'The sensation does not come from the sight of the object, but from the way it is *handled* and *physically* handled.'[24]

Looking after one's hands had became a theme for women's advice pages. In *Le Jardin de la beauté*, an article about hand care illustrated by five photographs by Kertész, author Jeanne Fernandez worried that 'there is relatively little time for women in France to look after their hands'. Krull would no doubt have been irritated to read that cars, which she so loved, were the great enemy of fine, white hands, these being 'meant for harmonious rest'.[25]

The heroine of *Twenty-Four Hours in the Life of a Woman*, a novella published in 1927 by Stefan Zweig, an old friend of Krull's, who has learned how to study hands rather than faces from her husband (who has a passion for palmistry), is in a casino watching the hands around the gaming table. She observes that 'If you watch from that angle, only the hands change – all those pale, moving, waiting hands around the green table ... You can tell everything from these hands, from the way they wait, they grab ... Almost all gamblers soon learn to control their faces ... but ... they forget their hands ... their hands shamelessly reveal their innermost secrets.'[26]

24 *Grand'Route* no. 1 (March 1930), p. 38; no. 5 (July 1930) for the plate.
25 Jeanne Fernandez, 'Les mains', in *Le Jardin de la beauté. Conseils à toutes les femmes* (published in *Le Jardin des modes*), 1931, p. 107.
26 Stefan Zweig, *Twenty-Fours in the Life of a Woman*, Paris, trans. Anthea Bell, Pushkin Press, 2006. My thanks to Judith Czernikow for reminding me of this passage.

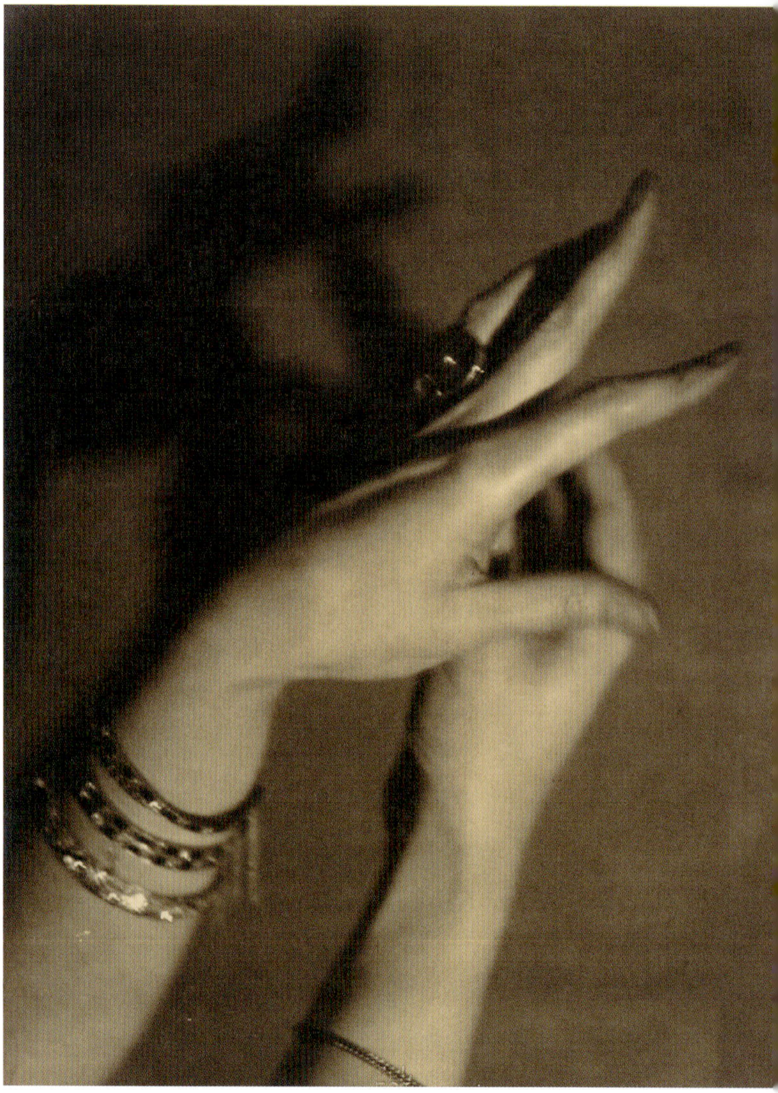

Hands with Shadow, 1928

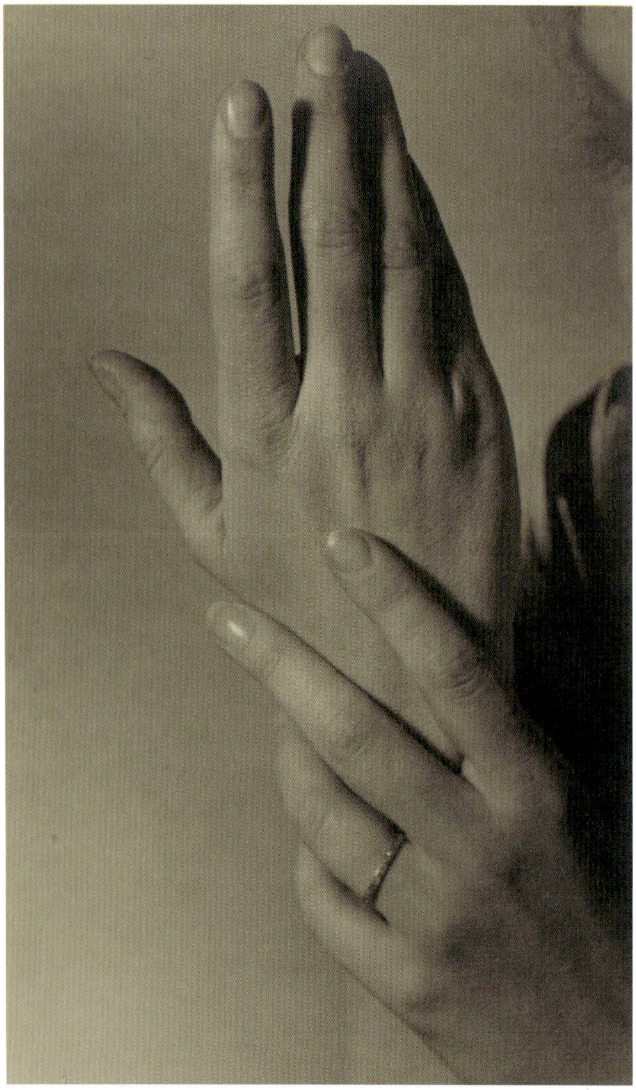

Hands, c. 1930

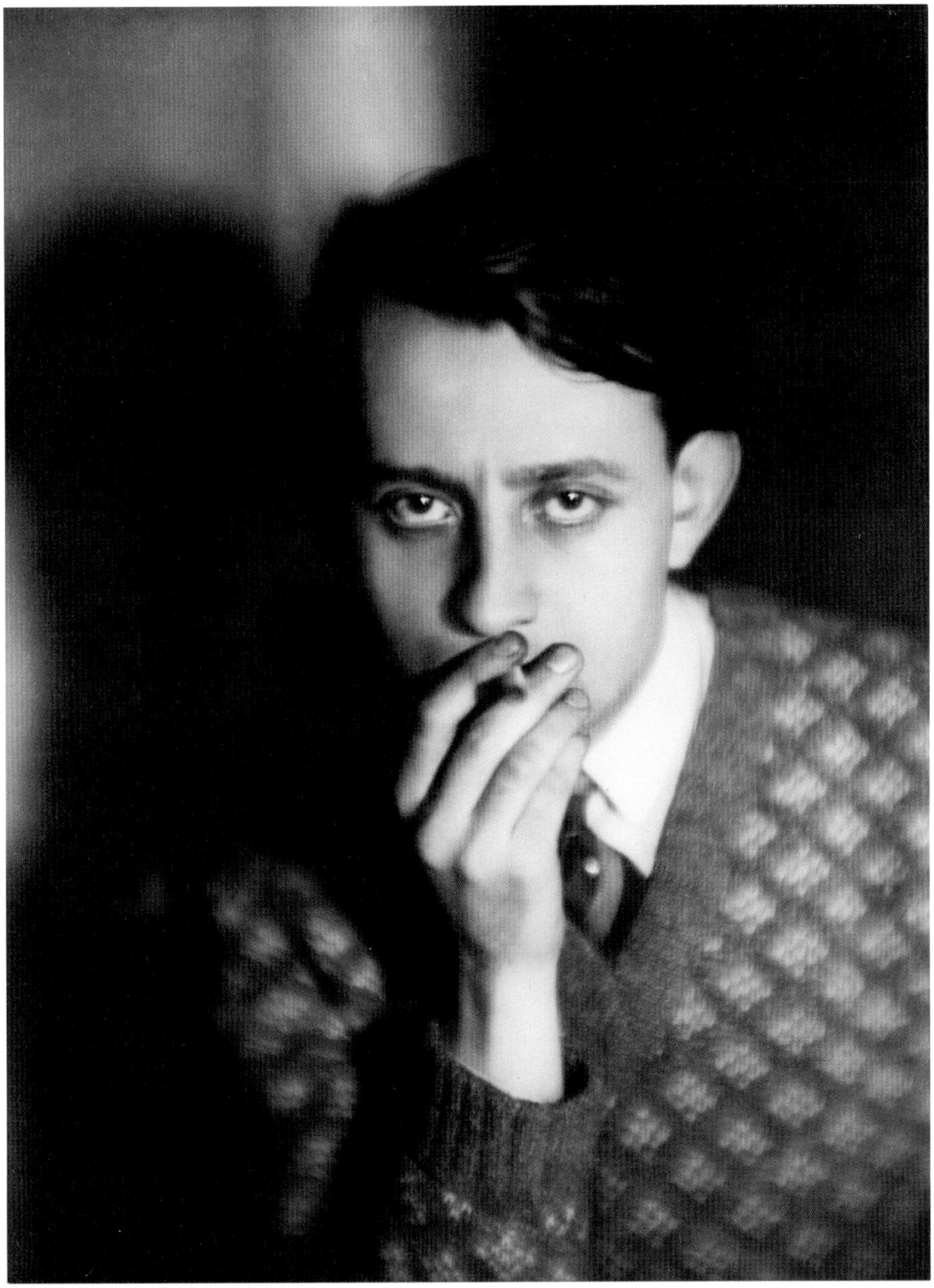

Portrait of André Malraux, 1930

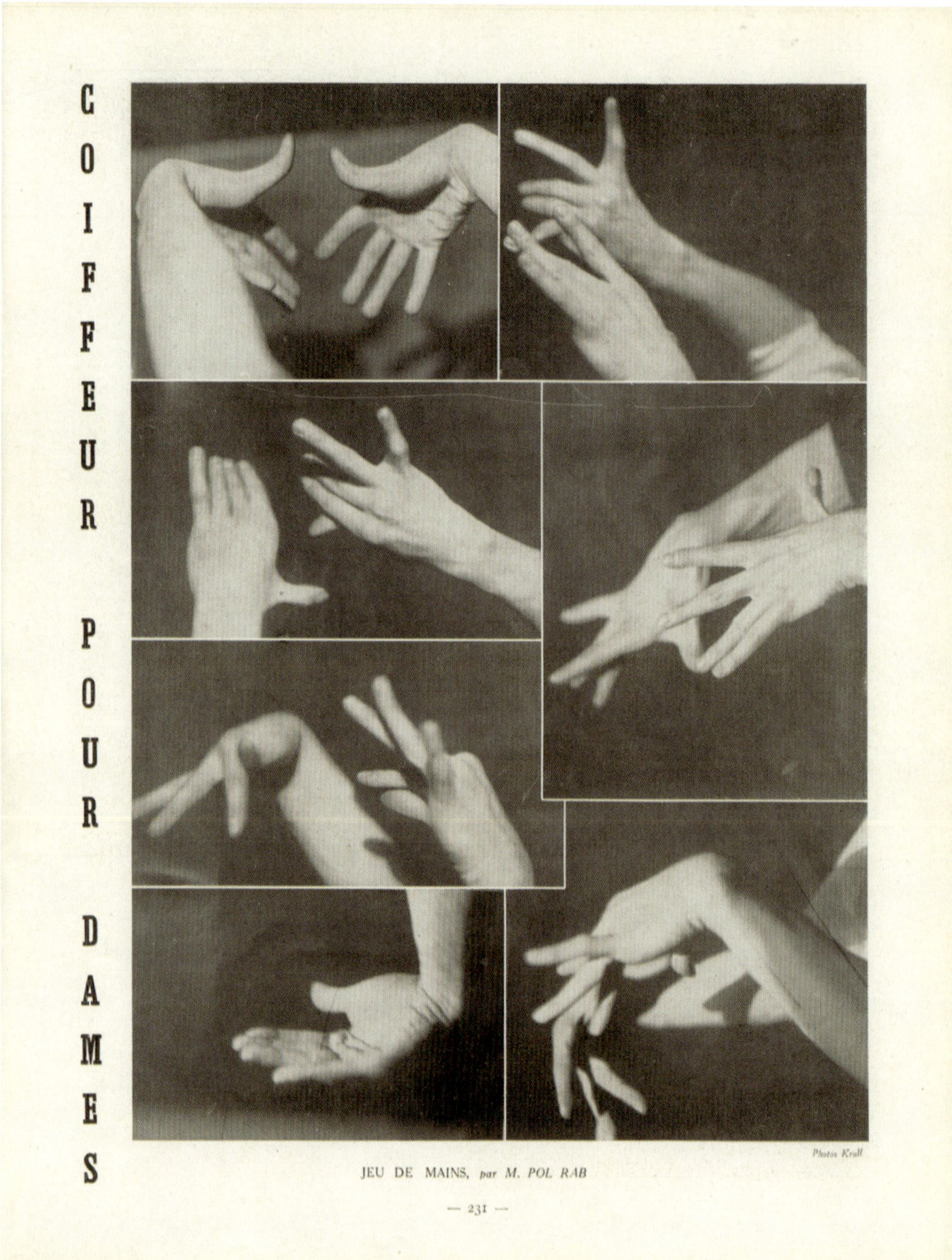

'Hand Gestures by M. Pol Rab', *Jazz*, 15 April 1929, p. 231

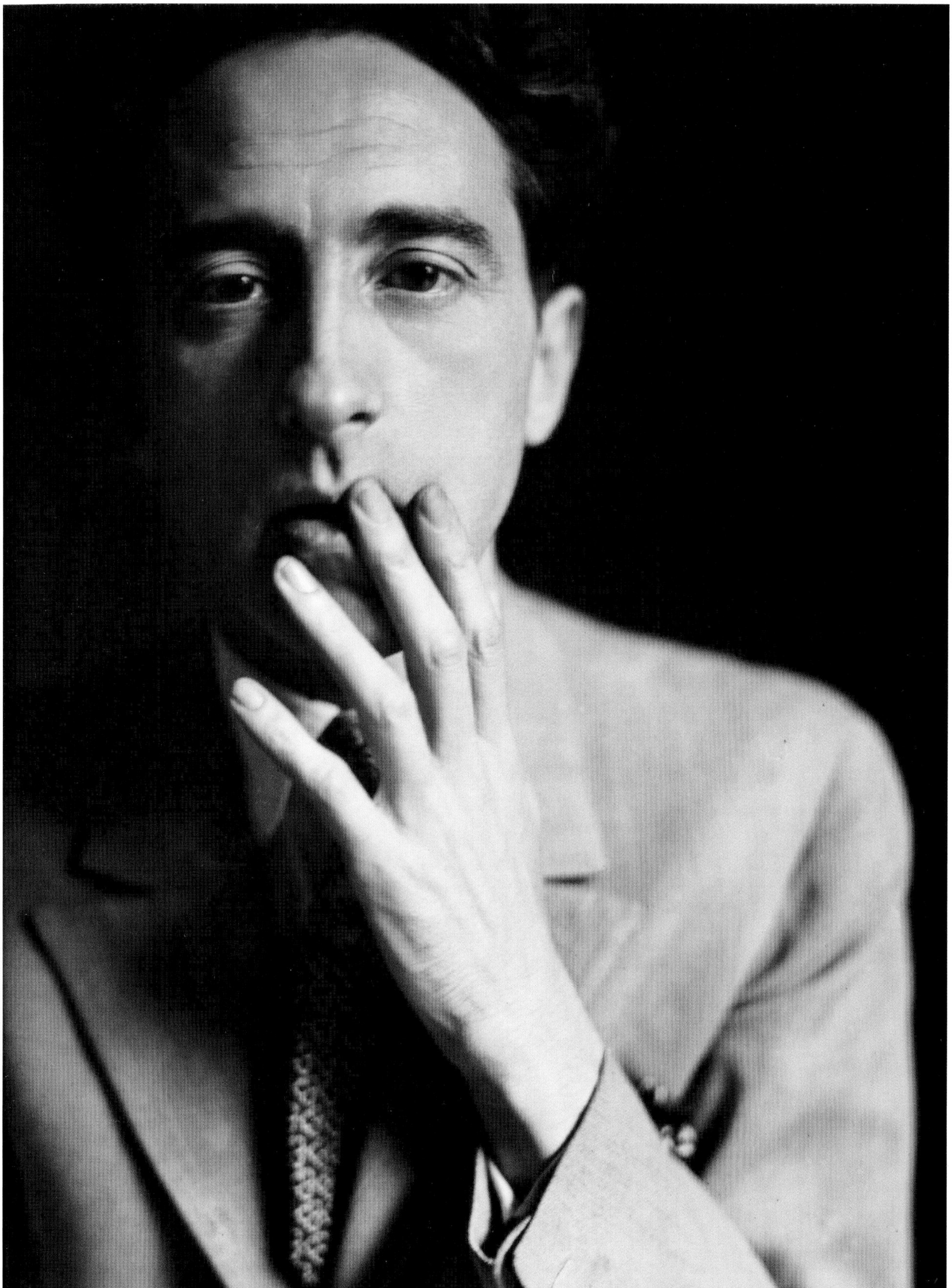

Jean Cocteau, 1929

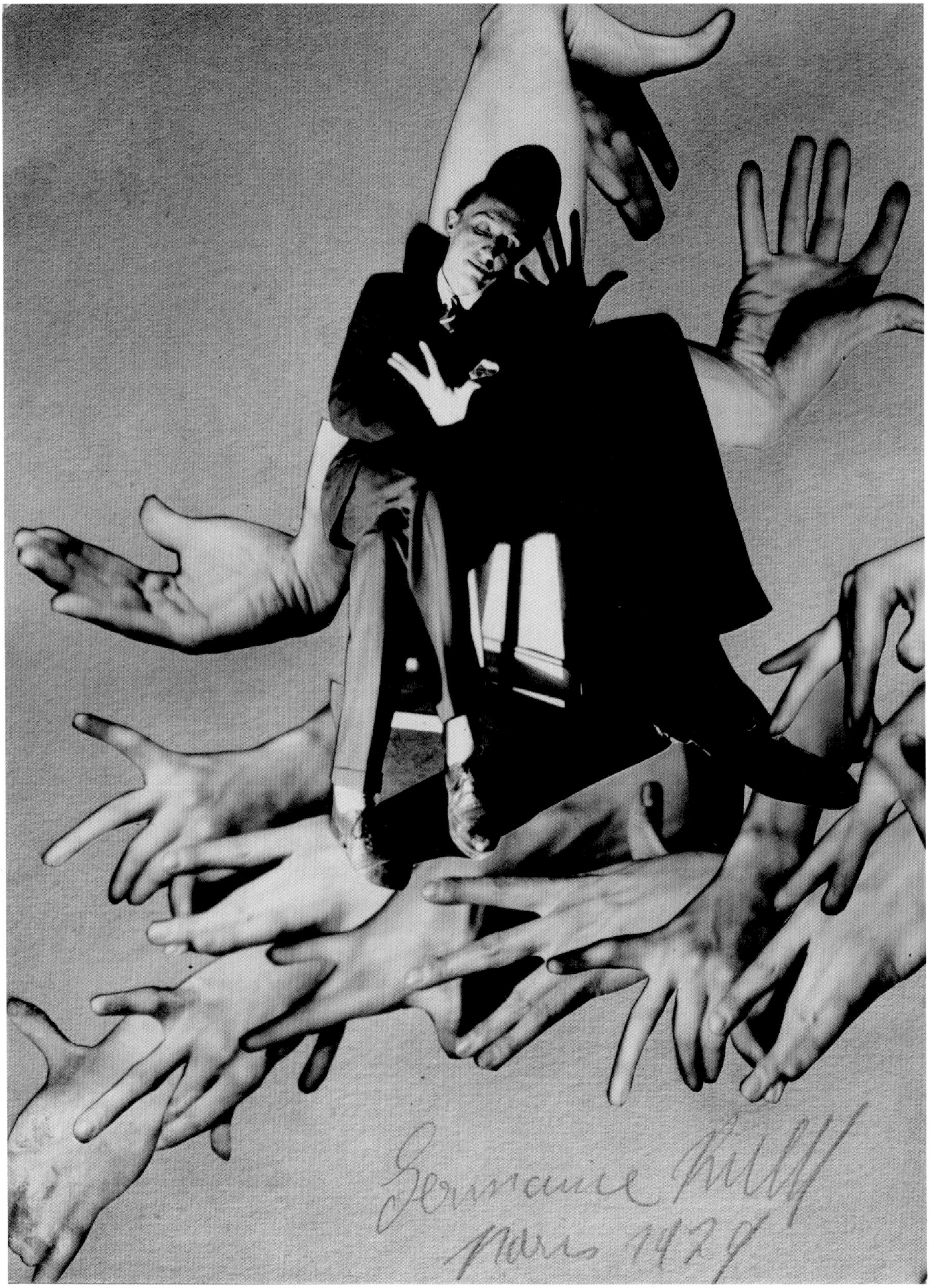

Pol Rab (Illustrator), Photomontage, 1929

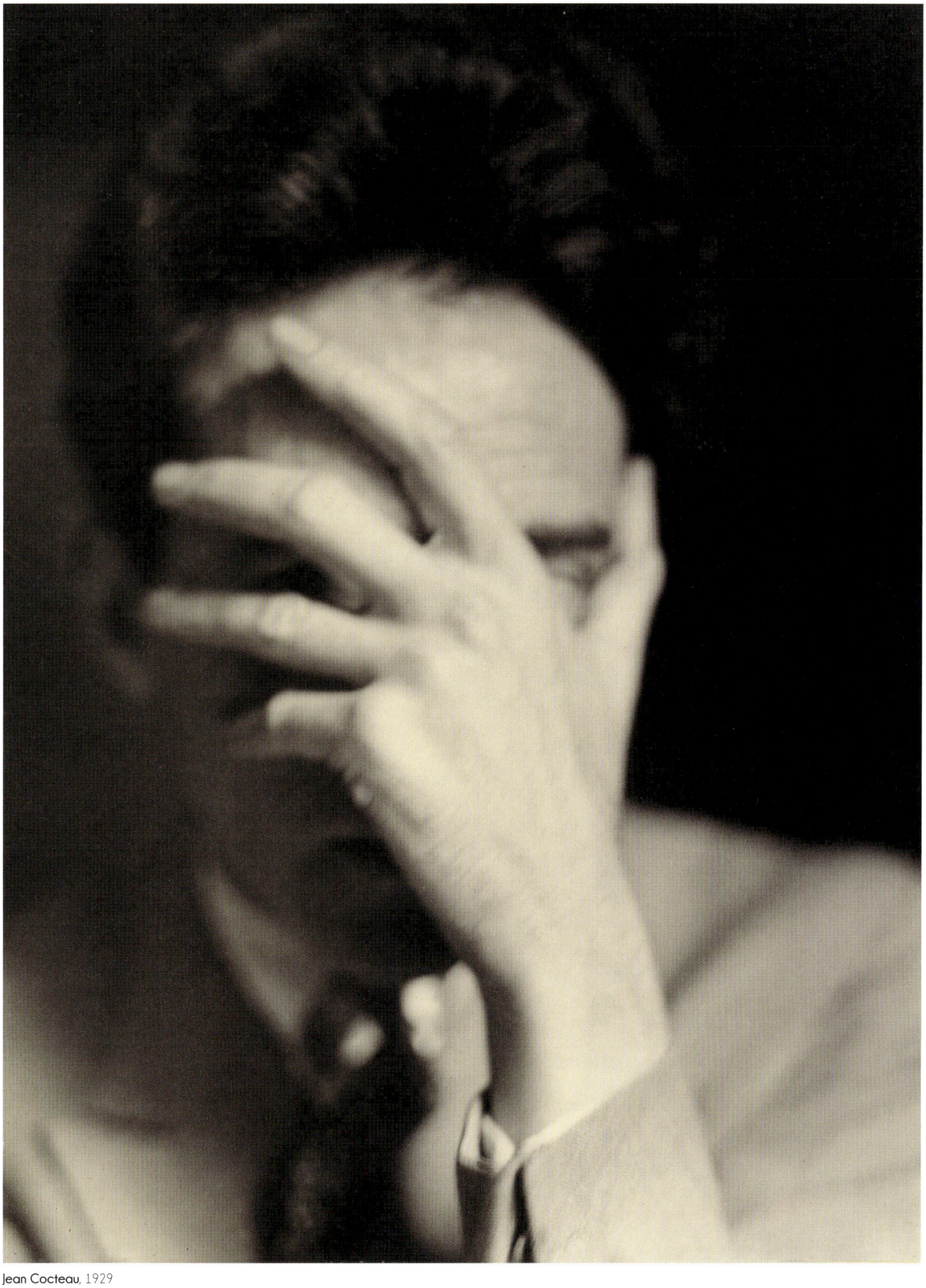

Jean Cocteau, 1929

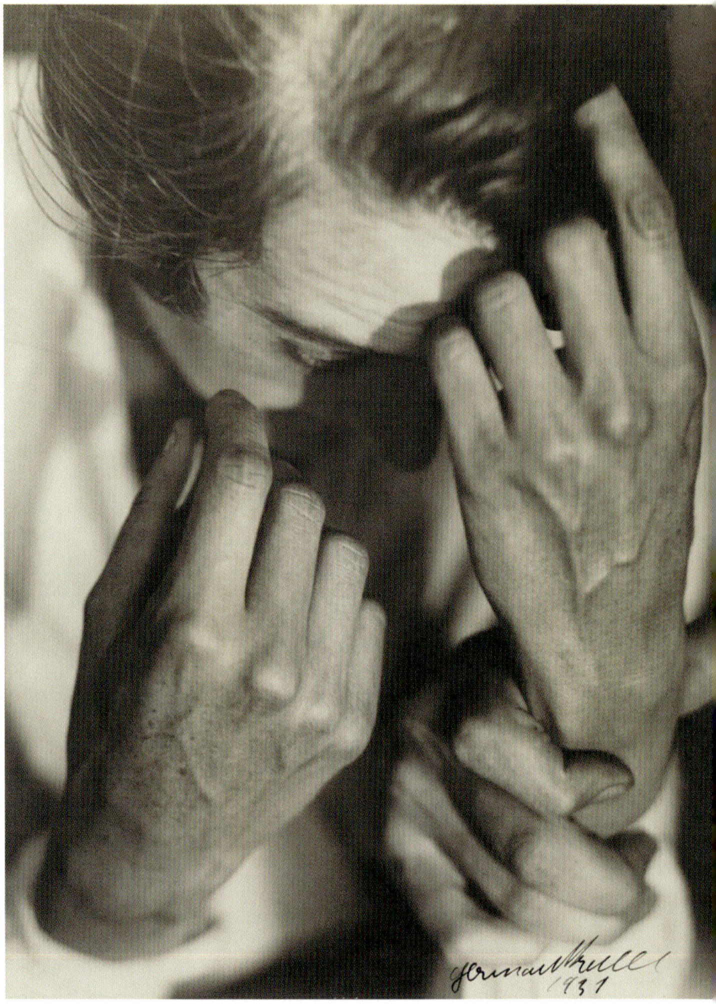

Face, Hands II, 1931

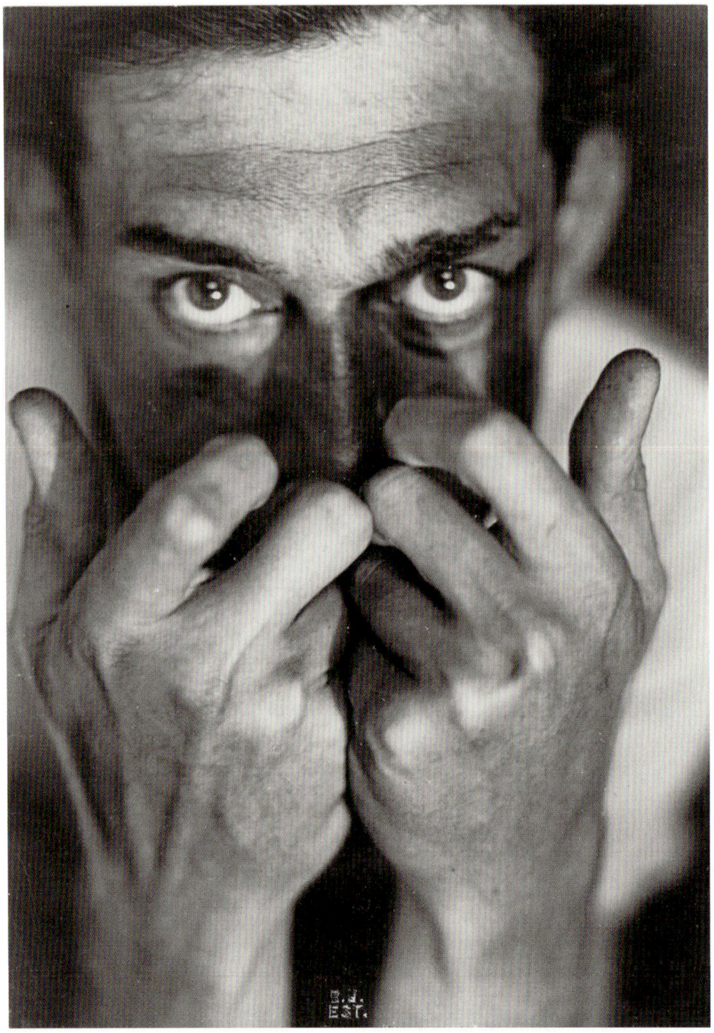

Portrait, 1930

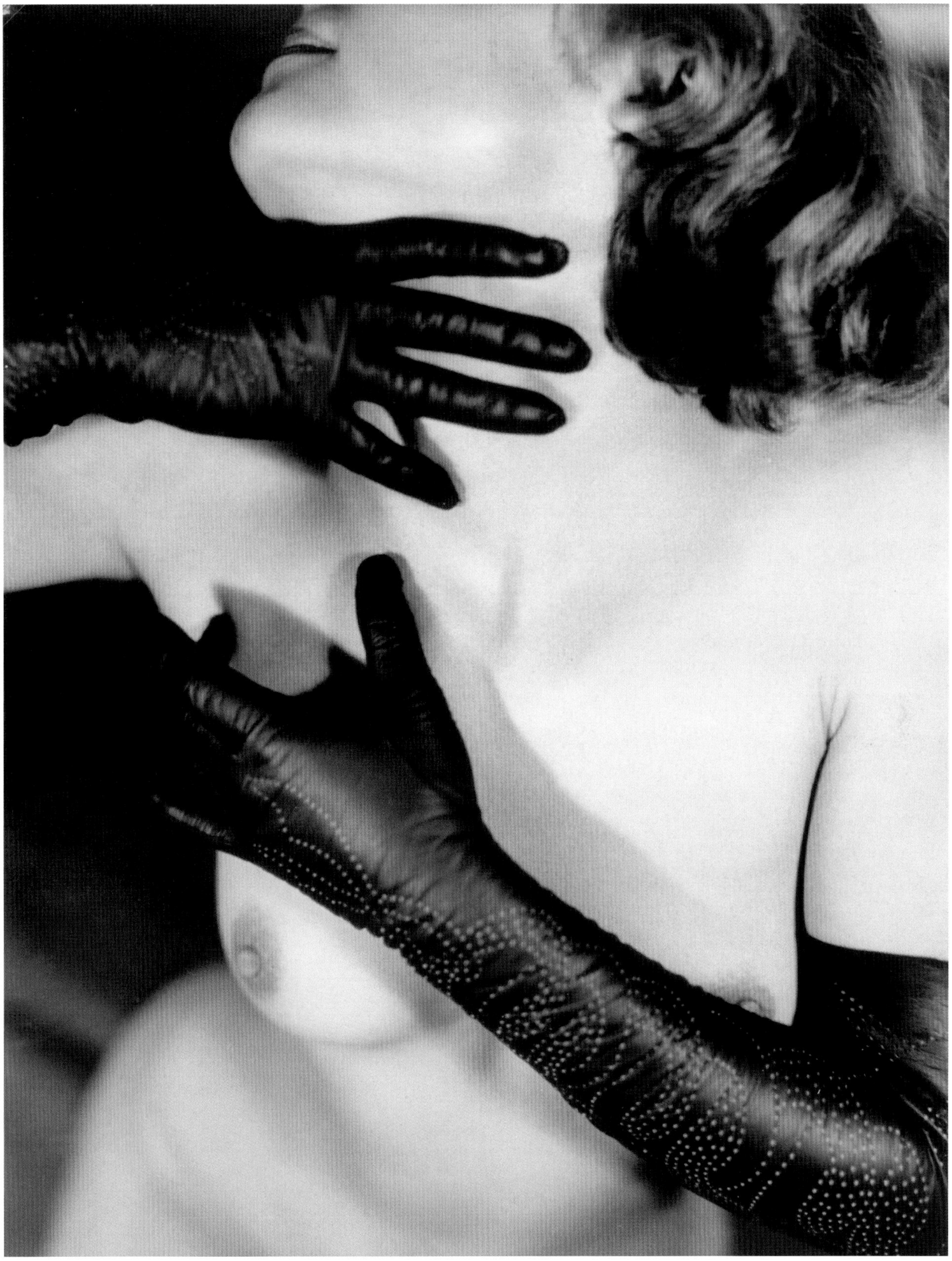

Nude with Black Gauntlets, c. 1931

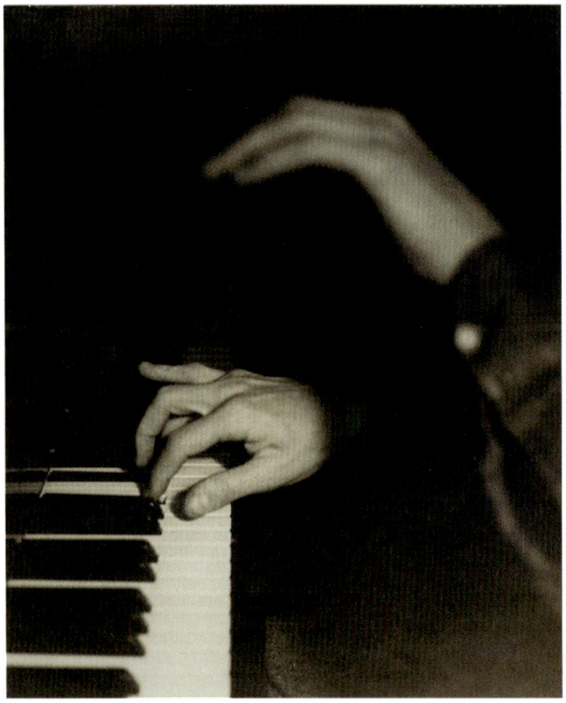

Hands of Brailowsky, c. 1935

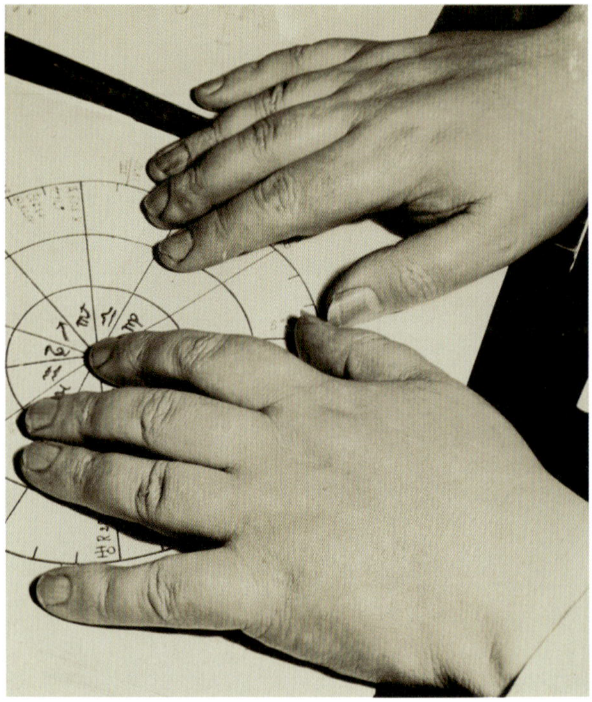

'Hands of Maurice Privat, Monte-Carlo', 1938

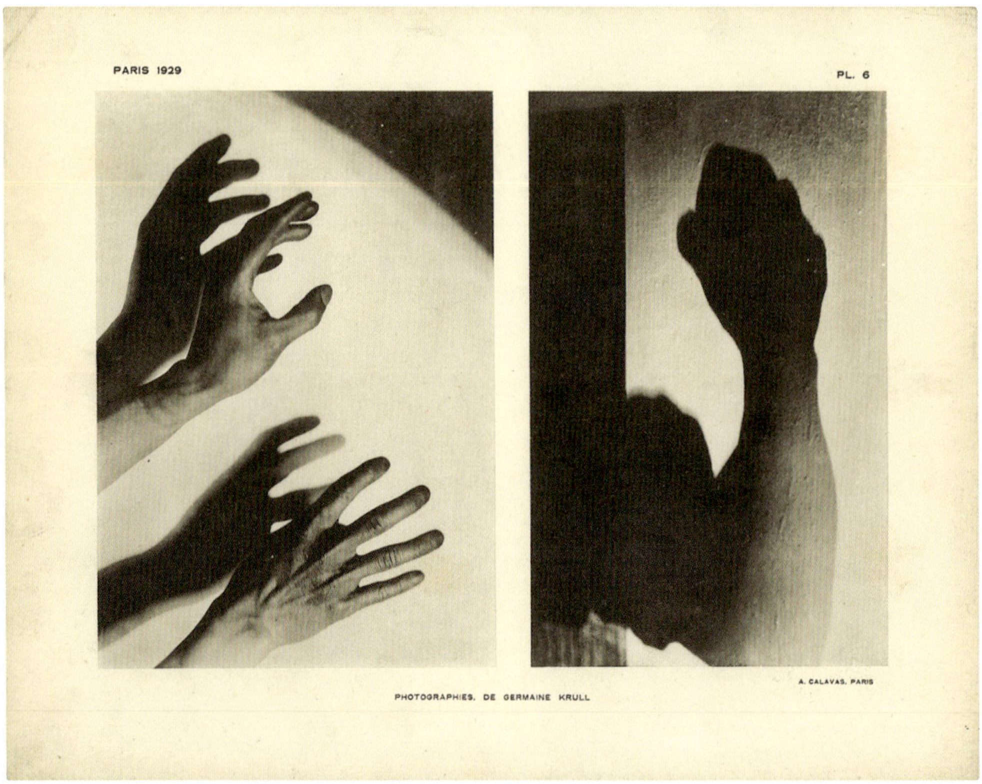

'Photographs by Germaine Krull', pl. 6 of portfolio *Paris 1929*, A. Calavas, Paris, 1930

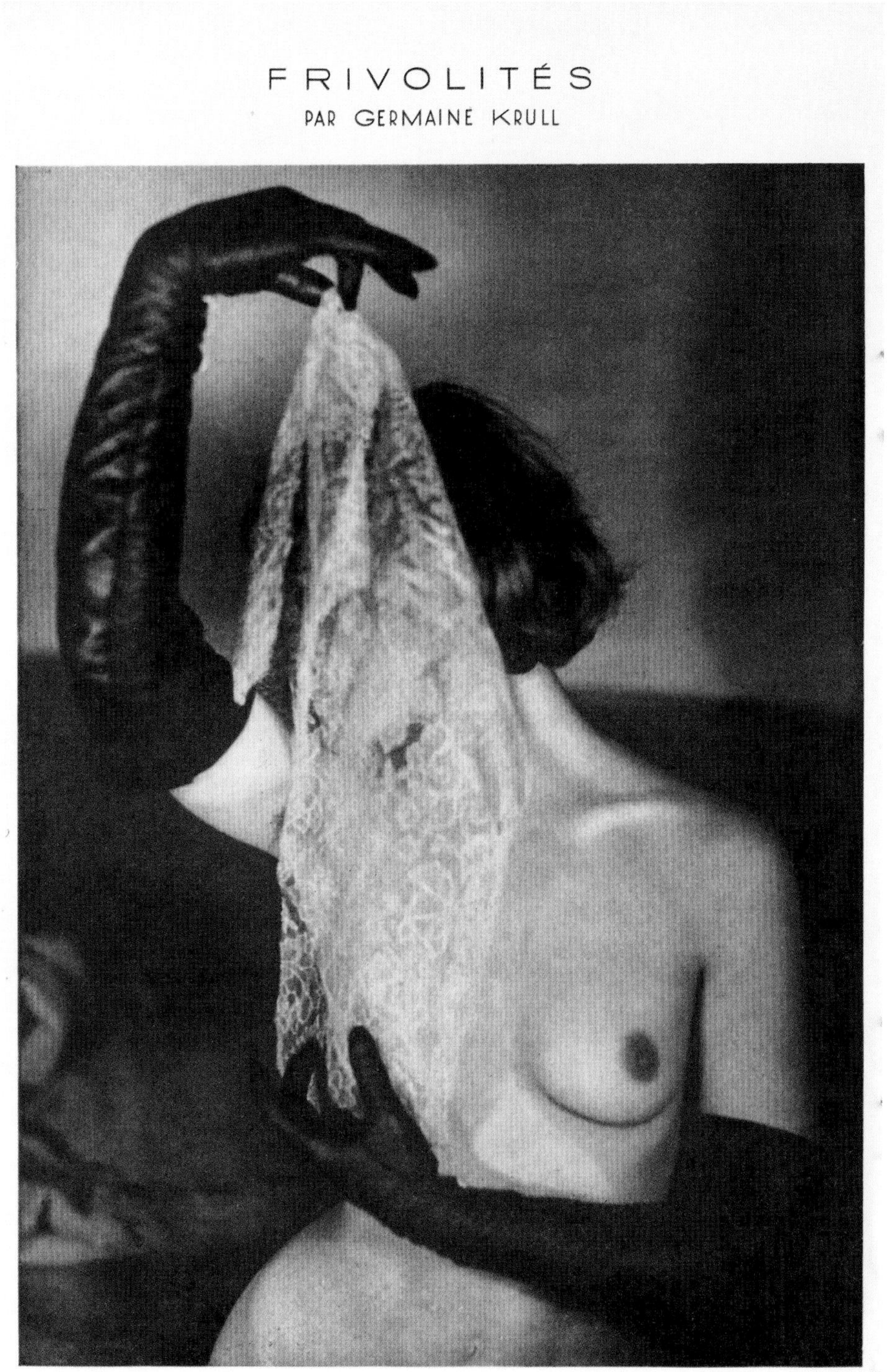

'Frivolities by Germaine Krull', *Allo Paris*, no. 10, March 1934, p. 4

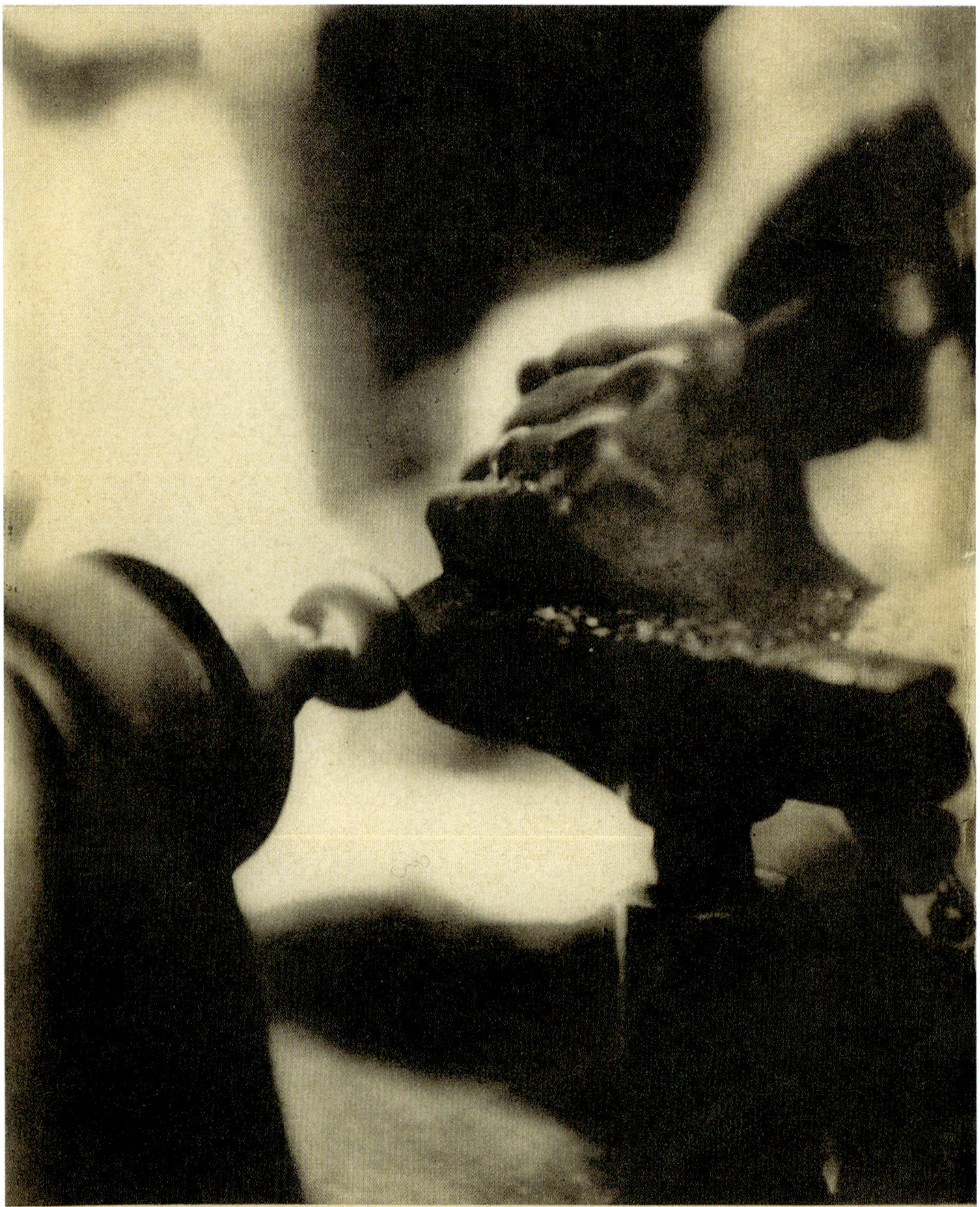

La Main de l'Homme

Photo Germaine Krull

'A Man's Hand', *Grand'Route*, no. 5, July 1930, p. 16

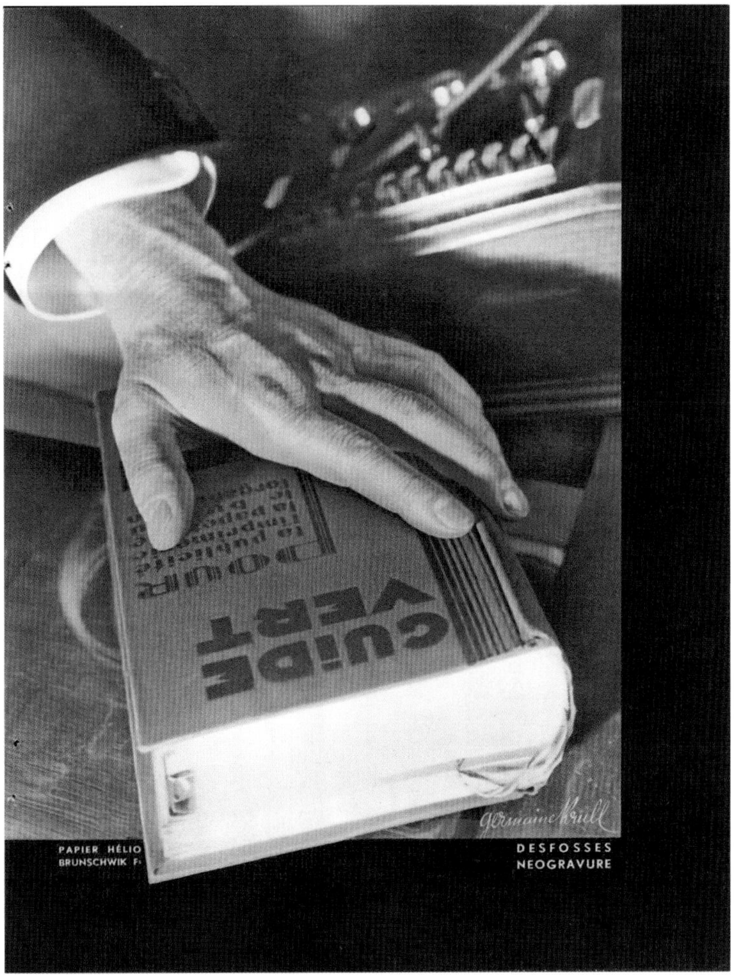

Advertisement for the *Guide Vert*, 1931

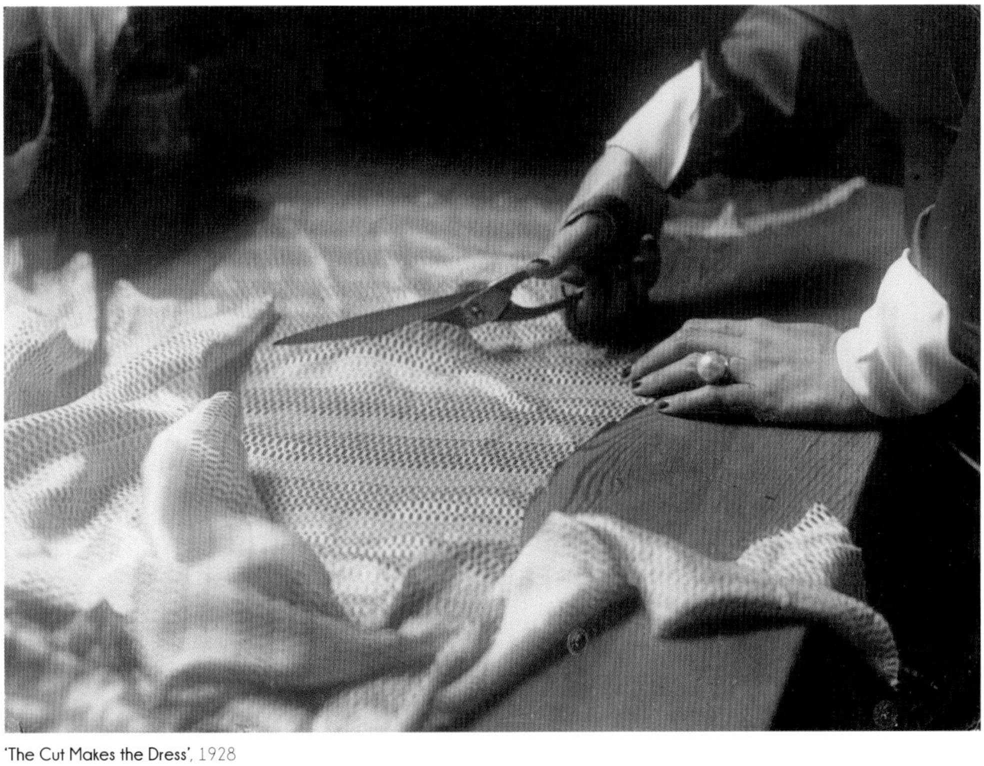

'The Cut Makes the Dress', 1928

LE COURRIER LITTÉRAIRE, 1930

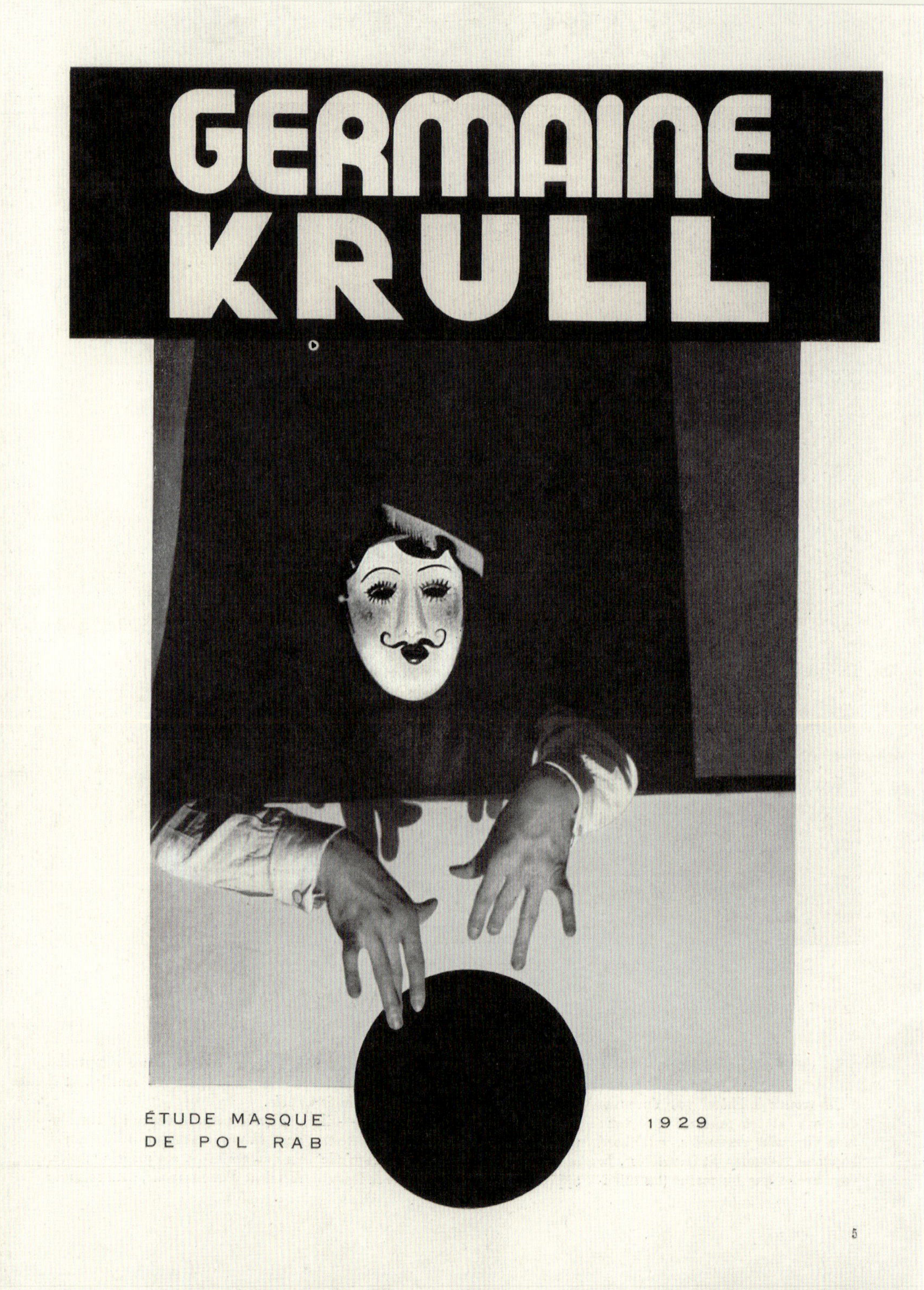

1 Issue 1 is dated March 1930.
2 Laurent Martin, 'De l'anarchisme à l'affairisme: les deux vies d'Eugène Merle, homme de presse (1884–1946)', *Revue historique* nos. 4, 123, 1999, pp. 789–807.
3 CEDG, pp. 43–45.
4 A set of twelve photographs 'provenance Eugène Merle' was exhibited at the Guillermo de Osma gallery, Madrid, in 2011. See *Germaine Krull: Metal y la fotografia industrial*, text by Juan Naranjo, Madrid, 2011. Four later came up for auction at Phillips, London, on 8 May 2013 (lot 39); six at Phillips, London, on 7 November 2013 (lot 100), same provenance given.

LE COURRIER LITTÉRAIRE was a short-lived modernist journal of art and literature. Published in early 1930, it got no further than two issues and these are absent from bibliographies and scarce in libraries. The second, dated April-May-June 1930 and printed in June 1930, contains a genuine, seventeen-page portfolio devoted to Krull's work. Rediscovered only now, these images are stunningly bold, even when compared to the kind of photography the journal claimed to support.

Le Courrier littéraire[1] was published and laid out by one Eugène Merle (1884–1946), a man of the press who had some success with the satirical weekly *Le Merle blanc*, founded in 1919, then launched *Paris Soir* in 1923 (this was bought by Jean Prouvost in 1930, after Merle got into trouble and ended up with a short prison sentence in 1929).[2] Merle went on to publish *Le Merle* in 1928–29, then *Le Merle littéraire*, which became *Le Courrier littéraire* in 1930. At the time, he was also director of the publishing house Éditions du Tambourin. Described as a man of 'shady dealings', Merle built his publishing success on the new advertising methods of the 1920s.

There is a long passage about Merle in *Click entre deux guerres*.[3] This 'extravagant character' was 'the most extraordinary man I ever met' – and '*Le Merle blanc* [was] a society and political gossip rag, wildly indiscreet, verging on blackmail.' With his 'skill at sinking politicians', was Merle an extortionist or merely a sordid adventurer on the make? Germaine recalls how she was invited and 'went with Renaud de Jouvenel in his open-top Bugatti for lunch at Merle's country house ... There were lots of people, really the Parisian smart set.' Champagne was served before lunch and the servants wore white gloves. 'Madame Merle is an extraordinary, fragile beauty, like a dream doll clad in an afternoon dress by Poiret.' Eugène Merle made his own onion soup, and then Germaine went around the upstairs rooms, which were all empty. 'A few days later', she concludes, '*Le Merle blanc* went bust and Merle disappeared from view'. This all seems to have taken place in late 1929 or early 1930, when Krull was part of 'Renaud's circle', yet she seems not to have remembered *Le Courrier littéraire*. This magazine, after all, was how she came to be anointed as an artist by Cocteau, but then it may also have irritated her by its casual approach to her photos. But then, was she even aware of its existence? The magazine was hard to come by and may well have been pulped in the case of bankruptcy. The letter from Cocteau to Krull published in this volume supports this hypothesis. Eugène Merle also had a collection of a dozen photographs from *Métal*.[4]

Merle's layout for the section dedicated to Krull – the typography of the first page, the choice of photos, the montage with black blocks of print (halftone process was used) – and the boldness and impertinence of the presentation all justify its publication here. The photographs sometimes overlap, making the images hard to read (this is the case for the full-height image of Cocteau), but the Constructivist influence, whether German or Soviet, is evident. The cover itself is close to the approach favoured by the Neoplasticists and Cercle et Carré (Mondrian, Van Doesburg, Vantongerloo). Twenty-four of Krull's photographs are reproduced, and a good number of them have never been seen anywhere else: a study of a mask by Pol Rab, a study of fabrics from 1926 (which could be connected to Sonia Delaunay), *The Hands of Titaÿna*,

Le Courrier littéraire, April-May-June 1930 (pp. 65-81 and pp.213-216)

a poster design from 1930, three views of roofs in Brittany and a *Portrait of Mme W.* We also find an image of Berthe Bovy in *La Voix humaine*, and two portraits of Cocteau, which explains the publication, as accompanying text, of his only letter to Krull, written on receiving the photos (the last page of this section is a facsimile of a page from this missive).[5] Three female nudes, two of them double exposures, are taken from the 1930 *Études de nu*, and another, also a double exposure, was never published anywhere else.

This issue of *Le Courrier littéraire* contains two other photographs by Krull (rails superimposed with a poem on metal by Chenal; and a portrait of Carlo Rim), both prominently positioned, two photos by Man Ray, a text by Robert Desnos, a rare photo by Sébastien, two articles by Carlo Rim about the Salon de l'Araignée and photography,[6] a big article about Soviet literature and another on film in Germany, illustrated by numerous montages of stills.[7] The artistic context created to frame Krull's work here is worthy of an international photographer being showcased at the 'Film und Foto' festival in 1929.

5 Reproduced in the appendices. The excerpt published in *Germaine Krull par Pierre Mac Orlan*, Paris: NRF, Gallimard ('Photographes nouveaux' series), 1931, p. 16, is dated April 1930.
6 In early 1930 Carlo Rim, former editor of *Jazz*, became editor-in-chief at *VU*, where he published a new version of this text on photography.
7 The photomontages and several illustrations are by Marcel Montagnier.

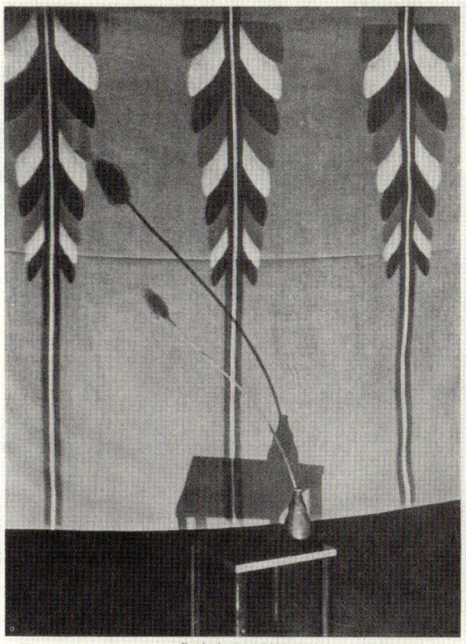

Etude de tissus 1926

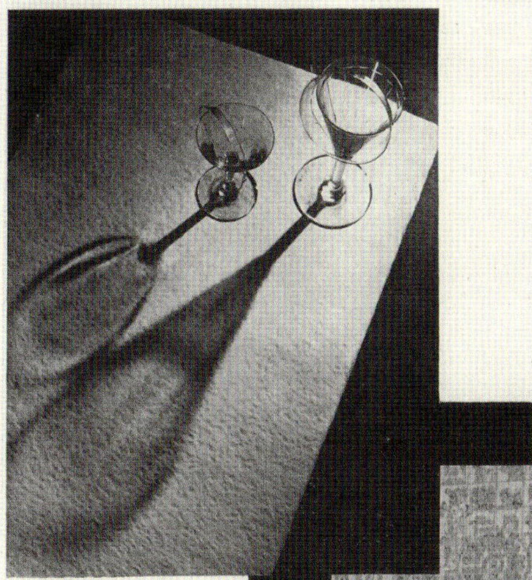

Etude 1930

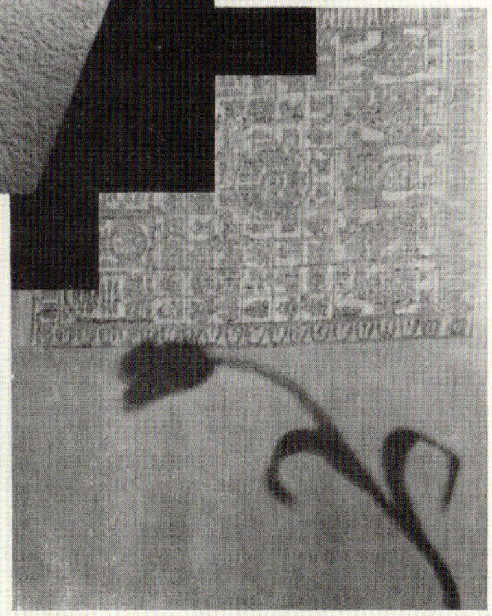

Etude de tissus 1926

Ma chère Germaine,

Je trouve à l'hôtel vos épreuves de Bovy et les miennes et je veux bien vite vous remercier. « D'abord les mains », comme dit Heurtebise. Je vous avoue que les mains (les miennes), je ne les reconnaissais pas. Je réagissais à l'inverse du pékinois d'une de mes amies. Le pékinois aime les mains de mon amie — il préfère sa main gauche — et déteste sa figure, ses jambes, etc.... Lorsqu'elle approche sa main gauche de sa figure, il imagine que la figure s'approche de la main pour la mordre, et il aboie.

J'avais peine à identifier ces longues choses nerveuses. Ensuite, j'ai vu que ces bêtes, ces plantes mortes, sortaient d'une manche, d'un costume

à moi et j'ai compris combien elles me ressemblaient plus qu'un visage. »

Berthe Bovy.

R. de Saint-Jean m'écrivait : *« Avez-vous les épreuves de Krull ? L'ombre de Bovy au téléphone ? On dirait une machine qui souffre. »*

Vous savez que la machine, je n'en suis pas idolâtre et que l'esclavage, même machinal, me répugne. Or, ce qui me touche, c'est la collaboration avec les machines. Elle s'impose. Chez

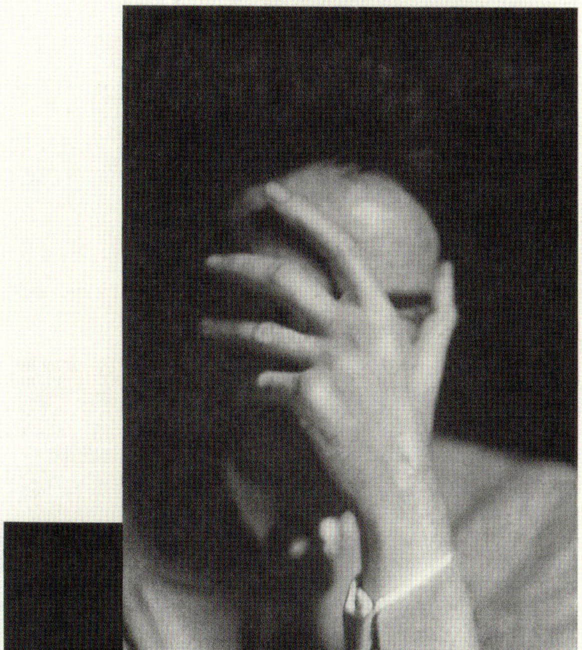

Jean Cocteau 1929

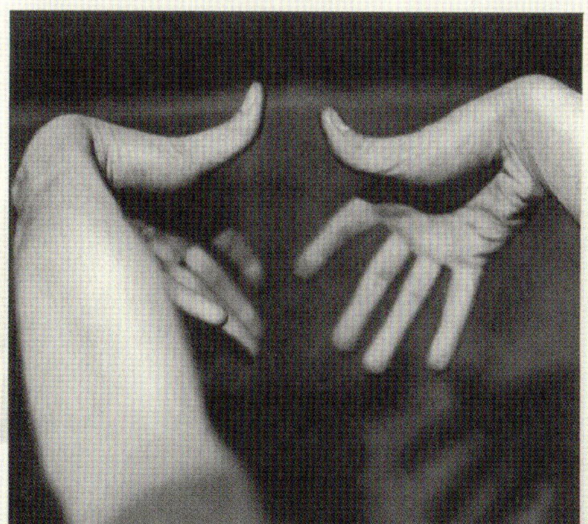

Les mains de Pol Rab 1929

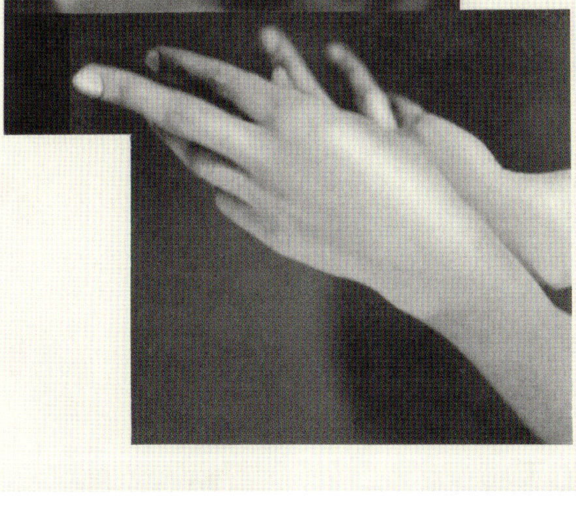

Les mains de Titayna 1929

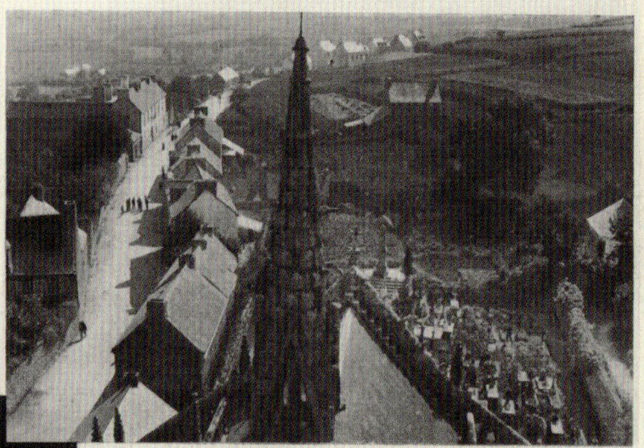

Bretagne 1929

chambre noire obtenez un monde neuf, un monde qui a traversé des mécanismes et une âme.

Cet individualisme de l'appareil offre un danger. Il est certain. Déjà, en 1912, j'envoyais le petit marchand japonais Takaïra prendre des kodaks de Versailles. Il emportait mon appareil. Il rapportait douze photographies japonaises du parc de Versailles.

Ce phénomène nous vaut un déluge de photographes. Incapables de s'exprimer par le pinceau ou par la plume, une foule d'esthètes s'exprime par l'entremise de l'appareil de prise de vues.

Il existe peu d'artistes nés sous le signe de la chambre noire, sous l'arc-en-ciel de la lentille, sous l'étoile de l'objectif. Vous êtes de cette petite troupe dont Man Ray ouvrait jadis la marche et dont le livre de Charles Peignot résume l'effort.

Vos épreuves de Bovy dans *La Voix Humaine* sont des chefs-d'œuvre. L'actrice n'a plus d'âge. Elle a cet âge du silence, du clair de lune, des décembres, des accidents d'automobile qui, une seconde après avoir eu lieu, prennent la grandeur d'une ruine d'Egypte. Ces larmes, ces mèches, ces membres épars, cette bouche-blessure, m'évoquent un souvenir de 1927. On démolissait les Arts Décoratifs. C'était l'été. Je longeais à midi, seul au monde, la palissade qui borde le quai des Invalides. Soudain, resté intact au fronton d'une espèce de temple en miettes, j'entendis un haut parleur, une voix terrible, une voix d'Œdipe (invisible parce qu'aveugle), déclamer les cours de la Bourse. L'effet était poignant, théâtral, inouï.

Ne croyez pas que je m'écarte de votre œuvre. Je tourne autour. Je cherche à vous communiquer ce que j'éprouve en face de ces documentaires d'une femme ravagée, d'une statue mise à la question.

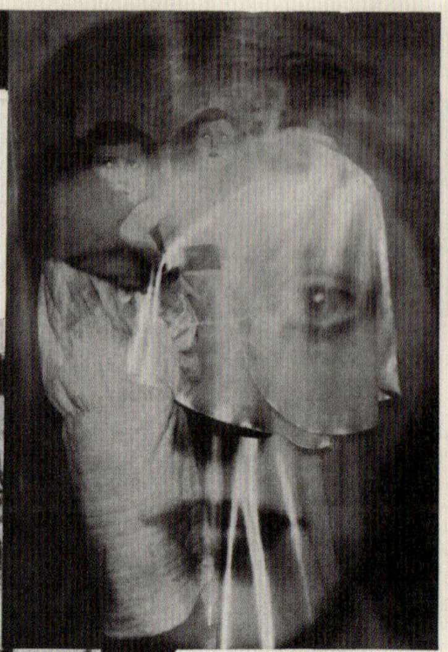

Vision 1930

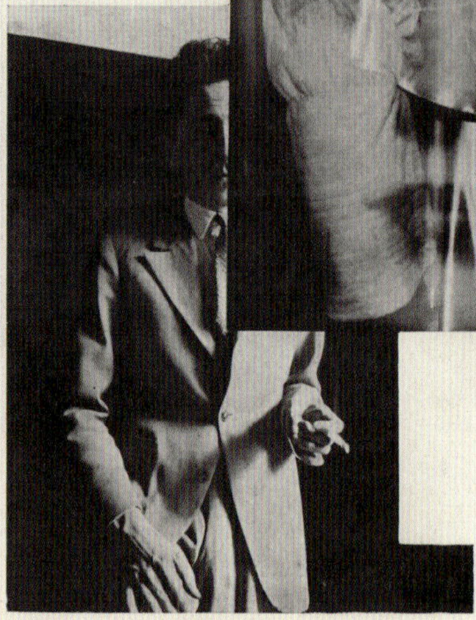

Jean Cocteau 1929

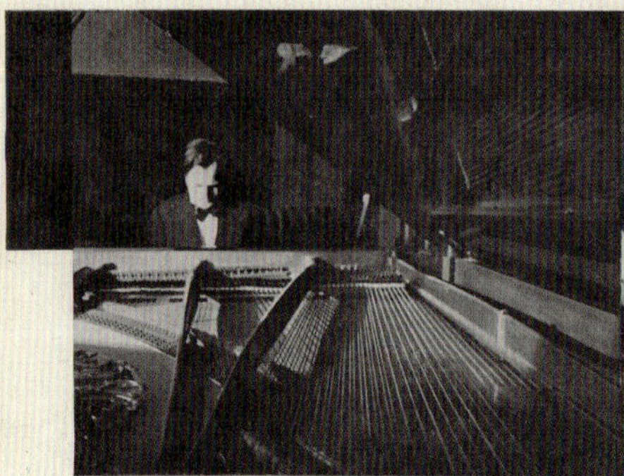

Walter Rummel 1929

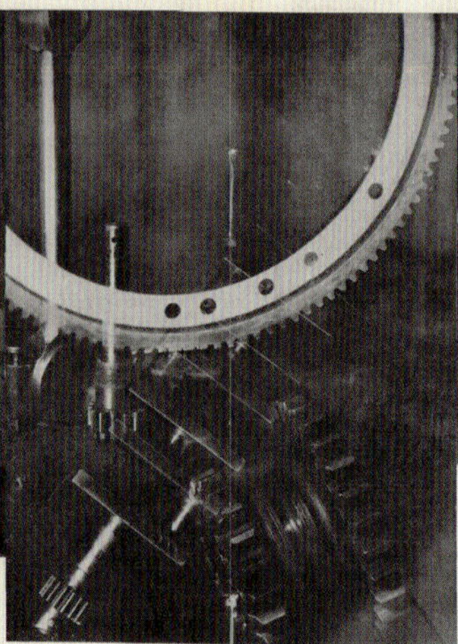

Projet d'affiche 1930

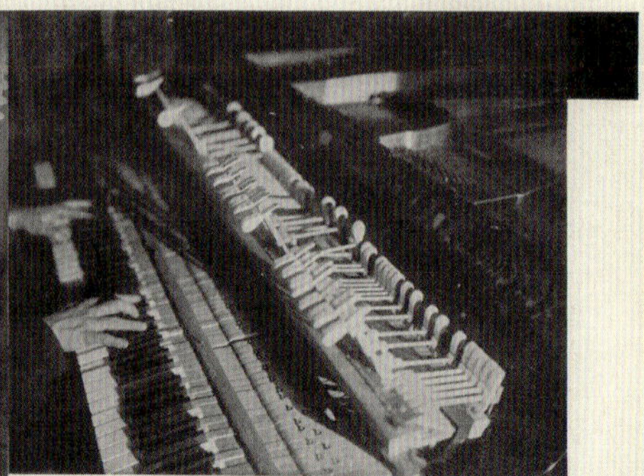

Les mains de Walter Rummel 1929

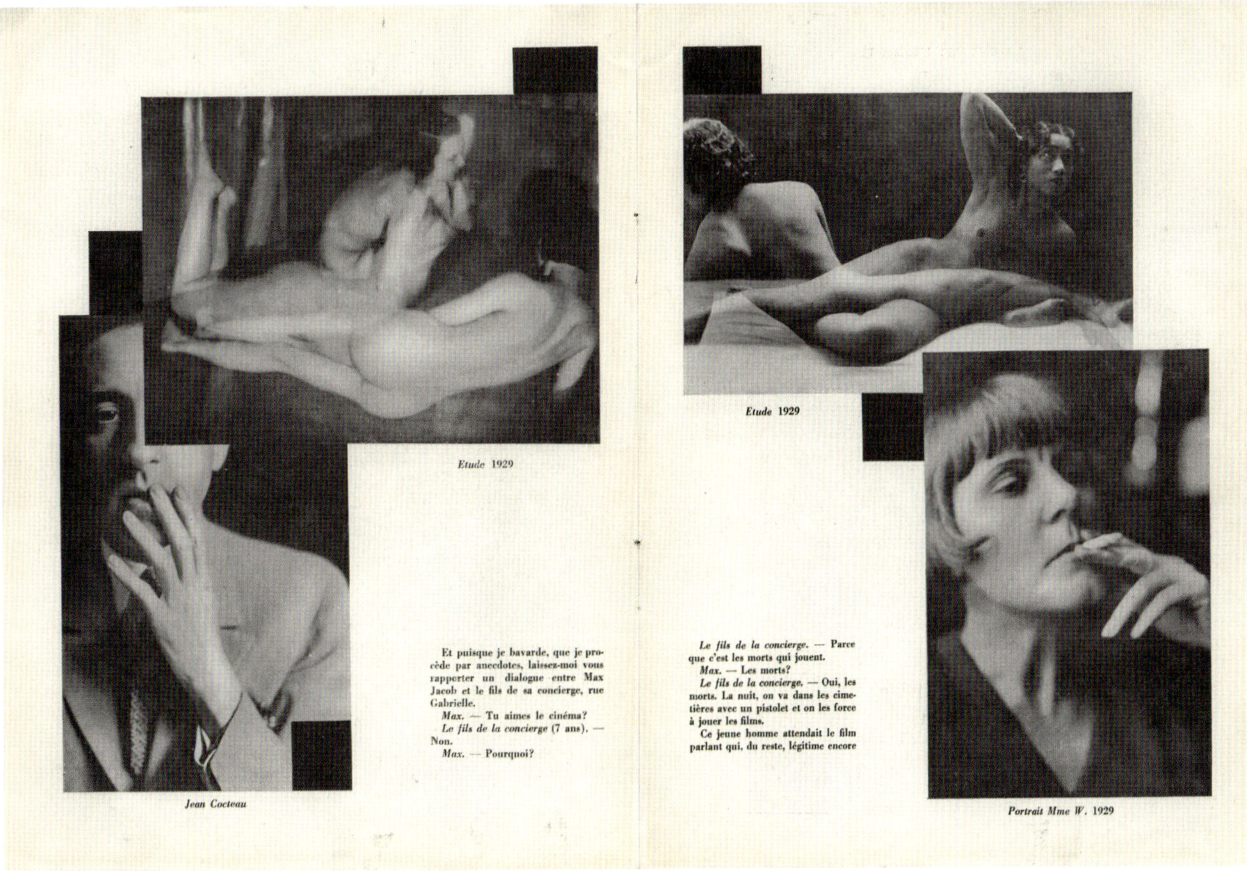

Etude 1929

Jean Cocteau

Et puisque je bavarde, que je procède par anecdotes, laissez-moi vous rapporter un dialogue entre Max Jacob et le fils de sa concierge, rue Gabrielle.

Max. — Tu aimes le cinéma?

Le fils de la concierge (7 ans). — Non.

Max. — Pourquoi?

Le fils de la concierge. — Parce que c'est les morts qui jouent.

Max. — Les morts?

Le fils de la concierge. — Oui, les morts. La nuit, on va dans les cimetières avec un pistolet et on les force à jouer les films.

Ce jeune homme attendait le film parlant qui, du reste, légitime encore

Etude 1929

Portrait Mme W. 1929

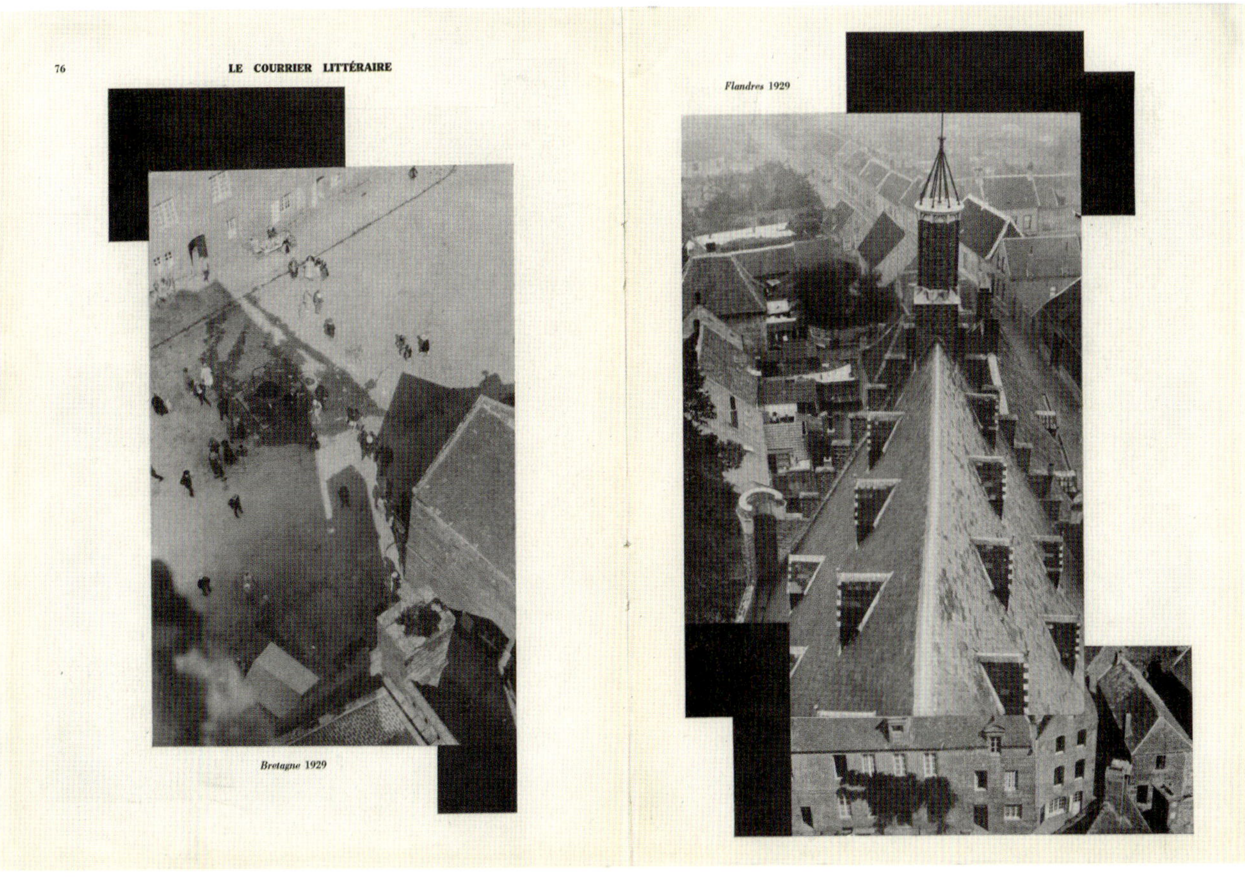

76 **LE COURRIER LITTÉRAIRE**

Bretagne 1929

Flandres 1929

78 LE COURRIER LITTÉRAIRE

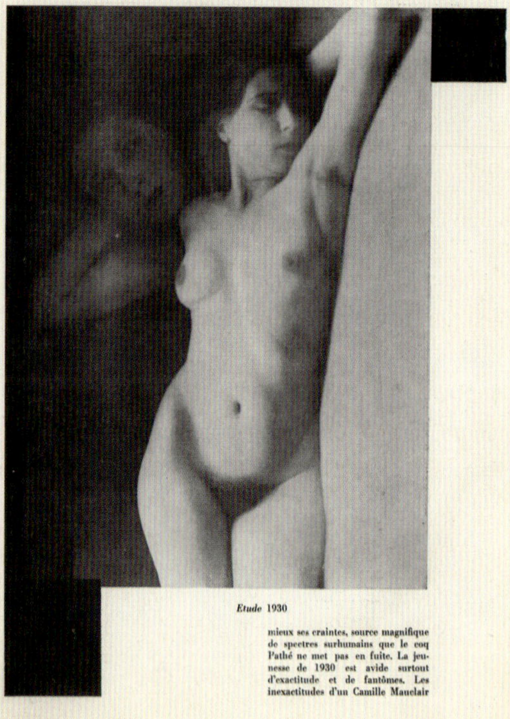

Etude 1930

mieux ses craintes, source magnifique de spectres surhumains que le coq Pathé ne met pas en fuite. La jeunesse de 1930 est avide surtout d'exactitude et de fantômes. Les inexactitudes d'un Camille Mauclair

LE COURRIER LITTÉRAIRE 79

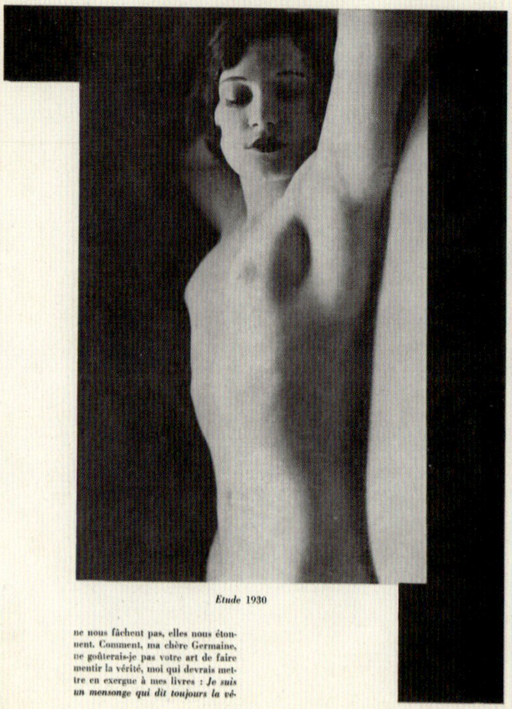

Etude 1930

ne nous fâchent pas, elles nous étonnent. Comment, ma chère Germaine, ne goûterais-je pas votre art de faire mentir la vérité, moi qui devrais mettre en exergue à mes livres : ***Je suis un mensonge qui dit toujours la vé-***

80 LE COURRIER LITTÉRAIRE

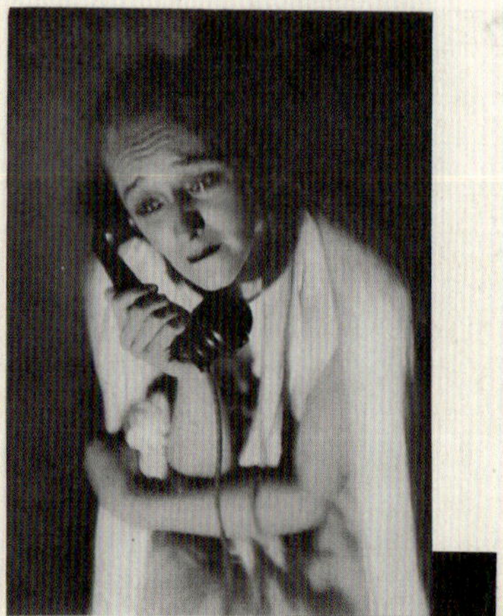

Berthe Bovy dans « La Voix Humaine » de Jean Cocteau 1930

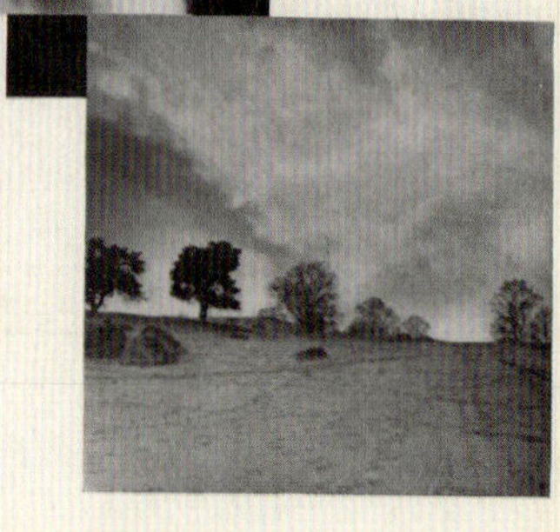

Ile-de-France 1930

rité, moi dont le plus vrai que le vrai reste la méthode profonde.

Je vous embrasse.

JEAN COCTEAU.

P.-S. — Vous devez savoir par Eisenstein que j'ai eu la chance de pouvoir le sauver. Il a donc obtenu son interrogatoire. La dernière lettre de B. est décisive. Je n'ai pu en parler l'autre soir, entre deux portes à la « Ligue générale ». J'étais trop ému.

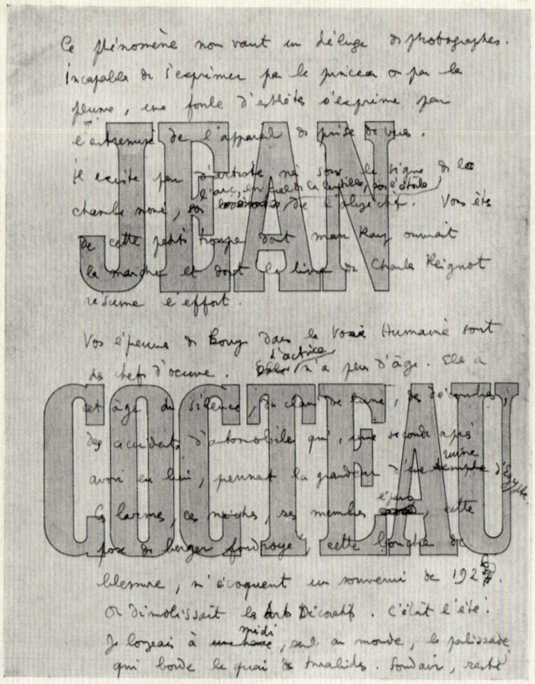

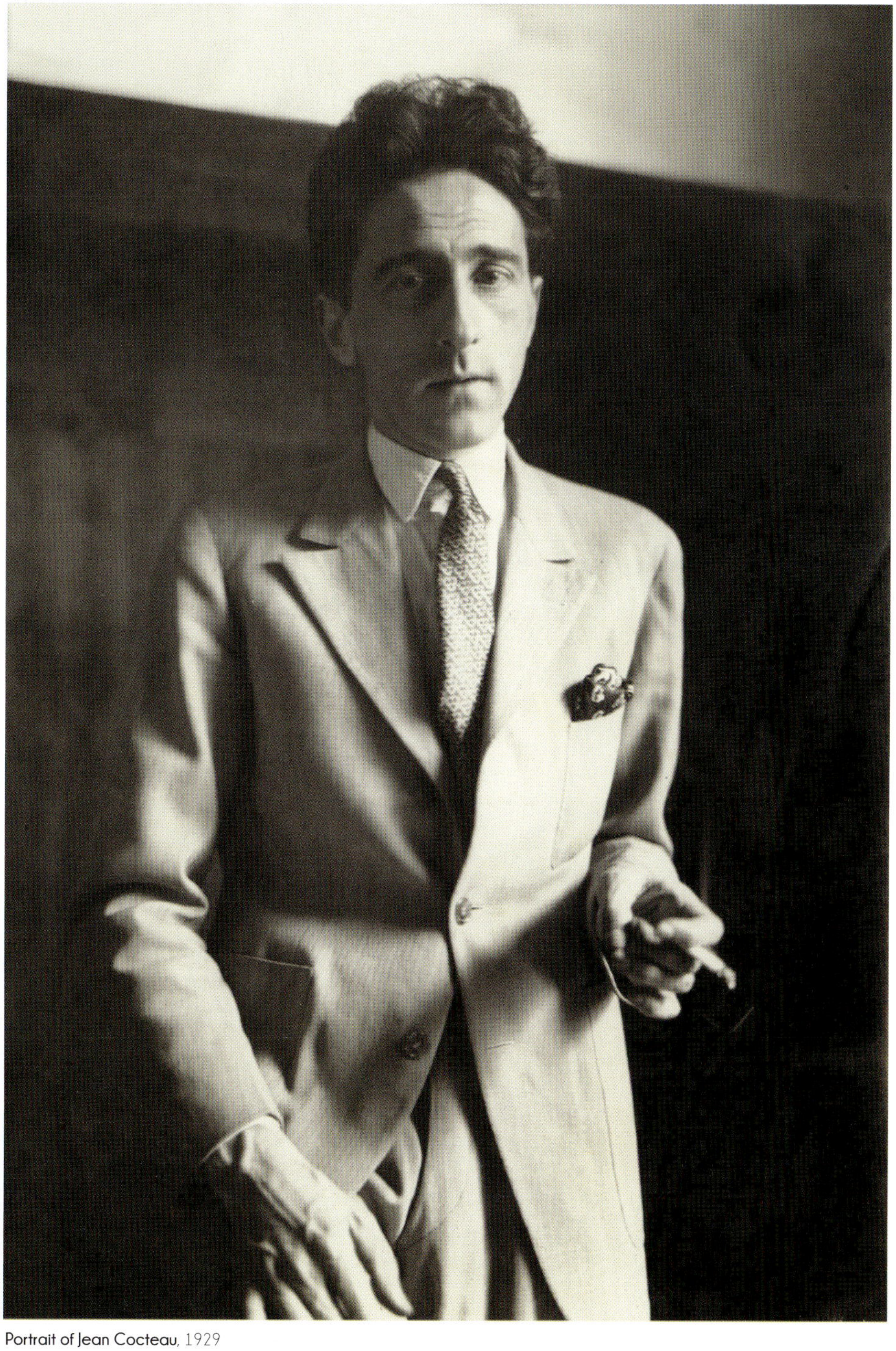

Portrait of Jean Cocteau, 1929

FREE SPIRIT

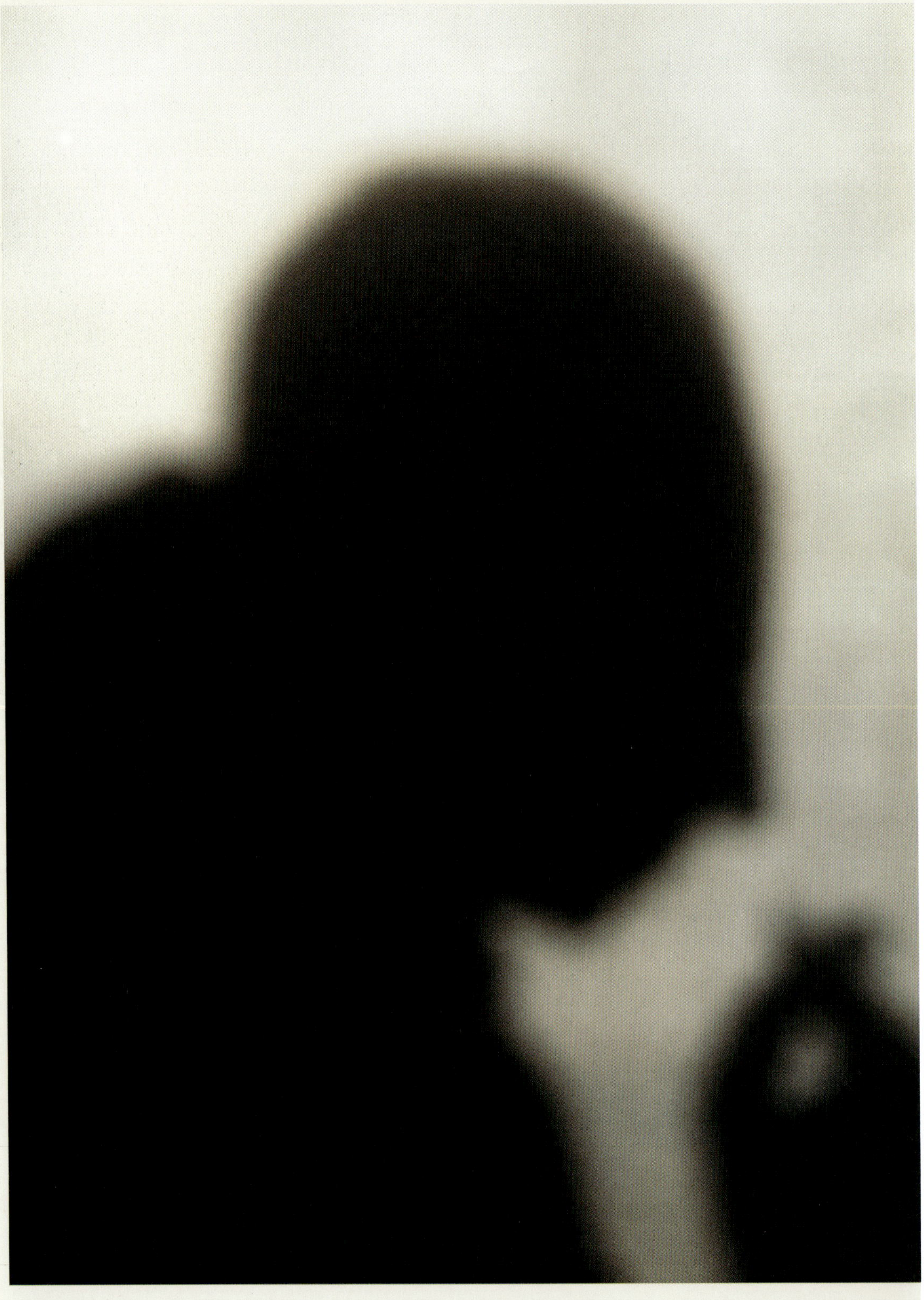

1 Destanque and Ivens, op. cit., p. 76.
2 CEDG, p. 54.
3 *Germaine Krull par Pierre Mac Orlan*, 'Photographes nouveaux' series, Paris: NRF, Gallimard, 1931, pp. 6–7.

'GERMAINE WAS A FORCE, and that force was disorderly. She wanted to be free, free of conventions in every area,' wrote Joris Ivens in his memoirs, looking back on their life together in 1925–1926.[1] How, in the space of a few years did this young woman with her painful and tormented past become one of the leading figures of the New Photography, that ephemeral constellation which cemented photography's place as an indispensable part of society and the media, and helped free it of its documentary function? She gave vent to this disorderliness where she was able – that is to say, in Paris, where she experienced the other forms of disorder that were bound up with the vivacity of the city and its extremely cosmopolitan artistic population. Germaine stood out at once among even the most intrepid photographers working in the city in 1928, and must have seemed eccentric to the writers and artists she frequented. Unlike Man Ray, she had no studio for portraits and, while working for magazines, did not make her living from topical events. 'My mind focused only on the visual side of things and was ill suited to the topical aspect.'[2] Whereas every image by her fellow proponents of the New Vision in photography invariably evokes the posture of the 'great photographer' or the 'artist photographer' who is aware of producing an œuvre, of belonging to one current or another, Krull's (abundant) memoirs mention no male or female colleague (apart from her companion Eli Lotar, and occasionally her friends Kertész and Man Ray) and no artistic movement that she might be associated with. They proffer no aesthetic considerations. Looking at her work, she does not seem concerned with the construction of the image in its rectangular frame. And when she tries to explain her creative ambitions in what is the only analytical text she wrote, the 1930 preface to *Études de nu*, her conclusion is the throwaway, 'because one summer morning [it] just appealed to me'. Her capacity for innovation was no less vital for all that. She found affinities with Lotar, for sure, and with the literary milieu they both frequented, as well as at Lucien Vogel's *VU*, an adventure that opened up a number of contradictory alternatives. Vogel forced her to reconcile the modernist vision of *Métal* and the verist approach imposed by photographic reportage and adopted by the writer or reporter signing the accompanying text.

Krull was supported in this approach by her writer, intellectual and publisher friends, who understood what photography could bring to literature and its impact on the imagination. Foremost among them was a man who was powerful and respected but also warm-hearted, Pierre Mac Orlan. Other members of this circle included Florent Fels, Carlo Rim, André Malraux, Jean Cocteau and Walter Benjamin, who came to Paris in 1926–1927. Krull, wrote Mac Orlan in his short preface to the little book of her work published by Malraux at the NRF in 1931, was 'an artist born to understand the effects of photography, which can reach to the furthest limits of the imagination ... Germaine Krull does not create easy anecdotes, but she makes visible the secret details that people do not always see.'[3]

Krull's maverick spirit, which was stimulated by the company she kept in Munich, Berlin, Amsterdam and Paris, is quite evident in many of her published photographs, and even more obvious in some of the unpublished ones that have only recently come to light, and that were also made with publication in mind. The point is that Krull did not work for exhibitions (of which there were few) or to sell to collectors (except for portraits). The places where she

'The Writer Rudolf Leonhard, Berlin', undated

preferred to work, such as flea markets, were likely to throw up surprising objects and situations, and to offer the kind of bizarre juxtapositions that had been the delight of the Surrealists only a few years earlier. Krull, though, always practised a 'realism' of vision: she meant to show reality as it was, a reality that was somewhat brutal because it was captured in the moment, on-site, without trying for elegance or refinement. 'There is a photographic reality that is definitely not "the real truth" but is more true than truth itself, like the poetic exaggeration of objective reality,' wrote Carlo Rim in *VU*. He was the magazine's editor at the time and familiar with Krull's reportage work.[4] The simple fact of photographic intervention (the lens, the photographic process, the positioning of the photographer, the framing) was enough to bestow on 'this or that familiar form ... a mysterious and troubling originality'.

VARIÉTÉS, AGAIN

It was in the Belgian journal *Variétés* that these resonances can be most fully perceived, and that Krull's images are most at home. One of the first photos she published here was a shop window with mannequins.[5] Writing about the windows of Le Printemps in Paris, the critic Paul Fierens spoke of 'Venus and the Mannequins'.[6] As we have seen, these mannequins were a favourite subject for those evoking the ambiguous relation between man and machine (robots). And they were a recurrent theme of the Surrealists. Not that Krull had any real links with Surrealism. She never talked about it and never mentioned or frequented the 'pure' Surrealists, nor were any of her photos championed by members of the movement (who in any case were very busy with their own internal divisions).

Writing in praise of Atget in 1928, Albert Valentin, who was both a follower of Surrealism and a pillar of *Variétés*, spoke of the 'unusual turn' taken by the 'petrified figuration' of photography in his work. He saw the approach being continued by 'young photographers' such as Krull, whom he named. In his view, the modernity of these views of Old Paris, the flea markets, the fairs and the 'Zone' invoked something mentally beyond the image: 'On Atget's sensitive paper there are only a few wretched buildings ... The rest, I tell you, is beyond, in the margins, in the watermark, in the mind, within reach of the least observant: one need only look.'[7] Writing later in a commentary on Krull's *100 × Paris,* Paul Fierens noted, 'One photographs mystery by aiming at reality, because mystery and reality are inseparable.'[8]

The issue of *Variétés* published on 15 October 1929 tackled witchcraft, religion and magic, and included the most unexpected of Krull's photos. There was a first section made up of a series of seven images on various beliefs and sects, then six other, more specific images in a section devoted to superstition.[9] Commissioned, no doubt, specially for the occasion, they are the most eloquent testimony to her whimsical spirit and to the photographic insolence that led her to cobble together an unlikely scene and capture it askew, quite innocently, 'as if you were there'. Because that was the point of the image: to give viewers the impression that they were taking part in these inaccessible micro-events: *The Open Umbrella, One Match for Three Cigarettes, Broken Mirror, Touch Wood, A Hat on the Bed, Fallen Scissors*. Two of these photographs were included in the four she gave *VU* to illustrate an issue on the same theme of 'Superstitions' a year later.[10] The other two were new, augmenting the series to eight images in all.

Krull's method was at its most absolute here. Here she was proceeding as was natural to her, free of affectation, because she constructed the photographic subject herself, without having to go and look for it, and determined the practical parameters for capturing it – the distance and lighting – in her characteristic, systematic deconstruction of the 'right image', of handsome, balanced photography. And she did this, as Mac Orlan emphasised, out of her love for things: 'Photographic vision attaches itself with great dexterity to the secret loves of things. It often exaggerates their tragic and fantastical aspect and makes sentimental investigations

4 Carlo Rim, 'Défense et illustration de la photographie', *VU* no. 214 (20 April 1932), p. 587.
5 *Variétés* 1, no. 6 (15 October 1928).
6 *Variétés* 1, no. 8 (15 December 1928).
7 Albert Valentin, 'Eugène Atget', *Variétés* 1, no. 8 (15 December 1928), pp. 403–407.
8 *Variétés* 2, no. 7 (15 November 1929), p. 508.
9 *Variétés* 2, no. 6 (15 October 1929), p. 428 a, b, c.
10 Sylviac, 'Superstitions', *VU* no. 143 (10 December 1930), pp. 1343–1345: four photos out of sixteen, as well as *A Piece of the Hanged Man's Noose* and *The Horseshoe*.

in the realm of shadow relatively easy.'[11] Krull took these photographs out of love for these machines, these objects or these beings, these rough or trivial forms that were manifestations of modernity and that they captured with great care.

Krull also made use of purely photographic artifices: photomontage, double exposure, camera shakiness, the blur from light saturation – all these were techniques that obscured the legibility of the image and therefore forced the viewer to *see* beyond the surface, using the imagination. *Ectoplasms: the Fortune Teller's Predictions* is not meant to be a photograph of a woman who happens to be a fortune teller, but to evoke fortune telling.[12] The eye is superimposed over the circle of an eyeglass, the hand speaks instead of the mouth. Mac Orlan uses the metaphor of the brain as a dark room where developing takes place, the place of self-revelation, speaking of 'The man who lives by his eye, who is dominated by his eye and who, alone in the dark room of his brain, under its red light, develops the candid film that he has recorded.'[13] Photography is neither an ersatz nor an additive to sight, and this was something Krull first realised with the pivoting cranes and the elevator bridge in Rotterdam. She would offer this amusing physics demonstration whenever she knew she had a receptive reader – the reader of *Variétés* or *Grand'Route*.

Several of her advertising images are double exposures (which were certainly not used): the woman's face prepared for Poiret (and eventually published in *Le Courrier littéraire* under the title *Vision 1930*), the study for Shell engine oil, the inside of a wireless. Likewise, her view of a foundry with sprays of molten metal is not easy to read.[14] In her portraits Krull made free use of the subject's cast shadow on a wall, a device she first adopted in 1926. In at least one case, her portrait of the German writer Rudolf Leonhard, who had lived in Paris in 1927, the shadow is all that remains of the subject.[15] This was a practice she shared with Kertész, but she was more systematic. In the model of professional studio portraiture that had general economic and social currency at the time, lighting was expected to be even and controlled; to go unnoticed. Krull delighted in breaking this code, just as she liked to go against the social order. In short, she reverted to the Mad Dog of Munich and Berlin. In those days, though, she photographed nudes in a kind of contrasting lighting derived from Pictorialism, according to which the technical instrument, the lamp, was meant not to be seen. But where this technical aspect was duly hidden in those earlier photos, in Paris it was to the fore, as part and parcel of the artisanal process. Once again, her mentor in this was no doubt Pierre Mac Orlan, whose frequent references to shadow ranged from the literal to the metaphorical, picturing it as something synonymous with the unknown, the dark, imaginary side of things. The close-up of Eisenstein's face, lit from below, obliges the viewer to go through a process of visual reconstitution similar to what happens when they see the Cubist deformations of Picasso. The image was even more radically cropped for its publication in *Grand'Route*. Krull was always ready to try disorienting optical effects, like the view of the inside of a conduit, and, when filming in a factory, welcomed the effects of camera movement and contre-jour in an image that writing on the back designates as 'fantastic forge'.[16]

'Photography . . . allies itself with singular power with all that constitutes the cerebral aspect of things, which is the only one that counts because that is what commands our sympathy or our antipathy.'[17] In an article about Krull for the entertainment magazine *La Rampe* published in 1931, journalist Jean Laurent emphasised her singularity: 'Everything interests her, but everything by her own measure.' And, in an apt comparison, he observed that 'Germaine Krull is a photographer the way Jean Cocteau is a poet.'[18] The nine accompanying photographs confirmed this eloquence.[19]

STRANGE AND FAMILIAR

Krull made use of numerous avant-garde techniques and practices and could be just as 'fantastical' when doing reportage or taking a photograph seemingly with no precise intention.

11 Preface to *Atget photographe de Paris*, Paris: Henri Jonquières, 1930.
12 *Variétés* 1, no. 9 (15 January 1929), p. 472.
13 *Masques sur mesure*, Paris: Gallimard, 1965, I, p. 128.
14 Citroën factories, Chalon-sur-Saône, Musée Nicéphore Niépce.
15 And the shadow of a woman's face in *La Chatte* by Colette, *Marianne* no. 28 (3 May 1933), p. 7.
16 The words are not in Krull's handwriting, however.
17 Pierre Mac Orlan, 'Photographie. Éléments de fantastique social', *Le Crapouillot*, January 1929, pp. 3–5.
18 Jean Laurent, 'Germaine Krull', *La Rampe*, 15 April–1 May 1931, pp. 27–30 and 54.
19 Two photographs of Berthe Bovy in *La Voix humaine*, *Walter Rummel at the Piano*, *Landscape*, *Nude*, *Circus Effect*, *The Eiffel Tower*, *Arthur Honegger*, *Variétés*.

The simple reason for this was that she had a very particular, spontaneous way of relating to her subject, without mental elaboration or anticipation. She placed her lens in the physiological position of the eye and simply followed her mood – or rather, her empathy. In this respect, her self-portrait with the Icarette is revelatory: it very exactly expresses the osmosis with the camera that is one of the ways of being for a photographer, and it also says that she is a woman, that she loves hands and that she is holding a cigarette. When she photographs an actor being made up she chooses the most extravagant situation, with the result that the viewer is uncertain about the nature of the scene. When she takes several portraits of Eugène Dabit at the Hôtel du Nord, in 1933 (the novel came out in 1929), she is not trying to illustrate the story but is using the setting to instil a strange atmosphere: Dabit in the embrasure of a small door up on the roof, Dabit at the end of a long, shadowy corridor, or on a soulless landing, a canary cage.[20] An unusual double page in *L'Art vivant* bearing the title 'Behind the Scenes' shows seven images taken backstage in theatres.[21] The subject and framing is disorienting, the settings uncertain and suffused with melancholy and disquiet. Faced with this image isolated by the camera, the viewer is uncertain about where they are. Whether responding to a magazine assignment or following her personal bent for collecting the weird and wonderful, Krull always listened to her instinct for revelatory disorder.

Pierre Bost, author of a portfolio of *Photographies modernes* (1930) and the leading analyst of the photography phenomenon at the time, insists on the 'photographic' component active in transforming reality into an image – the apparatus and the process – rather than on talent and style, as one would if discussing drawing. He was a fervent supporter of Krull and her method: 'Photographers understood that their instrument was perhaps, on the contrary, the most flexible of all, one that can allow itself the boldest fantasies with the object, without ever losing contact ... And so a familiar object appears to us in a new form, and our eyes are humiliated to have missed this form for so long, to have never grasped it before.'[22]

When Krull photographs simple railings in a Berlin courtyard at a slightly odd angle, what interests her is the discrepancy and the geometrical duplication of the railings. When she photographs what *Variétés* titles a 'Flemish River',[23] the mirror effect created by the water is like a Rorschach test inviting interpretation. When she photographs beams of wood floating outside a factory, her gaze homes in on the detail of the interlocking and she captures it in such a way that it becomes enigmatic for the viewer, inspiring suppressed visions that are 'irrefutable and yet inadmissible' (Pierre Bost).[24] 'The photographer's camera, which is an eye, and which is superior to the eye for the very reason that it is nothing other than an eye, reveals to us pure visual images that we have had time to forget since the day, as new-borns, when we first looked.' For Bost and for Krull, we may suppose that such was 'the role of photography: to isolate and make strange what is familiar'.

20 Paris, Bibliothèque Nationale de France.
21 'L'envers du décor', *L'Art vivant* no. 141 (1 November 1930), pp. 866–867.
22 Preface to *Photographies modernes*, Paris: A. Calavas, 1930.
23 *Variétés* 2, no. 10 (15 February 1930), p. 598.
24 A broader view is published in *Variétés* 2, no. 8 (15 December 1929), in 'Marines' section.

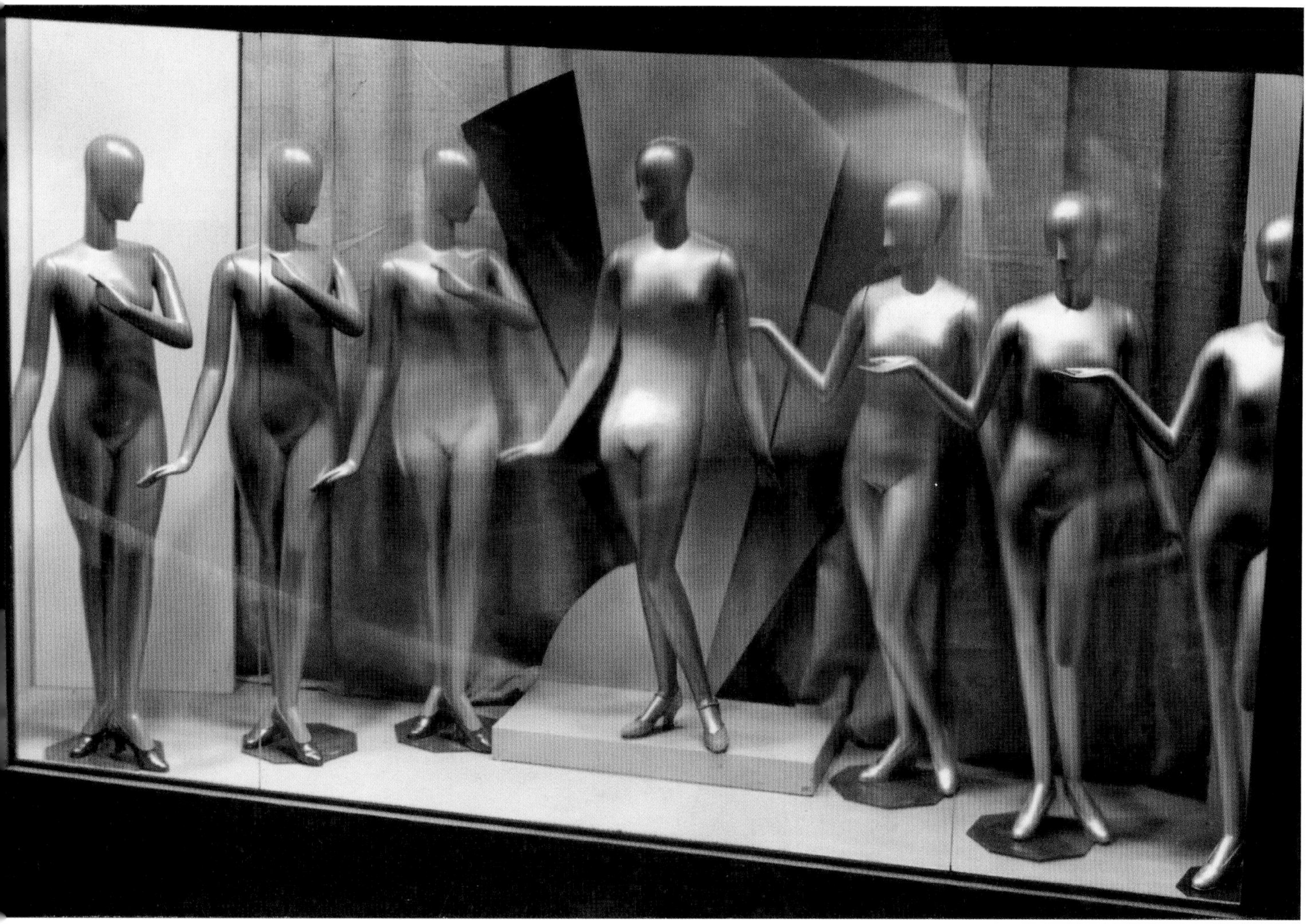

splays: Mannequins', 1928

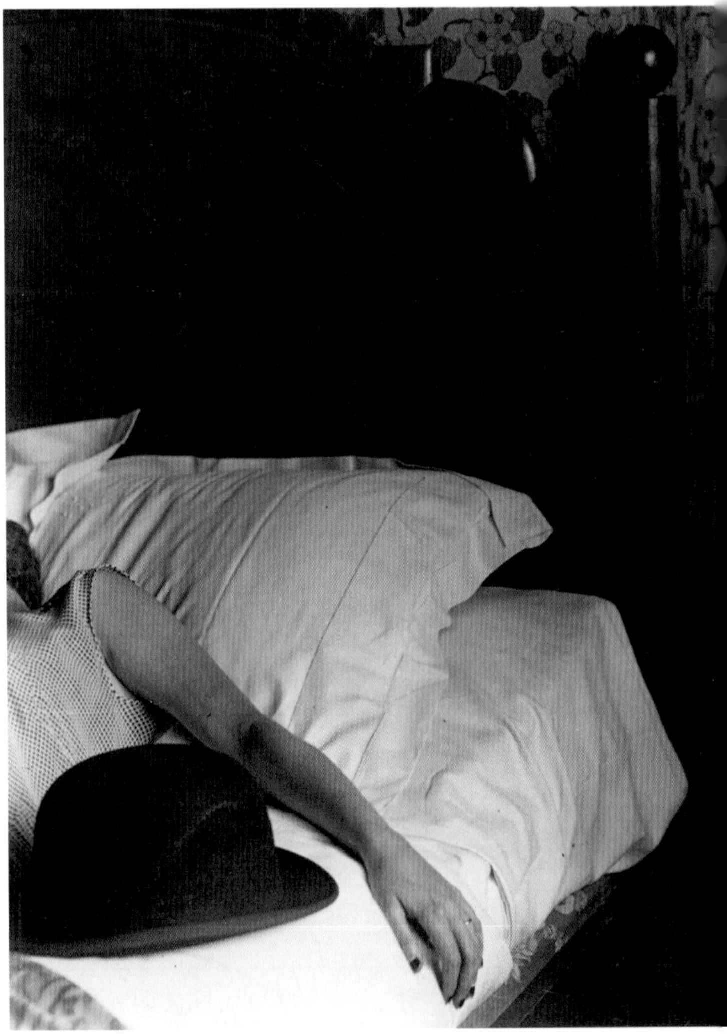

Superstitions: a Hat on the Bed, 1929

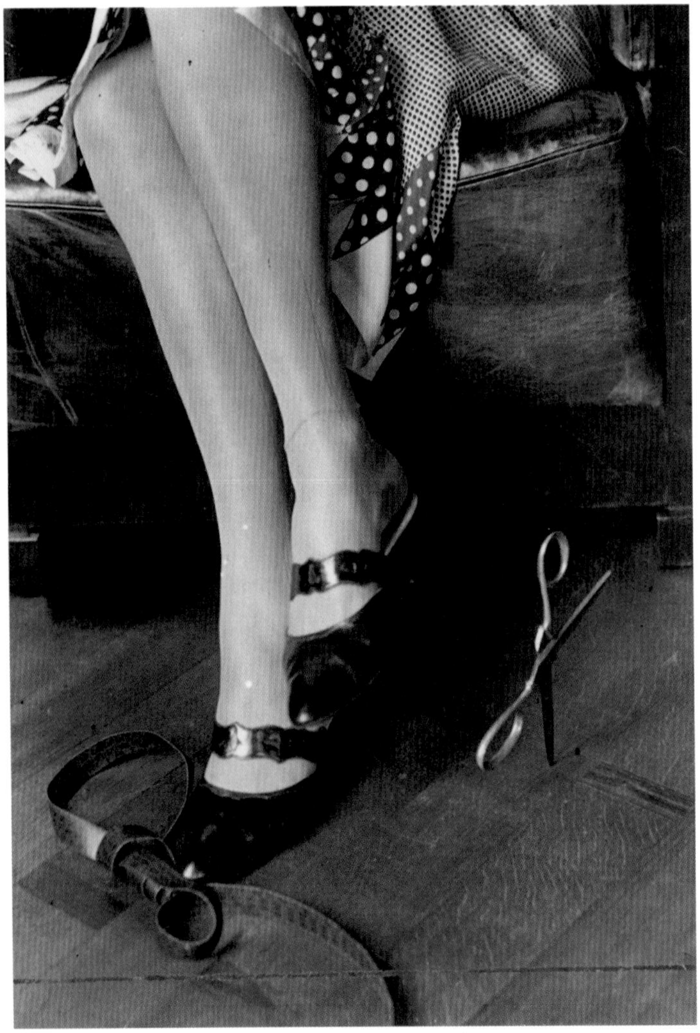

Superstitions: Fallen Scissors, 1929

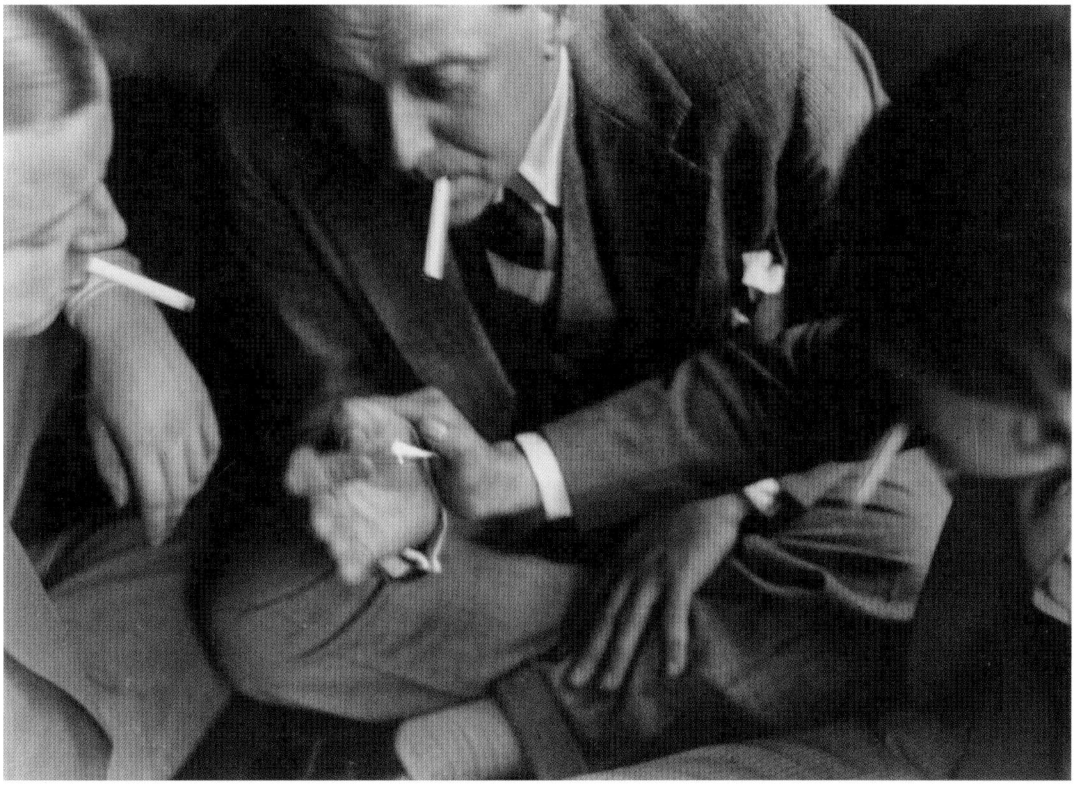

Superstition: One Match for Three Cigarettes, 1929

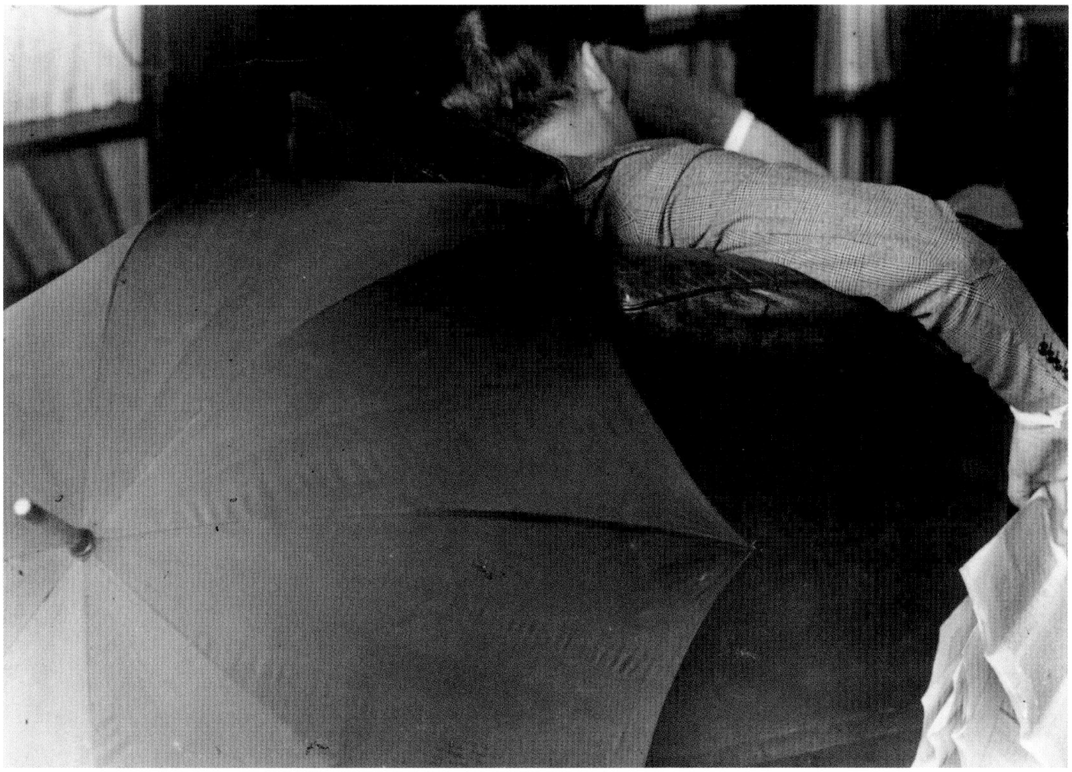

Superstitions: the Open Umbrella, 1929

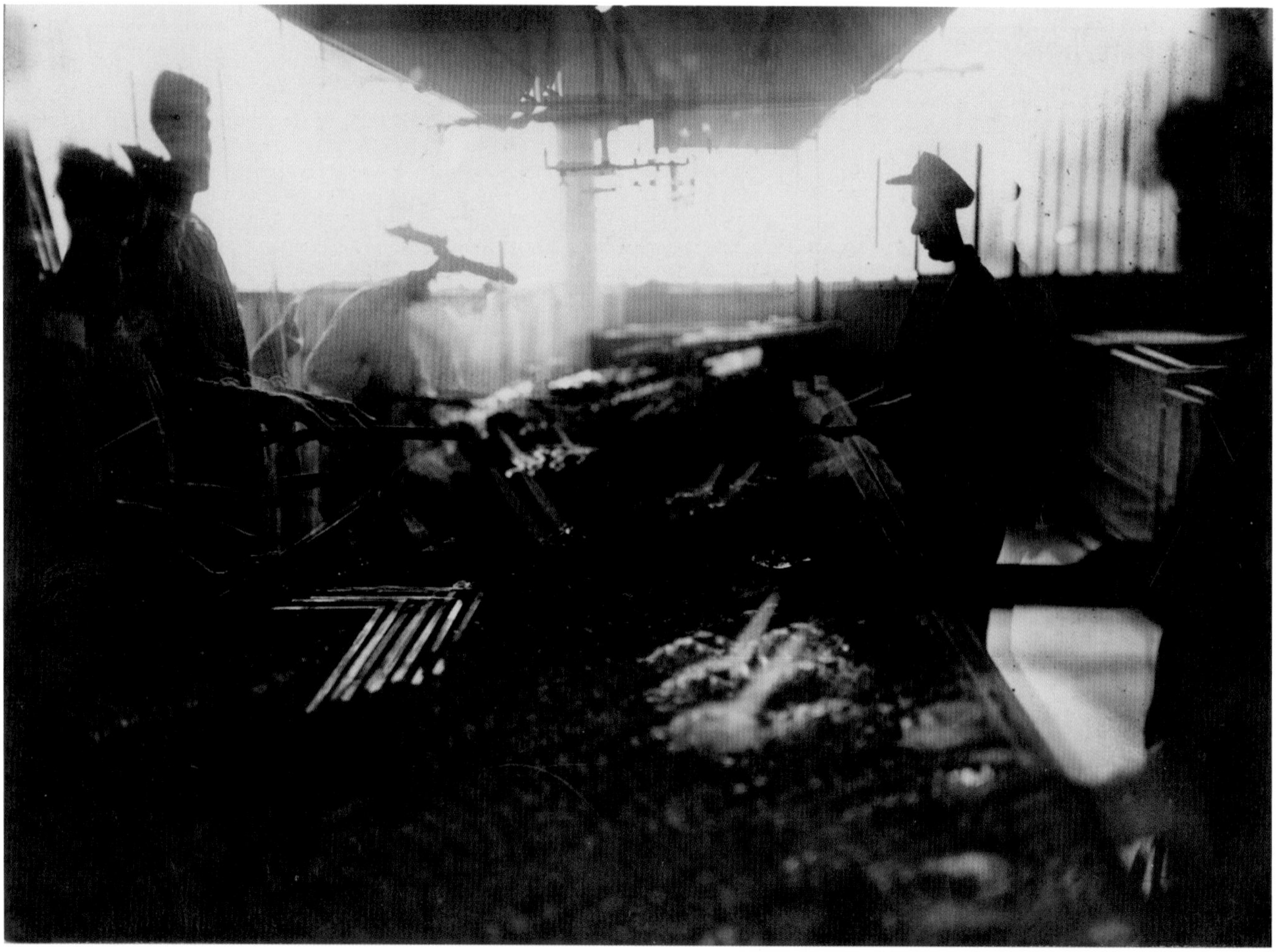

Fantastic Forge, c. 1929

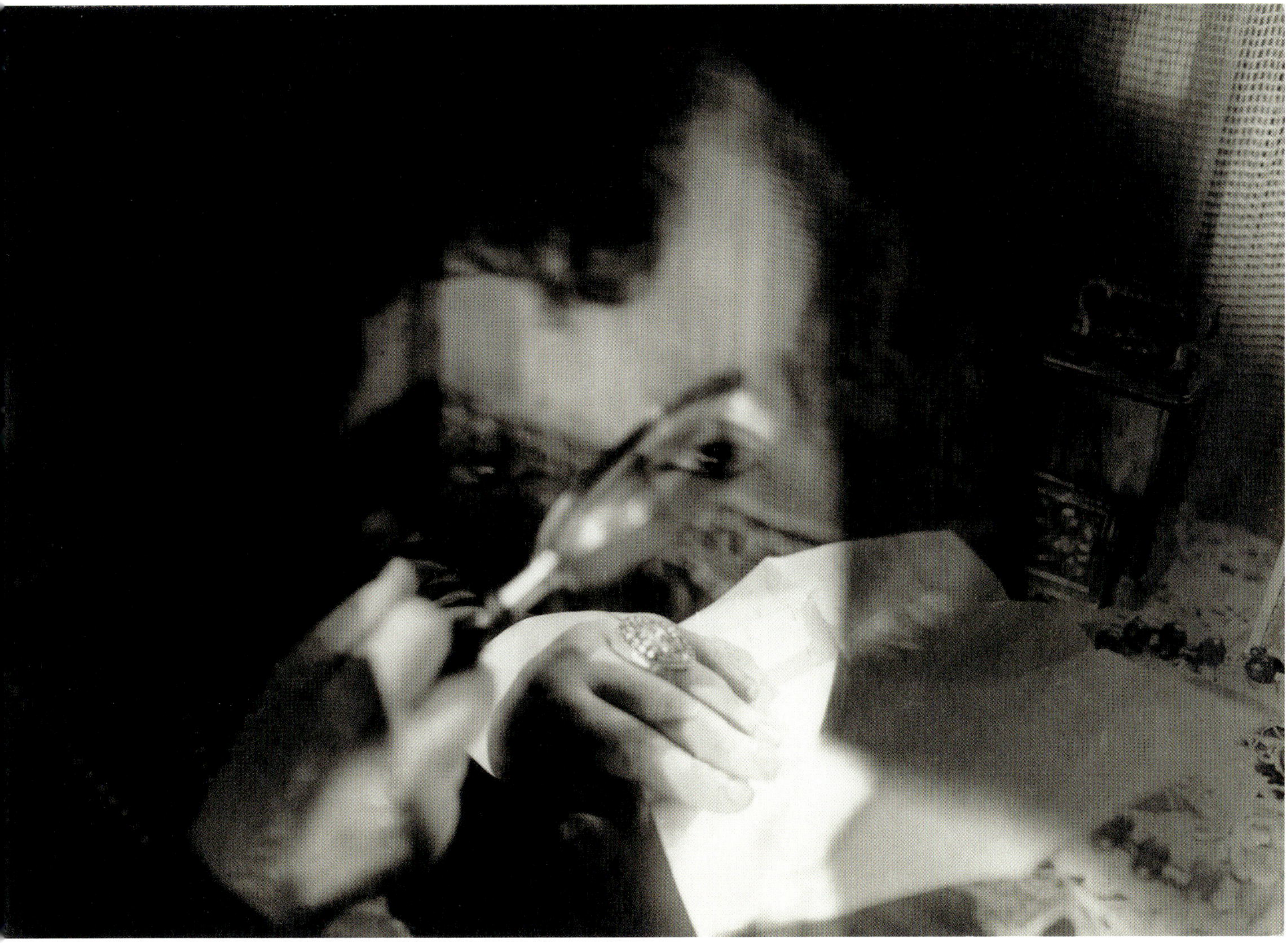

The Fortune Teller, 1928

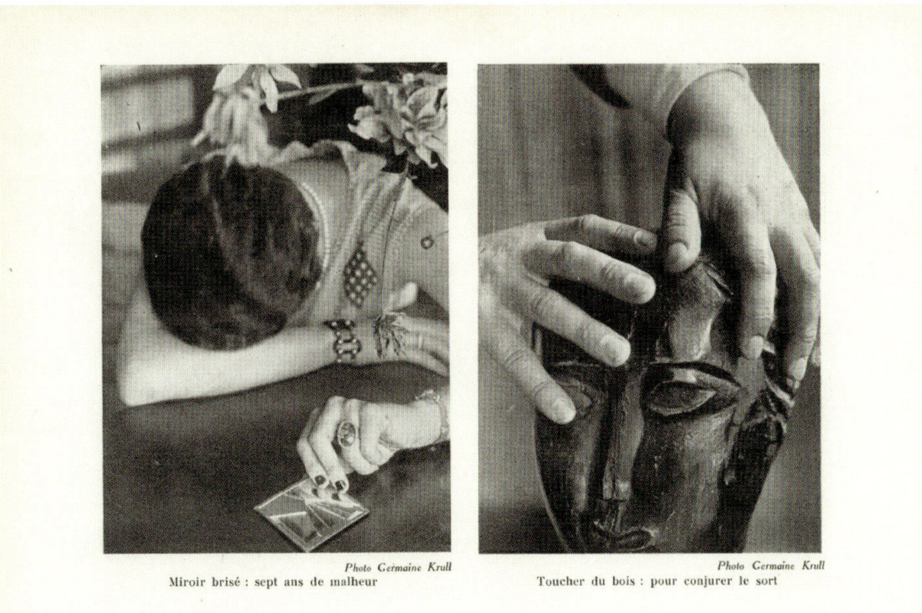

'Superstition: Broken Mirror; Touch Wood', *Variétés*, 2nd year, 6, 15 October 1929, p. 428b

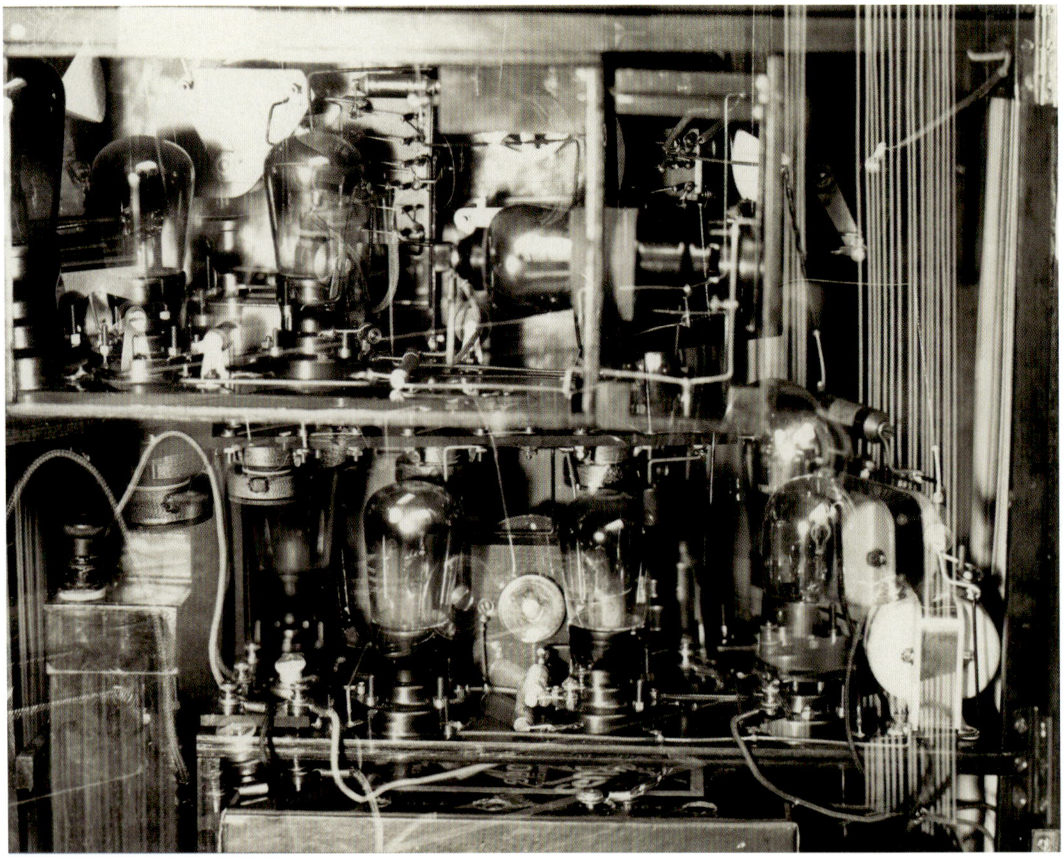

Inside of a Wireless, double exposure (advertisement idea), 1929

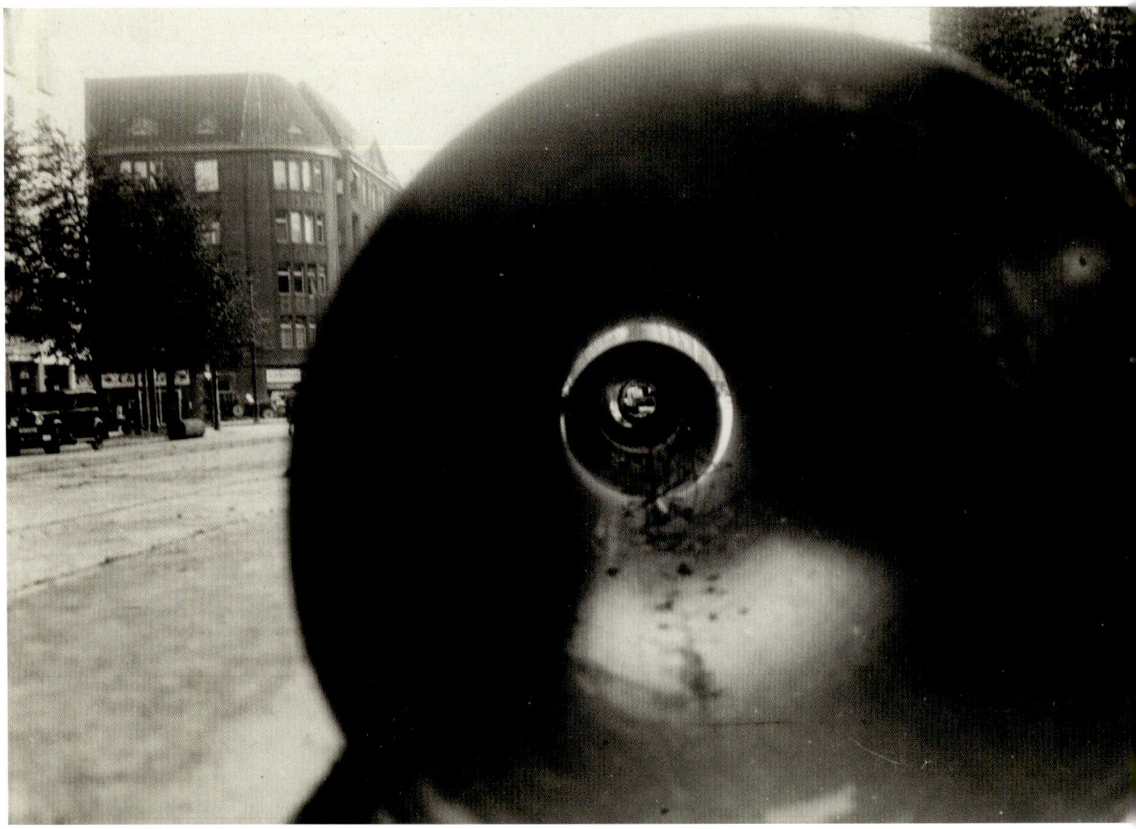

Untitled (Conduit), c. 1929

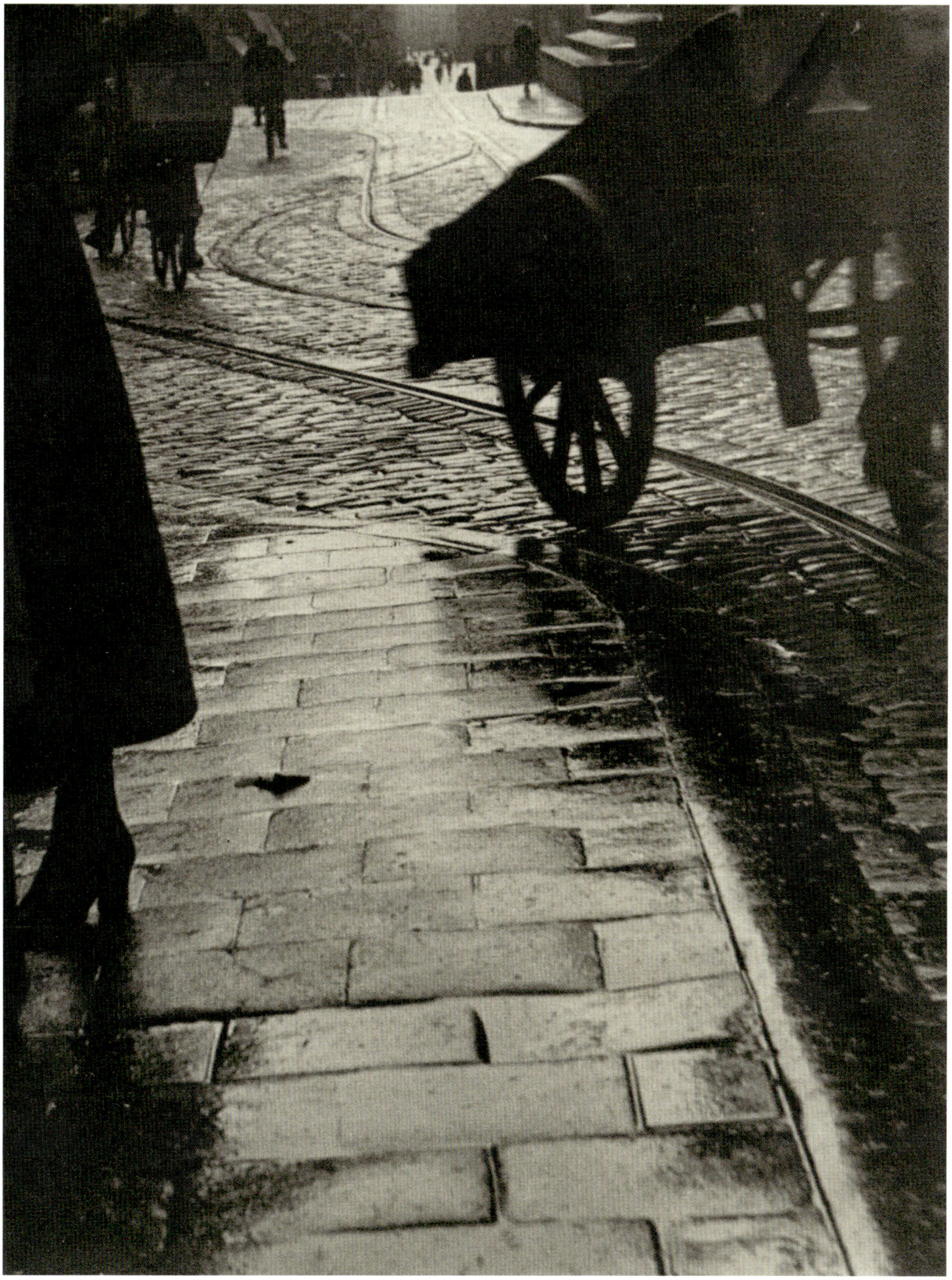

Belgium, c. 1926

L'ENVERS DU DÉCOR

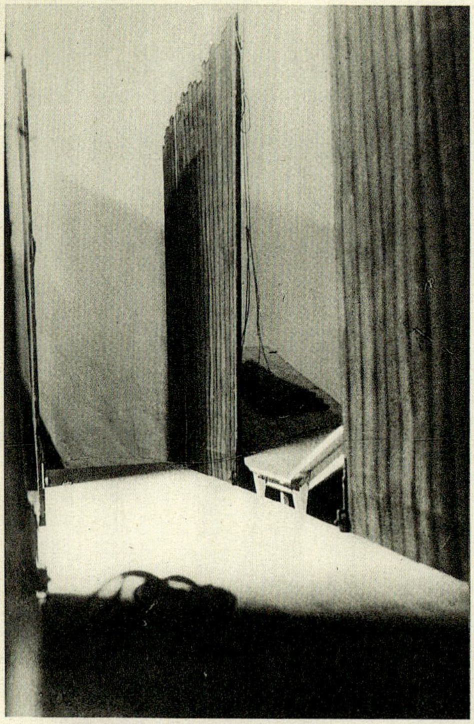

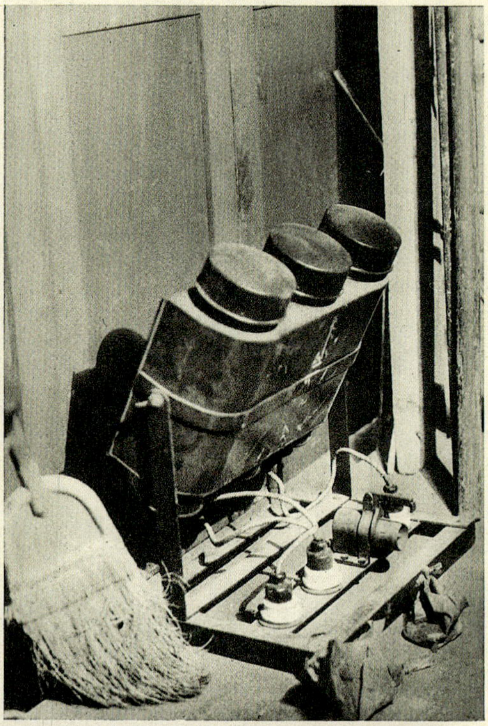

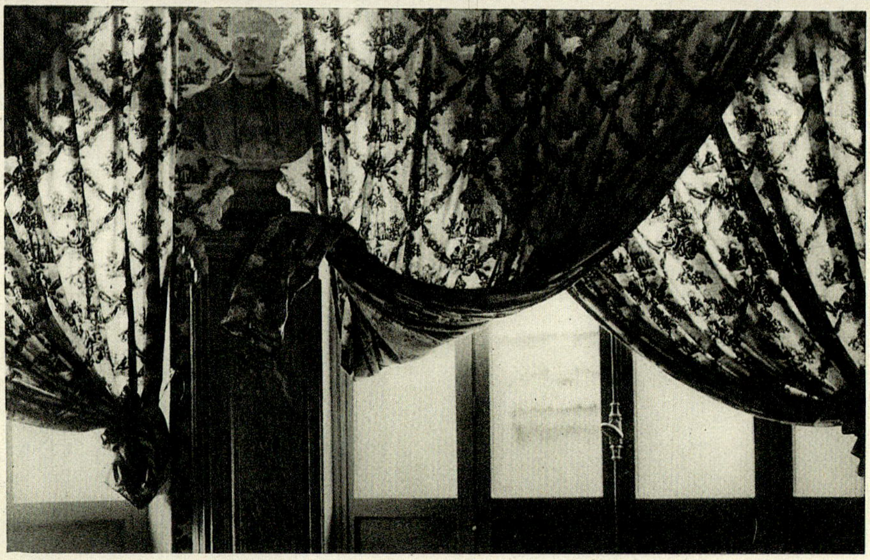

CES PHOTOGRAPHIES ET CELLES DE LA PAGE SUIVANTE SONT DE GERMAINE KRULL.

866

'Behind the Scenes', *L'Art vivant*, no. 141, 1 November 1930, pp. 866–867 (and facing page)

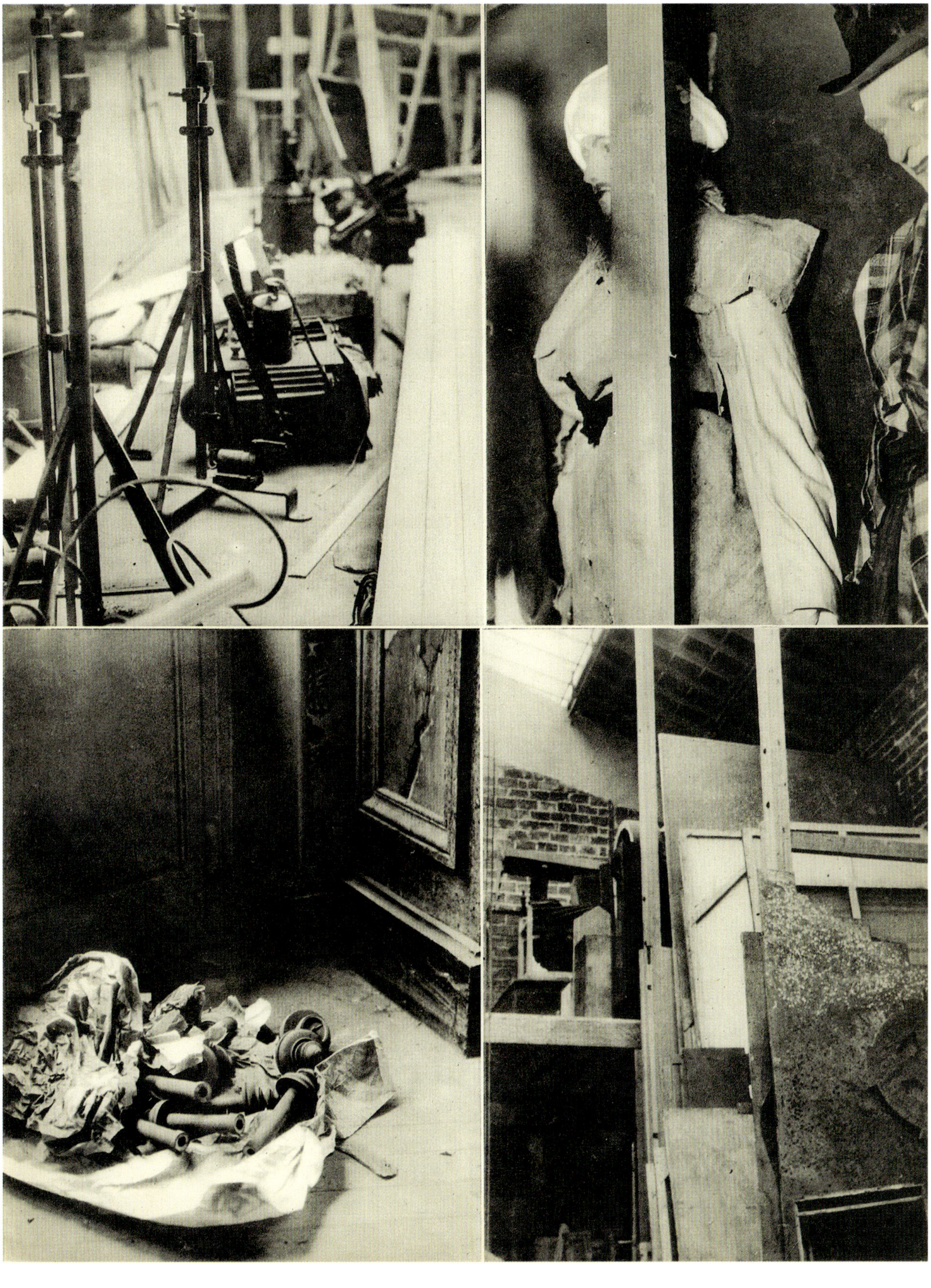

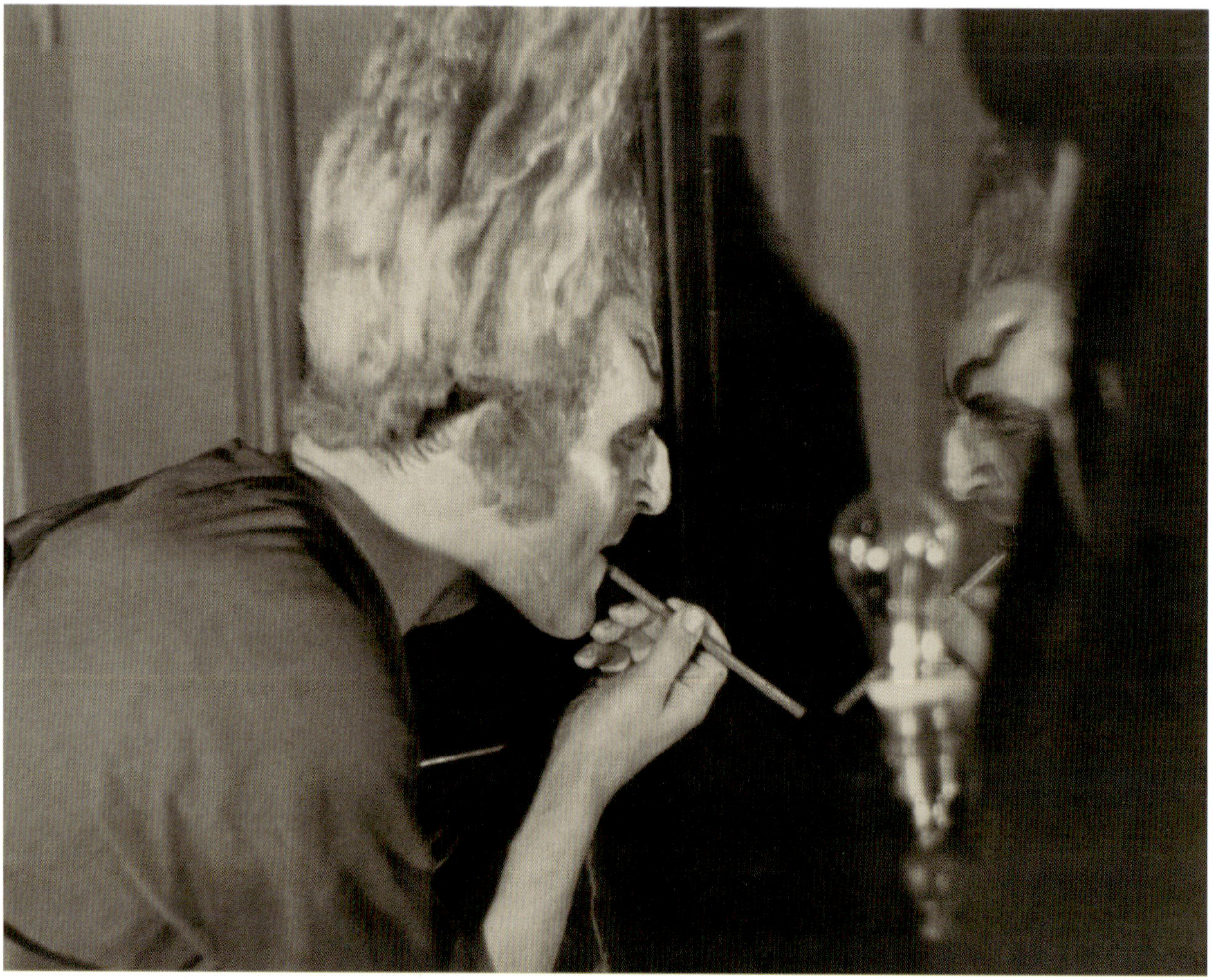

Mr Poeltzer Making Himself Up for Wagner's Ring Cycle at the Opéra de Monaco, 1935

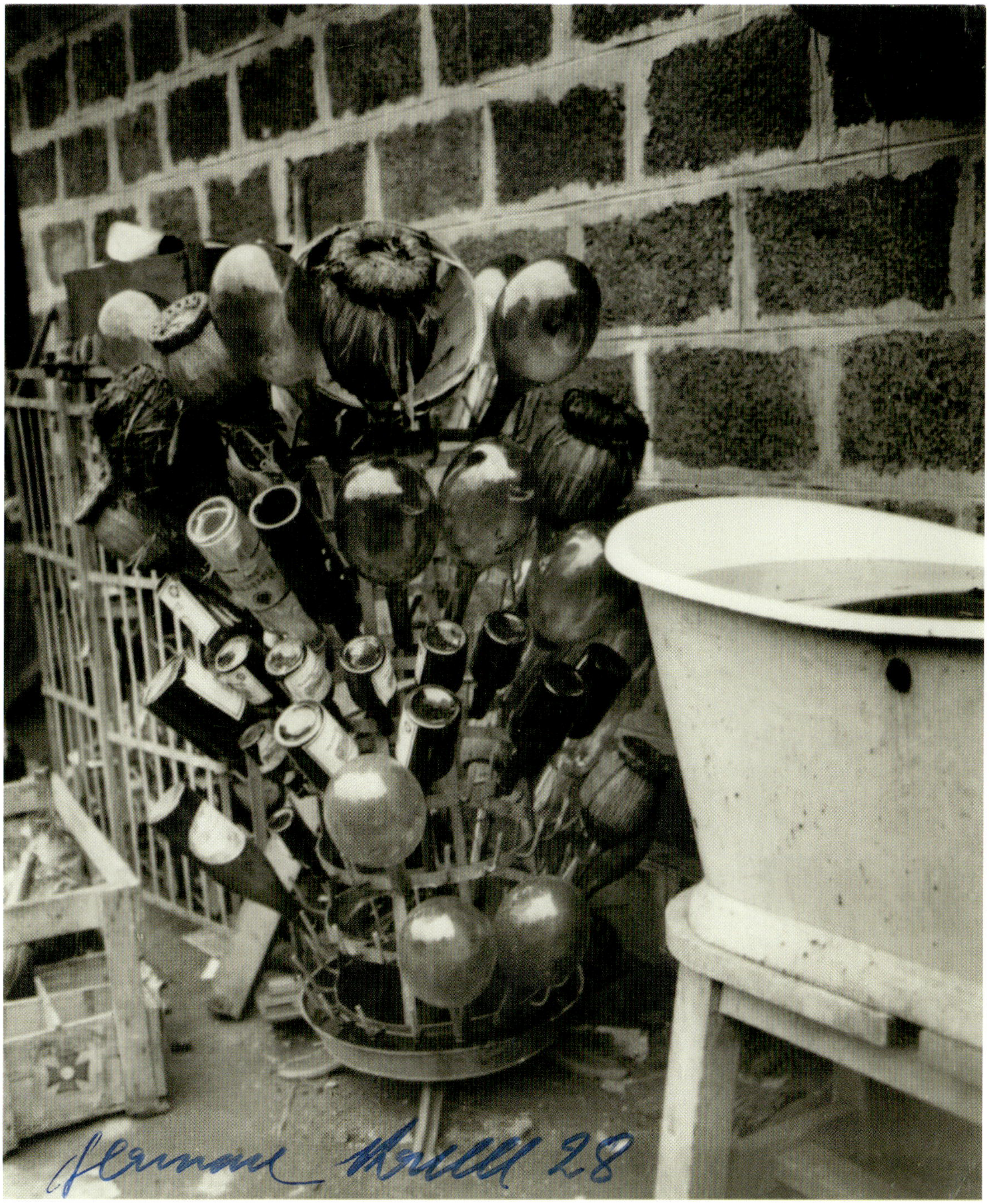

Flea Market, Paris, 1928

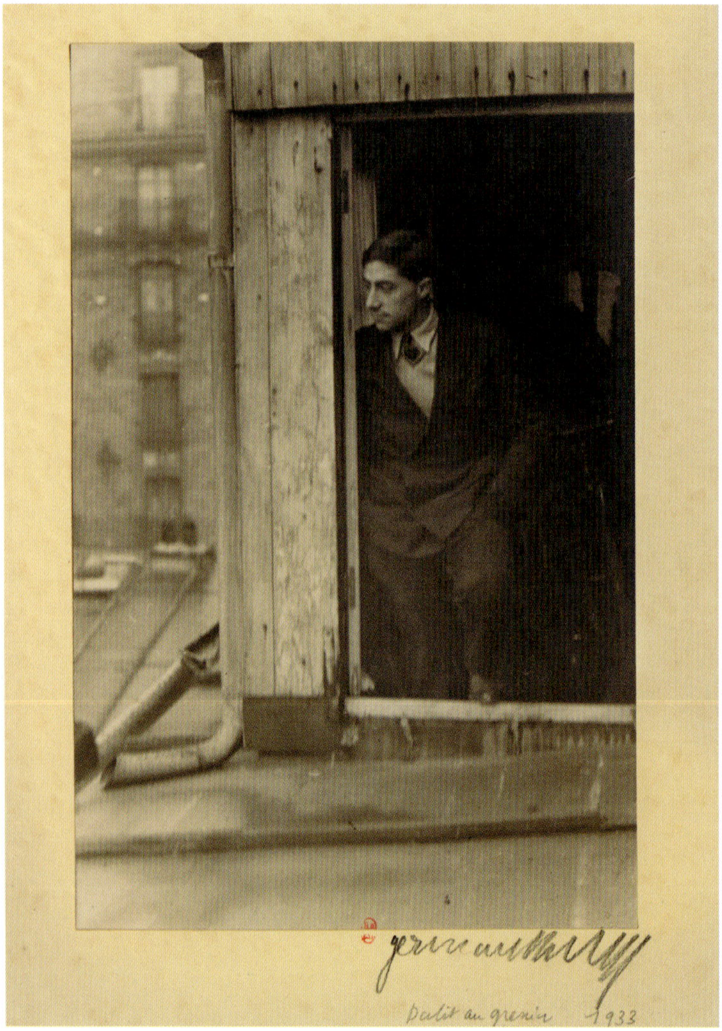

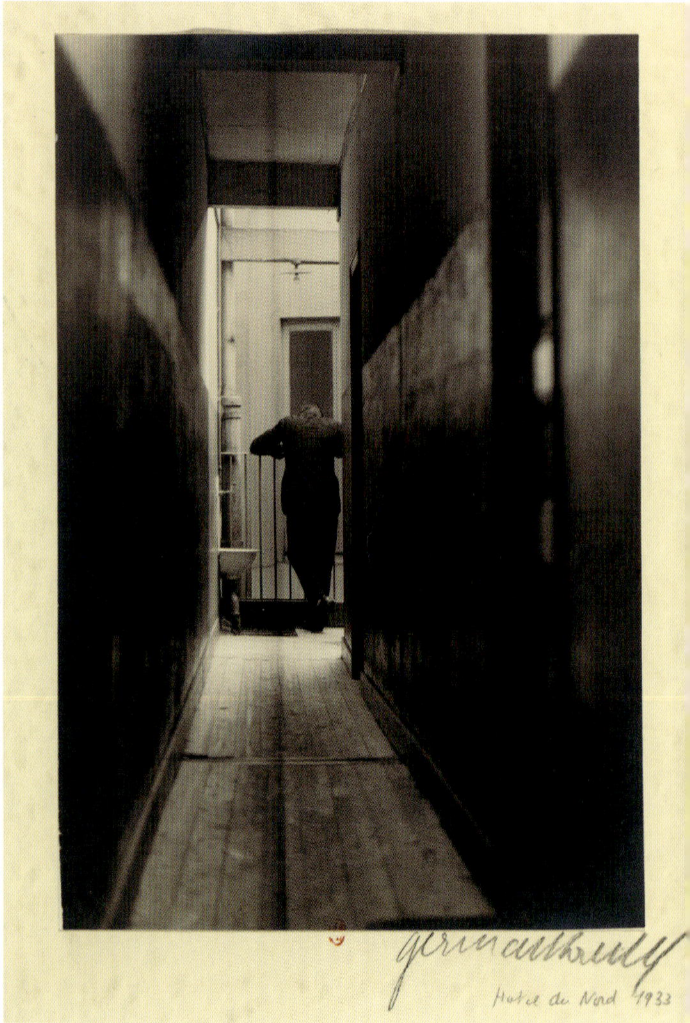

Hôtel du Nord, Eugène Dabit, 1933 (and right)

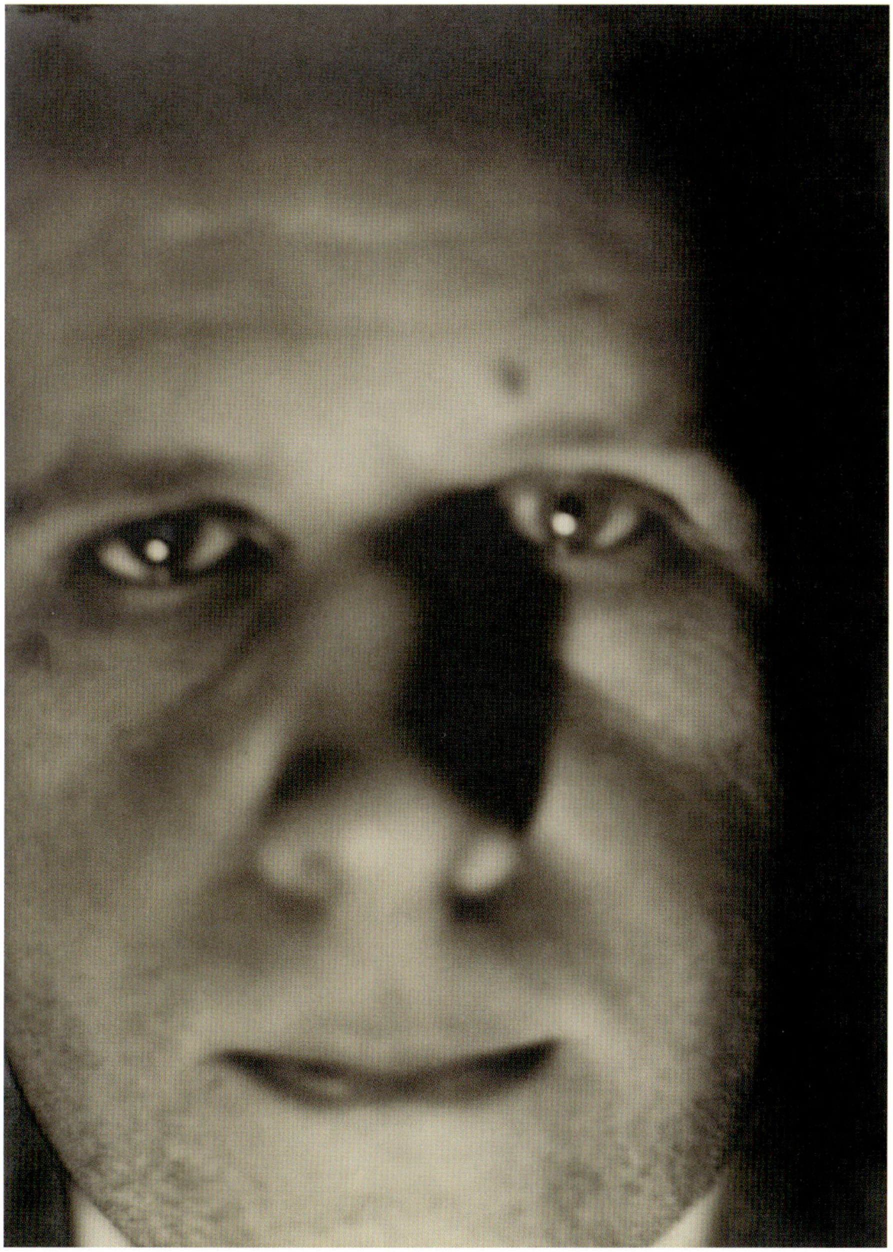

S. M. Eisenstein, 1930

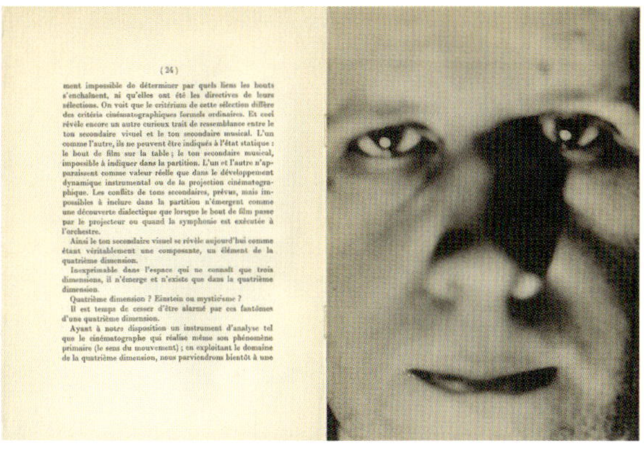

(24)

ment impossible de déterminer par quels liens les bouts s'enchaînent, ni qu'elles ont été les directives de leurs sélections. On voit que le critérium de cette sélection diffère des critéria cinématographiques formels ordinaires. Et ceci révèle encore un autre curieux trait de ressemblance entre le ton secondaire visuel et le ton secondaire musical. L'un comme l'autre, ils ne peuvent être indiqués à l'état statique : le bout de film sur la table ; le ton secondaire musical, impossible à indiquer dans la partition. L'un et l'autre n'apparaissent comme valeur réelle que dans le développement dynamique instrumental ou de la projection cinématographique. Les conflits de tons secondaires, prévus, mais impossibles à inclure dans la partition n'émergent comme une découverte dialectique que lorsque le bout de film passe par le projecteur ou quand la symphonie est exécutée à l'orchestre.

Ainsi le ton secondaire visuel se révèle aujourd'hui comme étant véritablement une composante, un élément de la quatrième dimension.

Inexprimable dans l'espace qui ne connaît que trois dimensions, il n'émerge et n'existe que dans la quatrième dimension.

Quatrième dimension ? Einstein ou mysticisme ?

Il est temps de cesser d'être alarmé par ces fantômes d'une quatrième dimension.

Ayant à notre disposition un instrument d'analyse tel que le cinématographe qui réalise même son phénomène primaire (le sens du mouvement) ; en exploitant le domaine de la quatrième dimension, nous parviendrons bientôt à une

Portrait of Eisenstein, *Grand'Route*, no. 3, May 1930, p. 24

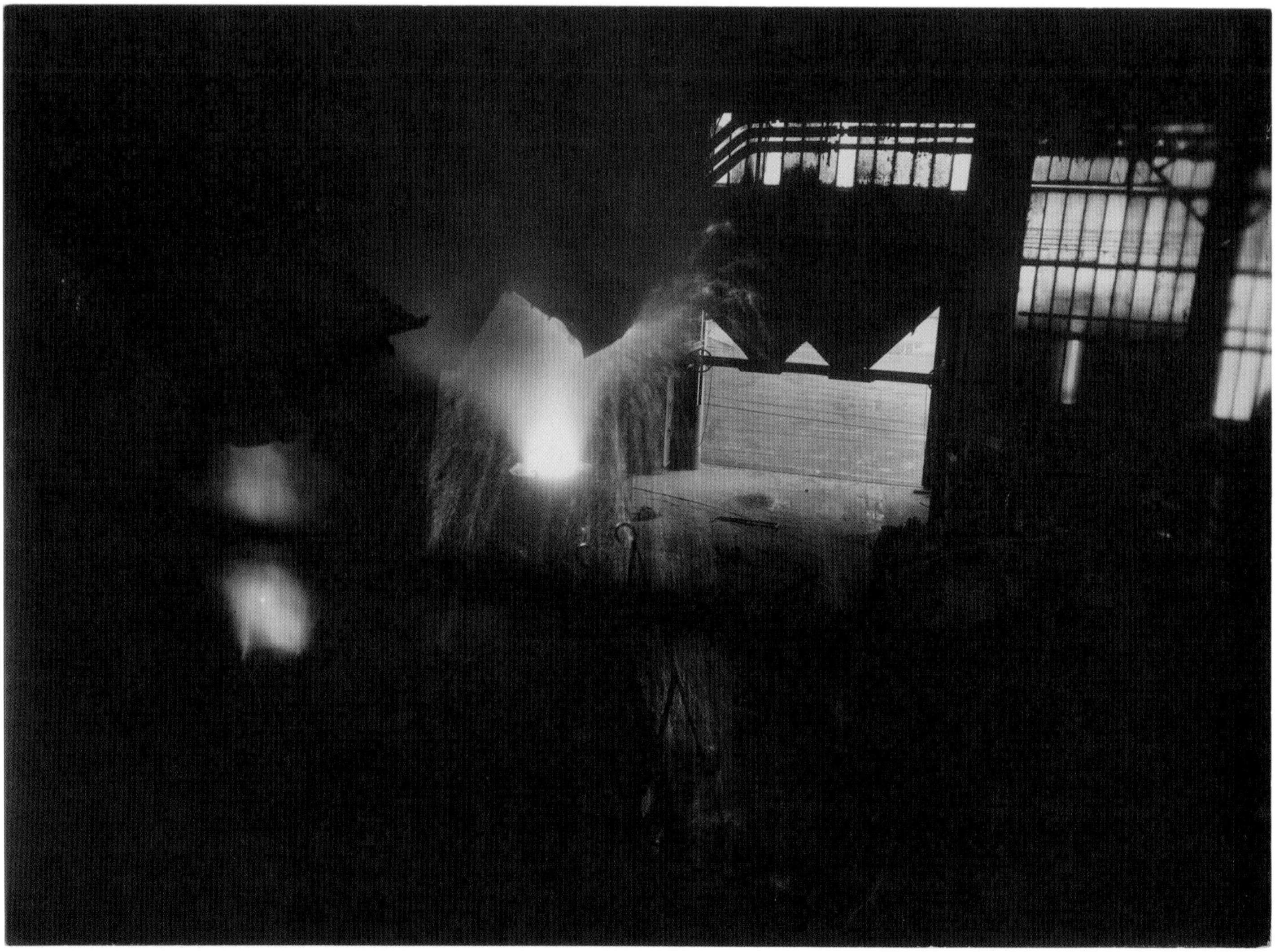

'Citroën', c. 1927

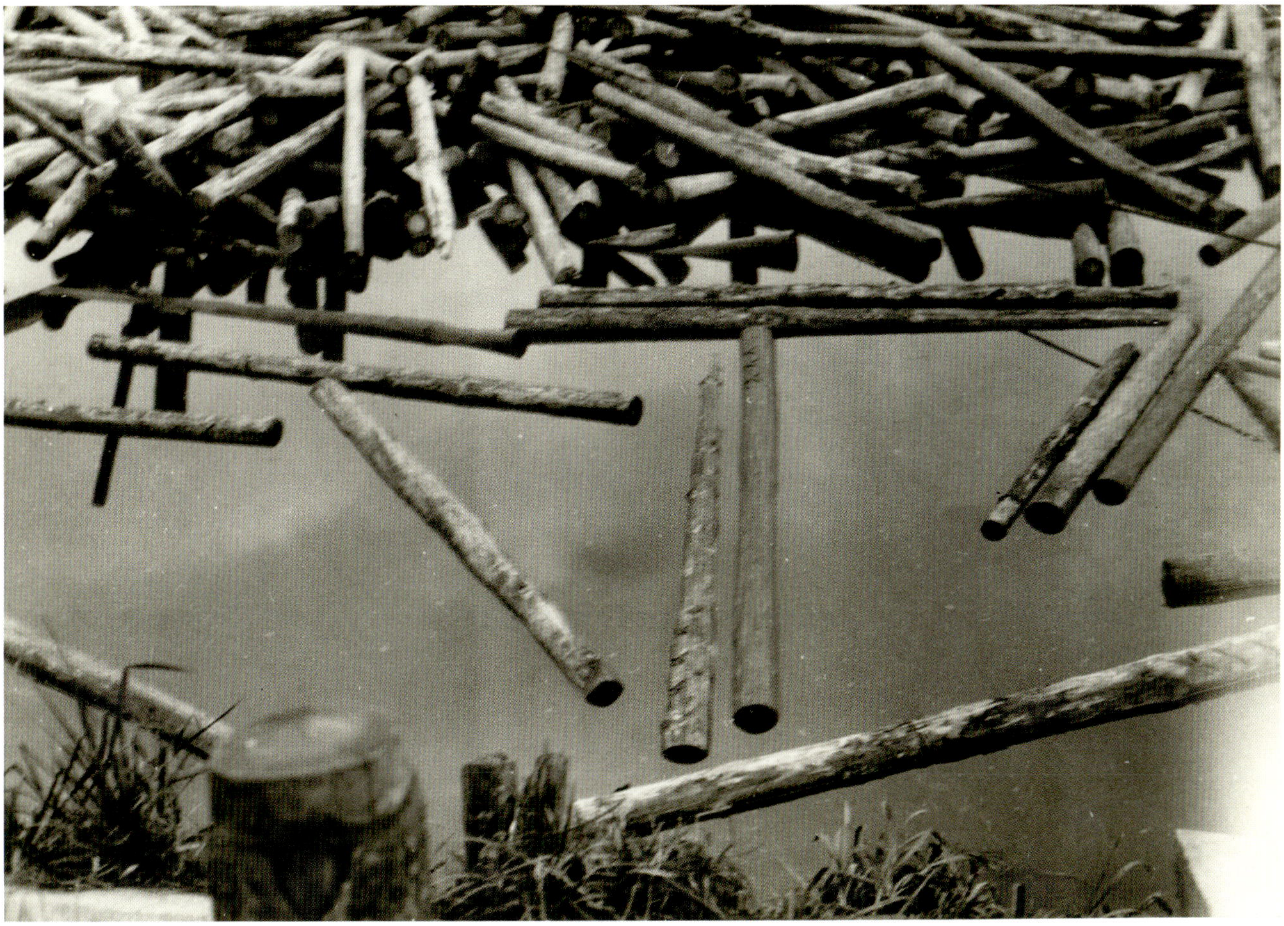

Floating Timber, 1929

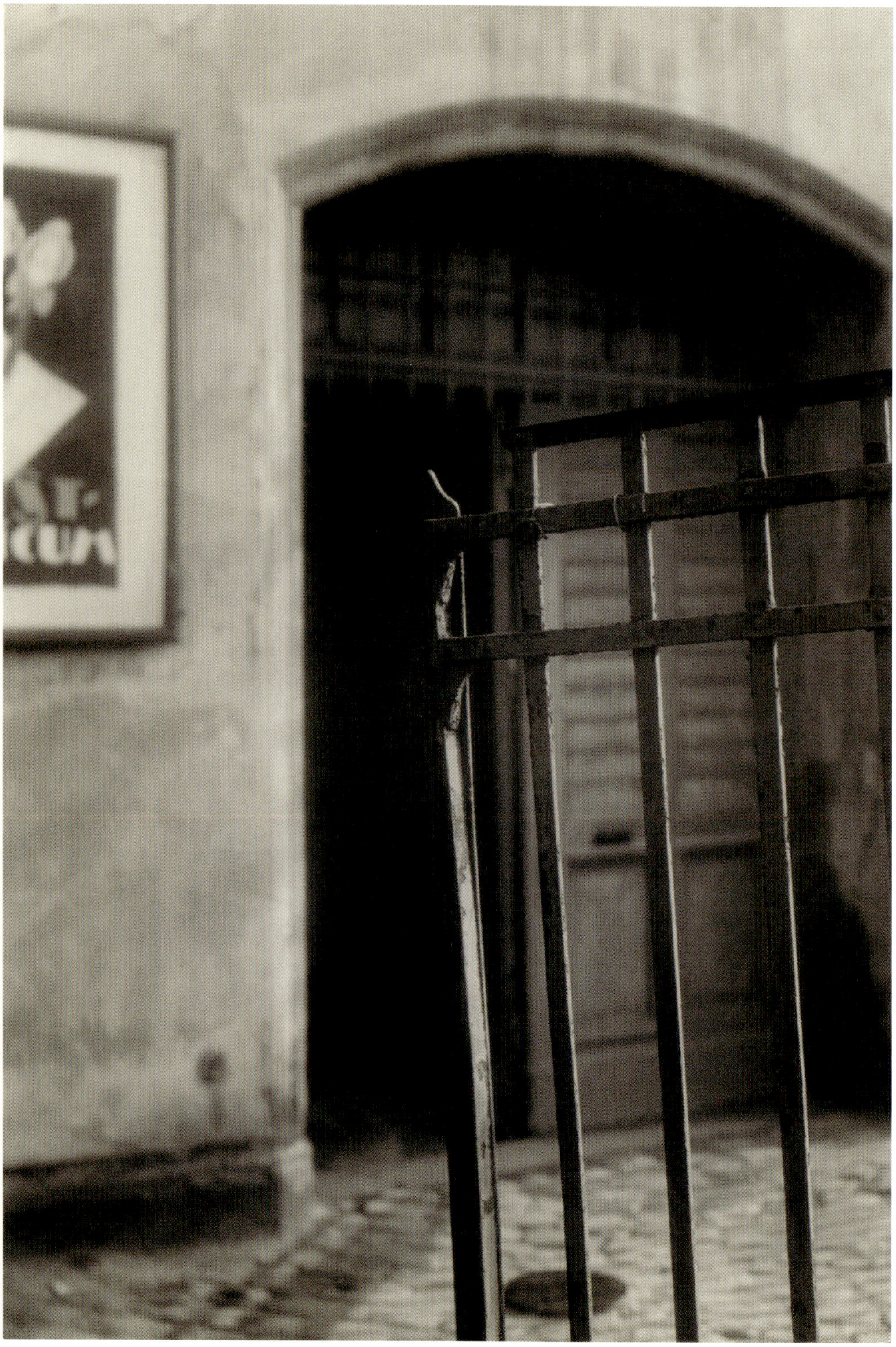

'Old Berlin', 1927

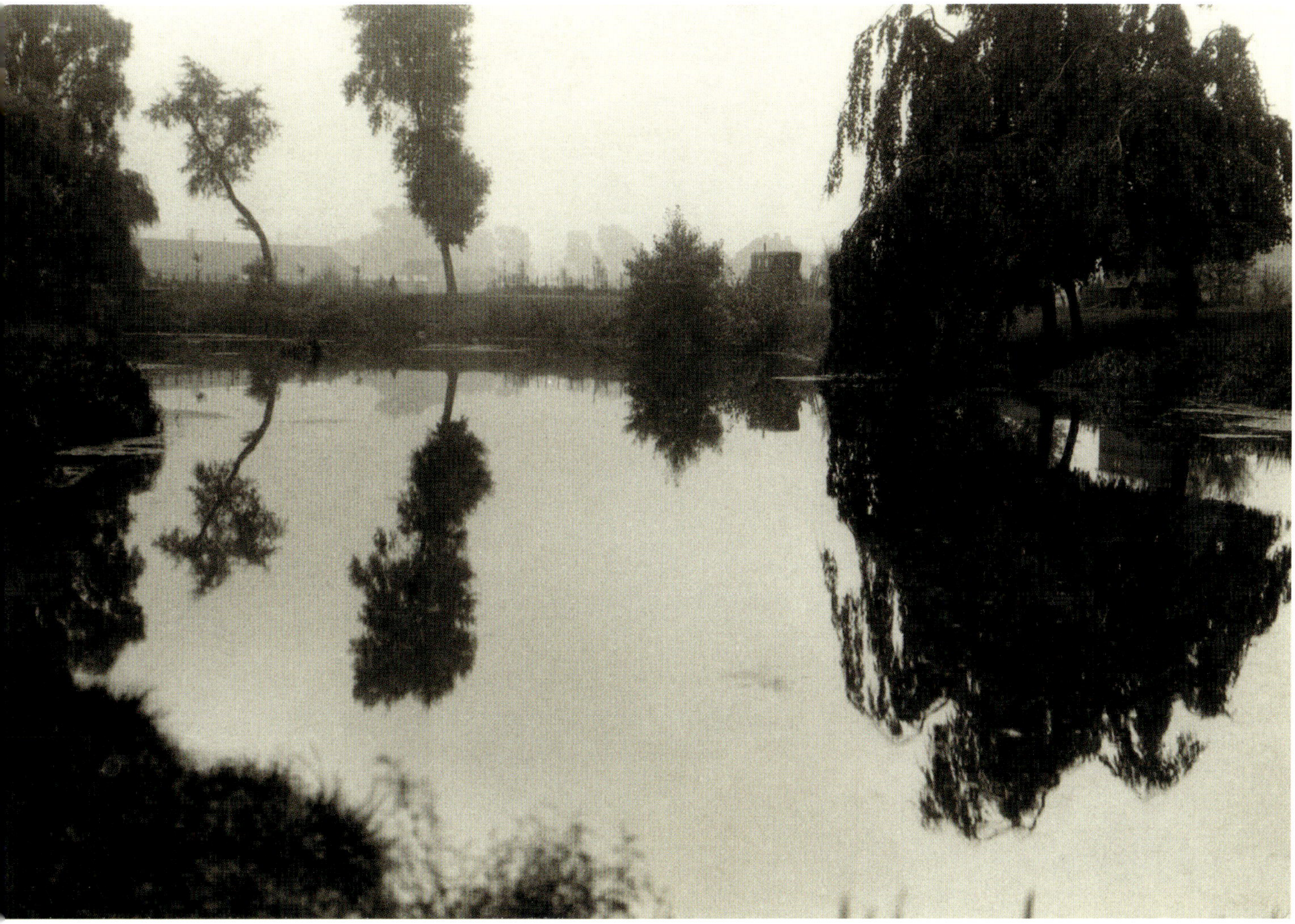

anders, Landscape, c. 1929

WAR

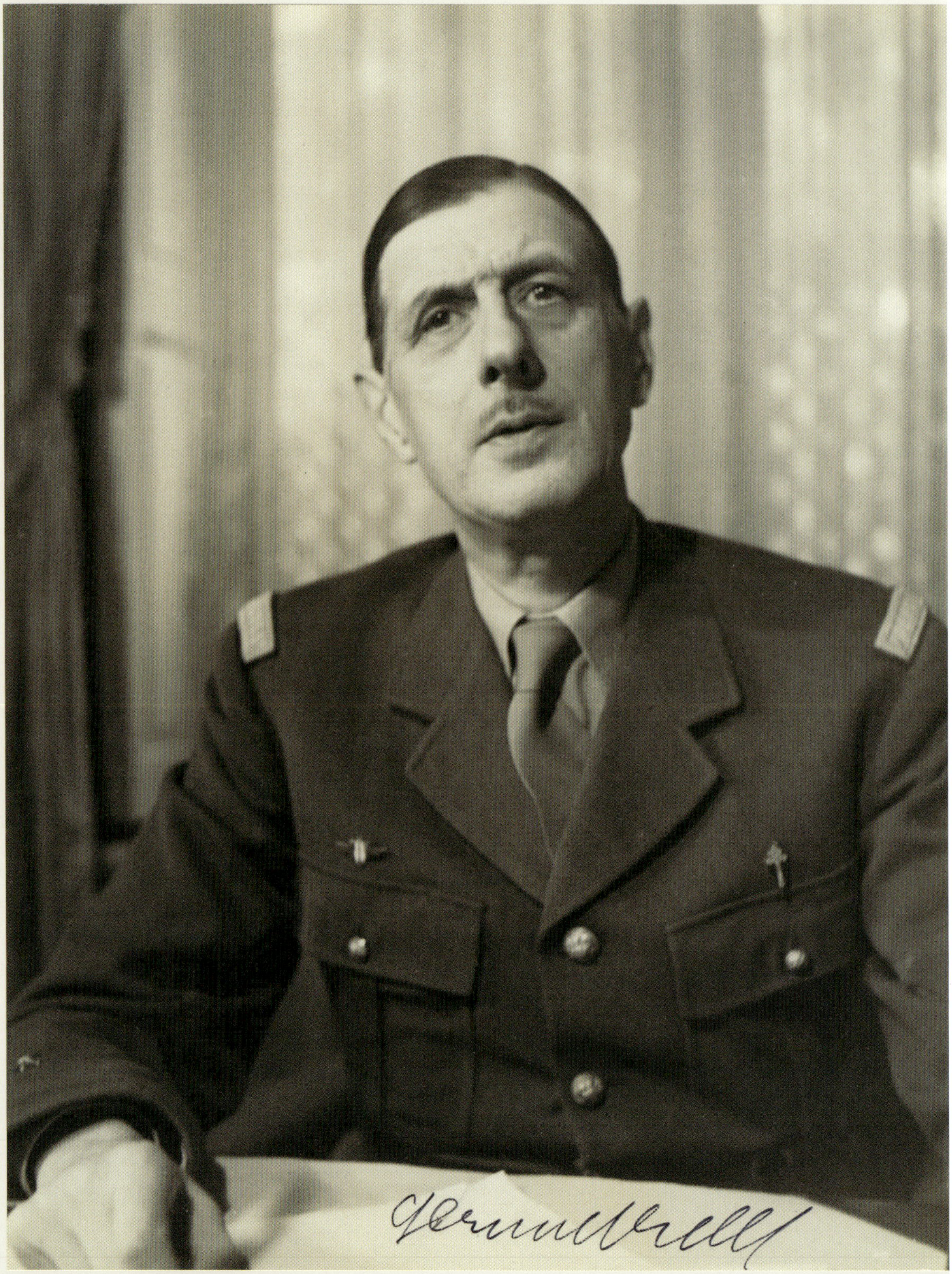

GERMAINE KRULL SPENT THE PHONEY WAR in Monte-Carlo with her friends the Privats. In June 1940 she was in the village of Flayosc, where she heard the call of 18 June. In Cannes she met up with Florent Fels, who urged her to sail to Brazil and from there to join Free France.[1] Visa duly obtained, she boarded the *Capitaine Paul-Lemerle* in Marseille. Sailing on this boat bound for Martinique were André Breton, Claude Lévi-Strauss, Wifredo Lam, Victor Serge (who became her friend, as did Jacques Rémy, as Raymond Assayas was pseudonymously known). Krull still had her Rollei and her Contax. Arriving in Martinique, they spent two weeks in a camp, after which some headed for New York while she and Rémy travelled to Saint-Laurent-du-Maroni. During their five days there she took photos of the area around the prison, doing a kind of report on the former convicts and their living conditions, and writing the text herself. She then moved on to Rio de Janeiro and contacted the French Committee with a view to continuing on to Brazzaville – a concern that fellow exiles in Brazil apparently deemed of lesser importance. She stayed in Rio for a year, was reunited with Jouvet and his band, and took photos that she exhibited and found ways of publishing. The result was another little book, about the old gold-mining town of Ouro Preto.[2] In August 1942 she finally set sail for Cape Town. The photos she left in Rio would eventually be lost.

She made it by train and boat to Brazzaville, where she was posted to Radio-Brazzaville. Its powerful transmitter sent out news reports from Free France, notably towards metropolitan France itself. She was a one-person photography service. 'We had to make people aware of the existence of Free France.'[3] The commander in chief was General Leclerc, 'who had an innate aversion to photographers'. Krull was asked to go out to Gabon, with a van and a driver, and equipped with a 'caisse-popote' ('tucker chest') for eating and sleeping. After Libreville (800 km), she took a flat-bottomed boat to Port-Gentil and photographed, successively, the cutters of okoumé wood, the production of rubber and the gold miners dredging riverbeds with their shovels, the idea always being to 'show the war effort'. She also wrote numerous texts relating to this reportage.[4] These photographs have survived in large numbers because they were widely distributed during and after the war – and generally credited to Krull – by the information department of French Forces in Free French Africa. She put on an exhibition of enlarged photos in Brazzaville, 'both of the virgin forest and of indigenous scenes which I know to be some of the best images I have made'.[5] Two other 'grand tours' of the bush followed, one in Ubangi-Shari, the other in Cameroun, on a rubber plantation.

Krull was now ordered to get to London. She travelled via Marrakech, where she photographed Churchill and de Gaulle. Finally, in early 1944, she was sent to Algiers. She spent a few months there, and had the emotional experience of doing a portrait of de Gaulle, who 'didn't like photographers' either. After that she was present for the 'southern landing' in August 1944 as war correspondent for a weekly paper in Algiers, alongside the American Sixth Army and the French First Army under General de Lattre de Tassigny. Advancing via Naples, Saint-Tropez

1 CEDG, pp. 78ff. The ambassador in Brazil reportedly collected all her books.
2 *Ouro Preto, Uma cidade antiga do Brasil, fotografias de Germaine Krull, prefácios de Raúl Lino e Ribeiro Couto*, Lisbon: Ediçoes Atlântico, Secçao Brasileira do Secretariado da Propaganda Nacional, 1943.
3 CEDG, p. 110.
4 GKN typescripts, Essen, and Institut Charles de Gaulle, Paris. Krull's reportage in Equatorial Africa is analysed by Thomas Schirmböck in 'Germaine Krull in Zentralafrika 1941–1943', *Frauen Kunst Wissenschaft*, H. 14, 1992, pp. 74–82.
5 CEDG, p. 124.

Charles de Gaulle, Algiers, 1943

and the Vercors, she reached Strasbourg in a few months, still working as a photojournalist, and witnessed the Battle of Alsace in late 1944. Finally, in March 1945 she crossed into Germany. The Nazi concentration camp of Vaihingen, near Stuttgart, was being liberated at the time.[6] 'The inmates were almost dying of typhus or hunger. I never thought it was possible to bring humanity so low.'[7]

The Battle of Alsace was chronicled in a little book illustrated by her photos,[8] published by her former lover, Jacques Haumont, whose bad luck with *La Route Paris–Biarritz* and *La Folle d'Itteville* had caused his bankruptcy back in 1931. During the war he had run an underground print operation. Another familiar face in the Alsace-Lorraine Brigade was Colonel Berger, aka André Malraux, with whom she would maintain a long-standing epistolary and sometimes political relationship.

6 Five of her photos were published in 'Au camp de l'épouvante', *Point de vue* no. 6 (27 April 1945), n.p.
7 CEDG, p. 130.
8 Roger Vailland, *La Bataille d'Alsace (novembre-décembre 1944)*, photographs by Germaine Krull, Paris: Jacques Haumont, 1945. See also about Germaine Krull's commitment, Hélène Terré, *Volontaires pour la France*, Paris, ministère de la Guerre, Imprimerie Sapho, 1946.

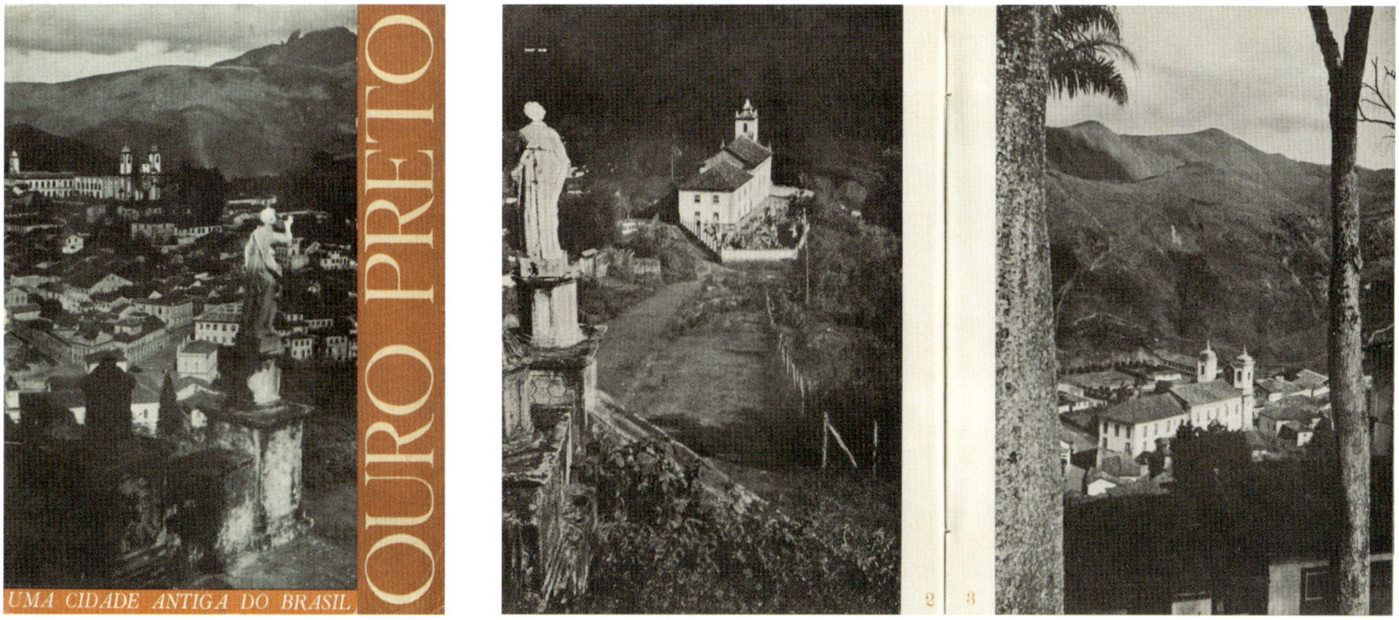

Ouro Preto, Uma Cidade Antiga do Brasil, Lisbon, Ediçoes Atlantico, 1943, cover and pp. 2–3

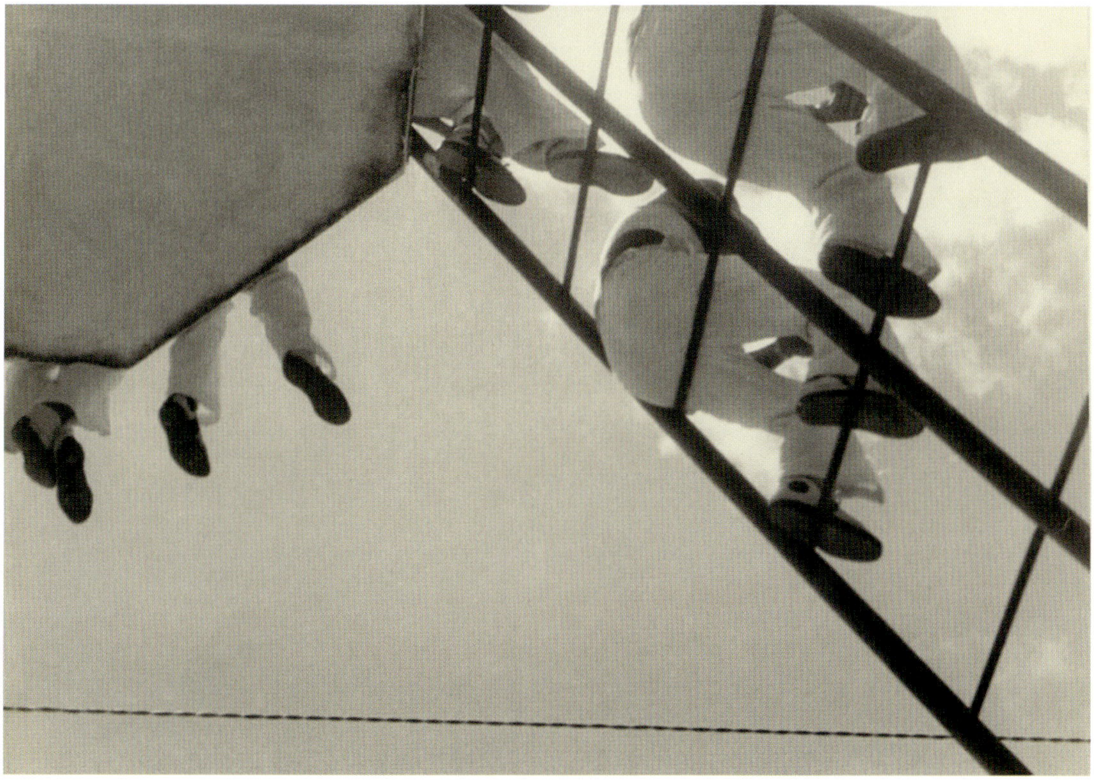

Brazil, 1941–1942

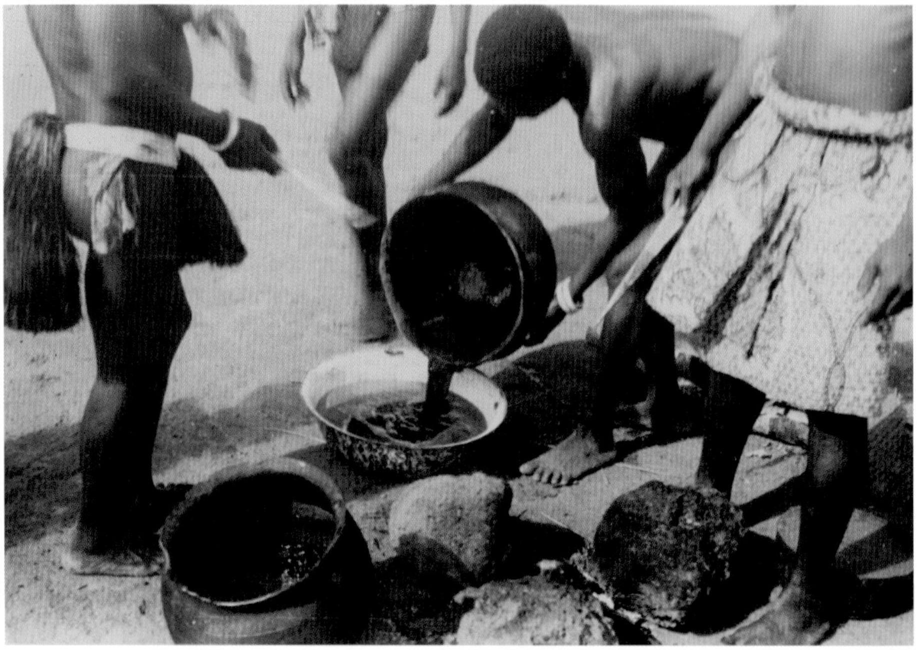

Ubangi-Shari, Bacaia, Making Wax, 1943

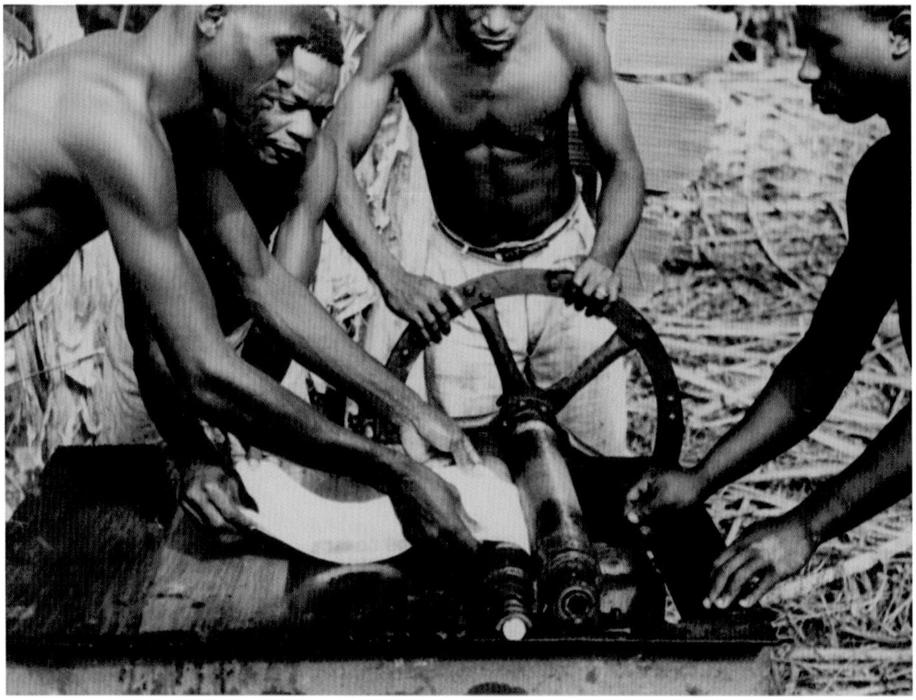

Gabon, Rubber Leaves, after Wringing, 1943

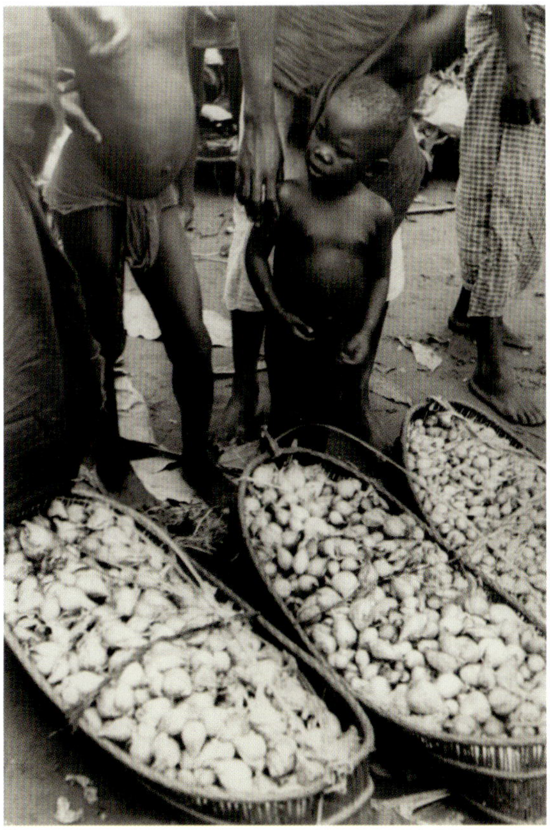

Loukouo, Congo, Market, 1943

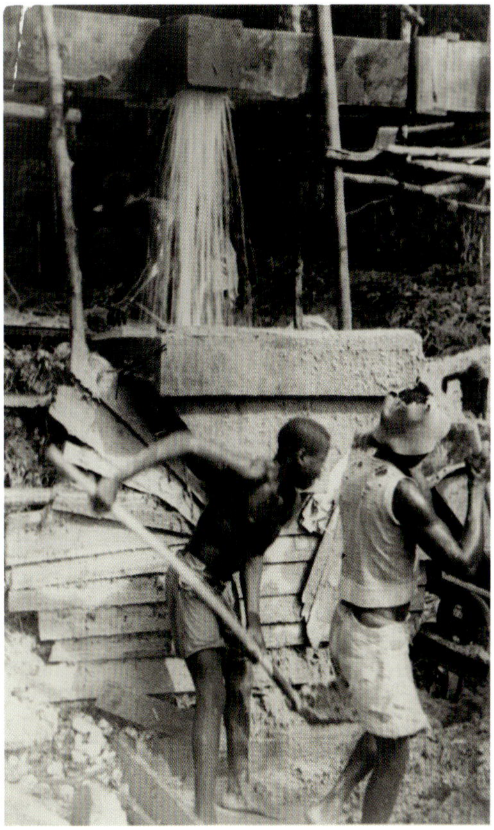

M'Vouti, Congo, Mine of M. Vigoureux, April 1943

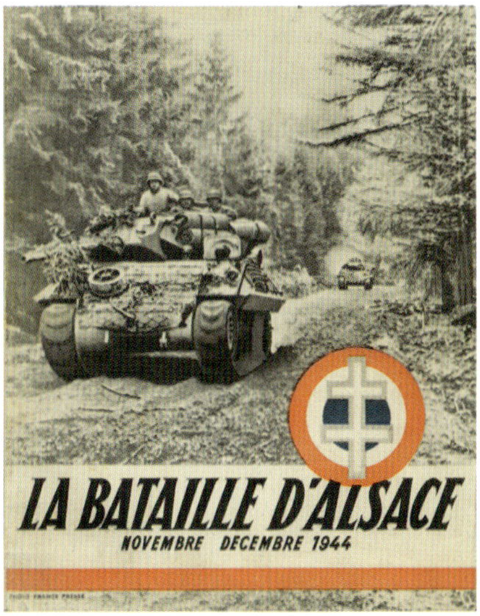

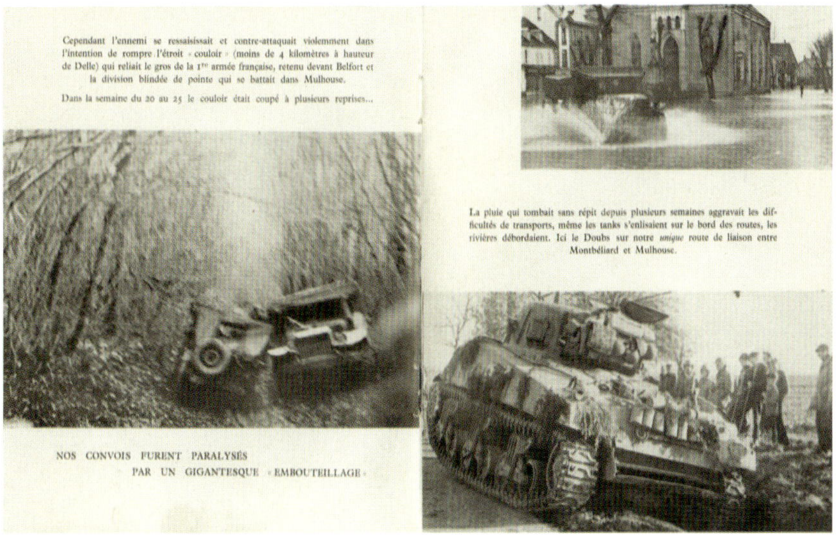

Cependant l'ennemi se ressaisissait et contre-attaquait violemment dans l'intention de rompre l'étroit « couloir » (moins de 4 kilomètres à hauteur de Delle) qui reliait le gros de la 1re armée française, retenu devant Belfort et la division blindée de pointe qui se battait dans Mulhouse.

Dans la semaine du 20 au 25 le couloir était coupé à plusieurs reprises...

NOS CONVOIS FURENT PARALYSÉS PAR UN GIGANTESQUE « EMBOUTEILLAGE »

La pluie qui tombait sans répit depuis plusieurs semaines aggravait les difficultés de transports, même les tanks s'enlisaient sur le bord des routes, les rivières débordaient. Ici le Doubs sur notre *unique* route de liaison entre Montbéliard et Mulhouse.

Roger Vailland, ***The Battle of Alsace (November-December 1944)***, Jacques Haumont, Paris, 1945

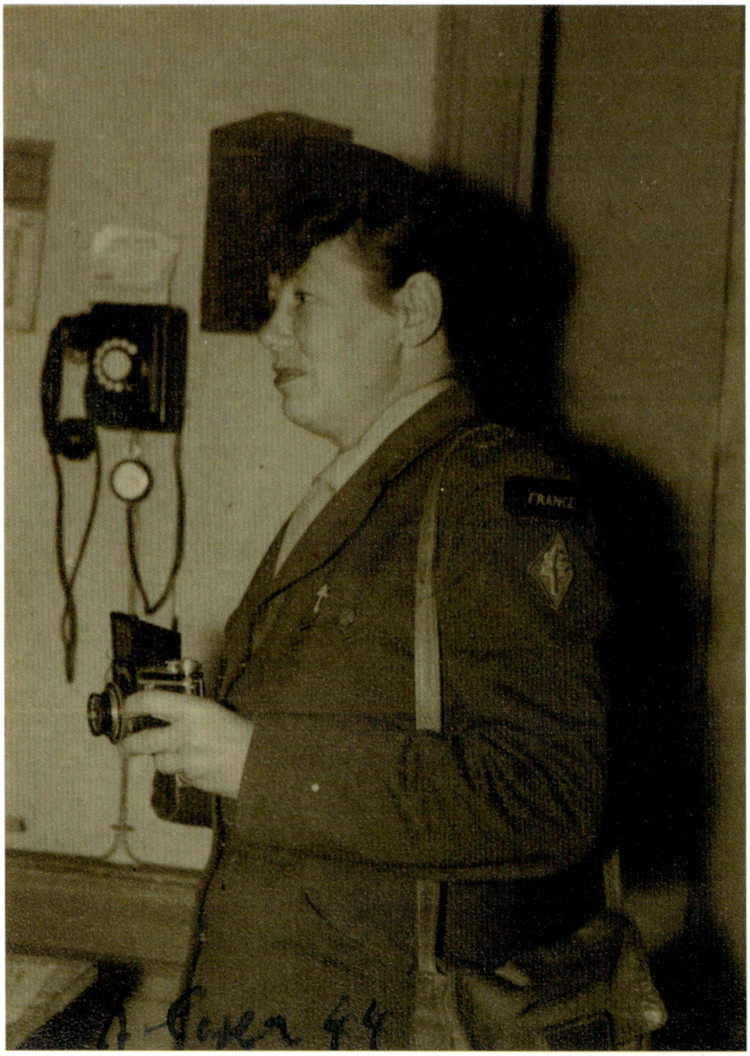

Unidentified photographer, **Portrait of Germaine Krull in the Uniform of the Free French Forces**, Algiers, 1944
'In the Camp of Horror', *Point de vue*, 1st year, no. 6, 27 April 1945, unpaginated (facing page)

AU CAMP DE L'ÉPOUVANTE

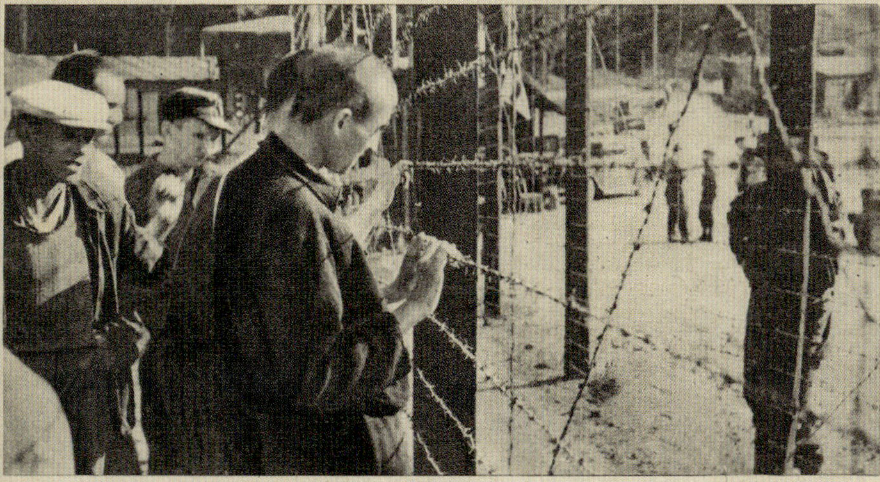

Ces déportés sont maintenant des hommes libres. Mais le typhus rôde, et, par mesure de précaution. ils ne peuvent sortir du camp qu'après la visite médicale.

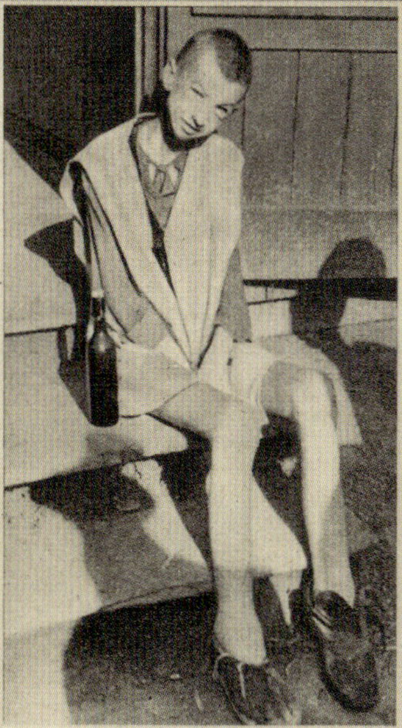

11 ans ! C'est l'âge qu'avait ce jeune déporté quand on l'amena au « Camp de la Mort ». Il ne sait plus sourire. il ne peut plus marcher sans aide.

AUSCHWITZ ! Ravensbrück ! Büchenwald ! Autant de noms qui évoquent les camps, lamentablement célèbres, de prisonniers ou de déportés. D'autres s'inscriront à la suite de l'effroyable liste, au fur et à mesure que les Alliés pénétreront plus avant en Allemagne.

Nous voulons aujourd'hui apporter un nouveau témoignage, irrécusable, des traitements qu'infligeaient les nazis à ceux qu'ils se refusaient à considérer comme des hommes.

Notre reporter nous a rapporté de Vaihingen des photos hallucinantes : toutes méritaient d'être publiées. Mais nous avons dû, faute de place, nous contenter d'en choisir quelques-unes.

Presque sans nourriture, sans soins, sans hygiène, des milliers de déportés de toutes nationalités étaient entassés dans ce « Camp de l'Epouvante », certains — les plus résistants — depuis six ans.

Peu d'entre eux avaient conservé assez de force pour crier leur joie à leurs libérateurs.

Ceux que la maladie a épargnés, aujourd'hui entourés de soins, reviennent lentement à la vie.

Demain, ils seront de retour chez eux. Puisse leur présence rappeler à ceux qui auraient tendance à l'oublier ce « slogan » plus nécessaire que jamais : « N'oubliez pas ! »

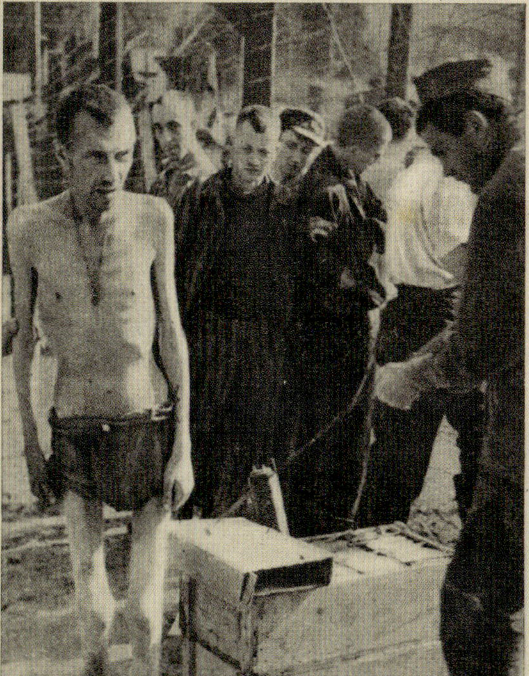

Un Français, ancien légionnaire, passe à la désinfection. Malgré son effroyable maigreur, ses premiers mots furent : « Dites à ma sœur que je tiens encore..., je tiendrai jusqu'au bout. »

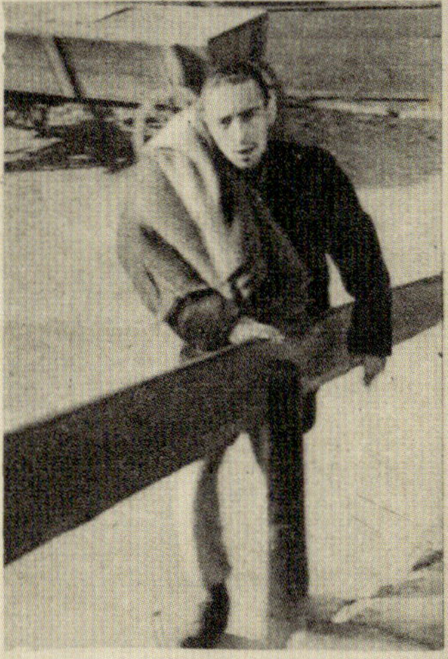

Pour aller au-devant des libérateurs, cet homme est obligé de s'appuyer....

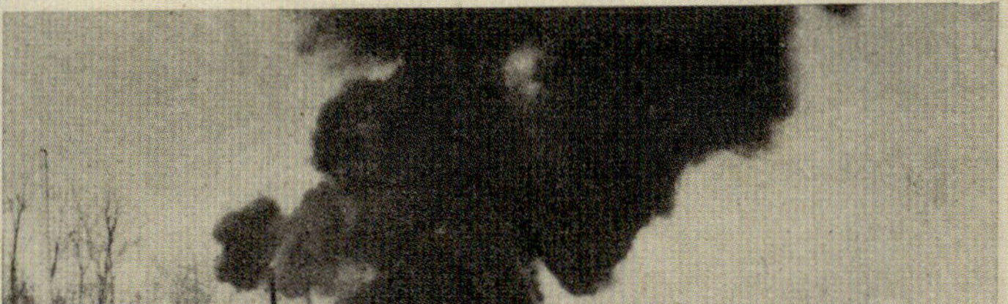

Première réaction... Dès qu'ils ont été libérés, les déportés qui pouvaient se traîner ont mis le feu aux baraquements des nazis. On purifie !

Ph. Germaine KRULL.

IN ASIA

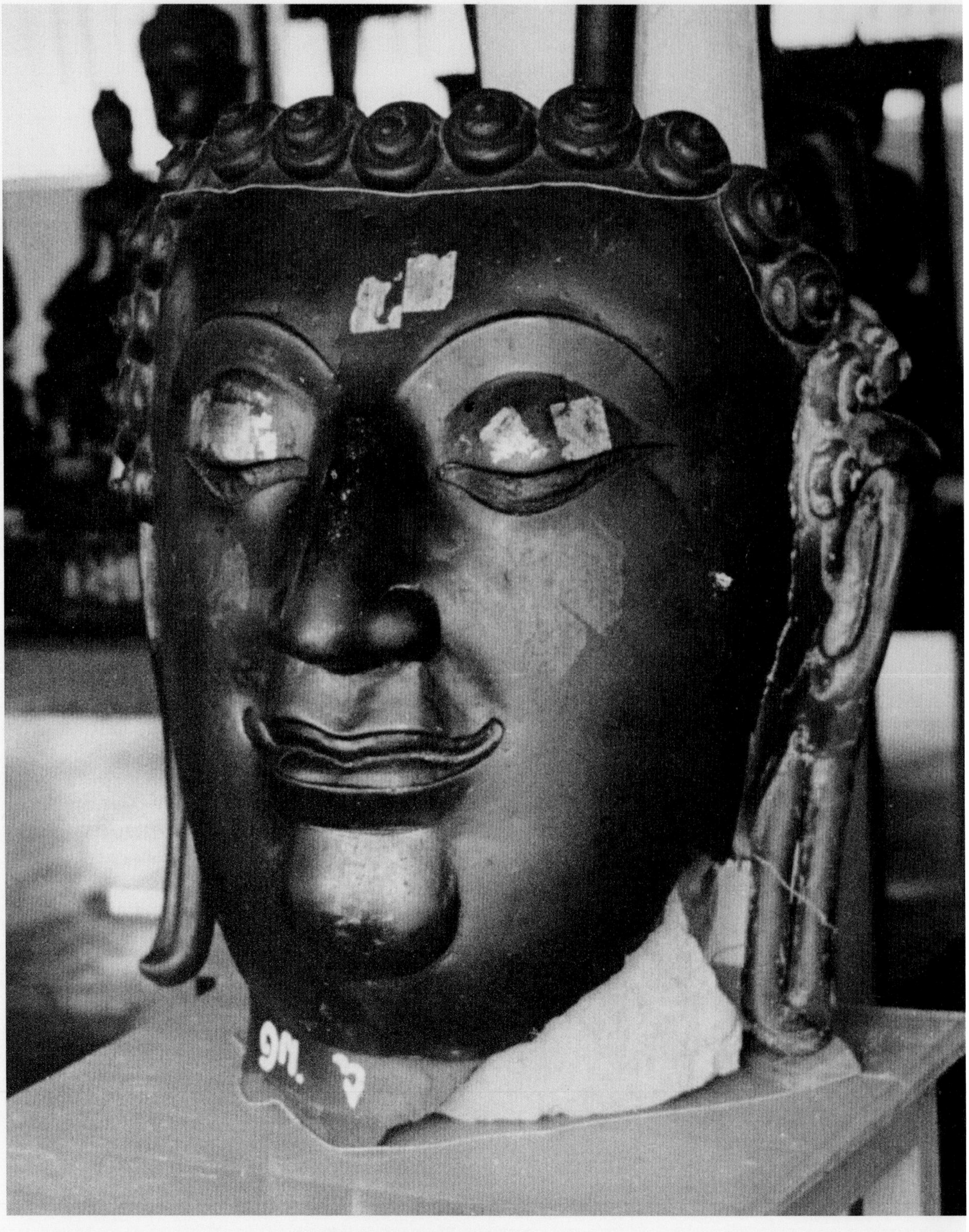

KRULL FELT UNCOMFORTABLE IN EUROPE. No sooner was she back in Germany than she asked to continue her work as a war correspondent in the Far East – Saigon, Jakarta, Burma and Thailand. She went by the name of Krull-Ivens, had Dutch nationality (by her marriage with Joris Ivens) and carried the card of the Agence d'Édition et de Presse. She was in permanent contact with her friend Malraux, who was Minister of Information in the provisional government under de Gaulle. The reports she sent back from Southeast Asia (Indochina) always made clear her own viewpoint on the situation. She was also in contact with Ho Chi Minh, much to the displeasure of Malraux and local French authorities ('Anyway, I was on the side of the Annamites!').[1] Eventually, caught between the two sides, she was forced to make a hasty departure from Saigon. De Gaulle had resigned in January 1946 and Malraux was no longer in the government. She still managed to publish one more article, 'Error in Laos',[2] in which she violently criticised the attitudes of the colonials. In Asia she was confronted with such realities in a way she hadn't been in Africa, but still responded with a certain innocence: 'Were the people sent out to the colonies really the right kind of Frenchmen?'[3] Krull now acted on a 'plan made with some friends' and, in partnership with an American acquaintance, took over the Oriental Hotel, the oldest establishment in Bangkok,[4] and the only one by the river. It had gone into steep decline after serving to billet troops, but the few weeks for which Krull promised to be involved turned into twenty years during which, as director, she added a new modern wing and made it one of the finest hotels in Asia.

Krull came back to Europe in around 1960. She saw her sister Berthe in Germany and met up with Malraux. While managing the hotel, she had started taking more and more photographs for her personal satisfaction. She began to document Buddhist culture, taking thousands of pictures of temples, statues and art objects in Burma and Thailand. There was a project with the famous 'Univers des Formes' series edited by Malraux at Gallimard, a global history of art based on his 'museum without walls' idea. In 1962 Krull signed a contract to provide the photographs for the Indochina volume. Malraux had been Minister of Cultural Affairs since 1959 and was increasingly busy. The guidance he sent was sparing to say the least. She took large numbers of photographs of Pagan, the city of a thousand temples, and in Cambodia, and sent Malraux 1,500 pictures so that he could make a selection. But the project was abandoned. Krull, though, still had plans for a photography book and decided to produce her own little volume on the old city of Chiang Mai, where she had a house.[5] This was self-published using funds accumulated at the Oriental Hotel. Its impeccable layout recalls her books from 1930–1931. In 1964 and 1966, she published two books of text (in English) illustrated by a few photographic plates: *Bangkok: Siam's City of Angels* and *Tales from Siam*.[6] But she continued to dream of the kind of publications she had made in the past. 'I was thinking about the beautiful pictures I could take, the beautiful albums and books I could illustrate, with thousands of temples to choose from, the exotic flowers, and the graceful girls. I had dreamed of putting out beautiful picture books, as I had in Brazil and France before the war.'[7]

1 VMD, p. 192.
2 Germaine Krull-Ivens, 'Error in Laos', *Far Eastern Survey*, XVI, no. 11 (4 June 1947), pp. 121–124.
3 VMD, p. 194.
4 Founded in 1876, now the Mandarin Oriental Hotel.
5 *Chiengmai*, pictures by Germaine Krull, commentary by Lotus, n.d., copyright 'Hôtel Oriental, Bangkok, Siam', fifty-four photographs.
6 Germaine Krull and Dorothea Melchers, *Bangkok: Siam's City of Angels*, London: Hale, 1964; Germaine Krull and Dorothea Melchers, *Tales from Siam*, London: Hale, 1966.
7 *Bangkok*, op. cit., p. 21.

Lamphun museum, Chiengsen head, Thailand, c. 1961

In 1966 she sold her shares in the Hotel Oriental and moved to Poissy, near Paris, for a year. It would seem she was planning to settle in France because she 'put all my things and the collection I had sent over from Bangkok in crates and kept in storage'.[8] She even started looking for a house in Provence.[9] Malraux had promised to help by finding her a position at the 'museum of popular arts', but her Dutch nationality ruled this out. He did, however, facilitate her first ever retrospective, held at the Cinémathèque Française–Musée du Cinéma (Palais de Chaillot), directed by Henri Langlois.[10] This featured enlargements of plates from *Métal* (1928) but not vintage prints, whose time had yet to come – and besides, 'I had never managed to find my prints from before the war.'[11] Krull also exhibited her efforts in colour, the Silpagrammes she developed with support from Kodak.

This sign of recognition was part of a general return to grace by major figures from the interwar years: in 1962 Man Ray's 'photographic oeuvre' had been shown at the Bibliothèque Nationale, which hosted a Brassaï retrospective in 1963. And that year also saw a slightly impromptu Kertész show in a foretaste of his MoMA retrospective in New York in 1964.

Feeling she was getting the cold shoulder from Malraux, Krull left Europe and settled near Dehradun (then Uttar Pradesh) in northern India, in 1968. She adopted the Buddhist way of life and frequented the many Tibetan exiles in the region. She met the Dalai Lama and joined Sakya Trizin's community, which became her 'family', and played an active role in running the school. Now at last she was able to publish another book of photographs (fifty-eight pages), *Tibetans in India*,[12] a 'homage to the wisdom of Tibet' that would, she hoped, help preserve 'the timeless spirituality of mankind'. She photographed Tibetan monastic structures in India, educational centres for refugees, manifestations of Tibetan culture and prominent figures such as the Dalai Lama and Sakya Trizin. Printed in India, the book lacked the quality of what was being done in Europe at a time when photography books were very much in vogue. Krull was deeply committed to her Buddhist community, but does not seem to have received much in exchange. She travelled frequently in the 1970s, notably to Paris, where she had prints made from her negatives.[13]

Krull dictated her memoir about her Parisian period, *Click entre deux guerres*, when staying in Zürich in 1976. A few years later she wrote *La Vie mène la danse*, which she completed in India in 1981. She fell ill in 1983 and managed to obtain assistance from the Ministry of Culture to return to Germany and be with her sister Berthe. She died there in Wetzlar on 30 July 1985. In 1995 her archives (Nachlass Germaine Krull) entered the Folkwang Museum, Essen, which now holds the rights. She left many unpublished writings, and a great number of photographs from her Asian period.

8 VMD, p. 244.
9 VMD, p. 242.
10 *Germaine Krull 1927–1967* (Paris, Cinémathèque Française–Musée du Cinéma, 1967), Paris: Cinémathèque Française, 1967.
11 VMD, p. 243. She had entrusted her negatives and prints to Lotar before the war. Krull and Lotar were still in contact and on good terms in the 1960s, but he did not know what had happened to them.
12 Germaine Krull, *Tibetans in India*, New Delhi: Allied Publishers Private Ltd., 1968. Fifty-eight photos, eight in colour. In the jacket text, Krull mentions that she was one of only two women war correspondents in Europe 'in 1946', and gives the list of her books from *Métal* onwards, but most of the dates are erroneous.
13 Responding to the general rediscovery of antique and modern photography, Ann and Jürgen Wilde in Cologne produced a facsimile edition of *Métal* in 2002.

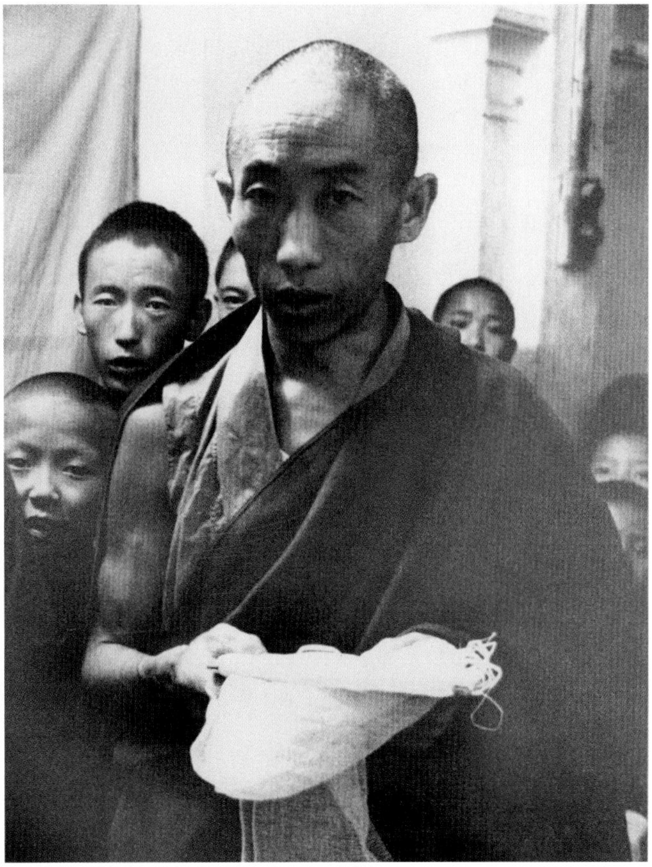

'Tibetan Religious Ceremony, Offering of the White Scarf', c. 1967

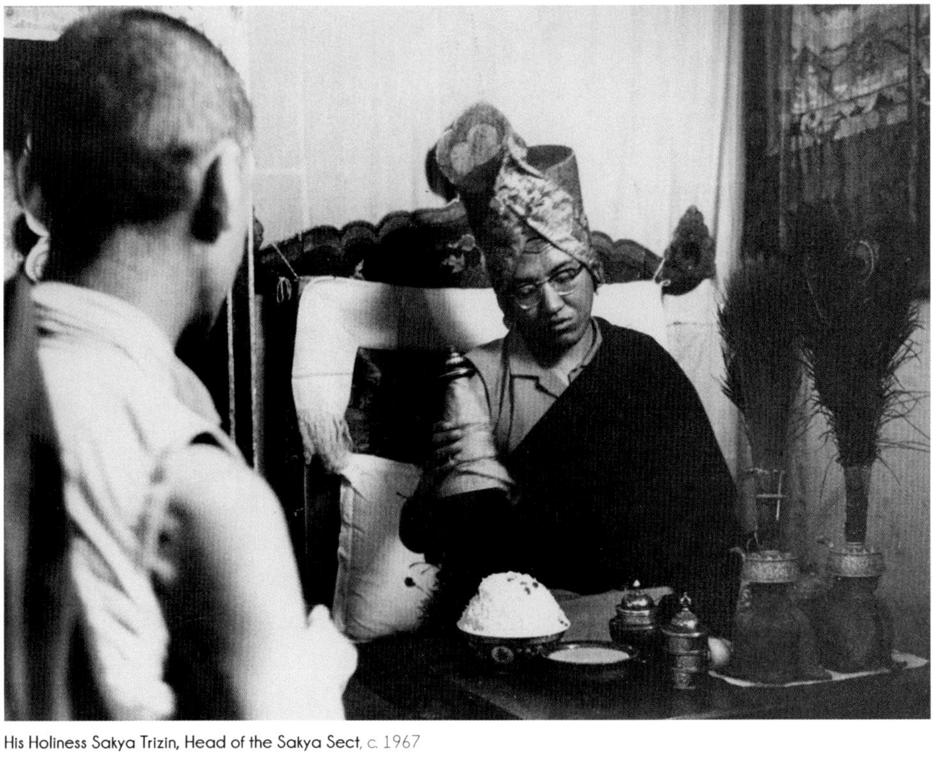

His Holiness Sakya Trizin, Head of the Sakya Sect, c. 1967

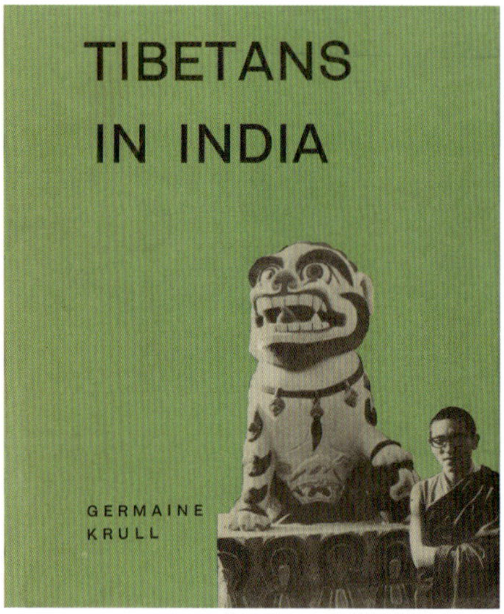

Germaine Krull, ***Tibetans in India***, New Delhi, Allied Publishers Private Ltd, 1968

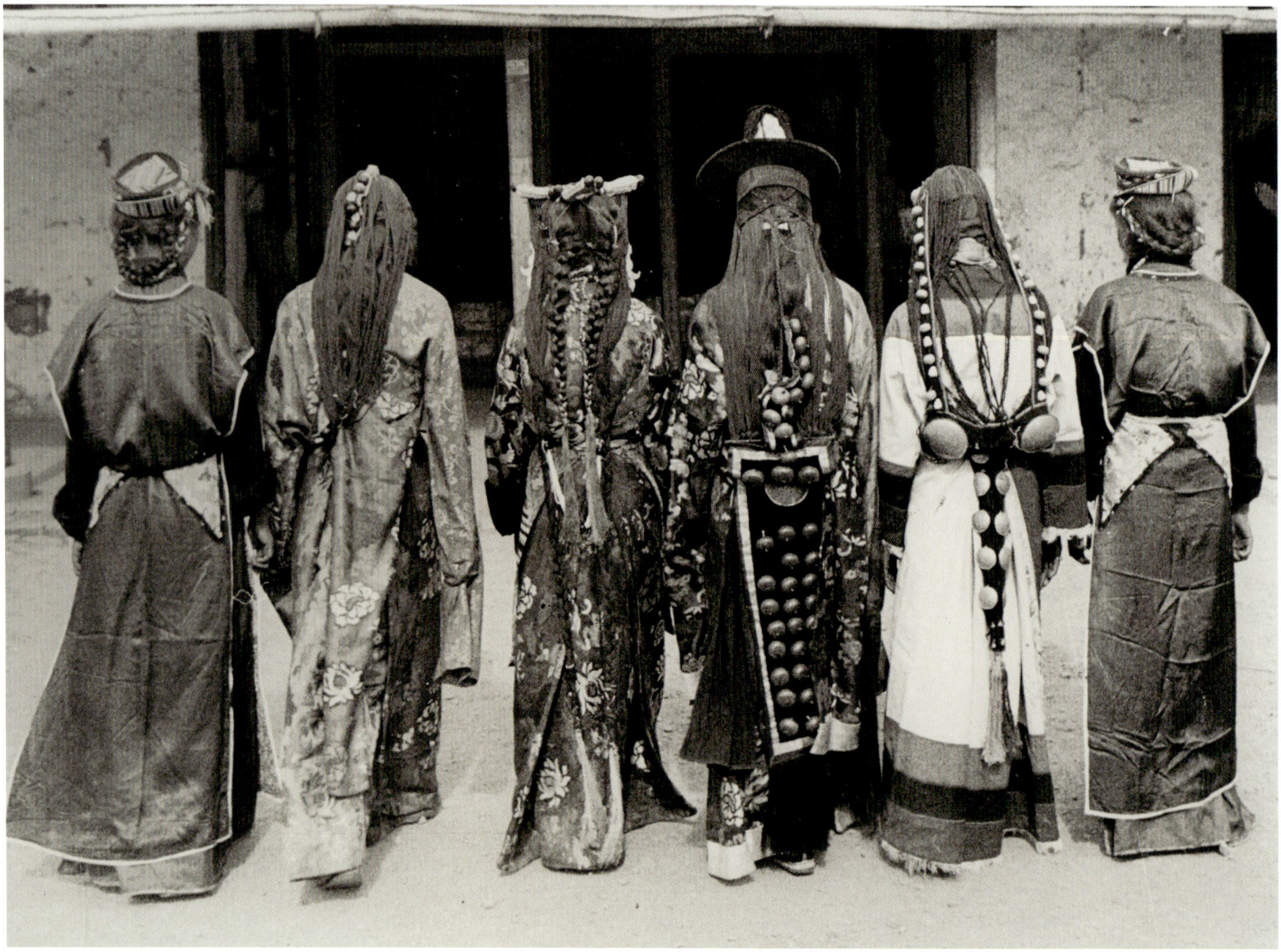

'Group of Tibetan Dancers', c. 1967

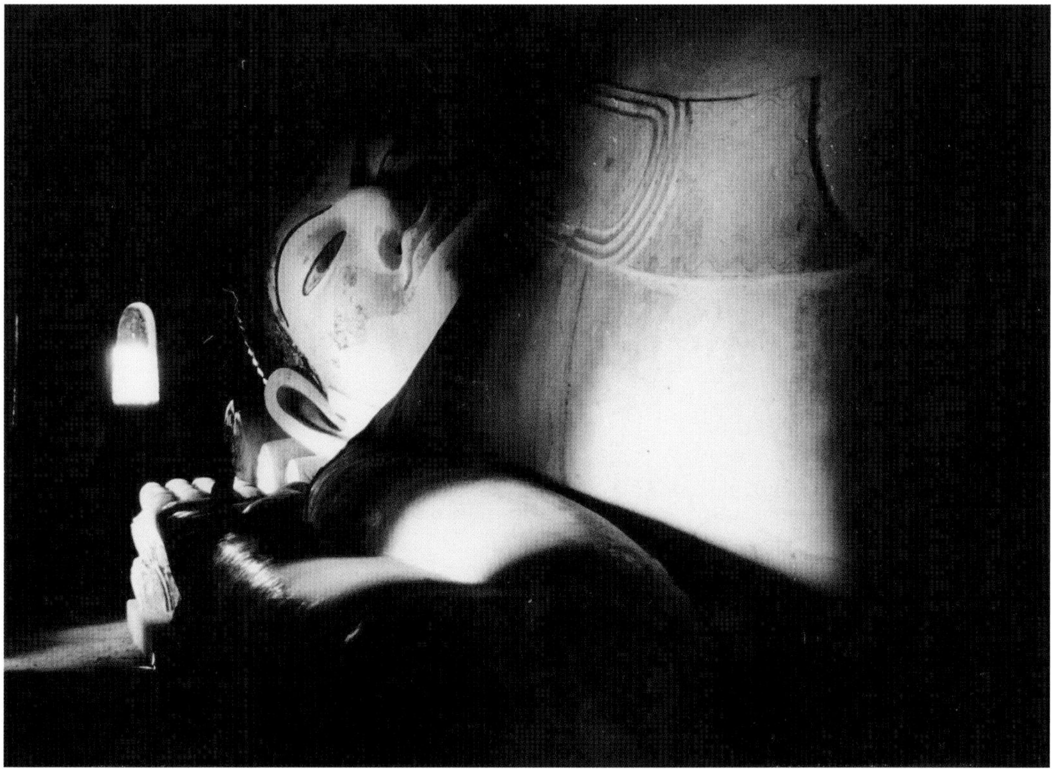

Pagan, Burma, Chinbinthalyang Temple, Reclining Buddha, c. 1961

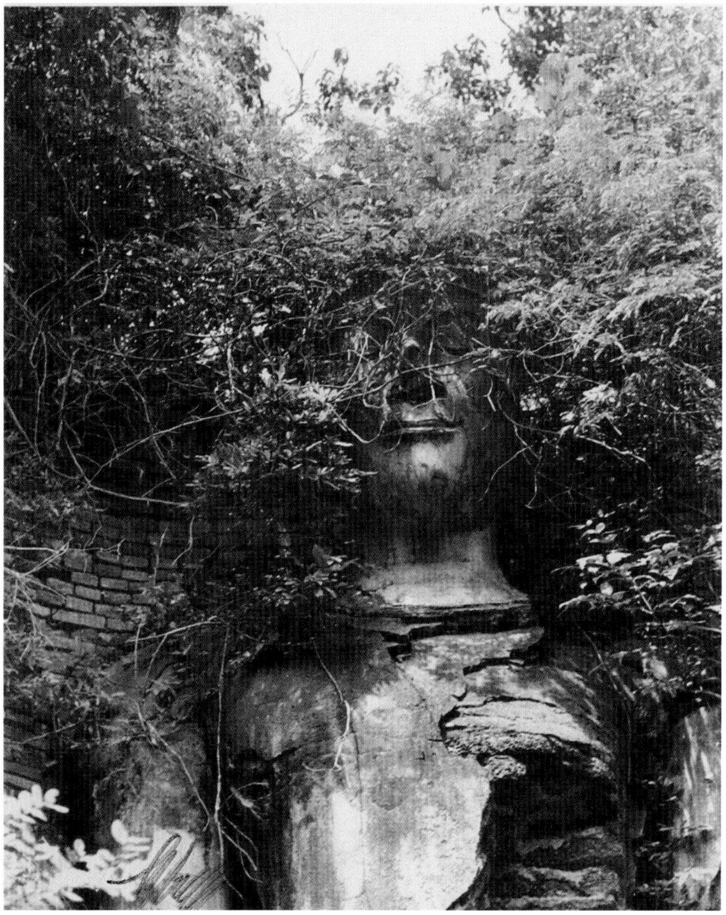

Wat Phra Lai, Chiang Mai, Thailand, 1961

GERMAINE KRULL, preface to *Études de nu*, Paris: Librairie des Arts Décoratifs, A. Calavas, 1930

"Re-forming Mirror"
Jean Cocteau

Taking photographs is a trade. / An artisan's trade. / A trade you learn, that you do well or less well, like any other trade.

Art exists in any craft that is done well. Because art is a choice.

The first science of the photographer is to know how to look. / One looks with one's eyes. The same world, seen through different eyes, is not exactly the same. / It is the world seen through a personality. / With one snap of the shutter, the lens registers the world from the outside, and the photographer from the inside.

The lens is an eye that is better made than the eye. / It deserves to see the world made better than the world, or made differently, which would already be a very good thing. / Each new angle itself multiplies the world.

The camera has no need to invent, to combine, to deceive. / It is not painting, or the imagination. /The photographer is a witness. / The witness of her era. / The true photographer is the witness of each day's events, a reporter. / It is natural that she does not always keep her eye at one-and-a-half metres off the ground. / But she must always think of the ground, of the grounding of today, of this morning, of this Thursday morning, of this day so beautiful we forget to enquire the name that it bears by chance. / The world. / The world of today.

And man who is merely one more moving object in the world, and in the times. And man, morally identical through time.

So why do nudes? / Because they have always been beautiful, and because one summer morning they just appealed to me.

Germaine Krull

LETTER FROM JEAN COCTEAU TO GERMAINE KRULL in *Le Courrier littéraire*, April-May-June 1930, pp. 66–81

My Dear Germaine,

At the hotel I found your prints of Bovy and of me and I am hastening to thank you. 'First the hands', as Heurtebise says. I must confess that I did not recognise these hands (my hands). I reacted in the opposite way to my friend's Pekinese. The Pekinese loves my friend's hands – the left hand especially – and hates her face, her legs, etc. When she puts her left hand up to her face, it imagines that her face is approaching the hand to bite it, and it barks. I found it hard to identify these long, nervous things. Then I saw that these beasts, these dead plants, were emerging from a sleeve, from one of my suits, and I understood that they looked more like me than a face.
Berthe Bovy.

R. de Saint-Jean wrote to me: 'Do you have Krull's prints? The shadow of Bovy on the telephone? It is like a suffering machine.'

You know that where machines are concerned I am no idolater and that slavery, even mechanical, repels me. What touches me is collaboration with machines. It imposes itself. At Columbia I refuse to let them take prints of my voice; in collaboration with the gramophone I create an unknown, new voice that is mordant as if issuing from a Greek mask.

Is that not your method? You are a re-forming mirror. You and the dark room obtain a new world, a world that has passed through mechanisms and a soul.

This individualism of the camera presents a danger. That is certain. Already, in 1912, I saw the little Japanese merchant Takaïra taking Kodaks of Versailles. He brought back twelve Japanese photographs of the park at Versailles.

This phenomenon is flooding us with photographs. Incapable of expressing themselves with the brush or pen, a host of aesthetes express themselves through the intermediary of the camera.

Few artists were born under the sign of the camera, under the rainbow of the object glass, under the star of the lens. You belong to that little troupe that Man Ray once set in train and whose effort is summed up in Charles Peignot's book.

Your prints of Bovy in *La Voix humaine* are masterpieces. The actress is ageless. She has that age of silence, moonlight, Decembers, car crashes that, a second after they occurred, acquire the grandeur of an Egyptian ruin. These tears, these locks of hair, this mouth/wound, bring back a memory from 1927. They were demolishing the Arts Décoratifs. It was summer. At midday, alone in the world, I was walking beside the fencing along the Quai des Invalides. Suddenly I heard a loudspeaker that had remained intact on the pediment of a kind of crumbling temple, a terrible voice, an Oedipal voice (invisible because blind) declaiming stock exchange prices. The effect was poignant, theatrical, utterly new.

Do not believe that I am turning away from your work here. I am turning to see it. I am trying to communicate to you what I feel when faced with these documentaries about a ravaged woman, a statue undergoing torture.

And since I am chatting, and proceeding by anecdotes, let me report a dialogue between Max Jacob and the son of his concierge in Rue Gabrielle.
Max. – Do you like cinema?
The concierge's son (7 years old). – No.
Max. – Why not?
The concierge's son. – Because the actors are dead people.
Max. – Dead people?
The concierge's son. – Yes, dead people. At night time they go into the cemeteries with a pistol and they force them to act in films.

This young man was waiting for talking films, which, as it happens, further justify his fears, as a magnificent source of superhuman spectres that the Pathé cockerel does not send running. The youth of 1930 is void, above all, of exactitude and ghosts. The inexactitudes of Camille Mauclair do not make us angry, they astonish us. How, my dear Germaine, could I not delight in your art which makes truth false, I who should put the words I am a lie who always tells the truth as the epigraph to all my books; I, whose deep method is truer than the true.

Warmest regards,

Jean Cocteau

P.S. – You must have heard from Eisenstein that I was luckily able to save him. And so he got his questioning in the end. B.'s last letter is decisive. I couldn't talk about it last night, in such hurried circumstances at 'The General Line'. I was too emotional.

PIERRE MAC ORLAN, preface to *Germaine Krull* by Pierre Mac Orlan, 'Photographes nouveaux' series, Paris: NRF Gallimard, 1931, pp. 3–8

Germaine Krull. The Feelings of the Street and the Accessories of the Street.
The photography that influenced at least a part of the German Expressionist movement seems to want to get involved with the lyrical inspiration of writers who sadly are still an enigma to the general public.

The mystery of things naturally resists human intelligence. It may sometimes be in cahoots with man's instincts, but he is defenceless before the mystery of the view camera. Photographic art is the great expressionist art of our day. At the same time, it is a good profession full of wiles and winsome naivety. This double personality is not without charm.

Meditation, even spontaneous, in front of certain photographic prints allows us to create other images – 'cerebral' images, as the little pimps in Rue de Lappe now say. These illustrations are the ones suited to the contemporary fantastic, which is a social fantastic that is at once barbaric and subtle.

Blood, which is perhaps the most terrifying element in this great age of enslavement to ill-known electricity, is a photographic detail. Most of the famous photos of our day can make us anticipate its appearance, without a need to take succour from the poetic texts that make our memory look like a provincial museum where the conservator is still a pink and chubby child.

A mixture of hereditary candour and vileness patiently acquired from the frequentation of men gives this awkward witness that is the photographic lens such a choice of experiences and conclusions that a family photograph album becomes something more moving than nature itself, for it becomes man's ally.

The enthusiasm for photographic expressionist art is not as recent as one could believe. In 1894 it was already being involved in combinations that may have been more plastic than poetic, but were clearly poetic. This was the age of Atget. He was no innocent, but a man who loved and was proficient at his craft. Around Georges Besson and Francis Jourdain there was wonder at the psychological mystery revealed by the silver bromide gelatine plate with the insouciance and perfidy of a magic mirror. Enthusiasm for this young art already wrinkled by experience did not reach beyond the dimensions of small journals.

The period was hardly going to associate with the scandalous cruelty of photography. That had to wait. The promises of a disquiet that began to spread in around 1910 were almost perfectly realised. The mechanical image showed men their true face, and if they were not all satisfied by it, inside, they were dazzled.

Among the works of all those who have been the lyrical and meticulous witnesses of the social picturesque since 1918, I particularly like those of Mme Germaine Krull, no doubt because we all have more or less the same reactions to certain visions which are plastic only by necessity.

Germaine Krull is Dutch. She is a Northern European and very much a Northern European, that is to say, an artist perfectly born to understand the effects of photography, whose complications can reach the furthest limits of the imagination.

This adroit and self-confident artist, who is a great reporter and a poet of everyday life, closely associates her personality with all the elements of steel and flesh that form and later serve to formulate the picturesque and the social fantastic of the contemporary period.

To the melancholy poetry that great journalists like Béraud, Dorgelès, Londres, Morand, Condroyer, G. Manue, Helsey and others impart to the world and its accelerating rhythm, photography – Krull's, for example – can adapt like a detail, a deep, ultimate song, a colour, words, a cry, whose resonance is almost unlimited. Her art strikes the intelligence. It is a loud shock, and all kinds of unacknowledged thoughts, even the most intimate ones, arise at the sly call of the secret elements on the plate.

Whether Krull transposes a machinescape into a kind of stunning symphony, or makes literary play with the lights of Paris between Place Pigalle and Place de la Bastille, she does not create easy anecdotes, but she makes visible the secret details that people do not always see, but that the light of her lens flushes out from their hiding place.

The Krull Paris is sometimes Carco's Paris, because on occasion it expands into the tenderness of regrets, but also the Paris of ghosts, of crimes and other events, and of the androids of prostitution.

It is a powerful and truly tragic commentary, for it contains an element of irresponsibility. This element intervenes only in the photographic sensations.

Germaine Krull is lettered. She too can 'throw a fresh rose' into a hall where giant milling machines are making engine blocks, but she can also adorn with a shiny turbine or a steamer funnel the sky of Paul and Virginie.

I like to imagine Krull in her studio, a cigarette between her lips, with a bit of smoke in her eyes. She knows that the street, which is the most securely closed domain of human thought, will reveal to her the shadow of its carriage entrances. Behind Krull and her lens, round like an octopus eye, the children of misfortune press around, jostle, moan, bicker and barge for position in front of the lens. Hold it!

This world grows calm and enters the silent accordion. Later, when the image appears on paper a known name will be given to these naked, aggressive objects.

PIERRE MAC ORLAN

TIMELINE

1897 On 29 November, birth of Germaine Krull in Wilda-Poznań in what is then Germany. The town is ceded to Poland in 1919.

1903–1912 The family travels a great deal, following the work of Germaine's father, an unstable and impecunious engineer: Bosnia, Paris (1906, the birthplace of Berthe, Germaine's younger sister), Slovenia, rural Bavaria and finally Munich, where her mother runs a boarding house.

1912–1915 Germaine lives a very free life at the boarding house. She has a first abortion. Her parents divorce.

1915–1917 She studies photography at the Lehr- und Versuchsanstalt für Photographie, Chemigraphie, Lichtdruck und Gravüre in Munich.

1917 Death of Germaine's father.

1917–1919 Germaine moves to Schwabing (Munich), where she mixes with artists, writers and the political thinker Kurt Eisner, who in November 1918 becomes the Prime Minister of the Free State of Bavaria. She befriends Max Horkheimer and Fritz Pollock.

1918 Her work features in a volume of female nudes (photogravures), *Der Akt*, published by Einhorn-Verlag.

1919 Kurt Eisner is assassinated on 21 February. Germaine is involved in the Bavarian Soviet Republic, playing a very active role alongside Moscow's envoy, Tobias Axelrod, and Kurt Adler (Samuel Levit). Travels to Budapest to seek support from Béla Kun's Hungarian Soviet Republic.

1920 Banned from Munich, Germaine and Kurt Adler arrive in Berlin in March.

1921–1922 She travels to Saint Petersburg and Moscow with Adler to attend the Congress of the Third International, where she hears Lenin's speech. The following day she is arrested and imprisoned in the Lubyanka, where she undergoes a fake execution. Betrayed by Adler but finally set free, she returns to Berlin in early 1922, suffering from typhus.

1922 Through Hans Basler, an acquaintance from Moscow, she is able to go into partnership with Gretel and Kurt Hübschmann, for whom she manages a photography studio in Berlin.

1923 In Berlin she meets Joris Ivens, the son of a Dutch supplier of cameras and photographic supplies.

1923–1924 Makes numerous studies of female nudes, including one of her sister Berthe (*Spuk* portfolio), a series with lesbian overtones (Siegert collection) and a more candidly erotic series, *Friends* (Ehrens collection).

1924 Stays with the parents of Joris Ivens.

1925 Liquidates the studio in Berlin and moves in with Ivens in Amsterdam. This is probably when she starts photographing port facilities, cranes and silos. Short sojourn in Paris with her friend Elsa.

1926 Travels to Paris. Charmed by the city where she lived as a child two decades earlier, Germaine Krull decides to live there. She opens a fashion photography studio backed by the Ivens family in association with Luigi Diaz. Works for Sonia Delaunay. The painter Robert Delaunay takes an interest in her photographs of iron structures, the *fers*.

1927 Meets Eli Lotar. They live together for two years. Lotar himself becomes a photographer and is attracted to cinema. In order to acquire Dutch nationality, Germaine Krull enters a marriage of convenience with Joris Ivens who, now a cineaste, is about to make the avant-garde film *The Bridge* (Rotterdam).

1928 On 28 March, a new photographic news magazine, *VU*, is launched by Lucien Vogel, who is familiar with the *fers*. He commissions her for modernist reportage, as he does Lotar and André Kertész. In May, Krull takes part in the Premier Salon Indépendant de la Photographie, the 'Salon de l'Escalier', alongside Man Ray, Kertész and Paul Outerbridge. This is the first French exhibition of modern photography. The publication of *Métal*, a portfolio of her views of metal structures, including the Eiffel Tower, makes her the most prominent avant-garde photographer in Paris. She also contributes to Mario von Bucovich's book *Paris*, published in Berlin.

1928–1931 Years of intense activity producing 'modern' reportage of the kind advocated by *VU* (tramps, October 1928), or more freely for the Surrealist-influenced Belgian periodical *Variétés*. Publishes in Carlo Rim's *Jazz*, and *L'Art vivant* edited by Florent Fels, one of her strongest supporters. Krull specialises in the Paris of working people, fairs, markets, bistros, balls, show business, the 'zone' and Paris by night. She frequents artists and writers, including Colette, Cocteau and Malraux. Travels to Brittany, Lorraine and the South of France.

1929 Takes part in Film und Foto (FiFo), the big international exhibition of the New Vision in Stuttgart. Publishes *100 × Paris* with Verlag der Reihe in Berlin. Advertisement for the Peugeot 201. She takes a growing interest in cars and develops a passion for 'the road'.

1930 Living with Philippe Lamour, publisher of *Grand'Route*. Publication of *Le Valois, illustrations de Germaine Krull, Comfort* and *Études de nu* portfolio. Contributes to *Visages de Paris* by André Warnod.

1931 With Jacques Haumont, her lover, she publishes *La Route Paris-Biarritz* and *La Folle d'Itteville* illustrating a Simenon novel. Gallimard publish *Germaine Krull par Pierre Mac Orlan*. Contribution to *La Route de Paris à la Méditerranée*.

1932 Illustrations to *La Chatte* by Colette for the weekly *Marianne*. Publication in *VU* of her photographs of the 'Women Workers of Paris' with texts by Emmanuel Berl.

1934 Writes memoirs of her turbulent youth, *Chien fou*, but fails to find a publisher.

1935 After almost two years without work, Germaine Krull moves to the Côte d'Azur. Is employed by the casino in Monte-Carlo. Publication of her book *Marseille*.

1937 Book: *Les Ballets de Monte-Carlo*. Mural photomontages at the Exposition Universelle in Paris.

1940 Takes the boat for Rio de Janeiro in Marseille, planning to serve Free France.

1942–1943 Directs the Free French photography service in Brazzaville. Propaganda reportage on production in French Equatorial Africa.

1943 Publication of her book *Ouro Preto*.

1944 Krull travels to Algiers and photographs De Gaulle. She is assigned as a reporter to the 'Southern Landing', via Italy and the Côte d'Azur, with the troops of De Lattre. Witnesses the Battle of Alsace.

1945 March: photographs the liberation of the Vaihingen camp. Publishes *La Bataille d'Alsace* with Jacques Haumont.

1946 Still as a reporter, she travels to Southeast Asia. There she becomes co-manager of the Oriental Hotel in Bangkok, which she turns into a major international hotel.

1960–1966 Travels, notably to France. Back in touch with the Malraux family and other old contacts. In the 1960s, Krull photographs thousands of monuments and statues in Thailand and Burma.

1962 Contract to do the photographs for the Southeast Asia volume in Malraux's sur 'L'Univers des Formes' series. This is never published.

1964 Publishes *Bangkok, Siam's City of Angels* with Dorothea Melchers.

1966 Sells her share in the Oriental Hotel, then returns briefly to Paris. Publication of *Tales from Siam* with Dorothea Melchers.

1967 Exhibition at the Cinémathèque Française–Musée du Cinéma in Paris, organised by Henri Langlois.

1968 Germaine Krull settles near Dehradun, in India, and works for the exiled Tibetans in Sakya Trizin's community. Publishes *Tibetans in India*.

1976 Dictates her memoirs, *Click entre deux guerres*.

1977 Exhibition at the Rheinisches Landesmuseum in Bonn.

1981 Finishes her autobiography, *La Vie mène la danse*.

1983 Returns to Germany and her sister Berthe.

1985 Dies in Wetzlar on 30 July.

BIBLIOGRAPHY

X ph. indicates the number of photographs by Germaine Krull.

PORTFOLIOS AND ALBUMS BY GERMAINE KRULL

Der Akt, Zwanzig photographische Aufnahmen weiblicher Körper nach der Natur, 1918, Erschienen im Einhorn-Verlag in Dachau bei München im fünften Kriegsjahre, 'Prof. J[osef]. Pesci, Bild 1, 3, 10, 14. W[anda]. v. Debschitz-Kunowski, Bild 2, 5, 6, 7, 8, 12, 17, 18, 20. L[ouisa]. G[ermaine]. Krull, Bild 4, 9, 11, 13, 15, 16, 19. Wiedergabe in Kupfer-Handpressendruck. Von Dieser Ausgabe wurden 50 exemplare auf echtem Japan in Halbleber gebunden'. Tipped-in heliogravures, a heliogravure mounted on the front cover.

Der Akt. Naturaufnahmen, Munich, Einhorn-Verlag in München, n.d. [c. 1918]. Tipped-in heliogravures, cover with flaps and title and mounted heliogravure (Fotomuseum München).

G. Krull, *Dämmerstunden. 6 Aufnahmen weiblicher Akte*, n.p., n.d. [c. 1923]. Original silver prints, label with printed title on the front cover.

Spuk, 8 Aufnahmen weiblicher Akte, Berlin, 1923. Original silver prints, cover with pink and black foliage, title on label, courtesy Johannes Faber Gallery, Vienna (same presentation as *Dämmerstunden*).

Akte, 12 silver prints, Dietmar Siegert collection, c. 1924.

Les amies, 11 silver prints, Susan Ehrens collection, c. 1924.

Kara-Mappe, Germaine Krull, Körperbildungsgruppen Adolf Koch, Aktkunstmappe 1, Burschen und Mädels, 6 Photo-Handabzüge, preface by Max Hodann, Leipzig, Ernst Oldenburg-Verlag, n.d. [1925]; *Aktkunstmappe II, Jungens*, 6 Photo-Handabzüge?, Leipzig, Ernst Oldenburg-Verlag, n.d. [1925].

Métal, preface by Florent Fels, Paris, Librairie des Arts Décoratifs, A. Calavas, 1928. Portfolio of 64 plates.

Études de nu by Germaine Krull, Paris, Librairie des Arts Décoratifs, A. Calavas, 1930. Portfolio of 24 plates.

BOOKS BY GERMAINE KRULL

Germaine Krull, *100 × Paris*, preface by Florent Fels, Berlin-Westend, Verlag der Reihe, 1929.

Le Valois by Gérard de Nerval, illustrated by Germaine Krull, Paris, Firmin-Didot et Cie, 1930. 48 ph.

La Route Paris-Biarritz, photographed by Germaine Krull, text by Claude Farrère, Paris, Éditions Jacques Haumont, 1931.

Georges Simenon and Germaine Krull, *La Folle d'Itteville*, Paris, Éditions Jacques Haumont ('Phototexte'), 1931.

Germaine Krull by Pierre Mac Orlan, Paris, NRF, Librairie Gallimard ('Photographes nouveaux' series), 1931.

Confort, texts by G. Lenôtre, Paul Reboux, Marcel Prévost and Pierre Mac Orlan, Versailles, SOC, Société Générale de Fonderie, 1931. Photographs attributable to Germaine Krull.

The Afghan Stuccos of the N.R.F. Collection, text by J. Strzygowsky, Paris, NRF, 1931. 46 ph.

Damia by Henri Béraud, Paris, Antoine Girard, n.d. [1933]. Brochure published for Columbia.

Marseille by Germaine Krull, text by André Suarès, Paris, Éditions d'Histoire et d'Art, Librairie Plon, Paris, 1935.

Germaine Krull, *Ballets de Monte-Carlo*, cover by Matisse, Nice, Marcel Roche, 1937.

Ouro Preto, Uma Cidade Antiga do Brasil, photographs by Germaine Krull, texts by Raul Lino and Ribeiro Couto, Lisbon, Edições Atlântico, 1943.

Roger Vailland, *La Bataille d'Alsace (November-December 1944)*, photographs by Germaine Krull, Paris, Jacques Haumont, 1945.

Chiengmai, pictures by Germaine Krull, commentary by Lotus, Bangkok, copyright Hotel Oriental, n.d. [c. 1960].

Germaine Krull and Dorothea Melchers, *Bangkok: Siam's City of Angels*, London, Robert Hale, 1964.

Germaine Krull and Dorothea Melchers, *Tales from Siam*, London, Robert Hale, 1966.

Germaine Krull, *Tibetans in India*, New Delhi, Allied Publishers Private Ltd., 1968.

MAJOR CONTRIBUTIONS BY GERMAINE KRULL

Mario von Bucovich, *Paris*, introduction by Paul Morand, Berlin, Albertus-Verlag, 1928; French edition, Henri Jonquières et Cie, Paris, n.d. [1928]; American edition, Random House, 1930.

Adolf Hallman, *Paris under 4 årstider*, Stockholm, Albert Bonniers Förlag, 1930.

André Warnod, *Visages de Paris*, preface by Jean de Castellane, Paris, Firmin-Didot et Cie, 1930.

Route de Paris à la Méditerranée, with texts by Paul Morand, Paris, Firmin-Didot et Cie, 1931.

AUTOBIOGRAPHY

Germaine Krull, *La vita conduce la danza*, Italian translation of 'La Vie mène la danse' (typescript of 1980–1981) by Giovanna Chiti, Florence, Giunti Gruppo Editoriale, 1992.

ARTICLE

Germaine Krull Ivens, 'Error in Laos', *Far Eastern Survey*, vol. XVI, no. 11, 4 June 1947, pp. 121–124.

GERMAINE KRULL'S MAJOR MANUSCRIPTS WRITTEN IN FRENCH

Germaine Krull archives (GK Nachlass), Museum Folkwang, Essen.

'Chien fou', 1934, unpublished (abbreviated CF).

'Hallo, Hallo, Brazzaville vous parle', c. 1943; English version with the title 'Hello! Hello! Brazzaville', translated by Margaret Nairn, unpublished.

'Click entre deux guerres', 1976, unpublished (abbreviated CEDG); German translation by Christel Klose, in Germaine Krull, *Fotografien 1922-1966*, Bonn, n.p., 1977.

'La vie mène la danse', 1980–1981, unpublished (abbreviated VMD); Italian version published as *La vita conduce la danza*, by Giovanna Chiti, Florence, Giunti Gruppo Editoriale, 1992.

ORIGINAL DOCUMENT

Ouvrières et midinettes au travail et au plaisir, original manuscript by Emmanuel Berl, 81 pages, 31 original photos, some by Germaine Krull, tipped in, November 1931 to May 1932, Paris, Bibliothèque Nationale de France, Département des Estampes et de la Photographie.

BOOK ILLUSTRATIONS

Peter Landow, *Natur und Kultur. Das Weib*, Berlin, Gesselschaft zur Verbreitung klassischer Kunst, 1925.

Nouvelles installations de la centrale d'Issy-les-Moulineaux, Paris, Compagnie Parisienne de Distribution d'Électricité, [5 June] 1929, 7 ph.

Jean Prévost, *Eiffel*, Paris, Les Éditions Rieder, 1929, pl. 43 to 48, 6 ph.

Rolf Voigt, *Hände, Eine Sammlung von Handabbildungen grosser Toter und Lebender*, Hamburg, Gebrüder Enoch Verlag, 1929, pl. 62: 'Blinder (Skapini)'.

Dr. W. Warstat, *Der schöne Akt, Bildmässige Aktphotographie ihre Ästhetik und Technik*, Berlin, Verlag Guido Hackebeil A.-G., 1929, Abb. 100 and 101, 2 ph.

200 vues de Paris, with comments by Robert Bonfils, Paris, Larousse, 1930 ('Guide des musées, monuments, etc.'), 2 ph., pp. 153, 155.

Arts et Métiers graphiques, annual volume *Photographie*: 1930: 2 ph., nos. 74 and 86; 1931: 2 ph., nos. 8 and 116; 1932: 1 ph., no. 66; 1933–1934: 1 ph., no. 90.

French-Cancan, texts by Paul Perret, Paris, Éditions de Paris, August 1930 ('Les Images de Paris, no. 2'), 17 ph. (the second part is illustrated with photos by Studio Marcello).

Pierre Mac Orlan, *Le Printemps*, Paris, Librairie Gallimard, 1930, photos attributable to Germaine Krull.

Mers, Marines, Marins, text by Paul Valéry, commentaries by Georges Dupuy, Paris, Firmin-Didot, 1930, 5 ph.

Paris 1929, preface by Antoine Roche, Paris, Librairie des Arts Décoratifs, A. Calavas, 1930, 2 ph.

Photographies modernes, presented by Pierre Bost, Paris, Librairie des Arts Décoratifs, A. Calavas, n.d. [1930].

Serge, *Vive le cirque*, Paris, Marcel Seheur, 1930.

Gonzague Truc, *Le Quartier Saint-Victor et le Jardin des Plantes*, Paris, Firmin-Didot, 1930, 3 ph., photographic insert.

Jeanne Fernandez, *Le jardin de la beauté. Conseils à toutes les femmes*, Paris, S. A. Le Jardin des modes, 1931, pp. 78, 81, 89, 3 ph.

La Leçon de travail dans un parc, Paris, Office d'Éditions d'Art pour les Laboratoires du Docteur Debat, n.d. [c. 1931], 1 photo and 2 photomontages attributable to Germaine Krull.

Studio D. P., brochure 8 p., Paris, Studio Deberny Peignot, reproducing Germaine Krull's advertisement for the Guide Vert, 1931.

Harold Clunn, *The Face of Paris*, London, Spring Books, 1933, 6 ph.

Georges Saint-Bonnet, *Scandales 33*, Paris, Paris Publications, 1933, 1 ph.

Jean Lasserre, *Paris-Misère*, Grenoble, B. Arthaud, 1935, full page p. 40 and back cover, 3 ph.

Georges Vallauris, *Orgies*, Paris, Les éditions du Vert-Logis, 1936.

Hélène Terré, *Volontaires pour la France*, Paris, Imprimerie Sapho – Ministère de la Guerre, 1946.

Berthe Bovy interprète La Voix humaine de Jean Cocteau, presented and produced by Pierre Hiégel, booklet in the Pathé DTX 288 record set, 1958, 4 ph.

FILMOGRAPHY

Six pour dix francs, 'Documentaire romancé', directed by Germaine Krull and Georges H. Patin, [1931], silent, 9 min, available for viewing at the Archives Françaises du Film, Bois d'Arcy.

Il partit pour un long voyage, directed by Germaine Krull and Georges H. Patin, 1932, sound, 11 min 20, original score by Jean Marcillac, available for viewing at the Archives Françaises du Film, Bois d'Arcy.

Autour de Brazzaville, directed by François Villiers, with the collaboration of Germaine Krull, text by Richard Francœur, 1943-1946, 25 min, available for viewing at the Archives Françaises du Film, Bois d'Arcy, and the CNC-Bnf.

L'Amitié noire, directed by François Villiers, with the collaboration by Germaine Krull and Pierre Bernard, text by Jean Cocteau, OFIC, 1946, 18 min, available for viewing at the Archives Françaises du Film, Bois d'Arcy, and the CNC-Bnf.

BOOKS ON GERMAINE KRULL

Germaine Krull 1927-1967, exhibition catalogue, Paris, Cinémathèque Française – Musée du Cinéma, 1967.

Germaine Krull, Fotografien 1922-1966, Bonn, Rheinisches Landesmuseum Bonn, Rheinland-Verlag GmbH Köln in Kommission bei Rudolf Habelt Verlag GmbH, 1977.

Germaine Krull, Photographie 1924-1936, text by Christian Bouqueret, Arles, Musée Réattu, Céret, Musée d'Art Moderne, Chalon-sur-Saône, Musée Nicéphore Niépce, 1988.

Kim Sichel, *Germaine Krull, Photographer of Modernity*, Cambridge, Mass., and London, The MIT Press, 1999; *Avant-garde als Abenteuer: Leben und Werk der Photographin Germaine Krull*, Munich, Schirmer Mosel, 1999.

Kim Sichel, *Germaine Krull à Monte-Carlo, The Monte Carlo Years*, Montreal, Montreal Museum of Fine Arts, 2006.

Germaine Krull: Metal y la fotografía industrial, text by Juan Naranjo, Madrid, Guillermo de Osma Galeria, 2011.

BOOKS AND ARTICLES ON GERMAINE KRULL, OR MENTIONING GERMAINE KRULL

Walter Benjamin, *Petite histoire de la photographie* (1931), translation by André Gunthert, in *Études photographiques*, no. 1, November 1996, pp. 6-39; original edition in *Literarische Welt*, 7th year, no. 38, 18 September 1931, no. 39, 25 September 1931, no. 40, 2 October 1931, in 2nd instalment no. 39, pp. 3-4, 2 ph.

Louis Aragon, 'Un "salon" photographique', *Commune, revue de l'Association des écrivains et des artistes révolutionnaires (AEAR)*, no. 22, June 1935, pp. 1189–1192 ('Documents de la vie sociale', photography exhibition, organised by the photographic department of the AEAR, at the Galerie La Pléiade, 73, boulevard Saint-Michel, Paris).

Hélène Terré, *Volontaires pour la France*, Paris, Imprimerie Sapho – Ministère de la Guerre, 1946.

'Une lettre de la célèbre photographe Germaine Krull: *Métal* (1925) et la suite', *Gazette des Beaux-Arts*, no. 1294, November 1976, p. 35.

Kim Sichel, *Photographs of Paris, 1928-1934: Brassaï, André Kertész, Germaine Krull and Man Ray*, PhD thesis, Yale University, Ann Arbor, UMI, 1986.

David Travis, 'In and of the Eiffel Tower', *Art Institute of Chicago Museum Studies*, vol. 13, no. 1, 1987, pp. 5-23.

Rudolf Herz and Dirk Halfbrodt, *Fotografie und Revolution. München 1918/19*, Berlin, Nishen Verlag, 1988.

Maria Morris Hambourg and Christopher Phillips, *The New Vision: Photography between the World Wars*, New York, Ford Motor Company Collection at The Metropolitan Museum of Art, 1989.

Kim Sichel, 'Les photographes étrangers à Paris durant l'entre-deux-guerres', in André Kaspi and Antoine Marès (eds.), *Le Paris des étrangers depuis un siècle*, Paris, Imprimerie Nationale, 1989, pp. 329-345.

Thomas Schirmböck, 'Germaine Krull in Zentralafrika 1941-1943', *Frauen Kunst Wissenschaft*, H. 14, 1992, pp. 74-82.

Ute Eskildsen (ed.), *Fotografieren hiess Teilnehmen: Fotografinnen der Weimarer Republik*, Düsseldorf, Richter Verlag, 1994.

Nathalie Raoux, 'Walter Benjamin, Gisèle Freund, Germaine Krull et Hélène Léger. Deutschland-Frankreich; Mann-Weib. Eine Folge von Briefen', *Revue germanique internationale*, no. 5, 1996, online: http://rgi.revues.org/570.

Christian Bouqueret, *Des années folles aux années noires. La Nouvelle Vision photographique en France, 1920-1940*, Paris, Marval, 1997.

Françoise Denoyelle, *La Lumière de Paris. I. Le Marché de la photographie 1919-1939. II. Les Usages de la photographie, 1919-1939*, Paris, L'Harmattan, 1997.

Olivia Lahs-Gonzalez and Lucy R. Lippard, *Defining Eye: Women Photographers of the 20th Century. Selection from the Helen Kornblum Collection*, Saint Louis, Saint Louis Art Museum, 1997.

André Stufkens, *Passages. Joris Ivens en de Kunst van deze eeuw*, Museum Het Walkhof/Europese Stichting Joris Ivens, Nijmegen, 1929.

Christian Bouqueret, *Les Femmes photographes de la Nouvelle Vision en France, 1920–1940*, Paris, Marval, 1998.

Inka Graeve, *Mechanismus und Ausdruck. Die Sammlung Ann und Jürgen Wilde. Fotografien aus dem 20. Jahrhundert*, Munich, Schirmer Mosel, 1999.

Ulrich Pohlmann and Rudolf Scheutle (eds.), *Lehrjahre-Lichtjahre: Die Münchner Fotoschule, 1900–2000*, Fotomuseum in Münchner Stadtmuseum, Munich, Schirmer Mosel, 2000.

Mark Antliff, 'Machines Primitives: Philippe Lamour, Germaine Krull and the Fascist Cult of Youth', *Qui Parle*, vol. 13, no. 1, 10 January 2001, pp. 57–102.

Cécile Godefroy, 'La photographie au service du simultanéisme', *Études photographiques*, no. 12, November 2002, online: http://etudesphotographiques.revues.org/322.

Unda Hörner, *Madame Man Ray: Fotografinnen der Avant-Garde in Paris*, Berlin, Ebersbach, 2002.

Jean-Robert Pitte, *Philippe Lamour, père de l'aménagement du territoire en France (1903–1992)*, Paris, Fayard, 2002.

Kim Sichel, 'Germaine Krull and L'Amitié Noire: World War II and French Colonialist Film', in Eleanor M. Hight and Gary D. Sampson (eds.), *Colonialist Photography: Imag(in)ing Race and Place*, London, Routledge, 2002, pp. 257–280.

Johan De Smet and Catherine Verleysen, *Variétés: Spiegel van de dolle jaren*, Ghent, Museum voor Schone Kunsten, 2004.

Sarah Kennel, 'Fantasies of the Street: Emigré Photography in Interwar Paris', *History of Photography*, vol. 29, no. 3, autumn 2005, pp. 287–300.

Mark Antliff, *Avant-Garde Fascism: The Mobilization of Myth, Art and Culture in France, 1909–1939*, Durham and London, Duke University Press, 2007.

Ulrike Rueckert, *'Die Fotografie ist ein schöner Beruf'. Das schillernde Leben der Germaine Krull*, Munich, Bayerischer Rundfunk, 2007.

Catherine Gonnard et Élisabeth Lebovici, *Femmes artistes / Artistes femmes, Paris, de 1880 à nos jours*, Paris, éditions Hazan, 2007.

David Campany, *Photography and Cinema*, London, Reaktion Books, 2008.

Herbert Molderings, *Die Moderne der Fotografie*, Hamburg, Philo Fine Arts, Fundus-Bücher, 2008.

Danièle Méaux, 'La tentative d'une forme policière alliant le texte et la photographie', *Dalhousie French Studies*, vol. 89, 'Voir le texte, lire l'image', winter 2009, pp. 11–18.

Marie-Hélène Dumas, *Lumières d'exil*, Paris, Éditions Joëlle Losfeld, 2009.

Margarete Gröner, Rudolf Scheutle and Ulrich Pohlmann (eds.), *Nude Visions: 150 Years of Nude Photography*, Heidelberg, Kehrer Verlag, 2009.

Camille Morineau and Annalisa Rimmaudo (eds.), *elles@centrepompidou: artistes femmes dans la collection du Musée national d'art moderne, Centre de création industrielle, Centre Pompidou*, Paris, Centre Pompidou, 2009.

Kristen Oehlrich, 'Images of Industry in the Twenties: Photography, Film, and Political Ideology', in Will Wright et al., *The Image of Technology*, Pueblo, Colorado State University, 2009, pp. 246–252.

Frank-Manuel Peter, 'The German Dance Archive, Cologne (Deutsches Tanzarchiv Köln)', *Dance Chronicle*, vol. 32, no. 3, 2009, pp. 476–489.

Unda Hörner, *Scharfsichtige Frauen. Fotografinnen der 20er und 30er Jahre in Paris*, Berlin, Ebersbach Verlag, 2010.

Petra Löffler, 'Picturing the Metropolis: Paris in the Eye of the Camera', in Elke Mettinger-Schartmann, Margaret Rubik and Jorg Türschmann (eds.), *Rive Gauche: Paris as a Site of Avant-Garde and Cultural Exchange in the 1920s*, Amsterdam, Rodopi, 2010.

Ursula Marx, Gudrun Schwarz, Michael Schwarz and Erdmut Wizisla (eds.), *Walter Benjamin. Archives. Images, textes et signes*, Paris, Klincksieck, 2011.

Elisabeth Otto and Vanessa Rocco, *The New Woman International: Representations in Photography and Film from the 1870s through the 1960s*, Ann Arbor, University of Michigan Press and the University of Michigan Library, 2011.

Quentin Bajac and Clément Chéroux (eds.), *Voici Paris. Modernités photographiques 1920–1950. La collection Christian Bouqueret*, Paris, Centre Pompidou, 2012.

Mattie Boom, 'Heavy Metal Beats Greyer Sky. Interpretations of the Netherlands by Foreign Photographers 1890–1930', *Depth of Field*, vol. 3, no. 1, December 2012, online: http://journal.depthoffield.eu/vol03/nr01/a03/en.

Christian Bouqueret, *Paris. Les Livres de photographie des années 1920 aux années 1950*, Paris, Gründ, 2012.

Xavier Canonne, 'Paul-Gustave Van Hecke et la photographie', in *L'Animateur d'art Paul-Gustave Van Hecke (1887–1967) et l'avant-garde, Cahiers des Musées royaux des Beaux-Arts de Belgique*, no. 12, March 2012, pp. 110–113.

John Abromeit, *Max Horkheimer and the Foundations of the Frankfurt School*, Cambridge, Mass., Cambridge University Press, 2013.

François Bon, Olivier Lugon and Philippe Simay, *Le Pont transbordeur de Marseille*, Paris, Institut National d'Histoire de l'Art, Collège International de Philosophie et Éditions Ophrys, 2013.

Damarice Amao, *Passion et désillusion. Eli Lotar (1905–1969). Contribution à une histoire des rapports entre les avant-gardes photographique et cinématographique à Paris dans l'entre-deux-guerres*, PhD thesis, art history, Université Paris IV, supervised by Arnauld Pierre, defended on 15 March 2014, unpublished.

Object: Photo. Modern Photographs: The Thomas Walter Collection 1909–1949, edited by Mitra Abbaspour, Lee Ann Daffner and Maria Morris Hambourg, essays by Quentin Bajac and Jim Coddington, New York, The Museum of Modern Art, 2014.

Kim Sichel, 'Contortions of Technique: Germaine Krull's Experimental Photography', in Mitra Abbaspour, Lee Ann Daffner and Maria Morris Hambourg (eds.), *Object: Photo. Modern Photographs: The Thomas Walther Collection 1909–1949. An Online Project of The Museum of Modern Art*, New York, The Museum of Modern Art, 2014, online: http://www.moma.org/ interactives/objectphoto/assets/essays/Sichel.pdf.

ILLUSTRATIONS IN MAGAZINES

Dr. A. Ponsel, 'Unter Kopfjägern', *UHU*, February 1926, pp. 69–75.

'Der Delaunay-Stil – die kommende Mode', *Illustrierte Beilage zum Berlin Börsen-Courier*, 14 March 1926.

'Maske zu Strawinskis "l'Histoire d'un soldat"', *Der Querschnitt*, 6, no. 12, December 1926, p. 918.

De Gemeenschap, nos. 10–11, 1927, back cover, 3 ph.

'Film, Bild und Rythmus' by Fritz Rosenfeld, *Filmliga*, 1, no. 10, April 1928, p. 7.

'Paris la nuit' by Joseph Kessel, *Détective*, 1, no. 3, 15 November 1928, p. 3, 3 ph.

Filmliga, 2, no. 5, February 1929, cover, 1 ph.

'Au son de l'accordéon' by Henri Danjou, *Détective*, 1, no. 47, 19 September 1929, pp. 12–13, 2 ph.

'Ombres de Paris', unpublished crime novel by Pierre Mac Orlan, *Détective*, no. 69, 20 February 1930, to no. 81, 15 May 1930, 7 p., in general 2 ph. by page.

Das Leben, 7. Jahrg., Nr. 10, April 1930, Windhunde, 2 ph.; Musik in Bildern, 5 ph.

'Ein javanischer Prinz tanzt', *Die Dame*, 14 April 1930, pp. 18–19.

'La photographie, art moderne' by Marcel Astruc, *Les Annales politiques et littéraires*, no. 2355, 1 April 1930, p. 335, 2 ph.

'Grands magasins. Enquête de Louis Roubaud et Francis Ambrière', *Les Annales politiques et littéraires*, no. 2385, 1 July 1930, pp. 17–24, 3 ph.; no. 2386, 15 July 1930, pp. 73–80, 9 ph.; no. 2387, 1 August 1930, pp. 113–120, 11 ph.; no. 2388, 15 August 1930, pp. 163–170, 7 ph.; no. 2389, 1 September 1930, pp. 201–207, 4 ph.; no. 2389, 15 September 1930, pp. 245–248, 0 ph.

Das Magazin, no. 78, February 1931, p. 5633, 'Bal Tabarin', 1 ph.

'Germaine Krull' by Jean Laurent, *La Rampe*, 15 April–1 May 1931, pp. 27–30 and p. 54; 9 ph.

'Pariser Colonial Austellung' by Ada Niel, *Die Dame*, no. 21, July 1931, pp. 4–7.

Modern Photography, special issue of *The Studio*, London, autumn 1931, pp. 58 and p. 97, 2 ph.

Le Sourire, Christmas 1932, 'Clochards', 3 ph; 'Le secret de polichinelle', 1 ph.

Heim, monthly review, no 4, 1932, 5 ph.

'La nuit des sept minutes', unpublished novel by Georges Simenon, *Marianne*, no. 23, 29 March 1933, p. 5; no. 24, 7 April 1933, p. 5; no. 25, 12 April 1933, p. 5, 9 ph.

'La Chatte', unpublished novel by Colette, *Marianne*, no. 25, 12 April 1933, p. 1 and p. 7; no. 26, 19 April 1933, p. 7; no. 27, 26 April 1933, p. 7; no. 28, 3 May 1933, p. 7; no. 29, 10 May 1933, p. 7; no. 30, 17 May 1933, p. 7; no. 31, 24 May 1933, p. 7; no. 32, 31 May 1933, p. 7; no. 33, 7 June 1933, p. 7, 27 ph.

'Bains de vapeur par Germaine Krull', *Le Sourire*, no. 839, 1 June 1933, p. 8, 5 ph.

'Repos par Germaine Krull', *Allo Paris*, no. 2, July 1933, no page numbers.

'Frivolités par Germaine Krull', *Allo Paris*, no. 10, March 1934, no page numbers [p. 4].

Miroir du monde, spring 1934, special issue, p. 5, 1 ph.; p. 8, 'Vénus 1934, la voluptueuse', 1 ph.; 'L'éclat emprunté' by Germaine Beaumont, pp. 15–16, 4 ph.

Le Sourire, no. 892, 7 June 1934, cover, 1 ph.; 'Dans l'intimité de Vénus (jambes)', Renée Dunan, 3 ph.; 'Avec le sourire', Pierre Humbourg, 1 ph.

Secrets de Paris, no. 6, October 1934, p. 253, 1 ph.

'Au camp de l'épouvante', *Point de vue*, no. 6, 27 April 1945, no page numbers ['Camp de Vaihingen' page].

MAGAZINES

The bibliography of *Art et Médecine* and *VU* was drawn up by the Musée Nicéphore Niépce in Chalon-sur-Saône. The bibliography of the other magazines is by the author.

ART ET MÉDECINE (1930–1936)

February 1931
'Lectures' by Dominique Pierre, p. 39, 1 ph. / 1.

June 1931
'... à l'aide d'un outillage puissant et original...', p. 1, 1 ph. / 1.
'Deux Auvergnes' by Henri Pourrat, pp. 18–24, 1 ph. / 10.

July 1931
'L'Âme de nos paysages' by Paul Volvenel, pp. 20–23, 1 ph. / 6.
'Rome en France' by Jean-Jacques Brousson, pp. 24–29, 10 ph. / 10.

October 1931
'Paname' by Francis Carco, pp. 42–45, 2 ph. / 5.
'Visages et paysages populaires de Paris' by Pierre Mac Orlan, pp. 46–49, 4 ph. / 7.

February 1932
'La Bretagne et les Bretons' by Charles Le Goffic, pp. 2–25, 7 ph. / 19.

March 1932
'Provence' by Gabriel Hanotaux, pp. 9–19, 5 ph. / 14.
'Les trois grandes beautés de la Méditerranée' by Louis Bertrand, pp. 20–25, 6 ph. / 8.
'Midi sévère' by Colette, pp. 26–29, 2 ph. / 5.

April 1932
'Discophilie' by Émile Vuillermoz, p. 45, 1 ph. / 1.

May 1932
'Discophilie' by Émile Vuillermoz, p. 44, 1 ph. / 1.

June 1932
'Ancien ou moderne' by Abel Bonnard, pp. 32–35, 3 ph. / 4.
'Lectures, Jacques de Lacretelle et Cie' by Pierre Dominique, p. 42, 1 ph. / 1.

July 1932
'L'Âme de l'Ile-de-France' by Abel Bonnard, pp. 12–21, 1 ph. / 12.
'Autour de ma maison' by Pierre Mac Orlan, pp. 36–39, 1 ph. / 4.
'Ah! Les beaux dimanches!' by Pierre Scize, pp. 40–41, 1 ph. / 1.

October 1932
'Chauffage électrique', p. 55, 1 ph. / 1.

July 1933
'Gloire de la cuisine' by Abel Bonnard, pp. 10–13, 1 ph. / 4.
'Propositions sur la cuisine française' by Georges Duhamel, pp. 14–17, 1 ph. / 4.

May 1934
'Cuisine 1934', p. 46, 1 ph. / 1.

May 1935
'L'avenir du théâtre d'Orange' by Jean Hervé and René Bruyez, pp. 30–33, 1 ph. / 4.

L'ART VIVANT (1928–1931)

no. 83, 1 June 1928
'Le premier salon indépendant de la photographie' by Florent Fels, pp. 444–445, 1 ph.

no. 91, 1 November 1928
Cover, 'Eiffel', 1 ph.
'Tour Eiffel sœur aînée des avions' by Marcelle Auclair, p. 743.
'Eiffel', pp. 756–757, 4 ph.

no. 104, 15 April 1929
'Vieux coins, vieilles boutiques' by Charles Fegdal, p. 313.
'Tableaux – Bric-à-brac – Curiosités' by Léo Larguier, p. 340.
'La Foire à la ferraille', p. 341, 2 ph.

no. 105, 1 May 1929
Cover, 'Lire dans ce numéro: Le métal inspirateur d'art', 1 ph.
'Le métal inspirateur d'art', pp. 368–369, 6 ph.

no. 109, 1 July 1929
'La photographie est-elle un art? Germaine Krull' by Jean Gallotti, p. 526.
'Les fleurs de Paris', 'Bouquet disposé par Germaine Krull', p. 527, 1 ph.
'Germaine Krull', p. 530, 2 ph.

no. 117, 1 November 1929
5 old photos of Paris, 'photo Krull', pp. 841–842, 5 ph.

no. 121, 1 January 1930
'Les quais de Seine', pp. 20–21, 5 ph.

no. 125, 1 March 1930
Advertisement for Firmin-Didot's *Images du monde*, p. 184, 1 ph.
'Les "Mannousch" de Bagnolet' by Charles Fegdal, p. 201; 'Les "Manousch" [*sic*] de Bagnolet', pp. 204–205, 4 ph.

no. 127, 1 April 1930
'Anticipations parisiennes', p. 289, 3 photomontages, 'Photographies G. Krull et Eli Lotar', combined with 'Anticipations parisiennes' by Charles Fegdal, p. 293.

no. 129, 1 May 1930
Cover: 'L'art à Java', 1 ph.
'Les danses javanaises', the dancer Mas Madjadjawa, p. 371, 2 ph.

no. 135, 1 August 1930
Cover, 'Curiosités photographiques', 1 ph.
Krull-Lotar.
p. 605, views of Paris, 2 ph.

no. 141, 1 November 1930
'L'envers du décor', pp. 866–867, 7 ph.
'Richesse plastique, jeu des ombres, étude de nu par Germaine Krull', p. 872, 1 ph.

no. 145, February 1931
Advertisement for *Images du monde*, 1 ph.

BIFUR (1929–1930)

no. 1, May 1929
pp. 24–25, 'Marché à Amsterdam', 1 ph.
pp. 152–153, 'Habitation du quartier gitan à Marseille', 'Amsterdam', 2 ph.

no. 2, July 1929
pp. 24-25, 'Histoire de marins', 1 ph.; 'Paysage', 1 ph.

no. 3, September 1929
pp. 24-25, 'La Bretagne pittoresque', 2 ph.

LE COURRIER LITTÉRAIRE (1930)

no. 2, April-May-June 1930
'Germaine Krull', with letter by Jean Cocteau, pp. 65-81, 24 ph.
Poem by Chenal with a photo by Krull, p. 17, 1 ph.
Carlo Rim photographed by Germaine Krull, p. 178, 1 ph.

GRAND'ROUTE (1930)

no. 1, March 1930
Cover, 1 ph.
'L'art mécanique' by Philippe Lamour, 1 full-page ph. p. 37

no. 2, April 1930 Cover, 1 ph.

no. 3, May 1930
Cover, 1 ph.
'Machinerie du Théâtre Pigalle, composition de Germaine Krull', 1 full-page ph. pp. 39-40
[Portrait d'Eisenstein], 1 full-page ph. pp. 24-25
Back cover, 1 ph.

no. 5, July 1930
'La Main de l'homme', 1 full-page ph. p. 16
Back cover, 1 ph.

L'IMAGE (1932-)

no. 2 Cover, 1 ph.

no. 3 'Le vrai visage du désert' by Léon Abensour, 7 ph.

no. 5 'Le marché aux oiseaux' by Lucie Porquerol, pp. 5-8, 9 ph.

no. 6 Cover, [woman with fan], 1 ph.

no. 7 Cover, [lock], 1 ph.

no. 8 'Femmes martyres' by R. Cardinne-Petit, pp. 4-7, 9 ph. Germaine Krull and Keystone

no. 12 Cover, [mother and child], 1 ph.

no. 13 Cover, 1 ph.

no. 15 Cover, [bar], 1 ph.

no. 16 [Marseille], 1 ph.

no. 19 'Heures de Paris: cinq à sept' by Georges Oudart, pp. 5-8, 11 ph. Germaine Krull and Schall

no. 28 [children]

no. 44 [barges]
Paris Magazine (1931-1939)

no. 5, January 1932 p. 52, 1 ph.

no. 17, January 1933 p. 19, 2 ph.

no. 37, September 1934 p. 551, 1 ph.

no. 40, December 1934 p. 717, 1 ph.

JAZZ (1928-1930)

no. 1, December 1928
'Port de Londres' by Pierre Mac Orlan, pp. 3-5, 4 ph.
'La tour Eiffel est-elle en péril?' by Jean Prévost, pp. 13-15, 4 ph.

no. 2, 15 January 1929
'Rue de Lappe' by Jacques Dyssord, pp. 51-54, 3 ph.
'Port d'Amsterdam' by Florent Fels, pp. 55-58, 7 ph.
'Fêtes foraines' by Henry Thétard, pp. 61-63, 1 ph.
'Le cinéma' by Pierre Scize, pp. 76-79, 3 ph.
Review of *Métal* by Pierre Bost, p. 90, 1 ph.

no. 4, 15 March 1929
'Hambourg' by Pierre Mac Orlan, pp. 151-156, 2 ph.

no. 5, 15 April 1929
'Coiffeur pour dames', 'Jeu de mains' by Pol Rab, p. 231, arrangement of 7 ph.
'Acier' by Florent Fels, pp. 232-234, 5 ph.

no. 6, 15 May 1929
Inside front cover, advertisement for *Eiffel* by Jean Prévost, 2 ph.

no. 7, 15 June 1929
'Joris Ivens' by Florent Fels, pp. 301-302, 2 uncredited ph.
'Marseille', pp. 313-314, 3 ph.
Review of *100 x Paris* by Pierre Bost, p. 335, 3 ph.
'Les disques' by Louis Laloy, p. 336, 1 ph.

no. 8, July-August 1929
'Toulon' by André Salmon, pp. 343-346, 3 ph.
'Ci-gît le café' by Jacques Dyssord, pp. 347-348, 3 ph.
'Paris by Night', pp. 371-373, 3 ph.
'Spectacles par Germaine Krull', p. 381, 2 ph.

no. 9, 15 September 1929
'Jean Cocteau, l'imposteur' by Paul Chauveau, pp. 421-422, 1 ph.

no. 10, 15 October 1929
'Trois nus par Germaine Krull', p. 443, 3 ph.
'Élégances et coquetteries intellectuelles', p. 454, 2 uncredited ph.

no. 12, 15 December 1929
Cover: 1 ph.
'Vieille et jeune Bretagne' by Pierre Mac Orlan, pp. 515-518, 3 ph.
'Port de Paris' by Louis Chéronnet, pp. 525-528, 1 ph.

no. 14, 15 February 1930
'Batoum' by André Beucler, pp. 605-607, 1 ph.
'Une femme élégante', p. 634, 1 ph.

no. 16, special issue
'Expédition à Vincennes' by René Maran, pp. 2-6, 3 ph.

no. 17, special issue (nudism)
Full-page selection of 6 ph. fragments of nudes, p. 26.
'Artifices par Paul Poiret', pp. 27-29, 1 ph.
'Rétrospective' by Paul Reboux, p. 39, 1 ph.

VARIÉTÉS (1928-1930)

Photographs are grouped in sections of four or eight pages with no page numbers. They are identified here by the page number of the preceding page and by the letters a to h.

1st year, no. 5, 15 September 1928
'Paysages de Paris': 'Vue prise de la tour Eiffel', p. 258c, 1 ph.
'Paysagistes': 'Robert Delaunay peignant son "paysage de Paris"', p. 258d, 1 ph.

1st year, no. 6, 15 October 1928
'Mannequins', p. 310b, 1 ph.
'La Goulue, ex-danseuse, étoile du cancan au Moulin Rouge à Paris', p. 326a, 1 ph.

1st year, no. 8, 15 December 1928
'La semaine du blanc', p. 414c, 1 ph.
'Grand magasin', p. 414d, 1 ph.
'Ferrailles au marché aux puces', p. 414e, 1 ph.
'Aux Halles de Paris', p. 414f, 2 ph.
'Maraicher', p. 414g, 1 ph.
'Clochards, par Germaine Krull', pp. 422a, 422b, 422c, 422d, 8 ph.
'Au bal musette de la rue de Lappe', p. 438b, 1 ph.
'Pignons de Paris': 'L'imprimerie de l'Horloge', p. 436h, 1 ph.

1st year, no. 9, 15 January 1929
'Mains': 'La lettre', p. 464a, 1 ph.
'Mains de femmes', p. 464b, 2 ph.
'Aveugles', p. 464d, 1 ph.
'Ectoplasmes': 'Les prédictions de la voyante', p. 472b, 1 ph.
'Extrait de "Métal", by Germaine Krull', p. 488c, 1 ph.
'Escalier en spirale', p. 488c, 1 ph.
'Germaine Krull chez les poètes du groupe "Chantiers": Joe Bousquet et René Nelli', p. 496h, 1 ph.

1st year, no. 11, 15 March 1929
'Beautés': 'Mécanique de la beauté', p. 612a, 1 ph.

1st year, no. 12, 15 April 1929
'Le jour des tulipes', p. 656c, 1 ph.
'Buveurs de bière au cabaret à Amsterdam', p. 656d, 1 ph.
'Les nouveaux quartiers d'Amsterdam': 'Architecte M. de Kler', p. 664c, 1 ph.
'Mâts métalliques à Amsterdam', p. 688b, 1 ph.
'Le stade olympique d'Amsterdam', p. 688e, 1 ph.
'Vieil Amsterdam': 'Voorburgval', 'Entrepôts au Prinzeneiland', p. 688f, 2 ph.
'Amsterdam', 'Rotterdam', p. 688g, 2 ph.
'Chaland passant devant Rotterdam', 'Moulin à Rotterdam', p. 688h, 2 ph.

2nd year, no. 1, 15 May 1929
'Bon pour la fille', p. 12g, 1 ph.
'Panoramas des ports': 'Rue du vieux port à Marseille', 'De la cathédrale d'Anvers', p. 28a, 2 ph.
'Géographies': 'Anvers', 'Hambourg', p. 28b, 2 ph.
'Londres', 'Rotterdam', p. 28c, 2 ph.
'À bord du croiseur': 'La lessive', 'Corvées', p. 28d, 2 ph.

2nd year, no. 2, 15 June 1929
'Les Champs-Élysées', p. 110b, 1 ph.
'Traversée de Paris', 'L'ombre de la colonne de Juillet sur la place de la Bastille', p. 110c, 2 ph.
'Place de l'Étoile', p. 110d, 1 ph.
Advertisement for '*Métal* danse des métaux nus', p. 128
Review of *100 x Paris*, pp. 142-143

2nd year, no. 3, 15 July 1929
'Les berges', p. 160b, 1 ph.
'La génération sacrifiée', p. 160c, 1 ph.
'Friture en plein vent', p. 160f, 1 ph.
'Le refuge', 'Gypsies', p. 160g, 2 ph.
'Les solitaires', p. 160h, 1 ph.
'Natures mortes': 'Photo de Germaine Krull', p. 192a, 1 ph.

2nd year, no. 4, 15 August 1929
'Les Blackbirds au Moulin Rouge': 'La danseuse Mary Clemans', 'Le danseur Earl Tucker', p. 256c, 2 ph.

2nd year, no. 6, 15 October 1929
'L'intérieur de la chapelle des divinistes et son fondateur M. Fortin', p. 416b, 2 ph.
'Temple antoiniste à Paris', 'Temple des théosophes à Paris', p. 416c, 2 ph.
'Quakeresses', p. 416e, 1 ph.
'La superstition': 'Le parapluie ouvert: malheur sur la maison', 'Du feu pour trois: mort du plus jeune', p. 428a, 2 ph.
'Miroir brisé: sept ans de malheur', 'Toucher du bois: pour conjurer le sort', p. 428b, 2 ph.
'Un chapeau sur un lit: infortune', 'Ciseaux fichés dans le sol: prospérité', p. 428c, 2 ph.
'Masque du Laos', p. 440f, 1 ph.
'Mascarade d'atelier', p. 440g, 1 ph.

2nd year, no. 7, 15 November 1929
'Automobiles': 'Une Bugatti au repos', p. 526a, 1 ph.
'Planche de bord d'une Peugeot', p. 526b, 1 ph.
'Le taxi', 'Le pare-chocs', p. 526d, 2 ph.
'Davia dans "Passionnément"', p. 534d, 1 ph.
'Couture': 'Les grandes mains', p. 534f, 2 ph.
'Silhouettes créées par Norine', p. 534g, 1 ph.
'Robes du soir de Norine', 'Ensemble de ville de Norine', p. 534h, 2 ph.

2nd year, no. 8, 15 December 1929
'Paysages méconnus', p. 558c, 1 ph.
n.t. [Bois flottants], p. 574d, 1 ph.
'Mélancolie des villes':
'Brest', p. 582d, 1 ph.
'Berlin', p. 582f, 1 ph.
'Amsterdam', p. 582g, 1 ph.

2nd year, no. 9, 15 January 1930
'Vie des machines':
p. 632a, 2 ph.
p. 632c, 2 ph.
p. 632d, 2 ph.
p. 632h, 2 ph.

2nd year, no. 10, 15 February 1930
'La Bretagne':
'Moulin de l'île d'Ouessant', 'La pointe du Raz', p. 698a, 2 ph.
'Pêcheur', p. 698b, 1 ph.
'Sur le marché à Quimper', 'Sur le quai à Douarnenez', p. 698c, 2 ph.
'À l'intérieur de l'île d'Ouessant', p. 698d, 2 ph.
'La Flandre':
'Philippine, port perdu', 'Damme, ferme des templiers', p. 698e, 2 ph.
'L'horloge du beffroi', 'Rue à Bruges', p. 698f, 2 ph.
'Damme encore', 'Et toujours la dentellière', p. 698g, 2 ph.
'Rivière flamande', 'Le long du canal de Bruges à l'écluse', p. 698h, 2 ph.
'Vitrines et étalages': 'Les mannequins', p. 722a, 1 ph.
'Le photographe Eli Lotar', 'Walter Ruttmann, réalisateur du film "La mélodie du monde"', p. 722g, 2 ph.

2nd year, no. 12, 15 April 1930
'Nourritures':
'Les choux-fleurs', p. 836a, 1 ph.
'Bouquet de légumes', p. 836b, 1 ph.
'Boucherie', p. 836c, 1 ph.

VU (1928-1940)

no. 1, 21 March 1928
'Vu cette semaine' by Henry Bidou, pp. 3-4, 1 ph. / 13.

no. 2, 28 March 1928
'Il y a des voix dans la lampe' by Florent Fels, p. 45, 1 ph. / 4.

no. 3, 4 April 1928
'Zozo Poulbot, humoriste de race', p. 61, 4 ph. / 4.

no. 4, 11 April 1928
'Fêtes foraines' by Edmond Gréville, pp. 92-93, 5 ph. / 5.

no. 6, 25 April 1928
'Comment j'ai volé la tête d'un bouddha d'Angkor' by Titaÿna, p. 165, 4 ph. / 4.

no. 10, 23 May 1928
'Vu dans le monde', p. 245, 1 ph. / 5.
'Un peu d'histoire olympique' by Lucien Gamblin, p. 248, 1 ph. / 3.
'On vend le château de Fleury-en-Bière' by Robert Linzeler, p. 263, 2 ph. / 2.

no. 11, 30 May 1928
'Dans toute sa force' by Florent Fels, p. 284, 3 ph. / 3.
'Paris - Cherbourg - Les Açores - L'Amérique' by J.-M. Texier, p. 287, 1 ph. / 2.

no. 12, 6 June 1928
'Les mystères de la foire aux puces' by Florent Fels, pp. 306-307, 7 ph. / 7.

no. 13, 13 June 1928
'Science et cuisine' by Jean Gallotti, p. 328, 2 ph. / 2.

no. 16, 4 July 1928
'La déroute des ailes blanches' by G. Dupuy, pp. 390-391, 1 ph. / 6.

no. 17, 11 July 1928
'Veille de revue', cover, 1 ph. / 1.
'La renaissance de la marine française' by Jean Fayard, pp. 402-403, 3 ph. / 8.

no. 19, 25 July 1928
'À Carcassonne le mirage des fêtes du bimillénaire', pp. 449-451, 7 ph. / 9.
'Les voyages présidentiels', p. 452, 1 ph. / 5.

no. 24, 29 August 1928
'Révolution armoricaine. L'autonomisme breton et ses joies' by Louis-Martin Chauffier, pp. 543-545, 10 ph. / 10.
'En Russie et en Italie', pp. 558-559, 3 ph. / 10.

no. 31, 17 October 1928
'Les clochards dans les bas-fonds de Paris' by Henri Danjou, pp. 688-690, 10 ph. / 10.

no. 33, 31 October 1928
'La Perle' by Jean d'Erleich, p. 728-730, 1 ph. / 8.

no. 38, 5 December 1928
'Un port moderne, une ville d'art: Anvers' by L. Léontin, pp. 834-835, 6 ph. / 6.

no. 42, 2 January 1929
'Religions inconnues' by Henri Danjou, pp. 908-910, 8 ph. / 8.

no. 44, 16 January 1929
'Les sauvetages de l'Armée du Salut' by Stella Croissant, pp. 38-39, 2 ph. / 10.

no. 47, 6 February 1929
'Le dernier interview de la Goulue', pp. 84-85, 2 ph. / 5.

no. 49, 20 February 1929
'Le pardon des Terre-Neuvas' by Marc d'Aubrive, pp. 130-131, 6 ph. / 6.

no. 50, 27 February 1929
'Une grande découverte artistique', pp. 147-148, 7 ph. / 7.

no. 52, 13 March 1929
'Les nuits lumineuses de Paris' by Edmond Wellhoff, pp. 190–191, 3 ph. / 6.

no. 53, 20 March 1929
'L'auto et son cœur' by E. Weiss, pp. 216–217, 1 ph. / 7.

no. 56, 10 April 1929
'La porte du monde: Marseille', pp. 276–278, 5 ph. / 10.

no. 62, 22 May 1929
'Beauté mon cher souci' by Jeanne Fernandez, pp. 411–414, 7 ph. / 11.

no. 64, 5 June 1929
'Vu en France', p. 438, 2 ph. / 3.
'Pour charmer les poissons, un étrange instrument de musique' by Jean Thomas, p. 444, 2 ph. / 2.

no. 69, 10 July 1929
'Vu cette semaine', p. 538, 1 ph. / 4.
'La comédie humaine de Courteline' by Edmond Wellhoff, pp. 543–544, 3 ph. / 5.

no. 70, 17 July 1929
'Magie noire', p. 574, 4 ph. / 4.

no. 71, 24 July 1929
'Examens: une maladie saisonnière' by Edmond Wellhoff, pp. 579–581, 2 ph. / 9.

no. 72, 31 July 1929
'La Grande Troménie au pays de Monsieur Saint-Ronan à Locronan' by Marc Daubrive, pp. 611–613, 7 ph. / 7.

no. 74, 14 August 1929
'Les maîtres de l'opinion: une journée de M. Léon Bailby, directeur de l'Intransigeant' by Edmond Wellhoff, pp. 639–641 and 648, 6 ph. / 6.

no. 77, 4 September 1929
'Au revoir Black Birds!', cover, 1 ph. / 1.
Untitled [news], p. 715, 1 ph. / 4.

no. 78, 11 September 1929
'10 jours chez Socrate ou Les entretiens de Pontigny' by Louis Martin-Chauffier, pp. 720–722, 10 ph. / 10.

no. 81, 2 October 1929
'Ligne, force, confort', pp. 781–783, 1 ph. / 11.

no. 85, 30 October 1929
'Les morts vont vite' by J. D., p. 890, 1 ph. / 4.

no. 93, 25 December 1929
'Les clous de l'année', pp. 1088–1089, 1 ph. / 11.

no. 94, 1 January 1930
'Tabarin' by Michel Georges-Michel, pp. 10–11, 4 ph. / 11.

no. 101, 19 February 1930
'Le scandale des Halles de Paris' by Florence Raymond, pp. 155–156, 1 ph. / 4.

no. 103, 5 March 1930
'L'Art nègre et océanien' by A. Level, pp. 186–187, 6 ph. / 9.

no. 119, 25 June 1930
'Les sardiniers du Finistère' by Marc Daubrive, pp. 622–623, 4 ph. / 6.

no. 120, 2 July 1930
'Thaumaturges? Non, médecins', cover, 1 ph. / 1.
'Thaumaturges? Non, médecins' by Jean Portail, pp. 635–638, 9 ph. / 9.

no. 121, 9 July 1930
'La fête des Espagnols à Saint-Tropez' by Philippe Lamaur, pp. 672–673, 7 ph. / 7.

no. 131, 17 September 1930
'Les Fêtes de Mistral à Maillane' by Jean-Jacques Brousson, pp. 918–919, 3 ph. / 11.

no. 139, 12 November 1930
'Témoignages de notre temps: Vive le cirque' by Serge, p. 1197, 1 ph. / 5.

no. 143, 10 December 1930
'Superstitions', pp. 1343–1345, 4 ph. / 16.

no. 144, 17 December 1930
'Échos photographiques', p. 1380, 1 ph. / 5.

no. 150, 28 January 1931
'Comment la portera-t-elle?', p. 119, 5 ph. / 5.

no. 151, 4 February 1931
'Une exposition d'art gothico-bouddhique' by André Malraux, pp. 161–162, 7 ph. / 7.

no. 155, 4 March 1931
'Route de Paris et de la Méditerranée' by Dr. Alfred Gradenwitz, p. 314, 1 ph. / 2.

no. 158, 25 March 1931
'Sing-Sing ou La maison des Trois Marches' by Georges Simenon, p. 409, 1 ph. / 1.

no. 185, 30 September 1931
'La Route…' by Hervé Lauwick, pp. 2279–2288, 1 ph. / 20.

no. 196, 16 December 1931
'Une grande leçon d'art chez Mercier Frères', p. 2755, 1 ph. / 4.

no. 200, 13 January 1932
'La fin des rentiers' by André Bouton, p. 58, 1 ph. / 5.

no. 201, 20 January 1932
'L'ameublement et la mode', p. 74, 2 ph. / 4.

no. 207, 2 March 1932
'Une exposition du mobilier', p. 280, 2 ph. / 4.
'Essai sur la France' by Ernest-Robert Curtius, pp. 282–283, 1 ph. / 3.

no. 247, 7 December 1932
'Les Ouvrières de Paris' by Emmanuel Berl, pp. 1925–1928, 11 ph. / 12.

no. 248, 14 December 1932
'Les Ouvrières de Paris' by Emmanuel Berl, pp. 2011–2014, 9 ph. / 10.

no. 250, 28 December 1932
'Les Ouvrières de Paris' by Emmanuel Berl, pp. 2079–2082, 3 ph. / 6.

no. 252, 11 January 1933
'Les Ouvrières de Paris' by Emmanuel Berl, pp. 43–47, 2 ph. / 11.

no. 263, 29 March 1933
'Quand l'amour s'installe' p. 452, 4 ph. / 5.

no. 276, 28 June 1933
'La journée d'un chien à Paris: un jet d'eau, du savon des mains expertes, chez le coiffeur' by Frank Nino, pp. 951–952, 5 ph. / 13.

no. 289 *bis*, 1 October 1933
'D'abord, rester sur la route!' by E.-H. Weiss, pp. 38–40, 1 ph. / 6.
'Prévoir les accidents c'est bien, vouloir les éviter serait mieux…' by Dr P. Béhague, p. 56, 1 ph. / 3.

no. 296, 15 November 1933
'Le Diable dans le bénitier du prophète: l'aventure héroï-comique d'une Française qui se fit musulmane, voulut aller à la Mecque et cependant n'y alla pas' by François Lassagne, pp. 1717–1719, 2 ph. / 7.

no. 299, 6 December 1933
'Les statues qui déménagent…', p. 1815, 3 ph. / 4.

no. 317, 11 April 1934
'Spectacles', p. 475, 2 ph. / 4.

no. 331, 18 July 1934
'Éden de banlieue' by Louis Chéronnet, pp. 902–903, 6 ph. / 6.
'Permanence du type populaire: les modèles des frères Le Nain' by Jean Gallotti, pp. 912–914, 6 ph. / 6.

no. 349, 21 November 1934
'L'ascète chez Gargantua' by Madeleine Jacob, pp. 1477–1479, 1 ph. / 9.

no. 419, 28 March 1936
'Religions multiples: course à la vérité' by Maurice Magre, pp. 44–46, 2 ph. / 9.

no. 460, 6 January 1937
'Théâtre' by R. Cardinne-Petit, p. 27, 1 ph. / 3.

LIST OF WORKS

Unless otherwise indicated, the photographs listed below are by Germaine Krull. Most of them did not originally carry captions and the 'titles' given here are taken from the documents or specify locations or subjects. The captions in inverted commas were written by Krull herself. Many of the photographs were dated after the event, by Krull or by others, and sometimes much later (1960s–1980s). The dates given here are therefore liable to be erroneous, including the ones written in Krull's own hand. Where the mistakes are obvious, I have tried to correct them by reference to biographical facts, publications or other information in my possession. Works maraked by an asterisk are not part of the exhibition.

LIKE A SONG, WORDS, A CRY

p. 8 **Rest on the Bank**, 1927, gelatin silver print, 22.3 × 16.9 cm. Stiftung Ann und Jürgen Wilde, Pinakothek der Moderne, Munich.

'MAD DOG'

p. 14 *Unidentified photographer, **Portrait of Germaine Krull**, 1916, gelatin silver print, 13,9 × 8,8 cm. Museum Folkwang, Essen.

p. 20 *Unidentified photographer, group portrait at Krull's school in **Munich** (Germaine is standing, second from the left), 1916, gelatin silver print, 8.9 × 11.5 cm. Museum Folkwang, Essen.

PHOTOGRAPHER

p. 21 **Portrait of Kurt Eisner**, 1917–1918, gelatin silver print. Münchner Stadtmuseum/ Sammlung Fotografie, Munich.

p. 22 Hans Basler, **Portrait of Germaine Krull**, Berlin, 1922, gelatin silver print, 15,9 × 22 cm; mounted on card. Museum Folkwang, Essen.

p. 30 Plate from **Dämmerstunden-6 Aufnahmen weiblicher Akte** [Twilight - 6 Female Nudes], 1918–1924, gelatin silver prints, 22.8 × 16 cm and 12 × 16.9 cm. Münchner Stadtmuseum/ Sammlung Fotografie, Munich.

p. 31 Plates of ***Der Akt, Zwanzig photographische Aufnahmen weiblicher Körper nach der Natur*** [The Nude, Twenty Photographs], 1918. Softbound volume, photogravure, 40.5 × 30.5 cm. Münchner Stadtmuseum/ Sammlung Fotografie, Munich.

p. 32, top ***Dance Study with Mask II**, from the *Spuk* portfolio, Berlin, 1923, mounted gelatin silver print, 21.1 × 16.5 cm (34 × 24 cm). Courtesy Galerie Johannes Faber.

p. 32, bottom Krull-Hübschmann (attributed to), **Reclining Nude**, 1919, gelatin silver print, 14.5 × 21 cm. Stiftung Ann und Jürgen Wilde, Pinakothek der Moderne, Munich.

p. 33 **Nudes**, 1924, gelatin silver print, 16.3 × 22.2 cm. Dietmar Siegert Collection.

p. 34 **The Dancer Jo Mihaly Dancing 'Revolution'**, 1925, gelatin silver print, 21.3 × 12.3 cm. Museum Folkwang, Essen.

p. 35, top Sonia Delaunay, 1925, gelatin silver print, 22.5 × 15.5 cm. Bibliothèque Nationale de France.

p. 35, bottom **Sonia Delaunay Showing One of Her Dresses**, 1925, gelatin silver print (one of two prints mounted on cardboard), 14 × 10 cm. Bibliothèque Nationale de France.

p. 36 **Demaria Wearing a Model by Sonia Delaunay**, 1926, gelatin silver print, 21.3 × 13.5 cm. Centre Pompidou, Paris. Musée National d'Art Moderne/Centre de Création Industrielle. Acquired with the support of Yves Rocher, 2011. Former Christian Bouqueret collection.

p. 37 **Lizica Codreano in a Dress by Sonia Delaunay**, 1926, gelatin silver print, 22.5 × 15.5 cm. Bibliothèque Nationale de France.

p. 38, Eli Lotar, **Portrait of Germaine Krull**, Paris, 1927, gelatin silver print, 17.5 × 21 cm. Museum Folkwang, Essen.

p. 39 **'Interior', Robert Delaunay**, 1926, gelatin silver print, 22.7 × 15.9 cm. Stiftung Ann und Jürgen Wilde, Pinakothek der Moderne, Munich.

p. 40 **Self-portrait**, Paris, 1927, gelatin silver print, 23.4 × 17.1 cm. Stiftung Ann und Jürgen Wilde, Pinakothek der Moderne, Munich.

1928: *VU* AND 'MY *FERS*'

p. 49 **'London'**, 1927, gelatin silver print, 15.8 × 10.8 cm. Stiftung Ann und Jürgen Wilde, Pinakothek der Moderne, Munich.

p. 50, top **Belfry**, c. 1928, gelatin silver print, 22.7 × 15.2 cm. Amsab-Institute of Social History, Ghent.

p. 50, bottom **'Flanders: the Belfry Clock'**, c. 1927, gelatin silver print, 22.4 × 15.8 cm. Amsab-Institute of Social History, Ghent.

p. 51, left **Eiffel Tower**, c. 1928, gelatin silver print, 22.8 × 15.5 cm. Museum Folkwang, Essen.

p. 51, right **Eiffel Tower**, 1927, gelatin silver print, 22 × 14.6 cm. Centre Pompidou, Paris. Musée National d'Art Moderne/Centre de Création Industrielle. Acquired with the support of Yves Rocher, 2011. Former Christian Bouqueret collection.

p. 52 **Eiffel Tower**, Paris, c. 1928, gelatin silver print, 21.5 × 15.1 cm. Museum Folkwang, Essen.

p. 53 **Bridge Crane, Rotterdam**, c. 1926, gelatin silver print, 21.9 × 15.3 cm. Stiftung Ann und Jürgen Wilde, Pinakothek der Moderne, Munich.

p. 54 **'Eiffel Tower'**, c. 1927, gelatin silver print, 21.6 × 15.7 cm. Amsab-Institute of Social History, Ghent.

p. 55 **'With All Its Strength'**, by Fels Florent, *VU*, no. 11 (30 May 1928), p. 284, 38 × 28 cm. Private collection.

p. 56, left **Grain silo, Rotterdam**, c. 1924, gelatin silver print, 37.1 × 27.2 cm. Stiftung Ann und Jürgen Wilde, Pinakothek der Moderne, Munich.

p. 56, right **Electricity Plant, Issy-les-Moulineaux**, 1928, gelatin silver print, 22.6 × 16.6 cm. Amsab-Institute of Social History, Ghent.

p. 57 **'Port St Malo'**, 1928, gelatin silver print, 20.3 × 14.6 cm. Amsab-Institute of Social History, Ghent.

pp. 58–59 ***Métal***, Paris, A. Calavas, 1928, portfolio, cover and plates in photogravure, 30 × 23.5 cm. Bouqueret-Rémy collection.

p. 60, top **'Eiffel'**, *L'Art vivant*, no. 91 (1 October 1928), pp. 75–77, 31.5 × 49 cm. Private collection.

p. 60, bottom **'Metal, Inspiration of Art'**, *L'Art vivant*, no. 105 (1 May 1930), pp. 368–369, 31.5 × 49 cm. Private collection.

p. 61 Germaine Krull, ***L'Art vivant***, no. 109 (1 July 1930), p. 530, 31.7 × 24.4 cm. Private collection.

p. 62, top **'A Modern Port, a Heritage City: Antwerp'**, *VU*, no. 38, 5 December 1928, 38 × 56 cm. Private collection.

p. 62, bottom **'Life of Machines'**, *Variétés*, 2nd year, no. 9 (15 January 1930), p. 632a, 18 × 25 cm. Private collection.

p. 63 top and bottom left **'Steel'**, *Jazz*, no. 5 (15 April 1929), by Florent Fels, pp. 232–234, 31.5 × 24.5 cm. Private collection.

p. 63, bottom right Cover of ***Jazz***, no. 12 (15 December 1929), 31.5 × 24.5 cm. Private collection.

REPORTAGE AND MAGAZINES

p. 64 **Self-portrait with Icarette, '1925'**, c. 1928, gelatin silver print, 23.6 × 17.5 cm. Centre Pompidou, Paris. Musée National d'Art Moderne/Centre de Création Industrielle. Acquired with the support of Yves Rocher, 2011. Former Christian Bouqueret collection.

p. 87 **Behind the Scenes at the Signature of the Briand-Kellogg Pact**, 1928, gelatin silver print, 14.5 × 21.3 cm. Centre Pompidou, Paris. Musée National d'Art Moderne/Centre de Création Industrielle. Acquired with the support of Yves Rocher, 2011. Former Christian Bouqueret collection.

p. 88 **Fair, Paris**, 1928, gelatin silver print, 21.9 × 15.2 cm. Stiftung Ann und Jürgen Wilde, Pinakothek der Moderne, Munich.

p. 89 **Big Dipper, Foire du Trône, Paris**, 1928, gelatin silver print, 21.7 × 14.5 cm. Private collection.

p. 90 **Big Dipper, Paris**, 1928, gelatin silver print, 21.7 × 14.4 cm. Museum Folkwang, Essen.

p. 91 **Big Dipper, Foire du Trône, Paris**, 1928, gelatin silver print, 22.9 × 15.6 cm. The Museum of Modern Art. Thomas Walther Collection. Gift of David H. McAlpin, by exchange.

p. 92, top **'Fairs'**, *VU*, no. 4 11 April 1928, pp. 92-93, 38 × 56 cm. Private Collection..

p. 92, bottom **'Mysteries of the Flea Fair'**, *VU*, no. 12, 6 June 1928, pp. 306-307, 38 × 56 cm. Private collection.

p. 93, left **'In a Courtyard, Rue des Rosiers', Flea Market, Paris**, 1928, gelatin silver print, 22.1 × 15.6 cm. Stiftung Ann und Jürgen Wilde, Pinakothek der Moderne, Munich.

p. 93, right **Flea Market in Paris, Old Iron**, 1928, gelatin silver print, 21.6 × 14.7 cm. Amsab-Institute of Social History, Ghent.

p. 94 **'Tramp'**, 1928, gelatin silver print, 21.7 × 14.4 cm. Museum Folkwang, Essen.

ép. 95 **'Homeless (under the Bridges)'**, 1928, gelatin silver print, 21 × 14.3 cm. Museum Folkwang, Essen.

p. 96 **'Tramps in the Lower Depths of Paris'**, *VU*, no. 31, 17 October 1928, pp. 688-690, 38 × 56 cm. Private collection.

p. 97, top **'Tramp'**, *Variétés*, 1st year, 8 15 December 1928, p. 422c, 21.7 × 14.5 cm. Private collection.

p. 97, bottom **'Tramps'**, *Variétés*, 1st year, 8 (15 December 1928), p. 422a, 21.7 × 14.5 cm. Private collection.

p. 98, left **London**, c. 1927, gelatin silver print, 20.9 × 14.9 cm. Amsab-Institute of Social History, Ghent.

p. 98, right **Market Scene**, c. 1928, gelatin silver print, 21.7 × 15 cm. Amsab-Institute of Social History, Ghent.

p. 99, top **Les Halles, Meats, Villette et Cie, Paris**, c. 1928. Gelatin silver print, 15.2 × 22.2 cm. Amsab-Institute of Social History, Ghent.

p. 99, bottom **Porcelain Window**, c. 1928, gelatin silver print, 14.6 × 16.1 cm. Amsab-Institute of Social History, Ghent.

p. 100, top **'The "Manouch" of Bagnolet'**, *L'Art vivant*, no. 125, 1 March 1930, 31.5 × 48 cm. Private collection.

p. 100, bottom **'At Les Halles in Paris'**, *Variétés*, 1st year, 8, 15 December 1928, pp. 414f, 21.7 × 14.5 cm. Private collection.

p. 101 **Les Halles at Night (with Van Ecke)**, 1928, gelatin silver print, 22 × 16.2 cm. Amsab-Institute of Social History, Ghent.

p. 102, left **The Dancer Earl Tucker, Blackbirds Revue at the Moulin Rouge**, 1929, gelatin silver print, 21.9 × 16.5 cm. Amsab-Institute of Social History, Ghent.

p. 102, right **The Dancer Earl Tucker, Blackbirds Revue at the Moulin Rouge**, 1929, gelatin silver print, 21.5 × 15.4 cm. Amsab-Institute of Social History, Ghent.

p. 103 **'Black Magic'**, *VU*, no. 70, 17 July 1929, p. 574, 38 × 28 cm. Private collection.

p. 104, top **'Gateway to the World: Marseille'**, *VU*, no. 56, 10 April 1929, pp. 276-278, 38 × 56 cm. Private collection.

p. 104, bottom **'The Three Great Beauties of the Mediterranean'**, *Art et Médecine*, March 1932, pp. 20-21, 30.8 × 48 cm. Private collection.

p. 105 **Marseille**, c. 1929. Gelatin silver print, 22.5 × 14.7 cm. Stiftung Ann und Jürgen Wilde, Pinakothek der Moderne, Munich.

p. 106, top **'The Terre-Neuvas Pilgrimage'**, *VU*, no. 49, 20 February 1929, pp. 130-131, 38 × 56 cm. Private collection.

p. 106, bottom **'The Day before the Review'**, *VU*, no. 17, 11 July 1928, pp. 402-403, 38 × 28 cm. Private collection.

p. 107, top **'Enduring Popular Types: the Modesl of the Le Nain Brothers'**, *VU*, no. 331, 18 July 1934, pp. 912-913, 38 × 28 cm. Private collection.

p. 107, bottom **'Suburban Eden'**, *VU*, no. 331, 18 July 1934, pp. 902-903, 38 × 56 cm. Private collection.

p. 108, top Colette, **'La Chatte'**, unpublished novel (details), *Marianne* no. 28, 3 May 1933, p. 7; no. 26, 19 April 1933, p. 7; no. 33, 7 June 1933, p. 7. Private collection.

p. 108, bottom **'Shadows of Paris'**, detective story by Pierre Mac Orlan serialised in *Détective*: no. 74, 27 March 1930, p. 7; no. 78, 24 April 1930, p. 7; no. 75, 3 April 1930, p. 7. Private collection.

p. 109, left and right **Comfort**, Société Générale de Fonderie, 1931, two pages, 31.8 × 24.2 cm. Private collection.

p. 110 **Place de la Bastille with shadow of the July Column**, 1928, gelatin silver print, 21.6 × 14.7 cm. Amsab-Institute of Social History, Ghent.

PARIS, PARIS

p. 118, top **The Grands Boulevards at the Haussmann crossroads, evening, Paris**, 1928, gelatin silver print, 11.8 × 9 cm. Private collection.

p. 118, bottom **'The Montmartre Fair at Night'**, 1928, gelatin silver print, 15 × 22.3 cm. Amsab-Institute of Social History, Ghent.

p. 119 **Au Bon Coin, Paris**, 1929, gelatin silver print, 14.2 × 10.5 cm. Bouqueret-Rémy collection.

p. 120, top **'The Bright Nights of Paris'**, *VU*, no. 52, 13 March 1929, pp. 190-191, 38 × 56 cm. Private collection.

p. 120, bottom **'The Banks of the Seine'**, *L'Art vivant*, no. 121, 1 January 1930, pp. 20, 21, 31.7 × 49.4 cm. Private collection.

p. 121, left **Linen Week in a Department Store, Le Printemps, Paris**, 1928, gelatin silver print, 22 × 14.9 cm. Amsab Institut d'Histoire Sociale, Ghent.

p. 121, right **A Department Store, Le Printemps, Paris**, 1928, gelatin silver print, 20.7 × 14.1 cm. Amsab-Institute of Social History, Ghent.

p. 122 **'Department Stores'**, *Les Annales*, 1930-1931, pp. 205, 168, 113, 78, 32 × 24 cm. Private collection.

p. 123 **Mannequins in a Shop Window**, 1930, gelatin silver print, 13.7 × 23.5 cm. Bouqueret-Rémy collection.

p. 124, top and bottom Mario von Bucovich, ***Paris***, Albertus-Verlag, Berlin, 1928, p. 12, 13, 183, 254, 29.2 × 21.8 cm. Private collection.

p. 125 **'Outside the Department Stores'**, c. 1929, gelatin silver print, 17.5 × 15.8 cm. Stiftung Ann und Jürgen Wilde, Pinakothek der Moderne, Munich.

pp. 126 and 127 Germaine Krull, ***100 × Paris***, Berlin-Westend, Verlag der Reihe, 1929, cover, pp. 66, 76, 80, 94, 24.3 × 17.3 cm. Private collection.

p. 128 **Rue Auber in Paris**, c. 1928, gelatin silver print, 16.9 × 22.9 cm. The Museum of Modern Art, New York Thomas Walther Collection. Gift of David H. McAlpin, by exchange.

p. 129 **Old Architecture: L'Horloge Print Works**, 1928, gelatin silver print, 21.9 × 15.2 cm. Amsab-Institute of Social History, Ghent.

pp. 130 and131 André Warnod, ***Visages de Paris***, Firmin-Didot, Paris, 1930, p. 5-6, 252, 264, 266-267, 274-275. Private collection.

pp. 132 and 133 Adolf Hallman, ***Paris under 4 Arstider***, Albert Bonniers Forlag, Stockholm, 1930. *The Zone*; p. 121, *Restaurant Maldoror*; p. 125, *Flea Market*; p. 135, *Staircase in Montmartre*, 23.2 × 15.6 cm. Private collection.

p. 134, top left **'New Images of Paris: Around Paris; the Shadow of the July Column'**, *Variétés*, 2nd year, 2, 15 June 1929, p. 110c, 21.7 × 14.5 cm. Private collection.

p. 134 top right **'Tomorrow's Paris'**, *L'Art vivant*, no 127, 1 April 1930, p. 289, 31.7 × 24.4 cm. Private collection.

p. 134, bottom **'Faces and Scenes of People's Paris'**, *Art et Médecine*, October 1931, pp. 48-49, 30.8 × 48 cm. Private collection.

p. 135 **Untitled**, 1930, photomontage. Gelatin silver print, 15 × 18.2 cm. Centre Pompidou, Paris. Musée National d'Art Moderne/Centre de Création Industrielle. Acquired with the support of Yves Rocher, 2011. Former Christian Bouqueret collection.

AUTOMOBILES, ON THE ROAD

p. 136 Unidentified photographer, **Monte-Carlo, Germaine Krull in Her Car**, 1937, gelatin silver print, 13 × 18.3 cm. Museum Folkwang, Essen.

p. 145 **Germaine Krull in Her Peugeot at Fontainebleau**, c. 1929, gelatin silver print, 17.2 × 15.2 cm. Stiftung Ann und Jürgen Wilde, Pinakothek der Moderne, Munich.

p. 146, left **Place Clichy**, 1928, gelatin silver print, 20.5 × 15.7 cm. Amsab-Institute of Social History, Ghent.

p. 146, right **'Traffic in Paris'**, 1926, gelatin silver print, 29.1 × 19.2 cm. Stiftung Ann und Jürgen Wilde, Pinakothek der Moderne, Munich.

p. 147, left **'Bugatti'**, c. 1928, gelatin silver print, 22.7 × 14.1 cm. Amsab-Institute of Social History, Ghent.

p. 147, right **The Bumper**, c. 1928, gelatin silver print, 22.7 × 15.8 cm. Amsab-Institute of Social History, Ghent.

p. 148, left **'The Road…'**, *VU*, no. 185, 30 September 1931, p. 2279, 38 × 28 cm. Private collection.

p. 148, right *VU*, no. 53, 20 March 1929, **'The Car at Heart'**, p. 216, 38 × 28 cm. Private collection.

p. 149 Peugeot advertising pull-out, **'La 201'**, 1929, 40 × 29 cm. Private collection.

p. 150, left ***Grand'Route***, no. 2, April 1930, cover, 22.3 × 16.8 cm. Private collection.

p. 150, right ***Grand'Route***, no. 3, May 1930, cover, 22.3 × 16.8 cm. Private collection.

p. 151 **Paris, Street Seen from Above**, 1928, gelatin silver print, 21.5 × 14.5 cm. Amsab-Institute of Social History, Ghent.

p. 152 ***Route de Paris à la Méditerranée***, Firmin-Didot et Cie, Paris, 1931, cover, pp. 5, 18, 44, 25 × 19.5 cm.

p. 153 **Route**, c. 1930, gelatin silver print, 20.4 × 15 cm. Bouqueret-Rémy collection.

pp. 154 and 155 ***Route de Paris-Biarritz***, Éditions Jacques Haumont, Paris, 1931, cover, pl. 1, pl. 14, pl. 22-23, pl. 44, pl. 86-87, 21.9 × 15 cm. Private collection.

p. 156 **A Country Road**, c. 1931, gelatin silver print, 14.9 × 14.1 cm. Centre Pompidou, Paris. Musée National d'Art Moderne/Centre de Création Industrielle. Acquired with the support of Yves Rocher, 2011. Former Christian Bouqueret collection.

p. 157 **Marseille**, June 1930, gelatin silver print, 21.2 × 15.3 cm. The Museum of Modern Art, New York. Thomas Walther Collection. Gift of Thomas Walther

pp. 158 and 159 ***Marseille par Germaine Krull***, Éditions d'Histoire et d'Art, Librairie Plon, Paris, 1935. Unpaginated, 29.2 × 22.5 cm. Private collection.

WOMEN

p. 160 **Advertisement design for Paul Poiret**, 1926, double exposure, gelatin silver print, 22 × 15.9 cm. Centre Pompidou, Paris. Musée National d'Art Moderne/Centre de Création Industrielle. Acquired with the support of Yves Rocher, 2011. Former Christian Bouqueret collection.

p. 174, left **Untitled**, c. 1927, gelatin silver print, 19.3 × 16.4 cm. Stiftung Ann und Jürgen Wilde, Pinakothek der Moderne, Munich.

p. 174, right **Model by Sonia Delaunay**, c. 1926, gelatin silver print (late print), 23 × 17.5 cm. Bibliothèque Nationale de France.

p. 175 **Mme Jacques Heim**, c. 1928, gelatin silver print, 20.4 × 16 cm. Musée National d'Art Moderne/Centre de Création Industrielle. Acquired with the support of Yves Rocher, 2011. Former Christian Bouqueret collection. Centre Pompidou, Paris.

p. 176 ***Germaine Krull par Pierre Mac Orlan***, 'Photographes nouveaux' by Pierre Mac Orlan, NRF, Gallimard, 1931, Paris, cover, pp. 5, 46, 60, 15.5 × 12 cm. Private collection.

p. 177 **Female Nude**, 1928, gelatin silver print, 21.6 × 14.4 cm. Centre Pompidou, Paris. Musée National d'Art Moderne/Centre de Création Industrielle. Acquired with the support of Yves Rocher, 2011. Former Christian Bouqueret collection.

p. 178 **Nude**, 1928, gelatin silver print, 17.6 × 12.6 cm. Bouqueret-Rémy collection.

p. 179 Plates of ***Études de nu***, A. Calavas, Paris, 1930, portfolio, photogravure plates, 22.5 × 16 cm. Bouqueret-Rémy collection.

p. 180, top **Germaine Beaumont**, 1930, gelatin silver print mounted on paper, 9 × 8.2 cm. Centre Pompidou, Paris. Musée National d'Art Moderne/Centre de Création Industrielle. Acquired with the support of Yves Rocher, 2011. Former Christian Bouqueret collection.

p. 180, bottom **Colette**, c. 1929, gelatin silver print, 19 × 17 cm. Bibliothèque Nationale de France.

p. 181, top left **'Au revoir Black Birds!'**, *VU*, no. 77, 4 September 1929, 38 × 28 cm. Private collection.

p. 181, top right **Photo 1931**, Arts et Métiers Graphiques, Paris, 1931, pl. 5, 31 × 24.5 cm. Private collection.

p. 181, bottom left ***Le Sourire***, no. 892 (7 June 1934), cover, 31.5 × 24.5 cm. Private collection.

p. 181, bottom right ***L'Image***, 1st year, no. 6, 1932, cover, 26 × 18 cm. Private collection.

pp. 182 and 183 **Berthe Bovy in La Voix humaine**, 1930, three gelatin silver prints. Maison Jean Cocteau, Milly-la-Forêt.

pp. 184 and 185 ***Damia*** by Henri Béraud, for Columbia, Antoine Girard, Paris, c. 1930, 21 × 21 cm. Private collection.

p. 186, top **Study for *La Folle d'Itteville***, 1931, gelatin silver print, 21.9 × 16.4 cm. Centre Pompidou, Paris. Musée National d'Art Moderne/Centre de Création Industrielle. Acquired with the support of Yves Rocher, 2011. Former Christian Bouqueret collection.

pp. 186 and 187, bottom ***La Folle d'Itteville*** by Georges Simenon and Germaine Krull, phototext. Éditions Jacques Haumont, Paris, 1931, 18 × 13.1 cm. Private collection.

pp. 186 and 187, top **Study for *La Folle d'Itteville***, 1931, gelatin silver print, 21.5 × 15.4 cm. The Museum of Modern Art, New York. Thomas Walther Collection. Gift of Thomas Walther.

p. 188 **Gibbs advertisement**, *L'Illustration*, no. 4533, 18 January 1930, 36.7 × 27.8 cm. Private collection.

p. 189, left **Assia Holding a Pot of Powder**, 1930, gelatin silver print, 19.9 × 16.1 cm. Centre Pompidou, Paris. Musée National d'Art Moderne/Centre de

Création Industrielle. Acquired with the support of Yves Rocher, 2011. Former Christian Bouqueret collection.

p. 189, right **Assia in Profile**, 1930, gelatin silver print, 22.2 × 15.8 cm. Bouqueret-Rémy collection.

pp. 190 and 191 top *VU*, **'Les ouvrières de Paris'** by Emmanuel Berl, no. 247, 7 December 1932, p. 1925; idem., pp. 1927-1928; no. 248, 14 December 1932, pp. 2012-2013; idem., p. 2014. 38 × 28 cm. Private collection.

p. 191, bottom **'Workers and Midinettes at Work and Play'**. Original manuscript by Emmanuel Berl, photograph by Germaine Krull, 1931-1932, 24.5 × 20 × 3.5 cm. Bibliothèque Nationale de France.

p. 192, top **'Tabarin'**, *VU*, no. 94, 1 January 1930, pp. 10-11, 38 × 28 cm. Private collection.

p. 192, bottom **'French Cancan'**, *Les images de Paris*, no. 2, August 1930, 23.9 × 15.5 cm. Münchner Stadtmuseum/Sammlung Fotografie, Munich.

p. 193 **'Venus 1934, the Voluptuous'**, *Miroir du monde*, special 'Spring Smiles' issue, 1934, 37 × 27 cm. Private collection.

'MY COLLECTION OF HANDS'

p. 194 Jean Privat, **Portrait of Germaine Krull**, c. 1939, gelatin silver print, 17.5 × 21 cm. Museum Folkwang, Essen.

p. 198, left **Hands**, c. 1930, gelatin silver print, 23.6 × 14.5 cm. Centre Pompidou, Paris. Musée National d'Art Moderne/Centre de Création Industrielle. Acquired in 1986.

p. 198, right **Hands with Shadow**, 1928, gelatin silver print, 22.5 × 17 cm. Bibliothèque Nationale de France.

p. 199 **Portrait of André Malraux**, 1930, gelatin silver print, 23 × 17.3 cm. Museum Folkwang, Essen.

p. 200 **'Hand Gestures by M. Pol Rab'**, *Jazz*, no. 15, April 1929, p. 231, 31.5 × 24.5 cm. Private collection.

p. 201 **Jean Cocteau**, 1929, print from 1976, gelatin silver print, 23.7 × 17.2 cm. Bouqueret-Rémy collection.

p. 202 **Pol Rab (Illustrator), Photomontage**, 1929, gelatin silver print, 19.5 × 14.5 cm. Amsab-Institute of Social History, Ghent.

p. 203 **Jean Cocteau**, 1929, gelatin silver print, 22.3 × 16.5 cm. The Museum of Modern Art, New York. Thomas Walther Collection. Gift of Thomas Walther.

p. 204, left **Portrait**, 1930, gelatin silver print, 19 × 17 cm. Bibliothèque Nationale de France.

p. 204, right **Face, Hands II**, 1931, gelatin silver print, 39.6 × 29.3 cm. Stiftung Ann und Jürgen Wilde, Pinakothek der Moderne, Munich.

p. 205 **Nude with Black Gauntlets**, c. 1931, gelatin silver print, 22.9 × 17.6 cm. Centre Pompidou, Paris. Musée National d'Art Moderne/Centre de Création Industrielle. Acquired in 1991.

p. 206, top left **Hands of Brailowsky**, c. 1935, gelatin silver print, 16 × 20.1 cm. Museum Folkwang, Essen.

p. 206, top right **'Hands of Maurice Privat, Monte-Carlo'**, 1938. Gelatin silver print, 16 × 20.1 cm. Museum Folkwang, Essen.

p. 206, bottom **'Photographs by Germaine Krull'**, pl. 6 of *Paris 1929*, A. Calavas, Paris, 1930, 22.4 × 29 cm. Private collection.

p. 207 **'Frivolities by Germaine Krull'**, *Allo Paris*, no. 10, March 1934, p. 4, 27.5 × 18.5 cm. Bouqueret-Rémy collection.

p. 208 **'A Man's Hand'**, *Grand'Route*, no. 5, July 1930, p. 16, 22.4 × 16.8 cm. Private collection.

p. 209, top **Advertisement for** *The Guide Vert*, 1931. Photogravure, 31.5 × 24.4 cm. Private collection.

p. 209, bottom **'The Cut Makes the Dress'**, 1928, gelatin silver print, 16.6 × 23 cm. Stiftung Ann und Jürgen Wilde, Pinakothek der Moderne, Munich.

LE COURRIER LITTÉRAIRE, 1930

pp. 210-216 ***Le Courrier littéraire***, April-May-June 1930, pp. 65-81, 32 × 24.2 cm. Private collection.

p. 217 **Portrait of Jean Cocteau**, 1929, gelatin silver print, 21.4 × 15 cm. Private collection.

FREE SPIRIT

p. 218 **'The Writer Rudolf Leonhard, Berlin'**, undated, gelatin silver print, 21.5 × 16 cm. Amsab-Institute of Social History, Ghent.

p. 223 **'Displays: Mannequins'**, 1928, gelatin silver print, 10.8 × 15.7 cm. Amsab-Institute of Social History, Ghent.

p. 224, left **Superstitions: Fallen Scissors**, 1929, gelatin silver print, 20.1 × 14.5 cm. Amsab-Institute of Social History, Ghent.

p. 224, right **Superstitions: a Hat on the Bed**, 1929, gelatin silver print, 18.1 × 13.5 cm. Amsab-Institute of Social History, Ghent.

p. 225, top **Superstition: One Match for Three Cigarettes**, 1929, gelatin silver print, 15.7 × 22.2 cm. Amsab-Institute of Social History, Ghent.

p. 225, bottom **Superstitions: the Open Umbrella**, 1929, gelatin silver print, 15.8 × 22.8 cm. Amsab-Institute of Social History, Ghent.

p. 226 **Fantastic Forge**, c. 1929, gelatin silver print, 15.9 × 22.3 cm. Amsab-Institute of Social History, Ghent.

p. 227, top **'The Fortune Teller'**, 1928, gelatin silver print, 15.6 × 22.4 cm. Amsab-Institute of Social History, Ghent.

p. 227, bottom **'Superstition: Broken Mirror; Touch Wood'**, *Variétés*, 2nd year, no. 6, 15 October 1929, p. 428b, 24.9 × 17.8 cm. Private collection.

p. 228, top **Inside of a Wireless**, double exposure (advertisement idea), 1929, gelatin silver print, 16 × 20.5 cm. Amsab-Institute of Social History, Ghent.

p. 228, bottom **Untitled (Conduit)**, c. 1929, gelatin silver print, 15.6 × 22.4 cm. Amsab-Institute of Social History, Ghent.

p. 229 **Belgium**, c. 1926, gelatin silver print, 21.2 × 16.3 cm. Stiftung Ann und Jürgen Wilde, Pinakothek der Moderne, Munich.

pp. 230 and 231 **'Behind the Scenes'**, *L'Art vivant*, no. 141, 1 November 1930, pp. 866-867, 31.5 × 24.4 cm. Private collection.

p. 232 **Mr. Poeltzer Making Himself Up for Wagner's Ring Cycle at the Opéra de Monaco**, 1935, gelatin silver print, 15.6 × 20 cm. Centre Pompidou, Paris. Musée National d'Art Moderne/Centre de Création Industrielle. Acquired with the support of Yves Rocher, 2011. Former Christian Bouqueret collection.

p. 233 **Flea Market, Paris**, 1928, gelatin silver print, 19.1 × 16.7 cm. Stiftung Ann und Jürgen Wilde, Pinakothek der Moderne, Munich.

p. 234, left **Hôtel du Nord, Eugène Dabit**, 1933, gelatin silver print mounted on cardboard, 23 × 15 cm. Bibliothèque Nationale de France.

p. 234, right **Hôtel du Nord, Eugène Dabit**, 1933, gelatin silver print mounted on cardboard, 23 × 15 cm. Bibliothèque Nationale de France.

p. 235, top **S. M. Eisenstein**, 1930, gelatin silver print, 23 × 17 cm. Centre Pompidou, Paris. Musée National d'Art Moderne/Centre de Création Industrielle. Acquired with the support of Yves Rocher, 2011. Former Christian Bouqueret collection.

p. 235, bottom **Portrait of Eisenstein**, *Grand'Route*, no. 3, May 1930, , p. 24, 22.2 × 16.8 cm. Private collection.

p. 236 **"Citroën'**, c. 1927, gelatin silver print, 16 × 22 cm. Musée Nicéphore Niépce, Chalon-sur-Saône.

p. 237 **Floating Timber**, 1929, gelatin silver print, 15.6 × 22.4 cm. Amsab-Institute of Social History, Ghent.

p. 238 **'Old Berlin'**, 1927, gelatin silver print, 22.9 × 15.6 cm. Amsab-Institute of Social History, Ghent.

p. 239 **Flanders, Landscape**, c. 1929, gelatin silver print, 15.4 × 22.6 cm. Amsab-Institute of Social History, Ghent.

WAR

p. 240 **Charles de Gaulle, Algiers**, 1943, gelatin silver print, 23.7 × 18.4 cm. Stiftung Ann und Jürgen Wilde, Pinakothek der Moderne, Munich.

p. 243, top left ***Ouro Preto, Uma Cidade do Brasil***, Ediçoes Atlantico, Lisbon, 1943, cover and pp. 2-3, 23.1 × 7.5 cm. Private collection.

p. 243, bottom **Brazil**, 1941-1942, gelatin silver print, 16.1 × 23.2 cm. Museum Folkwang, Essen.

p. 244, top **Ubangi-Shari, Bacaia, Making Wax**, 1943, gelatin silver print, 14.5 × 21.5 cm. Bibliothèque Nationale de France.

p. 244, bottom **Gabon, Rubber Leaves, after Wringing**, 1943, gelatin silver print, 16 × 21.5 cm. Bibliothèque Nationale de France.

p. 245, top left **Loukouo, Congo, Market**, 1943, gelatin silver print, 16.8 × 11.6 cm. Museum Folkwang, Essen.

p. 245, top right **M'Vouti, Congo, Mine of M. Vigoureux**, April 1943, gelatin silver print, 17.8 × 11.2 cm. Museum Folkwang, Essen.

p. 245, bottom Roger Vailland, ***The Battle of Alsace (November-December 1944)***, Jacques Haumont, Paris, 1945, 19 × 15.4 cm. Private collection.

p. 246 Unidentified photographer, **Portrait of Germaine Krull in the Uniform of the Free French Forces, Algiers**, 1944, gelatin silver print, 9.2 × 6.7 cm. Museum Folkwang, Essen.

p. 247 **'In the Camp of Horror'**, *Point de vue*, 1st year, no. 6, 27 April 1945, unpaginated, 36 × 26 cm. Private collection.

IN ASIA

p. 248 **Lamphun Museum, Chiengsen head, Thailand**, c. 1961. Gelatin silver print, 29.6 × 24.3 cm. Museum Folkwang, Essen.

p. 251, top **'Tibetan Religious Ceremony, Offering of the White Scarf**, c. 1960, gelatin silver print, 24.1 × 18.5 cm. Museum Folkwang, Essen.

p. 251, bottom **His Holiness Sakya Trizin, Head of the Sakya Sect**, c. 1965, gelatin silver print, 18.2 × 24.2 cm. Museum Folkwang, Essen.

p. 252, top Germaine Krull, ***Tibetans in India***, Allied Publishers Private Ltd, New Delhi, 1968, 26 × 22 cm. Private collection.

p. 252, bottom **'Group of Tibetan Dancers'**, c. 1965, gelatin silver print, 12.8 × 17.8 cm. Museum Folkwang, Essen.

p. 253, top **Pagan, Burma, Chinbinthalyang Temple, reclining Buddha**, c. 1961, gelatin silver print, 17.2 × 23.1 cm. Museum Folkwang, Essen.

p. 253, bottom **Wat Phra Lai, Chiang Mai, Thailand**, 1961, gelatin silver print, 29.3 × 24.3 cm. Museum Folkwang, Essen.

EXHIBITED WORKS NOT REPRODUCED

Unidentified photographer, **Germaine Krull with Camera**, c. 1934, gelatin silver print, 12.1 × 8.3 cm. Bouqueret-Rémy collection.

Blast Furnace, Pont-à-Mousson, 1926, gelatin silver print, 23.8 × 17.6. Stiftung Ann und Jürgen Wilde, Pinakothek der Moderne,

Blast Furnace, Pont-à-Mousson, 1926, gelatin silver print, 23.5 × 15.8. Stiftung Ann und Jürgen Wilde, Pinakothek der Moderne, Munich.

Rails, 1929, gelatin silver print, 23.7 × 15.8 cm. Bouqueret-Rémy collection.

Untitled, c. 1920, gelatin silver print, 19.3 × 16.4 cm. Stiftung Ann und Jürgen Wilde, Pinakothek der Moderne, Munich.

Roofs of Paris, c. 1929, gelatin silver print, 9 × 12.4 cm. Centre Pompidou, Paris. Musée National d'Art Moderne/Centre de Création Industrielle. Acquired with the support of Yves Rocher, 2011. Former Christian Bouqueret collection.

Study for *La Folle d'Itteville*, gelatin silver print, 15.3 × 11.3 cm. Private collection.

Brazzaville, Detail of the New Radio Brazzaville Radio Station, Ventilation by Compression, 1943, gelatin silver print, 17 × 11.5 cm. Bibliothèque Nationale de France.

Brazzaville, Warrior Dancer, 1943, gelatin silver print, 17.1 × 12.2 cm. Museum Folkwang, Essen.

This book is published on the occasion of the exhibition **'Germaine Krull (1897-1985). A photographer's journey'** presented at the Jeu de Paume, Paris (June 2-September 27, 2015), and at the Martin-Gropius-Bau, Berlin (October 15, 2015-January 31, 2016).

CURATOR OF THE EXHIBITION AND EDITOR OF THE CATALOGUE

Michel Frizot

JEU DE PAUME

Marta Gili, Director

Maryline Dunaud, General Secretary
Claude Bocage, Administration and Finances
Véronique Dabin, Exhibitions
Pierre-Yves Horel, Technical Services
Marta Ponsa, Public Programmes
Pascal Priest, Bookshop Manager
Anne Racine, Communications and Fundraising
Sabine Thiriot, Educational Programmes

Exhibition

Judith Czernichow, Exhibition Coordinator
Maddy Cougouluègnes, Registrar
Éric Michaux, Technical Coordinator

Catalogue

Muriel Rausch, Publications

EXHIBITION DESIGN

Nino Comba — n-worshop

The Jeu de Paume is supported by a grant from the French Ministère de la Culture et de la Communication.

Liberté • Égalité • Fraternité
République Française

Ministère Culture Communication

It is supported by Neuflize Vie and the Manufacture Jaeger-LeCoultre, its principal partners.

Neuflize Vie ABN AMRO   Jaeger-LeCoultre

ACKNOWLEDGMENTS

The Jeu de Paume and Michel Frizot would like to thank, first of all, the Museum Folkwang, Essen, holder of the estate of Germaine Krull, for giving us special access to its collection of archives, for its numerous loans, and for its collaboration throughout this project.
We especially thank the director Tobia Bezzola, Florian Ebner, the curator of the photography department, and Petra Steinhardt, associate researcher. We are also grateful to Amsab–the Institute of Social History in Ghent, for giving us access and permission to publish archives for the first time, and for their important loans, and especially the director Geert Van Goethem and head of the collections Hendrik Ollivier.
Our warm thanks also go to all the lenders for their generous contributions to this exhibition:

Bibliothèque Nationale de France, Paris (Sylvie Aubenas and Dominique Versavel);
Musée National d'Art Moderne/ Centre Pompidou, Paris (Clément Chéroux);
Münchner Stadtmuseum/Sammlung Fotografie, Munich (Dr Ulrich Pohlmann);
Pinakothek der Moderne, Stiftung Ann und Jürgen Wilde (Inka Graeve Ingelmann and Simone Foerster);
The Museum of Modern Art, New York;
Maison Jean Cocteau, Milly-la-Forêt;
Collection Bouqueret-Rémy;
Dietmar Siegert Collection;
CNC, Centre National du Cinéma et de l'Image Animée;
and all those who prefer to remain anonymous.

The Jeu de Paume and Michel Frizot are also grateful to Anne-Isabelle Vannier and Claire Hostalier at Éditions Hazan; to François Cheval, Sylvain Besson and Émilie Bernard, to the Musée Nicéphore Niépce, Chalon-sur-Saône; to Éric Rémy; to Galerie Johannes Faber, Vienna; to Yves Di Maria, Jean-Michel Duval and Cédric de Veigy.

The Jeu de Paume and Michel Frizot would like to pay tribute to Jean-François Barrielle, the director of Hazan, who died recently. He responded enthusiastically to this project. We also remember Christian Bouqueret († 2013), a great Germaine Krull expert, who gave Michel Frizot access to his documentation.

PHOTOGRAPHIC CREDITS

Figures refer to page numbers.

Amsab-Institute of Social History, Ghent: 50 (top and bottom), 54, 56 (right), 57, 93 (right), 98–99, 101, 102 (left and right), 110, 118 (bottom), 121 (left and right), 129, 146 (left), 147 (left and right), 151, 202, 218, 223, 224–225, 226, 227 (top), 228 (top and bottom), 237, 238, 239 – Bibliothèque Nationale de France: 35 (top and bottom), 37, 174 (right), 180 (bottom), 191 (bottom), 198 (left), 204 (left), 234 (left and right), 244 (top and bottom) – © Centre Pompidou, MNAM-CCI, Dist. RMN-Grand Palais / image Centre Pompidou, MNAM-CCI: 36, 51 (right), 64, 135, 175, 180 (top), 189 (left) / Georges Meguerditchian: 87, 156, 160, 232, 235 (top), front cover / Bertrand Prévost: 205 / Guy Carrard: 177, 186 (top) / Philippe Migeat: 198 (left) – Jean-Louis Losi: 58–59, 119, 123, 153, 178–179, 189 (right), 201, 207 – Maison Jean Cocteau, Milly-la-Forêt: 182–183 – Münchner Stadtmuseum / Sammlung Fotografie, München: 21, 30–31, 192 (bottom) – © Musée Nicéphore Niépce, Chalon-sur-Saône, 2015: 55, 62 (top), 92 (top and bottom), 96 (top and bottom), 103, 104 (top and bottom), 106 (top and bottom), 107 (top and bottom), 108 (bottom), 120 (top), 134 (bottom), 148 (left and right), 181 (top left), 190, 191 (top), 192 (top), 236 – Courtesy Galerie Johannes Faber: 32 (top) – Museum Folkwang, Essen: 14, 20, 22, 34, 38, 51 (left), 52, 90, 94, 95, 136, 194, 199, 206 (top, left and right), 243 (bottom), 245 (top, left and right), 246, 248, 251 (top and bottom), 252 (bottom), 253 (top and bottom) – © 2015. Digital Image, The Museum of Modern Art, New York/Scala, Florence: 91, 128, 157, 187 (top), 203, back cover – Courtesy Dietmar Siegert: 33 (top and bottom) – Stiftung Ann und Jürgen Wilde, Pinakothek der Moderne, Munich: 8, 32 (bottom), 39, 40, 49, 53, 56 (left), 88, 93 (left), 105, 125, 145, 146 (right), 174 (left), 204 (right), 209 (bottom), 229, 233, 240

Translations from French into English: Charles Penwarden and Deke Dusinberre
Translation from Spanish into English: Laura Suffield
Editorial coordination: Anne-Isabelle Vannier
Editing: Bernard Wooding
Graphic Design: Sylvie Milliet
Production: Claire Hostalier
Photoengraving: Litho Art New, Turin, Italy

www.editions-hazan.com
www.jeudepaume.org

ISBN: 9780300215151
Legal deposit: June 2015

Printed by Stamperia Artistica Nazionale, Trofarello, Italy

Library of Congress Control Number: 2015937163

A catalogue record for this book is available from The British Library